# Solutions Manual

## for

# Corporate Finance

## Tenth Edition

Stephen A. Ross
*Sloan School of Management*
*Massachusetts Institute of Technology*

Randolph W. Westerfield
*Marshall School of Business*
*University of Southern California*

Jeffrey Jaffe
*Wharton School of Business*
*University of Pennsylvania*

Prepared by
Joe Smolira
*Belmont University*

McGraw-Hill
Irwin

Solutions Manual for
CORPORATE FINANCE, Tenth Edition
Stephen A. Ross, Randolph W. Westerfield, and Jeffrey Jaffe

Published by McGraw-Hill/Irwin, an imprint of The McGraw-Hill Companies, Inc., 1221 Avenue of the
Americas, New York, NY 10020. Copyright © 2013, 2010 by The McGraw-Hill Companies, Inc. All rights reserved. Printed in the
United States of America.

1 2 3 4 5 6 7 8 9 0 QDB/QDB 1 0 9 8 7 6 5 4 3 2

ISBN: 978-0-07-751134-0
MHID: 0-07-751134-4


www.mhhe.com

# Table of Contents

**Chapter 1**    Introduction to Corporate Finance............................................................... 1-1

**Chapter 2**    Accounting Statements, Taxes, and Cash Flow....................................... 2-1

**Chapter 3**    Long-Term Financial Planning and Growth.............................................. 3-1

**Chapter 4**    Discounted Cash Flow Valuation............................................................. 4-1

**Chapter 5**    Net Present Value and Other Investment Criteria ................................... 5-1

**Chapter 6**    Making Capital Investment Decisions...................................................... 6-1

**Chapter 7**    Risk Analysis, Real Options, and Capital Budgeting............................... 7-1

**Chapter 8**    Interest Rates and Bond Valuation ......................................................... 8-1

**Chapter 9**    Stock Valuation ...................................................................................... 9-1

**Chapter 10**   Some Lessons from Capital Market History ........................................... 10-1

**Chapter 11**   Risk and Return: *The Capital Asset Pricing Model (CAPM)* ................. 11-1

**Chapter 12**   An Alternative View of Risk and Return: *The Arbitrage Pricing Theory*.............. 12-1

**Chapter 13**   Risk, Cost of Capital, and Capital Budgeting......................................... 13-1

**Chapter 14**   Corporate Financing Decisions and Efficient Capital Markets ............... 14-1

**Chapter 15**   Long-Term Financing: *An Introduction* ................................................ 15-1

**Chapter 16**   Capital Structure: *Basic Concepts* ........................................................ 16-1

**Chapter 17**   Capital Structure: *Limits to the Use of Debt* ........................................ 17-1

**Chapter 18**   Valuation and Capital Budgeting for the Levered Firm .......................... 18-1

**Chapter 19**   Dividends and Other Payouts ................................................................ 19-1

**Chapter 20**   Issuing Securities to the Public.............................................................. 20-1

**Chapter 21**   Leasing ................................................................................................... 21-1

**Chapter 22**   Options and Corporate Finance ............................................................. 22-1

**Chapter 23**   Options and Corporate Finance: *Extensions and Applications*.............. 23-1

**Chapter 24**   Warrants and Convertibles .................................................................... 24-1

iii

**Chapter 25**    Derivatives and Hedging Risk ................................................................. 25-1

**Chapter 26**    Short-Term Finance and Planning ........................................................... 26-1

**Chapter 27**    Cash Management ................................................................................... 27-1

**Chapter 28**    Credit and Inventory Management .......................................................... 28-1

**Chapter 29**    Mergers and Acquisitions ....................................................................... 29-1

**Chapter 30**    Financial Distress .................................................................................. 30-1

**Chapter 31**    International Corporate Finance .............................................................. 31-1

# CHAPTER 1
# INTRODUCTION TO CORPORATE FINANCE

**Answers to Concept Questions**

1.  In the corporate form of ownership, the shareholders are the owners of the firm. The shareholders elect the directors of the corporation, who in turn appoint the firm's management. This separation of ownership from control in the corporate form of organization is what causes agency problems to exist. Management may act in its own or someone else's best interests, rather than those of the shareholders. If such events occur, they may contradict the goal of maximizing the share price of the equity of the firm.

2.  Such organizations frequently pursue social or political missions, so many different goals are conceivable. One goal that is often cited is revenue minimization; i.e., provide whatever goods and services are offered at the lowest possible cost to society. A better approach might be to observe that even a not-for-profit business has equity. Thus, one answer is that the appropriate goal is to maximize the value of the equity.

3.  Presumably, the current stock value reflects the risk, timing, and magnitude of all future cash flows, both short-term *and* long-term. If this is correct, then the statement is false.

4.  An argument can be made either way. At the one extreme, we could argue that in a market economy, all of these things are priced. There is thus an optimal level of, for example, ethical and/or illegal behavior, and the framework of stock valuation explicitly includes these. At the other extreme, we could argue that these are non-economic phenomena and are best handled through the political process. A classic (and highly relevant) thought question that illustrates this debate goes something like this: "A firm has estimated that the cost of improving the safety of one of its products is $30 million. However, the firm believes that improving the safety of the product will only save $20 million in product liability claims. What should the firm do?"

5.  The goal will be the same, but the best course of action toward that goal may be different because of differing social, political, and economic institutions.

6.  The goal of management should be to maximize the share price for the current shareholders. If management believes that it can improve the profitability of the firm so that the share price will exceed $35, then they should fight the offer from the outside company. If management believes that this bidder or other unidentified bidders will actually pay more than $35 per share to acquire the company, then they should still fight the offer. However, if the current management cannot increase the value of the firm beyond the bid price, and no other higher bids come in, then management is not acting in the interests of the shareholders by fighting the offer. Since current managers often lose their jobs when the corporation is acquired, poorly monitored managers have an incentive to fight corporate takeovers in situations such as this.

**7.** We would expect agency problems to be less severe in other countries, primarily due to the relatively small percentage of individual ownership. Fewer individual owners should reduce the number of diverse opinions concerning corporate goals. The high percentage of institutional ownership might lead to a higher degree of agreement between owners and managers on decisions concerning risky projects. In addition, institutions may be better able to implement effective monitoring mechanisms on managers than can individual owners, based on the institutions' deeper resources and experiences with their own management.

**8.** The increase in institutional ownership of stock in the United States and the growing activism of these large shareholder groups may lead to a reduction in agency problems for U.S. corporations and a more efficient market for corporate control. However, this may not always be the case. If the managers of the mutual fund or pension plan are not concerned with the interests of the investors, the agency problem could potentially remain the same, or even increase since there is the possibility of agency problems between the fund and its investors.

**9.** How much is too much? Who is worth more, Larry Ellsion or Tiger Woods? The simplest answer is that there is a market for executives just as there is for all types of labor. Executive compensation is the price that clears the market. The same is true for athletes and performers. Having said that, one aspect of executive compensation deserves comment. A primary reason executive compensation has grown so dramatically is that companies have increasingly moved to stock-based compensation. Such movement is obviously consistent with the attempt to better align stockholder and management interests. In recent years, stock prices have soared, so management has cleaned up. It is sometimes argued that much of this reward is simply due to rising stock prices in general, not managerial performance. Perhaps in the future, executive compensation will be designed to reward only differential performance, i.e., stock price increases in excess of general market increases.

**10.** Maximizing the current share price is the same as maximizing the future share price at any future period. The value of a share of stock depends on all of the future cash flows of company. Another way to look at this is that, barring large cash payments to shareholders, the expected price of the stock must be higher in the future than it is today. Who would buy a stock for $100 today when the share price in one year is expected to be $80?

# CHAPTER 2
# ACCOUNTING STATEMENTS, TAXES, AND CASH FLOW

**Answers to Concepts Review and Critical Thinking Questions**

1. True. Every asset can be converted to cash at some price. However, when we are referring to a liquid asset, the added assumption that the asset can be quickly converted to cash at or near market value is important.

2. The recognition and matching principles in financial accounting call for revenues, and the costs associated with producing those revenues, to be "booked" when the revenue process is essentially complete, not necessarily when the cash is collected or bills are paid. Note that this way is not necessarily correct; it's the way accountants have chosen to do it.

3. The bottom line number shows the change in the cash balance on the balance sheet. As such, it is not a useful number for analyzing a company.

4. The major difference is the treatment of interest expense. The accounting statement of cash flows treats interest as an operating cash flow, while the financial cash flows treat interest as a financing cash flow. The logic of the accounting statement of cash flows is that since interest appears on the income statement, which shows the operations for the period, it is an operating cash flow. In reality, interest is a financing expense, which results from the company's choice of debt and equity. We will have more to say about this in a later chapter. When comparing the two cash flow statements, the financial statement of cash flows is a more appropriate measure of the company's performance because of its treatment of interest.

5. Market values can never be negative. Imagine a share of stock selling for –$20. This would mean that if you placed an order for 100 shares, you would get the stock along with a check for $2,000. How many shares do you want to buy? More generally, because of corporate and individual bankruptcy laws, net worth for a person or a corporation cannot be negative, implying that liabilities cannot exceed assets in market value.

6. For a successful company that is rapidly expanding, for example, capital outlays will be large, possibly leading to negative cash flow from assets. In general, what matters is whether the money is spent wisely, not whether cash flow from assets is positive or negative.

7. It's probably not a good sign for an established company to have negative cash flow from operations, but it would be fairly ordinary for a start-up, so it depends.

8. For example, if a company were to become more efficient in inventory management, the amount of inventory needed would decline. The same might be true if the company becomes better at collecting its receivables. In general, anything that leads to a decline in ending NWC relative to beginning would have this effect. Negative net capital spending would mean more long-lived assets were liquidated than purchased.

9. If a company raises more money from selling stock than it pays in dividends in a particular period, its cash flow to stockholders will be negative. If a company borrows more than it pays in interest and principal, its cash flow to creditors will be negative.

10. The adjustments discussed were purely accounting changes; they had no cash flow or market value consequences unless the new accounting information caused stockholders to revalue the derivatives.

**Solutions to Questions and Problems**

*NOTE: All end-of-chapter problems were solved using a spreadsheet. Many problems require multiple steps. Due to space and readability constraints, when these intermediate steps are included in this solutions manual, rounding may appear to have occurred. However, the final answer for each problem is found without rounding during any step in the problem.*

*Basic*

1. To find owners' equity, we must construct a balance sheet as follows:

| Balance Sheet | | | |
|---|---|---|---|
| CA | $ 5,700 | CL | $ 4,400 |
| NFA | 27,000 | LTD | 12,900 |
| | | OE | ?? |
| TA | $32,700 | TL & OE | $32,700 |

We know that total liabilities and owners' equity (TL & OE) must equal total assets of $32,700. We also know that TL & OE is equal to current liabilities plus long-term debt plus owner's equity, so owner's equity is:

OE = $32,700 – 12,900 – 4,400 = $15,400

NWC = CA – CL = $5,700 – 4,400 = $1,300

2. The income statement for the company is:

| Income Statement | |
|---|---|
| Sales | $387,000 |
| Costs | 175,000 |
| Depreciation | 40,000 |
| EBIT | $172,000 |
| Interest | 21,000 |
| EBT | $151,000 |
| Taxes | 52,850 |
| Net income | $ 98,150 |

One equation for net income is:

Net income = Dividends + Addition to retained earnings

Rearranging, we get:

Addition to retained earnings = Net income – Dividends
Addition to retained earnings = $98,150 – 30,000
Addition to retained earnings = $68,150

3.  To find the book value of current assets, we use: NWC = CA – CL. Rearranging to solve for current assets, we get:

CA = NWC + CL = $800,000 + 2,400,000 = $3,200,000

The market value of current assets and net fixed assets is given, so:

| | | | | |
|---|---|---|---|---|
| Book value CA | = $3,200,000 | | Market value CA | = $2,600,000 |
| Book value NFA | = $5,200,000 | | Market value NFA | = $6,500,000 |
| Book value assets | = $8,400,000 | | Market value assets | = $9,100,000 |

4.  Taxes = 0.15($50,000) + 0.25($25,000) + 0.34($25,000) + 0.39($273,000 – 100,000)
    Taxes = $89,720

The average tax rate is the total tax paid divided by net income, so:

Average tax rate = $89,720 / $273,000
Average tax rate = 32.86%

The marginal tax rate is the tax rate on the next $1 of earnings, so the marginal tax rate = 39%.

5.  To calculate OCF, we first need the income statement:

| Income Statement | |
|---|---|
| Sales | $18,700 |
| Costs | 10,300 |
| Depreciation | 1,900 |
| EBIT | $ 6,500 |
| Interest | 1,250 |
| Taxable income | $ 5,250 |
| Taxes | 2,100 |
| Net income | $ 3,150 |

OCF = EBIT + Depreciation – Taxes
OCF = $6,500 + 1,900 – 2,100
OCF = $6,300

6.  Net capital spending = $NFA_{end}$ – $NFA_{beg}$ + Depreciation
    Net capital spending = $1,690,000 – 1,420,000 + 145,000
    Net capital spending = $415,000

7. The long-term debt account will increase by $35 million, the amount of the new long-term debt issue. Since the company sold 10 million new shares of stock with a $1 par value, the common stock account will increase by $10 million. The capital surplus account will increase by $48 million, the value of the new stock sold above its par value. Since the company had a net income of $9 million, and paid $2 million in dividends, the addition to retained earnings was $7 million, which will increase the accumulated retained earnings account. So, the new long-term debt and stockholders' equity portion of the balance sheet will be:

| | |
|---|---|
| Long-term debt | $ 100,000,000 |
| Total long-term debt | $ 100,000,000 |
| | |
| Shareholders equity | |
| Preferred stock | $ 4,000,000 |
| Common stock ($1 par value) | 25,000,000 |
| Accumulated retained earnings | 142,000,000 |
| Capital surplus | 93,000,000 |
| Total equity | $ 264,000,000 |
| | |
| Total Liabilities & Equity | $ 364,000,000 |

8. Cash flow to creditors = Interest paid – Net new borrowing
Cash flow to creditors = $127,000 – (LTD$_{end}$ – LTD$_{beg}$)
Cash flow to creditors = $127,000 – ($1,520,000 – 1,450,000)
Cash flow to creditors = $127,000 – 70,000
Cash flow to creditors = $57,000

9. Cash flow to stockholders = Dividends paid – Net new equity
Cash flow to stockholders = $275,000 – [(Common$_{end}$ + APIS$_{end}$) – (Common$_{beg}$ + APIS$_{beg}$)]
Cash flow to stockholders = $275,000 – [($525,000 + 3,700,000) – ($490,000 + 3,400,000)]
Cash flow to stockholders = $275,000 – ($4,225,000 – 3,890,000)
Cash flow to stockholders = –$60,000

Note, APIS is the additional paid-in surplus.

10. Cash flow from assets $\quad$ = Cash flow to creditors + Cash flow to stockholders
$\quad$ = $57,000 – 60,000
$\quad$ = –$3,000

Cash flow from assets $\quad$ = OCF – Change in NWC – Net capital spending
–$3,000 $\quad$ = OCF – (–$87,000) – 945,000
OCF $\quad$ = $855,000

Operating cash flow $\quad$ = –$3,000 – 87,000 + 945,000
Operating cash flow $\quad$ = $855,000

## Intermediate

**11.** *a.* The accounting statement of cash flows explains the change in cash during the year. The accounting statement of cash flows will be:

### Statement of cash flows

*Operations*

| | |
|---|---:|
| Net income | $  95 |
| Depreciation | 90 |
| Changes in other current assets | (5) |
| Accounts payable | 10 |
| Total cash flow from operations | $  190 |

*Investing activities*

| | |
|---|---:|
| Acquisition of fixed assets | $  (110) |
| Total cash flow from investing activities | $  (110) |

*Financing activities*

| | |
|---|---:|
| Proceeds of long-term debt | $    5 |
| Dividends | (75) |
| Total cash flow from financing activities | ($    70) |

| | |
|---|---:|
| Change in cash (on balance sheet) | $    10 |

*b.* 
$$\begin{aligned}
\text{Change in NWC} &= \text{NWC}_{end} - \text{NWC}_{beg} \\
&= (\text{CA}_{end} - \text{CL}_{end}) - (\text{CA}_{beg} - \text{CL}_{beg}) \\
&= [(\$65 + 170) - 125] - [(\$55 + 165) - 115] \\
&= \$110 - 105 \\
&= \$5
\end{aligned}$$

*c.* To find the cash flow generated by the firm's assets, we need the operating cash flow, and the capital spending. So, calculating each of these, we find:

*Operating cash flow*

| | |
|---|---:|
| Net income | $ 95 |
| Depreciation | 90 |
| Operating cash flow | $185 |

Note that we can calculate OCF in this manner since there are no taxes.

*Capital spending*

| Ending fixed assets | $390 |
|---|---|
| Beginning fixed assets | (370) |
| Depreciation | 90 |
| Capital spending | $110 |

Now we can calculate the cash flow generated by the firm's assets, which is:

*Cash flow from assets*

| Operating cash flow | $ 185 |
|---|---|
| Capital spending | (110) |
| Change in NWC | (5) |
| Cash flow from assets | $ 70 |

12. With the information provided, the cash flows from the firm are the capital spending and the change in net working capital, so:

*Cash flows from the firm*

| Capital spending | $(21,000) |
|---|---|
| Additions to NWC | (1,900) |
| Cash flows from the firm | $(22,900) |

And the cash flows to the investors of the firm are:

*Cash flows to investors of the firm*

| Sale of long-term debt | (17,000) |
|---|---|
| Sale of common stock | (4,000) |
| Dividends paid | 14,500 |
| Cash flows to investors of the firm | $(6,500) |

**13.** *a.* The interest expense for the company is the amount of debt times the interest rate on the debt. So, the income statement for the company is:

| Income Statement | |
|---|---:|
| Sales | $1,060,000 |
| Cost of goods sold | 525,000 |
| Selling costs | 215,000 |
| Depreciation | 130,000 |
| EBIT | $ 190,000 |
| Interest | 56,000 |
| Taxable income | $ 134,000 |
| Taxes | 46,900 |
| Net income | $ 87,100 |

*b.* And the operating cash flow is:

OCF = EBIT + Depreciation – Taxes
OCF = $190,000 + 130,000 – 46,900
OCF = $273,100

**14.** To find the OCF, we first calculate net income.

| Income Statement | |
|---|---:|
| Sales | $185,000 |
| Costs | 98,000 |
| Depreciation | 16,500 |
| Other expenses | 6,700 |
| EBIT | $ 63,800 |
| Interest | 9,000 |
| Taxable income | $ 54,800 |
| Taxes | 19,180 |
| Net income | $ 35,620 |
| | |
| Dividends | $ 9,500 |
| Additions to RE | $ 26,120 |

*a.* OCF = EBIT + Depreciation – Taxes
OCF = $63,800 + 16,500 – 19,180
OCF = $61,120

*b.* CFC = Interest – Net new LTD
CFC = $9,000 – (–$7,100)
CFC = $16,100

Note that the net new long-term debt is negative because the company repaid part of its long-term debt.

*c.* CFS = Dividends – Net new equity
CFS = $9,500 – 7,550
CFS = $1,950

    *d.*    We know that CFA = CFC + CFS, so:

        CFA = $16,100 + 1,950 = $18,050

        CFA is also equal to OCF – Net capital spending – Change in NWC. We already know OCF. Net capital spending is equal to:

        Net capital spending = Increase in NFA + Depreciation
        Net capital spending = $26,100 + 16,500
        Net capital spending = $42,600

        Now we can use:

        CFA = OCF – Net capital spending – Change in NWC
        $18,050 = $61,120 – 42,600 – Change in NWC.

        Solving for the change in NWC gives $470, meaning the company increased its NWC by $470.

**15.**    The solution to this question works the income statement backwards. Starting at the bottom:

    Net income = Dividends + Addition to ret. earnings
    Net income = $1,570 + 4,900
    Net income = $6,470

    Now, looking at the income statement:

    EBT – (EBT × Tax rate) = Net income

    Recognize that EBT × tax rate is simply the calculation for taxes. Solving this for EBT yields:

    EBT = NI / (1– Tax rate)
    EBT = $6,470 / (1 – .35)
    EBT = $9,953.85

    Now we can calculate:

    EBIT = EBT + Interest
    EBIT = $9,953.85 + 1,840
    EBIT = $11,793.85

    The last step is to use:

    EBIT = Sales – Costs – Depreciation
    $11,793.85 = $41,000 – 26,400 – Depreciation
    Depreciation = $2,806.15

16. The market value of shareholders' equity cannot be negative. A negative market value in this case would imply that the company would pay you to own the stock. The market value of shareholders' equity can be stated as: Shareholders' equity = Max [(TA – TL), 0]. So, if TA is $12,400, equity is equal to $1,500, and if TA is $9,600, equity is equal to $0. We should note here that while the market value of equity cannot be negative, the book value of shareholders' equity can be negative.

17. *a.* Taxes Growth  = 0.15($50,000) + 0.25($25,000) + 0.34($86,000 – 75,000) = $17,490

   Taxes Income  = 0.15($50,000) + 0.25($25,000) + 0.34($25,000) + 0.39($235,000)
   $$+ 0.34($8,600,000 – 335,000)$$
   $$= $2,924,000$$

   *b.* Each firm has a marginal tax rate of 34% on the next $10,000 of taxable income, despite their different average tax rates, so both firms will pay an additional $3,400 in taxes.

18. *a.*

   | Income Statement | |
   | --- | --- |
   | Sales | $630,000 |
   | COGS | 470,000 |
   | A&S expenses | 95,000 |
   | Depreciation | 140,000 |
   | EBIT | ($ 75,000) |
   | Interest | 70,000 |
   | Taxable income | ($145,000) |
   | Taxes (35%) | 0 |
   | Net income | ($145,000) |

   *b.* OCF = EBIT + Depreciation – Taxes
   OCF = ($75,000) + 140,000 – 0
   OCF = $65,000

   *c.* Net income was negative because of the tax deductibility of depreciation and interest expense. However, the actual cash flow from operations was positive because depreciation is a non-cash expense and interest is a financing expense, not an operating expense.

19. A firm can still pay out dividends if net income is negative; it just has to be sure there is sufficient cash flow to make the dividend payments.

   Change in NWC = Net capital spending = Net new equity = 0. (Given)

   Cash flow from assets = OCF – Change in NWC – Net capital spending
   Cash flow from assets = $65,000 – 0 – 0 = $65,000

   Cash flow to stockholders = Dividends – Net new equity
   Cash flow to stockholders = $34,000 – 0 = $34,000

   Cash flow to creditors = Cash flow from assets – Cash flow to stockholders
   Cash flow to creditors = $65,000 – 34,000
   Cash flow to creditors = $31,000

Cash flow to creditors is also:

Cash flow to creditors = Interest – Net new LTD

So:

Net new LTD = Interest – Cash flow to creditors
Net new LTD = $70,000 – 31,000
Net new LTD = $39,000

**20.** *a.* The income statement is:

### Income Statement

| | |
|---|---:|
| Sales | $19,900 |
| Cost of good sold | 14,200 |
| Depreciation | 2,700 |
| EBIT | $ 3,000 |
| Interest | 670 |
| Taxable income | $ 2,330 |
| Taxes | 932 |
| Net income | $ 1,398 |

 *b.*   OCF = EBIT + Depreciation – Taxes
 OCF = $3,000 + 2,700 – 932
 OCF = $4,768

 *c.*   Change in NWC  = $NWC_{end} - NWC_{beg}$
  = $(CA_{end} - CL_{end}) - (CA_{beg} - CL_{beg})$
  = ($5,135 – 2,535) – ($4,420 – 2,470)
  = $2,600 – 1,950 = $650

 Net capital spending  = $NFA_{end} - NFA_{beg}$ + Depreciation
  = $16,770 – 15,340 + 2,700
  = $4,130

 CFA = OCF – Change in NWC – Net capital spending
  = $4,768 – 650 – 4,130
  = –$12

The cash flow from assets can be positive or negative, since it represents whether the firm raised funds or distributed funds on a net basis. In this problem, even though net income and OCF are positive, the firm invested heavily in both fixed assets and net working capital; it had to raise a net $12 in funds from its stockholders and creditors to make these investments.

 *d.*   Cash flow to creditors = Interest – Net new LTD
  = $670 – 0
  = $670

 Cash flow to stockholders = Cash flow from assets – Cash flow to creditors
  = –$12 – 670
  = –$682

We can also calculate the cash flow to stockholders as:

Cash flow to stockholders = Dividends − Net new equity

Solving for net new equity, we get:

Net new equity = $650 − (−682)
= $1,332

The firm had positive earnings in an accounting sense (NI > 0) and had positive cash flow from operations. The firm invested $650 in new net working capital and $4,130 in new fixed assets. The firm had to raise $12 from its stakeholders to support this new investment. It accomplished this by raising $1,332 in the form of new equity. After paying out $650 of this in the form of dividends to shareholders and $670 in the form of interest to creditors, $12 was left to meet the firm's cash flow needs for investment.

**21.** *a.*  Total assets 2011     = $936 + 4,176 = $5,112
Total liabilities 2011   = $382 + 2,160 = $2,542
Owners' equity 2011   = $5,112 − 2,542 = $2,570

Total assets 2012     = $1,015 + 4,896 = $5,911
Total liabilities 2012   = $416 + 2,477 = $2,893
Owners' equity 2012   = $5,911 − 2,893 = $3,018

*b.*  NWC 2011       = CA11 − CL11 = $936 − 382 = $554
NWC 2012       = CA12 − CL12 = $1,015 − 416 = $599
Change in NWC  = NWC12 − NWC11 = $599 − 554 = $45

*c.*  We can calculate net capital spending as:

Net capital spending = Net fixed assets 2012 − Net fixed assets 2011 + Depreciation
Net capital spending = $4,896 − 4,176 + 1,150
Net capital spending = $1,870

So, the company had a net capital spending cash flow of $1,870. We also know that net capital spending is:

Net capital spending  = Fixed assets bought − Fixed assets sold
$1,870              = $2,160 − Fixed assets sold
Fixed assets sold    = $2,160 − 1,870 = $290

To calculate the cash flow from assets, we must first calculate the operating cash flow. The operating cash flow is calculated as follows (you can also prepare a traditional income statement):

EBIT = Sales − Costs − Depreciation
EBIT = $12,380 − 5,776 − 1,150
EBIT = $5,454

EBT = EBIT – Interest
EBT = $5,454 – 314
EBT = $5,140

Taxes = EBT × .40
Taxes = $5,140 × .40
Taxes = $2,056

OCF = EBIT + Depreciation – Taxes
OCF = $5,454 + 1,150 – 2,056
OCF = $4,548

Cash flow from assets = OCF – Change in NWC – Net capital spending.
Cash flow from assets = $4,548 – 45 – 1,870
Cash flow from assets = $2,633

*d.*   Net new borrowing = LTD12 – LTD11
Net new borrowing = $2,477 – 2,160
Net new borrowing = $317

Cash flow to creditors = Interest – Net new LTD
Cash flow to creditors = $314 – 317
Cash flow to creditors = –$3

Net new borrowing = $317 = Debt issued – Debt retired
Debt retired = $432 – 317 = $115

**22.**

<u>Balance sheet as of Dec. 31, 2011</u>

| Cash | $ 4,109 | Accounts payable | $ 4,316 |
|---|---|---|---|
| Accounts receivable | 5,439 | Notes payable | 794 |
| Inventory | 9,670 | Current liabilities | $ 5,110 |
| Current assets | $19,218 | | |
| | | Long-term debt | $13,460 |
| Net fixed assets | $34,455 | Owners' equity | 35,103 |
| Total assets | $53,673 | Total liab. & equity | $53,673 |

<u>Balance sheet as of Dec. 31, 2012</u>

| Cash | $ 5,203 | Accounts payable | $ 4,185 |
|---|---|---|---|
| Accounts receivable | 6,127 | Notes payable | 746 |
| Inventory | 9,938 | Current liabilities | $ 4,931 |
| Current assets | $21,268 | | |
| | | Long-term debt | $16,050 |
| Net fixed assets | $35,277 | Owners' equity | 35,564 |
| Total assets | $56,545 | Total liab. & equity | $56,545 |

| 2011 Income Statement | | 2012 Income Statement | |
|---|---|---|---|
| Sales | $7,835.00 | Sales | $8,409.00 |
| COGS | 2,696.00 | COGS | 3,060.00 |
| Other expenses | 639.00 | Other expenses | 534.00 |
| Depreciation | 1,125.00 | Depreciation | 1,126.00 |
| EBIT | $3,375.00 | EBIT | $3,689.00 |
| Interest | 525.00 | Interest | 603.00 |
| EBT | $2,850.00 | EBT | $3,086.00 |
| Taxes | 969.00 | Taxes | 1,049.24 |
| Net income | $1,881.00 | Net income | $2,036.76 |
| | | | |
| Dividends | $ 956.00 | Dividends | $1,051.00 |
| Additions to RE | 925.00 | Additions to RE | 985.76 |

**23.** OCF = EBIT + Depreciation – Taxes
OCF = $3,689 + 1,126 – 1,049.24
OCF = $3,765.76

Change in NWC = $NWC_{end} - NWC_{beg}$ = $(CA - CL)_{end} - (CA - CL)_{beg}$
Change in NWC = ($21,268 – 4,931) – ($19,218 – 5,110)
Change in NWC = $2,229

Net capital spending = $NFA_{end} - NFA_{beg}$ + Depreciation
Net capital spending = $35,277 – 34,455 + 1,126
Net capital spending = $1,948

Cash flow from assets = OCF – Change in NWC – Net capital spending
Cash flow from assets = $3,765.76 – 2,229 – 1,948
Cash flow from assets = –$411.24

Cash flow to creditors = Interest – Net new LTD
Net new LTD = $LTD_{end} - LTD_{beg}$
Cash flow to creditors = $603 – ($16,050 – 13,460)
Cash flow to creditors = –$1,987

Net new equity = Common stock$_{end}$ – Common stock$_{beg}$
Common stock + Retained earnings = Total owners' equity
Net new equity = $(OE - RE)_{end} - (OE - RE)_{beg}$
Net new equity = $OE_{end} - OE_{beg} + RE_{beg} - RE_{end}$
$RE_{end} = RE_{beg}$ + Additions to RE
∴  Net new equity = $OE_{end} - OE_{beg} + RE_{beg} - (RE_{beg}$ + Additions to RE)
= $OE_{end} - OE_{beg}$ – Additions to RE
Net new equity = $35,564 – 35,103 – 985.76 = –$524.76

Cash flow to stockholders = Dividends – Net new equity
Cash flow to stockholders = $1,051– (–$524.76)
Cash flow to stockholders = $1,575.76

As a check, cash flow from assets is –$411.24

Cash flow from assets = Cash flow from creditors + Cash flow to stockholders
Cash flow from assets = –$1,987 + 1,575.76
Cash flow from assets = –$411.24

*Challenge*

**24.** We will begin by calculating the operating cash flow. First, we need the EBIT, which can be calculated as:

EBIT = Net income + Current taxes + Deferred taxes + Interest
EBIT = $173 + 98 + 19 + 48
EBIT = $338

Now we can calculate the operating cash flow as:

*Operating cash flow*

| | |
|---|---:|
| Earnings before interest and taxes | $338 |
| Depreciation | 94 |
| Current taxes | (98) |
| Operating cash flow | $334 |

The cash flow from assets is found in the investing activities portion of the accounting statement of cash flows, so:

*Cash flow from assets*

| | |
|---|---:|
| Acquisition of fixed assets | $215 |
| Sale of fixed assets | (23) |
| Capital spending | $192 |

The net working capital cash flows are all found in the operations cash flow section of the accounting statement of cash flows. However, instead of calculating the net working capital cash flows as the change in net working capital, we must calculate each item individually. Doing so, we find:

*Net working capital cash flow*

| | |
|---|---:|
| Cash | $14 |
| Accounts receivable | 18 |
| Inventories | (22) |
| Accounts payable | (17) |
| Accrued expenses | 9 |
| Notes payable | (6) |
| Other | (3) |
| NWC cash flow | ($ 7) |

Except for the interest expense and notes payable, the cash flow to creditors is found in the financing activities of the accounting statement of cash flows. The interest expense from the income statement is given, so:

*Cash flow to creditors*

| | |
|---|---|
| Interest | $ 48 |
| Retirement of debt | 162 |
| Debt service | $210 |
| Proceeds from sale of long-term debt | (116) |
| Total | $ 94 |

And we can find the cash flow to stockholders in the financing section of the accounting statement of cash flows. The cash flow to stockholders was:

*Cash flow to stockholders*

| | |
|---|---|
| Dividends | $ 86 |
| Repurchase of stock | 13 |
| Cash to stockholders | $ 99 |
| Proceeds from new stock issue | (44) |
| Total | $ 55 |

**25.** Net capital spending
$$= NFA_{end} - NFA_{beg} + Depreciation$$
$$= (NFA_{end} - NFA_{beg}) + (Depreciation + AD_{beg}) - AD_{beg}$$
$$= (NFA_{end} - NFA_{beg}) + AD_{end} - AD_{beg}$$
$$= (NFA_{end} + AD_{end}) - (NFA_{beg} + AD_{beg}) = FA_{end} - FA_{beg}$$

**26.** *a.* The tax bubble causes average tax rates to catch up to marginal tax rates, thus eliminating the tax advantage of low marginal rates for high income corporations.

   *b.* Assuming a taxable income of $335,000, the taxes will be:

Taxes = 0.15($50K) + 0.25($25K) + 0.34($25K) + 0.39($235K) = $113.9K

Average tax rate = $113.9K / $335K = 34%

The marginal tax rate on the next dollar of income is 34 percent.

For corporate taxable income levels of $335K to $10M, average tax rates are equal to marginal tax rates.

Taxes = 0.34($10M) + 0.35($5M) + 0.38($3.333M) = $6,416,667

Average tax rate = $6,416,667 / $18,333,334 = 35%

The marginal tax rate on the next dollar of income is 35 percent. For corporate taxable income levels over $18,333,334, average tax rates are again equal to marginal tax rates.

c.  Taxes      = 0.34($200K) = $68K = 0.15($50K) + 0.25($25K) + 0.34($25K) + X($100K);
    X($100K) = $68K − 22.25K = $45.75K
    X           = $45.75K / $100K
    X           = 45.75%

# CHAPTER 3
# LONG-TERM FINANCIAL PLANNING AND GROWTH

## Answers to Concepts Review and Critical Thinking Questions

1.  Time trend analysis gives a picture of changes in the company's financial situation over time. Comparing a firm to itself over time allows the financial manager to evaluate whether some aspects of the firm's operations, finances, or investment activities have changed. Peer group analysis involves comparing the financial ratios and operating performance of a particular firm to a set of peer group firms in the same industry or line of business. Comparing a firm to its peers allows the financial manager to evaluate whether some aspects of the firm's operations, finances, or investment activities are out of line with the norm, thereby providing some guidance on appropriate actions to take to adjust these ratios if appropriate. Both allow an investigation into what is different about a company from a financial perspective, but neither method gives an indication of whether the difference is positive or negative. For example, suppose a company's current ratio is increasing over time. It could mean that the company had been facing liquidity problems in the past and is rectifying those problems, or it could mean the company has become less efficient in managing its current accounts. Similar arguments could be made for a peer group comparison. A company with a current ratio lower than its peers could be more efficient at managing its current accounts, or it could be facing liquidity problems. Neither analysis method tells us whether a ratio is good or bad, both simply show that something is different, and tells us where to look.

2.  If a company is growing by opening new stores, then presumably total revenues would be rising. Comparing total sales at two different points in time might be misleading. Same-store sales control for this by only looking at revenues of stores open within a specific period.

3.  The reason is that, ultimately, sales are the driving force behind a business. A firm's assets, employees, and, in fact, just about every aspect of its operations and financing exist to directly or indirectly support sales. Put differently, a firm's future need for things like capital assets, employees, inventory, and financing are determined by its future sales level.

4.  Two assumptions of the sustainable growth formula are that the company does not want to sell new equity, and that financial policy is fixed. If the company raises outside equity, or increases its debt-equity ratio, it can grow at a higher rate than the sustainable growth rate. Of course, the company could also grow faster than its profit margin increases, if it changes its dividend policy by increasing the retention ratio, or its total asset turnover increases.

5. The sustainable growth rate is greater than 20 percent, because at a 20 percent growth rate the negative EFN indicates that there is excess financing still available. If the firm is 100 percent equity financed, then the sustainable and internal growth rates are equal and the internal growth rate would be greater than 20 percent. However, when the firm has some debt, the internal growth rate is always less than the sustainable growth rate, so it is ambiguous whether the internal growth rate would be greater than or less than 20 percent. If the retention ratio is increased, the firm will have more internal funding sources available, and it will have to take on more debt to keep the debt/equity ratio constant, so the EFN will decline. Conversely, if the retention ratio is decreased, the EFN will rise. If the retention rate is zero, both the internal and sustainable growth rates are zero, and the EFN will rise to the change in total assets.

6. Common-size financial statements provide the financial manager with a ratio analysis of the company. The common-size income statement can show, for example, that cost of goods sold as a percentage of sales is increasing. The common-size balance sheet can show a firm's increasing reliance on debt as a form of financing. Common-size statements of cash flows are not calculated for a simple reason: There is no possible denominator.

7. It would reduce the external funds needed. If the company is not operating at full capacity, it would be able to increase sales without a commensurate increase in fixed assets.

8. ROE is a better measure of the company's performance. ROE shows the percentage return for the year earned on shareholder investment. Since the goal of a company is to maximize shareholder wealth, this ratio shows the company's performance in achieving this goal over the period.

9. The EBITD/Assets ratio shows the company's operating performance before interest, taxes, and depreciation. This ratio would show how a company has controlled costs. While taxes are a cost, and depreciation and amortization can be considered costs, they are not as easily controlled by company management. Conversely, depreciation and amortization can be altered by accounting choices. This ratio only uses costs directly related to operations in the numerator. As such, it gives a better metric to measure management performance over a period than does ROA.

10. Long-term liabilities and equity are investments made by investors in the company, either in the form of a loan or ownership. Return on investment is intended to measure the return the company earned from these investments. Return on investment will be higher than the return on assets for a company with current liabilities. To see this, realize that total assets must equal total debt and equity, and total debt and equity is equal to current liabilities plus long-term liabilities plus equity. So, return on investment could be calculated as net income divided by total assets minus current liabilities.

11. Presumably not, but, of course, if the product had been *much* less popular, then a similar fate would have awaited due to lack of sales.

12. Since customers did not pay until shipment, receivables rose. The firm's NWC, but not its cash, increased. At the same time, costs were rising faster than cash revenues, so operating cash flow declined. The firm's capital spending was also rising. Thus, all three components of cash flow from assets were negatively impacted.

13. Financing possibly could have been arranged if the company had taken quick enough action. Sometimes it becomes apparent that help is needed only when it is too late, again emphasizing the need for planning.

14. All three were important, but the lack of cash or, more generally, financial resources, ultimately spelled doom. An inadequate cash resource is usually cited as the most common cause of small business failure.

15. Demanding cash upfront, increasing prices, subcontracting production, and improving financial resources via new owners or new sources of credit are some of the options. When orders exceed capacity, price increases may be especially beneficial.

## Solutions to Questions and Problems

*NOTE: All end-of-chapter problems were solved using a spreadsheet. Many problems require multiple steps. Due to space and readability constraints, when these intermediate steps are included in this solutions manual, rounding may appear to have occurred. However, the final answer for each problem is found without rounding during any step in the problem.*

### *Basic*

1. ROE = (PM)(TAT)(EM)
   ROE = (.043)(1.75)(1.55) = .1166 or 11.66%

2. The equity multiplier is:

   EM = 1 + D/E
   EM = 1 + 0.80 = 1.80

   One formula to calculate return on equity is:

   ROE = (ROA)(EM)
   ROE = 0.097(1.80) = .1746 or 17.46%

   ROE can also be calculated as:

   ROE = NI / TE

   So, net income is:

   NI = ROE(TE)
   NI = (.1746)($735,000) = $128,331

3. This is a multi-step problem involving several ratios. The ratios given are all part of the Du Pont Identity. The only Du Pont Identity ratio not given is the profit margin. If we know the profit margin, we can find the net income since sales are given.  So, we begin with the Du Pont Identity:

   ROE = 0.15 = (PM)(TAT)(EM) = (PM)(S / TA)(1 + D/E)

   Solving the Du Pont Identity for profit margin, we get:

   PM = [(ROE)(TA)] / [(1 + D/E)(S)]
   PM = [(0.15)($1,310)] / [(1 + 1.20)( $2,700)] = .0331

Now that we have the profit margin, we can use this number and the given sales figure to solve for net income:

PM = .0331 = NI / S
NI = .0331($2,700) = $89.32

4.  An increase of sales to $42,300 is an increase of:

Sales increase = ($42,300 – 37,300) / $37,300
Sales increase = .134 or 13.40%

Assuming costs and assets increase proportionally, the pro forma financial statements will look like this:

<u>Pro forma income statement</u>

| Sales | $42,300.00 |
|---|---|
| Costs | 29,258.45 |
| EBIT | 13,041.55 |
| Taxes (34%) | 4,434.13 |
| Net income | $ 8,607.43 |

<u>Pro forma balance sheet</u>

| Assets | $ 144,024.13 | Debt | $ 30,500.00 |
|---|---|---|---|
|  |  | Equity | 102,272.31 |
| Total | $ 144,024.13 | Total | $132,772.31 |

The payout ratio is constant, so the dividends paid this year is the payout ratio from last year times net income, or:

Dividends = ($2,500 / $7,590)($8,607.43)
Dividends = $2,835.12

The addition to retained earnings is:

Addition to retained earnings = $8,607.43 – 2,835.12
Addition to retained earnings = $5,772.31

And the new equity balance is:

Equity = $96,500 + 5,772.31
Equity = $102,272.31

So the EFN is:

EFN = Total assets – Total liabilities and equity
EFN = $144,024.13 – 132,772.31
EFN = $11,251.82

5. The maximum percentage sales increase without issuing new equity is the sustainable growth rate. To calculate the sustainable growth rate, we first need to calculate the ROE, which is:

ROE = NI / TE
ROE = $9,702 / $81,000
ROE = .1198

The plowback ratio, $b$, is one minus the payout ratio, so:

$b = 1 - .30$
$b = .70$

Now we can use the sustainable growth rate equation to get:

Sustainable growth rate = (ROE × b) / [1 − (ROE × b)]
Sustainable growth rate = [.1198(.70)] / [1 − .1198(.70)]
Sustainable growth rate = .0915 or 9.15%

So, the maximum dollar increase in sales is:

Maximum increase in sales = $54,000(.0915)
Maximum increase in sales = $4,941.96

6. We need to calculate the retention ratio to calculate the sustainable growth rate. The retention ratio is:

$b = 1 - .20$
$b = .80$

Now we can use the sustainable growth rate equation to get:

Sustainable growth rate = (ROE × $b$) / [1 − (ROE × $b$)]
Sustainable growth rate = [.13(.80)] / [1 − .13(.80)]
Sustainable growth rate = .1161 or 11.61%

7. We must first calculate the ROE using the Du Pont ratio to calculate the sustainable growth rate. The ROE is:

ROE = (PM)(TAT)(EM)
ROE = (.074)(2.20)(1.40)
ROE = .2279 or 22.79%

The plowback ratio is one minus the dividend payout ratio, so:

$b = 1 - .40$
$b = .60$

Now, we can use the sustainable growth rate equation to get:

Sustainable growth rate = (ROE × b) / [1 − (ROE × b)]
Sustainable growth rate = [.2279(.60)] / [1 − .2279(.60)]
Sustainable growth rate = .1584 or 15.84%

**8.** An increase of sales to $7,280 is an increase of:

Sales increase = ($7,280 − 6,500) / $6,500
Sales increase = .12 or 12%

Assuming costs and assets increase proportionally, the pro forma financial statements will look like this:

| Pro forma income statement | | | Pro forma balance sheet | | | |
|---|---|---|---|---|---|---|
| Sales | $ | 7,280 | Assets | $ 19,488 | Debt | $ 8,400 |
| Costs | | 5,958 | | | Equity | 10,322 |
| Net income | $ | 1,322 | Total | $ 19,488 | Total | $ 18,722 |

If no dividends are paid, the equity account will increase by the net income, so:

Equity = $9,000 + 1,322
Equity = $10,322

So the EFN is:

EFN = Total assets − Total liabilities and equity
EFN = $19,488 − 18,722 = $766

**9.** *a.* First, we need to calculate the current sales and change in sales. The current sales are next year's sales divided by one plus the growth rate, so:

Current sales = Next year's sales / (1 + g)
Current sales = $420,000,000 / (1 + .10)
Current sales = $381,818,182

And the change in sales is:

Change in sales = $420,000,000 − 381,818,182
Change in sales = $38,181,818

We can now complete the current balance sheet. The current assets, fixed assets, and short-term debt are calculated as a percentage of current sales. The long-term debt and par value of stock are given. The plug variable is the additions to retained earnings. So:

| Assets | | Liabilities and equity | |
|---|---|---|---|
| Current assets | $ 76,363,636 | Short-term debt | $ 57,272,727 |
| | | Long-term debt | $120,000,000 |
| Fixed assets | 286,363,636 | Common stock | $ 48,000,000 |
| | | Accumulated retained earnings | 137,454,545 |
| | | Total equity | $185,454,545 |
| Total assets | $362,727,273 | Total liabilities and equity | $362,727,273 |

b.  We can use the equation from the text to answer this question. The assets/sales and debt/sales are the percentages given in the problem, so:

$$EFN = \left(\frac{Assets}{Sales}\right) \times \Delta Sales - \left(\frac{Debt}{Sales}\right) \times \Delta Sales - (PM \times Projected\ sales) \times (1-d)$$

$EFN = (.20 + .75) \times \$38,181,818 - (.15 \times \$38,181,818) - [(.09 \times \$420,000,000) \times (1 - .30)]$

$EFN = \$4,085,455$

c.  The current assets, fixed assets, and short-term debt will all increase at the same percentage as sales. The long-term debt and common stock will remain constant. The accumulated retained earnings will increase by the addition to retained earnings for the year. We can calculate the addition to retained earnings for the year as:

Net income = Profit margin × Sales
Net income = .09($420,000,000)
Net income = $37,800,000

The addition to retained earnings for the year will be the net income times one minus the dividend payout ratio, which is:

Addition to retained earnings = Net income$(1 - d)$
Addition to retained earnings = $37,800,000$(1 - .30)$
Addition to retained earnings = $26,460,000

So, the new accumulated retained earnings will be:

Accumulated retained earnings = $137,454,545 + 26,460,000
Accumulated retained earnings = $163,914,545

The pro forma balance sheet will be:

| Assets | | Liabilities and equity | |
|---|---|---|---|
| Current assets | $ 84,000,000 | Short-term debt | $ 63,000,000 |
| | | Long-term debt | $120,000,000 |
| Fixed assets | $315,000,000 | Common stock | $ 48,000,000 |
| | | Accumulated retained earnings | 163,914,545 |
| | | Total equity | $211,914,545 |
| Total assets | $399,000,000 | Total liabilities and equity | $394,914,545 |

The EFN is:

EFN = Total assets – Total liabilities and equity
EFN = $399,000,000 – 394,914,545
EFN = $4,085,455

**10.** *a.* The sustainable growth is:

$$\text{Sustainable growth rate} = \frac{\text{ROE} \times b}{1 - \text{ROE} \times b}$$

where:

$b$ = Retention ratio = 1 – Payout ratio = .60

So:

$$\text{Sustainable growth rate} = \frac{.131 \times .60}{1 - .131 \times .60}$$

Sustainable growth rate = .0853 or 8.53%

*b.* It is possible for the sustainable growth rate and the actual growth rate to differ. If any of the actual parameters in the sustainable growth rate equation differs from those used to compute the sustainable growth rate, the actual growth rate will differ from the sustainable growth rate. Since the sustainable growth rate includes ROE in the calculation, this also implies that changes in the profit margin, total asset turnover, or equity multiplier will affect the sustainable growth rate.

*c.* The company can increase its growth rate by doing any of the following:

- Increase the debt-to-equity ratio by selling more debt or repurchasing stock.
- Increase the profit margin, most likely by better controlling costs.
- Decrease its total assets/sales ratio; in other words, utilize its assets more efficiently.
- Reduce the dividend payout ratio.

*Intermediate*

11. The solution requires substituting two ratios into a third ratio. Rearranging D/TA:

| Firm A | Firm B |
|---|---|
| D / TA = .35 | D / TA = .55 |
| (TA – E) / TA = .35 | (TA – E) / TA = .55 |
| (TA / TA) – (E / TA) = .35 | (TA / TA) – (E / TA) = .55 |
| 1 – (E / TA) = .35 | 1 – (E / TA) = .55 |
| E / TA = .65 | E / TA = .45 |
| E = .65(TA) | E = .45(TA) |

Rearranging ROA, we find:

| | |
|---|---|
| NI / TA = .09 | NI / TA = .07 |
| NI = .09(TA) | NI = .07(TA) |

Since ROE = NI / E, we can substitute the above equations into the ROE formula, which yields:

ROE = .09(TA) / .65(TA) = .09/.65 = 13.85%     ROE = .07(TA) / .45 (TA) = .07/.45 = 15.56%

12. PM = NI / S = –£37,543 / £345,182 = –.1088 or 10.88%

As long as both net income and sales are measured in the same currency, there is no problem; in fact, except for some market value ratios like EPS and BVPS, none of the financial ratios discussed in the text are measured in terms of currency. This is one reason why financial ratio analysis is widely used in international finance to compare the business operations of firms and/or divisions across national economic borders. The net income in dollars is:

NI = PM × Sales
NI = –0.1088($559,725) = –$60,877.32

13. *a.* The equation for external funds needed is:

$$EFN = \left( \frac{Assets}{Sales} \right) \times \Delta Sales - \left( \frac{Debt}{Sales} \right) \times \Delta Sales - (PM \times Projected\ sales) \times (1 - d)$$

where:

Assets/Sales = $24,800,000/$30,400,000 = 0.82
ΔSales = Current sales × Sales growth rate = $30,400,000(.15) = $4,560,000
Debt/Sales = $6,400,000/$30,400,000 = .2105
PM = Net income/Sales = $2,392,000/$30,400,000 = .0787
Projected sales = Current sales × (1 + Sales growth rate) = $30,400,000(1 + .15) = $34,960,000
*d* = Dividends/Net income = $956,800/$2,392,000 = .40

so:

EFN = (.82 × $4,560,000) – (.2105 × $4,560,000) – (.0787 × $34,960,000) × (1 – .40)
EFN = $1,109,520

b. The current assets, fixed assets, and short-term debt will all increase at the same percentage as sales. The long-term debt and common stock will remain constant. The accumulated retained earnings will increase by the addition to retained earnings for the year. We can calculate the addition to retained earnings for the year as:

Net income = Profit margin × Sales
Net income = .0787($34,960,000)
Net income = $2,750,800

The addition to retained earnings for the year will be the net income times one minus the dividend payout ratio, which is:

Addition to retained earnings = Net income$(1 - d)$
Addition to retained earnings = $2,750,800(1 - .40)
Addition to retained earnings = $1,650,480

So, the new accumulated retained earnings will be:

Accumulated retained earnings = $10,400,000 + 1,650,480
Accumulated retained earnings = $12,050,480

The pro forma balance sheet will be:

| Assets | | Liabilities and equity | |
|---|---|---|---|
| Current assets | $ 8,280,000 | Short-term debt | $ 7,360,000 |
| | | Long-term debt | $ 4,800,000 |
| Fixed assets | 20,240,000 | Common stock | $ 3,200,000 |
| | | Accumulated retained earnings | 12,050,480 |
| | | Total equity | $16,350,800 |
| Total assets | $28,520,000 | Total liabilities and equity | $27,410,800 |

The EFN is:

EFN = Total assets – Total liabilities and equity
EFN = $28,520,000 – 27,410,800
EFN = $1,109,520

c. The sustainable growth is:

$$\text{Sustainable growth rate} = \frac{\text{ROE} \times b}{1 - \text{ROE} \times b}$$

where:

ROE = Net income/Total equity = \$2,392,000/\$13,600,000 = .1759
b = Retention ratio = Retained earnings/Net income = \$1,435,200/\$2,392,000 = .60

So:

$$\text{Sustainable growth rate} = \frac{.1759 \times .60}{1 - .1759 \times .60}$$

Sustainable growth rate = .1180 or 11.80%

d. The company cannot just cut its dividends to achieve the forecast growth rate. As shown below, even with a zero dividend policy, the EFN will still be \$9,200.

| Assets | | Liabilities and equity | |
|--------|--|------------------------|--|
| Current assets | \$ 8,280,000 | Short-term debt | \$ 7,360,000 |
| | | Long-term debt | \$ 4,800,000 |
| Fixed assets | 20,240,000 | Common stock | \$ 3,200,000 |
| | | Accumulated retained earnings | 13,150,800 |
| | | Total equity | \$16,350,800 |
| Total assets | \$28,520,000 | Total liabilities and equity | \$28,510,800 |

The EFN is:

EFN = Total assets – Total liabilities and equity
EFN = \$28,520,000 – 28,510,800
EFN = \$9,200

The company does have several alternatives. It can increase its asset utilization and/or its profit margin. The company could also increase the debt in its capital structure. This will decrease the equity account, thereby increasing ROE.

14. This is a multi-step problem involving several ratios. It is often easier to look backward to determine where to start. We need receivables turnover to find days' sales in receivables. To calculate receivables turnover, we need credit sales, and to find credit sales, we need total sales. Since we are given the profit margin and net income, we can use these to calculate total sales as:

PM = 0.093 = NI / Sales = \$265,000 / Sales; Sales = \$2,849,462

Credit sales are 80 percent of total sales, so:

Credit sales = \$2,849,462(0.80) = \$2,279,570

Now we can find receivables turnover by:

Receivables turnover = Credit sales / Accounts receivable = \$2,279,570 / \$145,300 = 15.69 times

Days' sales in receivables = 365 days / Receivables turnover = 365 / 15.69 = 23.27 days

**15.** The solution to this problem requires a number of steps. First, remember that CA + NFA = TA. So, if we find the CA and the TA, we can solve for NFA. Using the numbers given for the current ratio and the current liabilities, we solve for CA:

CR = CA / CL
CA = CR(CL) = 1.25(\$950) = \$1,187.50

To find the total assets, we must first find the total debt and equity from the information given. So, we find the net income using the profit margin:

PM = NI / Sales
NI = Profit margin × Sales = .094(\$5,780) = \$543.32

We now use the net income figure as an input into ROE to find the total equity:

ROE = NI / TE
TE = NI / ROE = \$543.32 / .182 = \$2,985.27

Next, we need to find the long-term debt. The long-term debt ratio is:

Long-term debt ratio = 0.35 = LTD / (LTD + TE)

Inverting both sides gives:

1 / 0.35 = (LTD + TE) / LTD = 1 + (TE / LTD)

Substituting the total equity into the equation and solving for long-term debt gives the following:

1 + \$2,985.27 / LTD = 2.86
LTD = \$2,985.27 / 1.86 = \$1,607.46

Now, we can find the total debt of the company:

TD = CL + LTD = \$950 + 1,607.46 = \$2,557.46

And, with the total debt, we can find the TD&E, which is equal to TA:

TA = TD + TE = \$2,557.46 + 2,985.27 = \$5,542.73

And finally, we are ready to solve the balance sheet identity as:

NFA = TA – CA = \$5,542.73 – 1,187.50 = \$4,355.23

**16.** This problem requires you to work backward through the income statement. First, recognize that Net income = $(1 - t_C)$EBT. Plugging in the numbers given and solving for EBT, we get:

EBT = $8,320 / (1 – 0.34) = $12,606.06

Now, we can add interest to EBT to get EBIT as follows:

EBIT = EBT + Interest paid = $12,606.06 + 1,940 = $14,546.06

To get EBITD (earnings before interest, taxes, and depreciation), the numerator in the cash coverage ratio, add depreciation to EBIT:

EBITD = EBIT + Depreciation = $14,546.06 + 2,730 = $17,276.06

Now, simply plug the numbers into the cash coverage ratio and calculate:

Cash coverage ratio = EBITD / Interest = $17,276.06 / $1,940 = 8.91 times

**17.** We can start by multiplying ROE by Total assets / Total assets

$$\text{ROE} = \frac{\text{Net income}}{\text{Equity}} = \frac{\text{Net income}}{\text{Equity}} \times \frac{\text{Total assets}}{\text{Total assets}}$$

Rearranging, we get:

$$\text{ROE} = \frac{\text{Net income}}{\text{Total assets}} \times \frac{\text{Total assets}}{\text{Equity}}$$

Next, we can multiply by Sales / Sales, which yields:

$$\text{ROE} = \frac{\text{Net income}}{\text{Total assets}} \times \frac{\text{Equity}}{\text{Total assets}} \times \frac{\text{Sales}}{\text{Sales}}$$

Rearranging, we get:

$$\text{ROE} = \frac{\text{Net income}}{\text{Sales}} \times \frac{\text{Sales}}{\text{Total assets}} \times \frac{\text{Total assets}}{\text{Equity}}$$

Next, we can multiply the preceding three factor Du Pont equation by EBT / EBT, which yields:

$$\text{ROE} = \frac{\text{Net income}}{\text{Sales}} \times \frac{\text{Sales}}{\text{Total assets}} \times \frac{\text{Total assets}}{\text{Equity}} \times \frac{\text{EBT}}{\text{EBT}}$$

We can rearrange as:

$$\text{ROE} = \frac{\text{Net income}}{\text{EBT}} \times \frac{\text{EBT}}{\text{Sales}} \times \frac{\text{Sales}}{\text{Total assets}} \times \frac{\text{Total assets}}{\text{Equity}}$$

Finally, multiplying this equation EBIT / EBIT and rearranging yields:

$$\text{ROE} = \frac{\text{Net income}}{\text{EBT}} \times \frac{\text{EBT}}{\text{Sales}} \times \frac{\text{Sales}}{\text{Total assets}} \times \frac{\text{Total assets}}{\text{Equity}} \times \frac{\text{EBIT}}{\text{EBIT}}$$

$$ROE = \underbrace{\frac{\text{Net income}}{\text{EBT}}}_{(1)} \times \underbrace{\frac{\text{EBT}}{\text{EBIT}}}_{(2)} \times \underbrace{\frac{\text{EBIT}}{\text{Sales}}}_{(3)} \times \underbrace{\frac{\text{Sales}}{\text{Total assets}}}_{(4)} \times \underbrace{\frac{\text{Total assets}}{\text{Equity}}}_{(5)}$$

The interpretation of each term is as follows:

(1) This is the company's tax burden. This is the proportion of the company's profits retained after paying income taxes.
(2) This is the company's interest burden. It will be 1.00 for a company with no debt or financial leverage
(3) This is the company's operating profit margin. It is the operating profit before interest and taxes per dollar of sales.
(4) This is the company's operating efficiency as measured by dollar of sales per dollar of total assets.
(5) This is the company's financial leverage as measured by the equity multiplier.

**18.**

| | 2011 | Common size | 2012 | Common size | Common base year |
|---|---|---|---|---|---|
| **Assets** | | | | | |
| Current assets | | | | | |
| Cash | $ 8,014 | 2.86% | $ 9,954 | 3.13% | 1.2421 |
| Accounts receivable | 20,453 | 7.29% | 22,937 | 7.21% | 1.1214 |
| Inventory | 36,822 | 13.12% | 41,797 | 13.14% | 1.1351 |
| Total | $ 65,289 | 23.26% | $ 74,688 | 23.48% | 1.1440 |
| Fixed assets | | | | | |
| Net plant and equipment | 215,370 | 76.74% | 243,340 | 76.52% | 1.1299 |
| Total assets | $280,659 | 100% | $318,028 | 100% | 1.1331 |
| | | | | | |
| **Liabilities and Owners' Equity** | | | | | |
| Current liabilities | | | | | |
| Accounts payable | $ 40,898 | 14.57% | $ 45,884 | 14.43% | 1.1219 |
| Notes payable | 17,464 | 6.22% | 17,035 | 5.36% | 0.9754 |
| Total | $ 58,362 | 20.79% | $ 62,919 | 19.78% | 1.0781 |
| Long-term debt | 24,000 | 8.55% | 31,000 | 9.75% | 1.2917 |
| Owners' equity | | | | | |
| Common stock and paid-in surplus | $ 38,000 | 13.54% | $ 39,200 | 12.33% | 1.0316 |
| Accumulated retained earnings | 160,297 | 57.11% | 184,909 | 58.14% | 1.1535 |
| Total | $198,297 | 70.65% | $224,109 | 70.47% | 1.1302 |
| Total liabilities and owners' equity | $280,659 | 100% | $318,028 | 100% | 1.1331 |

The common-size balance sheet answers are found by dividing each category by total assets. For example, the cash percentage for 2011 is:

$8,014 / $280,659 = .0286 or 2.86%

This means that cash is 2.86% of total assets.

The common-base year answers for Question 18 are found by dividing each category value for 2012 by the same category value for 2011. For example, the cash common-base year number is found by:

$9,954 / $8,014 = 1.2421$

This means the cash balance in 2012 is 1.2421 times as large as the cash balance in 2011.

19. To determine full capacity sales, we divide the current sales by the capacity the company is currently using, so:

Full capacity sales = $725,000 / .90
Full capacity sales = $805,556

So, the dollar growth rate in sales is:

Sales growth = $805,556 – 725,000
Sales growth = $80,556

20. To find the new level of fixed assets, we need to find the current percentage of fixed assets to full capacity sales. Doing so, we find:

Fixed assets / Full capacity sales = $690,000 / $805,556
Fixed assets / Full capacity sales = .8566

Next, we calculate the total dollar amount of fixed assets needed at the new sales figure.

Total fixed assets = .8566($830,000)
Total fixed assets = $710,938

The new fixed assets necessary is the total fixed assets at the new sales figure minus the current level of fixed assets.

New fixed assets = $710,938 – 690,000
New fixed assets = $20,938

21. Assuming costs vary with sales and a 20 percent increase in sales, the pro forma income statement will look like this:

### MOOSE TOURS INC.
#### Pro Forma Income Statement

| | |
|---|---:|
| Sales | $ 1,003,320 |
| Costs | 780,840 |
| Other expenses | 20,520 |
| EBIT | $   201,960 |
| Interest | 12,600 |
| Taxable income | $   189,360 |
| Taxes(35%) | 66,276 |
| Net income | $   123,084 |

The payout ratio is constant, so the dividends paid this year is the payout ratio from last year times net income, or:

Dividends = ($30,300/$101,205)($123,084)
Dividends = $36,850

And the addition to retained earnings will be:

Addition to retained earnings = $123,084 – 36,850
Addition to retained earnings = $86,234

The new retained earnings on the pro forma balance sheet will be:

New retained earnings = $176,855 + 86,234
New retained earnings = $263,089

The pro forma balance sheet will look like this:

**MOOSE TOURS INC.**
Pro Forma Balance Sheet

| Assets | | | Liabilities and Owners' Equity | | |
|---|---|---|---|---|---|
| Current assets | | | Current liabilities | | |
| Cash | $ | 28,842 | Accounts payable | $ | 77,520 |
| Accounts receivable | | 46,398 | Notes payable | | 16,150 |
| Inventory | | 99,066 | Total | $ | 93,670 |
| Total | $ | 174,306 | Long-term debt | | 150,000 |
| Fixed assets | | | | | |
| Net plant and | | | Owners' equity | | |
| equipment | | 470,820 | Common stock and | | |
| | | | paid-in surplus | $ | 130,000 |
| | | | Retained earnings | | 263,089 |
| | | | Total | $ | 393,089 |
| | | | Total liabilities and owners' | | |
| Total assets | $ | 645,126 | equity | $ | 636,759 |

So the EFN is:

EFN = Total assets – Total liabilities and equity
EFN = $645,126 – 636,759
EFN = $8,367

22. First, we need to calculate full capacity sales, which is:

Full capacity sales = $836,100 / .80
Full capacity sales = $1,045,125

The full capacity ratio at full capacity sales is:

Full capacity ratio = Fixed assets / Full capacity sales
Full capacity ratio = \$392,350 / \$1,045,125
Full capacity ratio = .37541

The fixed assets required at full capacity sales is the full capacity ratio times the projected sales level:

Total fixed assets = .37541(\$1,003,320) = \$376,656

So, EFN is:

EFN = (\$174,306 + 376,656) − \$636,759 = −\$85,797

Note that this solution assumes that fixed assets are decreased (sold) so the company has a 100 percent fixed asset utilization. If we assume fixed assets are not sold, the answer becomes:

EFN = (\$174,306 + 392,350) − \$636,759 = −\$70,103

23. The D/E ratio of the company is:

D/E = (\$80,750 + 150,000) / \$306,855
D/E = .75198

So the new total debt amount will be:

New total debt = .75198(\$393,089)
New total debt = \$295,596

This is the new total debt for the company. Given that our calculation for EFN is the amount that must be raised externally and does not increase spontaneously with sales, we need to subtract the spontaneous increase in accounts payable. The new level of accounts payable will be the current accounts payable times the sales growth, or:

Spontaneous increase in accounts payable = \$64,600(.20)
Spontaneous increase in accounts payable = \$12,920

This means that \$12,920 of the new total debt is not raised externally. So, the debt raised externally, which will be the EFN is:

EFN = New total debt − (Beginning LTD + Beginning CL + Spontaneous increase in AP)
EFN = \$295,596 − (\$150,000 + 80,750 + 12,920) = \$51,926

The pro forma balance sheet with the new long-term debt will be:

MOOSE TOURS INC.
Pro Forma Balance Sheet

| Assets | | | Liabilities and Owners' Equity | | |
|---|---|---|---|---|---|
| **Current assets** | | | **Current liabilities** | | |
| Cash | $ | 28,842 | Accounts payable | $ | 77,520 |
| Accounts receivable | | 46,398 | Notes payable | | 16,150 |
| Inventory | | 99,066 | Total | $ | 93,670 |
| Total | $ | 174,306 | Long-term debt | | 201,926 |
| **Fixed assets** | | | | | |
| Net plant and equipment | | 470,820 | **Owners' equity** | | |
| | | | Common stock and paid-in surplus | $ | 130,000 |
| | | | Retained earnings | | 263,089 |
| | | | Total | $ | 393,089 |
| | | | Total liabilities and owners' | | |
| Total assets | $ | 645,126 | equity | $ | 688,685 |

The funds raised by the debt issue can be put into an excess cash account to make the balance sheet balance. The excess debt will be:

Excess debt = $645,126 – 688,685 = $43,559

To make the balance sheet balance, the company will have to increase its assets. We will put this amount in an account called excess cash, which will give us the following balance sheet:

MOOSE TOURS INC.
Pro Forma Balance Sheet

| Assets | | | Liabilities and Owners' Equity | | |
|---|---|---|---|---|---|
| **Current assets** | | | **Current liabilities** | | |
| Cash | $ | 28,842 | Accounts payable | $ | 77,520 |
| Excess cash | | 43,559 | | | |
| Accounts receivable | | 46,398 | Notes payable | | 16,150 |
| Inventory | | 99,066 | Total | $ | 93,670 |
| Total | $ | 217,865 | Long-term debt | | 201,926 |
| **Fixed assets** | | | | | |
| Net plant and equipment | | 470,820 | **Owners' equity** | | |
| | | | Common stock and paid-in surplus | $ | 130,000 |
| | | | Retained earnings | | 263,089 |
| | | | Total | $ | 393,089 |
| | | | Total liabilities and owners' | | |
| Total assets | $ | 688,685 | equity | $ | 688,685 |

The excess cash has an opportunity cost that we discussed earlier. Increasing fixed assets would also not be a good idea since the company already has enough fixed assets. A likely scenario would be the repurchase of debt and equity in its current capital structure weights. The company's debt-assets and equity-assets are:

Debt-assets = .75198 / (1 + .75198) = .43
Equity-assets = 1 / (1 + .75198) = .57

So, the amount of debt and equity needed will be:

Total debt needed = .43($645,126) = $276,900
Equity needed = .57($645,126) = $368,226

So, the repurchases of debt and equity will be:

Debt repurchase = ($93,670 + 201,926) – 276,900 = $18,696
Equity repurchase = $393,089 – 368,226 = $24,863

Assuming all of the debt repurchase is from long-term debt, and the equity repurchase is entirely from the retained earnings, the final pro forma balance sheet will be:

## MOOSE TOURS INC.
### Pro Forma Balance Sheet

| Assets | | | Liabilities and Owners' Equity | | |
|---|---|---|---|---|---|
| Current assets | | | Current liabilities | | |
| Cash | $ | 28,842 | Accounts payable | $ | 77,520 |
| Accounts receivable | | 46,398 | Notes payable | | 16,150 |
| Inventory | | 99,066 | Total | $ | 93,670 |
| Total | $ | 174,306 | Long-term debt | | 183,230 |
| Fixed assets | | | | | |
| Net plant and equipment | | 470,820 | Owners' equity | | |
| | | | Common stock and paid-in surplus | $ | 130,000 |
| | | | Retained earnings | | 238,226 |
| | | | Total | $ | 368,226 |
| | | | Total liabilities and owners' | | |
| Total assets | $ | 645,126 | equity | $ | 645,126 |

*Challenge*

24. The pro forma income statements for all three growth rates will be:

### MOOSE TOURS INC.
### Pro Forma Income Statement

|  | 15 % Sales Growth | 20% Sales Growth | 25% Sales Growth |
|---|---|---|---|
| Sales | $961,515 | $1,003,320 | $1,045,125 |
| Costs | 748,305 | 780,840 | 813,375 |
| Other expenses | 19,665 | 20,520 | 21,375 |
| EBIT | $193,545 | $ 201,960 | $ 210,375 |
| Interest | 12,600 | 12,600 | 12,600 |
| Taxable income | $180,945 | $ 189,360 | $ 197,775 |
| Taxes (35%) | 63,331 | 66,276 | 69,221 |
| Net income | $117,614 | $ 123,084 | $ 128,554 |
|  |  |  |  |
| Dividends | $ 35,213 | $ 36,850 | $ 38,488 |
| Add to RE | 82,401 | 86,234 | 90,066 |

We will calculate the EFN for the 15 percent growth rate first. Assuming the payout ratio is constant, the dividends paid will be:

Dividends = ($30,300/$936,100)($117,614)
Dividends = $35,213

And the addition to retained earnings will be:

Addition to retained earnings = $117,614 – 35,213
Addition to retained earnings = $82,401
The new retained earnings on the pro forma balance sheet will be:

New retained earnings = $176,855 + 82,401
New retained earnings = $259,256

The pro forma balance sheet will look like this:

*15% Sales Growth*:

MOOSE TOURS INC.
Pro Forma Balance Sheet

| Assets | | | Liabilities and Owners' Equity | | |
|---|---|---|---|---|---|
| Current assets | | | Current liabilities | | |
| Cash | $ | 27,640 | Accounts payable | $ | 74,290 |
| Accounts receivable | | 44,465 | Notes payable | | 16,150 |
| Inventory | | 94,938 | Total | $ | 90,440 |
| Total | $ | 167,043 | Long-term debt | $ | 150,000 |
| Fixed assets | | | | | |
| Net plant and equipment | | 451,203 | Owners' equity | | |
| | | | Common stock and paid-in surplus | $ | 130,000 |
| | | | Retained earnings | | 259,256 |
| | | | Total | $ | 389,256 |
| | | | Total liabilities and owners' | | |
| Total assets | $ | 618,246 | equity | $ | 629,696 |

So the EFN is:

EFN = Total assets – Total liabilities and equity
EFN = $618,246 – 629,696
EFN = –$11,451

At a 20 percent growth rate, and assuming the payout ratio is constant, the dividends paid will be:

Dividends = ($30,300/$101,205)($123,084)
Dividends = $36,850

And the addition to retained earnings will be:

Addition to retained earnings = $123,084 – 36,850
Addition to retained earnings = $86,234

The new retained earnings on the pro forma balance sheet will be:

New retained earnings = $176,855 + 86,234
New retained earnings = $263,089

The pro forma balance sheet will look like this:

*20% Sales Growth*:

**MOOSE TOURS INC.**
Pro Forma Balance Sheet

| Assets | | | Liabilities and Owners' Equity | | |
|---|---|---:|---|---|---:|
| Current assets | | | Current liabilities | | |
| Cash | $ | 28,842 | Accounts payable | $ | 77,520 |
| Accounts receivable | | 46,398 | Notes payable | | 16,150 |
| Inventory | | 99,066 | Total | $ | 93,670 |
| Total | $ | 174,306 | Long-term debt | | 150,000 |
| Fixed assets | | | | | |
| Net plant and | | | Owners' equity | | |
| equipment | | 470,820 | Common stock and | | |
| | | | paid-in surplus | $ | 130,000 |
| | | | Retained earnings | | 263,089 |
| | | | Total | $ | 393,089 |
| | | | Total liabilities and owners' | | |
| Total assets | $ | 645,126 | equity | $ | 636,759 |

So the EFN is:

EFN = Total assets – Total liabilities and equity
EFN = $645,126 – 636,759
EFN = $8,367

At a 25 percent growth rate, and assuming the payout ratio is constant, the dividends paid will be:

Dividends = ($30,300/$101,205)($128,554)
Dividends = $38,488

And the addition to retained earnings will be:

Addition to retained earnings = $128,554 – 38,488
Addition to retained earnings = $90,066

The new retained earnings on the pro forma balance sheet will be:

New retained earnings = $176,855 + 90,066
New retained earnings = $266,921

The pro forma balance sheet will look like this:

*25% Sales Growth*:

### MOOSE TOURS INC.
### Pro Forma Balance Sheet

| Assets | | | Liabilities and Owners' Equity | | |
|---|---|---|---|---|---|
| **Current assets** | | | **Current liabilities** | | |
| Cash | $ | 30,044 | Accounts payable | $ | 80,750 |
| Accounts receivable | | 48,331 | Notes payable | | 16,150 |
| Inventory | | 103,194 | Total | $ | 96,900 |
| Total | $ | 181,569 | Long-term debt | $ | 150,000 |
| **Fixed assets** | | | | | |
| Net plant and equipment | | 490,438 | **Owners' equity** | | |
| | | | Common stock and paid-in surplus | $ | 130,000 |
| | | | Retained earnings | | 266,921 |
| | | | Total | $ | 396,921 |
| | | | Total liabilities and owners' | | |
| Total assets | $ | 672,006 | equity | $ | 643,821 |

So the EFN is:

EFN = Total assets – Total liabilities and equity
EFN = $672,006 – 643,821
EFN = $28,186

**25.** The pro forma income statements for all three growth rates will be:

### MOOSE TOURS INC.
### Pro Forma Income Statement

| | 20% Sales Growth | 30% Sales Growth | 35% Sales Growth |
|---|---|---|---|
| Sales | $1,003,320 | $1,086,930 | $1,128,735 |
| Costs | 780,840 | 845,910 | 878,445 |
| Other expenses | 20,520 | 22,230 | 23,085 |
| EBIT | $ 201,960 | $ 218,790 | $ 227,205 |
| Interest | 12,600 | 12,600 | 12,600 |
| Taxable income | $ 189,360 | $ 206,190 | $ 214,605 |
| Taxes (35%) | 66,276 | 72,167 | 75,112 |
| Net income | $ 123,084 | $ 134,024 | $ 139,493 |
| | | | |
| Dividends | $ 36,850 | $ 40,126 | $ 41,763 |
| Add to RE | 86,234 | 93,898 | 97,730 |

At a 30 percent growth rate, and assuming the payout ratio is constant, the dividends paid will be:

Dividends = ($30,300/$101,205)($134,024)
Dividends = $40,126

And the addition to retained earnings will be:

Addition to retained earnings = $134,024 – 40,126
Addition to retained earnings = $93,898

The new addition to retained earnings on the pro forma balance sheet will be:

New addition to retained earnings = $176,855 + 93,898
New addition to retained earnings = $270,753

The new total debt will be:

New total debt = .75198($400,753)
New total debt = $301,260

So, the new long-term debt will be the new total debt minus the new short-term debt, or:

New long-term debt = $301,260 – 100,130
New long-term debt = $201,230

The pro forma balance sheet will look like this:

*Sales growth rate = 30% and debt/equity ratio = .75198:*

MOOSE TOURS INC.
Pro Forma Balance Sheet

| Assets | | | Liabilities and Owners' Equity | | |
|---|---|---|---|---|---|
| Current assets | | | Current liabilities | | |
| Cash | $ | 31,246 | Accounts payable | $ | 83,980 |
| Accounts receivable | | 50,265 | Notes payable | | 16,150 |
| Inventory | | 107,322 | Total | $ | 100,130 |
| Total | $ | 188,832 | Long-term debt | | 201,230 |
| Fixed assets | | | | | |
| Net plant and equipment | | 510,055 | Owners' equity | | |
| | | | Common stock and paid-in surplus | $ | 130,000 |
| | | | Retained earnings | | 270,753 |
| | | | Total | $ | 400,753 |
| | | | Total liabilities and owners' | | |
| Total assets | $ | 698,887 | equity | $ | 702,133 |

So the excess debt raised is:

Excess debt = $702,133 – 698,887
Excess debt = $3,226

At a 35 percent growth rate, and assuming the payout ratio is constant, the dividends paid will be:

Dividends = ($30,300/$101,205)($139,493)
Dividends = $41,763

And the addition to retained earnings will be:

Addition to retained earnings = $139,493 – 41,763
Addition to retained earnings = $97,730

The new retained earnings on the pro forma balance sheet will be:

New retained earnings = $176,855 + 97,730
New retained earnings = $274,585

The new total debt will be:

New total debt = .75198($404,585)
New total debt = $304,241

So, the new long-term debt will be the new total debt minus the new short-term debt, or:

New long-term debt = $304,241 – 103,360
New long-term debt = $200,881

*Sales growth rate = 35% and debt/equity ratio = .75198:*

## MOOSE TOURS INC.
### Pro Forma Balance Sheet

| Assets | | | Liabilities and Owners' Equity | | |
|---|---|---|---|---|---|
| Current assets | | | Current liabilities | | |
| Cash | $ | 32,447 | Accounts payable | $ | 87,210 |
| Accounts receivable | | 52,198 | Notes payable | | 16,150 |
| Inventory | | 111,449 | Total | $ | 103,360 |
| Total | $ | 196,094 | Long-term debt | $ | 200,881 |
| Fixed assets | | | | | |
| Net plant and equipment | | 529,673 | Owners' equity | | |
| | | | Common stock and paid-in surplus | $ | 130,000 |
| | | | Retained earnings | | 274,585 |
| | | | Total | $ | 404,585 |
| | | | Total liabilities and owners' | | |
| Total assets | $ | 725,767 | equity | $ | 708,826 |

So the excess debt raised is:

Excess debt = $708,826 – 725,767
Excess debt = –$16,940

At a 35 percent growth rate, the firm will need funds in the amount of $16,940 in addition to the external debt already raised. So, the EFN will be:

EFN = $50,881 + 16,940
EFN = $67,822

26. We need the ROE to calculate the sustainable growth rate. The ROE is:

ROE = (PM)(TAT)(EM)
ROE = (.053)(1 / 0.75)(1 + 0.40)
ROE = .0989 or 9.89%

Now, we can use the sustainable growth rate equation to find the retention ratio as:

Sustainable growth rate = (ROE × $b$) / [1 − (ROE × $b$)]
Sustainable growth rate = .12 = [.0989$b$] / [1 − .0989$b$]
$b$ = 1.08

This implies the payout ratio is:

Payout ratio = 1 − $b$
Payout ratio = 1 − 1.08
Payout ratio = −0.08

This is a dividend payout ratio of negative 8 percent, which is impossible. The growth rate is not consistent with the other constraints. The lowest possible payout rate is 0, which corresponds to retention ratio of 1, or total earnings retention.

The maximum sustainable growth rate for this company is:

Maximum sustainable growth rate = (ROE × $b$) / [1 − (ROE × $b$)]
Maximum sustainable growth rate = [.0989(1)] / [1 − .0989(1)]
Maximum sustainable growth rate = .1098 or 10.98%

27. We know that EFN is:

EFN = Increase in assets − Addition to retained earnings

The increase in assets is the beginning assets times the growth rate, so:

Increase in assets = A × $g$

The addition to retained earnings next year is the current net income times the retention ratio, times one plus the growth rate, so:

Addition to retained earnings = (NI × $b$)(1 + $g$)

And rearranging the profit margin to solve for net income, we get:

NI = PM(S)

Substituting the last three equations into the EFN equation we started with and rearranging, we get:

$EFN = A(g) - PM(S)b(1 + g)$
$EFN = A(g) - PM(S)b - [PM(S)b]g$
$EFN = - PM(S)b + [A - PM(S)b]g$

28. We start with the EFN equation we derived in Problem 27 and set it equal to zero:

$EFN = 0 = - PM(S)b + [A - PM(S)b]g$

Substituting the rearranged profit margin equation into the internal growth rate equation, we have:

Internal growth rate $= [PM(S)b] / [A - PM(S)b]$

Since:

$ROA = NI / A$
$ROA = PM(S) / A$

We can substitute this into the internal growth rate equation and divide both the numerator and denominator by A. This gives:

Internal growth rate $= \{[PM(S)b] / A\} / \{[A - PM(S)b] / A\}$
Internal growth rate $= b(ROA) / [1 - b(ROA)]$

To derive the sustainable growth rate, we must realize that to maintain a constant D/E ratio with no external equity financing, EFN must equal the addition to retained earnings times the D/E ratio:

$EFN = (D/E)[PM(S)b(1 + g)]$
$EFN = A(g) - PM(S)b(1 + g)$

Solving for g and then dividing numerator and denominator by A:

Sustainable growth rate $= PM(S)b(1 + D/E) / [A - PM(S)b(1 + D/E)]$
Sustainable growth rate $= [ROA(1 + D/E)b] / [1 - ROA(1 + D/E)b]$
Sustainable growth rate $= b(ROE) / [1 - b(ROE)]$

29. In the following derivations, the subscript "E" refers to end of period numbers, and the subscript "B" refers to beginning of period numbers. TE is total equity and TA is total assets.

For the sustainable growth rate:

Sustainable growth rate $= (ROE_E \times b) / (1 - ROE_E \times b)$
Sustainable growth rate $= (NI/TE_E \times b) / (1 - NI/TE_E \times b)$

We multiply this equation by:

$(TE_E / TE_E)$

Sustainable growth rate $= (NI / TE_E \times b) / (1 - NI / TE_E \times b) \times (TE_E / TE_E)$
Sustainable growth rate $= (NI \times b) / (TE_E - NI \times b)$

Recognize that the denominator is equal to beginning of period equity, that is:

$$(TE_E - NI \times b) = TE_B$$

Substituting this into the previous equation, we get:

Sustainable rate = $(NI \times b) / TE_B$

Which is equivalent to:

Sustainable rate = $(NI / TE_B) \times b$

Since $ROE_B = NI / TE_B$

The sustainable growth rate equation is:

Sustainable growth rate = $ROE_B \times b$

For the internal growth rate:

Internal growth rate = $(ROA_E \times b) / (1 - ROA_E \times b)$
Internal growth rate = $(NI / TA_E \times b) / (1 - NI / TA_E \times b)$

We multiply this equation by:

$(TA_E / TA_E)$

Internal growth rate = $(NI / TA_E \times b) / [(1 - NI / TA_E \times b) \times (TA_E / TA_E)]$
Internal growth rate = $(NI \times b) / (TA_E - NI \times b)$

Recognize that the denominator is equal to beginning of period assets, that is:

$$(TA_E - NI \times b) = TA_B$$

Substituting this into the previous equation, we get:

Internal growth rate = $(NI \times b) / TA_B$

Which is equivalent to:

Internal growth rate = $(NI / TA_B) \times b$

Since $ROA_B = NI / TA_B$

The internal growth rate equation is:

Internal growth rate = $ROA_B \times b$

**30.** Since the company issued no new equity, shareholders' equity increased by retained earnings. Retained earnings for the year were:

Retained earnings = NI – Dividends
Retained earnings = $90,000 – 43,000
Retained earnings = $47,000

So, the equity at the end of the year was:

Ending equity = $176,000 + 47,000
Ending equity = $223,000

The ROE based on the end of period equity is:

ROE = $90,000 / $223,000
ROE = 40.36%

The plowback ratio is:

Plowback ratio = Addition to retained earnings/NI
Plowback ratio = $47,000 / $90,000
Plowback ratio = .5222 or 52.22%

Using the equation presented in the text for the sustainable growth rate, we get:

Sustainable growth rate = (ROE × b) / [1 – (ROE × b)]
Sustainable growth rate = [.4036(.5222)] / [1 – .4036(.5222)]
Sustainable growth rate = .2108 or 21.08%

The ROE based on the beginning of period equity is

ROE = $90,000 / $176,000
ROE = .5114 or 51.14%

Using the shortened equation for the sustainable growth rate and the beginning of period ROE, we get:

Sustainable growth rate = ROE × b
Sustainable growth rate = .5114 × .5222
Sustainable growth rate = .2670 or 26.70%

Using the shortened equation for the sustainable growth rate and the end of period ROE, we get:

Sustainable growth rate = ROE × b
Sustainable growth rate = .4036 × .5222
Sustainable growth rate = .2108 or 21.08%

Using the end of period ROE in the shortened sustainable growth equation results in a growth rate that is too low. This will always occur whenever the equity increases. If equity increases, the ROE based on end of period equity is lower than the ROE based on the beginning of period equity. The ROE (and sustainable growth rate) in the abbreviated equation is based on equity that did not exist when the net income was earned.

# CHAPTER 4
# DISCOUNTED CASH FLOW VALUATION

## Answers to Concepts Review and Critical Thinking Questions

1. Assuming positive cash flows and interest rates, the future value increases and the present value decreases.

2. Assuming positive cash flows and interest rates, the present value will fall and the future value will rise.

3. The better deal is the one with equal installments.

4. Yes, they should. APRs generally don't provide the relevant rate. The only advantage is that they are easier to compute, but, with modern computing equipment, that advantage is not very important.

5. A freshman does. The reason is that the freshman gets to use the money for much longer before interest starts to accrue.

6. It's a reflection of the time value of money. TMCC gets to use the $24,099 immediately. If TMCC uses it wisely, it will be worth more than $100,000 in thirty years.

7. This will probably make the security less desirable. TMCC will only repurchase the security prior to maturity if it is to its advantage, i.e. interest rates decline. Given the drop in interest rates needed to make this viable for TMCC, it is unlikely the company will repurchase the security. This is an example of a "call" feature. Such features are discussed at length in a later chapter.

8. The key considerations would be: (1) Is the rate of return implicit in the offer attractive relative to other, similar risk investments? and (2) How risky is the investment; i.e., how certain are we that we will actually get the $100,000? Thus, our answer does depend on who is making the promise to repay.

9. The Treasury security would have a somewhat higher price because the Treasury is the strongest of all borrowers.

10. The price would be higher because, as time passes, the price of the security will tend to rise toward $100,000. This rise is just a reflection of the time value of money. As time passes, the time until receipt of the $100,000 grows shorter, and the present value rises. In 2019, the price will probably be higher for the same reason. We cannot be sure, however, because interest rates could be much higher, or TMCC's financial position could deteriorate. Either event would tend to depress the security's price.

**Solutions to Questions and Problems**

*NOTE: All-end-of chapter problems were solved using a spreadsheet. Many problems require multiple steps. Due to space and readability constraints, when these intermediate steps are included in this solutions manual, rounding may appear to have occurred. However, the final answer for each problem is found without rounding during any step in the problem.*

*Basic*

1.  The time line for the cash flows is:

0                                                                                              10
$5,000                                                                                         FV

The simple interest per year is:

$5,000 × .08 = $400

So, after 10 years, you will have:

$400 × 10 = $4,000 in interest.

The total balance will be $5,000 + 4,000 = $9,000

With compound interest, we use the future value formula:

$FV = PV(1 + r)^t$
$FV = \$5,000(1.08)^{10} = \$10,794.62$

The difference is:

$10,794.62 – 9,000 = $1,794.62

2.  To find the FV of a lump sum, we use:

$FV = PV(1 + r)^t$

*a.*

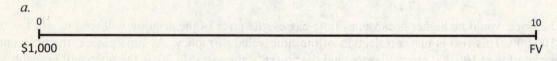

0                                                                                              10
$1,000                                                                                         FV

$FV = \$1,000(1.05)^{10}$    = $1,628.89

*b.*

0                                                                                              10
$1,000                                                                                         FV

$FV = \$1,000(1.10)^{10}$    = $2,593.74

*c.*

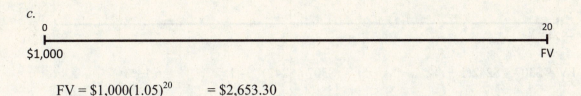

$$FV = \$1,000(1.05)^{20} \qquad = \$2,653.30$$

*d.* Because interest compounds on the interest already earned, the interest earned in part *c* is more than twice the interest earned in part *a*. With compound interest, future values grow exponentially.

3. To find the PV of a lump sum, we use:

$$PV = FV / (1 + r)^t$$

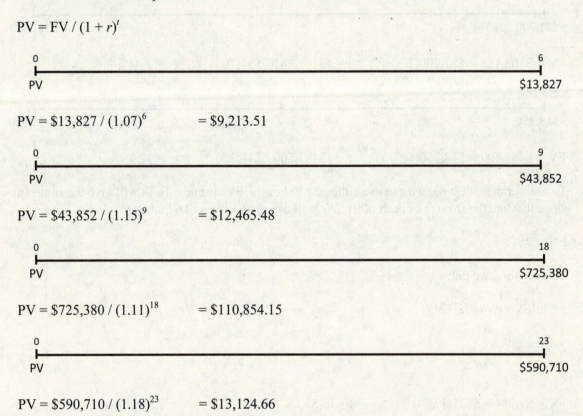

$$PV = \$13,827 / (1.07)^6 \qquad = \$9,213.51$$

$$PV = \$43,852 / (1.15)^9 \qquad = \$12,465.48$$

$$PV = \$725,380 / (1.11)^{18} \qquad = \$110,854.15$$

$$PV = \$590,710 / (1.18)^{23} \qquad = \$13,124.66$$

4. To answer this question, we can use either the FV or the PV formula. Both will give the same answer since they are the inverse of each other. We will use the FV formula, that is:

$$FV = PV(1 + r)^t$$

Solving for *r*, we get:

$$r = (FV / PV)^{1/t} - 1$$

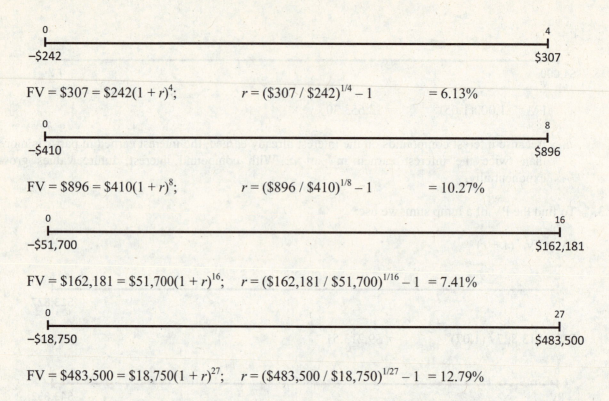

FV = $307 = $242(1 + r)^4$;     $r = ($307 / $242)^{1/4} - 1$     $= 6.13\%$

FV = $896 = $410(1 + r)^8$;     $r = ($896 / $410)^{1/8} - 1$     $= 10.27\%$

FV = $162,181 = $51,700(1 + r)^{16}$;     $r = ($162,181 / $51,700)^{1/16} - 1 = 7.41\%$

FV = $483,500 = $18,750(1 + r)^{27}$;     $r = ($483,500 / $18,750)^{1/27} - 1 = 12.79\%$

5.  To answer this question, we can use either the FV or the PV formula. Both will give the same answer since they are the inverse of each other. We will use the FV formula, that is:

$FV = PV(1 + r)^t$

Solving for $t$, we get:

$t = \ln(FV / PV) / \ln(1 + r)$

FV = $1,284 = $625(1.09)^t$;     $t = \ln($1,284/ $625) / \ln 1.09 = 8.35$ years

FV = $4,341 = $810(1.11)^t$;     $t = \ln($4,341/ $810) / \ln 1.11 = 16.09$ years

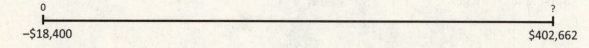

FV = $402,662 = $18,400(1.17)^t$;     $t = \ln($402,662 / $18,400) / \ln 1.17 = 19.65$ years

0                                                                    ?
├─────────────────────────────────────────────────────────┤
−$21,500                                                    $173,439

FV = $173,439 = $21,500(1.08)$^t$;     $t = \ln(\$173{,}439 \,/\, \$21{,}500) \,/\, \ln 1.08 = 27.13$ years

6.  To find the length of time for money to double, triple, etc., the present value and future value are irrelevant as long as the future value is twice the present value for doubling, three times as large for tripling, etc. To answer this question, we can use either the FV or the PV formula. Both will give the same answer since they are the inverse of each other. We will use the FV formula, that is:

$$FV = PV(1 + r)^t$$

Solving for $t$, we get:

$$t = \ln(FV \,/\, PV) \,/\, \ln(1 + r)$$

The length of time to double your money is:

0                                                                    ?
├─────────────────────────────────────────────────────────┤
−$1                                                          $2

FV = $2 = $1(1.08)$^t$
$t = \ln 2 \,/\, \ln 1.08 = 9.01$ years

The length of time to quadruple your money is:

0                                                                    ?
├─────────────────────────────────────────────────────────┤
−$1                                                          $4

FV = $4 = $1(1.08)$^t$
$t = \ln 4 \,/\, \ln 1.08 = 18.01$ years

Notice that the length of time to quadruple your money is twice as long as the time needed to double your money (the difference in these answers is due to rounding). This is an important concept of time value of money.

7.  The time line is:

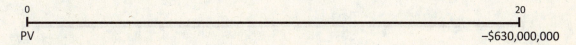

0                                                                    20
├─────────────────────────────────────────────────────────┤
PV                                                          −$630,000,000

To find the PV of a lump sum, we use:

$$PV = FV \,/\, (1 + r)^t$$
$$PV = \$630{,}000{,}000 \,/\, (1.071)^{20} = \$159{,}790{,}565.17$$

**8.** The time line is:

0                                                                                           4
−$1,680,000                                                                      $1,100,000

To answer this question, we can use either the FV or the PV formula. Both will give the same answer since they are the inverse of each other. We will use the FV formula, that is:

$FV = PV(1 + r)^t$

Solving for $r$, we get:

$r = (FV / PV)^{1/t} - 1$
$r = (\$1,100,000 / \$1,680,000)^{1/3} - 1 = -.1317 \text{ or } -13.17\%$

Notice that the interest rate is negative. This occurs when the FV is less than the PV.

**9.**

0        1
PV     $150    $150    $150    $150    ...    $150    $150    $150    $150    $150

A consol is a perpetuity. To find the PV of a perpetuity, we use the equation:

$PV = C / r$
$PV = \$150 / .046$
$PV = \$3,260.87$

**10.** To find the future value with continuous compounding, we use the equation:

$FV = PVe^{Rt}$

*a.*

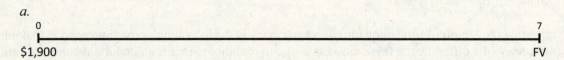

0                                                                                           7
$1,900                                                                                    FV

$FV = \$1,900e^{.12(7)} = \$4,401.10$

*b.*

0                                                                                           5
$1,900                                                                                    FV

$FV = \$1,900e^{.10(5)} = \$3,132.57$

*c.*

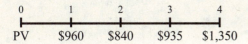

$$FV = \$1,900e^{.05(12)} = \$3,462.03$$

*d.*

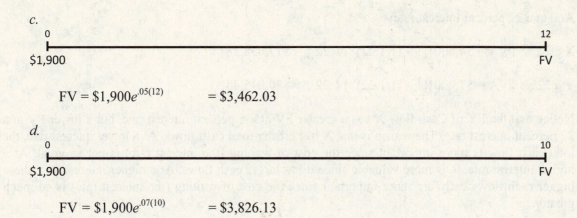

$$FV = \$1,900e^{.07(10)} = \$3,826.13$$

**11.** The time line is:

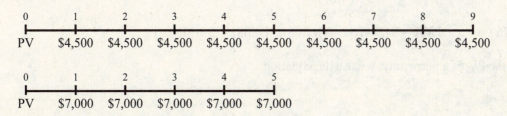

To solve this problem, we must find the PV of each cash flow and add them. To find the PV of a lump sum, we use:

$$PV = FV / (1 + r)^t$$

$$PV@10\% = \$960 / 1.10 + \$840 / 1.10^2 + \$935 / 1.10^3 + \$1,350 / 1.10^4 = \$3,191.49$$

$$PV@18\% = \$960 / 1.18 + \$840 / 1.18^2 + \$935 / 1.18^3 + \$1,350 / 1.18^4 = \$2,682.22$$

$$PV@24\% = \$960 / 1.24 + \$840 / 1.24^2 + \$935 / 1.24^3 + \$1,350 / 1.24^4 = \$2,381.91$$

**12.** The times lines are:

| 0 | 1 | 2 | 3 | 4 | 5 | 6 | 7 | 8 | 9 |
|---|---|---|---|---|---|---|---|---|---|
| PV | \$4,500 | \$4,500 | \$4,500 | \$4,500 | \$4,500 | \$4,500 | \$4,500 | \$4,500 | \$4,500 |

| 0 | 1 | 2 | 3 | 4 | 5 |
|---|---|---|---|---|---|
| PV | \$7,000 | \$7,000 | \$7,000 | \$7,000 | \$7,000 |

To find the PVA, we use the equation:

$$PVA = C(\{1 - [1/(1 + r)]^t\} / r )$$

At a 5 percent interest rate:

$$X@5\%: \quad PVA = \$4,500\{[1 - (1/1.05)^9] / .05\} = \$31,985.20$$

$$Y@5\%: \quad PVA = \$7,000\{[1 - (1/1.05)^5] / .05\} = \$30,306.34$$

And at a 22 percent interest rate:

X@22%: PVA = $4,500\{[1 - (1/1.22)^9] / .22\} = \$17,038.28$

Y@22%: PVA = $7,000\{[1 - (1/1.22)^5] / .22\} = \$20,045.48$

Notice that the PV of Cash flow X has a greater PV at a 5 percent interest rate, but a lower PV at a 22 percent interest rate. The reason is that X has greater total cash flows. At a lower interest rate, the total cash flow is more important since the cost of waiting (the interest rate) is not as great. At a higher interest rate, Y is more valuable since it has larger cash flows. At a higher interest rate, these bigger cash flows early are more important since the cost of waiting (the interest rate) is so much greater.

**13.** To find the PVA, we use the equation:

$$PVA = C(\{1 - [1/(1 + r)]^t\} / r)$$

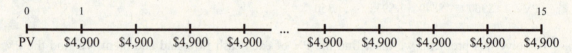

PVA@15 yrs:     PVA = $4,900\{[1 - (1/1.08)^{15}] / .08\} = \$41,941.45$

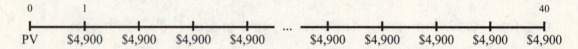

PVA@40 yrs:     PVA = $4,900\{[1 - (1/1.08)^{40}] / .08\} = \$58,430.61$

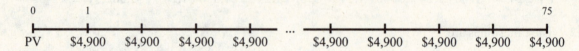

PVA@75 yrs:     PVA = $4,900\{[1 - (1/1.08)^{75}] / .08\} = \$61,059.31$

To find the PV of a perpetuity, we use the equation:

$$PV = C / r$$

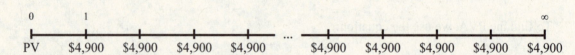

PV = $4,900 / .08$
PV = $\$61,250$

Notice that as the length of the annuity payments increases, the present value of the annuity approaches the present value of the perpetuity. The present value of the 75-year annuity and the present value of the perpetuity imply that the value today of all perpetuity payments beyond 75 years is only $190.69.

**14.** The time line is:

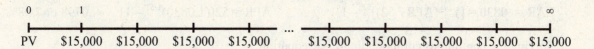

This cash flow is a perpetuity. To find the PV of a perpetuity, we use the equation:

$PV = C / r$
$PV = \$15,000 / .052 = \$288,461.54$

To find the interest rate that equates the perpetuity cash flows with the PV of the cash flows, we can use the PV of a perpetuity equation:

$PV = C / r$

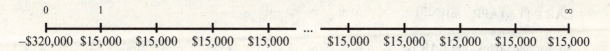

$\$320,000 = \$15,000 / r$

We can now solve for the interest rate as follows:

$r = \$15,000 / \$320,000 = .0469$ or 4.69%

**15.** For discrete compounding, to find the EAR, we use the equation:

$EAR = [1 + (APR / m)]^m - 1$

$EAR = [1 + (.07 / 4)]^4 - 1 \qquad = .0719$ or 7.19%

$EAR = [1 + (.16 / 12)]^{12} - 1 \quad = .1723$ or 17.23%

$EAR = [1 + (.11 / 365)]^{365} - 1 = .1163$ or 11.63%

To find the EAR with continuous compounding, we use the equation:

$EAR = e^r - 1$
$EAR = e^{.12} - 1 = .1275$ or 12.75%

**16.** Here, we are given the EAR and need to find the APR. Using the equation for discrete compounding:

$EAR = [1 + (APR / m)]^m - 1$

We can now solve for the APR. Doing so, we get:

$APR = m[(1 + EAR)^{1/m} - 1]$

$EAR = .0980 = [1 + (APR / 2)]^2 - 1 \qquad\qquad APR = 2[(1.0980)^{1/2} - 1] \qquad = .0957$ or 9.57%

$$EAR = .1960 = [1 + (APR / 12)]^{12} - 1 \qquad APR = 12[(1.1960)^{1/12} - 1] \quad = .1803 \text{ or } 18.03\%$$

$$EAR = .0830 = [1 + (APR / 52)]^{52} - 1 \qquad APR = 52[(1.0830)^{1/52} - 1] \quad = .0798 \text{ or } 7.98\%$$

Solving the continuous compounding EAR equation:

$$EAR = e^r - 1$$

We get:

$$APR = \ln(1 + EAR)$$
$$APR = \ln(1 + .1420)$$
$$APR = .1328 \text{ or } 13.28\%$$

17. For discrete compounding, to find the EAR, we use the equation:

$$EAR = [1 + (APR / m)]^m - 1$$

So, for each bank, the EAR is:

First National:   $EAR = [1 + (.1120 / 12)]^{12} - 1 = .1179 \text{ or } 11.79\%$

First United:    $EAR = [1 + (.1140 / 2)]^2 - 1 = .1172 \text{ or } 11.72\%$

A higher APR does not necessarily mean the higher EAR. The number of compounding periods within a year will also affect the EAR.

18. The cost of a case of wine is 10 percent less than the cost of 12 individual bottles, so the cost of a case will be:

Cost of case = (12)($10)(1 – .10)
Cost of case = $108

Now, we need to find the interest rate. The cash flows are an annuity due, so:

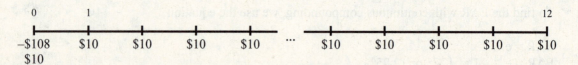

$$PVA = (1 + r) \, C(\{1 - [1/(1 + r)]^t \} / r)$$
$$\$108 = (1 + r) \, \$10(\{1 - [1 / (1 + r)^{12}] / r\})$$

Solving for the interest rate, we get:

$r = .0198$ or 1.98% per week

So, the APR of this investment is:

APR = .0198(52)
APR = 1.0277 or 102.77%

And the EAR is:

EAR = $(1 + .0198)^{52} - 1$
EAR = 1.7668 or 176.68%

The analysis appears to be correct. He really can earn about 177 percent buying wine by the case. The only question left is this: Can you really find a fine bottle of Bordeaux for $10?

19. The time line is:

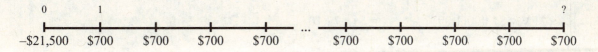

| 0 | 1 | | | | | | | | ? |
|---|---|---|---|---|---|---|---|---|---|
| –$21,500 | $700 | $700 | $700 | $700 | $700 | $700 | $700 | $700 | $700 |

Here, we need to find the length of an annuity. We know the interest rate, the PV, and the payments. Using the PVA equation:

PVA = $C(\{1 - [1/(1 + r)]^t\} / r)$
$21,500 = $700$\{[1 - (1/1.013)^t] / .013\}$

Now, we solve for $t$:

$1/1.013^t = 1 - [($21,500)(.013) / ($700)]$
$1.013^t = 1/(0.601) = 1.665$
$t = \ln 1.665 / \ln 1.013 = 39.46$ months

20. The time line is:

| 0 | 1 |
|---|---|
| $3 | $4 |

Here, we are trying to find the interest rate when we know the PV and FV. Using the FV equation:

FV = PV(1 + r)
$4 = $3(1 + r)
$r = 4/3 - 1 = 33.33\%$ per week

The interest rate is 33.33% per week. To find the APR, we multiply this rate by the number of weeks in a year, so:

APR = (52)33.33% = 1,733.33%

And using the equation to find the EAR:

$EAR = [1 + (APR / m)]^m - 1$
$EAR = [1 + .3333]^{52} - 1 = 313,916,515.69\%$

*Intermediate*

**21.** To find the FV of a lump sum with discrete compounding, we use:

$FV = PV(1 + r)^t$

*a.*

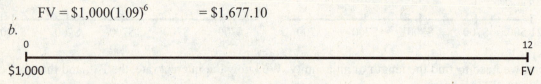

$FV = \$1,000(1.09)^6 \qquad = \$1,677.10$

*b.*

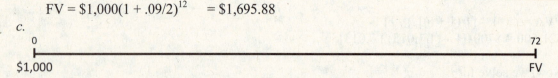

$FV = \$1,000(1 + .09/2)^{12} \qquad = \$1,695.88$

*c.*

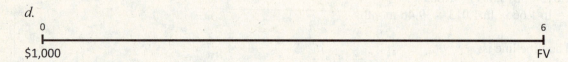

$FV = \$1,000(1 + .09/12)^{72} \qquad = \$1,712.55$

*d.*

0 ├──────────────────────────────────────── 6
$1,000                                      FV

To find the future value with continuous compounding, we use the equation:

$FV = PVe^{Rt}$
$FV = \$1,000e^{.09(6)} \qquad = \$1,716.01$

*e.* The future value increases when the compounding period is shorter because interest is earned on previously accrued interest. The shorter the compounding period, the more frequently interest is earned, and the greater the future value, assuming the same stated interest rate.

**22.** The total interest paid by First Simple Bank is the interest rate per period times the number of periods. In other words, the interest by First Simple Bank paid over 10 years will be:

$.05(10) = .5$

First Complex Bank pays compound interest, so the interest paid by this bank will be the FV factor of $1, or:

$$(1 + r)^{10}$$

Setting the two equal, we get:

$$(.05)(10) = (1 + r)^{10} - 1$$

$$r = 1.5^{1/10} - 1 = .0414 \text{ or } 4.14\%$$

23. Although the stock and bond accounts have different interest rates, we can draw one time line, but we need to remember to apply different interest rates. The time line is:

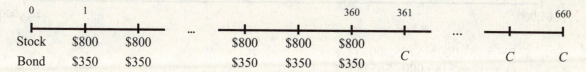

We need to find the annuity payment in retirement. Our retirement savings ends at the same time the retirement withdrawals begin, so the PV of the retirement withdrawals will be the FV of the retirement savings. So, we find the FV of the stock account and the FV of the bond account and add the two FVs.

Stock account: FVA = $800[\{[1 + (.11/12)]^{360} - 1\} / (.11/12)] = $2,243,615.79

Bond account: FVA = $350[\{[1 + (.06/12)]^{360} - 1\} / (.06/12)] = $351,580.26

So, the total amount saved at retirement is:

$2,243,615.79 + 351,580.26 = $2,595,196.05

Solving for the withdrawal amount in retirement using the PVA equation gives us:

PVA = $2,595,196.05 = C[1 - \{1 / [1 + (.08/12)]^{300}\} / (.08/12)]
C = $2,595,196.06 / 129.5645 = $20,030.14 withdrawal per month

24. The time line is:

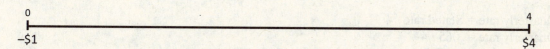

Since we are looking to quadruple our money, the PV and FV are irrelevant as long as the FV is four times as large as the PV. The number of periods is four, the number of quarters per year. So:

$$FV = \$4 = \$1(1 + r)^{(12/3)}$$
$$r = .4142 \text{ or } 41.42\%$$

**25.** Here, we need to find the interest rate for two possible investments. Each investment is a lump sum, so:

G:

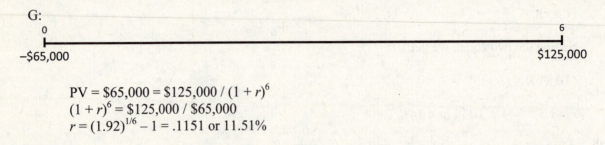

$$PV = \$65,000 = \$125,000 / (1 + r)^6$$
$$(1 + r)^6 = \$125,000 / \$65,000$$
$$r = (1.92)^{1/6} - 1 = .1151 \text{ or } 11.51\%$$

H:

$$PV = \$65,000 = \$185,000 / (1 + r)^{10}$$
$$(1 + r)^{10} = \$185,000 / \$65,000$$
$$r = (2.85)^{1/10} - 1 = .1103 \text{ or } 11.03\%$$

**26.** This is a growing perpetuity. The present value of a growing perpetuity is:

$$PV = C / (r - g)$$
$$PV = \$175,000 / (.10 - .035)$$
$$PV = \$2,692,307.69$$

It is important to recognize that when dealing with annuities or perpetuities, the present value equation calculates the present value one period before the first payment. In this case, since the first payment is in two years, we have calculated the present value one year from now. To find the value today, we simply discount this value as a lump sum. Doing so, we find the value of the cash flow stream today is:

$$PV = FV / (1 + r)^t$$
$$PV = \$2,692,307.69 / (1 + .10)^1$$
$$PV = \$2,447,552.45$$

**27.** The dividend payments are made quarterly, so we must use the quarterly interest rate. The quarterly interest rate is:

Quarterly rate = Stated rate / 4
Quarterly rate = .065 / 4
Quarterly rate = .01625

The time line is:

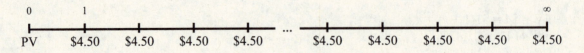

Using the present value equation for a perpetuity, we find the value today of the dividends paid must be:

PV = C / r
PV = $4.50 / .01625
PV = $276.92

28. The time line is:

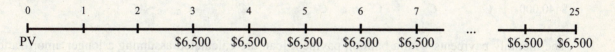

We can use the PVA annuity equation to answer this question. The annuity has 23 payments, not 22 payments. Since there is a payment made in Year 3, the annuity actually begins in Year 2. So, the value of the annuity in Year 2 is:

PVA = C({1 − [1/(1 + r)]$^t$ } / r )
PVA = $6,500({1 − [1/(1 + .07)]$^{23}$ } / .07)
PVA = $73,269.22

This is the value of the annuity one period before the first payment, or Year 2. So, the value of the cash flows today is:

PV = FV/(1 + r)$^t$
PV = $73,269.22 / (1 + .07)$^2$
PV = $63,996.17

29. The time line is:

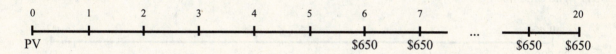

We need to find the present value of an annuity. Using the PVA equation, and the 13 percent interest rate, we get:

PVA = C({1 − [1/(1 + r)]$^t$ } / r )
PVA = $650({1 − [1/(1 + .13)]$^{15}$ } / .13)
PVA = $4,200.55

This is the value of the annuity in Year 5, one period before the first payment. Finding the value of this amount today, we find:

PV = FV/(1 + r)$^t$
PV = $4,200.55 / (1 + .11)$^5$
PV = $2,492.82

**30.** The amount borrowed is the value of the home times one minus the down payment, or:

Amount borrowed = $550,000(1 – .20)
Amount borrowed = $440,000

The time line is:

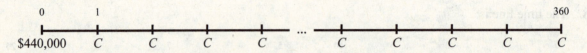

The monthly payments with a balloon payment loan are calculated assuming a longer amortization schedule, in this case, 30 years. The payments based on a 30-year repayment schedule would be:

PVA = $440,000 = $C(\{1 - [1 / (1 + .061/12)]^{360}\} / (.061/12))$
$C$ = $2,666.38

Now, at Year 8 (Month 96), we need to find the PV of the payments which have not been made. The time line is:

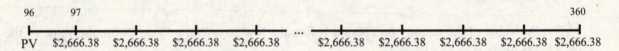

The balloon payment will be:

PVA = $2,666.38(\{1 - [1 / (1 + .061/12)]^{22(12)}\} / (.061/12))$
PVA = $386,994.11

**31.** The time line is:

Here, we need to find the FV of a lump sum, with a changing interest rate. We must do this problem in two parts. After the first six months, the balance will be:

FV = $7,500 [1 + (.024/12)]^6 = $7,590.45

This is the balance in six months. The FV in another six months will be:

FV = $7,590.45 [1 + (.18/12)]^6 = $8,299.73

The problem asks for the interest accrued, so, to find the interest, we subtract the beginning balance from the FV. The interest accrued is:

Interest = $8,299.73 – 7,500 = $799.73

**32.** The time line is:

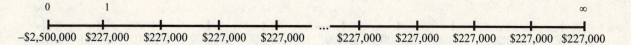

```
      0         1                                                                    ∞
      ├────────┼────────┼────────┼────────┼─ ... ─┼────────┼────────┼────────┼────────┤
-$2,500,000 $227,000 $227,000 $227,000 $227,000   $227,000 $227,000 $227,000 $227,000 $227,000
```

The company would be indifferent at the interest rate that makes the present value of the cash flows equal to the cost today. Since the cash flows are a perpetuity, we can use the PV of a perpetuity equation. Doing so, we find:

$PV = C / r$
$\$2,500,000 = \$227,000 / r$
$r = \$227,000 / \$2,500,000$
$r = .0908$ or $9.08\%$

**33.** The company will accept the project if the present value of the increased cash flows is greater than the cost. The cash flows are a growing perpetuity, so the present value is:

$PV = C \{[1/(r-g)] - [1/(r-g)] \times [(1+g)/(1+r)]^t\}$
$PV = \$21,000\{[1/(.10-.04)] - [1/(.10-.04)] \times [(1+.04)/(1+.10)]^5\}$
$PV = \$85,593.99$

The company should accept the project since the cost is less than the increased cash flows.

**34.** Since your salary grows at 4 percent per year, your salary next year will be:

Next year's salary $= \$65,000 (1 + .04)$
Next year's salary $= \$67,600$

This means your deposit next year will be:

Next year's deposit $= \$67,600(.05)$
Next year's deposit $= \$3,380$

Since your salary grows at 4 percent, you deposit will also grow at 4 percent. We can use the present value of a growing perpetuity equation to find the value of your deposits today. Doing so, we find:

$PV = C \{[1/(r-g)] - [1/(r-g)] \times [(1+g)/(1+r)]^t\}$
$PV = \$3,380\{[1/(.10-.04)] - [1/(.10-.04)] \times [(1+.04)/(1+.10)]^{40}\}$
$PV = \$50,357.59$

Now, we can find the future value of this lump sum in 40 years. We find:

$FV = PV(1+r)^t$
$FV = \$50,357.59(1+.10)^{40}$
$FV = \$2,279,147.23$

This is the value of your savings in 40 years.

**35.** The time line is:

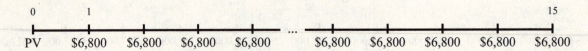

| 0 | 1 | | | | | | | | | 15 |
|---|---|---|---|---|---|---|---|---|---|---|
| PV | $6,800 | $6,800 | $6,800 | $6,800 | ... | $6,800 | $6,800 | $6,800 | $6,800 | $6,800 |

The relationship between the PVA and the interest rate is:

PVA falls as *r* increases, and PVA rises as *r* decreases
FVA rises as *r* increases, and FVA falls as *r* decreases

The present values of $6,800 per year for 15 years at the various interest rates given are:

$$\text{PVA@10\%} = \$6,800\{[1 - (1/1.10)^{15}]\,/\,.10\} = \$51,721.34$$

$$\text{PVA@5\%} = \$6,800\{[1 - (1/1.05)^{15}]\,/\,.05\} = \$70,581.67$$

$$\text{PVA@15\%} = \$6,800\{[1 - (1/1.15)^{15}]\,/\,.15\} = \$39,762.12$$

**36.** The time line is:

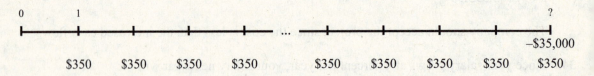

| 0 | 1 | | | | | | | | | ? |
|---|---|---|---|---|---|---|---|---|---|---|
| | $350 | $350 | $350 | $350 | ... | $350 | $350 | $350 | $350 | $350 |

−$35,000

Here, we are given the FVA, the interest rate, and the amount of the annuity. We need to solve for the number of payments. Using the FVA equation:

$$\text{FVA} = \$35,000 = \$350[\{[1 + (.10/12)]^{t} - 1\}\,/\,(.10/12)]$$

Solving for *t*, we get:

$$1.00833^{t} = 1 + [(\$35,000)(.10/12)\,/\,\$350]$$
$$t = \ln 1.83333\,/\,\ln 1.00833 = 73.04 \text{ payments}$$

**37.** The time line is:

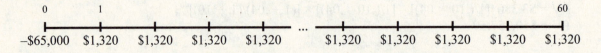

| 0 | 1 | | | | | | | | | 60 |
|---|---|---|---|---|---|---|---|---|---|---|
| −$65,000 | $1,320 | $1,320 | $1,320 | $1,320 | ... | $1,320 | $1,320 | $1,320 | $1,320 | $1,320 |

Here, we are given the PVA, number of periods, and the amount of the annuity. We need to solve for the interest rate. Using the PVA equation:

$$\text{PVA} = \$65,000 = \$1,320[\{1 - [1\,/\,(1 + r)]^{60}\}\,/\,r]$$

To find the interest rate, we need to solve this equation on a financial calculator, using a spreadsheet, or by trial and error. If you use trial and error, remember that increasing the interest rate lowers the PVA, and decreasing the interest rate increases the PVA. Using a spreadsheet, we find:

$r = 0.672\%$

The APR is the periodic interest rate times the number of periods in the year, so:

$APR = 12(0.672\%) = 8.07\%$

**38.** The time line is:

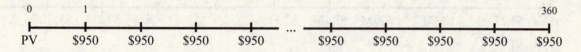

The amount of principal paid on the loan is the PV of the monthly payments you make. So, the present value of the $950 monthly payments is:

$PVA = \$950[(1 - \{1 / [1 + (.053/12)]\}^{360}) / (.053/12)] = \$171,077.26$

The monthly payments of $950 will amount to a principal payment of $171,077.26. The amount of principal you will still owe is:

$\$250,000 - 171,077.26 = \$78,922.74$

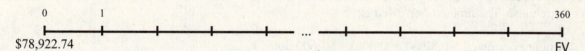

This remaining principal amount will increase at the interest rate on the loan until the end of the loan period. So the balloon payment in 30 years, which is the FV of the remaining principal will be:

Balloon payment $= \$78,922.74[1 + (.053/12)]^{360} = \$385,664.73$

**39.** The time line is:

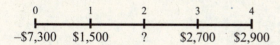

We are given the total PV of all four cash flows. If we find the PV of the three cash flows we know, and subtract them from the total PV, the amount left over must be the PV of the missing cash flow. So, the PV of the cash flows we know are:

PV of Year 1 CF: $\$1,500 / 1.08 = \$1,388.89$

PV of Year 3 CF: $\$2,700 / 1.08^3 = \$2,143.35$

PV of Year 4 CF: $\$2,900 / 1.08^4 = \$2,131.59$

So, the PV of the missing CF is:

$7,300 − 1,388.89 − 2,143.35 − 2,131.59 = $1,636.18

The question asks for the value of the cash flow in Year 2, so we must find the future value of this amount. The value of the missing CF is:

$1,636.18(1.08)^2 = $1,908.44

**40.** The time line is:

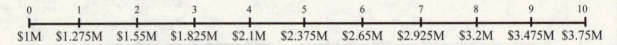

To solve this problem, we simply need to find the PV of each lump sum and add them together. It is important to note that the first cash flow of $1 million occurs today, so we do not need to discount that cash flow. The PV of the lottery winnings is:

$1,000,000 + $1,275,000/1.09 + $1,550,000/1.09^2 + $1,825,000/1.09^3 + $2,100,000/1.09^4 +
$2,375,000/1.09^5 + $2,650,000/1.09^6 + $2,925,000/1.09^7 + $3,200,000/1.09^8 +
$3,475,000/1.09^9 + $3,750,000/1.09^{10} = $15,885,026.33

**41.** Here, we are finding interest rate for an annuity cash flow. We are given the PVA, number of periods, and the amount of the annuity. We need to solve for the interest rate. We should also note that the PV of the annuity is not the amount borrowed since we are making a down payment on the warehouse. The amount borrowed is:

Amount borrowed = 0.80($4,500,000) = $3,600,000

The time line is:

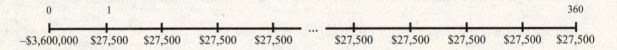

Using the PVA equation:

PVA = $3,600,000 = $27,500[{1 − [1 / (1 + r)]^{360}}/ r]

Unfortunately, this equation cannot be solved to find the interest rate using algebra. To find the interest rate, we need to solve this equation on a financial calculator, using a spreadsheet, or by trial and error. If you use trial and error, remember that increasing the interest rate decreases the PVA, and decreasing the interest rate increases the PVA. Using a spreadsheet, we find:

r = 0.702%

The APR is the monthly interest rate times the number of months in the year, so:

APR = 12(0.702%) = 8.43%

And the EAR is:

EAR = $(1 + .00702)^{12} - 1 = .0876$ or 8.76%

42. The time line is:

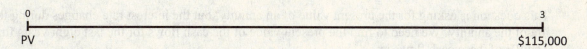

The profit the firm earns is just the PV of the sales price minus the cost to produce the asset. We find the PV of the sales price as the PV of a lump sum:

PV = $115,000 / $1.13^3$ = $79,700.77

And the firm's profit is:

Profit = $79,700.77 – 76,000 = $3,700.77

To find the interest rate at which the firm will break even, we need to find the interest rate using the PV (or FV) of a lump sum. Using the PV equation for a lump sum, we get:

$76,000 = $115,000 / $(1 + r)^3$
$r = ($115,000 / $76,000)^{1/3} - 1 = .1481$ or 14.81%

43. The time line is:

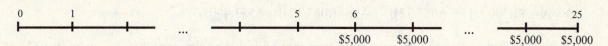

We want to find the value of the cash flows today, so we will find the PV of the annuity, and then bring the lump sum PV back to today. The annuity has 20 payments, so the PV of the annuity is:

PVA = $5,000\{[1 - (1/1.06)^{20}] / .06\}$ = $57,349.61

Since this is an ordinary annuity equation, this is the PV one period before the first payment, so it is the PV at $T = 5$. To find the value today, we find the PV of this lump sum. The value today is:

PV = $57,349.61 / $1.06^5$ = $42,854.96

**44.** The time line for the annuity is:

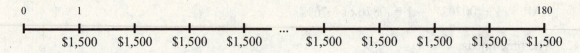

This question is asking for the present value of an annuity, but the interest rate changes during the life of the annuity. We need to find the present value of the cash flows for the last eight years first. The PV of these cash flows is:

$PVA_2 = \$1,500 \left[\{1 - 1 / [1 + (.06/12)]^{96}\} / (.06/12)\right] = \$114,142.83$

Note that this is the PV of this annuity exactly seven years from today. Now, we can discount this lump sum to today as well as finding the PV of the annuity for the first 7 years. The value of this cash flow today is:

$PV = \$114,142.83 / [1 + (.12/12)]^{84} + \$1,500 \left[\{1 - 1 / [1 + (.12/12)]^{84}\} / (.12/12)\right]$
$PV = \$134,455.36$

**45.** The time line for the annuity is:

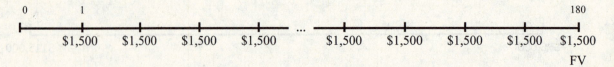

Here, we are trying to find the dollar amount invested today that will equal the FVA with a known interest rate, and payments. First, we need to determine how much we would have in the annuity account. Finding the FV of the annuity, we get:

$FVA = \$1,500 \left[\{[1 + (.087/12)]^{180} - 1\} / (.087/12)\right] = \$552,490.07$

Now, we need to find the PV of a lump sum that will give us the same FV. So, using the FV of a lump sum with continuous compounding, we get:

$FV = \$552,490.07 = PVe^{.08(15)}$
$PV = \$552,490.07e^{-1.20} = \$166,406.81$

**46.** The time line is:

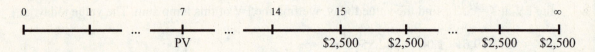

To find the value of the perpetuity at $T = 7$, we first need to use the PV of a perpetuity equation. Using this equation we find:

$PV = \$2,500 / .061 = \$40,983.61$

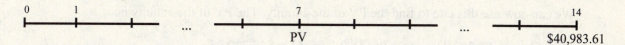

Remember that the PV of a perpetuity (and annuity) equations give the PV one period before the first payment, so, this is the value of the perpetuity at $t = 14$. To find the value at $t = 7$, we find the PV of this lump sum as:

PV = $40,983.61 / $1.061^7$ = $27,077.12

**47.** The time line is:

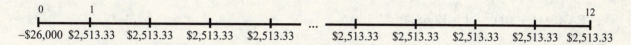

To find the APR and EAR, we need to use the actual cash flows of the loan. In other words, the interest rate quoted in the problem is only relevant to determine the total interest under the terms given. The interest rate for the cash flows of the loan is:

$$PVA = \$26{,}000 = \$2{,}513.33\{(1 - [1 / (1 + r)]^{12}) / r\}$$

Again, we cannot solve this equation for $r$, so we need to solve this equation on a financial calculator, using a spreadsheet, or by trial and error. Using a spreadsheet, we find:

$r = 2.361\%$ per month

So the APR is:

APR = 12(2.361%) = 28.33%

And the EAR is:

$$EAR = (1.02361)^{12} - 1 = 32.31\%$$

**48.** The time line is:

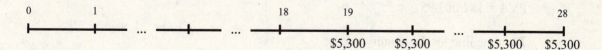

The cash flows in this problem are semiannual, so we need the effective semiannual rate. The interest rate given is the APR, so the monthly interest rate is:

Monthly rate = .12 / 12 = .01

To get the semiannual interest rate, we can use the EAR equation, but instead of using 12 months as the exponent, we will use 6 months. The effective semiannual rate is:

Semiannual rate = $(1.01)^6 - 1 = 6.15\%$

We can now use this rate to find the PV of the annuity. The PV of the annuity is:

PVA @ $t = 9$: $5,300\{[1 - (1 / 1.0615)^{10}] / .0615\} = \$38,729.05$

Note, that this is the value one period (six months) before the first payment, so it is the value at $t = 9$. So, the value at the various times the questions asked for uses this value 9 years from now.

PV @ $t = 5$: $\$38,729.05 / 1.0615^8 = \$24,022.10$

Note, that you can also calculate this present value (as well as the remaining present values) using the number of years. To do this, you need the EAR. The EAR is:

EAR $= (1 + .01)^{12} - 1 = 12.68\%$

So, we can find the PV at $t = 5$ using the following method as well:

PV @ $t = 5$: $\$38,729.05 / 1.1268^4 = \$24,022.10$

The value of the annuity at the other times in the problem is:

PV @ $t = 3$: $\$38,729.05 / 1.0615^{12} = \$18,918.99$
PV @ $t = 3$: $\$38,729.05 / 1.1268^6 = \$18,918.99$

PV @ $t = 0$: $\$38,729.05 / 1.0615^{18} = \$13,222.95$
PV @ $t = 0$: $\$38,729.05 / 1.1268^9 = \$13,222.95$

**49.** *a.* The time line for the ordinary annuity is:

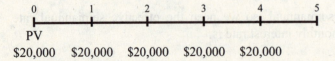

If the payments are in the form of an ordinary annuity, the present value will be:

PVA $= C(\{1 - [1/(1 + r)^t]\} / r ))$
PVA $= \$20,000[\{1 - [1 / (1 + .07)]^5\}/ .07]$
PVA $= \$82,003.95$

The time line for the annuity due is:

If the payments are an annuity due, the present value will be:

PVA$_{due} = (1 + r)$ PVA
PVA$_{due} = (1 + .07)\$82,003.95$
PVA$_{due} = \$87,744.23$

b.   The time line for the ordinary annuity is:

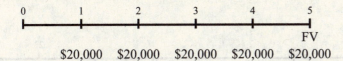

We can find the future value of the ordinary annuity as:

$FVA = C\{[(1 + r)^t - 1] / r\}$
$FVA = \$20,000\{[(1 + .07)^5 - 1] / .07\}$
$FVA = \$115,014.78$

The time line for the annuity due is:

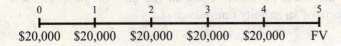

If the payments are an annuity due, the future value will be:

$FVA_{due} = (1 + r)\, FVA$
$FVA_{due} = (1 + .07)\$115,014.78$
$FVA_{due} = \$123,065.81$

c.   Assuming a positive interest rate, the present value of an annuity due will always be larger than the present value of an ordinary annuity. Each cash flow in an annuity due is received one period earlier, which means there is one period less to discount each cash flow. Assuming a positive interest rate, the future value of an ordinary due will always higher than the future value of an ordinary annuity. Since each cash flow is made one period sooner, each cash flow receives one extra period of compounding.

**50.**  The time line is:

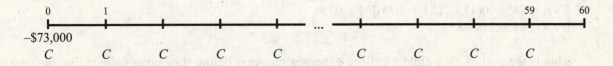

We need to use the PVA due equation, that is:

$PVA_{due} = (1 + r)\, PVA$

Using this equation:

$PVA_{due} = \$73,000 = [1 + (.0645/12)] \times C\{1 - 1 / [1 + (.0645/12)]^{60}\} / (.0645/12)$
$C = \$1,418.99$

Notice, to find the payment for the PVA due we simply compound the payment for an ordinary annuity forward one period.

*Challenge*

**51.** The time line is:

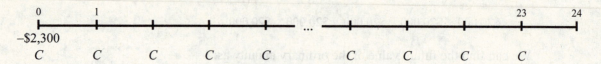

The monthly interest rate is the annual interest rate divided by 12, or:

Monthly interest rate = .104 / 12
Monthly interest rate = .00867

Now we can set the present value of the lease payments equal to the cost of the equipment, or $2,300. The lease payments are in the form of an annuity due, so:

$PVA_{due} = (1 + r)\ C(\{1 - [1/(1 + r)]^t\ \} / r\ )$
$\$2,300 = (1 + .00867)\ C(\{1 - [1/(1 + .00867)]^{24}\ \} / .00867\ )$
$C = \$105.64$

**52.** The time line is:

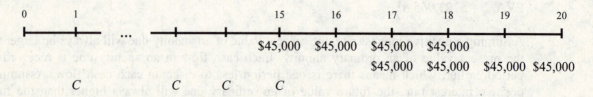

First, we will calculate the present value of the college expenses for each child. The expenses are an annuity, so the present value of the college expenses is:

$PVA = C(\{1 - [1/(1 + r)]^t\ \} / r\ )$
$PVA = \$45,000(\{1 - [1/(1 + .075)]^4\ \} / .075)$
$PVA = \$150,719.68$

This is the cost of each child's college expenses one year before they enter college. So, the cost of the oldest child's college expenses today will be:

$PV = FV/(1 + r)^t$
$PV = \$150,719.68/(1 + .075)^{14}$
$PV = \$54,758.49$

And the cost of the youngest child's college expenses today will be:

$PV = FV/(1 + r)^t$
$PV = \$150,719.68/(1 + .075)^{16}$
$PV = \$47,384.31$

Therefore, the total cost today of your children's college expenses is:

Cost today = $54,758.49 + 47,384.31
Cost today = $102,142.80

This is the present value of your annual savings, which are an annuity. So, the amount you must save each year will be:

PVA = $C(\{1 - [1/(1 + r)]^t\} / r)$
$102,142.80 = $C(\{1 - [1/(1 + .075)]^{15}\} / .075)$
$C$ = $11,571.48

53. The salary is a growing annuity, so we use the equation for the present value of a growing annuity. The salary growth rate is 3.5 percent and the discount rate is 9 percent, so the value of the salary offer today is:

PV = $C \{[1/(r - g)] - [1/(r - g)] \times [(1 + g)/(1 + r)]^t\}$
PV = $55,000$\{[1/(.09 - .035)] - [1/(.09 - .035)] \times [(1 + .035)/(1 + .09)]^{25}\}$
PV = $725,939.59

The yearly bonuses are 10 percent of the annual salary. This means that next year's bonus will be:

Next year's bonus = .10($55,000)
Next year's bonus = $5,500

Since the salary grows at 3.5 percent, the bonus will grow at 3.5 percent as well. Using the growing annuity equation, with a 3.5 percent growth rate and a 12 percent discount rate, the present value of the annual bonuses is:

PV = $C \{[1/(r - g)] - [1/(r - g)] \times [(1 + g)/(1 + r)]^t\}$
PV = $5,500$\{[1/(.09 - .035)] - [1/(.09 - .035)] \times [(1 + .035)/(1 + .09)]^{25}\}$
PV = $72,593.96

Notice the present value of the bonus is 10 percent of the present value of the salary. The present value of the bonus will always be the same percentage of the present value of the salary as the bonus percentage. So, the total value of the offer is:

PV = PV(Salary) + PV(Bonus) + Bonus paid today
PV = $725,939.59 + 72,593.96 + 10,000
PV = $808,533.55

54. Here, we need to compare two options. In order to do so, we must get the value of the two cash flow streams to the same time, so we will find the value of each today. We must also make sure to use the aftertax cash flows, since it is more relevant. For Option A, the aftertax cash flows are:

Aftertax cash flows = Pretax cash flows (1 – tax rate)
Aftertax cash flows = $250,000(1 – .28)
Aftertax cash flows = $180,000

So, the cash flows are:

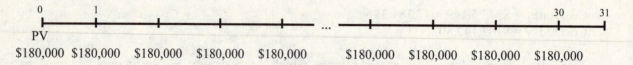

$180,000  $180,000  $180,000  $180,000  $180,000    $180,000  $180,000  $180,000  $180,000

The aftertax cash flows from Option A are in the form of an annuity due, so the present value of the cash flow today is:

$PVA_{due} = (1 + r)\, C(\{1 - [1/(1 + r)]^t\} / r)$
$PVA_{due} = (1 + .07)\, \$180{,}000(\{1 - [1/(1 + .07)]^{31}\} / .07)$
$PVA_{due} = \$2{,}413{,}627.41$

For Option B, the aftertax cash flows are:

Aftertax cash flows = Pretax cash flows (1 − tax rate)
Aftertax cash flows = $200,000(1 − .28)
Aftertax cash flows = $144,000

The cash flows are:

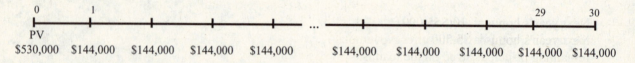

$530,000  $144,000  $144,000  $144,000  $144,000    $144,000  $144,000  $144,000  $144,000  $144,000

The aftertax cash flows from Option B are an ordinary annuity, plus the cash flow today, so the present value is:

$PV = C(\{1 - [1/(1 + r)]^t\} / r) + CF_0$
$PV = \$144{,}000\{1 - [1/(1 + .07)]^{30}\} / .07) + \$530{,}000$
$PV = \$2{,}316{,}901.93$

You should choose Option A because it has a higher present value on an aftertax basis.

55. We need to find the first payment into the retirement account. The present value of the desired amount at retirement is:

$PV = FV/(1 + r)^t$
$PV = \$2{,}000{,}000/(1 + .09)^{30}$
$PV = \$150{,}742.27$

This is the value today. Since the savings are in the form of a growing annuity, we can use the growing annuity equation and solve for the payment. Doing so, we get:

$PV = C\,\{[1/(r - g)] - [1/(r - g)] \times [(1 + g)/(1 + r)]^t\}$
$\$150{,}742.27 = C\{[1/(.09 - .03)] - [1/(.09 - .03)] \times [(1 + .03)/(1 + .09)]^{30}\}$
$C = \$11{,}069.69$

This is the amount you need to save next year. So, the percentage of your salary is:

Percentage of salary = $11,069.69/$70,000
Percentage of salary = .1581 or 15.81%

Note that this is the percentage of your salary you must save each year. Since your salary is increasing at 3 percent, and the savings are increasing at 3 percent, the percentage of salary will remain constant.

**56.** Since she put $1,000 down, the amount borrowed will be:

Amount borrowed = $30,000 – 1,000
Amount borrowed = $29,000

So, the monthly payments will be:

$PVA = C(\{1 - [1/(1 + r)]^t\} / r)$
$\$29{,}000 = C[\{1 - [1/(1 + .072/12)]^{60}\} / (.072/12)]$
$C = \$576.98$

The amount remaining on the loan is the present value of the remaining payments. Since the first payment was made on October 1, 2009, and she made a payment on October 1, 2011, there are 35 payments remaining, with the first payment due immediately. So, we can find the present value of the remaining 34 payments after November 1, 2011, and add the payment made on this date. So the remaining principal owed on the loan is:

$PV = C(\{1 - [1/(1 + r)]^t\} / r) + C_0$
$PV = \$576.98[\{1 - [1/(1 + .072/12)]^{34}\} / (.072/12)]$
$C = \$17{,}697.79$

She must also pay a one percent prepayment penalty and the payment due on November 1, 2011, so the total amount of the payment is:

Total payment = Balloon amount(1 + Prepayment penalty) + Current payment
Total payment = $17,697.79(1 + .01) + $576.98
Total payment = $18,451.74

**57.** The time line is:

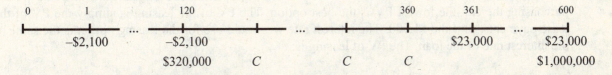

The cash flows for this problem occur monthly, and the interest rate given is the EAR. Since the cash flows occur monthly, we must get the effective monthly rate. One way to do this is to find the APR based on monthly compounding, and then divide by 12. So, the pre-retirement APR is:

$EAR = .11 = [1 + (APR / 12)]^{12} - 1;$ \qquad $APR = 12[(1.11)^{1/12} - 1] = 10.48\%$

And the post-retirement APR is:

$$EAR = .08 = [1 + (APR / 12)]^{12} - 1; \qquad APR = 12[(1.08)^{1/12} - 1] = 7.72\%$$

First, we will calculate how much he needs at retirement. The amount needed at retirement is the PV of the monthly spending plus the PV of the inheritance. The PV of these two cash flows is:

$$PVA = \$23,000\{1 - [1 / (1 + .0772/12)^{12(20)}]\} / (.0772/12) = \$2,807,787.80$$

$$PV = \$1,000,000 / (1 + .08)^{20} = \$214,548.21$$

So, at retirement, he needs:

$$\$2,807,787.80 + 214,548.21 = \$3,022,336.00$$

He will be saving $2,100 per month for the next 10 years until he purchases the cabin. The value of his savings after 10 years will be:

$$FVA = \$2,100[\{ 1 + (.1048/12)]^{12(10)} - 1\} / (.1048/12)] = \$442,239.69$$

After he purchases the cabin, the amount he will have left is:

$$\$442,239.69 - 320,000 = \$122,239.69$$

He still has 20 years until retirement. When he is ready to retire, this amount will have grown to:

$$FV = \$122,239.69[1 + (.1048/12)]^{12(20)} = \$985,534.47$$

So, when he is ready to retire, based on his current savings, he will be short:

$$\$3,022,336.00 - 985,534.47 = \$2,036,801.54$$

This amount is the FV of the monthly savings he must make between years 10 and 30. So, finding the annuity payment using the FVA equation, we find his monthly savings will need to be:

$$FVA = \$2,036,801.54 = C[\{ 1 + (.1048/12)]^{12(20)} - 1\} / (.1048/12)]$$
$$C = \$2,519.10$$

**58.** To answer this question, we should find the PV of both options, and compare them. Since we are purchasing the car, the lowest PV is the best option. The PV of the leasing is simply the PV of the lease payments, plus the $1,500. The interest rate we would use for the leasing option is the same as the interest rate of the loan. The PV of leasing is:

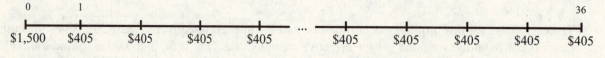

$$PV = \$1,500 + \$405\{1 - [1 / (1 + .06/12)^{12(3)}]\} / (.06/12) = \$14,812.76$$

The PV of purchasing the car is the current price of the car minus the PV of the resale price. The PV of the resale price is:

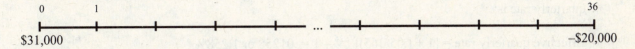

$$PV = \$20,000 / [1 + (.06/12)]^{12(3)} = \$16,712.90$$

The PV of the decision to purchase is:

$$\$31,000 - 16,712.90 = \$14,287.10$$

In this case, it is cheaper to buy the car than lease it since the PV of the leasing cash flows is lower. To find the breakeven resale price, we need to find the resale price that makes the PV of the two options the same. In other words, the PV of the decision to buy should be:

$$\$31,000 - PV \text{ of resale price} = \$14,812.76$$
$$PV \text{ of resale price} = \$16,187.24$$

The resale price that would make the PV of the lease versus buy decision equal is the FV of this value, so:

$$\text{Breakeven resale price} = \$16,187.24[1 + (.06/12)]^{12(3)} = \$19,370.95$$

**59.** To find the quarterly salary for the player, we first need to find the PV of the current contract. The cash flows for the contract are annual, and we are given a daily interest rate. We need to find the EAR so the interest compounding is the same as the timing of the cash flows. The EAR is:

$$EAR = [1 + (.05/365)]^{365} - 1 = 5.13\%$$

The PV of the current contract offer is the sum of the PV of the cash flows. So, the PV is:

$$PV = \$8,500,000 + \$3,900,000/1.0513 + \$4,600,000/1.0513^2 + \$5,300,000/1.0513^3$$
$$\quad + \$5,800,000/1.0513^4 + \$6,400,000/1.0513^5 + \$7,300,000/1.0513^6$$
$$PV = \$36,075,085.12$$

The player wants the contract increased in value by $1,500,000, so the PV of the new contract will be:

$$PV = \$36,075,085.12 + 1,500,000 = \$37,575,085.12$$

The player has also requested a signing bonus payable today in the amount of $10 million. We can simply subtract this amount from the PV of the new contract. The remaining amount will be the PV of the future quarterly paychecks.

$$\$37,575,085.12 - 10,000,000 = \$27,575,085.12$$

To find the quarterly payments, first realize that the interest rate we need is the effective quarterly rate. Using the daily interest rate, we can find the quarterly interest rate using the EAR equation, with the number of days being 91.25, the number of days in a quarter (365 / 4). The effective quarterly rate is:

Effective quarterly rate = $[1 + (.05/365)]^{91.25} - 1 = .01258$ or 1.258%

Now, we have the interest rate, the length of the annuity, and the PV. Using the PVA equation and solving for the payment, we get:

PVA = $27,575,085.12 = $C\{[1 - (1/1.01258)^{24}] / .01258\}$
C = $1,338,243.52

**60.** The time line for the cash flows is:

0                                                                                              1
├────────────────────────────────────────────────────────────────────────────────────────────┤
−$17,000                                                                                $20,000

To find the APR and EAR, we need to use the actual cash flows of the loan. In other words, the interest rate quoted in the problem is only relevant to determine the total interest under the terms given. The cash flows of the loan are the $20,000 you must repay in one year, and the $17,200 you borrow today. The interest rate of the loan is:

$20,000 = $17,000(1 + r)$
$r = ($20,000 / 17,000) - 1 = .1765$ or 17.65%

Because of the discount, you only get the use of $17,000, and the interest you pay on that amount is 17.65%, not 15%.

**61.** The time line is:

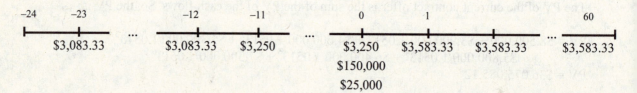

−24      −23              −12      −11                  0        1                      60
├─────────┼─── ... ───┼─────────┼─────── ... ───────┼────────┼─────────┼─── ... ───┤
  $3,083.33            $3,083.33  $3,250              $3,250   $3,583.33  $3,583.33  $3,583.33
                                                     $150,000
                                                     $25,000

Here, we have cash flows that would have occurred in the past and cash flows that would occur in the future. We need to bring both cash flows to today. Before we calculate the value of the cash flows today, we must adjust the interest rate, so we have the effective monthly interest rate. Finding the APR with monthly compounding and dividing by 12 will give us the effective monthly rate. The APR with monthly compounding is:

APR = $12[(1.09)^{1/12} - 1] = 8.65%$

To find the value today of the back pay from two years ago, we will find the FV of the annuity (salary), and then find the FV of the lump sum value of the salary. Doing so gives us:

FV = ($37,000/12) $[\{[ 1 + (.0865/12)]^{12} - 1\} / (.0865/12)] (1 + .09) = $41,967.73$

Notice we found the FV of the annuity with the effective monthly rate, and then found the FV of the lump sum with the EAR. Alternatively, we could have found the FV of the lump sum with the effective monthly rate as long as we used 12 periods. The answer would be the same either way.

Now, we need to find the value today of last year's back pay:

$$FVA = (\$39,000/12) \, [\{[1 + (.0865/12)]^{12} - 1\} / (.0865/12)] = \$40,583.72$$

Next, we find the value today of the five year's future salary:

$$PVA = (\$43,000/12)\{[\{1 - \{1 / [1 + (.0865/12)]^{12(5)}\}] / (.0865/12)\} = \$174,046.93$$

The value today of the jury award is the sum of salaries, plus the compensation for pain and suffering, and court costs. The award should be for the amount of:

Award = $41,967.73 + 40,583.72 + 174,046.93 + 150,000 + 25,000
Award = $431,598.39

As the plaintiff, you would prefer a lower interest rate. In this problem, we are calculating both the PV and FV of annuities. A lower interest rate will decrease the FVA, but increase the PVA. So, by a lower interest rate, we are lowering the value of the back pay. But, we are also increasing the PV of the future salary. Since the future salary is larger and has a longer time, this is the more important cash flow to the plaintiff.

62. Again, to find the interest rate of a loan, we need to look at the cash flows of the loan. Since this loan is in the form of a lump sum, the amount you will repay is the FV of the principal amount, which will be:

Loan repayment amount = $10,000(1.08) = $10,800

The amount you will receive today is the principal amount of the loan times one minus the points.

Amount received = $10,000(1 − .03) = $9,700

So, the time line is:

```
0                                                              9
├──────────────────────────────────────────────────────────────┤
−$9,700                                                    $10,800
```

Now, we simply find the interest rate for this PV and FV.

$10,800 = $9,700(1 + r)
$r = (\$10,800 / \$9,700) - 1 = .1134$ or 11.34%

With a quoted interest rate of 11 percent and two points, the EAR is:

Loan repayment amount = $10,000(1.11) = $11,100

Amount received = $10,000(1 − .02) = $9,800

$11,100 = $9,800(1 + r)$
$r = ($11,100 / $9,800) - 1 = .1327$ or 13.27%

The effective rate is not affected by the loan amount, since it drops out when solving for $r$.

**63.** First, we will find the APR and EAR for the loan with the refundable fee. Remember, we need to use the actual cash flows of the loan to find the interest rate. With the $2,400 application fee, you will need to borrow $202,400 to have $200,000 after deducting the fee. The time line is:

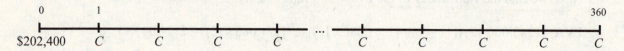

Solving for the payment under these circumstances, we get:

$PVA = $202,400 = C \{[1 - 1/(1.004417)^{360}]/.004417\}$ where $.004417 = .053/12$
$C = $1,123.94$

We can now use this amount in the PVA equation with the original amount we wished to borrow, $200,000.

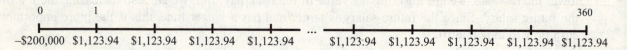

Solving for $r$, we find:

$PVA = $200,000 = $1,123.94[\{1 - [1 / (1 + r)]^{360}\} / r]$

Solving for $r$ with a spreadsheet, on a financial calculator, or by trial and error, gives:

$r = 0.4506\%$ per month

$APR = 12(0.4506\%) = 5.41\%$

$EAR = (1 + .004506)^{12} - 1 = .0554$ or 5.54%

With the nonrefundable fee, the APR of the loan is simply the quoted APR since the fee is not considered part of the loan. So:

$APR = 5.30\%$

$EAR = [1 + (.053/12)]^{12} - 1 = .0543$ or 5.43%

**64.** The time line is:

| 0 | 1 | | | | | | | | | 36 |
|---|---|---|---|---|---|---|---|---|---|---|
| –$1,000 | $45.64 | $45.64 | $45.64 | $45.64 | $45.64 | $45.64 | $45.64 | $45.64 | $45.64 |

Be careful of interest rate quotations. The actual interest rate of a loan is determined by the cash flows. Here, we are told that the PV of the loan is $1,000, and the payments are $45.64 per month for three years, so the interest rate on the loan is:

$$PVA = \$1,000 = \$45.64[ \; \{1 - [1 / (1 + r)]^{36} \} / r \; ]$$

Solving for $r$ with a spreadsheet, on a financial calculator, or by trial and error, gives:

$r = 2.98\%$ per month

$APR = 12(2.98\%) = 35.71\%$

$EAR = (1 + .0298)^{12} - 1 = .4218$ or $42.18\%$

It's called add-on interest because the interest amount of the loan is added to the principal amount of the loan before the loan payments are calculated.

**65.** We will calculate the number of periods necessary to repay the balance with no fee first. We simply need to use the PVA equation and solve for the number of payments.

Without fee and annual rate = 18.6%:

$$PVA = \$10,000 = \$200\{[1 - (1/1.0155)^t] / .0155 \} \text{ where } .0155 = .186/12$$

Solving for $t$, we get:

$t = \ln\{1 / [1 - (\$10,000/\$200)(.0155)]\} / \ln(1.0155)$
$t = \ln 4.4444 / \ln 1.0155$
$t = 96.98$ months

Without fee and annual rate = 8.2%:

$$PVA = \$10,000 = \$200\{[1 - (1/1.006833)^t] / .006833 \} \text{ where } .006833 = .082/12$$

Solving for $t$, we get:

$t = \ln\{1 / [1 - (\$10,000/\$200)(.006833)]\} / \ln(1.006833)$
$t = \ln 1.51899 / \ln 1.006833$
$t = 61.39$ months

Note that we do not need to calculate the time necessary to repay your current credit card with a fee since no fee will be incurred. The time to repay the new card with a transfer fee is:

With fee and annual rate = 8.20%:

$$PVA = \$10,200 = \$200\{ [1 - (1/1.006833)^t ] / .006833 \} \text{ where } .006833 = .082/12$$

Solving for $t$, we get:

$$t = \ln\{1 / [1 - (\$10,200/\$200)(.006833)]\} / \ln(1.006833)$$
$$t = \ln 1.53492 / \ln 1.006833$$
$$t = 62.92 \text{ months}$$

**66.** We need to find the FV of the premiums to compare with the cash payment promised at age 65. We have to find the value of the premiums at year 6 first since the interest rate changes at that time. So:

$$FV_1 = \$500(1.11)^5 = \$842.53$$

$$FV_2 = \$600(1.11)^4 = \$910.84$$

$$FV_3 = \$700(1.11)^3 = \$957.34$$

$$FV_4 = \$800(1.11)^2 = \$985.68$$

$$FV_5 = \$900(1.11)^1 = \$999.00$$

Value at year six = $842.53 + 910.84 + 957.34 + 985.68 + 999.00 + 1,000.00 = $5,695.39

Finding the FV of this lump sum at the child's 65th birthday:

$$FV = \$5,695.39(1.07)^{59} = \$308,437.08$$

The policy is not worth buying; the future value of the policy is $308,437.08, but the policy contract will pay off $275,000. The premiums are worth $33,437.08 more than the policy payoff.

Note, we could also compare the PV of the two cash flows. The PV of the premiums is:

$$PV = \$500/1.11 + \$600/1.11^2 + \$700/1.11^3 + \$800/1.11^4 + \$900/1.11^5 + \$1,000/1.11^6 = \$3,044.99$$

And the value today of the $275,000 at age 65 is:

$$PV = \$275,000/1.07^{59} = \$5,077.97$$

$$PV = \$5,077.97/1.11^6 = \$2,714.89$$

The premiums still have the higher cash flow. At time zero, the difference is $330.10. Whenever you are comparing two or more cash flow streams, the cash flow with the highest value at one time will have the highest value at any other time.

Here is a question for you: Suppose you invest $330.10, the difference in the cash flows at time zero, for six years at an 11 percent interest rate, and then for 59 years at a seven percent interest rate.

How much will it be worth? Without doing calculations, you know it will be worth $33,437.08, the difference in the cash flows at time 65!

67. Since the payments occur at six month intervals, we need to get the effective six-month interest rate. We can calculate the daily interest rate since we have an APR compounded daily, so the effective six-month interest rate is:

Effective six-month rate = $(1 + \text{Daily rate})^{180} - 1$
Effective six-month rate = $(1 + .09/360)^{180} - 1$
Effective six-month rate = $.0460$ or $4.60\%$

Now, we can use the PVA equation to find the present value of the semi-annual payments. Doing so, we find:

PVA = $C(\{1 - [1/(1 + r)]^t\} / r)$
PVA = $\$1,250,000(\{1 - [1/(1 + .0460]^{40}\} / .0460)$
PVA = $\$22,670,253.86$

This is the value six months from today, which is one period (six months) prior to the first payment. So, the value today is:

PV = $\$22,670,253.86 / (1 + .0460)$
PV = $\$21,672,827.50$

This means the total value of the lottery winnings today is:

Value of winnings today = $\$21,672,827.50 + 2,500,000$
Value of winnings today = $\$24,172,827.50$

You should not take the offer since the value of the offer is less than the present value of the payments.

68. Here, we need to find the interest rate that makes the PVA, the college costs, equal to the FVA, the savings. The PV of the college costs is:

PVA = $\$25,000[\{1 - [1/(1 + r)]^4\} / r]$

And the FV of the savings is:

FVA = $\$11,000\{[(1 + r)^6 - 1] / r\}$

Setting these two equations equal to each other, we get:

$\$25,000[\{1 - [1/(1 + r)]^4\} / r] = \$11,000\{[(1 + r)^6 - 1] / r\}$

Reducing the equation gives us:

$(1 + r)^{10} - 4.40(1 + r)^4 + 44.00 = 0$

Now, we need to find the root of this equation. We can solve using trial and error, a root-solving calculator routine, or a spreadsheet. Using a spreadsheet, we find:

$r = 8.54\%$

69. The time line is:

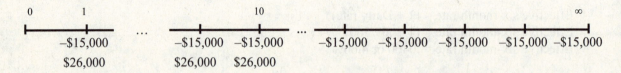

Here, we need to find the interest rate that makes us indifferent between an annuity and a perpetuity. To solve this problem, we need to find the PV of the two options and set them equal to each other. The PV of the perpetuity is:

$PV = \$15,000 / r$

And the PV of the annuity is:

$PVA = \$26,000[\{1 - [1 / (1 + r)]^{10} \} / r]$

Setting them equal and solving for $r$, we get:

$\$15,000 / r = \$26,000[\{1 - [1 / (1 + r)]^{10} \} / r]$
$\$15,000 / \$26,000 = 1 - [1 / (1 + r)]^{10}$
$.5769^{1/10} = 1 / (1 + r)$
$r = 1 / .5769^{1/10} - 1$
$r = .0898$ or $8.98\%$

70. The time line is:

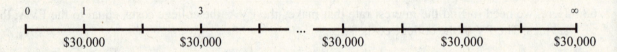

The cash flows in this problem occur every two years, so we need to find the effective two year rate. One way to find the effective two year rate is to use an equation similar to the EAR, except use the number of days in two years as the exponent. (We use the number of days in two years since it is daily compounding; if monthly compounding was assumed, we would use the number of months in two years.) So, the effective two-year interest rate is:

Effective 2-year rate $= [1 + (.13/365)]^{365(2)} - 1 = 29.69\%$

We can use this interest rate to find the PV of the perpetuity. Doing so, we find:

$PV = \$30,000 /.2969 = \$101,054.32$

This is an important point: Remember that the PV equation for a perpetuity (and an ordinary annuity) tells you the PV one period before the first cash flow. In this problem, since the cash flows are two years apart, we have found the value of the perpetuity one period (two years) before the first payment, which is one year ago. We need to compound this value for one year to find the value today. The value of the cash flows today is:

$$PV = \$101,054.32(1 + .13/365)^{365} = \$115,080.86$$

The second part of the question assumes the perpetuity cash flows begin in four years. In this case, when we use the PV of a perpetuity equation, we find the value of the perpetuity two years from today. So, the value of these cash flows today is:

$$PV = \$101,054.32 / (1 + .13/365)^{2(365)} = \$77,921.70$$

71. To solve for the PVA due:

$$PVA = \frac{C}{(1+r)} + \frac{C}{(1+r)^2} + .... + \frac{C}{(1+r)^t}$$

$$PVA_{due} = C + \frac{C}{(1+r)} + .... + \frac{C}{(1+r)^{t-1}}$$

$$PVA_{due} = (1+r)\left(\frac{C}{(1+r)} + \frac{C}{(1+r)^2} + .... + \frac{C}{(1+r)^t}\right)$$

$$PVA_{due} = (1+r)\,PVA$$

And the FVA due is:

$$FVA = C + C(1+r) + C(1+r)^2 + .... + C(1+r)^{t-1}$$
$$FVA_{due} = C(1+r) + C(1+r)^2 + .... + C(1+r)^t$$
$$FVA_{due} = (1+r)[C + C(1+r) + .... + C(1+r)^{t-1}]$$
$$FVA_{due} = (1+r)FVA$$

72. *a.* The APR is the interest rate per week times 52 weeks in a year, so:

$$APR = 52(7\%) = 364\%$$

$$EAR = (1 + .07)^{52} - 1 = 32.7253 \text{ or } 3,272.53\%$$

*b.* In a discount loan, the amount you receive is lowered by the discount, and you repay the full principal. With a 7 percent discount, you would receive \$9.30 for every \$10 in principal, so the weekly interest rate would be:

$$\$10 = \$9.30(1 + r)$$
$$r = (\$10 / \$9.30) - 1 = .0753 \text{ or } 7.53\%$$

Note the dollar amount we use is irrelevant. In other words, we could use $0.93 and $1, $93 and $100, or any other combination and we would get the same interest rate. Now we can find the APR and the EAR:

APR = 52(7.53%) = 391.40%

EAR = $(1 + .0753)^{52} - 1 = 42.5398$ or 4,253.98%

c. Using the cash flows from the loan, we have the PVA and the annuity payments and need to find the interest rate, so:

PVA = $68.92 = $25[{1 - [1 / (1 + r)]^4}/ r ]$

Using a spreadsheet, trial and error, or a financial calculator, we find:

$r$ = 16.75% per week

APR = 52(16.75%) = 871.002%

EAR = $1.1675^{52} - 1 = 3,142.1572$ or 314,215.72%

**73.** To answer this, we can diagram the perpetuity cash flows, which are: (Note, the subscripts are only to differentiate when the cash flows begin. The cash flows are all the same amount.)

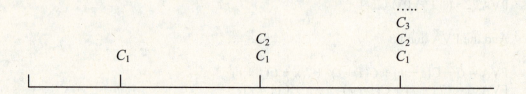

Thus, each of the increased cash flows is a perpetuity in itself. So, we can write the cash flows stream as:

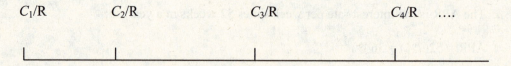

So, we can write the cash flows as the present value of a perpetuity with a perpetuity payment of:

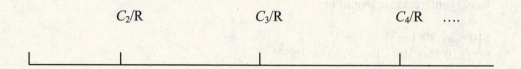

The present value of this perpetuity is:

$$PV = (C/R) / R = C/R^2$$

So, the present value equation of a perpetuity that increases by $C$ each period is:

$$PV = C/R + C/R^2$$

74. Since it is only an approximation, we know the Rule of 72 is exact for only one interest rate. Using the basic future value equation for an amount that doubles in value and solving for $t$, we find:

$$FV = PV(1 + R)^t$$
$$\$2 = \$1(1 + R)^t$$
$$\ln(2) = t \ln(1 + R)$$
$$t = \ln(2) / \ln(1 + R)$$

We also know the Rule of 72 approximation is:

$$t = 72 / R$$

We can set these two equations equal to each other and solve for R. We also need to remember that the exact future value equation uses decimals, so the equation becomes:

$$.72 / R = \ln(2) / \ln(1 + R)$$
$$0 = (.72 / R) / [ \ln(2) / \ln(1 + R)]$$

It is not possible to solve this equation directly for R, but using Solver, we find the interest rate for which the Rule of 72 is exact is 7.846894 percent.

75. We are only concerned with the time it takes money to double, so the dollar amounts are irrelevant. So, we can write the future value of a lump sum with continuously compounded interest as:

$$\$2 = \$1e^{Rt}$$
$$2 = e^{Rt}$$
$$Rt = \ln(2)$$
$$Rt = .693147$$
$$t = .693147 / R$$

Since we are using percentage interest rates while the equation uses decimal form, to make the equation correct with percentages, we can multiply by 100:

$$t = 69.3147 / R$$

**Calculator Solutions**

**1.**

| | N | I/Y | PV | PMT | FV |
|---|---|---|---|---|---|
| Enter | 10 | 8% | $5,000 | | |
| Solve for | | | | | $10,794.62 |

$10,794.62 − 9,000 = $1,794.62

**2.**

| | N | I/Y | PV | PMT | FV |
|---|---|---|---|---|---|
| Enter | 10 | 5% | $1,000 | | |
| Solve for | | | | | $1,628.89 |

| | N | I/Y | PV | PMT | FV |
|---|---|---|---|---|---|
| Enter | 10 | 10% | $1,000 | | |
| Solve for | | | | | $2,593.74 |

| | N | I/Y | PV | PMT | FV |
|---|---|---|---|---|---|
| Enter | 20 | 5% | $1,000 | | |
| Solve for | | | | | $2,653.30 |

**3.**

| | N | I/Y | PV | PMT | FV |
|---|---|---|---|---|---|
| Enter | 6 | 7% | | | $13,827 |
| Solve for | | | $9,213.51 | | |

| | N | I/Y | PV | PMT | FV |
|---|---|---|---|---|---|
| Enter | 9 | 15% | | | $43,852 |
| Solve for | | | $12,465.48 | | |

| | N | I/Y | PV | PMT | FV |
|---|---|---|---|---|---|
| Enter | 18 | 11% | | | $725,380 |
| Solve for | | | $110,854.15 | | |

| | N | I/Y | PV | PMT | FV |
|---|---|---|---|---|---|
| Enter | 23 | 18% | | | $590,710 |
| Solve for | | | $13,124.66 | | |

**4.**

| | N | I/Y | PV | PMT | FV |
|---|---|---|---|---|---|
| Enter | 4 | | $242 | | ±$307 |
| Solve for | | 6.13% | | | |

| Enter | 8 |  | $410 |  | ±$896 |
|---|---|---|---|---|---|
|  | **N** | **I/Y** | **PV** | **PMT** | **FV** |
| Solve for |  | 10.27% |  |  |  |

| Enter | 16 |  | $51,700 |  | ±$162,181 |
|---|---|---|---|---|---|
|  | **N** | **I/Y** | **PV** | **PMT** | **FV** |
| Solve for |  | 7.41% |  |  |  |

| Enter | 27 |  | $18,750 |  | ±$483,500 |
|---|---|---|---|---|---|
|  | **N** | **I/Y** | **PV** | **PMT** | **FV** |
| Solve for |  | 12.79% |  |  |  |

**5.**

| Enter |  | 9% | $625 |  | ±$1,284 |
|---|---|---|---|---|---|
|  | **N** | **I/Y** | **PV** | **PMT** | **FV** |
| Solve for | 8.35 |  |  |  |  |

| Enter |  | 11% | $810 |  | ±$4,341 |
|---|---|---|---|---|---|
|  | **N** | **I/Y** | **PV** | **PMT** | **FV** |
| Solve for | 16.09 |  |  |  |  |

| Enter |  | 17% | $18,400 |  | ±$402,662 |
|---|---|---|---|---|---|
|  | **N** | **I/Y** | **PV** | **PMT** | **FV** |
| Solve for | 19.65 |  |  |  |  |

| Enter |  | 8% | $21,500 |  | ±$173,439 |
|---|---|---|---|---|---|
|  | **N** | **I/Y** | **PV** | **PMT** | **FV** |
| Solve for | 27.13 |  |  |  |  |

**6.**

| Enter |  | 8% | $1 |  | ±$2 |
|---|---|---|---|---|---|
|  | **N** | **I/Y** | **PV** | **PMT** | **FV** |
| Solve for | 9.01 |  |  |  |  |

| Enter |  | 8% | $1 |  | ±$4 |
|---|---|---|---|---|---|
|  | **N** | **I/Y** | **PV** | **PMT** | **FV** |
| Solve for | 18.01 |  |  |  |  |

**7.**

| Enter | 20 | 7.1% |  |  | $630,000,000 |
|---|---|---|---|---|---|
|  | **N** | **I/Y** | **PV** | **PMT** | **FV** |
| Solve for |  |  | $159,790,565.17 |  |  |

**8.**

| | N | I/Y | PV | PMT | FV |
|---|---|---|---|---|---|
| Enter | 4 | | ±$1,680,000 | | $1,100,000 |
| Solve for | | −13.17% | | | |

**11.**

| CFo | $0 | | CFo | $0 | | CFo | $0 |
|---|---|---|---|---|---|---|---|
| C01 | $960 | | C01 | $960 | | C01 | $960 |
| F01 | 1 | | F01 | 1 | | F01 | 1 |
| C02 | $840 | | C02 | $840 | | C02 | $840 |
| F02 | 1 | | F02 | 1 | | F02 | 1 |
| C03 | $935 | | C03 | $935 | | C03 | $935 |
| F03 | 1 | | F03 | 1 | | F03 | 1 |
| C04 | $1,350 | | C04 | $1,350 | | C04 | $1,350 |
| F04 | 1 | | F04 | 1 | | F04 | 1 |

I = 10  
NPV CPT  
$3,191.49

I = 18  
NPV CPT  
$2,682.22

I = 24  
NPV CPT  
$2,381.91

**12.**

| | N | I/Y | PV | PMT | FV |
|---|---|---|---|---|---|
| Enter | 9 | 5% | | $4,500 | |
| Solve for | | | $31,985.20 | | |

| | N | I/Y | PV | PMT | FV |
|---|---|---|---|---|---|
| Enter | 5 | 5% | | $7,000 | |
| Solve for | | | $30,306.34 | | |

| | N | I/Y | PV | PMT | FV |
|---|---|---|---|---|---|
| Enter | 9 | 22% | | $4,500 | |
| Solve for | | | $17,038.28 | | |

| | N | I/Y | PV | PMT | FV |
|---|---|---|---|---|---|
| Enter | 5 | 22% | | $7,000 | |
| Solve for | | | $20,045.48 | | |

**13.**

| | N | I/Y | PV | PMT | FV |
|---|---|---|---|---|---|
| Enter | 15 | 8% | | $4,900 | |
| Solve for | | | $41,941.45 | | |

| | N | I/Y | PV | PMT | FV |
|---|---|---|---|---|---|
| Enter | 40 | 8% | | $4,900 | |
| Solve for | | | $58,430.61 | | |

| | | | | |
|---|---|---|---|---|
| Enter | 75 | 8% | | $4,900 | |
| | **N** | **I/Y** | **PV** | **PMT** | **FV** |
| Solve for | | | $61,059.31 | | |

**15.**

| | | | |
|---|---|---|---|
| Enter | 7% | | 4 |
| | **NOM** | **EFF** | **C/Y** |
| Solve for | | 7.19% | |

| | | | |
|---|---|---|---|
| Enter | 16% | | 12 |
| | **NOM** | **EFF** | **C/Y** |
| Solve for | | 17.23% | |

| | | | |
|---|---|---|---|
| Enter | 11% | | 365 |
| | **NOM** | **EFF** | **C/Y** |
| Solve for | | 11.63% | |

**16.**

| | | | |
|---|---|---|---|
| Enter | | 9.8% | 2 |
| | **NOM** | **EFF** | **C/Y** |
| Solve for | 9.57% | | |

| | | | |
|---|---|---|---|
| Enter | | 19.6% | 12 |
| | **NOM** | **EFF** | **C/Y** |
| Solve for | 18.03% | | |

| | | | |
|---|---|---|---|
| Enter | | 8.3% | 52 |
| | **NOM** | **EFF** | **C/Y** |
| Solve for | 7.98% | | |

**17.**

| | | | |
|---|---|---|---|
| Enter | 11.2% | | 12 |
| | **NOM** | **EFF** | **C/Y** |
| Solve for | | 11.79% | |

| | | | |
|---|---|---|---|
| Enter | 11.4% | | 2 |
| | **NOM** | **EFF** | **C/Y** |
| Solve for | | 11.72% | |

**18.** 2nd BGN  2nd SET

| | | | | |
|---|---|---|---|---|
| Enter | 12 | | $108 | ±$10 | |
| | **N** | **I/Y** | **PV** | **PMT** | **FV** |
| Solve for | | 1.98% | | | |

APR = 1.98% × 52 = 102.77%

| Enter | 102.77% | | 52 | | |
|---|---|---|---|---|---|
| | **NOM** | **EFF** | **C/Y** | | |
| Solve for | | 176.68% | | | |

**19.**

| Enter | | 1.3% | $21,500 | ±$700 | |
|---|---|---|---|---|---|
| | **N** | **I/Y** | **PV** | **PMT** | **FV** |
| Solve for | 39.46 | | | | |

**20.**

| Enter | 1,733.33% | | 52 | | |
|---|---|---|---|---|---|
| | **NOM** | **EFF** | **C/Y** | | |
| Solve for | | 313,916,515.69% | | | |

**21.**

| Enter | 6 | 9% | $1,000 | | |
|---|---|---|---|---|---|
| | **N** | **I/Y** | **PV** | **PMT** | **FV** |
| Solve for | | | | | $1,677.10 |

| Enter | 6 × 2 | 9%/2 | $1,000 | | |
|---|---|---|---|---|---|
| | **N** | **I/Y** | **PV** | **PMT** | **FV** |
| Solve for | | | | | $1,695.88 |

| Enter | 6 × 12 | 9%/12 | $1,000 | | |
|---|---|---|---|---|---|
| | **N** | **I/Y** | **PV** | **PMT** | **FV** |
| Solve for | | | | | $1,712.55 |

**23.** Stock account:

| Enter | 360 | 11% / 12 | | $800 | |
|---|---|---|---|---|---|
| | **N** | **I/Y** | **PV** | **PMT** | **FV** |
| Solve for | | | | | $2,243,615.79 |

Bond account:

| Enter | 360 | 6% / 12 | | $350 | |
|---|---|---|---|---|---|
| | **N** | **I/Y** | **PV** | **PMT** | **FV** |
| Solve for | | | | | $351,580.26 |

Savings at retirement = $2,243,615.79 + 351,580.26 = $2,595,196.05

| Enter | 300 | 8% / 12 | $2,595,196.05 | | |
|---|---|---|---|---|---|
| | **N** | **I/Y** | **PV** | **PMT** | **FV** |
| Solve for | | | | $20,030.14 | |

**24.**

| Enter | 12 / 3 | | ±$1 | | $4 |
|---|---|---|---|---|---|
| | **N** | **I/Y** | **PV** | **PMT** | **FV** |
| Solve for | | 41.42% | | | |

**25.**

| Enter | 6 | | ±$65,000 | | $125,000 |
|---|---|---|---|---|---|
| | **N** | **I/Y** | **PV** | **PMT** | **FV** |
| Solve for | | 11.51% | | | |

| Enter | 10 | | ±65,000 | | $185,000 |
|---|---|---|---|---|---|
| | **N** | **I/Y** | **PV** | **PMT** | **FV** |
| Solve for | | 11.03% | | | |

**28.**

| Enter | 23 | 7% | | $6,500 | |
|---|---|---|---|---|---|
| | **N** | **I/Y** | **PV** | **PMT** | **FV** |
| Solve for | | | $73,269.22 | | |

| Enter | 2 | 7% | | | $73,269.22 |
|---|---|---|---|---|---|
| | **N** | **I/Y** | **PV** | **PMT** | **FV** |
| Solve for | | | $63,996.17 | | |

**29.**

| Enter | 15 | 13% | | $650 | |
|---|---|---|---|---|---|
| | **N** | **I/Y** | **PV** | **PMT** | **FV** |
| Solve for | | | $4,200.55 | | |

| Enter | 5 | 11% | | | $4,200.55 |
|---|---|---|---|---|---|
| | **N** | **I/Y** | **PV** | **PMT** | **FV** |
| Solve for | | | $2,492.82 | | |

**30.**

| Enter | 360 | 6.1%/12 | .80($550,000) | | |
|---|---|---|---|---|---|
| | **N** | **I/Y** | **PV** | **PMT** | **FV** |
| Solve for | | | | $2,666.38 | |

| Enter | 22 × 12 | 6.1%/12 | | $2,666.38 | |
|---|---|---|---|---|---|
| | **N** | **I/Y** | **PV** | **PMT** | **FV** |
| Solve for | | | $386,994.11 | | |

**31.**

| Enter | 6 | 2.40% / 12 | $7,500 | | |
|---|---|---|---|---|---|
| | **N** | **I/Y** | **PV** | **PMT** | **FV** |
| Solve for | | | | | $7,590.45 |

| Enter | 6 | 18% / 12 | $7,590.45 | | |
|---|---|---|---|---|---|
| | **N** | **I/Y** | **PV** | **PMT** | **FV** |
| Solve for | | | | | $8,299.73 |

$8,299.73 − 7,500 = $799.73

**35.**

| Enter | 15 | 10% | | $6,800 | |
|---|---|---|---|---|---|
| | **N** | **I/Y** | **PV** | **PMT** | **FV** |
| Solve for | | | $51,721.34 | | |

| Enter | 15 | 5% | | $6,800 | |
|---|---|---|---|---|---|
| | **N** | **I/Y** | **PV** | **PMT** | **FV** |
| Solve for | | | $70,581.67 | | |

| Enter | 15 | 15% | | $6,800 | |
|---|---|---|---|---|---|
| | **N** | **I/Y** | **PV** | **PMT** | **FV** |
| Solve for | | | $39,762.12 | | |

**36.**

| Enter | | 10% / 12 | | ±$350 | $35,000 |
|---|---|---|---|---|---|
| | **N** | **I/Y** | **PV** | **PMT** | **FV** |
| Solve for | 73.04 | | | | |

**37.**

| Enter | 60 | | $65,000 | ±$1,320 | |
|---|---|---|---|---|---|
| | **N** | **I/Y** | **PV** | **PMT** | **FV** |
| Solve for | | 0.672% | | | |

$0.672\% \times 12 = 8.07\%$

**38.**

| Enter | 360 | 5.3% / 12 | | $950 | |
|---|---|---|---|---|---|
| | **N** | **I/Y** | **PV** | **PMT** | **FV** |
| Solve for | | | $171,077.26 | | |

$250,000 − 171,077.26 = $78,922.74

| Enter | 360 | 5.3% / 12 | $78,922.74 | | |
|---|---|---|---|---|---|
| | **N** | **I/Y** | **PV** | **PMT** | **FV** |
| Solve for | | | | | $385,664.73 |

**39.**

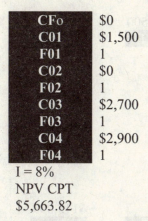

| | |
|---|---|
| CFo | $0 |
| C01 | $1,500 |
| F01 | 1 |
| C02 | $0 |
| F02 | 1 |
| C03 | $2,700 |
| F03 | 1 |
| C04 | $2,900 |
| F04 | 1 |

I = 8%
NPV CPT
$5,663.82

PV of missing CF = $7,300 − 5,663.82 = $1,636.18
Value of missing CF:

| | N | I/Y | PV | PMT | FV |
|---|---|---|---|---|---|
| Enter | 2 | 8% | $1,636.18 | | |
| Solve for | | | | | $1,908.44 |

**40.**

| | |
|---|---|
| CFo | $1,000,000 |
| C01 | $1,275,000 |
| F01 | 1 |
| C02 | $1,550,000 |
| F02 | 1 |
| C03 | $1,825,000 |
| F03 | 1 |
| C04 | $2,100,000 |
| F04 | 1 |
| C05 | $2,375,000 |
| F05 | 1 |
| C06 | $2,650,000 |
| F06 | 1 |
| C07 | $2,925,000 |
| F07 | 1 |
| C08 | $3,200,000 |
| F08 | 1 |
| C09 | $3,475,000 |
| F09 | 1 |
| C010 | $3,750,000 |

I = 9%
NPV CPT
$15,885,026.33

**41.**

| Enter | 360 | | .80($4,500,000) | ±$27,500 | |
|-------|-----|-----|-----------------|----------|-----|
| | **N** | **I/Y** | **PV** | **PMT** | **FV** |
| Solve for | | 0.702% | | | |

$$APR = 0.702\% \times 12 = 8.43\%$$

| Enter | 8.43% | | 12 |
|-------|-------|-----|-----|
| | **NOM** | **EFF** | **C/Y** |
| Solve for | | 8.76% | |

**42.**

| Enter | 3 | 13% | | | $115,000 |
|-------|---|-----|-----|-----|----------|
| | **N** | **I/Y** | **PV** | **PMT** | **FV** |
| Solve for | | | $79,700.77 | | |

$$Profit = \$79,700.77 - 76,000 = \$3,700.77$$

| Enter | 3 | | ±$76,000 | | $115,000 |
|-------|---|-----|----------|-----|----------|
| | **N** | **I/Y** | **PV** | **PMT** | **FV** |
| Solve for | | 14.81% | | | |

**43.**

| Enter | 20 | 7% | | $5,000 | |
|-------|----|----|-----|--------|-----|
| | **N** | **I/Y** | **PV** | **PMT** | **FV** |
| Solve for | | | $52,970.07 | | |

| Enter | 5 | 7% | | | $52,970.07 |
|-------|---|----|-----|-----|------------|
| | **N** | **I/Y** | **PV** | **PMT** | **FV** |
| Solve for | | | $37,766.93 | | |

**44.**

| Enter | 96 | 6% / 12 | | $1,500 | |
|-------|----|---------|-----|--------|-----|
| | **N** | **I/Y** | **PV** | **PMT** | **FV** |
| Solve for | | | $114,142.83 | | |

| Enter | 84 | 12% / 12 | | $1,500 | $114,142.83 |
|-------|----|----------|-----|--------|-------------|
| | **N** | **I/Y** | **PV** | **PMT** | **FV** |
| Solve for | | | $134,455.36 | | |

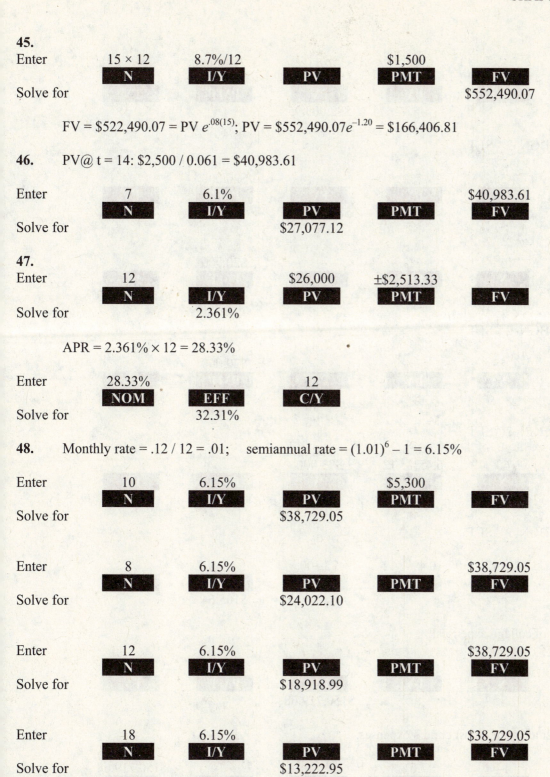

**45.**

| | N | I/Y | PV | PMT | FV |
|---|---|---|---|---|---|
| Enter | 15 × 12 | 8.7%/12 | | $1,500 | |
| Solve for | | | | | $552,490.07 |

$$FV = \$522,490.07 = PV\ e^{.08(15)};\ PV = \$552,490.07e^{-1.20} = \$166,406.81$$

**46.**  PV@ t = 14: $2,500 / 0.061 = $40,983.61

| | N | I/Y | PV | PMT | FV |
|---|---|---|---|---|---|
| Enter | 7 | 6.1% | | | $40,983.61 |
| Solve for | | | $27,077.12 | | |

**47.**

| | N | I/Y | PV | PMT | FV |
|---|---|---|---|---|---|
| Enter | 12 | | $26,000 | ±$2,513.33 | |
| Solve for | | 2.361% | | | |

APR = 2.361% × 12 = 28.33%

| | NOM | EFF | C/Y |
|---|---|---|---|
| Enter | 28.33% | | 12 |
| Solve for | | 32.31% | |

**48.**  Monthly rate = .12 / 12 = .01;    semiannual rate = $(1.01)^6 - 1 = 6.15\%$

| | N | I/Y | PV | PMT | FV |
|---|---|---|---|---|---|
| Enter | 10 | 6.15% | | $5,300 | |
| Solve for | | | $38,729.05 | | |

| | N | I/Y | PV | PMT | FV |
|---|---|---|---|---|---|
| Enter | 8 | 6.15% | | | $38,729.05 |
| Solve for | | | $24,022.10 | | |

| | N | I/Y | PV | PMT | FV |
|---|---|---|---|---|---|
| Enter | 12 | 6.15% | | | $38,729.05 |
| Solve for | | | $18,918.99 | | |

| | N | I/Y | PV | PMT | FV |
|---|---|---|---|---|---|
| Enter | 18 | 6.15% | | | $38,729.05 |
| Solve for | | | $13,222.95 | | |

**49.**

*a.*

| Enter | 5 | 7% | | $20,000 | |
|-------|---|-----|----|---------|----|
| | **N** | **I/Y** | **PV** | **PMT** | **FV** |
| Solve for | | | $82,003.95 | | |

2nd BGN 2nd SET

| Enter | 5 | 7% | | $20,000 | |
|-------|---|-----|----|---------|----|
| | **N** | **I/Y** | **PV** | **PMT** | **FV** |
| Solve for | | | $87,744.23 | | |

*b.*

| Enter | 5 | 7% | | $20,000 | |
|-------|---|-----|----|---------|----|
| | **N** | **I/Y** | **PV** | **PMT** | **FV** |
| Solve for | | | | | $115,014.78 |

2nd BGN 2nd SET

| Enter | 5 | 7% | | $20,000 | |
|-------|---|-----|----|---------|----|
| | **N** | **I/Y** | **PV** | **PMT** | **FV** |
| Solve for | | | | | $123,065.81 |

**50.** 2nd BGN 2nd SET

| Enter | 60 | 6.45% / 12 | $73,000 | | |
|-------|----|-----------|---------|----|----|
| | **N** | **I/Y** | **PV** | **PMT** | **FV** |
| Solve for | | | | $1,418.99 | |

**51.** 2nd BGN 2nd SET

| Enter | 2 × 12 | 10.4% / 12 | $2,300 | | |
|-------|--------|-----------|--------|----|----|
| | **N** | **I/Y** | **PV** | **PMT** | **FV** |
| Solve for | | | | $105.64 | |

**52.** PV of college expenses:

| Enter | 4 | 7.5% | | $45,000 | |
|-------|---|------|----|---------|----|
| | **N** | **I/Y** | **PV** | **PMT** | **FV** |
| Solve for | | | $150,719.68 | | |

Cost today of oldest child's expenses:

| Enter | 14 | 7.5% | | | $150,719.68 |
|-------|----|------|----|----|-------------|
| | **N** | **I/Y** | **PV** | **PMT** | **FV** |
| Solve for | | | $54,758.49 | | |

Cost today of youngest child's expenses:

| | N | I/Y | PV | PMT | FV |
|---|---|---|---|---|---|
| Enter | 16 | 7.5% | | | $150,719.68 |
| Solve for | | | $47,384.31 | | |

Total cost today = $54,758.49 + 47,384.31 = $102,142.80

| | N | I/Y | PV | PMT | FV |
|---|---|---|---|---|---|
| Enter | 15 | 7.5% | $102,142.80 | | |
| Solve for | | | | $11,571.48 | |

**54.** Option A:
Aftertax cash flows = Pretax cash flows(1 − tax rate)
Aftertax cash flows = $250,000(1 − .28)
Aftertax cash flows = $180,000

$2^{ND}$ BGN $2^{nd}$ SET

| | N | I/Y | PV | PMT | FV |
|---|---|---|---|---|---|
| Enter | 31 | 7% | | $180,000 | |
| Solve for | | | $2,413,627.41 | | |

Option B:
Aftertax cash flows = Pretax cash flows(1 − tax rate)
Aftertax cash flows = $200,000(1 − .28)
Aftertax cash flows = $144,000

$2^{ND}$ BGN $2^{nd}$ SET

| | N | I/Y | PV | PMT | FV |
|---|---|---|---|---|---|
| Enter | 30 | 7% | | $144,000 | |
| Solve for | | | $1,786,901.93 | | |

$1,786,901.93 + 530,000 = $2,316,901.93

**56.**

| | N | I/Y | PV | PMT | FV |
|---|---|---|---|---|---|
| Enter | 5 × 12 | 7.2% / 12 | $29,000 | | |
| Solve for | | | | $576.98 | |

| | N | I/Y | PV | PMT | FV |
|---|---|---|---|---|---|
| Enter | 34 | 7.2% / 12 | | $576.98 | |
| Solve for | | | $17,697.79 | | |

Total payment = Amount due(1 + Prepayment penalty) + Last payment
Total payment = $17,697.79(1 + .01) + $576.98
Total payment = $18,451.74

**57.** Pre-retirement APR:

| Enter | | 11% | 12 | | |
|---|---|---|---|---|---|
| | **NOM** | **EFF** | **C/Y** | | |
| Solve for | 10.48% | | | | |

Post-retirement APR:

| Enter | | 8% | 12 | | |
|---|---|---|---|---|---|
| | **NOM** | **EFF** | **C/Y** | | |
| Solve for | 7.72% | | | | |

At retirement, he needs:

| Enter | 240 | 7.72% / 12 | | $23,000 | $1,000,000 |
|---|---|---|---|---|---|
| | **N** | **I/Y** | **PV** | **PMT** | **FV** |
| Solve for | | | $3,022,336.00 | | |

In 10 years, his savings will be worth:

| Enter | 120 | 10.48% / 12 | | $2,100 | |
|---|---|---|---|---|---|
| | **N** | **I/Y** | **PV** | **PMT** | **FV** |
| Solve for | | | | | $442,239.69 |

After purchasing the cabin, he will have: $442,239.69 – 320,000 = $122,239.69

Each month between years 10 and 30, he needs to save:

| Enter | 240 | 10.48% / 12 | $122,239.69± | | $3,022,336.00 |
|---|---|---|---|---|---|
| | **N** | **I/Y** | **PV** | **PMT** | **FV** |
| Solve for | | | | –$2,519.10 | |

**58.** PV of purchase:

| Enter | 36 | 6% / 12 | | | $20,000 |
|---|---|---|---|---|---|
| | **N** | **I/Y** | **PV** | **PMT** | **FV** |
| Solve for | | | $16,712.90 | | |

$31,000 – 16,712.90 = $14,287.10

PV of lease:

| Enter | 36 | 6% / 12 | | $405 | |
|---|---|---|---|---|---|
| | **N** | **I/Y** | **PV** | **PMT** | **FV** |
| Solve for | | | $13,312.76 | | |

$13,312.76 + 1,500 = $14,812.76
Buy the car.

You would be indifferent when the PV of the two cash flows are equal. The present value of the purchase decision must be $14,812.76. Since the difference in the two cash flows is $31,000 – 14,812.76 = $16,187.24, this must be the present value of the future resale price of the car. The break-even resale price of the car is:

| | N | I/Y | PV | PMT | FV |
|---|---|---|---|---|---|
| Enter | 36 | 6% / 12 | $16,187.24 | | |
| Solve for | | | | | $19,370.95 |

**59.**

| | NOM | EFF | C/Y |
|---|---|---|---|
| Enter | 5% | | 365 |
| Solve for | | 5.13% | |

| | |
|---|---|
| CFo | $8,500,000 |
| C01 | $3,900,000 |
| F01 | 1 |
| C02 | $4,600,000 |
| F02 | 1 |
| C03 | $5,300,000 |
| F03 | 1 |
| C04 | $5,800,000 |
| F04 | 1 |
| C05 | $6,400,000 |
| F05 | 1 |
| C06 | $7,300,000 |
| F06 | 1 |

I = 5.13%
NPV CPT
$36,075,085.12

New contract value = $36,075,085.12 + 1,500,000 = $37,575,085.12

PV of payments = $37,575,085.12 – 10,000,000 = $27,575,085.12
Effective quarterly rate = $[1 + (.05/365)]^{91.25} - 1 = 1.258\%$

| | N | I/Y | PV | PMT | FV |
|---|---|---|---|---|---|
| Enter | 24 | 1.258% | $27,575,085.12 | | |
| Solve for | | | | $1,338,243.52 | |

**60.**

| | N | I/Y | PV | PMT | FV |
|---|---|---|---|---|---|
| Enter | 1 | | $17,000 | | ±$20,000 |
| Solve for | | 17.65% | | | |

**61.**

| | NOM | EFF | C/Y |
|---|---|---|---|
| Enter | | 9% | 12 |
| Solve for | 8.65% | | |

| Enter | 12 | 8.65% / 12 | | $37,000 / 12 | |
|---|---|---|---|---|---|
| | **N** | **I/Y** | **PV** | **PMT** | **FV** |
| Solve for | | | | | $38,502.50 |

| Enter | 1 | 9% | $38,502.50 | | |
|---|---|---|---|---|---|
| | **N** | **I/Y** | **PV** | **PMT** | **FV** |
| Solve for | | | | | $41,967.73 |

| Enter | 12 | 8.65% / 12 | | $39,000 / 12 | |
|---|---|---|---|---|---|
| | **N** | **I/Y** | **PV** | **PMT** | **FV** |
| Solve for | | | | | $40,583.72 |

| Enter | 60 | 8.65% / 12 | | $43,000 / 12 | |
|---|---|---|---|---|---|
| | **N** | **I/Y** | **PV** | **PMT** | **FV** |
| Solve for | | | $174,046.93 | | |

Award = $41,967.73 + 40,583.72 + 174,046.93 + 150,000 + 25,000 = $431,598.39

**62.**

| Enter | 1 | | $9,700 | | ±$10,800 |
|---|---|---|---|---|---|
| | **N** | **I/Y** | **PV** | **PMT** | **FV** |
| Solve for | | 11.34% | | | |

| Enter | 1 | | $9,800 | | ±$11,100 |
|---|---|---|---|---|---|
| | **N** | **I/Y** | **PV** | **PMT** | **FV** |
| Solve for | | 13.27% | | | |

**63.** Refundable fee: With the $2,400 application fee, you will need to borrow $202,400 to have $200,000 after deducting the fee. Solve for the payment under these circumstances.

| Enter | 30 × 12 | 5.39% / 12 | $202,400 | | |
|---|---|---|---|---|---|
| | **N** | **I/Y** | **PV** | **PMT** | **FV** |
| Solve for | | | | $1,123.94 | |

| Enter | 30 × 12 | | $200,000 | ±$1,123.94 | |
|---|---|---|---|---|---|
| | **N** | **I/Y** | **PV** | **PMT** | **FV** |
| Solve for | | 0.4506% | | | |

APR = 0.4506% × 12 = 5.41%

| Enter | 5.41% | | 12 |
|---|---|---|---|
| | **NOM** | **EFF** | **C/Y** |
| Solve for | | 5.54% | |

Without refundable fee: APR = 5.30%

| Enter | 5.30% | | 12 | | |
|-------|-------|-------|-----|-------|-------|
| | **NOM** | **EFF** | **C/Y** | | |
| Solve for | | 5.43% | | | |

**64.**

| Enter | 36 | | $1,000 | ±$45.64 | |
|-------|-----|-------|--------|---------|-------|
| | **N** | **I/Y** | **PV** | **PMT** | **FV** |
| Solve for | | 2.98% | | | |

APR = 2.98% × 12 = 35.71%

| Enter | 35.71% | | 12 | | |
|-------|--------|-------|-----|-------|-------|
| | **NOM** | **EFF** | **C/Y** | | |
| Solve for | | 42.18% | | | |

**65.**    Without fee:

| Enter | | 18.6% / 12 | $10,000 | ±$200 | |
|-------|-------|------------|---------|-------|-------|
| | **N** | **I/Y** | **PV** | **PMT** | **FV** |
| Solve for | 96.98 | | | | |

| Enter | | 8.2% / 12 | $10,000 | ±$200 | |
|-------|-------|-----------|---------|-------|-------|
| | **N** | **I/Y** | **PV** | **PMT** | **FV** |
| Solve for | 61.39 | | | | |

With fee:

| Enter | | 8.2% / 12 | $10,200 | ±$200 | |
|-------|-------|-----------|---------|-------|-------|
| | **N** | **I/Y** | **PV** | **PMT** | **FV** |
| Solve for | 62.92 | | | | |

**66.**    Value at Year 6:

| Enter | 5 | 11% | $500 | | |
|-------|-----|-----|------|-------|-------|
| | **N** | **I/Y** | **PV** | **PMT** | **FV** |
| Solve for | | | | | $842.53 |

| Enter | 4 | 11% | $600 | | |
|-------|-----|-----|------|-------|-------|
| | **N** | **I/Y** | **PV** | **PMT** | **FV** |
| Solve for | | | | | $910.84 |

| Enter | 3 | 11% | $700 | | |
|-------|-----|-----|------|-------|-------|
| | **N** | **I/Y** | **PV** | **PMT** | **FV** |
| Solve for | | | | | $957.34 |

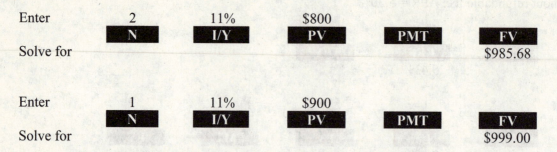

| Enter | 2 | 11% | $800 | | |
|---|---|---|---|---|---|
| | **N** | **I/Y** | **PV** | **PMT** | **FV** |
| Solve for | | | | | $985.68 |

| Enter | 1 | 11% | $900 | | |
|---|---|---|---|---|---|
| | **N** | **I/Y** | **PV** | **PMT** | **FV** |
| Solve for | | | | | $999.00 |

So, at Year 6, the value is: $842.53 + 910.84 + 957.34 + 985.68 + 999.00 + 1,000 = $5,695.39

At Year 65, the value is:

| Enter | 59 | 7% | $5,695.39 | | |
|---|---|---|---|---|---|
| | **N** | **I/Y** | **PV** | **PMT** | **FV** |
| Solve for | | | | | $308,437.08 |

The policy is not worth buying; the future value of the payments is $308,437.08 but the policy contract will pay off $275,000.

**67.** Effective six-month rate = $(1 + \text{Daily rate})^{180} - 1$
Effective six-month rate = $(1 + .09/360)^{180} - 1$
Effective six-month rate = .0460 or 4.60%

| Enter | 40 | 4.60% | | $1,250,000 | |
|---|---|---|---|---|---|
| | **N** | **I/Y** | **PV** | **PMT** | **FV** |
| Solve for | | | $22,670,253.86 | | |

| Enter | 1 | 4.60% | | | $22,670,253.86 |
|---|---|---|---|---|---|
| | **N** | **I/Y** | **PV** | **PMT** | **FV** |
| Solve for | | | $21,672,827.50 | | |

Value of winnings today = $22,670,253.86 + 2,500,000
Value of winnings today = $24,172,827.50

**68.**

| CFo | ±$11,000 |
|---|---|
| C01 | ±$11,000 |
| F01 | 5 |
| C02 | $25,000 |
| F02 | 4 |

IRR CPT
8.54%

**72.**

*a.*        APR = 7% × 52 = 364%

| | | | | | |
|---|---|---|---|---|---|
| Enter | 364% | | | 52 | |
| | **NOM** | **EFF** | | **C/Y** | |
| Solve for | | 3,272.53% | | | |

*b.*

| | | | | | | | | |
|---|---|---|---|---|---|---|---|---|
| Enter | 1 | | $9.30 | | | | ±$10.00 | |
| | **N** | **I/Y** | **PV** | | **PMT** | | **FV** | |
| Solve for | | 7.53% | | | | | | |

APR = 7.53% × 52 = 391.40%

| | | | | | |
|---|---|---|---|---|---|
| Enter | 391.40% | | | 52 | |
| | **NOM** | **EFF** | | **C/Y** | |
| Solve for | | 4,253.98% | | | |

*c.*

| | | | | | | |
|---|---|---|---|---|---|---|
| Enter | 4 | | $68.92 | | ±$25 | |
| | **N** | **I/Y** | **PV** | | **PMT** | **FV** |
| Solve for | | 16.75% | | | | |

APR = 16.75% × 52 = 871.00%

| | | | | | |
|---|---|---|---|---|---|
| Enter | 871.00% | | | 52 | |
| | **NOM** | **EFF** | | **C/Y** | |
| Solve for | | 314,215.72% | | | |

# CHAPTER 4, APPENDIX
# NET PRESENT VALUE: FIRST PRINCIPLES OF FINANCE

**Solutions to Questions and Problems**

*NOTE: All end-of-chapter problems were solved using a spreadsheet. Many problems require multiple steps. Due to space and readability constraints, when these intermediate steps are included in this solutions manual, rounding may appear to have occurred. However, the final answer for each problem is found without rounding during any step in the problem.*

1. The potential consumption for a borrower next year is the salary during the year, minus the repayment of the loan and interest to fund the current consumption. The amount that must be borrowed to fund this year's consumption is:

   Amount to borrow = $100,000 – 80,000 = $20,000

   Interest will be charged the amount borrowed, so the repayment of this loan next year will be:

   Loan repayment = $20,000(1.10) = $22,000

   So, the consumption potential next year is the salary minus the loan repayment, or:

   Consumption potential = $90,000 – 22,000 = $68,000

2. The potential consumption for a saver next year is the salary during the year, plus the savings from the current year and the interest earned. The amount saved this year is:

   Amount saved = $50,000 – 35,000 = $15,000

   The saver will earn interest over the year, so the value of the savings next year will be:

   Savings value in one year = $15,000(1.12) = $16,800

   So, the consumption potential next year is the salary plus the value of the savings, or:

   Consumption potential = $60,000 + 16,800 = $76,800

3. Financial markets arise to facilitate borrowing and lending between individuals. By borrowing and lending, people can adjust their pattern of consumption over time to fit their particular preferences. This allows corporations to accept all positive NPV projects, regardless of the inter-temporal consumption preferences of the shareholders.

4.  *a.*  The present value of labor income is the total of the maximum current consumption. So, solving for the interest rate, we find:

$86 = $40 + $50/(1 + R)
R = .0870 or 8.70%

*b.*  The NPV of the investment is the difference between the new maximum current consumption minus the old maximum current consumption, or:

NPV = $98 – 86 = $12

*c.*  The total maximum current consumption amount must be the present value of the equal annual consumption amount. If C is the equal annual consumption amount, we find:

$98 = C + C/(1 + R)
$98 = C + C/(1.0870)
C = $51.04

5.  *a.*  The market interest rate must be the increase in the maximum current consumption to the maximum consumption next year, which is:

Market interest rate = $90,000/$80,000 – 1 = 0.1250 or 12.50%

*b.*  Harry will invest $10,000 in financial assets and $30,000 in productive assets today.

*c.*  NPV = –$30,000 + $56,250/1.125
NPV = $20,000

# CHAPTER 5
# NET PRESENT VALUE AND OTHER INVESTMENT CRITERIA

## Answers to Concepts Review and Critical Thinking Questions

1. Assuming conventional cash flows, a payback period less than the project's life means that the NPV is positive for a zero discount rate, but nothing more definitive can be said. For discount rates greater than zero, the payback period will still be less than the project's life, but the NPV may be positive, zero, or negative, depending on whether the discount rate is less than, equal to, or greater than the IRR. The discounted payback includes the effect of the relevant discount rate. If a project's discounted payback period is less than the project's life, it must be the case that NPV is positive.

2. Assuming conventional cash flows, if a project has a positive NPV for a certain discount rate, then it will also have a positive NPV for a zero discount rate; thus, the payback period must be less than the project life. Since discounted payback is calculated at the same discount rate as is NPV, if NPV is positive, the discounted payback period must be less than the project's life. If NPV is positive, then the present value of future cash inflows is greater than the initial investment cost; thus, PI must be greater than 1. If NPV is positive for a certain discount rate $R$, then it will be zero for some larger discount rate $R^*$; thus, the IRR must be greater than the required return.

3.    *a.* Payback period is simply the accounting break-even point of a series of cash flows. To actually compute the payback period, it is assumed that any cash flow occurring during a given period is realized continuously throughout the period, and not at a single point in time. The payback is then the point in time for the series of cash flows when the initial cash outlays are fully recovered. Given some predetermined cutoff for the payback period, the decision rule is to accept projects that pay back before this cutoff, and reject projects that take longer to pay back. The worst problem associated with the payback period is that it ignores the time value of money. In addition, the selection of a hurdle point for the payback period is an arbitrary exercise that lacks any steadfast rule or method. The payback period is biased towards short-term projects; it fully ignores any cash flows that occur after the cutoff point.

   *b.* The IRR is the discount rate that causes the NPV of a series of cash flows to be identically zero. IRR can thus be interpreted as a financial break-even rate of return; at the IRR discount rate, the net value of the project is zero. The acceptance and rejection criteria are:

        If $C_0 < 0$ and all future cash flows are positive, accept the project if the internal rate of return is greater than or equal to the discount rate.
        If $C_0 < 0$ and all future cash flows are positive, reject the project if the internal rate of return is less than the discount rate.
        If $C_0 > 0$ and all future cash flows are negative, accept the project if the internal rate of return is less than or equal to the discount rate.
        If $C_0 > 0$ and all future cash flows are negative, reject the project if the internal rate of return is greater than the discount rate.

IRR is the discount rate that causes NPV for a series of cash flows to be zero. NPV is preferred in all situations to IRR; IRR can lead to ambiguous results if there are non-conventional cash flows, and it also may ambiguously rank some mutually exclusive projects. However, for stand-alone projects with conventional cash flows, IRR and NPV are interchangeable techniques.

    *c.*    The profitability index is the present value of cash inflows relative to the project cost. As such, it is a benefit/cost ratio, providing a measure of the relative profitability of a project. The profitability index decision rule is to accept projects with a PI greater than one, and to reject projects with a PI less than one. The profitability index can be expressed as: PI = (NPV + cost)/cost = 1 + (NPV/cost). If a firm has a basket of positive NPV projects and is subject to capital rationing, PI may provide a good ranking measure of the projects, indicating the "bang for the buck" of each particular project.

    *d.*    NPV is simply the present value of a project's cash flows, including the initial outlay. NPV specifically measures, after considering the time value of money, the net increase or decrease in firm wealth due to the project. The decision rule is to accept projects that have a positive NPV, and reject projects with a negative NPV. NPV is superior to the other methods of analysis presented in the text because it has no serious flaws. The method unambiguously ranks mutually exclusive projects, and it can differentiate between projects of different scale and time horizon. The only drawback to NPV is that it relies on cash flow and discount rate values that are often estimates and thus not certain, but this is a problem shared by the other performance criteria as well. A project with NPV = $2,500 implies that the total shareholder wealth of the firm will increase by $2,500 if the project is accepted.

**4.**    For a project with future cash flows that are an annuity:

Payback = I / C

And the IRR is:

$0 = -I + C / IRR$

Solving the IRR equation for IRR, we get:

IRR = C / I

Notice this is just the reciprocal of the payback. So:

IRR = 1 / PB

For long-lived projects with relatively constant cash flows, the sooner the project pays back, the greater is the IRR, and the IRR is approximately equal to the reciprocal of the payback period.

**5.**    There are a number of reasons. Two of the most important have to do with transportation costs and exchange rates. Manufacturing in the U.S. places the finished product much closer to the point of sale, resulting in significant savings in transportation costs. It also reduces inventories because goods spend less time in transit. Higher labor costs tend to offset these savings to some degree, at least compared to other possible manufacturing locations. Of great importance is the fact that manufacturing in the U.S. means that a much higher proportion of the costs are paid in dollars. Since sales are in dollars, the net effect is to immunize profits to a large extent against fluctuations in exchange rates. This issue is discussed in greater detail in the chapter on international finance.

6. The single biggest difficulty, by far, is coming up with reliable cash flow estimates. Determining an appropriate discount rate is also not a simple task. These issues are discussed in greater depth in the next several chapters. The payback approach is probably the simplest, followed by the AAR, but even these require revenue and cost projections. The discounted cash flow measures (discounted payback, NPV, IRR, and profitability index) are really only slightly more difficult in practice.

7. Yes, they are. Such entities generally need to allocate available capital efficiently, just as for-profits do. However, it is frequently the case that the "revenues" from not-for-profit ventures are not tangible. For example, charitable giving has real opportunity costs, but the benefits are generally hard to measure. To the extent that benefits are measurable, the question of an appropriate required return remains. Payback rules are commonly used in such cases. Finally, realistic cost/benefit analysis along the lines indicated should definitely be used by the U.S. government and would go a long way toward balancing the budget!

8. The statement is false. If the cash flows of Project B occur early and the cash flows of Project A occur late, then for a low discount rate the NPV of A can exceed the NPV of B. Observe the following example.

|  | $C_0$ | $C_1$ | $C_2$ | IRR | NPV @ 0% |
|---|---|---|---|---|---|
| Project A | –$1,000,000 | $      0 | $1,440,000 | 20% | $440,000 |
| Project B | –$2,000,000 | $2,400,000 | $      0 | 20% | 400,000 |

However, in one particular case, the statement is true for equally risky projects. If the lives of the two projects are equal and the cash flows of Project B are twice the cash flows of Project A in every time period, the NPV of Project B will be twice the NPV of Project A.

9. Although the profitability index (PI) is higher for Project B than for Project A, Project A should be chosen because it has the greater NPV. Confusion arises because Project B requires a smaller investment than Project A. Since the denominator of the PI ratio is lower for Project B than for Project A, B can have a higher PI yet have a lower NPV. Only in the case of capital rationing could the company's decision have been incorrect.

10. *a.* Project A would have a higher IRR since initial investment for Project A is less than that of Project B, if the cash flows for the two projects are identical.

   *b.* Yes, since both the cash flows as well as the initial investment are twice that of Project B.

11. Project B's NPV would be more sensitive to changes in the discount rate. The reason is the time value of money. Cash flows that occur further out in the future are always more sensitive to changes in the interest rate. This sensitivity is similar to the interest rate risk of a bond.

12. The MIRR is calculated by finding the present value of all cash outflows, the future value of all cash inflows to the end of the project, and then calculating the IRR of the two cash flows. As a result, the cash flows have been discounted or compounded by one interest rate (the required return), and then the interest rate between the two remaining cash flows is calculated. As such, the MIRR is not a true interest rate. In contrast, consider the IRR. If you take the initial investment, and calculate the future value at the IRR, you can replicate the future cash flows of the project exactly.

**13.** The statement is incorrect. It is true that if you calculate the future value of all intermediate cash flows to the end of the project at the required return, then calculate the NPV of this future value and the initial investment, you will get the same NPV. However, NPV says nothing about reinvestment of intermediate cash flows. The NPV is the present value of the project cash flows. What is actually done with those cash flows once they are generated is not relevant. Put differently, the value of a project depends on the cash flows generated by the project, not on the future value of those cash flows. The fact that the reinvestment "works" only if you use the required return as the reinvestment rate is also irrelevant simply because reinvestment is not relevant in the first place to the value of the project.

One caveat: Our discussion here assumes that the cash flows are truly available once they are generated, meaning that it is up to firm management to decide what to do with the cash flows. In certain cases, there may be a requirement that the cash flows be reinvested. For example, in international investing, a company may be required to reinvest the cash flows in the country in which they are generated and not "repatriate" the money. Such funds are said to be "blocked" and reinvestment becomes relevant because the cash flows are not truly available.

**14.** The statement is incorrect. It is true that if you calculate the future value of all intermediate cash flows to the end of the project at the IRR, then calculate the IRR of this future value and the initial investment, you will get the same IRR. However, as in the previous question, what is done with the cash flows once they are generated does not affect the IRR. Consider the following example:

|  | $C_0$ | $C_1$ | $C_2$ | IRR |
|---|---|---|---|---|
| Project A | –$100 | $10 | $110 | 10% |

Suppose this $100 is a deposit into a bank account. The IRR of the cash flows is 10 percent. Does the IRR change if the Year 1 cash flow is reinvested in the account, or if it is withdrawn and spent on pizza? No. Finally, consider the yield to maturity calculation on a bond. If you think about it, the YTM is the IRR on the bond, but no mention of a reinvestment assumption for the bond coupons is suggested. The reason is that reinvestment is irrelevant to the YTM calculation; in the same way, reinvestment is irrelevant in the IRR calculation. Our caveat about blocked funds applies here as well.

## Solutions to Questions and Problems

*NOTE: All end-of-chapter problems were solved using a spreadsheet. Many problems require multiple steps. Due to space and readability constraints, when these intermediate steps are included in this solutions manual, rounding may appear to have occurred. However, the final answer for each problem is found without rounding during any step in the problem.*

*Basic*

**1.** *a.* The payback period is the time that it takes for the cumulative undiscounted cash inflows to equal the initial investment.

Project A:

| | | |
|---|---|---|
| Cumulative cash flows Year 1 = $9,500 | = $9,500 |
| Cumulative cash flows Year 2 = $9,500 + 6,000 | = $15,500 |

Companies can calculate a more precise value using fractional years. To calculate the fractional payback period, find the fraction of year 2's cash flows that is needed for the company to have cumulative undiscounted cash flows of $15,000. Divide the difference between the initial investment and the cumulative undiscounted cash flows as of year 1 by the undiscounted cash flow of year 2.

Payback period = 1 + ($15,000 − 9,500) / $6,000
Payback period = 1.917 years

Project B:

| | |
|---|---|
| Cumulative cash flows Year 1 = $10,500 | = $10,500 |
| Cumulative cash flows Year 2 = $10,500 + 7,000 | = $17,500 |
| Cumulative cash flows Year 3 = $10,500 + 7,000 + 6,000 | = $23,500 |

To calculate the fractional payback period, find the fraction of year 3's cash flows that is needed for the company to have cumulative undiscounted cash flows of $18,000. Divide the difference between the initial investment and the cumulative undiscounted cash flows as of year 2 by the undiscounted cash flow of year 3.

Payback period = 2 + ($18,000 − 10,500 − 7,000) / $6,000
Payback period = 2.083 years

Since project A has a shorter payback period than project B has, the company should choose project A.

b.  Discount each project's cash flows at 15 percent. Choose the project with the highest NPV.

Project A:
$NPV = -\$15,000 + \$9,500 / 1.15 + \$6,000 / 1.15^2 + \$2,400 / 1.15^3$
$NPV = -\$624.23$

Project B:
$NPV = -\$18,000 + \$10,500 / 1.15 + \$7,000 / 1.15^2 + \$6,000 / 1.15^3$
$NPV = \$368.54$

The firm should choose Project B since it has a higher NPV than Project A has.

2.  To calculate the payback period, we need to find the time that the project has taken to recover its initial investment. The cash flows in this problem are an annuity, so the calculation is simpler. If the initial cost is $3,400, the payback period is:

Payback = 3 + ($680 / $840) = 3.81 years

There is a shortcut to calculate the payback period if the future cash flows are an annuity. Just divide the initial cost by the annual cash flow. For the $3,400 cost, the payback period is:

Payback = $3,400 / $840 = 3.81 years

For an initial cost of $4,800, the payback period is:

Payback = $4,800 / $840 = 5.71 years

The payback period for an initial cost of $7,300 is a little trickier. Notice that the total cash inflows after eight years will be:

Total cash inflows = 8($840) = $6,720

If the initial cost is $7,300, the project never pays back. Notice that if you use the shortcut for annuity cash flows, you get:

Payback = $7,300 / $840 = 8.69 years

This answer does not make sense since the cash flows stop after eight years, so there is no payback period.

3. When we use discounted payback, we need to find the value of all cash flows today. The value today of the project cash flows for the first four years is:

Value today of Year 1 cash flow = $5,000/1.14 = $4,385.96
Value today of Year 2 cash flow = $5,500/1.14$^2$ = $4,232.07
Value today of Year 3 cash flow = $6,000/1.14$^3$ = $4,049.83
Value today of Year 4 cash flow = $7,000/1.14$^4$ = $4,144.56

To find the discounted payback, we use these values to find the payback period. The discounted first year cash flow is $4,385.96, so the discounted payback for an initial cost of $8,000 is:

Discounted payback = 1 + ($8,000 – 4,385.96)/$4,232.07 = 1.85 years

For an initial cost of $12,000, the discounted payback is:

Discounted payback = 2 + ($12,000 – 4,385.96 – 4,232.07)/$4,049.83 = 2.84 years

Notice the calculation of discounted payback. We know the payback period is between two and three years, so we subtract the discounted values of the Year 1 and Year 2 cash flows from the initial cost. This is the numerator, which is the discounted amount we still need to make to recover our initial investment. We divide this amount by the discounted amount we will earn in Year 3 to get the fractional portion of the discounted payback.

If the initial cost is $16,000, the discounted payback is:

Discounted payback = 3 + ($16,000 – 4,385.96 – 4,232.07 – 4,049.83) / $4,144.56 = 3.80 years

4. To calculate the discounted payback, discount all future cash flows back to the present, and use these discounted cash flows to calculate the payback period. To find the fractional year, we divide the amount we need to make in the last year to payback the project by the amount we will make. Doing so, we find:

R = 0%:  3 + ($3,600 / $3,800) = 3.95 years
       Discounted payback = Regular payback = 3.95 years

R = 10%: $\$3,800/1.10 + \$3,800/1.10^2 + \$3,800/1.10^3 + \$3,800/1.10^4 + \$3,800/1.10^5 = \$14,404.99$
$\qquad \$3,800/1.10^6 = \$2,145.00$
$\qquad$ Discounted payback = $5 + (\$15,000 - 14,404.99) / \$2,145.00 = 5.28$ years

R = 15%: $\$3,800/1.15 + \$3,800/1.15^2 + \$3,800/1.15^3 + \$3,800/1.15^4 + \$3,800/1.15^5 + \$3,800/1.15^6$
$\qquad = \$14,381.03$; The project never pays back.

5.  The IRR is the interest rate that makes the NPV of the project equal to zero. So, the equation that defines the IRR for this project is:

$0 = C_0 + C_1 / (1 + IRR) + C_2 / (1 + IRR)^2 + C_3 / (1 + IRR)^3$
$0 = -\$20,000 + \$8,500/(1 + IRR) + \$10,200/(1 + IRR)^2 + \$6,200/(1 + IRR)^3$

Using a spreadsheet, financial calculator, or trial and error to find the root of the equation, we find that:

IRR = 12.41%

Since the IRR is greater than the required return we would accept the project.

6.  The IRR is the interest rate that makes the NPV of the project equal to zero. So, the equation that defines the IRR for this Project A is:

$0 = C_0 + C_1 / (1 + IRR) + C_2 / (1 + IRR)^2 + C_3 / (1 + IRR)^3$
$0 = -\$5,300 + \$2,000/(1 + IRR) + \$2,800/(1 + IRR)^2 + \$1,600/(1 + IRR)^3$

Using a spreadsheet, financial calculator, or trial and error to find the root of the equation, we find that:

IRR = 10.38%

And the IRR for Project B is:

$0 = C_0 + C_1 / (1 + IRR) + C_2 / (1 + IRR)^2 + C_3 / (1 + IRR)^3$
$0 = -\$2,900 + \$1,100/(1 + IRR) + \$1,800/(1 + IRR)^2 + \$1,200/(1 + IRR)^3$

Using a spreadsheet, financial calculator, or trial and error to find the root of the equation, we find that:

IRR = 19.16%

7.  The profitability index is defined as the PV of the cash inflows divided by the PV of the cash outflows. The cash flows from this project are an annuity, so the equation for the profitability index is:

PI = $C(PVIFA_{R,t}) / C_0$
PI = $\$84,000(PVIFA_{13\%,7}) / \$385,000$
PI = 0.965

**8.** *a.* The profitability index is the present value of the future cash flows divided by the initial cost. So, for Project Alpha, the profitability index is:

$PI_{Alpha} = [\$1,200 / 1.10 + \$1,100 / 1.10^2 + \$900 / 1.10^3] / \$2,300 = 1.164$

And for Project Beta the profitability index is:

$PI_{Beta} = [\$800 / 1.10 + \$2,300 / 1.10^2 + \$2,900 / 1.10^3] / \$3,900 = 1.233$

    *b.* According to the profitability index, you would accept Project Beta. However, remember the profitability index rule can lead to an incorrect decision when ranking mutually exclusive projects.

### Intermediate

**9.** *a.* To have a payback equal to the project's life, given $C$ is a constant cash flow for N years:

$C = I/N$

    *b.* To have a positive NPV, $I < C\,(PVIFA_{R\%,\,N})$. Thus, $C > I / (PVIFA_{R\%,\,N})$.

    *c.* Benefit $= C\,(PVIFA_{R\%,\,N}) = 2 \times$ costs $= 2I$
$C = 2I / (PVIFA_{R\%,\,N})$

**10.** *a.* The IRR is the interest rate that makes the NPV of the project equal to zero. So, the equation that defines the IRR for this project is:

$0 = C_0 + C_1 / (1 + IRR) + C_2 / (1 + IRR)^2 + C_3 / (1 + IRR)^3 + C_4 / (1 + IRR)^4$
$0 = \$7,000 - \$3,700 / (1 + IRR) - \$2,400 / (1 + IRR)^2 - \$1,500 / (1 + IRR)^3$
     $- \$1,200 / (1 + IRR)^4$

Using a spreadsheet, financial calculator, or trial and error to find the root of the equation, we find that:

IRR = 12.40%

    *b.* This problem differs from previous ones because the initial cash flow is positive and all future cash flows are negative. In other words, this is a financing-type project, while previous projects were investing-type projects. For financing situations, accept the project when the IRR is less than the discount rate. Reject the project when the IRR is greater than the discount rate.

IRR = 12.40%
Discount Rate = 10%

IRR > Discount Rate

Reject the offer when the discount rate is less than the IRR.

c.  Using the same reason as part *b.*, we would accept the project if the discount rate is 20 percent.

IRR = 12.40%
Discount Rate = 20%

IRR < Discount Rate

Accept the offer when the discount rate is greater than the IRR.

d.  The NPV is the sum of the present value of all cash flows, so the NPV of the project if the discount rate is 10 percent will be:

$$NPV = \$7,000 - \$3,700 / 1.1 - \$2,400 / 1.1^2 - \$1,500 / 1.1^3 - \$1,200 / 1.1^4$$
$$NPV = -\$293.70$$

When the discount rate is 10 percent, the NPV of the offer is –$293.70. Reject the offer.

And the NPV of the project if the discount rate is 20 percent will be:

$$NPV = \$7,000 - \$3,700 / 1.2 - \$2,400 / 1.2^2 - \$1,500 / 1.2^3 - \$1,200 / 1.2^4$$
$$NPV = \$803.24$$

When the discount rate is 20 percent, the NPV of the offer is $803.24. Accept the offer.

e.  Yes, the decisions under the NPV rule are consistent with the choices made under the IRR rule since the signs of the cash flows change only once.

11.  a.  The IRR is the interest rate that makes the NPV of the project equal to zero. So, the IRR for each project is:

Deepwater Fishing IRR:

$$0 = C_0 + C_1 / (1 + IRR) + C_2 / (1 + IRR)^2 + C_3 / (1 + IRR)^3$$
$$0 = -\$950,000 + \$370,000 / (1 + IRR) + \$510,000 / (1 + IRR)^2 + \$420,000 / (1 + IRR)^3$$

Using a spreadsheet, financial calculator, or trial and error to find the root of the equation, we find that:

IRR = 17.07%

Submarine Ride IRR:

$$0 = C_0 + C_1 / (1 + IRR) + C_2 / (1 + IRR)^2 + C_3 / (1 + IRR)^3$$
$$0 = -\$1,850,000 + \$900,000 / (1 + IRR) + \$800,000 / (1 + IRR)^2 + \$750,000 / (1 + IRR)^3$$

Using a spreadsheet, financial calculator, or trial and error to find the root of the equation, we find that:

IRR = 16.03%

Based on the IRR rule, the deepwater fishing project should be chosen because it has the higher IRR.

b.  To calculate the incremental IRR, we subtract the smaller project's cash flows from the larger project's cash flows. In this case, we subtract the deepwater fishing cash flows from the submarine ride cash flows. The incremental IRR is the IRR of these incremental cash flows. So, the incremental cash flows of the submarine ride are:

|  | Year 0 | Year 1 | Year 2 | Year 3 |
|---|---|---|---|---|
| Submarine Ride | −$1,850,000 | $900,000 | $800,000 | $750,000 |
| Deepwater Fishing | −950,000 | 370,000 | 510,000 | 420,000 |
| Submarine − Fishing | −$ 900,000 | $530,000 | $290,000 | $330,000 |

Setting the present value of these incremental cash flows equal to zero, we find the incremental IRR is:

$$0 = C_0 + C_1 / (1 + IRR) + C_2 / (1 + IRR)^2 + C_3 / (1 + IRR)^3$$
$$0 = -\$900,000 + \$530,000 / (1 + IRR) + \$290,000 / (1 + IRR)^2 + \$330,000 / (1 + IRR)^3$$

Using a spreadsheet, financial calculator, or trial and error to find the root of the equation, we find that:

Incremental IRR = 14.79%

For investing-type projects, accept the larger project when the incremental IRR is greater than the discount rate. Since the incremental IRR, 14.79%, is greater than the required rate of return of 14 percent, choose the submarine ride project. Note that this is not the choice when evaluating only the IRR of each project. The IRR decision rule is flawed because there is a scale problem. That is, the submarine ride has a greater initial investment than does the deepwater fishing project. This problem is corrected by calculating the IRR of the incremental cash flows, or by evaluating the NPV of each project.

c.  The NPV is the sum of the present value of the cash flows from the project, so the NPV of each project will be:

Deepwater fishing:

$$NPV = -\$950,000 + \$370,000 / 1.14 + \$510,000 / 1.14^2 + \$420,000 / 1.14^3$$
$$NPV = \$50,477.88$$

Submarine ride:

$$NPV = -\$1,850,000 + \$900,000 / 1.14 + \$800,000 / 1.14^2 + \$750,000 / 1.14^3$$
$$NPV = \$61,276.34$$

Since the NPV of the submarine ride project is greater than the NPV of the deepwater fishing project, choose the submarine ride project. The incremental IRR rule is always consistent with the NPV rule.

**12.** *a.*   The profitability index is the PV of the future cash flows divided by the initial investment. The cash flows for both projects are an annuity, so:

$PI_I = \$18,000(PVIFA_{10\%,3}) / \$30,000 = 1.492$

$PI_{II} = \$7,500(PVIFA_{10\%,3}) / \$12,000 = 1.554$

The profitability index decision rule implies that we accept project II, since $PI_{II}$ is greater than the $PI_I$.

*b.*   The NPV of each project is:

$NPV_I = -\$30,000 + \$18,000(PVIFA_{10\%,3}) = \$14,763.34$

$NPV_{II} = -\$12,000 + \$7,500(PVIFA_{10\%,3}) = \$6,651.39$

The NPV decision rule implies accepting Project I, since the $NPV_I$ is greater than the $NPV_{II}$.

*c.*   Using the profitability index to compare mutually exclusive projects can be ambiguous when the magnitudes of the cash flows for the two projects are of different scales. In this problem, project I is 2.5 times as large as project II and produces a larger NPV, yet the profitability index criterion implies that project II is more acceptable.

**13.** *a.*   The equation for the NPV of the project is:

$NPV = -\$85,000,000 + \$125,000,000/1.1 - \$15,000,000/1.1^2 = \$16,239,669.42$

The NPV is greater than 0, so we would accept the project.

*b.*   The equation for the IRR of the project is:

$0 = -\$85,000,000 + \$125,000,000/(1+IRR) - \$15,000,000/(1+IRR)^2$

From Descartes' rule of signs, we know there are two IRRs since the cash flows change signs twice. From trial and error, the two IRRs are:

$IRR = 33.88\%, -86.82\%$

When there are multiple IRRs, the IRR decision rule is ambiguous. Both IRRs are correct; that is, both interest rates make the NPV of the project equal to zero. If we are evaluating whether or not to accept this project, we would not want to use the IRR to make our decision.

**14.** *a.*   The payback period is the time that it takes for the cumulative undiscounted cash inflows to equal the initial investment.

Board game:

Cumulative cash flows Year 1 = $600            = $600
Cumulative cash flows Year 2 = $600 + 450     = $1,050

Payback period = 1 + $150 / $450            = 1.33 years

DVD:

Cumulative cash flows Year 1 = $1,300           = $1,300
Cumulative cash flows Year 2 = $1,300 + 850 = $2,150

Payback period = 1 + ($1,800 – 1,300) / $850
Payback period = 1.59 years

Since the board game has a shorter payback period than the DVD project, the company should choose the board game.

b.   The NPV is the sum of the present value of the cash flows from the project, so the NPV of each project will be:

Board game:

NPV = –$750 + $600 / 1.10 + $450 / 1.10$^2$ + $120 / 1.10$^3$
NPV = $257.51

DVD:

NPV = –$1,850 + $1,300 / 1.10 + $850 / 1.10$^2$ + $350 / 1.10$^3$
NPV = $347.26

Since the NPV of the DVD is greater than the NPV of the board game, choose the DVD.

c.   The IRR is the interest rate that makes the NPV of a project equal to zero. So, the IRR of each project is:

Board game:

$0 = -\$750 + \$600 / (1 + IRR) + \$450 / (1 + IRR)^2 + \$120 / (1 + IRR)^3$

Using a spreadsheet, financial calculator, or trial and error to find the root of the equation, we find that:

IRR = 33.79%

DVD:

$0 = -\$1,850 + \$1,300 / (1 + IRR) + \$850 / (1 + IRR)^2 + \$350 / (1 + IRR)^3$

Using a spreadsheet, financial calculator, or trial and error to find the root of the equation, we find that:

IRR = 23.31%

Since the IRR of the board game is greater than the IRR of the DVD, IRR implies we choose the board game. Note that this is the choice when evaluating only the IRR of each project. The IRR decision rule is flawed because there is a scale problem. That is, the DVD has a greater initial investment than does the board game. This problem is corrected by calculating the IRR of the incremental cash flows, or by evaluating the NPV of each project.

*d.* To calculate the incremental IRR, we subtract the smaller project's cash flows from the larger project's cash flows. In this case, we subtract the board game cash flows from the DVD cash flows. The incremental IRR is the IRR of these incremental cash flows. So, the incremental cash flows of the DVD are:

|  | Year 0 | Year 1 | Year 2 | Year 3 |
|---|---|---|---|---|
| DVD | −$1,800 | $1,300 | $850 | $350 |
| Board game | −750 | 600 | 450 | 120 |
| DVD – Board game | −$1,050 | $ 700 | $400 | $230 |

Setting the present value of these incremental cash flows equal to zero, we find the incremental IRR is:

$$0 = C_0 + C_1 / (1 + IRR) + C_2 / (1 + IRR)^2 + C_3 / (1 + IRR)^3$$
$$0 = -\$1,050 + \$700 / (1 + IRR) + \$400 / (1 + IRR)^2 + \$230 / (1 + IRR)^3$$

Using a spreadsheet, financial calculator, or trial and error to find the root of the equation, we find that:

Incremental IRR = 15.86%

For investing-type projects, accept the larger project when the incremental IRR is greater than the discount rate. Since the incremental IRR, 15.86%, is greater than the required rate of return of 10 percent, choose the DVD project.

15. *a.* The profitability index is the PV of the future cash flows divided by the initial investment. The profitability index for each project is:

$PI_{CDMA} = [\$11,000,000 / 1.10 + \$7,500,000 / 1.10^2 + \$2,500,000 / 1.10^3] / \$8,000,000 = 2.26$

$PI_{G4} = [\$10,000,000 / 1.10 + \$25,000,000 / 1.10^2 + \$20,000,000 / 1.10^3] / \$12,000,000 = 3.73$

$PI_{Wi\text{-}Fi} = [\$18,000,000 / 1.10 + \$32,000,000 / 1.10^2 + \$20,000,000 / 1.10^3] / \$20,000,000 = 2.89$

The profitability index implies we accept the G4 project. Remember this is not necessarily correct because the profitability index does not necessarily rank projects with different initial investments correctly.

*b.* The NPV of each project is:

$NPV_{CDMA} = -\$8,000,000 + \$11,000,000 / 1.10 + \$7,500,000 / 1.10^2 + \$2,500,000 / 1.10^3$
$NPV_{CDMA} = \$10,076,634.11$

$NPV_{G4} = -\$12,000,000 + \$10,000,000 / 1.10 + \$25,000,000 / 1.10^2 + \$20,000,000 / 1.10^3$
$NPV_{G4} = \$32,778,362.13$

$NPV_{Wi-Fi} = -\$20,000,000 + \$18,000,000 / 1.10 + \$32,000,000 / 1.10^2 + \$20,000,000 / 1.10^3$
$NPV_{Wi-Fi} = \$37,836,213.37$

NPV implies we accept the Wi-Fi project since it has the highest NPV. This is the correct decision if the projects are mutually exclusive.

c.   We would like to invest in all three projects since each has a positive NPV. If the budget is limited to $20 million, we can only accept the CDMA project and the G4 project, or the Wi-Fi project. NPV is additive across projects and the company. The total NPV of the CDMA project and the G4 project is:

$NPV_{CDMA \text{ and } G4} = \$10,076,634.11 + 32,778,362.13$
$NPV_{CDMA \text{ and } G4} = \$42,854,996.24$

This is greater than the Wi-Fi project, so we should accept the CDMA project and the G4 project.

16.   a.   The payback period is the time that it takes for the cumulative undiscounted cash inflows to equal the initial investment.

AZM Mini-SUV:

Cumulative cash flows Year 1 = $320,000              = $320,000
Cumulative cash flows Year 2 = $320,000 + 180,000   = $500,000

Payback period = 1+ $130,000 / $180,000 = 1.72 years

AZF Full-SUV:

Cumulative cash flows Year 1 = $350,000                        = $350,000
Cumulative cash flows Year 2 = $350,000 + 420,000              = $770,000
Cumulative cash flows Year 2 = $350,000 + 420,000 + 290,000    = $1,060,000

Payback period = 2+ $30,000 / $290,000 = 2.10 years

Since the AZM has a shorter payback period than the AZF, the company should choose the AZM. Remember the payback period does not necessarily rank projects correctly.

b.   The NPV of each project is:

$NPV_{AZM} = -\$450,000 + \$320,000 / 1.10 + \$180,000 / 1.10^2 + \$150,000 / 1.10^3$
$NPV_{AZM} = \$102,366.64$

$NPV_{AZF} = -\$800,000 + \$350,000 / 1.10 + \$420,000 / 1.10^2 + \$290,000 / 1.10^3$
$NPV_{AZF} = \$83,170.55$

The NPV criteria implies we accept the AZM because it has the highest NPV.

c.   The IRR is the interest rate that makes the NPV of the project equal to zero. So, the IRR of the AZM is:

$$0 = -\$450,000 + \$320,000 / (1 + IRR) + \$180,000 / (1 + IRR)^2 + \$150,000 / (1 + IRR)^3$$

Using a spreadsheet, financial calculator, or trial and error to find the root of the equation, we find that:

$IRR_{AZM} = 24.65\%$

And the IRR of the AZF is:

$$0 = -\$800,000 + \$350,000 / (1 + IRR) + \$420,000 / (1 + IRR)^2 + \$290,000 / (1 + IRR)^3$$

Using a spreadsheet, financial calculator, or trial and error to find the root of the equation, we find that:

$IRR_{AZF} = 15.97\%$

The IRR criteria implies we accept the AZM because it has the highest IRR. Remember the IRR does not necessarily rank projects correctly.

d.   Incremental IRR analysis is not necessary. The AZM has the smallest initial investment, and the largest NPV, so it should be accepted.

17. a.   The profitability index is the PV of the future cash flows divided by the initial investment. The profitability index for each project is:

$PI_A = [\$110,000 / 1.12 + \$110,000 / 1.12^2] / \$150,000 = 1.24$

$PI_B = [\$200,000 / 1.12 + \$200,000 / 1.12^2] / \$300,000 = 1.13$

$PI_C = [\$120,000 / 1.12 + \$90,000 / 1.12^2] / \$150,000 = 1.19$

b.   The NPV of each project is:

$NPV_A = -\$150,000 + \$110,000 / 1.12 + \$110,000 / 1.12^2$
$NPV_A = \$35,905.61$

$NPV_B = -\$300,000 + \$200,000 / 1.12 + \$200,000 / 1.12^2$
$NPV_B = \$38,010.20$

$NPV_C = -\$150,000 + \$120,000 / 1.12 + \$90,000 / 1.12^2$
$NPV_C = \$28,890.31$

c.   Accept projects A, B, and C. Since the projects are independent, accept all three projects because the respective profitability index of each is greater than one.

d.  Accept Project B. Since the Projects are mutually exclusive, choose the Project with the highest PI, while taking into account the scale of the Project. Because Projects A and C have the same initial investment, the problem of scale does not arise when comparing the profitability indices. Based on the profitability index rule, Project C can be eliminated because its PI is less than the PI of Project A. Because of the problem of scale, we cannot compare the PIs of Projects A and B. However, we can calculate the PI of the incremental cash flows of the two projects, which are:

| Project | $C_0$ | $C_1$ | $C_2$ |
|---------|-------|-------|-------|
| B – A   | –$150,000 | $90,000 | $90,000 |

When calculating incremental cash flows, remember to subtract the cash flows of the project with the smaller initial cash outflow from those of the project with the larger initial cash outflow. This procedure insures that the incremental initial cash outflow will be negative. The incremental PI calculation is:

$PI(B – A) = [\$90,000 / 1.12 + \$90,000 / 1.12^2] / \$150,000$
$PI(B – A) = 1.014$

The company should accept Project B since the PI of the incremental cash flows is greater than one.

e.  Remember that the NPV is additive across projects. Since we can spend $450,000, we could take two of the projects. In this case, we should take the two projects with the highest NPVs, which are Project B and Project A.

18.  a.  The payback period is the time that it takes for the cumulative undiscounted cash inflows to equal the initial investment.

Dry Prepeg:

Cumulative cash flows Year 1 = $1,100,000        = $1,100,000
Cumulative cash flows Year 2 = $1,100,000 + 900,000 = $2,000,000

Payback period = 1 + ($600,000/$900,000) = 1.67 years

Solvent Prepeg:

Cumulative cash flows Year 1 = $375,000          = $375,000
Cumulative cash flows Year 2 = $375,000 + 600,000 = $975,000

Payback period = 1 + ($375,000/$600,000) = 1.63 years

Since the solvent prepeg has a shorter payback period than the dry prepeg, the company should choose the solvent prepeg. Remember the payback period does not necessarily rank projects correctly.

*b.* The NPV of each project is:

$NPV_{Dry\ prepeg} = -\$1,700,000 + \$1,100,000 / 1.10 + \$900,000 / 1.10^2 + \$750,000 / 1.10^3$
$NPV_{Dry\ prepeg} = \$607,287.75$

$NPV_{Solvent\ perpeg} = -\$750,000 + \$375,000 / 1.10 + \$600,000 / 1.10^2 + \$390,000 / 1.10^3$
$NPV_{Solvent\ prepeg} = \$379,789.63$

The NPV criteria implies accepting the dry prepeg because it has the highest NPV.

*c.* The IRR is the interest rate that makes the NPV of the project equal to zero. So, the IRR of the dry prepeg is:

$0 = -\$1,700,000 + \$1,100,000 / (1 + IRR) + \$900,000 / (1 + IRR)^2 + \$750,000 / (1 + IRR)^3$

Using a spreadsheet, financial calculator, or trial and error to find the root of the equation, we find that:

$IRR_{Dry\ prepeg} = 30.90\%$

And the IRR of the solvent prepeg is:

$0 = -\$750,000 + \$375,000 / (1 + IRR) + \$600,000 / (1 + IRR)^2 + \$390,000 / (1 + IRR)^3$

Using a spreadsheet, financial calculator, or trial and error to find the root of the equation, we find that:

$IRR_{Solvent\ prepeg} = 36.51\%$

The IRR criteria implies accepting the solvent prepeg because it has the highest IRR. Remember the IRR does not necessarily rank projects correctly.

*d.* Incremental IRR analysis is necessary. The solvent prepeg has a higher IRR, but is relatively smaller in terms of investment and NPV. In calculating the incremental cash flows, we subtract the cash flows from the project with the smaller initial investment from the cash flows of the project with the large initial investment, so the incremental cash flows are:

| | Year 0 | Year 1 | Year 2 | Year 3 |
|---|---|---|---|---|
| Dry prepeg | −$1,700,000 | $1,100,000 | $900,000 | $750,000 |
| Solvent prepeg | −750,000 | 375,000 | 600,000 | 390,000 |
| Dry prepeg – Solvent prepeg | −$ 950,000 | $ 725,000 | $300,000 | $360,000 |

Setting the present value of these incremental cash flows equal to zero, we find the incremental IRR is:

$0 = -\$950,000 + \$725,000 / (1 + IRR) + \$300,000 / (1 + IRR)^2 + \$360,000 / (1 + IRR)^3$

Using a spreadsheet, financial calculator, or trial and error to find the root of the equation, we find that:

Incremental IRR = 25.52%

For investing-type projects, we accept the larger project when the incremental IRR is greater than the discount rate. Since the incremental IRR, 25.52%, is greater than the required rate of return of 10 percent, we choose the dry prepeg.

**19.** *a.* The payback period is the time that it takes for the cumulative undiscounted cash inflows to equal the initial investment.

NP-30:

| | |
|---|---|
| Cumulative cash flows Year 1 = $185,000 | = $185,000 |
| Cumulative cash flows Year 2 = $185,000 + 185,000 | = $370,000 |
| Cumulative cash flows Year 3 = $185,000 + 185,000 + 185,000 | = $555,000 |

Payback period = 2 + ($180,000/$185,000) = 2.97 years

NX-20:

| | |
|---|---|
| Cumulative cash flows Year 1 = $100,000 | = $100,000 |
| Cumulative cash flows Year 2 = $100,000 + 110,000 | = $210,000 |
| Cumulative cash flows Year 3 = $100,000 + 110,000 + 121,000 | = $331,000 |
| Cumulative cash flows Year 4 = $100,000 + 110,000 + 121,000 + 133,100 | = $464,100 |

Payback period = 3 + ($19,000/$133,100) = 3.14 years

Since the NP-30 has a shorter payback period than the NX-20, the company should choose the NP-30. Remember the payback period does not necessarily rank projects correctly.

*b.* The IRR is the interest rate that makes the NPV of the project equal to zero, so the IRR of each project is:

NP-30:

$$0 = -\$550,000 + \$185,000(\{1 - [1/(1 + IRR)^5]\} / IRR)$$

Using a spreadsheet, financial calculator, or trial and error to find the root of the equation, we find that:

$IRR_{NP-30} = 20.27\%$

And the IRR of the NX-20 is:

$$0 = -\$350,000 + \$100,000 / (1 + IRR) + \$110,000 / (1 + IRR)^2 + \$121,000 / (1 + IRR)^3 + \$133,100 / (1 + IRR)^4 + \$146,410 / (1 + IRR)^5$$

Using a spreadsheet, financial calculator, or trial and error to find the root of the equation, we find that:

$IRR_{NX-20} = 20.34\%$

The IRR criteria implies accepting the NX-20.

c.   The profitability index is the present value of all subsequent cash flows, divided by the initial investment, so the profitability index of each project is:

$PI_{NP-30} = (\$185,000\{[1 - (1/1.15)^5]/.15\})/\$550,000$
$PI_{NP-30} = 1.128$

$PI_{NX-20} = [\$100,000/1.15 + \$110,000/1.15^2 + \$121,000/1.15^3 + \$133,100/1.15^4 + \$146,410/1.15^5]/\$350,000$
$PI_{NX-20} = 1.139$

The PI criteria implies accepting the NX-20.

d.   The NPV of each project is:

$NPV_{NP-30} = -\$550,000 + \$185,000\{[1 - (1/1.15)^5]/.15\}$
$NPV_{NP-30} = \$70,148.69$

$NPV_{NX-20} = -\$350,000 + \$100,000/1.15 + \$110,000/1.15^2 + \$121,000/1.15^3 + \$133,100/1.15^4 + \$146,410/1.15^5$
$NPV_{NX-20} = \$48,583.79$

The NPV criteria implies accepting the NP-30.

## Challenge

20.  The equation for the IRR of the project is:

$0 = -\$75,000 + \$155,000/(1+IRR) - \$65,000/(1+IRR)^2$

From Descartes' Rule of Signs, we know there are either zero IRRs or two IRRs since the cash flows change signs twice. We can rewrite this equation as:

$0 = -\$75,000 + \$155,000X - \$65,000X^2$
   where $X = 1/(1+IRR)$

This is a quadratic equation. We can solve for the roots of this equation with the quadratic formula:

$$X = \frac{-b \pm \sqrt{b^2 - 4ac}}{2a}$$

Remember that the quadratic formula is written as:

$0 = aX^2 + bX + c$

In this case, the equation is:

$0 = -\$65,000X^2 + \$155,000X - \$75,000$

$$X = \frac{-155,000 \pm \sqrt{(155,000)^2 - 4(-75,000)(-65,000)}}{2(-65,000)}$$

$$X = \frac{-155,000 \pm \sqrt{4,525,000,000}}{2(-65,000)}$$

$$X = \frac{-155,000 \pm 67,268.12}{-130,000}$$

Solving the quadratic equation, we find two Xs:

X = 0.6749, 1.7098

Since:

X = 1 / (1 + IRR)
1.7098 = 1 / (1 + IRR)
IRR = −.4151 or − 41.51%

And:

X = 1 / (1 + IRR)
0.6749 = 1 / (1 + IRR)
IRR = 0.4818 or 48.18%

To find the maximum (or minimum) of a function, we find the derivative and set it equal to zero. The derivative of this IRR function is:

$0 = -\$155,000(1 + IRR)^{-2} + \$130,000(1 + IRR)^{-3}$
$\quad -\$155,000(1 + IRR)^{-2} = \$130,000(1 + IRR)^{-3}$
$\quad -\$155,000(1 + IRR)^{3} = \$130,000(1 + IRR)^{2}$
$\quad -\$155,000(1 + IRR) = \$130,000$
IRR = \$130,000/\$155,000 − 1
IRR = − .1613 or −16.13%

To determine if this is a maximum or minimum, we can find the second derivative of the IRR function. If the second derivative is positive, we have found a minimum and if the second derivative is negative we have found a maximum. Using the reduced equation above, that is:

−\$155,000(1 + IRR) = \$130,000

The second derivative is −\$262,722.18, therefore we have a maximum.

21. Given the six-year payback, the worst case is that the payback occurs at the end of the sixth year. Thus, the worst case:

$$NPV = -\$434,000 + \$434,000/1.12^6 = -\$214,122.09$$

The best case has infinite cash flows beyond the payback point. Thus, the best-case NPV is infinite.

22. The equation for the IRR of the project is:

$$0 = -\$1,008 + \$5,724/(1 + IRR) - \$12,140/(1 + IRR)^2 + \$11,400/(1 + IRR)^3 - \$4,000/(1 + IRR)^4$$

Using Descartes' rule of signs, from looking at the cash flows we know there are four IRRs for this project. Even with most computer spreadsheets, we have to do some trial and error. From trial and error, IRRs of 25%, 33.33%, 42.86%, and 66.67% are found.

We would accept the project when the NPV is greater than zero. See for yourself that the NPV is greater than zero for required returns between 25% and 33.33% or between 42.86% and 66.67%.

23. *a.* Here the cash inflows of the project go on forever, which is a perpetuity. Unlike ordinary perpetuity cash flows, the cash flows here grow at a constant rate forever, which is a growing perpetuity. The PV of the future cash flows from the project is:

PV of cash inflows = $C_1/(R - g)$
PV of cash inflows = $\$290,000/(.11 - .05) = \$4,833,333.33$

NPV is the PV of the outflows minus by the PV of the inflows, so the NPV is:

NPV of the project = $-\$3,900,000 + 4,833,333.33 = \$933,333.33$

The NPV is positive, so we would accept the project.

*b.* Here we want to know the minimum growth rate in cash flows necessary to accept the project. The minimum growth rate is the growth rate at which we would have a zero NPV. The equation for a zero NPV, using the equation for the PV of a growing perpetuity is:

$$0 = -\$3,900,000 + \$290,000/(.11 - g)$$

Solving for $g$, we get:

$$g = 3.56\%$$

24. *a.* The project involves three cash flows: the initial investment, the annual cash inflows, and the abandonment costs. The mine will generate cash inflows over its 11-year economic life. To express the PV of the annual cash inflows, apply the growing annuity formula, discounted at the IRR and growing at eight percent.

PV(Cash Inflows) = $C \{[1/(r - g)] - [1/(r - g)] \times [(1 + g)/(1 + r)]^t\}$
PV(Cash Inflows) = $\$345,000\{[1/(IRR - .08)] - [1/(IRR - .08)] \times [(1 + .08)/(1 + IRR)]^{11}\}$

At the end of 11 years, the company will abandon the mine, incurring a $400,000 charge. Discounting the abandonment costs back 11 years at the IRR to express its present value, we get:

$$PV(\text{Abandonment}) = C_{11} / (1 + IRR)^{11}$$
$$PV(\text{Abandonment}) = -\$400,000 / (1+ IRR)^{11}$$

So, the IRR equation for this project is:

$$0 = -\$2,400,000 + \$345,000\{[1/(IRR-.08)] - [1/(IRR-.08)] \times [(1+.08)/(1+IRR)]^{11}\}$$
$$-\$400,000 / (1+ IRR)^{11}$$

Using a spreadsheet, financial calculator, or trial and error to find the root of the equation, we find that:

$$IRR = 14.74\%$$

b.  Yes. Since the mine's IRR exceeds the required return of 10 percent, the mine should be opened. The correct decision rule for an investment-type project is to accept the project if the IRR is greater than the discount rate. Although it appears there is a sign change at the end of the project because of the abandonment costs, the last cash flow is actually positive because of the operating cash flow in the last year.

25. First, we need to find the future value of the cash flows for the one year in which they are blocked by the government. So, reinvesting each cash inflow for one year, we find:

Year 2 cash flow = $285,000(1.04) = $296,400
Year 3 cash flow = $345,000(1.04) = $358,800
Year 4 cash flow = $415,000(1.04) = $431,600
Year 5 cash flow = $255,000(1.04) = $265,200

So, the NPV of the project is:

$$NPV = -\$950,000 + \$296,400/1.11^2 + \$358,800/1.11^3 + \$431,600/1.11^4 + \$265,200/1.11^5$$
$$NPV = -\$5,392.06$$

And the IRR of the project is:

$$0 = -\$950,000 + \$296,400/(1+IRR)^2 + \$358,800/(1+IRR)^3 + \$431,600/(1+IRR)^4$$
$$+ \$265,200/(1+IRR)^5$$

Using a spreadsheet, financial calculator, or trial and error to find the root of the equation, we find that:

$$IRR = 10.81\%$$

While this may look like a MIRR calculation, it is not a MIRR, rather it is a standard IRR calculation. Since the cash inflows are blocked by the government, they are not available to the company for a period of one year. Thus, all we are doing is calculating the IRR based on when the cash flows actually occur for the company.

**26.** *a.*    We can apply the growing perpetuity formula to find the PV of stream *A*. The perpetuity formula values the stream as of one year before the first payment. Therefore, the growing perpetuity formula values the stream of cash flows as of year 2. Next, discount the PV as of the end of year 2 back two years to find the PV as of today, year 0. Doing so, we find:

$$PV(A) = [C_3 / (R - g)] / (1 + R)^2$$
$$PV(A) = [\$8,900 / (0.12 - 0.04)] / (1.12)^2$$
$$PV(A) = \$88,687.82$$

We can apply the perpetuity formula to find the PV of stream *B*. The perpetuity formula discounts the stream back to year 1, one period prior to the first cash flow. Discount the PV as of the end of year 1 back one year to find the PV as of today, year 0. Doing so, we find:

$$PV(B) = [C_2 / R] / (1 + R)$$
$$PV(B) = [-\$10,000 / 0.12] / (1.12)$$
$$PV(B) = -\$74,404.76$$

*b.*    If we combine the cash flow streams to form Project C, we get:

$$\text{Project A} = [C_3 / (R - G)] / (1 + R)^2$$

$$\text{Project B} = [C_2 / R] / (1 + R)$$

$$\text{Project C} = \text{Project } A + \text{Project } B$$
$$\text{Project C} = [C_3 / (R - g)] / (1 + R)^2 + [C_2 / R] / (1 + R)$$
$$0 = [\$8,900 / (IRR - .04)] / (1 + IRR)^2 + [-\$10,000 / IRR] / (1 + IRR)$$

Using a spreadsheet, financial calculator, or trial and error to find the root of the equation, we find that:

$$IRR = 16.80\%$$

*c.*    The correct decision rule for an investing-type project is to accept the project if the discount rate is below the IRR. Since there is one IRR, a decision can be made. At a point in the future, the cash flows from stream *A* will be greater than those from stream *B*. Therefore, although there are many cash flows, there will be only one change in sign. When the sign of the cash flows change more than once over the life of the project, there may be multiple internal rates of return. In such cases, there is no correct decision rule for accepting and rejecting projects using the internal rate of return.

**27.** To answer this question, we need to examine the incremental cash flows. To make the projects equally attractive, Project Billion must have a larger initial investment. We know this because the subsequent cash flows from Project Billion are larger than the subsequent cash flows from Project Million. So, subtracting the Project Million cash flows from the Project Billion cash flows, we find the incremental cash flows are:

| Year | Incremental cash flows |
|------|------------------------|
| 0 | $-I_0 + \$1{,}200$ |
| 1 | 240 |
| 2 | 240 |
| 3 | 400 |

Now we can find the present value of the subsequent incremental cash flows at the discount rate, 12 percent. The present value of the incremental cash flows is:

$$PV = \$1{,}200 + \$240 \, / \, 1.12 + \$240 \, / \, 1.12^2 + \$400 \, / \, 1.12^3$$
$$PV = \$1{,}890.32$$

So, if $I_0$ is greater than $\$1,890.32$, the incremental cash flows will be negative. Since we are subtracting Project Million from Project Billion, this implies that for any value over $\$1,890.32$ the NPV of Project Billion will be less than that of Project Million, so $I_0$ must be less than $\$1,890.32$.

**28.** The IRR is the interest rate that makes the NPV of the project equal to zero. So, the IRR of the project is:

$$0 = \$20{,}000 - \$26{,}000 \, / \, (1 + IRR) + \$13{,}000 \, / \, (1 + IRR)^2$$

Even though it appears there are two IRRs, a spreadsheet, financial calculator, or trial and error will not give an answer. The reason is that there is no real IRR for this set of cash flows. If you examine the IRR equation, what we are really doing is solving for the roots of the equation. Going back to high school algebra, in this problem we are solving a quadratic equation. In case you don't remember, the quadratic equation is:

$$x = \frac{-b \pm \sqrt{b^2 - 4ac}}{2a}$$

In this case, the equation is:

$$x = \frac{-(-26{,}000) \pm \sqrt{(-26{,}000)^2 - 4(20{,}000)(13{,}000)}}{2(20{,}000)}$$

The square root term works out to be:

$$676{,}000{,}000 - 1{,}040{,}000{,}000 = -364{,}000{,}000$$

The square root of a negative number is a complex number, so there is no real number solution, meaning the project has no real IRR.

## Calculator Solutions

**1.** *b.*   *Project A*

| | |
|---|---|
| CFo | –$15,000 |
| C01 | $9,500 |
| F01 | 1 |
| C02 | $6,000 |
| F02 | 1 |
| C03 | $2,400 |
| F03 | 1 |

I = 15%
NPV CPT
–$624.23

| | |
|---|---|
| CFo | –$18,000 |
| C01 | $10,500 |
| F01 | 1 |
| C02 | $7,000 |
| F02 | 1 |
| C03 | $6,000 |
| F03 | 1 |

I = 15%
NPV CPT
$368.54

**5.**

| | |
|---|---|
| CFo | –$20,000 |
| C01 | $8,500 |
| F01 | 1 |
| C02 | $10,200 |
| F02 | 1 |
| C03 | $6,200 |
| F03 | 1 |

IRR CPT
12.41%

**6.**   *Project A*

| | |
|---|---|
| CFo | –$5,300 |
| C01 | $2,000 |
| F01 | 1 |
| C02 | $2,800 |
| F02 | 1 |
| C03 | $1,600 |
| F03 | 1 |

IRR CPT
10.38%

*Project B*

| | |
|---|---|
| CFo | –$2,900 |
| C01 | $1,100 |
| F01 | 1 |
| C02 | $1,800 |
| F02 | 1 |
| C03 | $1,200 |
| F03 | 1 |

IRR CPT
19.16%

**7.**

| | |
|---|---|
| CFo | 0 |
| C01 | $84,000 |
| F01 | 7 |

I = 13%
NPV CPT
$371,499.28

PI = $371,499.28 / $385,000 = 0.965

**10.**

| | |
|---|---|
| CF0 | $7,000 |
| C01 | −$3,700 |
| F01 | 1 |
| C02 | −$2,400 |
| F02 | 1 |
| C03 | −$1,500 |
| F03 | 1 |
| C04 | −$1,200 |
| F04 | 1 |
| IRR CPT | |
| 12.40% | |

| | |
|---|---|
| CF0 | $7,000 |
| C01 | −$3,700 |
| F01 | 1 |
| C02 | −$2,400 |
| F02 | 1 |
| C03 | −$1,500 |
| F03 | 1 |
| C04 | −$1,200 |
| F04 | 1 |
| I = 10% | |
| NPV CPT | |
| −$293.70 | |

| | |
|---|---|
| CF0 | $7,000 |
| C01 | −$3,700 |
| F01 | 1 |
| C02 | −$2,400 |
| F02 | 1 |
| C03 | −$1,500 |
| F03 | 1 |
| C04 | −$1,200 |
| F04 | 1 |
| I = 20% | |
| NPV CPT | |
| $803.24 | |

**11.** *a.*

*Deepwater fishing*

| | |
|---|---|
| CF0 | −$950,000 |
| C01 | $370,000 |
| F01 | 1 |
| C02 | $510,000 |
| F02 | 1 |
| C03 | $420,000 |
| F03 | 1 |
| IRR CPT | |
| 17.07% | |

*Submarine ride*

| | |
|---|---|
| CF0 | −$1,850,000 |
| C01 | $900,000 |
| F01 | 1 |
| C02 | $800,000 |
| F02 | 1 |
| C03 | $750,000 |
| F03 | 1 |
| IRR CPT | |
| 16.03% | |

*b.*

| | |
|---|---|
| CF0 | −$900,000 |
| C01 | $530,000 |
| F01 | 1 |
| C02 | $290,000 |
| F02 | 1 |
| C03 | $330,000 |
| F03 | 1 |
| IRR CPT | |
| 14.79% | |

c.   *Deepwater fishing*          *Submarine ride*

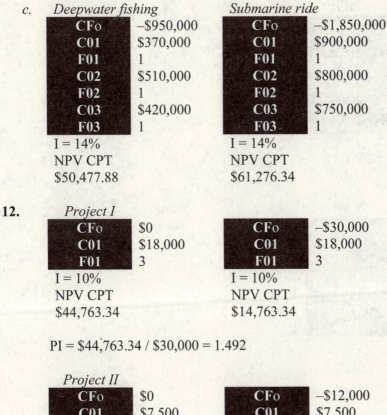

| CF₀ | –$950,000 |
|------|-----------|
| C01 | $370,000 |
| F01 | 1 |
| C02 | $510,000 |
| F02 | 1 |
| C03 | $420,000 |
| F03 | 1 |

I = 14%
NPV CPT
$50,477.88

| CF₀ | –$1,850,000 |
|------|-----------|
| C01 | $900,000 |
| F01 | 1 |
| C02 | $800,000 |
| F02 | 1 |
| C03 | $750,000 |
| F03 | 1 |

I = 14%
NPV CPT
$61,276.34

**12.**   *Project I*

| CF₀ | $0 |
|------|-----|
| C01 | $18,000 |
| F01 | 3 |

I = 10%
NPV CPT
$44,763.34

| CF₀ | –$30,000 |
|------|-----------|
| C01 | $18,000 |
| F01 | 3 |

I = 10%
NPV CPT
$14,763.34

PI = $44,763.34 / $30,000 = 1.492

*Project II*

| CF₀ | $0 |
|------|-----|
| C01 | $7,500 |
| F01 | 3 |

I = 10%
NPV CPT
$18,651.39

| CF₀ | –$12,000 |
|------|-----------|
| C01 | $7,500 |
| F01 | 3 |

I = 10%
NPV CPT
$6,651.39

PI = $18,651.39 / $12,000 = 1.554

**13.**

| CF₀ | –$85,000,000 |
|------|-----------|
| C01 | $125,000,000 |
| F01 | 1 |
| C02 | –$15,000,000 |
| F02 | 1 |

I = 10%
NPV CPT
$16,239,669.42

| CF₀ | –$85,000,000 |
|------|-----------|
| C01 | $125,000,000 |
| F01 | 1 |
| C02 | –$15,000,000 |
| F02 | 1 |

IRR CPT
33.88%

Financial calculators will only give you one IRR, even if there are multiple IRRs. Using trial and error, or a root solving calculator, the other IRR is –86.82%.

**14.** *b.*

| Board game | | DVD | |
|---|---|---|---|
| CF₀ | −$750 | CF₀ | −$1,800 |
| C01 | $600 | C01 | $1,300 |
| F01 | 1 | F01 | 1 |
| C02 | $450 | C02 | $850 |
| F02 | 1 | F02 | 1 |
| C03 | $120 | C03 | $350 |
| F03 | 1 | F03 | 1 |

I = 10%           I = 10%
NPV CPT          NPV CPT
$257.51           $347.26

*c.*

| Board game | | DVD | |
|---|---|---|---|
| CF₀ | −$750 | CF₀ | −$1,800 |
| C01 | $600 | C01 | $1,300 |
| F01 | 1 | F01 | 1 |
| C02 | $450 | C02 | $850 |
| F02 | 1 | F02 | 1 |
| C03 | $120 | C03 | $350 |
| F03 | 1 | F03 | 1 |

IRR CPT           IRR CPT
33.79%           23.31%

*d.*

| CF₀ | −$1,050 |
|---|---|
| C01 | $700 |
| F01 | 1 |
| C02 | $400 |
| F02 | 1 |
| C03 | $230 |
| F03 | 1 |

IRR CPT
15.86%

**15.** *a.*

| CDMA | | G4 | | Wi-Fi | |
|---|---|---|---|---|---|
| CF₀ | 0 | CF₀ | 0 | CF₀ | 0 |
| C01 | $11,000,000 | C01 | $10,000,000 | C01 | $18,000,000 |
| F01 | 1 | F01 | 1 | F01 | 1 |
| C02 | $7,500,000 | C02 | $25,000,000 | C02 | $32,000,000 |
| F02 | 1 | F02 | 1 | F02 | 1 |
| C03 | $2,500,000 | C03 | $20,000,000 | C03 | $20,000,000 |
| F03 | 1 | F03 | 1 | F03 | 1 |

I = 10%              I = 10%              I = 10%
NPV CPT             NPV CPT             NPV CPT
$18,076,634.11       $44,778,362.13       $57,836,213.37

$PI_{CDMA}$ = $18,076,634.11 / $8,000,000 = 2.26
$PI_{G4}$ = $44,778,362.13 / $12,000,000 = 3.73
$PI_{Wi-Fi}$ = $57,836,213.37 / $20,000,000 = 2.89

*b.*

| CDMA | | G4 | | Wi-Fi | |
|------|------|------|------|------|------|
| **CFo** | −$8,000,000 | **CFo** | −$12,000,000 | **CFo** | −$20,000,000 |
| **C01** | $11,000,000 | **C01** | $10,000,000 | **C01** | $18,000,000 |
| **F01** | 1 | **F01** | 1 | **F01** | 1 |
| **C02** | $7,500,000 | **C02** | $25,000,000 | **C02** | $32,000,000 |
| **F02** | 1 | **F02** | 1 | **F02** | 1 |
| **C03** | $2,500,000 | **C03** | $20,000,000 | **C03** | $20,000,000 |
| **F03** | 1 | **F03** | 1 | **F03** | 1 |

CDMA: $I = 10\%$, NPV CPT $10,076,634.11

G4: $I = 10\%$, NPV CPT $32,778,362.13

Wi-Fi: $I = 10\%$, NPV CPT $37,836,213.37

**16.** *b.*

| AZM | | AZF | |
|------|------|------|------|
| **CFo** | −$450,000 | **CFo** | −$800,000 |
| **C01** | $320,000 | **C01** | $350,000 |
| **F01** | 1 | **F01** | 1 |
| **C02** | $180,000 | **C02** | $420,000 |
| **F02** | 1 | **F02** | 1 |
| **C03** | $150,000 | **C03** | $290,000 |
| **F03** | 1 | **F03** | 1 |

AZM: $I = 10\%$, NPV CPT $102,366.64

AZF: $I = 10\%$, NPV CPT $83,170.55

*c.*

| AZM | | AZF | |
|------|------|------|------|
| **CFo** | −$450,000 | **CFo** | −$800,000 |
| **C01** | $320,000 | **C01** | $350,000 |
| **F01** | 1 | **F01** | 1 |
| **C02** | $180,000 | **C02** | $420,000 |
| **F02** | 1 | **F02** | 1 |
| **C03** | $150,000 | **C03** | $290,000 |
| **F03** | 1 | **F03** | 1 |

AZM: IRR CPT 24.65%

AZF: IRR CPT 15.97%

**17.** *a.*

| Project A | | Project B | | Project C | |
|------|------|------|------|------|------|
| **CFo** | 0 | **CFo** | 0 | **CFo** | 0 |
| **C01** | $110,000 | **C01** | $200,000 | **C01** | $120,000 |
| **F01** | 1 | **F01** | 1 | **F01** | 1 |
| **C02** | $110,000 | **C02** | $200,000 | **C02** | $90,000 |
| **F02** | 1 | **F02** | 1 | **F02** | 1 |

Project A: $I = 12\%$, NPV CPT $185,905.61

Project B: $I = 12\%$, NPV CPT $338,010.20

Project C: $I = 12\%$, NPV CPT $178,890.31

$PI_A = \$185,905.61 / \$150,000 = 1.24$

$PI_B = \$338,010.20 / \$300,000 = 1.13$

$PI_C = \$178,890.31 / \$150,000 = 1.19$

b.

| Project A | | | Project B | | | Project C | |
|---|---|---|---|---|---|---|---|
| **CFo** | –$150,000 | | **CFo** | –$300,000 | | **CFo** | –$150,000 |
| **C01** | $110,000 | | **C01** | $200,000 | | **C01** | $120,000 |
| **F01** | 1 | | **F01** | 1 | | **F01** | 1 |
| **C02** | $110,000 | | **C02** | $200,000 | | **C02** | $90,000 |
| **F02** | 1 | | **F02** | 1 | | **F02** | 1 |

I = 12%  
NPV CPT  
$35,905.61

I = 12%  
NPV CPT  
$38,010.20

I = 12%  
NPV CPT  
$28,890.31

**18.** b.

| Dry prepeg | | | Solvent prepeg | |
|---|---|---|---|---|
| **CFo** | –$1,700,000 | | **CFo** | –$750,000 |
| **C01** | $1,100,000 | | **C01** | $375,000 |
| **F01** | 1 | | **F01** | 1 |
| **C02** | $900,000 | | **C02** | $600,000 |
| **F02** | 1 | | **F02** | 1 |
| **C03** | $750,000 | | **C03** | $390,0000 |
| **F03** | 1 | | **F03** | 1 |

I = 10%  
NPV CPT  
$607,287.75

I = 10%  
NPV CPT  
$379,789.63

c.

| Dry prepeg | | | Solvent prepeg | |
|---|---|---|---|---|
| **CFo** | –$1,700,000 | | **CFo** | –$750,000 |
| **C01** | $1,100,000 | | **C01** | $375,000 |
| **F01** | 1 | | **F01** | 1 |
| **C02** | $900,000 | | **C02** | $600,000 |
| **F02** | 1 | | **F02** | 1 |
| **C03** | $750,000 | | **C03** | $390,0000 |
| **F03** | 1 | | **F03** | 1 |

IRR CPT  
30.90%

IRR CPT  
36.51%

d.

| | |
|---|---|
| **CFo** | –$950,000 |
| **C01** | $725,000 |
| **F01** | 1 |
| **C02** | $300,000 |
| **F02** | 1 |
| **C03** | $360,000 |
| **F03** | 1 |

IRR CPT  
25.52%

**19.** *b.*

| *NP-30* | |
|---|---|
| **CFo** | –$550,000 |
| **C01** | $185,000 |
| **F01** | 5 |
| **C02** | |
| **F02** | |
| **C03** | |
| **F03** | |
| **C04** | |
| **F04** | |
| **C05** | |
| **F05** | |

IRR CPT
20.27%

| *NX-20* | |
|---|---|
| **CFo** | –$350,000 |
| **C01** | $100,000 |
| **F01** | 1 |
| **C02** | $110,000 |
| **F02** | 1 |
| **C03** | $121,000 |
| **F03** | 1 |
| **C04** | $133,100 |
| **F04** | 1 |
| **C05** | $146,410 |
| **F05** | 1 |

IRR CPT
20.34%

*c.*

| *NP-30* | |
|---|---|
| **CFo** | –$550,000 |
| **C01** | $185,000 |
| **F01** | 5 |
| **C02** | |
| **F02** | |
| **C03** | |
| **F03** | |
| **C04** | |
| **F04** | |
| **C05** | |
| **F05** | |

I = 15%
NPV CPT
$620,148.69

| *NX-20* | |
|---|---|
| **CFo** | –$350,000 |
| **C01** | $100,000 |
| **F01** | 1 |
| **C02** | $110,000 |
| **F02** | 1 |
| **C03** | $121,000 |
| **F03** | 1 |
| **C04** | $133,100 |
| **F04** | 1 |
| **C05** | $146,410 |
| **F05** | 1 |

I = 15%
NPV CPT
$398,583.79

$PI_{NP-30} = \$620,148.69 / \$550,000 = 1.128$
$PI_{NX-20} = \$398,583.79 / \$350,000 = 1.139$

*d.*

| *NP-30* | |
|---|---|
| **CFo** | –$550,000 |
| **C01** | $185,000 |
| **F01** | 5 |
| **C02** | |
| **F02** | |
| **C03** | |
| **F03** | |
| **C04** | |
| **F04** | |
| **C05** | |
| **F05** | |

I = 15%
NPV CPT
$70,148.66

| *NX-20* | |
|---|---|
| **CFo** | –$350,000 |
| **C01** | $100,000 |
| **F01** | 1 |
| **C02** | $110,000 |
| **F02** | 1 |
| **C03** | $121,000 |
| **F03** | 1 |
| **C04** | $133,100 |
| **F04** | 1 |
| **C05** | $146,410 |
| **F05** | 1 |

I = 15%
NPV CPT
$48,583.79

**28.**

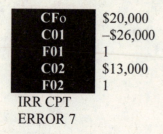

| | |
|---|---|
| CFo | $20,000 |
| C01 | –$26,000 |
| F01 | 1 |
| C02 | $13,000 |
| F02 | 1 |

IRR CPT

ERROR 7

# CHAPTER 6
# MAKING CAPITAL INVESTMENT DECISIONS

**Answers to Concepts Review and Critical Thinking Questions**

1.  In this context, an opportunity cost refers to the value of an asset or other input that will be used in a project. The relevant cost is what the asset or input is actually worth today, not, for example, what it cost to acquire.

2.  *a.*  Yes, the reduction in the sales of the company's other products, referred to as erosion, should be treated as an incremental cash flow. These lost sales are included because they are a cost (a revenue reduction) that the firm must bear if it chooses to produce the new product.

    *b.*  Yes, expenditures on plant and equipment should be treated as incremental cash flows. These are costs of the new product line. However, if these expenditures have already occurred (and cannot be recaptured through a sale of the plant and equipment), they are sunk costs and are not included as incremental cash flows.

    *c.*  No, the research and development costs should not be treated as incremental cash flows. The costs of research and development undertaken on the product during the past three years are sunk costs and should not be included in the evaluation of the project. Decisions made and costs incurred in the past cannot be changed. They should not affect the decision to accept or reject the project.

    *d.*  Yes, the annual depreciation expense must be taken into account when calculating the cash flows related to a given project. While depreciation is not a cash expense that directly affects cash flow, it decreases a firm's net income and hence, lowers its tax bill for the year. Because of this depreciation tax shield, the firm has more cash on hand at the end of the year than it would have had without expensing depreciation.

    *e.*  No, dividend payments should not be treated as incremental cash flows. A firm's decision to pay or not pay dividends is independent of the decision to accept or reject any given investment project. For this reason, dividends are not an incremental cash flow to a given project. Dividend policy is discussed in more detail in later chapters.

    *f.*  Yes, the resale value of plant and equipment at the end of a project's life should be treated as an incremental cash flow. The price at which the firm sells the equipment is a cash inflow, and any difference between the book value of the equipment and its sale price will create accounting gains or losses that result in either a tax credit or liability.

    *g.*  Yes, salary and medical costs for production employees hired for a project should be treated as incremental cash flows. The salaries of all personnel connected to the project must be included as costs of that project.

3.    Item (a) is a relevant cost because the opportunity to sell the land is lost if the new golf club is produced. Item (b) is also relevant because the firm must take into account the erosion of sales of existing products when a new product is introduced. If the firm produces the new club, the earnings from the existing clubs will decrease, effectively creating a cost that must be included in the decision. Item (c) is not relevant because the costs of research and development are sunk costs. Decisions made in the past cannot be changed. They are not relevant to the production of the new club.

4.    For tax purposes, a firm would choose MACRS because it provides for larger depreciation deductions earlier. These larger deductions reduce taxes, but have no other cash consequences. Notice that the choice between MACRS and straight-line is purely a time value issue; the total depreciation is the same, only the timing differs.

5.    It's probably only a mild over-simplification. Current liabilities will all be paid, presumably. The cash portion of current assets will be retrieved. Some receivables won't be collected, and some inventory will not be sold, of course. Counterbalancing these losses is the fact that inventory sold above cost (and not replaced at the end of the project's life) acts to increase working capital. These effects tend to offset one another.

6.    Management's discretion to set the firm's capital structure is applicable at the firm level. Since any one particular project could be financed entirely with equity, another project could be financed with debt, and the firm's overall capital structure would remain unchanged. Financing costs are not relevant in the analysis of a project's incremental cash flows according to the stand-alone principle.

7.    The EAC approach is appropriate when comparing mutually exclusive projects with different lives that will be replaced when they wear out. This type of analysis is necessary so that the projects have a common life span over which they can be compared. For example, if one project has a three-year life and the other has a five-year life, then a 15-year horizon is the minimum necessary to place the two projects on an equal footing, implying that one project will be repeated five times and the other will be repeated three times. Note the shortest common life may be quite long when there are more than two alternatives and/or the individual project lives are relatively long. Assuming this type of analysis is valid implies that the project cash flows remain the same over the common life, thus ignoring the possible effects of, among other things: (1) inflation, (2) changing economic conditions, (3) the increasing unreliability of cash flow estimates that occur far into the future, and (4) the possible effects of future technology improvement that could alter the project cash flows.

8.    Depreciation is a non-cash expense, but it is tax-deductible on the income statement. Thus depreciation causes taxes paid, an actual cash outflow, to be reduced by an amount equal to the depreciation tax shield, $t_cD$. A reduction in taxes that would otherwise be paid is the same thing as a cash inflow, so the effects of the depreciation tax shield must be added in to get the total incremental aftertax cash flows.

9.    There are two particularly important considerations. The first is erosion. Will the "essentialized" book simply displace copies of the existing book that would have otherwise been sold? This is of special concern given the lower price. The second consideration is competition. Will other publishers step in and produce such a product? If so, then any erosion is much less relevant. A particular concern to book publishers (and producers of a variety of other product types) is that the publisher only makes money from the sale of new books. Thus, it is important to examine whether the new book would displace sales of used books (good from the publisher's perspective) or new books (not good). The concern arises any time there is an active market for used product.

10. Definitely. The damage to Porsche's reputation is a factor the company needed to consider. If the reputation was damaged, the company would have lost sales of its existing car lines.

11. One company may be able to produce at lower incremental cost or market better. Also, of course, one of the two may have made a mistake!

12. Porsche would recognize that the outsized profits would dwindle as more products come to market and competition becomes more intense.

**Solutions to Questions and Problems**

*NOTE: All end-of-chapter problems were solved using a spreadsheet. Many problems require multiple steps. Due to space and readability constraints, when these intermediate steps are included in this solutions manual, rounding may appear to have occurred. However, the final answer for each problem is found without rounding during any step in the problem.*

*Basic*

1. Using the tax shield approach to calculating OCF, we get:

   $OCF = (Sales - Costs)(1 - t_C) + t_C Depreciation$
   $OCF = [(\$4.75 \times 1,500) - (\$2.30 \times 1,500)](1 - 0.34) + 0.34(\$9,000/5)$
   $OCF = \$3,037.50$

   So, the NPV of the project is:

   $NPV = -\$9,000 + \$3,037.50(PVIFA_{14\%,5})$
   $NPV = \$1,427.98$

2. We will use the bottom-up approach to calculate the operating cash flow for each year. We also must be sure to include the net working capital cash flows each year. So, the net income and total cash flow each year will be:

|  | | Year 1 | Year 2 | Year 3 | Year 4 |
|---|---|---|---|---|---|
| Sales | | $12,500 | $13,000 | $13,500 | $10,500 |
| Costs | | 2,700 | 2,800 | 2,900 | 2,100 |
| Depreciation | | 6,000 | 6,000 | 6,000 | 6,000 |
| EBT | | $ 3,800 | $ 4,200 | $ 4,600 | $ 2,400 |
| Tax | | 1,292 | 1,428 | 1,564 | 816 |
| Net income | | $ 2,508 | $ 2,772 | $ 3,036 | $ 1,584 |
| | | | | | |
| OCF | 0 | $ 8,508 | $ 8,772 | $ 9,036 | $ 7,584 |
| Capital spending | –$24,000 | 0 | 0 | 0 | 0 |
| NWC | –300 | –350 | –400 | –300 | 1,350 |
| Incremental cash flow | –$24,300 | $ 8,158 | $ 8,372 | $ 8,736 | $ 8,934 |

The NPV for the project is:

$$NPV = -\$24,300 + \$8,158 / 1.12 + \$8,372 / 1.12^2 + \$8,736 / 1.12^3 + \$8,934 / 1.12^4$$
$$NPV = \$1,553.87$$

3.  Using the tax shield approach to calculating OCF, we get:

$$OCF = (Sales - Costs)(1 - t_C) + t_C Depreciation$$
$$OCF = (\$1,120,000 - 480,000)(1 - 0.35) + 0.35(\$1,400,000/3)$$
$$OCF = \$579,333.33$$

So, the NPV of the project is:

$$NPV = -\$1,400,000 + \$579,333.33(PVIFA_{12\%,3})$$
$$NPV = -\$8,539.09$$

4.  The cash outflow at the beginning of the project will increase because of the spending on NWC. At the end of the project, the company will recover the NWC, so it will be a cash inflow. The sale of the equipment will result in a cash inflow, but we also must account for the taxes which will be paid on this sale. So, the cash flows for each year of the project will be:

| Year | Cash Flow | |
|------|-----------|---|
| 0 | – $1,685,000 | = –$1,400,000 – 285,000 |
| 1 | 579,333.33 | |
| 2 | 579,333.33 | |
| 3 | 1,010,583.33 | = $579,333.33 + 285,000 + 225,000 + (0 – 225,000)(.35) |

And the NPV of the project is:

$$NPV = -\$1,685,000 + \$579,333.33(PVIFA_{12\%,2}) + (\$1,010,583.33 / 1.12^3)$$
$$NPV = \$13,416.15$$

5.  First we will calculate the annual depreciation for the equipment necessary for the project. The depreciation amount each year will be:

Year 1 depreciation = $1,400,000(0.3333) = $466,620
Year 2 depreciation = $1,400,000(0.4445) = $622,300
Year 3 depreciation = $1,400,000(0.1481) = $207,340

So, the book value of the equipment at the end of three years, which will be the initial investment minus the accumulated depreciation, is:

Book value in 3 years = $1,400,000 – ($466,620 + 622,300 + 207,340)
Book value in 3 years = $103,740

The asset is sold at a gain to book value, so this gain is taxable.

Aftertax salvage value = $225,000 + ($103,740 – 225,000)(0.35)
Aftertax salvage value = $182,559

To calculate the OCF, we will use the tax shield approach, so the cash flow each year is:

$$OCF = (Sales - Costs)(1 - t_C) + t_C Depreciation$$

| Year | Cash Flow | |
|------|-----------|---|
| 0 | – $1,685,000 | = –$1,400,000 – 285,000 |
| 1 | 579,317 | = ($640,000)(.65) + 0.35($466,620) |
| 2 | 633,805 | = ($640,000)(.65) + 0.35($622,300) |
| 3 | 956,128 | = ($640,000)(.65) + 0.35($207,340) + $182,559 + 285,000 |

Remember to include the NWC cost in Year 0, and the recovery of the NWC at the end of the project. The NPV of the project with these assumptions is:

$$NPV = - \$1,685,000 + \$579,317/1.12 + \$633,805/1.12^2 + \$956,128/1.12^3$$
$$NPV = \$18,065.81$$

6. First, we will calculate the annual depreciation of the new equipment. It will be:

Annual depreciation charge = $670,000/5
Annual depreciation charge = $134,000

The aftertax salvage value of the equipment is:

Aftertax salvage value = $50,000(1 – 0.35)
Aftertax salvage value = $32,500

Using the tax shield approach, the OCF is:

OCF = $240,000(1 – 0.35) + 0.35($134,000)
OCF = $202,900

Now we can find the project IRR. There is an unusual feature that is a part of this project. Accepting this project means that we will reduce NWC. This reduction in NWC is a cash inflow at Year 0. This reduction in NWC implies that when the project ends, we will have to increase NWC. So, at the end of the project, we will have a cash outflow to restore the NWC to its level before the project. We also must include the aftertax salvage value at the end of the project. The IRR of the project is:

$$NPV = 0 = -\$670,000 + 85,000 + \$202,900(PVIFA_{IRR\%,5})$$
$$+ [(\$202,900 + 32,500 - 85,000) / (1+IRR)^5]$$

IRR = 20.06%

7. First, we will calculate the annual depreciation of the new equipment. It will be:

Annual depreciation = $375,000/5
Annual depreciation = $75,000

Now, we calculate the aftertax salvage value. The aftertax salvage value is the market price minus (or plus) the taxes on the sale of the equipment, so:

Aftertax salvage value = $MV + (BV - MV)t_c$

Very often, the book value of the equipment is zero as it is in this case. If the book value is zero, the equation for the aftertax salvage value becomes:

Aftertax salvage value = $MV + (0 - MV)t_c$
Aftertax salvage value = $MV(1 - t_c)$

We will use this equation to find the aftertax salvage value since we know the book value is zero. So, the aftertax salvage value is:

Aftertax salvage value = $\$40,000(1 - 0.34)$
Aftertax salvage value = $\$26,400$

Using the tax shield approach, we find the OCF for the project is:

OCF = $\$105,000(1 - 0.34) + 0.34(\$75,000)$
OCF = $\$94,800$

Now we can find the project NPV. Notice that we include the NWC in the initial cash outlay. The recovery of the NWC occurs in Year 5, along with the aftertax salvage value.

NPV = $-\$375,000 - 28,000 + \$94,800(PVIFA_{10\%,5}) + [(\$26,400 + 28,000) / 1.1^5]$
NPV = $-\$9,855.29$

8.  To find the BV at the end of four years, we need to find the accumulated depreciation for the first four years. We could calculate a table with the depreciation each year, but an easier way is to add the MACRS depreciation amounts for each of the first four years and multiply this percentage times the cost of the asset. We can then subtract this from the asset cost. Doing so, we get:

$BV_4$ = $\$7,100,000 - 7,100,000(0.2000 + 0.3200 + 0.1920 + 0.1152)$
$BV_4$ = $\$1,226,880$

The asset is sold at a gain to book value, so this gain is taxable.

Aftertax salvage value = $\$1,400,000 + (\$1,226,880 - 1,400,000)(.35)$
Aftertax salvage value = $\$1,339,408$

9.  We will begin by calculating the initial cash outlay, that is, the cash flow at Time 0. To undertake the project, we will have to purchase the equipment and increase net working capital. So, the cash outlay today for the project will be:

| | |
|---|---|
| Equipment | −$3,800,000 |
| NWC | −150,000 |
| Total | −$3,950,000 |

Using the bottom-up approach to calculating the operating cash flow, we find the operating cash flow each year will be:

| | |
|---|---|
| Sales | $2,500,000 |
| Costs | 625,000 |
| Depreciation | 950,000 |
| EBT | $ 925,000 |
| Tax | 323,750 |
| Net income | $ 601,250 |

The operating cash flow is:

OCF = Net income + Depreciation
OCF = $601,250 + 950,000
OCF = $1,551,250

To find the NPV of the project, we add the present value of the project cash flows. We must be sure to add back the net working capital at the end of the project life, since we are assuming the net working capital will be recovered. So, the project NPV is:

NPV = –$3,950,000 + $1,551,250(PVIFA$_{16\%,4}$) + $150,000 / 1.16$^4$
NPV = $473,521.38

10. We will need the aftertax salvage value of the equipment to compute the EAC. Even though the equipment for each product has a different initial cost, both have the same salvage value. The aftertax salvage value for both is:

Both cases: aftertax salvage value = $20,000(1 – 0.35) = $13,000

To calculate the EAC, we first need the OCF and NPV of each option. The OCF and NPV for Techron I is:

OCF = – $35,000(1 – 0.35) + 0.35($215,000/3) = $2,333.33

NPV = –$215,000 + $2,333.33(PVIFA$_{12\%,3}$) + ($13,000/1.12$^3$) = –$200,142.58

EAC = –$200,142.58 / (PVIFA$_{12\%,3}$) = –$83,329.16

And the OCF and NPV for Techron II is:

OCF = – $44,000(1 – 0.35) + 0.35($270,000/5) = –$9,700

NPV = –$270,000 – $9,700(PVIFA$_{12\%,5}$) + ($13,000/1.12$^5$) = –$297,589.78

EAC = –$297,589.78 / (PVIFA$_{12\%,5}$) = –$82,554.30

The two milling machines have unequal lives, so they can only be compared by expressing both on an equivalent annual basis, which is what the EAC method does. Thus, you prefer the Techron II because it has the lower (less negative) annual cost.

*Intermediate*

11. First, we will calculate the depreciation each year, which will be:

$D_1 = \$640{,}000(0.2000) = \$128{,}000$
$D_2 = \$640{,}000(0.3200) = \$204{,}800$
$D_3 = \$640{,}000(0.1920) = \$122{,}880$
$D_4 = \$640{,}000(0.1150) = \$73{,}728$

The book value of the equipment at the end of the project is:

$BV_4 = \$640{,}000 - (\$128{,}000 + 204{,}800 + 122{,}880 + 73{,}728) = \$110{,}592$

The asset is sold at a loss to book value, so this creates a tax refund.
After-tax salvage value = $\$70{,}000 + (\$110{,}592 - 70{,}000)(0.35) = \$84{,}207.20$

So, the OCF for each year will be:

$OCF_1 = \$270{,}000(1 - 0.35) + 0.35(\$128{,}000) = \$220{,}300.00$
$OCF_2 = \$270{,}000(1 - 0.35) + 0.35(\$204{,}800) = \$247{,}180.00$
$OCF_3 = \$270{,}000(1 - 0.35) + 0.35(\$122{,}880) = \$218{,}508.00$
$OCF_4 = \$270{,}000(1 - 0.35) + 0.35(\$73{,}728) = \$201{,}304.80$

Now we have all the necessary information to calculate the project NPV. We need to be careful with the NWC in this project. Notice the project requires $20,000 of NWC at the beginning, and $3,500 more in NWC each successive year. We will subtract the $20,000 from the initial cash flow and subtract $3,500 each year from the OCF to account for this spending. In Year 4, we will add back the total spent on NWC, which is $30,500. The $3,500 spent on NWC capital during Year 4 is irrelevant. Why? Well, during this year the project required an additional $3,500, but we would get the money back immediately. So, the net cash flow for additional NWC would be zero. With all this, the equation for the NPV of the project is:

$$NPV = -\$640{,}000 - 20{,}000 + (\$220{,}300 - 3{,}500)/1.14 + (\$247{,}180 - 3{,}500)/1.14^2$$
$$+ (\$218{,}508 - 3{,}500)/1.14^3 + (\$201{,}304.80 + 30{,}500 + 84{,}207.20)/1.14^4$$
$$NPV = \$49{,}908.03$$

12. If we are trying to decide between two projects that will not be replaced when they wear out, the proper capital budgeting method to use is NPV. Both projects only have costs associated with them, not sales, so we will use these to calculate the NPV of each project. Using the tax shield approach to calculate the OCF, the NPV of System A is:

$OCF_A = -\$85{,}000(1 - 0.34) + 0.34(\$290{,}000/4)$
$OCF_A = -\$31{,}450$

$NPV_A = -\$290{,}000 - \$31{,}450(PVIFA_{11\%,\,4})$
$NPV_A = -\$387{,}571.92$

And the NPV of System B is:

$OCF_B = -\$75,000(1 - 0.34) + 0.34(\$405,000/6)$
$OCF_B = -\$26,550$

$NPV_B = -\$405,000 - \$26,550(PVIFA_{11\%, 6})$
$NPV_B = -\$517,320.78$

If the system will not be replaced when it wears out, then System A should be chosen, because it has the less negative NPV.

13.  If the equipment will be replaced at the end of its useful life, the correct capital budgeting technique is EAC. Using the NPVs we calculated in the previous problem, the EAC for each system is:

$EAC_A = - \$387,571.92 / (PVIFA_{11\%, 4})$
$EAC_A = -\$124,924.64$

$EAC_B = - \$517,320.78 / (PVIFA_{11\%, 6})$
$EAC_B = -\$122,282.51$

If the conveyor belt system will be continually replaced, we should choose System B since it has the less negative EAC.

14.  Since we need to calculate the EAC for each machine, sales are irrelevant. EAC only uses the costs of operating the equipment, not the sales. Using the bottom up approach, or net income plus depreciation, method to calculate OCF, we get:

|  | Machine A | Machine B |
|---|---|---|
| Variable costs | -$4,200,000 | -$3,600,000 |
| Fixed costs | -195,000 | -165,000 |
| Depreciation | -483,333 | -633,333 |
| EBT | -$4,878,333 | -$4,398,333 |
| Tax | 1,707,417 | 1,539,417 |
| Net income | -$3,170,917 | -$2,858,917 |
| + Depreciation | 483,333 | 633,333 |
| OCF | -$2,687,583 | -$2,225,583 |

The NPV and EAC for Machine A is:

$NPV_A = -\$2,900,000 - \$2,687,583(PVIFA_{10\%, 6})$
$NPV_A = -\$14,605,126.07$

$EAC_A = - \$14,605,126.07 / (PVIFA_{10\%, 6})$
$EAC_A = -\$3,353,444.74$

And the NPV and EAC for Machine B is:

$NPV_B = -\$5,700,000 - 2,225,583(PVIFA_{10\%,9})$
$NPV_B = -\$18,517,187.42$

$EAC_B = -\$18,517,187.42 / (PVIFA_{10\%,9})$
$EAC_B = -\$3,215,334.41$

You should choose Machine B since it has a less negative EAC.

**15.** When we are dealing with nominal cash flows, we must be careful to discount cash flows at the nominal interest rate, and we must discount real cash flows using the real interest rate. Project A's cash flows are in real terms, so we need to find the real interest rate. Using the Fisher equation, the real interest rate is:

$1 + R = (1 + r)(1 + h)$
$1.13 = (1 + r)(1 + .04)$
$r = .0865$ or $8.65\%$

So, the NPV of Project A's real cash flows, discounting at the real interest rate, is:

$NPV = -\$50,000 + \$30,000 / 1.0865 + \$25,000 / 1.0865^2 + \$20,000 / 1.0865^3$
$NPV = \$14,378.65$

Project B's cash flow are in nominal terms, so the NPV discounted at the nominal interest rate is:

$NPV = -\$65,000 + \$29,000 / 1.13 + \$38,000 / 1.13^2 + \$41,000 / 1.13^3$
$NPV = \$18,838.35$

We should accept Project B if the projects are mutually exclusive since it has the highest NPV.

**16.** To determine the value of a firm, we can simply find the present value of the firm's future cash flows. No depreciation is given, so we can assume depreciation is zero. Using the tax shield approach, we can find the present value of the aftertax revenues, and the present value of the aftertax costs. The required return, growth rates, price, and costs are all given in real terms. Subtracting the costs from the revenues will give us the value of the firm's cash flows. We must calculate the present value of each separately since each is growing at a different rate. First, we will find the present value of the revenues. The revenues in year 1 will be the number of bottles sold, times the price per bottle, or:

Aftertax revenue in year 1 in real terms = $(2,800,000 \times \$1.25)(1 - 0.34)$
Aftertax revenue in year 1 in real terms = $\$2,310,000$

Revenues will grow at six percent per year in real terms forever. Apply the growing perpetuity formula, we find the present value of the revenues is:

PV of revenues = $C_1 / (R - g)$
PV of revenues = $\$2,310,000 / (0.10 - 0.06)$
PV of revenues = $\$57,750,000$

The real aftertax costs in year 1 will be:

Aftertax costs in year 1 in real terms = (2,800,000 × $0.90)(1 – 0.34)
Aftertax costs in year 1 in real terms = $1,663,200

Costs will grow at five percent per year in real terms forever. Applying the growing perpetuity formula, we find the present value of the costs is:

PV of costs = $C_1 / (R - g)$
PV of costs = $1,663,200 / (0.10 – 0.05)
PV of costs = $33,264,000

Now we can find the value of the firm, which is:

Value of the firm = PV of revenues – PV of costs
Value of the firm = $57,750,000 – 33,264,000
Value of the firm = $24,486,000

17. To calculate the nominal cash flows, we increase each item in the income statement by the inflation rate, except for depreciation. Depreciation is a nominal cash flow, so it does not need to be adjusted for inflation in nominal cash flow analysis. Since the resale value is given in nominal terms as of the end of year 5, it does not need to be adjusted for inflation. Also, no inflation adjustment is needed for net working capital since it already expressed in nominal terms. Note that an increase in required net working capital is a negative cash flow whereas a decrease in required net working capital is a positive cash flow. We first need to calculate the taxes on the salvage value. Remember, to calculate the taxes paid (or tax credit) on the salvage value, we take the book value minus the market value, times the tax rate, which, in this case, would be:

Taxes on salvage value = $(BV - MV)t_C$
Taxes on salvage value = ($0 – 45,000)(.34)
Taxes on salvage value = –$15,300

So, the nominal aftertax salvage value is:

| | |
|---|---|
| Market price | $45,000 |
| Tax on sale | −15,300 |
| Aftertax salvage value | $29,700 |

Now we can find the nominal cash flows each year using the income statement. Doing so, we find:

|  | Year 0 | Year 1 | Year 2 | Year 3 | Year 4 | Year 5 |
|---|---|---|---|---|---|---|
| Sales |  | $245,000 | $252,350 | $259,921 | $267,718 | $275,750 |
| Expenses |  | 70,000 | 72,100 | 74,263 | 76,491 | 78,786 |
| Depreciation |  | 73,000 | 73,000 | 73,000 | 73,000 | 73,000 |
| EBT |  | $102,000 | $107,250 | $112,658 | $118,227 | $123,964 |
| Tax |  | 34,680 | 36,465 | 38,304 | 40,197 | 42,148 |
| Net income |  | $ 67,320 | $ 70,785 | $ 74,354 | $ 78,030 | $ 81,816 |
| OCF |  | $140,320 | $143,785 | $147,354 | $151,030 | $154,816 |
|  |  |  |  |  |  |  |
| Capital spending | –$365,000 |  |  |  |  | 29,700 |
| NWC | –10,000 |  |  |  |  | 10,000 |
| Total cash flow | –$375,000 | $140,320 | $143,785 | $147,354 | $151,030 | $194,516 |

18. The present value of the company is the present value of the future cash flows generated by the company. Here we have real cash flows, a real interest rate, and a real growth rate. The cash flows are a growing perpetuity, with a negative growth rate. Using the growing perpetuity equation, the present value of the cash flows is:

$PV = C_1 / (R - g)$
$PV = \$190,000 / [.11 - (-.04)]$
$PV = \$1,266,666.67$

19. To find the EAC, we first need to calculate the NPV of the incremental cash flows. We will begin with the aftertax salvage value, which is:

$\text{Taxes on salvage value} = (BV - MV)t_C$
$\text{Taxes on salvage value} = (\$0 - 18,000)(.34)$
$\text{Taxes on salvage value} = -\$6,120$

| Market price | $18,000 |
|---|---|
| Tax on sale | –6,120 |
| Aftertax salvage value | $11,880 |

Now we can find the operating cash flows. Using the tax shield approach, the operating cash flow each year will be:

$OCF = -\$8,600(1 - 0.34) + 0.34(\$94,000/3)$
$OCF = \$4,977.33$

So, the NPV of the cost of the decision to buy is:

$NPV = -\$94,000 + \$4,977.33(PVIFA_{12\%, 3}) + (\$11,880/1.12^3)$
$NPV = -\$73,589.34$

In order to calculate the equivalent annual cost, set the NPV of the equipment equal to an annuity with the same economic life. Since the project has an economic life of three years and is discounted at 12 percent, set the NPV equal to a three-year annuity, discounted at 12 percent.

$$EAC = -\$73,589.34 / (PVIFA_{12\%,3})$$
$$EAC = -\$30,638.84$$

20. We will calculate the aftertax salvage value first. The aftertax salvage value of the equipment will be:

Taxes on salvage value $= (BV - MV)t_C$
Taxes on salvage value $= (\$0 - 60,000)(.34)$
Taxes on salvage value $= -\$20,400$

| | |
|---|---|
| Market price | $60,000 |
| Tax on sale | –20,400 |
| Aftertax salvage value | $39,600 |

Next, we will calculate the initial cash outlay, that is, the cash flow at Time 0. To undertake the project, we will have to purchase the equipment. The new project will decrease the net working capital, so this is a cash inflow at the beginning of the project. So, the cash outlay today for the project will be:

| | |
|---|---|
| Equipment | –$360,000 |
| NWC | 80,000 |
| Total | –$280,000 |

Now we can calculate the operating cash flow each year for the project. Using the bottom up approach, the operating cash flow will be:

| | |
|---|---|
| Saved salaries | $105,000 |
| Depreciation | 72,000 |
| EBT | $ 33,000 |
| Taxes | 11,220 |
| Net income | $ 21,780 |

And the OCF will be:

$$OCF = \$21,780 + 72,000$$
$$OCF = \$93,780$$

Now we can find the NPV of the project. In Year 5, we must replace the saved NWC, so:

$$NPV = -\$280,000 + \$93,780(PVIFA_{12\%,\,5}) + (\$39,600 - 80,000) / 1.12^5$$
$$NPV = \$35,131.87$$

**21.** Replacement decision analysis is the same as the analysis of two competing projects, in this case, keep the current equipment, or purchase the new equipment. We will consider the purchase of the new machine first.

Purchase new machine:

The initial cash outlay for the new machine is the cost of the new machine, plus the increased net working capital. So, the initial cash outlay will be:

| | |
|---|---|
| Purchase new machine | –$18,000,000 |
| Net working capital | –250,000 |
| Total | –$18,250,000 |

Next, we can calculate the operating cash flow created if the company purchases the new machine. The saved operating expense is an incremental cash flow. Additionally, the reduced operating expense is a cash inflow, so it should be treated as such in the income statement. The pro forma income statement, and adding depreciation to net income, the annual operating cash flow created by purchasing the new machine will be:

| | |
|---|---|
| Operating expense | $6,700,000 |
| Depreciation | 4,500,000 |
| EBT | $2,200,000 |
| Taxes | 858,000 |
| Net income | $1,342,000 |
| OCF | $5,842,000 |

So, the NPV of purchasing the new machine, including the recovery of the net working capital, is:

$$NPV = -\$18,250,000 + \$5,842,000(PVIFA_{10\%,4}) + \$250,000 / 1.10^4$$
$$NPV = \$439,107.30$$

And the IRR is:

$$0 = -\$18,250,000 + \$5,842,000(PVIFA_{IRR,4}) + \$250,000 / (1 + IRR)^4$$

Using a spreadsheet or financial calculator, we find the IRR is:

$$IRR = 11.10\%$$

Now we can calculate the decision to keep the old machine:

Keep old machine:

The initial cash outlay for the old machine is the market value of the old machine, including any potential tax consequence. The decision to keep the old machine has an opportunity cost, namely, the company could sell the old machine. Also, if the company sells the old machine at its current value, it will receive a tax benefit. Both of these cash flows need to be included in the analysis. So, the initial cash flow of keeping the old machine will be:

| | |
|---|---|
| Keep machine | −$4,500,000 |
| Taxes | −585,000 |
| Total | −$5,085,000 |

Next, we can calculate the operating cash flow created if the company keeps the old machine. There are no incremental cash flows from keeping the old machine, but we need to account for the cash flow effects of depreciation. The income statement, adding depreciation to net income to calculate the operating cash flow will be:

| | |
|---|---|
| Depreciation | $1,500,000 |
| EBT | −$1,500,000 |
| Taxes | −585,000 |
| Net income | −$ 915,000 |
| OCF | $ 585,000 |

So, the NPV of the decision to keep the old machine will be:

$$NPV = -\$5,085,000 + \$585,000(PVIFA_{10\%,4})$$
$$NPV = -\$3,230,628.71$$

And the IRR is:

$$0 = -\$5,085,000 + \$585,000(PVIFA_{IRR,4})$$

Using a spreadsheet or financial calculator, we find the IRR is:

$$IRR = -25.15\%$$

There is another way to analyze a replacement decision that is often used. It is an incremental cash flow analysis of the change in cash flows from the existing machine to the new machine, assuming the new machine is purchased. In this type of analysis, the initial cash outlay would be the cost of the new machine, the increased NWC, and the cash inflow (including any applicable taxes) of selling the old machine. In this case, the initial cash flow under this method would be:

| | |
|---|---|
| Purchase new machine | –$18,000,000 |
| Net working capital | –250,000 |
| Sell old machine | 4,500,000 |
| Taxes on old machine | 585,000 |
| Total | –$13,165,000 |

The cash flows from purchasing the new machine would be the saved operating expenses. We would also need to include the change in depreciation. The old machine has a depreciation of $1.5 million per year, and the new machine has a depreciation of $4.5 million per year, so the increased depreciation will be $3 million per year. The pro forma income statement and operating cash flow under this approach will be:

| | |
|---|---|
| Operating expense savings | $6,700,000 |
| Depreciation | 3,000,000 |
| EBT | $3,700,000 |
| Taxes | 1,443,000 |
| Net income | $2,257,000 |
| OCF | $5,257,000 |

The NPV under this method is:

$$NPV = -\$13,165,000 + \$5,257,000(PVIFA_{10\%, 4}) + \$250,000 / 1.10^4$$
$$NPV = \$3,669,736.02$$

And the IRR is:

$$0 = -\$13,165,000 + \$5,257,000(PVIFA_{IRR, 4}) + \$250,000 / (1 + IRR)^4$$

Using a spreadsheet or financial calculator, we find the IRR is:

$$IRR = 22.23\%$$

So, this analysis still tells us the company should purchase the new machine. This is really the same type of analysis we originally did. Consider this: Subtract the NPV of the decision to keep the old machine from the NPV of the decision to purchase the new machine. You will get:

$$Differential\ NPV = \$439,107.30 - (-\$3,230,628.71) = \$3,669,736.02$$

This is the exact same NPV we calculated when using the second analysis method.

**22.** We can find the NPV of a project using nominal cash flows or real cash flows. Either method will result in the same NPV. For this problem, we will calculate the NPV using both nominal and real cash flows. The initial investment in either case is $270,000 since it will be spent today. We will begin with the nominal cash flows. The revenues and production costs increase at different rates, so we must be careful to increase each at the appropriate growth rate. The nominal cash flows for each year will be:

|  | Year 0 | Year 1 | Year 2 | Year 3 |
|---|---|---|---|---|
| Revenues | | $105,000.00 | $110,250.00 | $115,762.50 |
| Costs | | $ 30,000.00 | 31,800.00 | 33,708.00 |
| Depreciation | | 38,571.43 | 38,571.43 | 38,571.43 |
| EBT | | $ 36,428.57 | $ 39,878.57 | $ 43,483.07 |
| Taxes | | 12,385.71 | 13,558.71 | 14,784.24 |
| Net income | | $ 24,042.86 | $ 26,319.86 | $ 28,698.83 |
| OCF | | $ 62,614.29 | $ 64,891.29 | $ 67,270.26 |
| | | | | |
| Capital spending | −$270,000 | | | |
| | | | | |
| Total cash flow | −$270,000 | $ 62,614.29 | $ 64,891.29 | $ 67,270.26 |

|  | Year 4 | Year 5 | Year 6 | Year 7 |
|---|---|---|---|---|
| Revenues | $121,550.63 | $127,628.16 | $134,009.56 | $140,710.04 |
| Costs | 35,730.48 | 37,874.31 | 40,146.77 | 42,555.57 |
| Depreciation | 38,571.43 | 38,571.43 | 38,571.43 | 38,571.43 |
| EBT | $ 47,248.72 | $ 51,182.42 | $ 55,291.37 | $ 59,583.04 |
| Taxes | 16,064.56 | 17,402.02 | 18,799.07 | 20,258.23 |
| Net income | $ 31,184.15 | $ 33,780.40 | $ 36,492.30 | $ 39,324.81 |
| OCF | $ 69,755.58 | $ 72,351.83 | $ 75,063.73 | $ 77,896.24 |
| | | | | |
| Capital spending | | | | |
| | | | | |
| Total cash flow | $ 69,755.58 | $ 72,351.83 | $ 75,063.73 | $ 77,896.24 |

Now that we have the nominal cash flows, we can find the NPV. We must use the nominal required return with nominal cash flows. Using the Fisher equation to find the nominal required return, we get:

$$(1 + R) = (1 + r)(1 + h)$$
$$(1 + R) = (1 + .08)(1 + .05)$$
$$R = .1340 \text{ or } 13.40\%$$

So, the NPV of the project using nominal cash flows is:

NPV = –$270,000 + $62,614.29 / 1.1340 + $64,891.29 / $1.1340^2$ + $67,270.26 / $1.1340^3$
    + $69,755.58 / $1.1340^4$ + $72,351.83 / $1.1340^5$ + $75,063.73 / $1.1340^6$ + $77,896.24 / $1.1340^7$
NPV = $30,170.71

We can also find the NPV using real cash flows and the real required return. This will allow us to find the operating cash flow using the tax shield approach. Both the revenues and expenses are growing annuities, but growing at different rates. This means we must find the present value of each separately. We also need to account for the effect of taxes, so we will multiply by one minus the tax rate. So, the present value of the aftertax revenues using the growing annuity equation is:

PV of aftertax revenues = $C \{[1/(r-g)] - [1/(r-g)] \times [(1+g)/(1+r)]^t\}(1-t_C)$
PV of aftertax revenues = $105,000\{[1/(.134-.05)] - [1/(.134-.05)] \times [(1+.05)/(1+.134)]^7\}(1-.34)$
PV of aftertax revenues = $343,620.42

And the present value of the aftertax costs will be:

PV of aftertax costs = $C \{[1/(r-g)] - [1/(r-g)] \times [(1+g)/(1+r)]^t\}(1-t_C)$
PV of aftertax costs = $30,000\{[1/(.134-.06)] - [1/(.134-.06)] \times [(1+.06)/(1+.134)]^7\}(1-.34)$
PV of aftertax costs = $100,734.11

Now we need to find the present value of the depreciation tax shield. The depreciation amount in the first year is a real value, so we can find the present value of the depreciation tax shield as an ordinary annuity using the real required return. So, the present value of the depreciation tax shield will be:

PV of depreciation tax shield = ($270,000/7)(.34)(PVIFA$_{13.40\%,7}$)
PV of depreciation tax shield = $57,284.40

Using the present value of the real cash flows to find the NPV, we get:

NPV = Initial cost + PV of revenues – PV of costs + PV of depreciation tax shield
NPV = –$270,000 + $343,620.42 – 100,734.11 + 57,284.40
NPV = $30,170.71

Notice, the NPV using nominal cash flows or real cash flows is identical, which is what we would expect.

23.  Here we have a project in which the quantity sold each year increases. First, we need to calculate the quantity sold each year by increasing the current year's quantity by the growth rate. So, the quantity sold each year will be:

Year 1 quantity = 7,000
Year 2 quantity = 7,000(1 + .08) = 7,560
Year 3 quantity = 7,560(1 + .08) = 8,165
Year 4 quantity = 8,165(1 + .08) = 8,818
Year 5 quantity = 8,818(1 + .08) = 9,523

Now we can calculate the sales revenue and variable costs each year. The pro forma income statements and operating cash flow each year will be:

| | Year 0 | Year 1 | Year 2 | Year 3 | Year 4 | Year 5 |
|---|---|---|---|---|---|---|
| Revenues | | $336,000.00 | $362,880.00 | $391,910.40 | $423,263.23 | $457,124.29 |
| Fixed costs | | 95,000.00 | 95,000.00 | 95,000.00 | 95,000.00 | 95,000.00 |
| Variable costs | | 140,000.00 | 151,200.00 | 163,296.00 | 176,359.68 | 190,468.45 |
| Depreciation | | 35,000.00 | 35,000.00 | 35,000.00 | 35,000.00 | 35,000.00 |
| EBT | | $ 66,000.00 | $ 81,680.00 | $ 98,614.40 | $116,903.55 | $136,655.84 |
| Taxes | | 22,440.00 | 27,771.20 | 33,528.90 | 39,747.21 | 46,462.98 |
| Net income | | $ 43,560.00 | $ 53,908.80 | $ 65,085.50 | $ 77,156.34 | $ 90,192.85 |
| OCF | | $ 78,560.00 | $ 88,908.80 | $100,085.50 | $112,156.34 | $125,192.85 |
| | | | | | | |
| Capital spending | –$175,000 | | | | | |
| NWC | –35,000 | | | | | 35,000 |
| | | | | | | |
| Total cash flow | –$210,000 | $ 78,560.00 | $ 88,908.80 | $100,085.50 | $112,156.34 | $160,192.85 |

So, the NPV of the project is:

$$NPV = -\$210,000 + 75,860 / 1.25 + \$88,908.80 / 1.25^2 + \$100,085.50 / 1.25^3 + \$112,156.34 / 1.25^4 + \$160,192.85 / 1.25^5$$
$$NPV = \$59,424.64$$

We could also have calculated the cash flows using the tax shield approach, with growing annuities and ordinary annuities. The sales and variable costs increase at the same rate as sales, so both are growing annuities. The fixed costs and depreciation are both ordinary annuities. Using the growing annuity equation, the present value of the revenues is:

$$PV \text{ of revenues} = C \{[1/(r-g)] - [1/(r-g)] \times [(1+g)/(1+r)]^t\}$$
$$PV \text{ of revenues} = \$336,000\{[1/(.25-.08)] - [1/(.25-.08)] \times [(1+.08)/(1+.25)]^5\}$$
$$PV \text{ of revenues} = \$1,024,860.43$$

And the present value of the variable costs will be:

$$PV \text{ of variable costs} = C \{[1/(r-g)] - [1/(r-g)] \times [(1+g)/(1+r)]^t\}$$
$$PV \text{ of variable costs} = \$140,000\{[1/(.25-.08)] - [1/(.25-.08)] \times [(1+.08)/(1+.25)]^5\}$$
$$PV \text{ of variable costs} = \$427,025.18$$

The fixed costs and depreciation are both ordinary annuities. The present value of each is:

$$PV \text{ of fixed costs} = C(\{1 - [1/(1+r)]^t\}/r)$$
$$PV \text{ of fixed costs} = \$95,000(PVIFA_{25\%, 5})$$
$$PV \text{ of fixed costs} = \$255,481.60$$

PV of depreciation = $C(\{1 - [1/(1 + r)]^t\} / r)$
PV of depreciation = $\$35,000(PVIFA_{25\%, 5})$
PV of depreciation = $\$94,124.80$

Now, we can use the depreciation tax shield approach to find the NPV of the project, which is:

NPV = –$210,000 + ($1,024,860.43 – 427,025.18 – 255,481.60)(1 – .34) + ($94,124.80)(.34)
        + $35,000 / $1.25^5$
NPV = $59,424.64

24. We will begin by calculating the aftertax salvage value of the equipment at the end of the project's life. The aftertax salvage value is the market value of the equipment minus any taxes paid (or refunded), so the aftertax salvage value in four years will be:

Taxes on salvage value = $(BV – MV)t_C$
Taxes on salvage value = ($0 – 300,000)(.38)
Taxes on salvage value = –$114,000

| | |
|---|---|
| Market price | $300,000 |
| Tax on sale | –114,000 |
| Aftertax salvage value | $186,000 |

Now we need to calculate the operating cash flow each year. Note, we assume that the net working capital cash flow occurs immediately. Using the bottom up approach to calculating operating cash flow, we find:

| | Year 0 | Year 1 | Year 2 | Year 3 | Year 4 |
|---|---|---|---|---|---|
| Revenues | | $1,842,500 | $2,062,500 | $2,502,500 | $1,705,000 |
| Fixed costs | | 350,000 | 350,000 | 350,000 | 350,000 |
| Variable costs | | 276,375 | 309,375 | 375,375 | 255,750 |
| Depreciation | | 1,033,230 | 1,377,950 | 459,110 | 229,710 |
| EBT | | $ 182,895 | $ 25,175 | $1,318,015 | $ 869,540 |
| Taxes | | 69,500 | 9,567 | 500,846 | 330,425 |
| Net income | | $ 113,395 | $ 15,609 | $ 817,169 | $ 539,115 |
| OCF | | $1,146,625 | $1,393,559 | $1,276,279 | $ 768,825 |
| | | | | | |
| Capital spending | –$3,100,000 | | | | 186,000 |
| Land | –900,000 | | | | 1,200,000 |
| NWC | –120,000 | | | | 120,000 |
| | | | | | |
| Total cash flow | –$4,120,000 | $1,146,625 | $1,393,559 | $1,276,279 | $2,274,825 |

Notice the calculation of the cash flow at time 0. The capital spending on equipment and investment in net working capital are cash outflows. The aftertax selling price of the land is also a cash outflow. Even though no cash is actually spent on the land because the company already owns it, the aftertax cash flow from selling the land is an opportunity cost, so we need to include it in the analysis. With all the project cash flows, we can calculate the NPV, which is:

$$NPV = -\$4,120,000 + \$1,146,625 / 1.13 + \$1,393,559 / 1.13^2 + \$1,246,279 / 1.13^3$$
$$+ \$2,274,825 / 1.13^4$$
$$NPV = \$265,791.25$$

The company should accept the new product line.

25. Replacement decision analysis is the same as the analysis of two competing projects, in this case, keep the current equipment, or purchase the new equipment. We will consider the purchase of the new machine first.

Purchase new machine:

The initial cash outlay for the new machine is the cost of the new machine. We can calculate the operating cash flow created if the company purchases the new machine. The maintenance cost is an incremental cash flow, so using the pro forma income statement, and adding depreciation to net income, the operating cash flow created each year by purchasing the new machine will be:

| Maintenance cost | $ 330,000 |
|---|---|
| Depreciation | 860,000 |
| EBT | −$1,190,000 |
| Taxes | −476,000 |
| Net income | −$ 714,000 |
| OCF | $ 146,000 |

Notice the taxes are negative, implying a tax credit. The new machine also has a salvage value at the end of five years, so we need to include this in the cash flows analysis. The aftertax salvage value will be:

| Sell machine | $800,000 |
|---|---|
| Taxes | −320,000 |
| Total | $480,000 |

The NPV of purchasing the new machine is:

$$NPV = -\$4,300,000 + \$146,000(PVIFA_{8\%,\,5}) + \$480,000 / 1.08^5$$
$$NPV = -\$3,390,384.40$$

Notice the NPV is negative. This does not necessarily mean we should not purchase the new machine. In this analysis, we are only dealing with costs, so we would expect a negative NPV. The revenue is not included in the analysis since it is not incremental to the machine. Similar to an EAC analysis, we will use the machine with the least negative NPV. Now we can calculate the decision to keep the old machine:

Keep old machine:

The initial cash outlay for the keeping the old machine is the market value of the old machine, including any potential tax. The decision to keep the old machine has an opportunity cost, namely, the company could sell the old machine. Also, if the company sells the old machine at its current value, it will incur taxes. Both of these cash flows need to be included in the analysis. So, the initial cash flow of keeping the old machine will be:

| | |
|---|---|
| Keep machine | –$2,200,000 |
| Taxes | 320,000 |
| Total | –$1,880,000 |

Next, we can calculate the operating cash flow created if the company keeps the old machine. We need to account for the cost of maintenance, as well as the cash flow effects of depreciation. The pro forma income statement, adding depreciation to net income to calculate the operating cash flow will be:

| | |
|---|---|
| Maintenance cost | $ 845,000 |
| Depreciation | 280,000 |
| EBT | –$1,125,000 |
| Taxes | –450,000 |
| Net income | –$ 675,000 |
| OCF | –$ 395,000 |

The old machine also has a salvage value at the end of five years, so we need to include this in the cash flows analysis. The aftertax salvage value will be:

| | |
|---|---|
| Sell machine | $120,000 |
| Taxes | –48,000 |
| Total | $ 72,000 |

So, the NPV of the decision to keep the old machine will be:

$$NPV = -\$1,880,000 - \$395,000(PVIFA_{8\%, 5}) + \$72,000 / 1.08^5$$
$$NPV = -\$3,408,118.47$$

The company should buy the new machine since it has a greater NPV.

There is another way to analyze a replacement decision that is often used. It is an incremental cash flow analysis of the change in cash flows from the existing machine to the new machine, assuming the new machine is purchased. In this type of analysis, the initial cash outlay would be the cost of the new machine, and the cash inflow (including any applicable taxes) of selling the old machine. In this case, the initial cash flow under this method would be:

| | |
|---|---|
| Purchase new machine | –$4,300,000 |
| Sell old machine | 2,200,000 |
| Taxes on old machine | –320,000 |
| Total | –$2,420,000 |

The cash flows from purchasing the new machine would be the difference in the operating expenses. We would also need to include the change in depreciation. The old machine has a depreciation of $280,000 per year, and the new machine has a depreciation of $860,000 per year, so the increased depreciation will be $580,000 per year. The pro forma income statement and operating cash flow under this approach will be:

| | |
|---|---|
| Maintenance cost | –$515,000 |
| Depreciation | 580,000 |
| EBT | –$ 65,000 |
| Taxes | –26,000 |
| Net income | –$ 39,000 |
| OCF | $541,000 |

The salvage value of the differential cash flow approach is more complicated. The company will sell the new machine, and incur taxes on the sale in five years. However, we must also include the lost sale of the old machine. Since we assumed we sold the old machine in the initial cash outlay, we lose the ability to sell the machine in five years. This is an opportunity loss that must be accounted for. So, the salvage value is:

| | |
|---|---|
| Sell machine | $800,000 |
| Taxes | –320,000 |
| Lost sale of old | –120,000 |
| Taxes on lost sale of old | 48,000 |
| Total | $408,000 |

The NPV under this method is:

$$NPV = -\$2,420,000 + \$541,000(PVIFA_{8\%, 5}) + \$408,000 / 1.08$$
$$NPV = \$17,734.07$$

So, this analysis still tells us the company should purchase the new machine. This is really the same type of analysis we originally did. Consider this: Subtract the NPV of the decision to keep the old machine from the NPV of the decision to purchase the new machine. You will get:

$$\text{Differential NPV} = -\$3,390,384.40 - (-3,408,118.47) = \$17,734.07$$

This is the exact same NPV we calculated when using the second analysis method.

26. Here we are comparing two mutually exclusive assets, with inflation. Since each will be replaced when it wears out, we need to calculate the EAC for each. We have real cash flows. Similar to other capital budgeting projects, when calculating the EAC, we can use real cash flows with the real interest rate, or nominal cash flows and the nominal interest rate. Using the Fisher equation to find the real required return, we get:

$$(1 + R) = (1 + r)(1 + h)$$
$$(1 + .14) = (1 + r)(1 + .05)$$
$$r = .0857 \text{ or } 8.57\%$$

This is the interest rate we need to use with real cash flows. We are given the real aftertax cash flows for each asset, so the NPV for the XX40 is:

NPV = –$900 – $120(PVIFA$_{8.57\%,3}$)
NPV = –$1,206.09

So, the EAC for the XX40 is:

–$1,206.09 = EAC(PVIFA$_{8.57\%,3}$)
EAC = –$472.84

And the EAC for the RH45 is:

NPV = –$1,400 – $95(PVIFA$_{8.57\%,5}$)
NPV = –$1,773.66

–$1,773.66 = EAC(PVIFA$_{8.57\%,5}$)
EAC = –$450.94

The company should choose the RH45 because it has the greater EAC.

27. The project has a sales price that increases at 5 percent per year, and a variable cost per unit that increases at 6 percent per year. First, we need to find the sales price and variable cost for each year. The table below shows the price per unit and the variable cost per unit each year.

|  | Year 1 | Year 2 | Year 3 | Year 4 | Year 5 |
|---|---|---|---|---|---|
| Sales price | $40.00 | $42.00 | $44.10 | $46.31 | $48.62 |
| Cost per unit | $15.00 | $15.90 | $16.85 | $17.87 | $18.94 |

Using the sales price and variable cost, we can now construct the pro forma income statement for each year. We can use this income statement to calculate the cash flow each year. We must also make sure to include the net working capital outlay at the beginning of the project, and the recovery of the net working capital at the end of the project. The pro forma income statement and cash flows for each year will be:

|  | Year 0 | Year 1 | Year 2 | Year 3 | Year 4 | Year 5 |
|---|---|---|---|---|---|---|
| Revenues |  | $800,000.00 | $840,000.00 | $882,000.00 | $926,100.00 | $972,405.00 |
| Fixed costs |  | 195,000.00 | 195,000.00 | 195,000.00 | 195,000.00 | 195,000.00 |
| Variable costs |  | 300,000.00 | 318,000.00 | 337,080.00 | 357,304.80 | 378,743.09 |
| Depreciation |  | 195,000.00 | 195,000.00 | 195,000.00 | 195,000.00 | 195,000.00 |
| EBT |  | $110,000.00 | $132,000.00 | $154,920.00 | $178,795.20 | $203,661.91 |
| Taxes |  | 37,400.00 | 44,880.00 | 52,672.80 | 60,790.37 | 69,245.05 |
| Net income |  | $ 72,600.00 | $ 87,120.00 | $102,247.20 | $118,004.83 | $134,416.86 |
| OCF |  | $267,600.00 | $282,120.00 | $297,247.20 | $313,004.83 | $329,416.86 |
|  |  |  |  |  |  |  |
| Capital spending | –$ 975,000 |  |  |  |  |  |
| NWC | –25,000 |  |  |  |  | 25,000 |
|  |  |  |  |  |  |  |
| Total cash flow | –$1,000,000 | $267,600.00 | $282,120.00 | $297,247.20 | $313,004.83 | $354,416.86 |

With these cash flows, the NPV of the project is:

$$NPV = -\$1,000,000 + \$267,600 / 1.11 + \$282,120 / 1.11^2 + \$297,247.20 / 1.11^3$$
$$+ \$313,004.83 / 1.11^4 + \$354,416.86 / 1.11^5$$
$$NPV = \$103,915.73$$

We could also answer this problem using the depreciation tax shield approach. The revenues and variable costs are growing annuities, growing at different rates. The fixed costs and depreciation are ordinary annuities. Using the growing annuity equation, the present value of the revenues is:

$$PV \text{ of revenues} = C\ \{[1/(r-g)] - [1/(r-g)] \times [(1+g)/(1+r)]^t\}$$
$$PV \text{ of revenues} = \$800,000\{[1/(.11-.05)] - [1/(.11-.05)] \times [(1+.05)/(1+.11)]^5\}$$
$$PV \text{ of revenues} = \$3,234,520.16$$

And the present value of the variable costs will be:

$$PV \text{ of variable costs} = C\ \{[1/(r-g)] - [1/(r-g)] \times [(1+g)/(1+r)]^t\}$$
$$PV \text{ of variable costs} = \$300,000\{[1/(.11-.06)] - [1/(.11-.06)] \times [(1+.06)/(1+.11)]^5\}$$
$$PV \text{ of variable costs} = \$1,234,969.52$$

The fixed costs and depreciation are both ordinary annuities. The present value of each is:

$$PV \text{ of fixed costs} = C(\{1 - [1/(1+r)]^t\}\ /\ r)$$
$$PV \text{ of fixed costs} = \$195,000(\{1 - [1/(1+.11)]^5\}\ /\ .11)$$
$$PV \text{ of fixed costs} = \$720,699.92$$

$$PV \text{ of depreciation} = C(\{1 - [1/(1+r)]^t\}\ /\ r)$$
$$PV \text{ of depreciation} = \$195,000(\{1 - [1/(1+.11)]^5\}\ /\ .11)$$
$$PV \text{ of depreciation} = \$720,699.92$$

Now, we can use the depreciation tax shield approach to find the NPV of the project, which is:

$$NPV = -\$1,000,000 + (\$3,234,520.16 - 1,234,696.52 - 720,699.92)(1 - .34) + (\$720,699.92)(.34)$$
$$+ \$25,000 / 1.11^5$$
$$NPV = \$103,915.73$$

*Challenge*

28. Probably the easiest OCF calculation for this problem is the bottom up approach, so we will construct an income statement for each year. Beginning with the initial cash flow at time zero, the project will require an investment in equipment. The project will also require an investment in NWC of $1,500,000. So, the cash flow required for the project today will be:

| | |
|---|---|
| Capital spending | −$23,000,000 |
| Change in NWC | −1,500,000 |
| Total cash flow | −$24,500,000 |

Now we can begin the remaining calculations. Sales figures are given for each year, along with the price per unit. The variable costs per unit are used to calculate total variable costs, and fixed costs are given at $2,400,000 per year. To calculate depreciation each year, we use the initial equipment cost of $23 million, times the appropriate MACRS depreciation each year. The remainder of each income statement is calculated below. Notice at the bottom of the income statement we added back depreciation to get the OCF for each year. The section labeled "Net cash flows" will be discussed below:

| Year | 1 | 2 | 3 | 4 | 5 |
|---|---|---|---|---|---|
| Ending book value | $19,713,300 | $14,080,600 | $10,057,900 | $ 7,185,200 | $ 5,131,300 |
| | | | | | |
| Sales | $28,635,000 | $31,740,000 | $35,880,000 | $33,810,000 | $28,980,000 |
| Variable costs | 15,770,000 | 17,480,000 | 19,760,000 | 18,620,000 | 15,960,000 |
| Fixed costs | 2,400,000 | 2,400,000 | 2,400,000 | 2,400,000 | 2,400,000 |
| Depreciation | 3,286,700 | 5,632,700 | 4,022,700 | 2,872,700 | 2,053,900 |
| EBIT | 7,178,300 | 6,227,300 | 9,697,300 | 9,917,300 | 8,566,100 |
| Taxes | 2,512,405 | 2,179,555 | 3,394,055 | 3,471,055 | 2,998,135 |
| Net income | 4,665,895 | 4,047,745 | 6,303,245 | 6,446,245 | 5,567,965 |
| Depreciation | 3,286,700 | 5,632,700 | 4,022,700 | 2,872,700 | 2,053,900 |
| Operating cash flow | $ 7,952,595 | $ 9,680,445 | $10,325,945 | $ 9,318,945 | $ 7,621,865 |
| | | | | | |
| *Net cash flows* | | | | | |
| Operating cash flow | $ 7,952,595 | $ 9,680,445 | $10,325,945 | $ 9,318,945 | $ 7,621,865 |
| Change in NWC | −465,750 | −621,000 | 310,500 | 724,500 | 1,551,750 |
| Capital spending | | | | | 4,785,955 |
| Total cash flow | $ 7,486,845 | $ 9,059,445 | $10,636,445 | $10,043,445 | $13,959,570 |

After we calculate the OCF for each year, we need to account for any other cash flows. The other cash flows in this case are NWC cash flows and capital spending, which is the aftertax salvage of the equipment. The required NWC is 15 percent of the sales increase in the next year. We will work through the NWC cash flow for Year 1. The total NWC in Year 1 will be 15 percent of sales increase from Year 1 to Year 2, or:

Increase in NWC for Year 1 = .15($31,740,000 – 28,635,000)
Increase in NWC for Year 1 = $465,750

Notice that the NWC cash flow is negative. Since the sales are increasing, we will have to spend more money to increase NWC. In Year 4, the NWC cash flow is positive since sales are declining. And, in Year 5, the NWC cash flow is the recovery of all NWC the company still has in the project.

To calculate the aftertax salvage value, we first need the book value of the equipment. The book value at the end of the five years will be the purchase price, minus the total depreciation. So, the ending book value is:

Ending book value = $23,000,000 – ($3,286,700 + 5,632,700 + 4,022,700 + 2,872,700 + 2,053,900)
Ending book value = $5,131,300

The market value of the used equipment is 20 percent of the purchase price, or $4.6 million, so the aftertax salvage value will be:

Aftertax salvage value = $4,600,000 + ($5,131,300 – 4,600,000)(.35)
Aftertax salvage value = $4,785,955

The aftertax salvage value is included in the total cash flows as capital spending. Now we have all of the cash flows for the project. The NPV of the project is:

$$NPV = -\$24,500,000 + \$7,486,845/1.18 + \$9,059,445/1.18^2 + \$10,636,445/1.18^3$$
$$+ \$10,043,445/1.18^4 + \$13,959,570/1.18^5$$
NPV = $6,106,958.94

And the IRR is:

$$IRR = 0 = -\$24,500,000 + \$7,486,845/(1 + IRR) + \$9,059,445/(1 + IRR)^2 + \$10,636,445/(1 + IRR)^3$$
$$+ \$10,043,445/(1 + IRR)^4 + \$13,959,570/(1 + IRR)^5$$
IRR = 27.54%

We should accept the project.

29. To find the initial pretax cost savings necessary to buy the new machine, we should use the tax shield approach to find the OCF. We begin by calculating the depreciation each year using the MACRS depreciation schedule. The depreciation each year is:

$D_1 = \$640,000(0.3333) = \$213,312$
$D_2 = \$640,000(0.4445) = \$284,480$
$D_3 = \$640,000(0.1481) = \$94,784$
$D_4 = \$640,000(0.0741) = \$47,424$

Using the tax shield approach, the OCF each year is:

$OCF_1 = (S - C)(1 - 0.35) + 0.35(\$213,312)$
$OCF_2 = (S - C)(1 - 0.35) + 0.35(\$284,480)$
$OCF_3 = (S - C)(1 - 0.35) + 0.35(\$94,784)$
$OCF_4 = (S - C)(1 - 0.35) + 0.35(\$47,424)$
$OCF_5 = (S - C)(1 - 0.35)$

Now we need the aftertax salvage value of the equipment. The aftertax salvage value is:

After-tax salvage value = $\$60,000(1 - 0.35) = \$39,000$

To find the necessary cost reduction, we must realize that we can split the cash flows each year. The OCF in any given year is the cost reduction (S – C) times one minus the tax rate, which is an annuity for the project life, and the depreciation tax shield. To calculate the necessary cost reduction, we would require a zero NPV. The equation for the NPV of the project is:

$$NPV = 0 = -\$640,000 - 55,000 + (S - C)(0.65)(PVIFA_{12\%,5}) + 0.35(\$213,312/1.12$$
$$+ \$284,480/1.12^2 + \$94,784/1.12^3 + \$47,424/1.12^4) + (\$55,000 + 39,000)/1.12^5$$

Solving this equation for the sales minus costs, we get:

$(S - C)(0.65)(PVIFA_{12\%, 5}) = \$461,465.41$
$(S - C) = \$196,946.15$

**30.** To find the bid price, we need to calculate all other cash flows for the project, and then solve for the bid price. The aftertax salvage value of the equipment is:

Aftertax salvage value = $\$150,000(1 - 0.35) = \$97,500$

Now we can solve for the necessary OCF that will give the project a zero NPV. The equation for the NPV of the project is:

$$NPV = 0 = -\$1,800,000 - 130,000 + OCF(PVIFA_{14\%,5}) + [(\$130,000 + 97,500) / 1.14^5]$$

Solving for the OCF, we find the OCF that makes the project NPV equal to zero is:

OCF = $\$1,811,843.63 / PVIFA_{14\%,5} = \$527,760.24$

The easiest way to calculate the bid price is the tax shield approach, so:

$OCF = \$527,760.24 = [(P - v)Q - FC](1 - t_C) + t_C D$
$\$527,760.24 = [(P - \$8.50)(140,000) - \$265,000](1 - 0.35) + 0.35(\$1,800,000/5)$
$P = \$14.81$

**31.** *a.* This problem is basically the same as the previous problem, except that we are given a sales price. The cash flow at Time 0 for all three parts of this question will be:

| Capital spending | –$1,800,000 |
|---|---|
| Change in NWC | –130,000 |
| Total cash flow | –$1,930,000 |

We will use the initial cash flow and the salvage value we already found in that problem. Using the bottom up approach to calculating the OCF, we get:

*Assume price per unit = $16 and units/year = 140,000*

| Year | 1 | 2 | 3 | 4 | 5 |
|---|---|---|---|---|---|
| Sales | $2,240,000 | $2,240,000 | $2,240,000 | $2,240,000 | $2,240,000 |
| Variable costs | 1,190,000 | 1,190,000 | 1,190,000 | 1,190,000 | 1,190,000 |
| Fixed costs | 265,000 | 265,000 | 265,000 | 265,000 | 265,000 |
| Depreciation | 360,000 | 360,000 | 360,000 | 360,000 | 360,000 |
| EBIT | $ 425,000 | $ 425,000 | $ 425,000 | $ 425,000 | $ 425,000 |
| Taxes (35%) | 148,750 | 148,750 | 148,750 | 148,750 | 148,750 |
| Net Income | $ 276,250 | $ 276,250 | $ 276,250 | $ 276,250 | $ 276,250 |
| Depreciation | 360,000 | 360,000 | 360,000 | 360,000 | 360,000 |
| Operating CF | $ 636,250 | $ 636,250 | $ 636,250 | $ 636,250 | $ 636,250 |

| Year | 1 | 2 | 3 | 4 | 5 |
|---|---|---|---|---|---|
| Operating CF | $636,250 | $636,250 | $636,250 | $636,250 | $636,250 |
| Change in NWC | | | | | 130,000 |
| Capital spending | | | | | 97,500 |
| Total CF | $636,250 | $636,250 | $636,250 | $636,250 | $863,750 |

With these cash flows, the NPV of the project is:

$$NPV = -\$1,800,000 - 130,000 + \$636,250(PVIFA_{14\%,\,5}) + [(\$130,000 + 97,500) / 1.14^5]$$
$$NPV = \$372,454.14$$

If the actual price is above the bid price that results in a zero NPV, the project will have a positive NPV. As for the cartons sold, if the number of cartons sold increases, the NPV will increase, and if the costs increase, the NPV will decrease.

*b.* To find the minimum number of cartons sold to still breakeven, we need to use the tax shield approach to calculating OCF, and solve the problem similar to finding a bid price. Using the initial cash flow and salvage value we already calculated, the equation for a zero NPV of the project is:

$$NPV = 0 = -\$1,800,000 - 130,000 + OCF(PVIFA_{14\%,5}) + [(\$130,000 + 97,500) / 1.14^5]$$

So, the necessary OCF for a zero NPV is:

$$OCF = \$1,811,843.63 / PVIFA_{14\%,\,5} = \$527,760.24$$

Now we can use the tax shield approach to solve for the minimum quantity as follows:

$$\text{OCF} = \$527{,}760.24 = [(P - v)Q - FC](1 - t_C) + t_C D$$
$$\$527{,}760.24 = [(\$16.00 - 8.50)Q - 265{,}000](1 - 0.35) + 0.35(\$1{,}800{,}000/5)$$
$$Q = 117{,}746$$

As a check, we can calculate the NPV of the project with this quantity. The calculations are:

| Year | 1 | 2 | 3 | 4 | 5 |
|---|---|---|---|---|---|
| Sales | $1,883,931 | $1,883,931 | $1,883,931 | $1,883,931 | $1,883,931 |
| Variable costs | 1,000,838 | 1,000,838 | 1,000,838 | 1,000,838 | 1,000,838 |
| Fixed costs | 265,000 | 265,000 | 265,000 | 265,000 | 265,000 |
| Depreciation | 360,000 | 360,000 | 360,000 | 360,000 | 360,000 |
| EBIT | $ 258,093 | $ 258,093 | $ 258,093 | $ 258,093 | $ 258,093 |
| Taxes (35%) | 90,332 | 90,332 | 90,332 | 90,332 | 90,332 |
| Net Income | $ 167,760 | $ 167,760 | $ 167,760 | $ 167,760 | $ 167,760 |
| Depreciation | 360,000 | 360,000 | 360,000 | 360,000 | 360,000 |
| Operating CF | $ 527,760 | $ 527,760 | $ 527,760 | $ 527,760 | $ 527,760 |

| Year | 1 | 2 | 3 | 4 | 5 |
|---|---|---|---|---|---|
| Operating CF | $527,760 | $527,760 | $527,760 | $527,760 | $527,760 |
| Change in NWC | 0 | 0 | 0 | 0 | 130,000 |
| Capital spending | 0 | 0 | 0 | 0 | 97,500 |
| Total CF | $527,760 | $527,760 | $527,760 | $527,760 | $755,260 |

$$\text{NPV} = -\$1{,}800{,}000 - 130{,}000 + \$527{,}760\,(\text{PVIFA}_{14\%,5}) + [(\$130{,}000 + 97{,}500)\,/\,1.14^5] \approx \$0$$

Note that the NPV is not exactly equal to zero because we had to round the number of cartons sold; you cannot sell one-half of a carton.

c.  To find the highest level of fixed costs and still breakeven, we need to use the tax shield approach to calculating OCF, and solve the problem similar to finding a bid price. Using the initial cash flow and salvage value we already calculated, the equation for a zero NPV of the project is:

$$\text{NPV} = 0 = -\$1{,}800{,}000 - 130{,}000 + \text{OCF}(\text{PVIFA}_{14\%,5}) + [(\$130{,}000 + 97{,}500)\,/\,1.14^5]$$
$$\text{OCF} = \$1{,}811{,}843.63\,/\,\text{PVIFA}_{14\%,\,5} = \$527{,}760.24$$

Notice this is the same OCF we calculated in part *b*. Now we can use the tax shield approach to solve for the maximum level of fixed costs as follows:

$$\text{OCF} = \$527{,}760.24 = [(P-v)Q - FC](1 - t_C) + t_C D$$
$$\$527{,}760.24 = [(\$16.00 - \$8.50)(140{,}000) - FC](1 - 0.35) + 0.35(\$1{,}800{,}000/5)$$
$$FC = \$431{,}907.33$$

As a check, we can calculate the NPV of the project with this quantity. The calculations are:

| Year | 1 | 2 | 3 | 4 | 5 |
|---|---|---|---|---|---|
| Sales | $2,240,000 | $2,240,000 | $2,240,000 | $2,240,000 | $2,240,000 |
| Variable costs | 1,190,000 | 1,190,000 | 1,190,000 | 1,190,000 | 1,190,000 |
| Fixed costs | 431,907 | 431,907 | 431,907 | 431,907 | 431,907 |
| Depreciation | 360,000 | 360,000 | 360,000 | 360,000 | 360,000 |
| EBIT | $ 258,093 | $ 258,093 | $ 258,093 | $ 258,093 | $ 258,093 |
| Taxes (35%) | 90,332 | 90,332 | 90,332 | 90,332 | 90,332 |
| Net Income | $ 167,760 | $ 167,760 | $ 167,760 | $ 167,760 | $ 167,760 |
| Depreciation | 360,000 | 360,000 | 360,000 | 360,000 | 360,000 |
| Operating CF | $ 527,760 | $ 527,760 | $ 527,760 | $ 527,760 | $ 527,760 |

| Year | 1 | 2 | 3 | 4 | 5 |
|---|---|---|---|---|---|
| Operating CF | $527,760 | $527,760 | $527,760 | $527,760 | $527,760 |
| Change in NWC | 0 | 0 | 0 | 0 | 130,000 |
| Capital spending | 0 | 0 | 0 | 0 | 97,500 |
| Total CF | $527,760 | $527,760 | $527,760 | $527,760 | $755,260 |

$$\text{NPV} = -\$1,800,000 - 130,000 + \$527,760(\text{PVIFA}_{14\%,5}) + [(\$130,000 + 97,500) / 1.14^5] \approx \$0$$

32. We need to find the bid price for a project, but the project has extra cash flows. Since we don't already produce the keyboard, the sales of the keyboard outside the contract are relevant cash flows. Since we know the extra sales number and price, we can calculate the cash flows generated by these sales. The cash flow generated from the sale of the keyboard outside the contract is:

| | Year 1 | Year 2 | Year 3 | Year 4 |
|---|---|---|---|---|
| Sales | $820,000 | $2,460,000 | $2,870,000 | $1,435,000 |
| Variable costs | 420,000 | 1,260,000 | 1,470,000 | 735,000 |
| EBT | $400,000 | $1,200,000 | $1,400,000 | $ 700,000 |
| Tax | 160,000 | 480,000 | 560,000 | 280,000 |
| Net income (and OCF) | $240,000 | $ 720,000 | $ 840,000 | $ 420,000 |

So, the addition to NPV of these market sales is:

NPV of market sales = $240,000/1.13 + $720,000/1.13$^2$ + $840,000/1.13$^3$ + $420,000/1.13$^4$
NPV of market sales = $1,616,010.99

You may have noticed that we did not include the initial cash outlay, depreciation, or fixed costs in the calculation of cash flows from the market sales. The reason is that it is irrelevant whether or not we include these here. Remember that we are not only trying to determine the bid price, but we are also determining whether or not the project is feasible. In other words, we are trying to calculate the NPV of the project, not just the NPV of the bid price. We will include these cash flows in the bid price calculation. Whether we include these costs in this initial calculation is irrelevant since you will come up with the same bid price if you include these costs in this calculation, or if you include them in the bid price calculation.

Next, we need to calculate the aftertax salvage value, which is:

Aftertax salvage value = $200,000(1 − .40) = $120,000

Instead of solving for a zero NPV as is usual in setting a bid price, the company president requires an NPV of $100,000, so we will solve for a NPV of that amount. The NPV equation for this project is (remember to include the NWC cash flow at the beginning of the project, and the NWC recovery at the end):

$$NPV = \$100,000 = -\$3,400,000 - 75,000 + 1,616,010.99 + OCF\ (PVIFA_{13\%,\,4}) + [(\$120,000 + 75,000)\ /\ 1.13^4]$$

Solving for the OCF, we get:

$$OCF = \$1,839,391.85\ /\ PVIFA_{13\%,4} = \$618,392.87$$

Now we can solve for the bid price as follows:

$$OCF = \$618,392.87 = [(P - v)Q - FC\ ](1 - t_C) + t_C D$$
$$\$618,392.87 = [(P - \$105)(15,000) - \$700,000](1 - 0.40) + 0.40(\$3,400,000/4)$$
$$P = \$182.60$$

33.  *a.*   Since the two computers have unequal lives, the correct method to analyze the decision is the EAC. We will begin with the EAC of the new computer. Using the depreciation tax shield approach, the OCF for the new computer system is:

$$OCF = (\$85,000)(1 - .38) + (\$580,000\ /\ 5)(.38) = \$96,780$$

Notice that the costs are positive, which represents a cash inflow. The costs are positive in this case since the new computer will generate a cost savings. The only initial cash flow for the new computer is the cost of $780,000. We next need to calculate the aftertax salvage value, which is:

Aftertax salvage value = $130,000(1 − .38) = $80,600

Now we can calculate the NPV of the new computer as:

$$NPV = -\$580,000 + \$96,780(PVIFA_{14\%,\,5}) + \$80,600\ /\ 1.14^5$$
$$NPV = -\$205,885.31$$

And the EAC of the new computer is:

$$EAC = -\ \$205,885.31\ /\ (PVIFA_{14\%,\,5}) = -\$59,971.00$$

Analyzing the old computer, the only OCF is the depreciation tax shield, so:

$$OCF = \$90,000(.38) = \$34,200$$

The initial cost of the old computer is a little trickier. You might assume that since we already own the old computer there is no initial cost, but we can sell the old computer, so there is an opportunity cost. We need to account for this opportunity cost. To do so, we will calculate the aftertax salvage value of the old computer today. We need the book value of the old computer to do so. The book value is not given directly, but we are told that the old computer has depreciation of $90,000 per year for the next three years, so we can assume the book value is the total amount of depreciation over the remaining life of the system, or $270,000. So, the aftertax salvage value of the old computer is:

Aftertax salvage value = $230,000 + ($270,000 – 230,000)(.38) = $245,200

This is the initial cost of the old computer system today because we are forgoing the opportunity to sell it today. We next need to calculate the aftertax salvage value of the computer system in two years since we are "buying" it today. The aftertax salvage value in two years is:

Aftertax salvage value = $60,000 + ($90,000 – 60,000)(.38) = $71,400

Now we can calculate the NPV of the old computer as:

NPV = –$245,200 + $34,200(PVIFA$_{14\%,2}$) + 71,400 / $1.14^2$
NPV = –$133,944.23

And the EAC of the old computer is:

EAC = – $133,944.23 / (PVIFA$_{14\%,2}$) = –$81,342.95

If we are going to replace the system in two years no matter what our decision today, we should instead replace it today since the EAC is lower.

b.  If we are only concerned with whether or not to replace the machine now, and are not worrying about what will happen in two years, the correct analysis is NPV. To calculate the NPV of the decision on the computer system now, we need the difference in the total cash flows of the old computer system and the new computer system. From our previous calculations, we can say the cash flows for each computer system are:

| $t$ | New computer | Old computer | Difference |
|---|---|---|---|
| 0 | –$580,000 | $245,200 | –$334,800 |
| 1 | 96,780 | –34,200 | 62,580 |
| 2 | 96,780 | –105,600 | –8,820 |
| 3 | 96,780 | 0 | 96,780 |
| 4 | 96,780 | 0 | 96,780 |
| 5 | 177,380 | 0 | 177,380 |

Since we are only concerned with marginal cash flows, the cash flows of the decision to replace the old computer system with the new computer system are the differential cash flows. The NPV of the decision to replace, ignoring what will happen in two years is:

NPV = –$334,800 + $62,580/1.14 – $8,820/$1.14^2$ + $96,780/$1.14^3$ + $96,780/$1.14^4$
        + $177,380/$1.14^5$
NPV = –$71,941.08

If we are not concerned with what will happen in two years, we should not replace the old computer system.

**34.** To answer this question, we need to compute the NPV of all three alternatives, specifically, continue to rent the building, Project A, or Project B. We would choose the project with the highest NPV. If all three of the projects have a positive NPV, the project that is more favorable is the one with the highest NPV

There are several important cash flows we should not consider in the incremental cash flow analysis. The remaining fraction of the value of the building and depreciation are not incremental and should not be included in the analysis of the two alternatives. The $1,450,000 purchase price of the building is a same for all three options and should be ignored. In effect, what we are doing is finding the NPV of the future cash flows of each option, so the only cash flow today would be the building modifications needed for Project A and Project B. If we did include these costs, the effect would be to lower the NPV of all three options by the same amount, thereby leading to the same conclusion. The cash flows from renting the building after year 15 are also irrelevant. No matter what the company chooses today, it will rent the building after year 15, so these cash flows are not incremental to any project.

We will begin by calculating the NPV of the decision of continuing to rent the building first.

Continue to rent:

| | |
|---|---|
| Rent | $61,000 |
| Taxes | 20,740 |
| Net income | $40,260 |

Since there is no incremental depreciation, the operating cash flow is simply the net income. So, the NPV of the decision to continue to rent is:

$$NPV = \$40,260(PVIFA_{12\%,\ 15})$$
$$NPV = \$274,205.40$$

Product A:

Next, we will calculate the NPV of the decision to modify the building to produce Product A. The income statement for this modification is the same for the first 14 years, and in Year 15, the company will have an additional expense to convert the building back to its original form. This will be an expense in Year 15, so the income statement for that year will be slightly different. The cash flow at time zero will be the cost of the equipment, and the cost of the initial building modifications, both of which are depreciable on a straight-line basis. So, the pro forma cash flows for Product A are:

Initial cash outlay:

| | |
|---|---|
| Building modifications | –$  95,000 |
| Equipment | –195,000 |
| Total cash flow | –$280,000 |

|  | Years 1-14 | Year 15 |
|---|---|---|
| Revenue | $180,000 | $180,000 |
| Expenditures | 70,000 | 70,000 |
| Depreciation | 19,333 | 19,333 |
| Restoration cost | 0 | 55,000 |
| EBT | $ 90,667 | $ 35,667 |
| Tax | 30,827 | 12,127 |
| NI | $ 59,840 | $ 23,540 |
| OCF | $ 79,173 | $ 42,873 |

The OCF each year is net income plus depreciation. So, the NPV for modifying the building to manufacture Product A is:

$$NPV = -\$280,000 + \$79,173(PVIFA_{12\%, 14}) + \$42,873 / 1.12^{15}$$
$$NPV = \$242,606.97$$

Product B:

Now we will calculate the NPV of the decision to modify the building to produce Product B. The income statement for this modification is the same for the first 14 years, and in year 15, the company will have an additional expense to convert the building back to its original form. This will be an expense in year 15, so the income statement for that year will be slightly different. The cash flow at time zero will be the cost of the equipment, and the cost of the initial building modifications, both of which are depreciable on a straight-line basis. So, the pro forma cash flows for Product B are:

Initial cash outlay:

| Building modifications | –$125,000 |
|---|---|
| Equipment | –230,000 |
| Total cash flow | –$355,000 |

|  | Years 1-14 | Year 15 |
|---|---|---|
| Revenue | $215,000 | $215,000 |
| Expenditures | 90,000 | 90,000 |
| Depreciation | 23,667 | 23,667 |
| Restoration cost | 0 | 80,000 |
| EBT | $101,333 | $ 21,333 |
| Tax | 34,453 | 7,253 |
| NI | $ 66,880 | $ 14,080 |
| OCF | $ 90,547 | $ 37,747 |

The OCF each year is net income plus depreciation. So, the NPV for modifying the building to manufacture Product B is:

$$NPV = -\$355,000 + \$90,547(PVIFA_{12\%,14}) + \$37,747 / 1.12^{15}$$
$$NPV = \$252,054.71$$

Since renting has the highest NPV, the company should continue to rent the building.

We could have also done the analysis as the incremental cash flows between Product A and continuing to rent the building, and the incremental cash flows between Product B and continuing to rent the building. The results of this type of analysis would be:

NPV of differential cash flows between Product A and continuing to rent:

$NPV = NPV_{Product A} - NPV_{Rent}$
$NPV = \$242,606.97 - 274,205.40$
$NPV = -\$31,598.43$

NPV of differential cash flows between Product B and continuing to rent:

$NPV = NPV_{Product B} - NPV_{Rent}$
$NPV = \$252,054.71 - 274,205.40$
$NPV = -\$22,150.69$

Since the differential NPV of both products and renting is negative, the company should continue to rent, which is the same as our original result.

35. The discount rate is expressed in real terms, and the cash flows are expressed in nominal terms. We can answer this question by converting all of the cash flows to real dollars. We can then use the real interest rate. The real value of each cash flow is the present value of the year 1 nominal cash flows, discounted back to the present at the inflation rate. So, the real value of the revenue and costs will be:

Revenue in real terms = $\$265,000 / 1.06 = \$250,000.00$
Labor costs in real terms = $\$185,000 / 1.06 = \$174,528.30$
Other costs in real terms = $\$55,000 / 1.06 = \$51,886.79$
Lease payment in real terms = $\$90,000 / 1.06 = \$84,905.66$

Revenues, labor costs, and other costs are all growing perpetuities. Each has a different growth rate, so we must calculate the present value of each separately. Using the real required return, the present value of each of these is:

$PV_{Revenue} = \$250,000.00 / (0.10 - 0.04) = \$4,166,666.67$
$PV_{Labor costs} = \$174,528.30 / (0.10 - 0.03) = \$2,493,261.46$
$PV_{Other costs} = \$51,886.79 / (0.10 - 0.01) = \$576,519.92$

The lease payments are constant in nominal terms, so they are declining in real terms by the inflation rate. Therefore, the lease payments form a growing perpetuity with a negative growth rate. The real present value of the lease payments is:

$PV_{Lease payments} = \$84,905.66 / [0.10 - (-0.06)] = \$530,660.38$

Now we can use the tax shield approach to calculate the net present value. Since there is no investment in equipment, there is no depreciation; therefore, no depreciation tax shield, so we will ignore this in our calculation. This means the cash flows each year are equal to net income. There is also no initial cash outlay, so the NPV is the present value of the future aftertax cash flows. The NPV of the project is:

$$NPV = (PV_{Revenue} - PV_{Labor\ costs} - PV_{Other\ costs} - PV_{Lease\ payments})(1 - t_C)$$
$$NPV = (\$4,166,666.67 - 2,493,261.46 - 576,519.92 - 530,660.38)(1 - .34)$$
$$NPV = \$373,708.45$$

Alternatively, we could have solved this problem by expressing everything in nominal terms. This approach yields the same answer as given above. However, in this case, the computation would have been impossible. The reason is that we are dealing with growing perpetuities. In other problems, when calculating the NPV of nominal cash flows, we could simply calculate the nominal cash flow each year since the cash flows were finite. Because of the perpetual nature of the cash flows in this problem, we cannot calculate the nominal cash flows each year until the end of the project. When faced with two alternative approaches, where both are equally correct, always choose the simplest one.

**36.** We are given the real revenue and costs, and the real growth rates, so the simplest way to solve this problem is to calculate the NPV with real values. While we could calculate the NPV using nominal values, we would need to find the nominal growth rates, and convert all values to nominal terms. The real labor costs will increase at a real rate of two percent per year, and the real energy costs will increase at a real rate of three percent per year, so the real costs each year will be:

|  | Year 1 | Year 2 | Year 3 | Year 4 |
|---|---|---|---|---|
| Real labor cost each year | $15.75 | $16.07 | $16.39 | $16.71 |
| Real energy cost each year | $ 3.80 | $ 3.91 | $ 4.03 | $ 4.15 |

Remember that the depreciation tax shield also affects a firm's aftertax cash flows. The present value of the depreciation tax shield must be added to the present value of a firm's revenues and expenses to find the present value of the cash flows related to the project. The depreciation the firm will recognize each year is:

Annual depreciation = Investment / Economic Life
Annual depreciation = $165,000,000 / 4
Annual depreciation = $41,250,000

Depreciation is a nominal cash flow, so to find the real value of depreciation each year, we discount the real depreciation amount by the inflation rate. Doing so, we find the real depreciation each year is:

Year 1 real depreciation = $41,250,000 / 1.05 = $39,285,714.29
Year 2 real depreciation = $41,250,000 / 1.05$^2$ = $37,414,965.99
Year 3 real depreciation = $41,250,000 / 1.05$^3$ = $35,633,300.94
Year 4 real depreciation = $41,250,000 / 1.05$^4$ = $33,936,477.09

Now we can calculate the pro forma income statement each year in real terms. We can then add back depreciation to net income to find the operating cash flow each year. Doing so, we find the cash flow of the project each year is:

| | Year 0 | Year 1 | Year 2 | Year 3 | Year 4 |
|---|---|---|---|---|---|
| Revenues | | $69,300,000.00 | $74,250,000.00 | $84,150,000.00 | $79,200,000.00 |
| Labor cost | | 17,640,000.00 | 19,278,000.00 | 22,285,368.00 | 21,393,953.28 |
| Energy cost | | 798,000.00 | 880,650.00 | 1,028,012.10 | 996,567.02 |
| Depreciation | | 39,285,714.29 | 37,414,965.99 | 35,633,300.94 | 33,936,477.09 |
| EBT | | $11,576,285.71 | $16,676,384.01 | $25,203,318.96 | $22,873,002.61 |
| Taxes | | 3,935,937.14 | 5,669,970.56 | 8,569,128.45 | 7,776,820.89 |
| Net income | | $ 7,640,348.57 | $11,006,413.45 | $16,634,190.51 | $15,096,181.72 |
| OCF | | $46,926,062.86 | $48,421,379.44 | $52,267,491.45 | $49,032,658.81 |
| Capital spending | −$165,000,000 | | | | |
| Total CF | −$165,000,000 | $46,926,062.86 | $48,421,379.44 | $52,267,491.45 | $49,032,658.81 |

We can use the total cash flows each year to calculate the NPV, which is:

$$NPV = -\$165,000,000 + \$46,926,062.86 / 1.04 + \$48,421,379.44 / 1.04^2 + \$52,267,491.45 / 1.04^3 + \$49,032,658.81 / 1.04^4$$
$$NPV = \$13,268,433.31$$

37. Here we have the sales price and production costs in real terms. The simplest method to calculate the project cash flows is to use the real cash flows. In doing so, we must be sure to adjust the depreciation, which is in nominal terms. We could analyze the cash flows using nominal values, which would require calculating the nominal discount rate, nominal price, and nominal production costs. This method would be more complicated, so we will use the real numbers. We will first calculate the NPV of the headache only pill.

Headache only:

We can find the real revenue and production costs by multiplying each by the units sold. We must be sure to discount the depreciation, which is in nominal terms. We can then find the pro forma net income, and add back depreciation to find the operating cash flow. Discounting the depreciation each year by the inflation rate, we find the following cash flows each year:

| | Year 1 | Year 2 | Year 3 |
|---|---|---|---|
| Sales | $25,050,000 | $25,050,000 | $25,050,000 |
| Production costs | 12,300,000 | 12,300,000 | 12,300,000 |
| Depreciation | 7,443,366 | 7,226,569 | 7,016,086 |
| EBT | $ 5,306,634 | $ 5,523,431 | $ 5,733,914 |
| Tax | 1,804,256 | 1,877,967 | 1,949,531 |
| Net income | $ 3,502,379 | $ 3,645,465 | $ 3,784,383 |
| OCF | $10,945,744 | $10,872,033 | $10,800,469 |

And the NPV of the headache only pill is:

NPV = –$23,000,000 + $10,945,744 / 1.07 + $10,872,033 / $1.07^2$ + $10,800,469 / $1.07^3$
NPV = $5,542,122.70

Headache and arthritis:

For the headache and arthritis pill project, the equipment has a salvage value. We will find the aftertax salvage value of the equipment first, which will be:

| Market value | $1,000,000 |
|---|---|
| Taxes | –340,000 |
| Total | $ 660,000 |

Remember, to calculate the taxes on the equipment salvage value, we take the book value minus the market value, times the tax rate. Using the same method as the headache only pill, the cash flows each year for the headache and arthritis pill will be:

|  | Year 1 | Year 2 | Year 3 |
|---|---|---|---|
| Sales | $37,575,000 | $37,575,000 | $37,575,000 |
| Production costs | 20,925,000 | 20,925,000 | 20,925,000 |
| Depreciation | 10,355,987 | 10,054,356 | 9,761,511 |
| EBT | $ 6,294,013 | $ 6,595,644 | $ 6,888,489 |
| Tax | 2,139,964 | 2,242,519 | 2,342,086 |
| Net income | $ 4,154,049 | $ 4,353,125 | $ 4,546,403 |
| OCF | $14,510,036 | $14,407,481 | $14,307,914 |

So, the NPV of the headache and arthritis pill is:

NPV = –$32,000,000 + $14,510,036 / 1.07 + $14,407,481 / $1.07^2$ + ($14,307,914 + 660,000) / $1.07^3$
NPV = $6,363,109.18

The company should manufacture the headache and arthritis remedy since the project has a higher NPV.

38. Since the project requires an initial investment in inventory as a percentage of sales, we will calculate the sales figures for each year first. The incremental sales will include the sales of the new table, but we also need to include the lost sales of the existing model. This is an erosion cost of the new table. The lost sales of the existing table are constant for every year, but the sales of the new table change every year. So, the total incremental sales figure for the five years of the project will be:

|  | Year 1 | Year 2 | Year 3 | Year 4 | Year 5 |
|---|---|---|---|---|---|
| New | $10,980,000 | $11,895,000 | $15,250,000 | $14,335,000 | $12,810,000 |
| Lost sales | –1,125,000 | –1,125,000 | –1,125,000 | –1,125,000 | –1,125,000 |
| Total | $ 9,855,000 | $10,770,000 | $14,125,000 | $13,210,000 | $11,685,000 |

Now we will calculate the initial cash outlay that will occur today. The company has the necessary production capacity to manufacture the new table without adding equipment today. So, the equipment will not be purchased today, but rather in two years. The reason is that the existing capacity is not being used. If the existing capacity were being used, the new equipment would be required, so it would be a cash flow today. The old equipment would have an opportunity cost if it could be sold. As there is no discussion that the existing equipment could be sold, we must assume it cannot be sold. The only initial cash flow is the cost of the inventory. The company will have to spend money for inventory in the new table, but will be able to reduce inventory of the existing table. So, the initial cash flow today is:

| New table | –$1,098,000 |
|-----------|-------------|
| Old table | 112,500 |
| Total | –$ 985,500 |

In year 2, the company will have a cash outflow to pay for the cost of the new equipment. Since the equipment will be purchased in two years rather than now, the equipment will have a higher salvage value. The book value of the equipment in five years will be the initial cost, minus the accumulated depreciation, or:

Book value = $18,000,000 – 2,572,200 – 4,408,200 – 3,148,200
Book value = $7,871,400

The taxes on the salvage value will be:

Taxes on salvage = ($7,871,400 – 7,400,000)(.40)
Taxes on salvage = $188,560

So, the aftertax salvage value of the equipment in five years will be:

| Sell equipment | $7,400,000 |
|----------------|-----------|
| Taxes | 188,560 |
| Salvage value | $7,588,560 |

Next, we need to calculate the variable costs each year. The variable costs of the lost sales are included as a variable cost savings, so the variable costs will be:

| | Year 1 | Year 2 | Year 3 | Year 4 | Year 5 |
|---|--------|--------|--------|--------|--------|
| New | $4,941,000 | $5,352,750 | $6,862,500 | $6,450,750 | $5,764,500 |
| Lost sales | –450,000 | –450,000 | –450,000 | –450,000 | –450,000 |
| Variable costs | $4,491,000 | $4,902,750 | $6,412,500 | $6,000,750 | $5,314,500 |

Now we can prepare the rest of the pro forma income statements for each year. The project will have no incremental depreciation for the first two years as the equipment is not purchased for two years. Adding back depreciation to net income to calculate the operating cash flow, we get:

|  | Year 1 | Year 2 | Year 3 | Year 4 | Year 5 |
|---|---|---|---|---|---|
| Sales | $9,855,000 | $10,770,000 | $14,125,000 | $13,210,000 | $11,685,000 |
| VC | 4,491,000 | 4,902,750 | 6,412,500 | 6,000,750 | 5,314,500 |
| Fixed costs | 1,900,000 | 1,900,000 | 1,900,000 | 1,900,000 | 1,900,000 |
| Dep. | 0 | 0 | 2,572,200 | 4,408,200 | 3,148,200 |
| EBT | $3,464,000 | $3,967,250 | $3,240,300 | $901,050 | $1,322,300 |
| Tax | 1,385,600 | 1,586,900 | 1,296,120 | 360,420 | 528,920 |
| NI | $2,078,400 | $2,380,350 | $1,944,180 | $540,630 | $793,380 |
| +Dep. | 0 | 0 | 2,572,200 | 4,408,200 | 3,148,200 |
| OCF | $2,078,400 | $2,380,350 | $4,516,380 | $4,948,830 | $3,941,580 |

Next, we need to account for the changes in inventory each year. The inventory is a percentage of sales. The way we will calculate the change in inventory is the beginning of period inventory minus the end of period inventory. The sign of this calculation will tell us whether the inventory change is a cash inflow, or a cash outflow. The inventory each year, and the inventory change, will be:

|  | Year 1 | Year 2 | Year 3 | Year 4 | Year 5 |
|---|---|---|---|---|---|
| Beginning | $1,098,000 | $1,189,500 | $1,525,000 | $1,433,500 | $1,281,000 |
| Ending | 1,189,500 | 1,525,000 | 1,433,500 | 1,281,000 | 0 |
| Change | –$91,500 | –$335,500 | $91,500 | $152,500 | $1,281,000 |

Notice that we recover the remaining inventory at the end of the project. The total cash flows for the project will be the sum of the operating cash flow, the capital spending, and the inventory cash flows, so:

|  | Year 1 | Year 2 | Year 3 | Year 4 | Year 5 |
|---|---|---|---|---|---|
| OCF | $2,078,400 | $2,380,350 | $4,516,380 | $4,948,830 | $3,941,580 |
| Equipment | 0 | –18,000,000 | 0 | 0 | 7,588,560 |
| Inventory | –91,500 | –335,500 | 91,500 | 152,500 | 1,281,000 |
| Total | $1,986,900 | –$15,955,150 | $4,607,880 | $5,101,330 | $12,811,140 |

The NPV of the project, including the inventory cash flow at the beginning of the project, will be:

$$NPV = -\$985,500 + \$1,986,900 / 1.11 - \$15,955,150 / 1.11^2 + \$4,607,880 / 1.11^3$$
$$+ \$5,101,330 / 1.11^4 + \$12,811,140 / 1.11^5$$
$$NPV = \$2,187,376.60$$

The company should go ahead with the new table.

b.   You can perform an IRR analysis, and would expect to find three IRRs since the cash flows change signs three times.

c.   The profitability index is intended as a "bang for the buck" measure; that is, it shows how much shareholder wealth is created for every dollar of initial investment. This is usually a good measure of the investment since most projects have conventional cash flows. In this case, the largest investment is not at the beginning of the project, but later in its life, so while the interpretation is the same, it really does not measure the bang for the dollar invested.

# CHAPTER 7
# RISK ANALYSIS, REAL OPTIONS, AND CAPITAL BUDGETING

**Answers to Concepts Review and Critical Thinking Questions**

1. Forecasting risk is the risk that a poor decision is made because of errors in projected cash flows. The danger is greatest with a new product because the cash flows are probably harder to predict.

2. With a sensitivity analysis, one variable is examined over a broad range of values. With a scenario analysis, all variables are examined for a limited range of values.

3. It is true that if average revenue is less than average cost, the firm is losing money. This much of the statement is therefore correct. At the margin, however, accepting a project with marginal revenue in excess of its marginal cost clearly acts to increase operating cash flow.

4. From the shareholder perspective, the financial break-even point is the most important. A project can exceed the accounting and cash break-even points but still be below the financial break-even point. This causes a reduction in shareholder (your) wealth.

5. The project will reach the cash break-even first, the accounting break-even next and finally the financial break-even. For a project with an initial investment and sales afterwards, this ordering will always apply. The cash break-even is achieved first since it excludes depreciation. The accounting break-even is next since it includes depreciation. Finally, the financial break-even, which includes the time value of money, is achieved.

6. Traditional NPV analysis is often too conservative because it ignores profitable options such as the ability to expand the project if it is profitable, or abandon the project if it is unprofitable. The option to alter a project when it has already been accepted has a value, which increases the NPV of the project.

7. The type of option most likely to affect the decision is the option to expand. If the country just liberalized its markets, there is likely the potential for growth. First entry into a market, whether an entirely new market, or with a new product, can give a company name recognition and market share. This may make it more difficult for competitors entering the market.

8. Sensitivity analysis can determine how the financial break-even point changes when some factors (such as fixed costs, variable costs, or revenue) change.

9. There are two sources of value with this decision to wait. The price of the timber can potentially increase, and the amount of timber will almost definitely increase, barring a natural catastrophe or forest fire. The option to wait for a logging company is quite valuable, and companies in the industry have models to estimate the future growth of a forest depending on its age.

**10.** When the additional analysis has a negative NPV. Since the additional analysis is likely to occur almost immediately, this means when the benefits of the additional analysis outweigh the costs. The benefits of the additional analysis are the reduction in the possibility of making a bad decision. Of course, the additional benefits are often difficult, if not impossible, to measure, so much of this decision is based on experience.

**Solutions to Questions and Problems**

*NOTE: All end-of-chapter problems were solved using a spreadsheet. Many problems require multiple steps. Due to space and readability constraints, when these intermediate steps are included in this solutions manual, rounding may appear to have occurred. However, the final answer for each problem is found without rounding during any step in the problem.*

*Basic*

**1.** *a.* To calculate the accounting breakeven, we first need to find the depreciation for each year. The depreciation is:

Depreciation = $644,000/8
Depreciation = $80,500 per year

And the accounting breakeven is:

$Q_A$ = ($725,000 + 80,500)/($37 − 21)
$Q_A$ = 50,344 units

*b.* We will use the tax shield approach to calculate the OCF. The OCF is:

$OCF_{base}$ = [(P − v)Q − FC](1 − $t_c$) + $t_c$D
$OCF_{base}$ = [($37 − 21)(70,000) − $725,000](0.65) + 0.35($80,500)
$OCF_{base}$ = $284,925

Now we can calculate the NPV using our base-case projections. There is no salvage value or NWC, so the NPV is:

$NPV_{base}$ = −$644,000 + $284,925(PVIFA$_{15\%,8}$)
$NPV_{base}$ = $634,550.08

To calculate the sensitivity of the NPV to changes in the quantity sold, we will calculate the NPV at a different quantity. We will use sales of 71,000 units. The OCF at this sales level is:

$OCF_{new}$ = [($37 − 21)(71,000) − $725,000](0.65) + 0.35($80,500)
$OCF_{new}$ = $295,325

And the NPV is:

$NPV_{new}$ = −$644,000 + $295,325(PVIFA$_{15\%,8}$)
$NPV_{new}$ = $681,218.22

So, the change in NPV for every unit change in sales is:

$\Delta NPV/\Delta S = (\$634,550.08 - 681,218.22)/(70,000 - 71,000)$
$\Delta NPV/\Delta S = +\$46.668$

If sales were to drop by 500 units, then NPV would drop by:

NPV drop = $46.668(500) = \$23,334.07$

You may wonder why we chose 71,000 units. Because it doesn't matter! Whatever sales number we use, when we calculate the change in NPV per unit sold, the ratio will be the same.

c.   To find out how sensitive OCF is to a change in variable costs, we will compute the OCF at a variable cost of $22. Again, the number we choose to use here is irrelevant: We will get the same ratio of OCF to a one dollar change in variable cost no matter what variable cost we use. So, using the tax shield approach, the OCF at a variable cost of $22 is:

$OCF_{new} = [(\$37 - 22)(70,000) - 725,000](0.65) + 0.35(\$80,500)$
$OCF_{new} = \$239,425$

So, the change in OCF for a $1 change in variable costs is:

$\Delta OCF/\Delta v = (\$284,925 - 239,425)/(\$21 - 22)$
$\Delta OCF/\Delta v = -\$45,500$

If variable costs decrease by $1 then, OCF would increase by $45,500

2.   We will use the tax shield approach to calculate the OCF for the best- and worst-case scenarios. For the best-case scenario, the price and quantity increase by 10 percent, so we will multiply the base case numbers by 1.1, a 10 percent increase. The variable and fixed costs both decrease by 10 percent, so we will multiply the base case numbers by .9, a 10 percent decrease. Doing so, we get:

$OCF_{best} = \{[(\$37)(1.1) - (\$21)(0.9)](70,000)(1.1) - \$725,000(0.9)\}(0.65) + 0.35(\$80,500)$
$OCF_{best} = \$695,140$

The best-case NPV is:

$NPV_{best} = -\$644,000 + \$695,140(PVIFA_{15\%,8})$
$NPV_{best} = \$2,475,316.67$

For the worst-case scenario, the price and quantity decrease by 10 percent, so we will multiply the base case numbers by .9, a 10 percent decrease. The variable and fixed costs both increase by 10 percent, so we will multiply the base case numbers by 1.1, a 10 percent increase. Doing so, we get:

$OCF_{worst} = \{[(\$37)(0.9) - (\$21)(1.1)](70,000)(0.9) - \$725,000(1.1)\}(0.65) + 0.35(\$80,500)$
$OCF_{worst} = -\$72,510$

The worst-case NPV is:

$NPV_{worst} = -\$644,000 - \$72,510(PVIFA_{15\%,8})$
$NPV_{worst} = -\$969,375.68$

3.  We can use the accounting breakeven equation:

$Q_A = (FC + D)/(P - v)$

to solve for the unknown variable in each case. Doing so, we find:

(1):  $Q_A = 95,300 = (\$820,000 + D)/(\$41 - 30)$
    $D = \$228,300$

(2):  $Q_A = 143,806 = (\$2,750,000 + 1,150,000)/(P - \$56)$
    $P = \$83.12$

(3):  $Q_A = 7,835 = (\$160,000 + 105,000)/(\$97 - v)$
    $v = \$63.18$

4.  When calculating the financial breakeven point, we express the initial investment as an equivalent annual cost (EAC). Dividing the initial investment by the five-year annuity factor, discounted at 12 percent, the EAC of the initial investment is:

$EAC = $ Initial Investment $/ PVIFA_{12\%,5}$
$EAC = \$390,000 / 3.60478$
$EAC = \$108,189.80$

Note that this calculation solves for the annuity payment with the initial investment as the present value of the annuity. In other words:

$PVA = C(\{1 - [1/(1 + R)]^t\} / R)$
$\$390,000 = C\{[1 - (1/1.12)^5] / .12\}$
$C = \$108,189.80$

The annual depreciation is the cost of the equipment divided by the economic life, or:

Annual depreciation $= \$390,000 / 5$
Annual depreciation $= \$78,000$

Now we can calculate the financial breakeven point. The financial breakeven point for this project is:

$Q_F = [EAC + FC(1 - t_C) - D(t_C)] / [(P - VC)(1 - t_C)]$
$Q_F = [\$108,189.80 + \$280,000(1 - 0.34) - \$78,000(0.34)] / [(\$25 - 11)(1 - 0.34)]$
$Q_F = 28,838.72$ or about 28,839 units

5.  If we purchase the machine today, the NPV is the cost plus the present value of the increased cash flows, so:

$NPV_0 = -\$2,900,000 + \$475,000(PVIFA_{9\%,10})$
$NPV_0 = \$148,387.41$

We should not necessarily purchase the machine today. We would want to purchase the machine when the NPV is the highest. So, we need to calculate the NPV each year. The NPV each year will be the cost plus the present value of the increased cash savings. We must be careful, however. In order to make the correct decision, the NPV for each year must be taken to a common date. We will discount all of the NPVs to today. Doing so, we get:

Year 1: $NPV_1 = [-\$2,690,000 + \$475,000(PVIFA_{9\%,9})] / 1.12$
$NPV_1 = \$157,742.27$

Year 2: $NPV_2 = [-\$2,480,000 + \$475,000(PVIFA_{9\%,8})] / 1.12^2$
$NPV_2 = \$149,039.08$

Year 3: $NPV_3 = [-\$2,270,000 + \$475,000(PVIFA_{9\%,7})] / 1.12^3$
$NPV_3 = \$120,652.60$

Year 4: $NPV_4 = [-\$2,270,000 + \$475,000(PVIFA_{9\%,6})] / 1.12^4$
$NPV_4 = -\$139,188.67$

Year 5: $NPV_5 = [-\$2,270,000 + \$475,000(PVIFA_{9\%,5})] / 1.12^5$
$NPV_5 = -\$422,415.65$

Year 6: $NPV_6 = [-\$2,270,000 + \$475,000(PVIFA_{9\%,4})] / 1.12^6$
$NPV_6 = -\$731,133.06$

The company should purchase the machine one year from now when the NPV is the highest.

6.  We need to calculate the NPV of the two options, go directly to market now, or utilize test marketing first. The NPV of going directly to market now is:

$NPV = C_{Success}$ (Prob. of Success) $+$ $C_{Failure}$ (Prob. of Failure)
$NPV = \$34,000,000(0.50) + \$12,000,000(0.50)$
$NPV = \$23,000,000$

Now we can calculate the NPV of test marketing first. Test marketing requires a $1.5 million cash outlay. Choosing the test marketing option will also delay the launch of the product by one year. Thus, the expected payoff is delayed by one year and must be discounted back to year 0.

$NPV = C_0 + \{[C_{Success}$ (Prob. of Success)$] + [C_{Failure}$ (Prob. of Failure)$]\} / (1 + R)^t$
$NPV = -\$1,300,000 + \{[\$34,000,000 (0.80)] + [\$12,000,000 (0.20)]\} / 1.11$
$NPV = \$25,366,666.67$

The company should test market first with the product since that option has the highest expected payoff.

7.  We need to calculate the NPV of each option, and choose the option with the highest NPV. So, the NPV of going directly to market is:

$NPV = C_{Success}$ (Prob. of Success)
$NPV = \$1,900,000 (0.50)$
$NPV = \$950,000$

The NPV of the focus group is:

$$\text{NPV} = C_0 + C_{\text{Success}}\,(\text{Prob. of Success})$$
$$\text{NPV} = -\$175{,}000 + \$1{,}900{,}000\,(0.65)$$
$$\text{NPV} = \$1{,}060{,}000$$

And the NPV of using the consulting firm is:

$$\text{NPV} = C_0 + C_{\text{Success}}\,(\text{Prob. of Success})$$
$$\text{NPV} = -\$390{,}000 + \$1{,}900{,}000\,(0.85)$$
$$\text{NPV} = \$1{,}130{,}000$$

The firm should use the consulting firm since that option has the highest NPV.

8.  The company should analyze both options, and choose the option with the greatest NPV. So, if the company goes to market immediately, the NPV is:

$$\text{NPV} = C_{\text{Success}}\,(\text{Prob. of Success}) + C_{\text{Failure}}\,(\text{Prob. of Failure})$$
$$\text{NPV} = \$19{,}000{,}000(.55) + \$6{,}000{,}000(.45)$$
$$\text{NPV} = \$13{,}150{,}000$$

Customer segment research requires a $1.2 million cash outlay. Choosing the research option will also delay the launch of the product by one year. Thus, the expected payoff is delayed by one year and must be discounted back to year 0. So, the NPV of the customer segment research is:

$$\text{NPV} = C_0 + \{[C_{\text{Success}}\,(\text{Prob. of Success})] + [C_{\text{Failure}}\,(\text{Prob. of Failure})]\} / (1+R)^t$$
$$\text{NPV} = -\$1{,}200{,}000 + \{[\$19{,}000{,}000\,(0.70)] + [\$6{,}000{,}000\,(0.30)]\} / 1.15$$
$$\text{NPV} = \$11{,}930{,}434.78$$

The company should go to market now since it has the largest NPV.

9.  *a.*  The accounting breakeven is the aftertax sum of the fixed costs and depreciation charge divided by the aftertax contribution margin (selling price minus variable cost). So, the accounting breakeven level of sales is:

$$Q_A = [(\text{FC} + \text{Depreciation})(1 - t_C)] / [(P - \text{VC})(1 - t_C)]$$
$$Q_A = [(\$375{,}000 + \$840{,}000/7)\,(1 - 0.35)] / [(\$35 - 6.10)\,(1 - 0.35)]$$
$$Q_A = 17{,}128.03 \text{ or about } 17{,}128 \text{ units}$$

*b.*  When calculating the financial breakeven point, we express the initial investment as an equivalent annual cost (EAC). Dividing the initial investment by the seven-year annuity factor, discounted at 15 percent, the EAC of the initial investment is:

$$\text{EAC} = \text{Initial Investment} / \text{PVIFA}_{15\%,7}$$
$$\text{EAC} = \$840{,}000 / 4.1604$$
$$\text{EAC} = \$201{,}902.71$$

Note that this calculation solves for the annuity payment with the initial investment as the present value of the annuity. In other words:

$$PVA = C(\{1 - [1/(1 + R)]^t\} / R)$$
$$\$840,000 = C\{[1 - (1/1.15)^7] / .15\}$$
$$C = \$201,902.71$$

Now we can calculate the financial breakeven point. The financial breakeven point for this project is:

$$Q_F = [EAC + FC(1 - t_C) - D(t_C)] / [(P - VC)(1 - t_C)]$$
$$Q_F = [\$201,902.71 + \$375,000(.65) - (\$840,000/7)(.35)] / [(\$35 - 6.10)(.65)]$$
$$Q_F = 21,488.03 \text{ or about } 21,488 \text{ units}$$

**10.** When calculating the financial breakeven point, we express the initial investment as an equivalent annual cost (EAC). Dividing the initial investment by the five-year annuity factor, discounted at 8 percent, the EAC of the initial investment is:

$$EAC = \text{Initial Investment} / PVIFA_{8\%,5}$$
$$EAC = \$575,000 / 3.99271$$
$$EAC = \$144,012.46$$

Note that this calculation solves for the annuity payment with the initial investment as the present value of the annuity. In other words:

$$PVA = C(\{1 - [1/(1 + R)]^t\} / R)$$
$$\$575,000 = C\{[1 - (1/1.08)^5] / .08\}$$
$$C = \$144,012.46$$

The annual depreciation is the cost of the equipment divided by the economic life, or:

$$\text{Annual depreciation} = \$575,000 / 5$$
$$\text{Annual depreciation} = \$115,000$$

Now we can calculate the financial breakeven point. The financial breakeven point for this project is:

$$Q_F = [EAC + FC(1 - t_C) - D(t_C)] / [(P - VC)(1 - t_C)]$$
$$Q_F = [\$144,012.46 + \$165,000(1 - 0.34) - \$115,000(0.34)] / [(\$60 - 14)(1 - 0.34)]$$
$$Q_F = 7,042.57 \text{ or about } 7,043 \text{ units}$$

*Intermediate*

**11.** *a.* At the accounting breakeven, the IRR is zero percent since the project recovers the initial investment. The payback period is N years, the length of the project since the initial investment is exactly recovered over the project life. The NPV at the accounting breakeven is:

$$NPV = I [(I/N)(PVIFA_{R\%,N}) - 1]$$

b.  At the cash breakeven level, the IRR is –100 percent, the payback period is negative, and the NPV is negative and equal to the initial cash outlay.

c.  The definition of the financial breakeven is where the NPV of the project is zero. If this is true, then the IRR of the project is equal to the required return. It is impossible to state the payback period, except to say that the payback period must be less than the length of the project. Since the discounted cash flows are equal to the initial investment, the undiscounted cash flows are greater than the initial investment, so the payback must be less than the project life.

**12.** Using the tax shield approach, the OCF at 90,000 units will be:

$OCF = [(P - v)Q - FC](1 - t_C) + t_C(D)$
$OCF = [(\$37 - 23)(90,000) - 195,000](0.66) + 0.34(\$480,000/4)$
$OCF = \$743,700$

We will calculate the OCF at 91,000 units. The choice of the second level of quantity sold is arbitrary and irrelevant. No matter what level of units sold we choose we will still get the same sensitivity. So, the OCF at this level of sales is:

$OCF = [(\$37 - 23)(91,000) - 195,000](0.66) + 0.34(\$480,000/4)$
$OCF = \$752,940$

The sensitivity of the OCF to changes in the quantity sold is:

$Sensitivity = \Delta OCF/\Delta Q = (\$743,700 - 752,940)/(90,000 - 91,000)$
$\Delta OCF/\Delta Q = +\$9.24$

OCF will increase by \$9.24 for every additional unit sold.

**13.** *a.*  The base-case, best-case, and worst-case values are shown below. Remember that in the best-case, unit sales increase, while costs decrease. In the worst-case, unit sales, and costs increase.

| Scenario | Unit sales | Variable cost | Fixed costs |
|---|---|---|---|
| Base | 450 | $15,400 | $610,000 |
| Best | 495 | $13,860 | $549,000 |
| Worst | 405 | $16,940 | $671,000 |

Using the tax shield approach, the OCF and NPV for the base case estimate are:

$OCF_{base} = [(\$18,000 - 15,400)(450) - \$610,000](0.65) + 0.35(\$820,000/4)$
$OCF_{base} = \$435,750$

$NPV_{base} = -\$820,000 + \$435,750(PVIFA_{15\%,4})$
$NPV_{base} = \$424,056.82$

The OCF and NPV for the worst case estimate are:

$OCF_{worst} = [(\$18,000 - 16,940)(405) - \$671,000](0.65) + 0.35(\$820,000/4)$
$OCF_{worst} = -\$85,355$

$NPV_{worst} = -\$820,000 - \$85,355(PVIFA_{15\%,4})$
$NPV_{worst} = -\$1,063,686.68$

And the OCF and NPV for the best case estimate are:

$OCF_{best} = [(\$18,000 - 13,860)(495) - \$549,000](0.65) + 0.35(\$820,000/4)$
$OCF_{best} = \$1,046,945$

$NPV_{best} = -\$820,000 + \$1,046,945(PVIFA_{15\%,4})$
$NPV_{best} = \$2,169,005.32$

b.  To calculate the sensitivity of the NPV to changes in fixed costs, we choose another level of fixed costs. We will use fixed costs of \$620,000. The OCF using this level of fixed costs and the other base case values with the tax shield approach, we get:

$OCF = [(\$18,000 - 15,400)(450) - \$620,000](0.65) + 0.35(\$820,000/4)$
$OCF = \$429,250$

And the NPV is:

$NPV = -\$820,000 + \$429,250(PVIFA_{15\%,4})$
$NPV = \$405,499.46$

The sensitivity of NPV to changes in fixed costs is:

$\Delta NPV/\Delta FC = (\$424,056.82 - 405,499.46)/(\$610,000 - 620,000)$
$\Delta NPV/\Delta FC = -\$1.856$

For every dollar FC increase, NPV falls by \$1.86.

c.  The accounting breakeven is:

$Q_A = (FC + D)/(P - v)$
$Q_A = [\$610,000 + (\$820,000/4)]/(\$18,000 - 15,400)$
$Q_A = 313.46$ or about 313 units

14. The marketing study and the research and development are both sunk costs and should be ignored. We will calculate the sales and variable costs first. Since we will lose sales of the expensive clubs and gain sales of the cheap clubs, these must be accounted for as erosion. The total sales for the new project will be:

Sales
| | | |
|---|---|---|
| New clubs | $\$875 \times 60,000 =$ | \$52,500,000 |
| Exp. clubs | $\$1,100 \times (-12,000) =$ | -13,200,000 |
| Cheap clubs | $\$400 \times 15,000 =$ | 6,000,000 |
| | | \$45,300,000 |

For the variable costs, we must include the units gained or lost from the existing clubs. Note that the variable costs of the expensive clubs are an inflow. If we are not producing the sets any more, we will save these variable costs, which is an inflow. So:

| Var. costs | | |
|---|---|---|
| New clubs | $-\$430 \times 60{,}000 =$ | $-\$25{,}800{,}000$ |
| Exp. clubs | $-\$620 \times (-12{,}000) =$ | $7{,}440{,}000$ |
| Cheap clubs | $-\$210 \times 15{,}000 =$ | $-3{,}150{,}000$ |
| | | $-\$21{,}510{,}000$ |

The pro forma income statement will be:

| | |
|---|---|
| Sales | $45,300,000 |
| Variable costs | 21,510,000 |
| Fixed costs | 9,300,000 |
| Depreciation | 4,200,000 |
| EBT | $10,290,000 |
| Taxes | 4,116,000 |
| Net income | $ 6,174,000 |

Using the bottom up OCF calculation, we get:

OCF = NI + Depreciation = $6,174,000 + 4,200,000
OCF = $10,374,000

So, the payback period is:

Payback period = 2 + $10,052,000/$10,374,000
Payback period = 2.969 years

The NPV is:

$$NPV = -\$29{,}400{,}000 - 1{,}400{,}000 + \$10{,}374{,}000(PVIFA_{14\%,7}) + \$1{,}400{,}000/1.14^7$$
$$NPV = \$14{,}246{,}366.65$$

And the IRR is:

$$IRR = -\$29{,}400{,}000 - 1{,}400{,}000 + \$10{,}374{,}000(PVIFA_{IRR\%,7}) + \$1{,}400{,}000/(1 + IRR)^7$$
$$IRR = 27.89\%$$

15. The upper and lower bounds for the variables are:

| | Base Case | Best Case | Worst Case |
|---|---|---|---|
| Unit sales (new) | 60,000 | 66,000 | 54,000 |
| Price (new) | $     875 | $     963 | $     788 |
| VC (new) | $     430 | $     387 | $     473 |
| Fixed costs | $9,300,000 | $8,370,000 | $10,230,000 |
| Sales lost (expensive) | 12,000 | 10,800 | 13,200 |
| Sales gained (cheap) | 15,000 | 16,500 | 13,500 |

Best-case

We will calculate the sales and variable costs first. Since we will lose sales of the expensive clubs and gain sales of the cheap clubs, these must be accounted for as erosion. The total sales for the new project will be:

Sales
| | | |
|---|---|---|
| New clubs | $963 \times 66,000 =$ | $63,525,500 |
| Exp. clubs | $1,100 \times (-10,800) =$ | $-11,880,000 |
| Cheap clubs | $400 \times 16,500 =$ | 6,600,000 |
| | | $58,245,000 |

For the variable costs, we must include the units gained or lost from the existing clubs. Note that the variable costs of the expensive clubs are an inflow. If we are not producing the sets any more, we will save these variable costs, which is an inflow. So:

Var. costs
| | | |
|---|---|---|
| New clubs | $-\$387 \times 66,000 =$ | $-\$25,542,000 |
| Exp. clubs | $-\$620 \times (-10,800) =$ | 6,696,000 |
| Cheap clubs | $-\$210 \times 16,500 =$ | $-3,465,000 |
| | | $-\$22,311,000 |

The pro forma income statement will be:

| | |
|---|---|
| Sales | $58,245,000 |
| Variable costs | 22,311,000 |
| Fixed costs | 8,370,000 |
| Depreciation | 4,200,000 |
| EBT | $23,364,000 |
| Taxes | 9,345,600 |
| Net income | $14,018,400 |

Using the bottom up OCF calculation, we get:

OCF = Net income + Depreciation = $14,018,400 + 4,200,000
OCF = $18,218,400

And the best-case NPV is:

$$NPV = -\$29,400,000 - 1,400,000 + \$18,218,400(PVIFA_{14\%,7}) + 1,400,000/1.14^7$$
NPV = $47,885,545.13

Worst-case
We will calculate the sales and variable costs first. Since we will lose sales of the expensive clubs and gain sales of the cheap clubs, these must be accounted for as erosion. The total sales for the new project will be:

Sales
New clubs $788 \times 54,000 = \$42,525,000$
Exp. clubs $\$1,100 \times (-13,200) = -14,520,000$
Cheap clubs $\$400 \times 13,500 = \underline{5,400,000}$
$\$33,405,000$

For the variable costs, we must include the units gained or lost from the existing clubs. Note that the variable costs of the expensive clubs are an inflow. If we are not producing the sets any more, we will save these variable costs, which is an inflow. So:

Var. costs
New clubs $-\$473 \times 54,000 = -\$25,542,000$
Exp. clubs $-\$620 \times (-13,200) = 8,184,000$
Cheap clubs $-\$210 \times 13,500 = \underline{-2,835,000}$
$-\$20,193,000$

The pro forma income statement will be:

| | |
|---|---|
| Sales | $33,405,000 |
| Variable costs | 20,193,000 |
| Costs | 10,230,000 |
| Depreciation | 4,200,000 |
| EBT | –$ 1,218,000 |
| Taxes | –487,200  *assumes a tax credit |
| Net income | –$ 730,800 |

Using the bottom up OCF calculation, we get:

OCF = NI + Depreciation = –$730,800 + 4,200,000
OCF = $3,469,200

And the worst-case NPV is:

NPV = –$29,400,000 – 1,400,000 + $3,469,200(PVIFA$_{14\%,7}$) + 1,400,000/1.14$^7$
NPV = –$15,363,520.60

**16.** To calculate the sensitivity of the NPV to changes in the price of the new club, we simply need to change the price of the new club. We will choose $880, but the choice is irrelevant as the sensitivity will be the same no matter what price we choose.

We will calculate the sales and variable costs first. Since we will lose sales of the expensive clubs and gain sales of the cheap clubs, these must be accounted for as erosion. The total sales for the new project will be:

Sales
| | | |
|---|---|---|
| New clubs | $880 × 60,000 = | $52,800,000 |
| Exp. clubs | $1,100 × (– 12,000) = | –13,200,000 |
| Cheap clubs | $400 × 15,000 = | 6,000,000 |
| | | $45,600,000 |

For the variable costs, we must include the units gained or lost from the existing clubs. Note that the variable costs of the expensive clubs are an inflow. If we are not producing the sets any more, we will save these variable costs, which is an inflow. So:

Var. costs
| | | |
|---|---|---|
| New clubs | –$430 × 60,000 = | –$25,800,000 |
| Exp. clubs | –$620 × (–12,000) = | 7,440,000 |
| Cheap clubs | –$210 × 15,000 = | –3,150,000 |
| | | –$21,510,000 |

The pro forma income statement will be:

| | |
|---|---|
| Sales | $45,600,000 |
| Variable costs | 21,510,000 |
| Fixed costs | 9,300,000 |
| Depreciation | 4,200,000 |
| EBT | $10,590,000 |
| Taxes | 4,236,000 |
| Net income | $ 6,354,000 |

Using the bottom up OCF calculation, we get:

OCF = NI + Depreciation = $6,354,000 + 4,200,000
OCF = $10,554,000

And the NPV is:

NPV = –$29,400,000 – 1,400,000 + $10,554,000(PVIFA$_{14\%,7}$) + 1,400,000/1.14$^7$
NPV = $15,018,261.52

So, the sensitivity of the NPV to changes in the price of the new club is:

$\Delta NPV/\Delta P = (\$14,246,366.65 - 15,018,261.52)/(\$875 - 880)$
$\Delta NPV/\Delta P = \$154,378.97$

For every dollar increase (decrease) in the price of the clubs, the NPV increases (decreases) by $154,378.97.

To calculate the sensitivity of the NPV to changes in the quantity sold of the new club, we simply need to change the quantity sold. We will choose 65,000 units, but the choice is irrelevant as the sensitivity will be the same no matter what quantity we choose.

We will calculate the sales and variable costs first. Since we will lose sales of the expensive clubs and gain sales of the cheap clubs, these must be accounted for as erosion. The total sales for the new project will be:

| Sales | | |
|---|---|---|
| New clubs | $875 × 65,000 = | $56,875,000 |
| Exp. clubs | $1,100 × (– 12,000) = | –13,200,000 |
| Cheap clubs | $400 × 15,000 = | 6,000,000 |
| | | $49,675,000 |

For the variable costs, we must include the units gained or lost from the existing clubs. Note that the variable costs of the expensive clubs are an inflow. If we are not producing the sets any more, we will save these variable costs, which is an inflow. So:

| Var. costs | | |
|---|---|---|
| New clubs | –$390 × 65,000 = | –$27,950,000 |
| Exp. clubs | –$620 × (–12,000) = | 7,440,000 |
| Cheap clubs | –$210 × 15,000 = | –3,150,000 |
| | | –$23,660,000 |

The pro forma income statement will be:

| | |
|---|---|
| Sales | $49,675,000 |
| Variable costs | 23,660,000 |
| Fixed costs | 9,300,000 |
| Depreciation | 4,200,000 |
| EBT | $12,515,000 |
| Taxes | 5,006,000 |
| Net income | $ 7,509,000 |

Using the bottom up OCF calculation, we get:

OCF = NI + Depreciation = $7,509,000 + 4,200,000
OCF = $11,709,000

The NPV at this quantity is:

NPV = –$29,400,000 – $1,400,000 + $11,709,000(PVIFA$_{14\%,7}$) + $1,400,000/1.14$^7$
NPV = $19,971,253.61

So, the sensitivity of the NPV to changes in the quantity sold is:

ΔNPV/ΔQ = ($14,246,366.65 – 19,971,253.61)/(60,000 – 65,000)
ΔNPV/ΔQ = $1,144.98

For an increase (decrease) of one set of clubs sold per year, the NPV increases (decreases) by $1,144.98.

17. *a.* The base-case NPV is:

NPV = –$1,350,000 + $315,000(PVIFA$_{16\%,10}$)
NPV = $172,466.66

*b.* We would abandon the project if the cash flow from selling the equipment is greater than the present value of the future cash flows. We need to find the sale quantity where the two are equal, so:

$950,000 = ($35)Q(PVIFA$_{16\%,9}$)
Q = $950,000/[$35(4.6065)]
Q = 5,892

Abandon the project if Q < 5,892 units, because the NPV of abandoning the project is greater than the NPV of the future cash flows.

*c.* The $950,000 is the market value of the project. If you continue with the project in one year, you forego the $950,000 that could have been used for something else.

18. *a.* If the project is a success, present value of the future cash flows will be:

PV future CFs = $35(11,000)(PVIFA$_{16\%,9}$)
PV future CFs = $1,773,519.39

From the previous question, if the quantity sold is 4,000, we would abandon the project, and the cash flow would be $950,000. Since the project has an equal likelihood of success or failure in one year, the expected value of the project in one year is the average of the success and failure cash flows, plus the cash flow in one year, so:

Expected value of project at year 1 = [($1,773,519.39 + $950,000)/2] + $315,000
Expected value of project at year 1 = $1,676,759.70

The NPV is the present value of the expected value in one year plus the cost of the equipment, so:

NPV = –$1,350,000 + ($1,676,759.70)/1.16
NPV = $95,482.50

b.  If we couldn't abandon the project, the present value of the future cash flows when the quantity is 4,000 will be:

PV future CFs = $35(4,000)(PVIFA$_{16\%,9}$)
PV future CFs = $644,916.14

The gain from the option to abandon is the abandonment value minus the present value of the cash flows if we cannot abandon the project, so:

Gain from option to abandon = $950,000 – 644,916.14
Gain from option to abandon = $305,083.86

We need to find the value of the option to abandon times the likelihood of abandonment. So, the value of the option to abandon today is:

Option value = (.50)($305,083.86)/1.16
Option value = $131,501.66

19. If the project is a success, present value of the future cash flows will be:

PV future CFs = $35(22,000)(PVIFA$_{16\%,9}$)
PV future CFs = $3,547,038.78

If the sales are only 4,000 units, from Problem #17, we know we will abandon the project, with a value of $950,000. Since the project has an equal likelihood of success or failure in one year, the expected value of the project in one year is the average of the success and failure cash flows, plus the cash flow in one year, so:

Expected value of project at year 1 = [($3,547,038.78 + $950,000)/2] + $315,000
Expected value of project at year 1 = $2,563,519.39

The NPV is the present value of the expected value in one year plus the cost of the equipment, so:

NPV = –$1,350,000 + $2,563,519.39/1.16
NPV = $859,930.51

The gain from the option to expand is the present value of the cash flows from the additional units sold, so:

Gain from option to expand = $35(11,000)(PVIFA$_{16\%,9}$)
Gain from option to expand = $1,773,519.39

We need to find the value of the option to expand times the likelihood of expansion. We also need to find the value of the option to expand today, so:

Option value = (.50)($1,773,519.39)/1.16
Option value = $764,448.01

**20.** *a.* The accounting breakeven is the aftertax sum of the fixed costs and depreciation charge divided by the contribution margin (selling price minus variable cost). In this case, there are no fixed costs, and the depreciation is the entire price of the press in the first year. So, the accounting breakeven level of sales is:

$Q_A = [(FC + D)(1 - t_C)] / [(P - VC)(1 - t_C)]$
$Q_A = [(\$0 + 5,600)(1 - 0.30)] / [(\$10 - 4.50)(1 - 0.30)]$
$Q_A = 1,018.18$ or about 1,018 units

*b.* When calculating the financial breakeven point, we express the initial investment as an equivalent annual cost (EAC). The initial investment is the $15,000 in licensing fees. Dividing the initial investment by the three-year annuity factor, discounted at 12 percent, the EAC of the initial investment is:

EAC = Initial Investment / $PVIFA_{12\%,3}$
EAC = $15,000 / 2.4018
EAC = $6,245.23

Note, this calculation solves for the annuity payment with the initial investment as the present value of the annuity, in other words:

$PVA = C(\{1 - [1/(1 + R)]^t\} / R)$
$\$15,000 = C\{[1 - (1/1.12)^3] / .12\}$
$C = \$6,245.23$

Now we can calculate the financial breakeven point. Notice that there are no fixed costs or depreciation. The financial breakeven point for this project is:

$Q_F = [EAC + FC(1 - t_C) - D(t_C)] / [(P - VC)(1 - t_C)]$
$Q_F = (\$6,245.23 + 0 - 0) / [(\$10 - 4.50)(.70)]$
$Q_F = 1,622.14$ or about 1,622 units

**21.** The payoff from taking the lump sum is $10,000, so we need to compare this to the expected payoff from taking one percent of the profit. The decision tree for the movie project is:

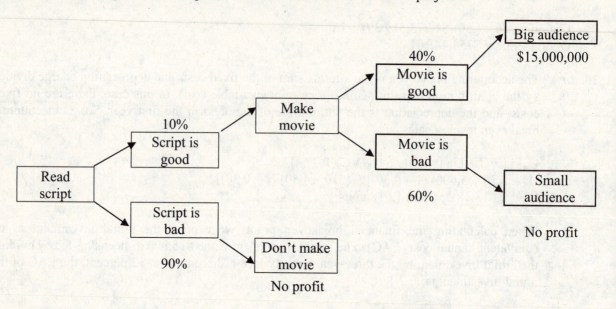

The value of one percent of the profits is as follows. There is a 40 percent probability the movie is good, and the audience is big, so the expected value of this outcome is:

Value = $15,000,000 × .40
Value = $6,000,000

The value if the movie is good, and has a big audience, assuming the script is good is:

Value = $6,000,000 × .10
Value = $600,000

This is the expected value for the studio, but the screenwriter will only receive one percent of this amount, so the payment to the screenwriter will be:

Payment to screenwriter = $600,000 × .01
Payment to screenwriter = $6,000

The screenwriter should take the upfront offer of $10,000.

**22.** We can calculate the value of the option to wait as the difference between the NPV of opening the mine today and the NPV of waiting one year to open the mine. The remaining life of the mine is:

48,000 ounces / 6,000 ounces per year = 8 years

This will be true no matter when you open the mine. The aftertax cash flow per year if opened today is:

CF = 6,000($1,400) = $8,400,000

So, the NPV of opening the mine today is:

NPV = –$34,000,000 + $8,400,000(PVIFA$_{12\%,8}$)
NPV = $7,728,174.04

If you open the mine in one year, the cash flow will be either:

CF$_{Up}$ = 6,000($1,600) = $9,600,000 per year
CF$_{Down}$ = 6,000($1,300) = $7,800,000 per year

The PV of these cash flows is:

Price increase CF = $9,600,000(PVIFA$_{12\%,8}$) = $47,689,341.76
Price decrease CF = $7,800,000(PVIFA$_{12\%,8}$) = $38,747,590.18

So, the NPV is one year will be:

NPV = –$34,000,000 + [.60($47,689,341.76) + .40($38,747,590.18)]
NPV = $10,112,641.13

And the NPV today is:

NPV today = $10,112,641.13 / 1.12
NPV today = $9,029,143.87

So, the value of the option to wait is:

Option value = $9,029,143.87 – 7,728,174.04
Option value = $1,300,969.82

**23.** *a.* The NPV of the project is sum of the present value of the cash flows generated by the project. The cash flows from this project are an annuity, so the NPV is:

$$NPV = -\$51,000,000 + \$10,500,000(PVIFA_{13\%,10})$$
$$NPV = \$5,975,556.50$$

*b.* The company should abandon the project if the PV of the revised cash flows for the next nine years is less than the project's aftertax salvage value. Since the option to abandon the project occurs in year 1, discount the revised cash flows to year 1 as well. To determine the level of expected cash flows below which the company should abandon the project, calculate the equivalent annual cash flows the project must earn to equal the aftertax salvage value. We will solve for $C_2$, the revised cash flow beginning in year 2. So, the revised annual cash flow below which it makes sense to abandon the project is:

$$\text{Aftertax salvage value} = C_2(PVIFA_{13\%,9})$$
$$\$31,000,000 = C_2(PVIFA_{13\%,9})$$
$$C_2 = \$31,000,000 \,/\, PVIFA_{13\%,9}$$
$$C_2 = \$6,040,935.96$$

**24.** *a.* The NPV of the project is sum of the present value of the cash flows generated by the project. The annual cash flow for the project is the number of units sold times the cash flow per unit, which is:

$$\text{Annual cash flow} = 15(\$305,000)$$
$$\text{Annual cash flow} = \$4,575,000$$

The cash flows from this project are an annuity, so the NPV is:

$$NPV = -\$15,000,000 + \$4,575,000(PVIFA_{16\%,5})$$
$$NPV = -\$20,106.53$$

*b.* The company will abandon the project if unit sales are not revised upward. If the unit sales are revised upward, the aftertax cash flows for the project over the last four years will be:

$$\text{New annual cash flow} = 20(\$305,000)$$
$$\text{New annual cash flow} = \$6,100,000$$

The NPV of the project will be the initial cost, plus the expected cash flow in year one based on 15 unit sales projection, plus the expected value of abandonment, plus the expected value of expansion. We need to remember that the abandonment value occurs in year 1, and the present value of the expansion cash flows are in year one, so each of these must be discounted back to today. So, the project NPV under the abandonment or expansion scenario is:

$$NPV = -\$15,000,000 + \$4,575,000 \,/\, 1.16 + .50(\$11,000,000) \,/\, 1.16$$
$$+ \,[.50(\$6,100,000)(PVIFA_{16\%,4})] \,/\, 1.16$$
$$NPV = \$1,042,630.13$$

**25.** To calculate the unit sales for each scenario, we multiply the market sales times the company's market share. We can then use the quantity sold to find the revenue each year, and the variable costs each year. After doing these calculations, we will construct the pro forma income statement for each scenario. We can then find the operating cash flow using the bottom up approach, which is net income plus depreciation. Doing so, we find:

|  | *Pessimistic* | *Expected* | *Optimistic* |
|---|---|---|---|
| Units per year | 21,000 | 27,600 | 36,250 |
| Revenue | $3,150,000.00 | $4,278,000.00 | $5,836,250.00 |
| Variable costs | 2,184,000.00 | 2,732,400.00 | 3,552,500.00 |
| Fixed costs | 965,000.00 | 920,000.00 | 890,000.00 |
| Depreciation | 316,666.67 | 300,000.00 | 283,333.33 |
| EBT | –$ 315,666.67 | $ 325,600.00 | $1,110,416.67 |
| Tax | –126,266.67 | 130,240.00 | 444,166.67 |
| Net income | –$ 189,400.00 | $ 195,360.00 | $ 666,250.00 |
| OCF | $ 127,266.67 | $ 495,360.00 | $ 949,583.33 |

Note that under the pessimistic scenario, the taxable income is negative. We assumed a tax credit in the case. Now we can calculate the NPV under each scenario, which will be:

$$NPV_{Pessimistic} = -\$1,900,000 + \$127,266.67(PVIFA_{13\%,6})$$
$$NPV = -\$1,391,245.16$$

$$NPV_{Expected} = -\$1,800,000 + \$495,360(PVIFA_{13\%,6})$$
$$NPV = \$180,226.26$$

$$NPV_{Optimistic} = -\$1,700,000 + \$949,583.33(PVIFA_{13\%,6})$$
$$NPV = \$2,096,006.65$$

The NPV under the pessimistic scenario is negative, but the company should probably accept the project.

*Challenge*

**26.** *a.* Using the tax shield approach, the OCF is:

OCF = [($345 – 285)(35,000) – $495,000](0.62) + 0.38($2,900,000/5)
OCF = $1,215,500

And the NPV is:

$$NPV = -\$2,900,000 - 450,000 + \$1,215,500(PVIFA_{13\%,5})$$
$$+ [\$450,000 + 300,000(1 - .38)]/1.13^5$$
$$NPV = \$1,270,389.92$$

    *b.*    In the worst-case, the OCF is:

$$OCF_{worst} = \{[(\$345)(0.9) - 285](35,000) - \$495,000\}(0.62) + 0.38(\$3,335,000/5)$$
$$OCF_{worst} = \$499,910$$

And the worst-case NPV is:

$$NPV_{worst} = -\$3,335,000 - 450,000(1.05) + \$499,910(PVIFA_{13\%,5}) +$$
$$[\$450,000(1.05) + 300,000(0.85)(1 - .38)]/1.13^5$$
$$NPV_{worst} = -\$1,706,936.50$$

The best-case OCF is:

$$OCF_{best} = \{[\$345(1.1) - 285](35,000) - \$495,000\}(0.62) + 0.38(\$2,465,000/5)$$
$$OCF_{best} = \$1,931,090$$

And the best-case NPV is:

$$NPV_{best} = -\$2,465,000 - \$450,000(0.95) + \$1,931,090(PVIFA_{13\%,5}) +$$
$$[\$450,000(0.95) + 300,000(1.15)(1 - .38)]/1.13^5$$
$$NPV_{best} = \$4,247,716.34$$

**27.** To calculate the sensitivity to changes in quantity sold, we will choose a quantity of 36,000. The OCF at this level of sales is:

$$OCF = [(\$345 - 285)(36,000) - \$495,000](0.62) + 0.38(\$2,900,000/5)$$
$$OCF = \$1,252,700$$

The sensitivity of changes in the OCF to quantity sold is:

$$\Delta OCF/\Delta Q = (\$1,215,500 - 1,252,700)/(35,000 - 36,000)$$
$$\Delta OCF/\Delta Q = +\$37.20$$

The NPV at this level of sales is:

$$NPV = -\$2,900,000 - 450,000 + \$1,252,700(PVIFA_{13\%,5}) + [\$450,000 + 300,000(1 - .38)]/1.13^5$$
$$NPV = \$1,401,230.92$$

And the sensitivity of NPV to changes in the quantity sold is:

$$\Delta NPV/\Delta Q = (\$1,270,389.92 - 1,401,230.92)/(35,000 - 36,000)$$
$$\Delta NPV/\Delta Q = +\$130.84$$

You wouldn't want the quantity to fall below the point where the NPV is zero. We know the NPV changes $130.84 for every unit sale, so we can divide the NPV for 35,000 units by the sensitivity to get a change in quantity. Doing so, we get:

$$\$1,270,389.92 = \$130.84 \, (\Delta Q)$$
$$\Delta Q = 9,709$$

For a zero NPV, sales would have to decrease 9,709 units, so the minimum quantity is:

$Q_{Min} = 35,000 - 9,709$
$Q_{Min} = 25,291$

28. We will use the bottom up approach to calculate the operating cash flow. Assuming we operate the project for all four years, the cash flows are:

| Year | 0 | 1 | 2 | 3 | 4 |
|---|---|---|---|---|---|
| Sales | | $6,850,000 | $6,850,000 | $6,850,000 | $6,850,000 |
| Operating costs | | 2,800,000 | 2,800,000 | 2,800,000 | 2,800,000 |
| Depreciation | | 2,000,000 | 2,000,000 | 2,000,000 | 2,000,000 |
| EBT | | $2,050,000 | $2,050,000 | $2,050,000 | $2,050,000 |
| Tax | | 779,000 | 779,000 | 779,000 | 779,000 |
| Net income | | $1,271,000 | $1,271,000 | $1,271,000 | $1,271,000 |
| +Depreciation | | 2,000,000 | 2,000,000 | 2,000,000 | 2,000,000 |
| Operating CF | | $3,271,000 | $3,271,000 | $3,271,000 | $3,271,000 |
| | | | | | |
| Change in NWC | –$ 950,000 | 0 | 0 | 0 | $ 950,000 |
| Capital spending | –8,000,000 | 0 | 0 | 0 | 0 |
| Total cash flow | –$8,950,000 | $3,271,000 | $3,271,000 | $3,271,000 | $4,221,000 |

There is no salvage value for the equipment. The NPV is:

$NPV = -\$8,950,000 + \$3,271,000(PVIFA_{16\%,3}) + \$4,221,000/1.16^4$
$NPV = \$727,525.41$

The cash flows if we abandon the project after one year are:

| Year | 0 | 1 |
|---|---|---|
| Sales | | $6,850,000 |
| Operating costs | | 2,800,000 |
| Depreciation | | 2,000,000 |
| EBT | | $2,050,000 |
| Tax | | 779,000 |
| Net income | | $1,271,000 |
| +Depreciation | | 2,000,000 |
| Operating CF | | $3,271,000 |
| | | |
| Change in NWC | –$ 950,000 | $ 950,000 |
| Capital spending | –8,000,000 | 5,442,000 |
| Total cash flow | –$8,950,000 | $9,663,000 |

The book value of the equipment is:

Book value = $8,000,000 – (1)($8,000,000/4)
Book value = $6,000,000

So the taxes on the salvage value will be:

Taxes = ($6,000,000 – 5,100,000)(.38)
Taxes = $342,000

This makes the aftertax salvage value:

Aftertax salvage value = $5,100,000 + 342,000
Aftertax salvage value = $5,442,000

The NPV if we abandon the project after one year is:

NPV = –$8,950,000 + $9,663,000/1.16
NPV = –$619,827.59

If we abandon the project after two years, the cash flows are:

| Year | 0 | 1 | 2 |
|---|---|---|---|
| Sales | | $6,850,000 | $6,850,000 |
| Operating costs | | 2,800,000 | 2,800,000 |
| Depreciation | | 2,000,000 | 2,000,000 |
| EBT | | $2,050,000 | $2,050,000 |
| Tax | | 779,000 | 779,000 |
| Net income | | $1,271,000 | $1,271,000 |
| +Depreciation | | 2,000,000 | 2,000,000 |
| Operating CF | | $3,271,000 | $3,271,000 |
| | | | |
| Change in NWC | –$  950,000 | 0 | 950,000 |
| Capital spending | –8,000,000 | 0 | 3,876,000 |
| Total cash flow | –$8,950,000 | $3,271,000 | $8,097,000 |

The book value of the equipment is:

Book value = $8,000,000 – (2)($8,000,000/4)
Book value = $4,000,000

So the taxes on the salvage value will be:

Taxes = ($4,000,000 – 3,800,000)(.38)
Taxes = $76,000

This makes the aftertax salvage value:

Aftertax salvage value = $3,800,000 + 76,000
Aftertax salvage value = $3,876,000

The NPV if we abandon the project after two years is:

NPV = –$8,950,000 + $3,271,000/1.16 + $8,097,000/1.16$^2$
NPV = –$112,782.40

If we abandon the project after three years, the cash flows are:

| Year | 0 | 1 | 2 | 3 |
|------|---|---|---|---|
| Sales | | $6,850,000 | $6,850,000 | $6,850,000 |
| Operating costs | | 2,800,000 | 2,800,000 | 2,800,000 |
| Depreciation | | 2,000,000 | 2,000,000 | 2,000,000 |
| EBT | | $2,050,000 | $2,050,000 | $2,050,000 |
| Tax | | 779,000 | 779,000 | 779,000 |
| Net income | | $1,271,000 | $1,271,000 | $1,271,000 |
| +Depreciation | | 2,000,000 | 2,000,000 | 2,000,000 |
| Operating CF | | $3,271,000 | $3,271,000 | $3,271,000 |
| | | | | |
| Change in NWC | –$ 950,000 | 0 | 0 | 950,000 |
| Capital spending | –8,000,000 | 0 | 0 | 2,744,000 |
| Total cash flow | –$8,950,000 | $3,271,000 | $3,271,000 | $6,965,000 |

The book value of the equipment is:

Book value = $8,000,000 – (3)($8,000,000/4)
Book value = $2,000,000

So the taxes on the salvage value will be:

Taxes = ($2,000,000 – 3,200,000)(.38)
Taxes = –$456,000

This makes the aftertax salvage value:

Aftertax salvage value = $3,200,000 – 456,000
Aftertax salvage value = $2,744,000

The NPV if we abandon the project after two years is:

$$NPV = -\$8,950,000 + \$3,271,000(PVIFA_{16\%,2}) + \$6,965,000/1.16^3$$
$$NPV = \$762,894.13$$

We should abandon the equipment after three years since the NPV of abandoning the project after three years has the highest NPV.

**29.** *a.* The NPV of the project is sum of the present value of the cash flows generated by the project. The cash flows from this project are an annuity, so the NPV is:

$$NPV = -\$7,000,000 + \$1,300,000(PVIFA_{10\%,10})$$
$$NPV = \$987,937.24$$

*b.* The company will abandon the project if the value of abandoning the project is greater than the value of the future cash flows. The present value of the future cash flows if the company revises its sales downward will be:

PV of downward revision = $\$285,000(PVIFA_{10\%,9})$
PV of downward revision = $\$1,641,321.79$

Since this is greater than the value of abandoning the project, the company should continue in one year. So, the revised NPV of the project will be the initial cost, plus the expected cash flow in year one based on upward sales projection, plus the expected downward revision. We need to remember that the abandonment value occurs in year 1, and the present value of the expansion cash flows are in year one, so each of these must be discounted back to today. So, the project NPV under the abandonment or expansion scenario is:

$$NPV = -\$7,000,000 + \$1,300,000 / 1.10 + .50(\$2,600,000) / 1.10$$
$$+ [.50(\$2,200,000)(PVIFA_{10\%,9})] / 1.10$$
$$NPV = \$1,122,660.18$$

**30.** First, determine the cash flow from selling the old harvester. When calculating the salvage value, remember that tax liabilities or credits are generated on the difference between the resale value and the book value of the asset. Using the original purchase price of the old harvester to determine annual depreciation, the annual depreciation for the old harvester is:

$Depreciation_{Old} = \$65,000 / 15$
$Depreciation_{Old} = \$4,333.33$

Since the machine is five years old, the firm has accumulated five annual depreciation charges, reducing the book value of the machine. The current book value of the machine is equal to the initial purchase price minus the accumulated depreciation, so:

Book value = Initial Purchase Price – Accumulated Depreciation
Book value = $\$65,000 - (\$4,333.333 \times 5 \text{ years})$
Book value = $\$43,333.33$

Since the firm is able to resell the old harvester for $21,000, which is less than the $43,333 book value of the machine, the firm will generate a tax credit on the sale. The aftertax salvage value of the old harvester will be:

Aftertax salvage value = Market value + $t_C$(Book value – Market value)
Aftertax salvage value = $21,000 + .34($43,333.33 – 21,000)
Aftertax salvage value = $28,593.33

Next, we need to calculate the incremental depreciation. We need to calculate the depreciation tax shield generated by the new harvester less the forgone depreciation tax shield from the old harvester. Let $P$ be the break-even purchase price of the new harvester. So, we find:

Depreciation tax shield$_{New}$ = (Initial Investment / Economic Life) $\times t_C$
Depreciation tax shield$_{New}$ = ($P$ / 10) (.34)

And the depreciation tax shield on the old harvester is:

Depreciation tax shield$_{Old}$ = ($65,000 / 15) (.34)
Depreciation tax shield$_{Old}$ = ($4,333.33)(0.34)

So, the incremental depreciation tax, which is the depreciation tax shield from the new harvester, minus the depreciation tax shield from the old harvester, is:

Incremental depreciation tax shield = ($P$ / 10)(.34) – ($4,333.33)(.34)
Incremental depreciation tax shield = ($P$ / 10 – $4,333.33)(.34)

The present value of the incremental depreciation tax shield will be:

PV$_{Depreciation\ tax\ shield}$ = ($P$ / 10)(.34)(PVIFA$_{15\%,10}$) – $4,333.33(.34)(PVIFA$_{15\%,10}$)

The new harvester will generate year-end pre-tax cash flow savings of $12,000 per year for 10 years. We can find the aftertax present value of the cash flows savings as:

PV$_{Ssavings}$ = $C_1(1 – t_C)$(PVIFA$_{15\%,10}$)
PV$_{Ssavings}$ = $13,000(1 – 0.34)(PVIFA$_{15\%,10}$)
PV$_{Ssavings}$ = $43,061.03

The break-even purchase price of the new harvester is the price, $P$, which makes the NPV of the machine equal to zero.

NPV = –$P$ + Salvage value$_{Old}$ + PV$_{Depreciation\ tax\ shield}$ + PV$_{Savings}$
$0 = –$P$ + $28,593.33 + ($P$ / 10)(.34)(PVIFA$_{15\%,10}$) – $4,333.33(.34)(PVIFA$_{15\%,10}$) + $43,061.03
$P$ – ($P$ / 10)(.34)(PVIFA$_{15\%,10}$) = $71,654.36 – $4,333.33(.34)(PVIFA$_{15\%,10}$)
$P$[1 – (1 / 10)(.34)(PVIFA$_{15\%,10}$)] = $64,260.05
$P$ = $77,481.32

# CHAPTER 8
# INTEREST RATES AND BOND VALUATION

## Answers to Concept Questions

1. No. As interest rates fluctuate, the value of a Treasury security will fluctuate. Long-term Treasury securities have substantial interest rate risk.

2. All else the same, the Treasury security will have lower coupons because of its lower default risk, so it will have greater interest rate risk.

3. No. If the bid were higher than the ask, the implication would be that a dealer was willing to sell a bond and immediately buy it back at a higher price. How many such transactions would you like to do?

4. Prices and yields move in opposite directions. Since the bid price must be lower, the bid yield must be higher.

5. Bond issuers look at outstanding bonds of similar maturity and risk. The yields on such bonds are used to establish the coupon rate necessary for a particular issue to initially sell for par value. Bond issuers also simply ask potential purchasers what coupon rate would be necessary to attract them. The coupon rate is fixed and simply determines what the bond's coupon payments will be. The required return is what investors actually demand on the issue, and it will fluctuate through time. The coupon rate and required return are equal only if the bond sells for exactly at par.

6. Yes. Some investors have obligations that are denominated in dollars; i.e., they are nominal. Their primary concern is that an investment provides the needed nominal dollar amounts. Pension funds, for example, often must plan for pension payments many years in the future. If those payments are fixed in dollar terms, then it is the nominal return on an investment that is important.

7. Companies pay to have their bonds rated simply because unrated bonds can be difficult to sell; many large investors are prohibited from investing in unrated issues.

8. Treasury bonds have no credit risk since it is backed by the U.S. government, so a rating is not necessary. Junk bonds often are not rated because there would be no point in an issuer paying a rating agency to assign its bonds a low rating (it's like paying someone to kick you!).

9. The term structure is based on pure discount bonds. The yield curve is based on coupon-bearing issues.

10. Bond ratings have a subjective factor to them. Split ratings reflect a difference of opinion among credit agencies.

**11.** As a general constitutional principle, the federal government cannot tax the states without their consent if doing so would interfere with state government functions. At one time, this principle was thought to provide for the tax-exempt status of municipal interest payments. However, modern court rulings make it clear that Congress can revoke the municipal exemption, so the only basis now appears to be historical precedent. The fact that the states and the federal government do not tax each other's securities is referred to as "reciprocal immunity."

**12.** Lack of transparency means that a buyer or seller can't see recent transactions, so it is much harder to determine what the best bid and ask prices are at any point in time.

**13.** When the bonds are initially issued, the coupon rate is set at auction so that the bonds sell at par value. The wide range of coupon rates shows the interest rate when each bond was issued. Notice that interest rates have evidently declined. Why?

**14.** Companies charge that bond rating agencies are pressuring them to pay for bond ratings. When a company pays for a rating, it has the opportunity to make its case for a particular rating. With an unsolicited rating, the company has no input.

**15.** A 100-year bond looks like a share of preferred stock. In particular, it is a loan with a life that almost certainly exceeds the life of the lender, assuming that the lender is an individual. With a junk bond, the credit risk can be so high that the borrower is almost certain to default, meaning that the creditors are very likely to end up as part owners of the business. In both cases, the "equity in disguise" has a significant tax advantage.

**16.** *a.* The bond price is the present value of the cash flows from a bond. The YTM is the interest rate used in valuing the cash flows from a bond.

    *b.* If the coupon rate is higher than the required return on a bond, the bond will sell at a premium, since it provides periodic income in the form of coupon payments in excess of that required by investors on other similar bonds. If the coupon rate is lower than the required return on a bond, the bond will sell at a discount since it provides insufficient coupon payments compared to that required by investors on other similar bonds. For premium bonds, the coupon rate exceeds the YTM; for discount bonds, the YTM exceeds the coupon rate, and for bonds selling at par, the YTM is equal to the coupon rate.

    *c.* Current yield is defined as the annual coupon payment divided by the current bond price. For premium bonds, the current yield exceeds the YTM, for discount bonds the current yield is less than the YTM, and for bonds selling at par value, the current yield is equal to the YTM. In all cases, the current yield plus the expected one-period capital gains yield of the bond must be equal to the required return.

**17.** A long-term bond has more interest rate risk compared to a short-term bond, all else the same. A low coupon bond has more interest rate risk than a high coupon bond, all else the same. When comparing a high coupon, long-term bond to a low coupon, short-term bond, we are unsure which has more interest rate risk. Generally, the maturity of a bond is a more important determinant of the interest rate risk, so the long-term, high coupon bond probably has more interest rate risk. The exception would be if the maturities are close, and the coupon rates are vastly different.

## Solutions to Questions and Problems

*NOTE: All end-of-chapter problems were solved using a spreadsheet. Many problems require multiple steps. Due to space and readability constraints, when these intermediate steps are included in this solutions manual, rounding may appear to have occurred. However, the final answer for each problem is found without rounding during any step in the problem.*

*NOTE: Most problems do not explicitly list a par value for bonds. Even though a bond can have any par value, in general, corporate bonds in the United States will have a par value of $1,000. We will use this par value in all problems unless a different par value is explicitly stated.*

### Basic

1. The price of a pure discount (zero coupon) bond is the present value of the par value. Remember, even though there are no coupon payments, the periods are semiannual to stay consistent with coupon bond payments. So, the price of the bond for each YTM is:

   a. $P = \$1,000/(1 + .05/2)^{30} = \$476.74$

   b. $P = \$1,000/(1 + .10/2)^{30} = \$231.38$

   c. $P = \$1,000/(1 + .15/2)^{30} = \$114.22$

2. The price of any bond is the PV of the interest payment, plus the PV of the par value. Notice this problem assumes a semiannual coupon. The price of the bond at each YTM will be:

   a. $P = \$35(\{1 - [1/(1 + .035)]^{30}\} / .035) + \$1,000[1 / (1 + .035)^{30}]$
   $P = \$1,000.00$
   When the YTM and the coupon rate are equal, the bond will sell at par.

   b. $P = \$35(\{1 - [1/(1 + .045)]^{30}\} / .045) + \$1,000[1 / (1 + .045)^{30}]$
   $P = \$837.11$
   When the YTM is greater than the coupon rate, the bond will sell at a discount.

   c. $P = \$35(\{1 - [1/(1 + .025)]^{30}\} / .025) + \$1,000[1 / (1 + .025)^{30}]$
   $P = \$1,209.30$
   When the YTM is less than the coupon rate, the bond will sell at a premium.

3. Here we are finding the YTM of a semiannual coupon bond. The bond price equation is:

   $P = \$1,050 = \$32(PVIFA_{R\%,26}) + \$1,000(PVIF_{R\%,26})$

   Since we cannot solve the equation directly for $R$, using a spreadsheet, a financial calculator, or trial and error, we find:

   $R = 2.923\%$

   Since the coupon payments are semiannual, this is the semiannual interest rate. The YTM is the APR of the bond, so:

   $YTM = 2 \times 2.923\% = 5.85\%$

4. Here we need to find the coupon rate of the bond. All we need to do is to set up the bond pricing equation and solve for the coupon payment as follows:

$$P = \$1,060 = C(PVIFA_{3.8\%,23}) + \$1,000(PVIF_{3.8\%,23})$$

Solving for the coupon payment, we get:

$$C = \$41.96$$

Since this is the semiannual payment, the annual coupon payment is:

$$2 \times \$41.96 = \$83.92$$

And the coupon rate is the annual coupon payment divided by par value, so:

Coupon rate = $83.92 / $1,000 = .0839 or 8.39%

5. The price of any bond is the PV of the interest payment, plus the PV of the par value. The fact that the bond is denominated in euros is irrelevant. Notice this problem assumes an annual coupon. The price of the bond will be:

$$P = €45(\{1 - [1/(1 + .039)]^{19}\} / .039) + €1,000[1 / (1 + .039)^{19}]$$
$$P = €1,079.48$$

6. Here we are finding the YTM of an annual coupon bond. The fact that the bond is denominated in yen is irrelevant. The bond price equation is:

$$P = ¥92,000 = ¥2,800(PVIFA_{R\%,21}) + ¥100,000(PVIF_{R\%,21})$$

Since we cannot solve the equation directly for $R$, using a spreadsheet, a financial calculator, or trial and error, we find:

$$R = 3.34\%$$

Since the coupon payments are annual, this is the yield to maturity.

7. The approximate relationship between nominal interest rates ($R$), real interest rates ($r$), and inflation ($h$) is:

$$R = r + h$$

Approximate $r$ = .045 – .021 = .024 or 2.40%

The Fisher equation, which shows the exact relationship between nominal interest rates, real interest rates, and inflation is:

$$(1 + R) = (1 + r)(1 + h)$$

$$(1 + .045) = (1 + r)(1 + .021)$$

Exact $r$ = [(1 + .045) / (1 + .021)] – 1 = .0235 or 2.35%

8. The Fisher equation, which shows the exact relationship between nominal interest rates, real interest rates, and inflation, is:

$(1 + R) = (1 + r)(1 + h)$

$R = (1 + .024)(1 + .031) – 1 = .0557$ or 5.57%

9. The Fisher equation, which shows the exact relationship between nominal interest rates, real interest rates, and inflation, is:

$(1 + R) = (1 + r)(1 + h)$

$h = [(1 + .14) / (1 + .10)] – 1 = .0364$ or 3.64%

10. The Fisher equation, which shows the exact relationship between nominal interest rates, real interest rates, and inflation, is:

$(1 + R) = (1 + r)(1 + h)$

$r = [(1 + .125) / (1.053)] – 1 = .0684$ or 6.84%

11. The coupon rate, located in the first column of the quote is 4.750%. The bid price is:

Bid price = 109:11 = 109 11/32 = 109.34375% × $1,000 = $1,093.4375

The previous day's ask price is found by:

Previous day's asked price = Today's asked price – Change = 119 13/32 – (–11/32) = 119 24/32

The previous day's price in dollars was:

Previous day's dollar price = 109.7500% × $1,000 = $1,097.5000

12. This is a premium bond because it sells for more than 100% of face value. The current yield is:

Current yield = Annual coupon payment / Asked price = $43.75/$1,023.7500 = .0427 or 4.27%

The YTM is located under the "Asked yield" column, so the YTM is 4.2306%.

The bid-ask spread is the difference between the bid price and the ask price, so:

Bid-Ask spread = 102:12 – 102:11 = 1/32

**13.** Zero coupon bonds are priced with semiannual compounding to correspond with coupon bonds. The price of the bond when purchased was:

$$P_0 = \$1,000 / (1 + .035)^{50}$$
$$P_0 = \$179.05$$

And the price at the end of one year is:

$$P_0 = \$1,000 / (1 + .035)^{48}$$
$$P_0 = \$191.81$$

So, the implied interest, which will be taxable as interest income, is:

Implied interest = $\$191.81 - 179.05$
Implied interest = $\$12.75$

*Intermediate*

**14.** Here we are finding the YTM of semiannual coupon bonds for various maturity lengths. The bond price equation is:

$$P = C(PVIFA_{R\%,t}) + \$1,000(PVIF_{R\%,t})$$

Miller Corporation bond:

$P_0 = \$40(PVIFA_{3\%,26}) + \$1,000(PVIF_{3\%,26}) = \$1,178.77$
$P_1 = \$40(PVIFA_{3\%,24}) + \$1,000(PVIF_{3\%,24}) = \$1,169.36$
$P_3 = \$40(PVIFA_{3\%,20}) + \$1,000(PVIF_{3\%,20}) = \$1,148.77$
$P_8 = \$40(PVIFA_{3\%,10}) + \$1,000(PVIF_{3\%,10}) = \$1,085.30$
$P_{12} = \$40(PVIFA_{3\%,2}) + \$1,000(PVIF_{3\%,2}) = \$1,019.13$
$P_{13} = \$1,000$

Modigliani Company bond:

$P_0 = \$30(PVIFA_{4\%,26}) + \$1,000(PVIF_{4\%,26}) = \$840.17$
$P_1 = \$30(PVIFA_{4\%,24}) + \$1,000(PVIF_{4\%,24}) = \$847.53$
$P_3 = \$30(PVIFA_{4\%,20}) + \$1,000(PVIF_{4\%,20}) = \$864.10$
$P_8 = \$30(PVIFA_{4\%,10}) + \$1,000(PVIF_{4\%,10}) = \$918.89$
$P_{12} = \$30(PVIFA_{4\%,2}) + \$1,000(PVIF_{4\%,2}) = \$981.14$
$P_{13} = \$1,000$

All else held equal, the premium over par value for a premium bond declines as maturity approaches, and the discount from par value for a discount bond declines as maturity approaches. This is called "pull to par." In both cases, the largest percentage price changes occur at the shortest maturity lengths.

Also, notice that the price of each bond when no time is left to maturity is the par value, even though the purchaser would receive the par value plus the coupon payment immediately. This is because we calculate the clean price of the bond.

15. Any bond that sells at par has a YTM equal to the coupon rate. Both bonds sell at par, so the initial YTM on both bonds is the coupon rate, 7 percent. If the YTM suddenly rises to 9 percent:

$P_{Laurel}$ = $35(PVIFA_{4.5\%,4})$ + $1,000(PVIF_{4.5\%,4})$ = $964.12

$P_{Hardy}$ = $35(PVIFA_{4.5\%,30})$ + $1,000(PVIF_{4.5\%,30})$ = $837.11

The percentage change in price is calculated as:

Percentage change in price = (New price – Original price) / Original price

$\Delta P_{Laurel}\%$ = ($964.12 – 1,000) / $1,000 = –0.0359 or –3.59%

$\Delta P_{Hardy}\%$ = ($837.11 – 1,000) / $1,000 = –0.1629 or –16.29%

If the YTM suddenly falls to 5 percent:

$P_{Laurel}$ = $35(PVIFA_{2.5\%,4})$ + $1,000(PVIF_{2.5\%,4})$ = $1,037.62

$P_{Hardy}$ = $35(PVIFA_{2.5\%,30})$ + $1,000(PVIF_{2.5\%,30})$ = $1,209.30

$\Delta P_{Laurel}\%$ = ($1,037.62 – 1,000) / $1,000 = +0.0376 or 3.76%

$\Delta P_{Hardy}\%$ = ($1,209.30 – 1,000) / $1,000 = +0.2093 or 20.93%

All else the same, the longer the maturity of a bond, the greater is its price sensitivity to changes in interest rates. Notice also that for the same interest rate change, the gain from a decline in interest rates is larger than the loss from the same magnitude change. For a plain vanilla bond, this is always true.

16. Initially, at a YTM of 10 percent, the prices of the two bonds are:

$P_{Faulk}$ = $30(PVIFA_{5\%,24})$ + $1,000(PVIF_{5\%,24})$ = $724.03

$P_{Gonas}$ = $70(PVIFA_{5\%,24})$ + $1,000(PVIF_{5\%,24})$ = $1,275.97

If the YTM rises from 10 percent to 12 percent:

$P_{Faulk}$ = $30(PVIFA_{6\%,24})$ + $1,000(PVIF_{6\%,24})$ = $623.49

$P_{Gonas}$ = $70(PVIFA_{6\%,24})$ + $1,000(PVIF_{6\%,24})$ = $1,125.50

The percentage change in price is calculated as:

Percentage change in price = (New price – Original price) / Original price

$\Delta P_{Faulk}\%$ = ($623.49 – 724.03) / $724.03 = –0.1389 or –13.89%
$\Delta P_{Gonas}\%$ = ($1,125.50 – 1,275.97) / $1,275.97 = –0.1179 or –11.79%

If the YTM declines from 10 percent to 8 percent:

$$P_{Faulk} = \$30(PVIFA_{4\%,24}) + \$1,000(PVIF_{4\%,24}) = \$847.53$$

$$P_{Gonas} = \$70(PVIFA_{4\%,24}) + \$1,000(PVIF_{4\%,24}) = \$1,457.41$$

$$\Delta P_{Faulk}\% = (\$847.53 - 724.03) / \$724.03 = +0.1706 \text{ or } 17.06\%$$

$$\Delta P_{Gonas}\% = (\$1,457.41 - 1,275.97) / \$1,275.97 = +0.1422 \text{ or } 14.22\%$$

All else the same, the lower the coupon rate on a bond, the greater is its price sensitivity to changes in interest rates.

17. The bond price equation for this bond is:

$$P_0 = \$1,050 = \$31(PVIFA_{R\%,18}) + \$1,000(PVIF_{R\%,18})$$

Using a spreadsheet, financial calculator, or trial and error we find:

$$R = 2.744\%$$

This is the semiannual interest rate, so the YTM is:

$$YTM = 2 \times 2.744\% = 5.49\%$$

The current yield is:

Current yield = Annual coupon payment / Price = $62 / $1,050 = .0590 or 5.90%

The effective annual yield is the same as the EAR, so using the EAR equation from the previous chapter:

Effective annual yield = $(1 + 0.02744)^2 - 1 = .0556$ or 5.56%

18. The company should set the coupon rate on its new bonds equal to the required return. The required return can be observed in the market by finding the YTM on outstanding bonds of the company. So, the YTM on the bonds currently sold in the market is:

$$P = \$1,063 = \$35(PVIFA_{R\%,40}) + \$1,000(PVIF_{R\%,40})$$

Using a spreadsheet, financial calculator, or trial and error we find:

$$R = 3.218\%$$

This is the semiannual interest rate, so the YTM is:

$$YTM = 2 \times 3.218\% = 6.44\%$$

19. Accrued interest is the coupon payment for the period times the fraction of the period that has passed since the last coupon payment. Since we have a semiannual coupon bond, the coupon payment per six months is one-half of the annual coupon payment. There are two months until the next coupon payment, so four months have passed since the last coupon payment. The accrued interest for the bond is:

Accrued interest = $68/2 × 4/6 = $22.67

And we calculate the clean price as:

Clean price = Dirty price − Accrued interest = $950 − 22.67 = $927.33

20. Accrued interest is the coupon payment for the period times the fraction of the period that has passed since the last coupon payment. Since we have a semiannual coupon bond, the coupon payment per six months is one-half of the annual coupon payment. There are four months until the next coupon payment, so two months have passed since the last coupon payment. The accrued interest for the bond is:

Accrued interest = $59/2 × 2/6 = $9.83

And we calculate the dirty price as:

Dirty price = Clean price + Accrued interest = $1,053 + 9.83 = $1,062.83

21. To find the number of years to maturity for the bond, we need to find the price of the bond. Since we already have the coupon rate, we can use the bond price equation, and solve for the number of years to maturity. We are given the current yield of the bond, so we can calculate the price as:

Current yield = .0842 = $90/$P_0$
$P_0$ = $90/.0842 = $1,068.88

Now that we have the price of the bond, the bond price equation is:

P = $1,068.88 = $90\{[(1 − (1/1.0781)^t)] / .0781\} + $1,000/1.0781^t

We can solve this equation for $t$ as follows:

$1,068.88 (1.0781)^t = $1,152.37 (1.0781)^t − 1,152.37 + 1,000
152.37 = 83.49(1.0781)^t
1.8251 = 1.0781^t
$t$ = log 1.8251 / log 1.0781 = 8.0004 ≈ 8 years

The bond has 8 years to maturity.

22. The bond has 9 years to maturity, so the bond price equation is:

P = $1,053.12 = $36.20(PVIFA$_{R\%,18}$) + $1,000(PVIF$_{R\%,18}$)

Using a spreadsheet, financial calculator, or trial and error we find:

$R$ = 3.226%

This is the semiannual interest rate, so the YTM is:

YTM = 2 × 3.226% = 6.45%

The current yield is the annual coupon payment divided by the bond price, so:

Current yield = $72.40 / $1,053.12 = .0687 or 6.87%

**23.** We found the maturity of a bond in Problem 21. However, in this case, the maturity is indeterminate. A bond selling at par can have any length of maturity. In other words, when we solve the bond pricing equation as we did in Problem 21, the number of periods can be any positive number.

**24.** The price of a zero coupon bond is the PV of the par, so:

*a.* $P_0 = \$1,000/1.035^{50} = \$179.05$

*b.* In one year, the bond will have 24 years to maturity, so the price will be:

$P_1 = \$1,000/1.035^{48} = \$191.81$

The interest deduction is the price of the bond at the end of the year, minus the price at the beginning of the year, so:

Year 1 interest deduction = $191.81 – 179.05 = $12.75

The price of the bond when it has one year left to maturity will be:

$P_{24} = \$1,000/1.035^2 = \$933.51$

Year 25 interest deduction = $1,000 – 933.51 = $66.49

*c.* Previous IRS regulations required a straight-line calculation of interest. The total interest received by the bondholder is:

Total interest = $1,000 – 179.05 = $820.95

The annual interest deduction is simply the total interest divided by the maturity of the bond, so the straight-line deduction is:

Annual interest deduction = $820.95 / 25 = $32.84

*d.* The company will prefer straight-line methods when allowed because the valuable interest deductions occur earlier in the life of the bond.

**25.** *a.*  The coupon bonds have a 6 percent coupon which matches the 6 percent required return, so they will sell at par. The number of bonds that must be sold is the amount needed divided by the bond price, so:

Number of coupon bonds to sell = $45,000,000 / $1,000 = 45,000

The number of zero coupon bonds to sell would be:

Price of zero coupon bonds = $1,000/1.03^{60} = $169.73

Number of zero coupon bonds to sell = $45,000,000 / $169.73 = 265,122

*b.*  The repayment of the coupon bond will be the par value plus the last coupon payment times the number of bonds issued. So:

Coupon bonds repayment = 45,000($1,030) = $46,350,000

The repayment of the zero coupon bond will be the par value times the number of bonds issued, so:

Zeroes: repayment = 265,122($1,000) = $265,122,140

*c.*  The total coupon payment for the coupon bonds will be the number bonds times the coupon payment. For the cash flow of the coupon bonds, we need to account for the tax deductibility of the interest payments. To do this, we will multiply the total coupon payment times one minus the tax rate. So:

Coupon bonds: (45,000)($60)(1–.35) = $1,755,000 cash outflow

Note that this is cash outflow since the company is making the interest payment.

For the zero coupon bonds, the first year interest payment is the difference in the price of the zero at the end of the year and the beginning of the year. The price of the zeroes in one year will be:

$P_1 = $1,000/1.03^{58} = $180.07

The year 1 interest deduction per bond will be this price minus the price at the beginning of the year, which we found in part *b*, so:

Year 1 interest deduction per bond = $180.07 – 169.73 = $10.34

The total cash flow for the zeroes will be the interest deduction for the year times the number of zeroes sold, times the tax rate. The cash flow for the zeroes in year 1 will be:

Cash flows for zeroes in Year 1 = (265,122)($10.34)(.35) = $959,175.00

Notice the cash flow for the zeroes is a cash inflow. This is because of the tax deductibility of the imputed interest expense. That is, the company gets to write off the interest expense for the year even though the company did not have a cash flow for the interest expense. This reduces the company's tax liability, which is a cash inflow.

During the life of the bond, the zero generates cash inflows to the firm in the form of the interest tax shield of debt. We should note an important point here: If you find the PV of the cash flows from the coupon bond and the zero coupon bond, they will be the same. This is because of the much larger repayment amount for the zeroes.

*Challenge*

26. To find the capital gains yield and the current yield, we need to find the price of the bond. The current price of Bond P and the price of Bond P in one year is:

P:    $P_0 = \$90(\text{PVIFA}_{7\%,10}) + \$1,000(\text{PVIF}_{7\%,10}) = \$1,140.47$

$P_1 = \$90(\text{PVIFA}_{7\%,9}) + \$1,000(\text{PVIF}_{7\%,9}) = \$1,130.30$

Current yield = $90 / $1,140.47 = .0789 or 7.89%

The capital gains yield is:

Capital gains yield = (New price – Original price) / Original price

Capital gains yield = ($1,130.30 – 1,140.47) / $1,140.47 = –0.0089 or –0.89%

The current price of Bond D and the price of Bond D in one year is:

D:    $P_0 = \$50(\text{PVIFA}_{7\%,10}) + \$1,000(\text{PVIF}_{7\%,10}) = \$859.53$

$P_1 = \$50(\text{PVIFA}_{7\%,9}) + \$1,000(\text{PVIF}_{7\%,9}) = \$869.70$

Current yield = $50 / $859.53 = 0.0582 or 5.82%

Capital gains yield = ($869.70 – 859.53) / $859.53 = 0.0118 or 1.18%

All else held constant, premium bonds pay a high current income while having price depreciation as maturity nears; discount bonds pay a lower current income but have price appreciation as maturity nears. For either bond, the total return is still 7%, but this return is distributed differently between current income and capital gains.

27. *a.*    The rate of return you expect to earn if you purchase a bond and hold it until maturity is the YTM. The bond price equation for this bond is:

$P_0 = \$930 = \$56(\text{PVIFA}_{R\%,10}) + \$1,000(\text{PVIF}_{R\%,10})$

Using a spreadsheet, financial calculator, or trial and error we find:

$R = \text{YTM} = 6.58\%$

b.    To find our HPY, we need to find the price of the bond in two years. The price of the bond in two years, at the new interest rate, will be:

$$P_2 = \$56(\text{PVIFA}_{5.58\%,8}) + \$1,000(\text{PVIF}_{5.58\%,8}) = \$1,001.44$$

To calculate the HPY, we need to find the interest rate that equates the price we paid for the bond with the cash flows we received. The cash flows we received were $90 each year for two years, and the price of the bond when we sold it. The equation to find our HPY is:

$$P_0 = \$930 = \$56(\text{PVIFA}_{R\%,2}) + \$1,001.44(\text{PVIF}_{R\%,2})$$

Solving for $R$, we get:

$$R = \text{HPY} = 9.68\%$$

The realized HPY is greater than the expected YTM when the bond was bought because interest rates dropped by 1 percent; bond prices rise when yields fall.

28.  The price of any bond (or financial instrument) is the PV of the future cash flows. Even though Bond M makes different coupons payments, to find the price of the bond, we just find the PV of the cash flows. The PV of the cash flows for Bond M is:

$$P_M = \$800(\text{PVIFA}_{4\%,16})(\text{PVIF}_{4\%,12}) + \$1,000(\text{PVIFA}_{4\%,12})(\text{PVIF}_{4\%,28}) + \$30,000(\text{PVIF}_{4\%,40})$$
$$P_M = \$15,200.77$$

Notice that for the coupon payments of $800, we found the PVA for the coupon payments, and then discounted the lump sum back to today.

Bond N is a zero coupon bond with a $30,000 par value; therefore, the price of the bond is the PV of the par, or:

$$P_N = \$30,000(\text{PVIF}_{4\%,40}) = \$6,248.67$$

29.  In general, this is not likely to happen, although it can (and did). The reason this bond has a negative YTM is that it is a callable U.S. Treasury bond. Market participants know this. Given the high coupon rate of the bond, it is extremely likely to be called, which means the bondholder will not receive all the cash flows promised. A better measure of the return on a callable bond is the yield to call (YTC). The YTC calculation is the basically the same as the YTM calculation, but the number of periods is the number of periods until the call date. If the YTC were calculated on this bond, it would be positive.

30.  To find the present value, we need to find the real weekly interest rate. To find the real return, we need to use the effective annual rates in the Fisher equation. So, we find the real EAR is:

$(1 + R) = (1 + r)(1 + h)$
$1 + .069 = (1 + r)(1 + .032)$
$r = .0359$ or $3.59\%$

Now, to find the weekly interest rate, we need to find the APR. Using the equation for discrete compounding:

$$EAR = [1 + (APR / m)]^m - 1$$

We can solve for the APR. Doing so, we get:

$$APR = m[(1 + EAR)^{1/m} - 1]$$
$$APR = 52[(1 + .0359)^{1/52} - 1]$$
$$APR = .0352 \text{ or } 3.52\%$$

So, the weekly interest rate is:

Weekly rate = APR / 52
Weekly rate = .0352 / 52
Weekly rate = .0007 or 0.07%

Now we can find the present value of the cost of the roses. The real cash flows are an ordinary annuity, discounted at the real interest rate. So, the present value of the cost of the roses is:

$$PVA = C(\{1 - [1/(1 + r)]^t \} / r)$$
$$PVA = \$8(\{1 - [1/(1 + .0007)]^{30(52)}\} / .0007)$$
$$PVA = \$7,702.30$$

31. To answer this question, we need to find the monthly interest rate, which is the APR divided by 12. We also must be careful to use the real interest rate. The Fisher equation uses the effective annual rate, so, the real effective annual interest rates, and the monthly interest rates for each account are:

Stock account:
$$(1 + R) = (1 + r)(1 + h)$$
$$1 + .12 = (1 + r)(1 + .04)$$
$$r = .0769 \text{ or } 7.69\%$$

$$APR = m[(1 + EAR)^{1/m} - 1]$$
$$APR = 12[(1 + .0769)^{1/12} - 1]$$
$$APR = .0743 \text{ or } 7.43\%$$

Monthly rate = APR / 12
Monthly rate = .0743 / 12
Monthly rate = .0062 or 0.62%

Bond account:
$$(1 + R) = (1 + r)(1 + h)$$
$$1 + .07 = (1 + r)(1 + .04)$$
$$r = .0288 \text{ or } 2.88\%$$

$$APR = m[(1 + EAR)^{1/m} - 1]$$
$$APR = 12[(1 + .0288)^{1/12} - 1]$$
$$APR = .0285 \text{ or } 2.85\%$$

Monthly rate = APR / 12
Monthly rate = .0285 / 12
Monthly rate = .0024 or 0.24%

Now we can find the future value of the retirement account in real terms. The future value of each account will be:

Stock account:
$FVA = C \{(1 + r)^t - 1] / r\}$
$FVA = \$900\{[(1 + .0062)^{360} - 1] / .0062]\}$
$FVA = \$1,196,731.96$

Bond account:
$FVA = C \{(1 + r)^t - 1] / r\}$
$FVA = \$300\{[(1 + .0024)^{360} - 1] / .0024]\}$
$FVA = \$170,316.78$

The total future value of the retirement account will be the sum of the two accounts, or:

Account value = $1,196,731.96 + 170,316.78
Account value = $1,367,048.74

Now we need to find the monthly interest rate in retirement. We can use the same procedure that we used to find the monthly interest rates for the stock and bond accounts, so:

$(1 + R) = (1 + r)(1 + h)$
$1 + .08 = (1 + r)(1 + .04)$
$r = .0385$ or 3.85%

$APR = m[(1 + EAR)^{1/m} - 1]$
$APR = 12[(1 + .0385)^{1/12} - 1]$
$APR = .0378$ or 3.78%

Monthly rate = APR / 12
Monthly rate = .0378 / 12
Monthly rate = .0031 or 0.31%

Now we can find the real monthly withdrawal in retirement. Using the present value of an annuity equation and solving for the payment, we find:

$PVA = C(\{1 - [1/(1 + r)]^t\} / r)$
$\$1,367,048.74 = C(\{1 - [1/(1 + .0031)]^{300}\} / .0031)$
$C = \$7,050.75$

This is the real dollar amount of the monthly withdrawals. The nominal monthly withdrawals will increase by the inflation rate each month. To find the nominal dollar amount of the last withdrawal, we can increase the real dollar withdrawal by the inflation rate. We can increase the real withdrawal by the effective annual inflation rate since we are only interested in the nominal amount of the last withdrawal. So, the last withdrawal in nominal terms will be:

$$FV = PV(1 + r)^t$$
$$FV = \$7,050.75(1 + .04)^{(30 + 25)}$$
$$FV = \$60,963.34$$

32. In this problem, we need to calculate the future value of the annual savings after the five years of operations. The savings are the revenues minus the costs, or:

Savings = Revenue − Costs

Since the annual fee and the number of members are increasing, we need to calculate the effective growth rate for revenues, which is:

Effective growth rate = $(1 + .06)(1 + .03) - 1$
Effective growth rate = .0918 or 9.18%

The revenue for the current year is the number of members times the annual fee, or:

Current revenue = 600($500)
Current revenue = $300,000

The revenue will grow at 9.18 percent, and the costs will grow at 2 percent, so the savings each year for the next five years will be:

| Year | Revenue | Costs | Savings |
|---|---|---|---|
| 1 | $327,540.00 | $127,500.00 | $200,040.00 |
| 2 | 357,608.17 | 130,050.00 | 227,558.17 |
| 3 | 390,436.60 | 132,651.00 | 257,785.60 |
| 4 | 426,278.68 | 135,304.02 | 290,974.66 |
| 5 | 465,411.07 | 138,010.10 | 327,400.96 |

Now we can find the value of each year's savings using the future value of a lump sum equation, so:

$$FV = PV(1 + r)^t$$

| Year | | Future Value |
|---|---|---|
| 1 | $200,040.00(1 + .09)^4 =$ | $ 282,372.79 |
| 2 | $227,558.17(1 + .09)^3 =$ | 294,694.43 |
| 3 | $257,785.60(1 + .09)^2 =$ | 306,275.07 |
| 4 | $290,974.66(1 + .09)^1 =$ | 317,162.38 |
| 5 | | 327,400.96 |
| Total future value of savings = | | $1,527,905.64 |

He will spend $500,000 on a luxury boat, so the value of his account will be:

Value of account = $1,527,905.64 − 500,000
Value of account = $1,027,905.64

Now we can use the present value of an annuity equation to find the payment. Doing so, we find:

$PVA = C(\{1 − [1/(1 + r)]^t \} / r )$
$\$1,027,905.64 = C(\{1 − [1/(1 + .09)]^{25} \} / .09)$
$C = \$104,647.22$

## Calculator Solutions

**1.**

*a.*

| Enter | 30 | 2.5% | | | $1,000 |
|---|---|---|---|---|---|
| | **N** | **I/Y** | **PV** | **PMT** | **FV** |
| Solve for | | | $476.74 | | |

*b.*

| Enter | 30 | 5% | | | $1,000 |
|---|---|---|---|---|---|
| | **N** | **I/Y** | **PV** | **PMT** | **FV** |
| Solve for | | | $231.38 | | |

*c.*

| Enter | 30 | 7.5% | | | $1,000 |
|---|---|---|---|---|---|
| | **N** | **I/Y** | **PV** | **PMT** | **FV** |
| Solve for | | | $114.22 | | |

**2.**

*a.*

| Enter | 30 | 3.5% | | $35 | $1,000 |
|---|---|---|---|---|---|
| | **N** | **I/Y** | **PV** | **PMT** | **FV** |
| Solve for | | | $1,000.00 | | |

*b.*

| Enter | 30 | 4.5% | | $35 | $1,000 |
|---|---|---|---|---|---|
| | **N** | **I/Y** | **PV** | **PMT** | **FV** |
| Solve for | | | $837.11 | | |

*c.*

| Enter | 30 | 2.5% | | $35 | $1,000 |
|---|---|---|---|---|---|
| | **N** | **I/Y** | **PV** | **PMT** | **FV** |
| Solve for | | | $1,209.30 | | |

**3.**

| Enter | 26 | | ±$1,050 | $32 | $1,000 |
|---|---|---|---|---|---|
| | **N** | **I/Y** | **PV** | **PMT** | **FV** |
| Solve for | | 2.923% | | | |

2.923% × 2 = 5.85%

**4.**

| Enter | 23 | 3.8% | ±$1,060 | | $1,000 |
|---|---|---|---|---|---|
| | **N** | **I/Y** | **PV** | **PMT** | **FV** |
| Solve for | | | | $41.96 | |

$41.96 × 2 = $83.92
$83.92 / $1,000 = 8.39%

**5.**

| Enter | 19 | 3.90% | | €45 | €1,000 |
|---|---|---|---|---|---|
| | **N** | **I/Y** | **PV** | **PMT** | **FV** |
| Solve for | | | €1,079.48 | | |

**6.**

| Enter | 21 | | ±¥92,000 | ¥2,800 | ¥100,000 |
|---|---|---|---|---|---|
| | **N** | **I/Y** | **PV** | **PMT** | **FV** |
| Solve for | | 3.34% | | | |

**13.**

$P_0$

| Enter | 50 | 3.5% | | | $1,000 |
|---|---|---|---|---|---|
| | **N** | **I/Y** | **PV** | **PMT** | **FV** |
| Solve for | | | $179.05 | | |

$P_1$

| Enter | 48 | 3.5% | | | $1,000 |
|---|---|---|---|---|---|
| | **N** | **I/Y** | **PV** | **PMT** | **FV** |
| Solve for | | | $191.81 | | |

$191.81 - 179.05 = $12.75

**14.**    Miller Corporation

$P_0$

| Enter | 26 | 3% | | $40 | $1,000 |
|---|---|---|---|---|---|
| | **N** | **I/Y** | **PV** | **PMT** | **FV** |
| Solve for | | | $1,178.77 | | |

$P_1$

| Enter | 24 | 3% | | $40 | $1,000 |
|---|---|---|---|---|---|
| | **N** | **I/Y** | **PV** | **PMT** | **FV** |
| Solve for | | | $1,169.36 | | |

$P_3$

| Enter | 20 | 3% | | $40 | $1,000 |
|---|---|---|---|---|---|
| | **N** | **I/Y** | **PV** | **PMT** | **FV** |
| Solve for | | | $1,148.77 | | |

$P_8$

| Enter | 10 | 3% | | $40 | $1,000 |
|---|---|---|---|---|---|
| | **N** | **I/Y** | **PV** | **PMT** | **FV** |
| Solve for | | | $1,085.30 | | |

$P_{12}$

| Enter | 2 | 3% | | $40 | $1,000 |
|---|---|---|---|---|---|
| | **N** | **I/Y** | **PV** | **PMT** | **FV** |
| Solve for | | | $1,019.13 | | |

Modigliani Company

$P_0$

| Enter | 26 | 4% | | $30 | $1,000 |
|-------|-----|------|------|------|--------|
| | **N** | **I/Y** | **PV** | **PMT** | **FV** |
| Solve for | | | $840.17 | | |

$P_1$

| Enter | 24 | 4% | | $30 | $1,000 |
|-------|-----|------|------|------|--------|
| | **N** | **I/Y** | **PV** | **PMT** | **FV** |
| Solve for | | | $847.53 | | |

$P_3$

| Enter | 20 | 4% | | $30 | $1,000 |
|-------|-----|------|------|------|--------|
| | **N** | **I/Y** | **PV** | **PMT** | **FV** |
| Solve for | | | $864.10 | | |

$P_8$

| Enter | 10 | 4% | | $30 | $1,000 |
|-------|-----|------|------|------|--------|
| | **N** | **I/Y** | **PV** | **PMT** | **FV** |
| Solve for | | | $918.89 | | |

$P_{12}$

| Enter | 2 | 4% | | $30 | $1,000 |
|-------|-----|------|------|------|--------|
| | **N** | **I/Y** | **PV** | **PMT** | **FV** |
| Solve for | | | $981.14 | | |

**15.** If both bonds sell at par, the initial YTM on both bonds is the coupon rate, 7 percent. If the YTM suddenly rises to 9 percent:

$P_{Laurel}$

| Enter | 4 | 4.5% | | $35 | $1,000 |
|-------|-----|------|------|------|--------|
| | **N** | **I/Y** | **PV** | **PMT** | **FV** |
| Solve for | | | $964.12 | | |

$\Delta P_{Laurel}\% = (\$964.12 - 1,000) / \$1,000 = -3.59\%$

$P_{Hardy}$

| Enter | 30 | 4.5% | | $35 | $1,000 |
|-------|-----|------|------|------|--------|
| | **N** | **I/Y** | **PV** | **PMT** | **FV** |
| Solve for | | | $837.11 | | |

$\Delta P_{Hardy}\% = (\$837.11 - 1,000) / \$1,000 = -16.29\%$

If the YTM suddenly falls to 5 percent:

$P_{Laurel}$

| Enter | 4 | 2.5% | | $35 | $1,000 |
|-------|-----|------|------|------|--------|
| | **N** | **I/Y** | **PV** | **PMT** | **FV** |
| Solve for | | | $1,037.62 | | |

$\Delta P_{Laurel} \% = (\$1,037.62 - 1,000) / \$1,000 = + 3.76\%$

$P_{Hardy}$

| | N | I/Y | PV | PMT | FV |
|---|---|---|---|---|---|
| Enter | 30 | 2.5% | | $35 | $1,000 |
| Solve for | | | $1,209.93 | | |

$\Delta P_{Hardy}\% = (\$1,209.93 - 1,000) / \$1,000 = +20.93\%$

All else the same, the longer the maturity of a bond, the greater is its price sensitivity to changes in interest rates.

**16.** Initially, at a YTM of 10 percent, the prices of the two bonds are:

$P_{Faulk}$

| | N | I/Y | PV | PMT | FV |
|---|---|---|---|---|---|
| Enter | 24 | 5% | | $30 | $1,000 |
| Solve for | | | $724.03 | | |

$P_{Gonas}$

| | N | I/Y | PV | PMT | FV |
|---|---|---|---|---|---|
| Enter | 24 | 5% | | $70 | $1,000 |
| Solve for | | | $1,275.97 | | |

If the YTM rises from 10 percent to 12 percent:

$P_{Faulk}$

| | N | I/Y | PV | PMT | FV |
|---|---|---|---|---|---|
| Enter | 24 | 6% | | $30 | $1,000 |
| Solve for | | | $623.49 | | |

$\Delta P_{Faulk}\% = (\$623.49 - 724.03) / \$724.03 = -13.89\%$

$P_{Gonas}$

| | N | I/Y | PV | PMT | FV |
|---|---|---|---|---|---|
| Enter | 24 | 6% | | $70 | $1,000 |
| Solve for | | | $1,125.50 | | |

$\Delta P_{Gonas}\% = (\$1,125.50 - 1,275.97) / \$1,275.97 = -11.79\%$

If the YTM declines from 10 percent to 8 percent:

$P_{Faulk}$

| | N | I/Y | PV | PMT | FV |
|---|---|---|---|---|---|
| Enter | 24 | 4% | | $30 | $1,000 |
| Solve for | | | $847.53 | | |

$\Delta P_{Faulk}\% = (\$847.53 - 724.03) / \$724.03 = +17.06\%$

$P_{Gonas}$

| | N | I/Y | PV | PMT | FV |
|---|---|---|---|---|---|
| Enter | 24 | 4% | | $70 | $1,000 |
| Solve for | | | $1,457.41 | | |

$\Delta P_{Gonas}\% = (\$1,457.41 - 1,275.97) / \$1,275.97 = +14.22\%$

All else the same, the lower the coupon rate on a bond, the greater is its price sensitivity to changes in interest rates.

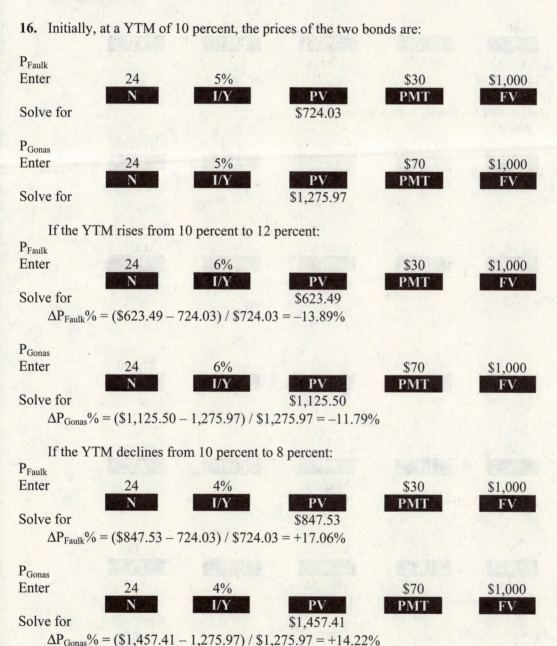
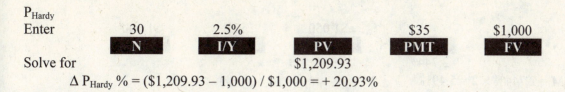

**17.**

| Enter | 18 | | ±$1,050 | $31 | $1,000 |
|---|---|---|---|---|---|
| | **N** | **I/Y** | **PV** | **PMT** | **FV** |
| Solve for | | 2.744% | | | |

YTM = 2.744% × 2 = 5.49%

**18.** The company should set the coupon rate on its new bonds equal to the required return; the required return can be observed in the market by finding the YTM on outstanding bonds of the company.

| Enter | 40 | | ±$1,063 | $35 | $1,000 |
|---|---|---|---|---|---|
| | **N** | **I/Y** | **PV** | **PMT** | **FV** |
| Solve for | | 3.218% | | | |

3.218% × 2 = 6.44%

**21.** Current yield = .0842 = $90/$P_0$ ; $P_0$ = $1,068.88

| Enter | | 7.81% | ±$1,068.88 | $90 | $1,000 |
|---|---|---|---|---|---|
| | **N** | **I/Y** | **PV** | **PMT** | **FV** |
| Solve for | 8.0004 | | | | |

8 years

**22.**

| Enter | 18 | | ±$1,053.12 | $36.20 | $1,000 |
|---|---|---|---|---|---|
| | **N** | **I/Y** | **PV** | **PMT** | **FV** |
| Solve for | | 3.226% | | | |

3.226% × 2 = 6.45%

**24.**

*a.* $P_0$

| Enter | 50 | 7%/2 | | | $1,000 |
|---|---|---|---|---|---|
| | **N** | **I/Y** | **PV** | **PMT** | **FV** |
| Solve for | | | $179.05 | | |

*b.* $P_1$

| Enter | 48 | 7%/2 | | | $1,000 |
|---|---|---|---|---|---|
| | **N** | **I/Y** | **PV** | **PMT** | **FV** |
| Solve for | | | $191.81 | | |

year 1 interest deduction = $191.81 − 179.05 = $12.75

$P_{24}$

| Enter | 2 | 7%/2% | | | $1,000 |
|---|---|---|---|---|---|
| | **N** | **I/Y** | **PV** | **PMT** | **FV** |
| Solve for | | | $933.51 | | |

year 25 interest deduction = $1,000 − 933.51 = $66.49

*c.* Total interest = $1,000 – 179.05 = $820.95
Annual interest deduction = $820.95 / 25 = $32.84

*d.* The company will prefer straight-line method when allowed because the valuable interest deductions occur earlier in the life of the bond.

25. *a.* The coupon bonds have a 6% coupon rate, which matches the 6% required return, so they will sell at par; # of bonds = $45,000,000/$1,000 = 45,000.

For the zeroes:

| | | | | | |
|---|---|---|---|---|---|
| Enter | 60 | 6%/2 | | | $1,000 |
| | **N** | **I/Y** | **PV** | **PMT** | **FV** |
| Solve for | | | $169.73 | | |

$45,000,000/$169.73 = 265,122 will be issued.

*b.* Coupon bonds: repayment = 45,000($1,030) = $46,350,000
Zeroes: repayment = 265,122($1,000) = $265,122,140

*c.* Coupon bonds: (45,000)($60)(1 –.35) = $1,755,000 cash outflow
Zeroes:

| | | | | | |
|---|---|---|---|---|---|
| Enter | 58 | 6%/2 | | | $1,000 |
| | **N** | **I/Y** | **PV** | **PMT** | **FV** |
| Solve for | | | $180.07 | | |

year 1 interest deduction = $180.07 – 169.73 = $10.34
(265,122)($10.34)(.35) = $959,175.00 cash inflow
During the life of the bond, the zero generates cash inflows to the firm in the form of the interest tax shield of debt.

**26.**
Bond P
$P_0$

| | | | | | |
|---|---|---|---|---|---|
| Enter | 10 | 7% | | $90 | $1,000 |
| | **N** | **I/Y** | **PV** | **PMT** | **FV** |
| Solve for | | | $1,140.47 | | |

$P_1$

| | | | | | |
|---|---|---|---|---|---|
| Enter | 9 | 7% | | $90 | $1,000 |
| | **N** | **I/Y** | **PV** | **PMT** | **FV** |
| Solve for | | | $1,130.30 | | |

Current yield = $90 / $1,140.47 = 7.89%
Capital gains yield = ($1,130.30 – 1,140.47) / $1,140.47 = –0.89%

Bond D
$P_0$

| | | | | | |
|---|---|---|---|---|---|
| Enter | 10 | 7% | | $50 | $1,000 |
| | **N** | **I/Y** | **PV** | **PMT** | **FV** |
| Solve for | | | $859.53 | | |

$P_1$

Enter

| 9 | 7% | | $50 | $1,000 |
|---|---|---|---|---|
| **N** | **I/Y** | **PV** | **PMT** | **FV** |

Solve for | | | $869.70 | | |

Current yield = $50 / $859.53 = 5.82%

Capital gains yield = ($869.70 − 859.53) / $859.53 = +1.18%

All else held constant, premium bonds pay a higher current income while having price depreciation as maturity nears; discount bonds pay a lower current income but have price appreciation as maturity nears. For either bond, the total return is still 7%, but this return is distributed differently between current income and capital gains.

**27.**

*a.*

Enter

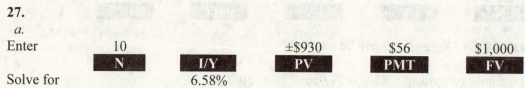

| 10 | | ±$930 | $56 | $1,000 |
|---|---|---|---|---|
| **N** | **I/Y** | **PV** | **PMT** | **FV** |

Solve for | | 6.58% | | | |

This is the rate of return you expect to earn on your investment when you purchase the bond.

*b.*

Enter

| 8 | 5.58% | | $56 | $1,000 |
|---|---|---|---|---|
| **N** | **I/Y** | **PV** | **PMT** | **FV** |

Solve for | | | $1,001.44 | | |

The HPY is:

Enter

| 2 | | ±$930 | $56 | $1,001.44 |
|---|---|---|---|---|
| **N** | **I/Y** | **PV** | **PMT** | **FV** |

Solve for | | 9.68% | | | |

The realized HPY is greater than the expected YTM when the bond was bought because interest rates dropped by 1 percent; bond prices rise when yields fall.

**28.**

$P_M$

| CFo | $0 |
|---|---|
| C01 | $0 |
| F01 | 12 |
| C02 | $800 |
| F02 | 16 |
| C03 | $1,000 |
| F03 | 11 |
| C04 | $31,000 |
| F04 | 1 |

I = 4%

NPV CPT

$15,200.77

$P_N$

| Enter | 40 | 4% | | | $30,000 |
|---|---|---|---|---|---|
| | **N** | **I/Y** | **PV** | **PMT** | **FV** |
| Solve for | | | $6,248.67 | | |

**31.**

Real return for stock account: $1 + .12 = (1 + r)(1 + .04)$; $r = 7.6923\%$

| Enter | | 7.6923% | 12 |
|---|---|---|---|
| | **NOM** | **EFF** | **C/Y** |
| Solve for | 7.4337% | | |

Real return for bond account: $1 + .07 = (1 + r)(1 + .04)$; $r = 2.8846\%$

| Enter | | 2.8846% | 12 |
|---|---|---|---|
| | **NOM** | **EFF** | **C/Y** |
| Solve for | 2.8472% | | |

Real return post-retirement: $1 + .08 = (1 + r)(1 + .04)$; $r = 3.8462\%$

| Enter | | 3.8462% | 12 |
|---|---|---|---|
| | **NOM** | **EFF** | **C/Y** |
| Solve for | 3.7800% | | |

Stock portfolio value:

| Enter | 12 × 30 | 7.4337% / 12 | | $800 | |
|---|---|---|---|---|---|
| | **N** | **I/Y** | **PV** | **PMT** | **FV** |
| Solve for | | | | | $1,196,731.96 |

Bond portfolio value:

| Enter | 12 × 30 | 2.8472% / 12 | | $400 | |
|---|---|---|---|---|---|
| | **N** | **I/Y** | **PV** | **PMT** | **FV** |
| Solve for | | | | | $170,316.78 |

Retirement value = $1,196,731.96 + 170,316.78 = $1,367,048.74

Retirement withdrawal:

| Enter | 25 × 12 | 3.7800% / 12 | $1,367,048.74 | | |
|---|---|---|---|---|---|
| | **N** | **I/Y** | **PV** | **PMT** | **FV** |
| Solve for | | | | $7,050.75 | |

The last withdrawal in real terms is:

| Enter | 30 + 25 | 4% | $7,050.75 | | |
|---|---|---|---|---|---|
| | **N** | **I/Y** | **PV** | **PMT** | **FV** |
| Solve for | | | | | $60,963.34 |

**32.**

Future value of savings:

Year 1:

| | N | I/Y | PV | PMT | FV |
|---|---|---|---|---|---|
| Enter | 4 | 9% | $200,040 | | |
| Solve for | | | | | $282,372.79 |

Year 2:

| | N | I/Y | PV | PMT | FV |
|---|---|---|---|---|---|
| Enter | 3 | 9% | $227,558.17 | | |
| Solve for | | | | | $294,694.43 |

Year 3:

| | N | I/Y | PV | PMT | FV |
|---|---|---|---|---|---|
| Enter | 2 | 9% | $257,785.60 | | |
| Solve for | | | | | $306,275.07 |

Year 4:

| | N | I/Y | PV | PMT | FV |
|---|---|---|---|---|---|
| Enter | 1 | 9% | $290,974.66 | | |
| Solve for | | | | | $317,162.38 |

Future value = $282,372.79 + 294,694.43 + 306,275.07 + 317,162.38 + 327,400.96
Future value = $1,527,905.64

He will spend $500,000 on a luxury boat, so the value of his account will be:

Value of account = $1,527,905.64 − 500,000
Value of account = $1,027,905.64

| | N | I/Y | PV | PMT | FV |
|---|---|---|---|---|---|
| Enter | 25 | 9% | $1,027,905.64 | | |
| Solve for | | | | $104,647.22 | |

# CHAPTER 9
# STOCK VALUATION

**Answers to Concept Questions**

1. The value of any investment depends on the present value of its cash flows; i.e., what investors will actually receive. The cash flows from a share of stock are the dividends.

2. Investors believe the company will eventually start paying dividends (or be sold to another company).

3. In general, companies that need the cash will often forgo dividends since dividends are a cash expense. Young, growing companies with profitable investment opportunities are one example; another example is a company in financial distress. This question is examined in depth in a later chapter.

4. The general method for valuing a share of stock is to find the present value of all expected future dividends. The dividend growth model presented in the text is only valid (i) if dividends are expected to occur forever; that is, the stock provides dividends in perpetuity, and (ii) if a constant growth rate of dividends occurs forever. A violation of the first assumption might be a company that is expected to cease operations and dissolve itself some finite number of years from now. The stock of such a company would be valued by applying the general method of valuation explained in this chapter. A violation of the second assumption might be a start-up firm that isn't currently paying any dividends, but is expected to eventually start making dividend payments some number of years from now. This stock would also be valued by the general dividend valuation method explained in this chapter.

5. The common stock probably has a higher price because the dividend can grow, whereas it is fixed on the preferred. However, the preferred is less risky because of the dividend and liquidation preference, so it is possible the preferred could be worth more, depending on the circumstances.

6. The two components are the dividend yield and the capital gains yield. For most companies, the capital gains yield is larger. This is easy to see for companies that pay no dividends. For companies that do pay dividends, the dividend yields are rarely over five percent and are often much less.

7. Yes. If the dividend grows at a steady rate, so does the stock price. In other words, the dividend growth rate and the capital gains yield are the same.

8. The three factors are: 1) The company's future growth opportunities. 2) The company's level of risk, which determines the interest rate used to discount cash flows. 3) The accounting method used.

9. It wouldn't seem to be. Investors who don't like the voting features of a particular class of stock are under no obligation to buy it.

10. Presumably, the current stock value reflects the risk, timing and magnitude of all future cash flows, both short-term and long-term. If this is correct, then the statement is false.

**Solutions to Questions and Problems**

*NOTE: All end-of-chapter problems were solved using a spreadsheet. Many problems require multiple steps. Due to space and readability constraints, when these intermediate steps are included in this solutions manual, rounding may appear to have occurred. However, the final answer for each problem is found without rounding during any step in the problem.*

*Basic*

1. The constant dividend growth model is:

   $P_t = D_t \times (1 + g) / (R - g)$

   So, the price of the stock today is:

   $P_0 = D_0 (1 + g) / (R - g) = \$1.90 (1.05) / (.11 - .05) = \$37.63$

   The dividend at year 4 is the dividend today times the FVIF for the growth rate in dividends and four years, so:

   $P_3 = D_3 (1 + g) / (R - g) = D_0 (1 + g)^4 / (R - g) = \$1.90 (1.05)^4 / (.11 - .05) = \$43.56$

   We can do the same thing to find the dividend in Year 16, which gives us the price in Year 15, so:

   $P_{15} = D_{15} (1 + g) / (R - g) = D_0 (1 + g)^{16} / (R - g) = \$1.90 (1.05)^{16} / (.11 - .05) = \$78.22$

   There is another feature of the constant dividend growth model: The stock price grows at the dividend growth rate. So, if we know the stock price today, we can find the future value for any time in the future we want to calculate the stock price. In this problem, we want to know the stock price in three years, and we have already calculated the stock price today. The stock price in three years will be:

   $P_3 = P_0(1 + g)^3 = \$37.63(1 + .05)^3 = \$43.56$

   And the stock price in 15 years will be:

   $P_{15} = P_0(1 + g)^{15} = \$37.63(1 + .05)^{15} = \$78.22$

2. We need to find the required return of the stock. Using the constant growth model, we can solve the equation for *R*. Doing so, we find:

   $R = (D_1 / P_0) + g = (\$3.20 / \$63.50) + .06 = .1104$, or 11.04%

3.  The dividend yield is the dividend next year divided by the current price, so the dividend yield is:

    Dividend yield = $D_1 / P_0$ = \$3.20 / \$63.50 = .0504, or 5.04%

    The capital gains yield, or percentage increase in the stock price, is the same as the dividend growth rate, so:

    Capital gains yield = 6%

4.  Using the constant growth model, we find the price of the stock today is:

    $P_0 = D_1 / (R - g)$ = \$2.65 / (.11 − .0475) = \$42.40

5.  The required return of a stock is made up of two parts: The dividend yield and the capital gains yield. So, the required return of this stock is:

    $R$ = Dividend yield + Capital gains yield = .043 + .064 = .1070, or 10.70%

6.  We know the stock has a required return of 11.5 percent, and the dividend and capital gains yield are equal, so:

    Dividend yield = 1/2(.115) = .0575 = Capital gains yield

    Now we know both the dividend yield and capital gains yield. The dividend is simply the stock price times the dividend yield, so:

    $D_1$ = .0575(\$72) = \$4.14

    This is the dividend next year. The question asks for the dividend this year. Using the relationship between the dividend this year and the dividend next year:

    $D_1 = D_0(1 + g)$

    We can solve for the dividend that was just paid:

    \$4.14 = $D_0$ (1 + .0575)

    $D_0$ = \$4.14 / 1.0575 = \$3.91

7.  The price of any financial instrument is the PV of the future cash flows. The future dividends of this stock are an annuity for 12 years, so the price of the stock is the PVA, which will be:

    $P_0$ = \$9(PVIFA$_{10\%,12}$) = \$61.32

8.  The price of a share of preferred stock is the dividend divided by the required return. This is the same equation as the constant growth model, with a dividend growth rate of zero percent. Remember that most preferred stock pays a fixed dividend, so the growth rate is zero. Using this equation, we find the price per share of the preferred stock is:

    $R = D/P_0$ = \$5.90/\$87 = .0678, or 6.78%

**9.** The growth rate of earnings is the return on equity times the retention ratio, so:

$g = ROE \times b$
$g = .16(.80)$
$g = .1280$, or 12.80%

To find next year's earnings, we simply multiply the current earnings times one plus the growth rate, so:

Next year's earnings = Current earnings$(1 + g)$
Next year's earnings = $34,000,000(1 + .1280)$
Next year's earnings = $38,352,000

**10.** Using the equation to calculate the price of a share of stock with the PE ratio:

P = Benchmark PE ratio × EPS

So, with a PE ratio of 18, we find:

P = 18($1.75)
P = $31.50

And with a PE ratio of 21, we find:

P = 21($1.75)
P = $36.75

*Intermediate*

**11.** This stock has a constant growth rate of dividends, but the required return changes twice. To find the value of the stock today, we will begin by finding the price of the stock at Year 6, when both the dividend growth rate and the required return are stable forever. The price of the stock in Year 6 will be the dividend in Year 7, divided by the required return minus the growth rate in dividends. So:

$P_6 = D_6 (1 + g) / (R - g) = D_0 (1 + g)^7 / (R - g) = \$3.10(1.06)^7 / (.11 - .06) = \$93.23$

Now we can find the price of the stock in Year 3. We need to find the price here since the required return changes at that time. The price of the stock in Year 3 is the PV of the dividends in Years 4, 5, and 6, plus the PV of the stock price in Year 6. The price of the stock in Year 3 is:

$P_3 = \$3.10(1.06)^4 / 1.13 + \$3.10(1.06)^5 / 1.13^2 + \$3.10(1.06)^6 / 1.13^3 + \$93.23 / 1.13^3$
$P_3 = \$74.37$

Finally, we can find the price of the stock today. The price today will be the PV of the dividends in Years 1, 2, and 3, plus the PV of the stock in Year 3. The price of the stock today is:

$P_0 = \$3.10(1.06) / 1.15 + \$3.10(1.06)^2 / (1.15)^2 + \$3.10(1.06)^3 / (1.15)^3 + \$74.37 / (1.15)^3$
$P_0 = \$56.82$

**12.** Here we have a stock that pays no dividends for 10 years. Once the stock begins paying dividends, it will have a constant growth rate of dividends. We can use the constant growth model at that point. It is important to remember that the general form of the constant dividend growth formula is:

$$P_t = [D_t \times (1 + g)] / (R - g)$$

This means that since we will use the dividend in Year 10, we will be finding the stock price in Year 9. The dividend growth model is similar to the PVA and the PV of a perpetuity: The equation gives you the PV one period before the first payment. So, the price of the stock in Year 9 will be:

$$P_9 = D_{10} / (R - g) = \$15.00 / (.13 - .055) = \$200$$

The price of the stock today is simply the PV of the stock price in the future. We simply discount the future stock price at the required return. The price of the stock today will be:

$$P_0 = \$200 / 1.13^9 = \$66.58$$

**13.** The price of a stock is the PV of the future dividends. This stock is paying five dividends, so the price of the stock is the PV of these dividends using the required return. The price of the stock is:

$$P_0 = \$15 / 1.12 + \$18 / 1.12^2 + \$21 / 1.12^3 + \$24 / 1.12^4 + \$27 / 1.12^5 = \$73.26$$

**14.** With differential dividends, we find the price of the stock when the dividends level off at a constant growth rate, and then find the PV of the future stock price, plus the PV of all dividends during the differential growth period. The stock begins constant growth in Year 5, so we can find the price of the stock in Year 4, one year before the constant dividend growth begins, as:

$$P_4 = D_4 (1 + g) / (R - g) = \$2.75(1.05) / (.13 - .05) = \$36.09$$

The price of the stock today is the PV of the first four dividends, plus the PV of the Year 4 stock price. So, the price of the stock today will be:

$$P_0 = \$10 / 1.13 + \$7 / 1.13^2 + \$6 / 1.13^3 + (\$2.75 + 36.09) / 1.13^4 = \$42.31$$

**15.** With differential dividends, we find the price of the stock when the dividends level off at a constant growth rate, and then find the PV of the future stock price, plus the PV of all dividends during the differential growth period. The stock begins constant growth in Year 4, so we can find the price of the stock in Year 3, one year before the constant dividend growth begins as:

$$P_3 = D_3 (1 + g) / (R - g) = D_0 (1 + g_1)^3 (1 + g_2) / (R - g_2) = \$2.80(1.20)^3(1.05) / (.12 - .05) = \$72.58$$

The price of the stock today is the PV of the first three dividends, plus the PV of the Year 3 stock price. The price of the stock today will be:

$$P_0 = \$2.80(1.20) / 1.12 + \$2.80(1.20)^2 / 1.12^2 + \$2.80(1.20)^3 / 1.12^3 + \$72.58 / 1.12^3$$
$$P_0 = \$61.32$$

**16.** Here we need to find the dividend next year for a stock experiencing differential growth. We know the stock price, the dividend growth rates, and the required return, but not the dividend. First, we need to realize that the dividend in Year 3 is the current dividend times the FVIF. The dividend in Year 3 will be:

$$D_3 = D_0 (1.30)^3$$

And the dividend in Year 4 will be the dividend in Year 3 times one plus the growth rate, or:

$$D_4 = D_0 (1.30)^3 (1.18)$$

The stock begins constant growth after the $4^{th}$ dividend is paid, so we can find the price of the stock in Year 4 as the dividend in Year 5, divided by the required return minus the growth rate. The equation for the price of the stock in Year 4 is:

$$P_4 = D_4 (1 + g) / (R - g)$$

Now we can substitute the previous dividend in Year 4 into this equation as follows:

$$P_4 = D_0 (1 + g_1)^3 (1 + g_2) (1 + g_3) / (R - g_3)$$

$$P_4 = D_0 (1.30)^3 (1.18) (1.08) / (.11 - .08) = 93.33 D_0$$

When we solve this equation, we find that the stock price in Year 4 is 93.33 times as large as the dividend today. Now we need to find the equation for the stock price today. The stock price today is the PV of the dividends in Years 1, 2, 3, and 4, plus the PV of the Year 4 price. So:

$$P_0 = D_0(1.30)/1.11 + D_0(1.30)^2/1.11^2 + D_0(1.30)^3/1.11^3 + D_0(1.30)^3(1.18)/1.11^4 + 93.33D_0/1.11^4$$

We can factor out $D_0$ in the equation, and combine the last two terms. Doing so, we get:

$$P_0 = \$65.00 = D_0\{1.30/1.11 + 1.30^2/1.11^2 + 1.30^3/1.11^3 + [(1.30)^3(1.18) + 93.33] / 1.11^4\}$$

Reducing the equation even further by solving all of the terms in the braces, we get:

$$\$65 = \$74.43 D_0$$

$$D_0 = \$65.00 / \$74.43 = \$0.87$$

This is the dividend today, so the projected dividend for the next year will be:

$$D_1 = \$0.87(1.30) = \$1.14$$

**17.** The constant growth model can be applied even if the dividends are declining by a constant percentage, just make sure to recognize the negative growth. So, the price of the stock today will be:

$$P_0 = D_0 (1 + g) / (R - g) = \$9(1 - .04) / [(.11 - (-.04)] = \$57.60$$

**18.** We are given the stock price, the dividend growth rate, and the required return, and are asked to find the dividend. Using the constant dividend growth model, we get:

$$P_0 = \$58.32 = D_0\,(1 + g) / (R - g)$$

Solving this equation for the dividend gives us:

$$D_0 = \$58.32(.115 - .05) / (1.05) = \$3.61$$

**19.** The price of a share of preferred stock is the dividend payment divided by the required return. We know the dividend payment in Year 5, so we can find the price of the stock in Year 4, one year before the first dividend payment. Doing so, we get:

$$P_4 = \$8.00 / .056 = \$142.86$$

The price of the stock today is the PV of the stock price in the future, so the price today will be:

$$P_0 = \$142.86 / (1.056)^4 = \$114.88$$

**20.** The dividend yield is the annual dividend divided by the stock price, so:

Dividend yield = Dividend / Stock price
.019 = Dividend / $26.18
Dividend = $0.50

The "Net Chg" of the stock shows the stock decreased by $0.13 on this day, so the closing stock price yesterday was:

Yesterday's closing price = $26.18 – (–0.13) = $26.31

To find the net income, we need to find the EPS. The stock quote tells us the P/E ratio for the stock is 23. Since we know the stock price as well, we can use the P/E ratio to solve for EPS as follows:

P/E = 23 = Stock price / EPS = $26.18 / EPS

EPS = $26.18 / 23 = $1.138

We know that EPS is just the total net income divided by the number of shares outstanding, so:

EPS = NI / Shares = $1.138 = NI / 25,000,000

NI = $1.138(25,000,000) = $28,456,522

**21.** To find the number of shares owned, we can divide the amount invested by the stock price. The share price of any financial asset is the present value of the cash flows, so, to find the price of the stock we need to find the cash flows. The cash flows are the two dividend payments plus the sale price. We also need to find the aftertax dividends since the assumption is all dividends are taxed at the same rate for all investors. The aftertax dividends are the dividends times one minus the tax rate, so:

Year 1 aftertax dividend = $2.25(1 − .28)
Year 1 aftertax dividend = $1.62

Year 2 aftertax dividend = $2.40(1 − .28)
Year 2 aftertax dividend = $1.73

We can now discount all cash flows from the stock at the required return. Doing so, we find the price of the stock is:

$P = \$1.62/1.15 + \$1.73/(1.15)^2 + \$65/(1+.15)^3$
$P = \$45.45$

The number of shares owned is the total investment divided by the stock price, which is:

Shares owned = $100,000 / $45.45
Shares owned = 2,200.03

**22.** Here we have a stock paying a constant dividend for a fixed period, and an increasing dividend thereafter. We need to find the present value of the two different cash flows using the appropriate quarterly interest rate. The constant dividend is an annuity, so the present value of these dividends is:

$PVA = C(PVIFA_{R,t})$
$PVA = \$0.80(PVIFA_{2.5\%,12})$
$PVA = \$8.21$

Now we can find the present value of the dividends beyond the constant dividend phase. Using the present value of a growing annuity equation, we find:

$P_{12} = D_{13} / (R − g)$
$P_{12} = \$0.80(1 + .01) / (.025 − .01)$
$P_{12} = \$53.87$

This is the price of the stock immediately after it has paid the last constant dividend. So, the present value of the future price is:

$PV = \$53.87 / (1 + .025)^{12}$
$PV = \$40.05$

The price today is the sum of the present value of the two cash flows, so:

$P_0 = \$8.21 + 40.05$
$P_0 = \$48.26$

**23.** Here we need to find the dividend next year for a stock with nonconstant growth. We know the stock price, the dividend growth rates, and the required return, but not the dividend. First, we need to realize that the dividend in Year 3 is the constant dividend times the FVIF. The dividend in Year 3 will be:

$D_3 = D(1.04)$

The equation for the stock price will be the present value of the constant dividends, plus the present value of the future stock price, or:

$P_0 = D / 1.11 + D/1.11^2 + D(1.04)/(.11 - .04)]/1.11^2$
$\$45 = D / 1.11 + D/1.11^2 + D(1.04)/(.11 - .04)]/1.11^2$

We can factor out $D_0$ in the equation. Doing so, we get:

$\$45 = D\{1/1.11 + 1/1.11^2 + [(1.04)/(.11 - .04)] / 1.11^2\}$

Reducing the equation even further by solving all of the terms in the braces, we get:

$\$45 = D(13.7709)$

$D = \$45 / 13.7709 = \$3.27$

**24.** The required return of a stock consists of two components, the capital gains yield and the dividend yield. In the constant dividend growth model (growing perpetuity equation), the capital gains yield is the same as the dividend growth rate, or algebraically:

$R = D_1/P_0 + g$

We can find the dividend growth rate by the growth rate equation, or:

$g = ROE \times b$
$g = .13 \times .70$
$g = .0910$, or 9.10%

This is also the growth rate in dividends. To find the current dividend, we can use the information provided about the net income, shares outstanding, and payout ratio. The total dividends paid is the net income times the payout ratio. To find the dividend per share, we can divide the total dividends paid by the number of shares outstanding. So:

Dividend per share = (Net income × Payout ratio) / Shares outstanding
Dividend per share = ($18,000,000 × .30) / 2,000,000
Dividend per share = $2.70

Now we can use the initial equation for the required return. We must remember that the equation uses the dividend in one year, so:

$R = D_1/P_0 + g$
$R = \$2.70(1 + .0910)/\$93 + .0910$
$R = .1227$, or 12.27%

**25.** First, we need to find the annual dividend growth rate over the past four years. To do this, we can use the future value of a lump sum equation, and solve for the interest rate. Doing so, we find the dividend growth rate over the past four years was:

$FV = PV(1 + R)^t$
$\$1.77 = \$1.35(1 + R)^4$
$R = (\$1.77 / \$1.35)^{1/4} - 1$
$R = .0701$, or 7.01%

We know the dividend will grow at this rate for five years before slowing to a constant rate indefinitely. So, the dividend amount in seven years will be:

$D_7 = D_0(1 + g_1)^5(1 + g_2)^2$
$D_7 = \$1.77(1 + .0701)^5(1 + .05)^2$
$D_7 = \$2.74$

**26.**   *a.*   We can find the price of all the outstanding company stock by using the dividends the same way we would value an individual share. Since earnings are equal to dividends, and there is no growth, the value of the company's stock today is the present value of a perpetuity, so:

$P = D / R$
$P = \$950,000 / .12$
$P = \$7,916,666.67$

The price-earnings ratio is the stock price divided by the current earnings, so the price-earnings ratio of each company with no growth is:

P/E = Price / Earnings
P/E = \$7,916,666.67 / \$950,000
P/E = 8.33 times

   *b.*   Since the earnings have increased, the price of the stock will increase. The new price of the outstanding company stock is:

$P = D / R$
$P = (\$950,000 + 100,000) / .12$
$P = \$8,750,000$

The price-earnings ratio is the stock price divided by the current earnings, so the price-earnings with the increased earnings is:

P/E = Price / Earnings
P/E = \$8,750,000 / \$950,000
P/E = 9.21 times

   *c.*   Since the earnings have increased, the price of the stock will increase. The new price of the outstanding company stock is:

$P = D / R$
$P = (\$950,000 + 200,000) / .12$
$P = \$9,583,333.33$

The price-earnings ratio is the stock price divided by the current earnings, so the price-earnings with the increased earnings is:

P/E = Price / Earnings
P/E = \$9,583,333.33 / \$950,000
P/E = 10.09 times

27.  *a.*  If the company does not make any new investments, the stock price will be the present value of the constant perpetual dividends. In this case, all earnings are paid as dividends, so, applying the perpetuity equation, we get:

P = Dividend / R
P = \$9.40 / .12
P = \$78.33

*b.*  The investment is a one-time investment that creates an increase in EPS for two years. To calculate the new stock price, we need the cash cow price plus the NPVGO. In this case, the NPVGO is simply the present value of the investment plus the present value of the increases in EPS. So, the NPVGO will be:

$NPVGO = C_1 / (1 + R) + C_2 / (1 + R)^2 + C_3 / (1 + R)^3$
$NPVGO = -\$1.95 / 1.12 + \$2.75 / 1.12^2 + \$3.05 / 1.12^3$
NPVGO = \$2.62

So, the price of the stock if the company undertakes the investment opportunity will be:

P = \$78.33 + 2.62
P = \$80.96

*c.*  After the project is over, and the earnings increase no longer exists, the price of the stock will revert back to \$78.33, the value of the company as a cash cow.

28.  *a.*  The price of the stock is the present value of the dividends. Since earnings are equal to dividends, we can find the present value of the earnings to calculate the stock price. Also, since we are excluding taxes, the earnings will be the revenues minus the costs. We simply need to find the present value of all future earnings to find the price of the stock. The present value of the revenues is:

$PV_{Revenue} = C_1 / (R - g)$
$PV_{Revenue} = \$7,500,000(1 + .05) / (.13 - .05)$
$PV_{Revenue} = \$98,437,500$

And the present value of the costs will be:

$PV_{Costs} = C_1 / (R - g)$
$PV_{Costs} = \$3,400,000(1 + .05) / (.13 - .05)$
$PV_{Costs} = \$44,625,000$

Since there are no taxes, the present value of the company's earnings and dividends will be:

$PV_{Dividends} = \$98,437,500 - 44,625,000$
$PV_{Dividends} = \$53,812,500$

Note that since revenues and costs increase at the same rate, we could have found the present value of future dividends as the present value of current dividends. Doing so, we find:

$D_0 = Revenue_0 - Costs_0$
$D_0 = \$7,500,000 - 3,400,000$
$D_0 = \$4,100,000$

Now, applying the growing perpetuity equation, we find:

$PV_{Dividends} = C_1 / (R - g)$
$PV_{Dividends} = \$4,100,000(1 + .05) / (.13 - .05)$
$PV_{Dividends} = \$53,812,500$

This is the same answer we found previously. The price per share of stock is the total value of the company's stock divided by the shares outstanding, or:

$P = $ Value of all stock / Shares outstanding
$P = \$53,812,500 / 1,000,000$
$P = \$53.81$

b.  The value of a share of stock in a company is the present value of its current operations, plus the present value of growth opportunities. To find the present value of the growth opportunities, we need to discount the cash outlay in Year 1 back to the present, and find the value today of the increase in earnings. The increase in earnings is a perpetuity, which we must discount back to today. So, the value of the growth opportunity is:

$NPVGO = C_0 + C_1 / (1 + R) + (C_2 / R) / (1 + R)$
$NPVGO = -\$17,000,000 - \$6,000,000 / (1 + .13) + (\$4,200,000 / .13) / (1 + .13)$
$NPVGO = \$6,281,143.64$

To find the value of the growth opportunity on a per share basis, we must divide this amount by the number of shares outstanding, which gives us:

$NPVGO_{Per\ share} = \$6,821,143.64 / 1,000,000$
$NPVGO_{Per\ share} = \$6.28$

The stock price will increase by $6.28 per share. The new stock price will be:

New stock price = $53.81 + 6.28
New stock price = $60.09

**29.** *a.* If the company continues its current operations, it will not grow, so we can value the company as a cash cow. The total value of the company as a cash cow is the present value of the future earnings, which are a perpetuity, so:

Cash cow value of company = $C / R$
Cash cow value of company = $71,000,000 / .12
Cash cow value of company = $591,666,666.67

The value per share is the total value of the company divided by the shares outstanding, so:

Share price = $591,666,666.67 / 15,000,000
Share price = $39.44

*b.* To find the value of the investment, we need to find the NPV of the growth opportunities. The initial cash flow occurs today, so it does not need to be discounted. The earnings growth is a perpetuity. Using the present value of a perpetuity equation will give us the value of the earnings growth one period from today, so we need to discount this back to today. The NPVGO of the investment opportunity is:

NPVGO = $C_0 + C_1 / (1 + R) + (C_2 / R) / (1 + R)$
NPVGO = –$16,000,000 – 5,000,000 / (1 + .12) + ($11,000,000 / .12) / (1 + .12)
NPVGO = $61,380,952.38

*c.* The price of a share of stock is the cash cow value plus the NPVGO. We have already calculated the NPVGO for the entire project, so we need to find the NPVGO on a per share basis. The NPVGO on a per share basis is the NPVGO of the project divided by the shares outstanding, which is:

NPVGO per share = $61,380,952.38 / 15,000,000
NPVGO per share = $4.09

This means the per share stock price if the company undertakes the project is:

Share price = Cash cow price + NPVGO per share
Share price = $39.44 + 4.09
Share price = $43.54

**30.** *a.* Using the equation to calculate the price of a share of stock with the PE ratio:

P = Benchmark PE ratio × EPS

So, with a PE ratio of 21, we find:

P = 21($2.35)
P = $49.35

*b.* First, we need to find the earnings per share next year, which will be:

$EPS_1 = EPS_0(1 + g)$
$EPS_1$ = $2.35(1 + .07)
$EPS_1$ = $2.51

Using the equation to calculate the price of a share of stock with the PE ratio:

$P_1$ = Benchmark PE ratio × $EPS_1$
$P_1$ = 21($2.51)
$P_1$ = $52.80

c. To find the implied return over the next year, we calculate the return as:

$R = (P_1 - P_0) / P_0$
$R = ($52.80 - 49.35) / $49.35$
$R$ = .07, or 7%

Notice that the return is the same as the growth rate in earnings. Assuming a stock pays no dividends and the PE ratio is constant, this will always be true when using price ratios to evaluate the price of a share of stock.

31. We need to find the enterprise value of the company. We can calculate EBITDA as sales minus costs, so:

EBITDA = Sales – Costs
EBITDA = $28,000,000 – 12,000,000
EBITDA = $16,000,000

Solving the EV/EBITDA multiple for enterprise value, we find:

Enterprise value = $16,000,000(7.5)
Enterprise value = $120,000,000

The total value of equity is the enterprise value minus any outstanding debt and cash, so:

Equity value = Enterprise value – Debt – Cash
Equity value = $120,000,000 – 54,000,000 – 18,000,000
Equity value = $48,000,000

So, the price per share is:

Stock price = $48,000,000 / 950,000
Stock price = $50.53

**32.** *a.* To value the stock today, we first need to calculate the cash flows for the next 6 years. The sales, costs, and net investment all grow by same rate, namely 14 percent, 12 percent, 10 percent, 8 percent, respectively, for the following 4 years, then 6 percent indefinitely. So, the cash flows for each year will be:

|  | Year 1 | Year 2 | Year 3 | Year 4 | Year 5 | Year 6 |
|---|---|---|---|---|---|---|
| Sales | $145,000,000 | $165,300,000 | $185,136,000 | $203,649,600 | $219,941,568 | $233,138,062 |
| Costs | 81,000,000 | 92,340,000 | 103,420,800 | 113,762,880 | 122,863,910 | 130,235,745 |
| EBT | $ 64,000,000 | $ 72,960,000 | $ 81,715,200 | $ 89,886,720 | $ 97,077,658 | $102,902,317 |
| Taxes | 25,600,000 | 29,184,000 | 32,686,080 | 35,954,688 | 38,831,063 | 41,160,927 |
| Net income | $ 38,400,000 | $ 43,776,000 | $ 49,029,120 | $ 53,932,032 | $ 58,246,595 | $ 61,741,390 |
| Investment | 15,000,000 | 17,100,000 | 19,152,000 | 21,067,200 | 22,752,576 | 24,117,731 |
| Cash flow | $ 23,400,000 | $ 26,676,000 | $ 29,877,120 | $ 32,864,832 | $ 35,494,019 | $ 37,623,660 |

To find the terminal value of the company in Year 6, we can discount the Year 7 cash flows as a growing perpetuity, which will be:

Terminal value = $37,623,660(1 + .06) / (.13 – .06)
Terminal value = $569,729,704

So, the value of the company today is:

Company value today = $23,400,000 / 1.13 + $26,676,000 / $1.13^2$ + $29,877,120 / $1.13^3$
    + $32,864,832 / $1.13^4$ + 35,494,019 / $1.13^5$ + ($37,623,660 + 569,729,704) / $1.13^6$
Company value today = $393,449,950

Dividing the company value by the shares outstanding to get the share price we get:

Share price = $393,449,950 / 5,500,000
Share price = $71.54

*b.* In this case, we are going to use the PE multiple to find the terminal value. All of the cash flows from part *a* will remain the same. So, the terminal value in Year 6 is:

Terminal value = 11($61,741,390)
Terminal value = $679,155,293

Under this assumption for the terminal value, the value of the company today is:

Company value today = $23,400,000 / 1.13 + $26,676,000 / $1.13^2$ + $29,877,120 / $1.13^3$
    + $32,864,832 / $1.13^4$ + 35,494,019 / $1.13^5$ + ($37,623,660 + 679,155,293) / $1.13^6$
Company value today = $446,009,087

Dividing the company value by the shares outstanding to get the share price we get:

Share price = $446,009,087 / 5,500,000
Share price = $81.09

*Challenge*

33. We are asked to find the dividend yield and capital gains yield for each of the stocks. All of the stocks have a 17 percent required return, which is the sum of the dividend yield and the capital gains yield. To find the components of the total return, we need to find the stock price for each stock. Using this stock price and the dividend, we can calculate the dividend yield. The capital gains yield for the stock will be the total return (required return) minus the dividend yield.

W:   $P_0 = D_0(1 + g) / (R - g) = \$3.50(1.085)/(.17 - .085) = \$44.68$

Dividend yield $= D_1/P_0 = 3.50(1.085)/\$44.68 = .085$, or 8.5%

Capital gains yield $= .17 - .085 = .085$, or 8.5%

X:   $P_0 = D_0(1 + g) / (R - g) = \$3.50/(.17 - 0) = \$20.59$

Dividend yield $= D_1/P_0 = \$3.50/\$20.59 = .17$, or 17%

Capital gains yield $= .17 - .17 = 0\%$

Y:   $P_0 = D_0(1 + g) / (R - g) = \$3.50(1 - .05)/(.17 + .05) = \$15.11$

Dividend yield $= D_1/P_0 = \$3.50(0.95)/\$15.11 = .22$, or 22%

Capital gains yield $= .17 - .22 = -.05$, or –5%

Z:   $P_2 = D_2(1 + g) / (R - g) = D_0(1 + g_1)^2(1 + g_2)/(R - g_2) = \$3.50(1.30)^2(1.08)/(.17 - .08)$
     $P_2 = \$70.98$

   $P_0 = \$3.50(1.30) / (1.17) + \$3.50 (1.30)^2 / (1.17)^2 + \$70.98 / (1.17)^2$
   $P_0 = \$60.06$

Dividend yield $= D_1/P_0 = \$3.50(1.30)/\$60.06 = .0758$, or 7.58%

Capital gains yield $= .17 - .0758 = .0942$, or 9.42%

In all cases, the required return is 17 percent, but the return is distributed differently between current income and capital gains. High-growth stocks have an appreciable capital gains component but a relatively small current income yield; conversely, mature, negative-growth stocks provide a high current income but also price depreciation over time.

34. *a.*   Using the constant growth model, the price of the stock paying annual dividends will be:

   $P_0 = D_0(1 + g) / (R - g) = \$3.20(1.05)/(.11 - .05) = \$56.00$

b.  If the company pays quarterly dividends instead of annual dividends, the quarterly dividend will be one-fourth of annual dividend, or:

Quarterly dividend: $3.20(1.05)/4 = $0.84

To find the equivalent annual dividend, we must assume that the quarterly dividends are reinvested at the required return. We can then use this interest rate to find the equivalent annual dividend. In other words, when we receive the quarterly dividend, we reinvest it at the required return on the stock. So, the effective quarterly rate is:

Effective quarterly rate: $1.11^{.25} - 1 = .0264$, or 2.64%

The effective annual dividend will be the FVA of the quarterly dividend payments at the effective quarterly required return. In this case, the effective annual dividend will be:

Effective $D_1 = $0.84(FVIFA_{2.64\%,4}) = $3.50$

Now, we can use the constant growth model to find the current stock price as:

$P_0 = $3.50/(.11 - .05) = $58.26$

Note that we cannot simply find the quarterly effective required return and growth rate to find the value of the stock. This would assume the dividends increased each quarter, not each year.

35. a.  If the company does not make any new investments, the stock price will be the present value of the constant perpetual dividends. In this case, all earnings are paid as dividends, so, applying the perpetuity equation, we get:

P = Dividend / R
P = $8.50 / .12
P = $70.83

b.  The investment occurs every year in the growth opportunity, so the opportunity is a growing perpetuity. So, we first need to find the growth rate. The growth rate is:

g = Retention Ratio × Return on Retained Earnings
g = 0.20 × 0.10
g = 0.02, or 2.00%

Next, we need to calculate the NPV of the investment. During Year 3, 20 percent of the earnings will be reinvested. Therefore, $1.70 is invested ($8.50 × .20). One year later, the shareholders receive a return of 10 percent on the investment, or $0.17 ($1.70 × .10), in perpetuity. The perpetuity formula values that stream as of Year 3. Since the investment opportunity will continue indefinitely and grows at 2 percent, apply the growing perpetuity formula to calculate the NPV of the investment as of Year 2. Discount that value back two years to today.

NPVGO = [(Investment + Return / R) / (R − g)] / (1 + R)^2
NPVGO = [(−$1.70 + $0.17 / .12) / (0.12 − 0.02)] / (1.12)^2
NPVGO = −$2.26

The value of the stock is the PV of the firm without making the investment plus the NPV of the investment, or:

P = PV(EPS) + NPVGO
P = $70.83 – 2.26
P = $68.57

c. Zero percent! There is no retention ratio which would make the project profitable for the company. If the company retains more earnings, the growth rate of the earnings on the investment will increase, but the project will still not be profitable. Since the return of the project is less than the required return on the company stock, the project is never worthwhile. In fact, the more the company retains and invests in the project, the less valuable the stock becomes.

**36.** Here we have a stock with differential growth, but the dividend growth changes every year for the first four years. We can find the price of the stock in Year 3 since the dividend growth rate is constant after the third dividend. The price of the stock in Year 3 will be the dividend in Year 4, divided by the required return minus the constant dividend growth rate. So, the price in Year 3 will be:

$P_3 = \$3.85(1.20)(1.15)(1.10)(1.05) / (.13 - .05) = \$76.71$

The price of the stock today will be the PV of the first three dividends, plus the PV of the stock price in Year 3, so:

$P_0 = \$3.85(1.20)/(1.13) + \$3.85(1.20)(1.15)/1.13^2 + \$3.85(1.20)(1.15)(1.10)/1.13^3$
     $+ \$76.71/1.13^3$
$P_0 = \$65.46$

**37.** Here we want to find the required return that makes the PV of the dividends equal to the current stock price. The equation for the stock price is:

$P = \$3.85(1.20)/(1 + R) + \$3.85(1.20)(1.15)/(1 + R)^2 + \$3.85(1.20)(1.15)(1.10)/(1 + R)^3$
   $+ [\$3.85(1.20)(1.15)(1.10)(1.05)/(R - .05)]/(1 + R)^3 = \$78.43$

We need to find the roots of this equation. Using spreadsheet, trial and error, or a calculator with a root solving function, we find that:

$R = .1169$, or 11.69%

**38.** In this problem, growth is occurring from two different sources: The learning curve and the new project. We need to separately compute the value from the two different sources. First, we will compute the value from the learning curve, which will increase at 5 percent. All earnings are paid out as dividends, so we find the earnings per share are:

$EPS_1$ = Earnings/total number of outstanding shares
$EPS_1 = (\$18,000,000 \times 1.05) / 7,500,000$
$EPS_1 = \$2.52$

From the NPVGO model:

$P = E/(R - g) + \text{NPVGO}$
$P = \$2.52/(0.10 - 0.05) + \text{NPVGO}$
$P = \$50.40 + \text{NPVGO}$

Now we can compute the NPVGO of the new project to be launched two years from now. The earnings per share two years from now will be:

$\text{EPS}_2 = \$2.52(1 + .05)$
$\text{EPS}_2 = \$2.646$

Therefore, the initial investment in the new project will be:

Initial investment = .30($2.646)
Initial investment = $0.79

The earnings per share of the new project is a perpetuity, with an annual cash flow of:

Increased EPS from project = $6,500,000 / 7,500,000 shares
Increased EPS from project = $0.87

So, the value of all future earnings in year 2, one year before the company realizes the earnings, is:

$PV = \$0.87 / .10$
$PV = \$8.67$

Now, we can find the NPVGO per share of the investment opportunity in year 2, which will be:

$\text{NPVGO}_2 = -\$0.79 + 8.67$
$\text{NPVGO}_2 = \$7.87$

The value of the NPVGO today will be:

$\text{NPVGO} = \$7.87 / (1 + .10)^2$
$\text{NPVGO} = \$6.51$

Plugging in the NPVGO model we get;

$P = \$50.40 + 6.51$
$P = \$56.91$

Note that you could also value the company and the project with the values given, and then divide the final answer by the shares outstanding. The final answer would be the same.

# CHAPTER 10
# SOME LESSONS FROM CAPITAL MARKET HISTORY

## Answers to Concepts Review and Critical Thinking Questions

1.  They all wish they had! Since they didn't, it must have been the case that the stellar performance was not foreseeable, at least not by most.

2.  As in the previous question, it's easy to see after the fact that the investment was terrible, but it probably wasn't so easy ahead of time.

3.  No, stocks are riskier. Some investors are highly risk averse, and the extra possible return doesn't attract them relative to the extra risk.

4.  Unlike gambling, the stock market is a positive sum game; everybody can win. Also, speculators provide liquidity to markets and thus help to promote efficiency.

5.  T-bill rates were highest in the early eighties. This was during a period of high inflation and is consistent with the Fisher effect.

6.  Before the fact, for most assets, the risk premium will be positive; investors demand compensation over and above the risk-free return to invest their money in the risky asset. After the fact, the observed risk premium can be negative if the asset's nominal return is unexpectedly low, the risk-free return is unexpectedly high, or if some combination of these two events occurs.

7.  Yes, the stock prices are currently the same. Below is a diagram that depicts the stocks' price movements. Two years ago, each stock had the same price, $P_0$. Over the first year, General Materials' stock price increased by 10 percent, or $(1.1) \times P_0$. Standard Fixtures' stock price declined by 10 percent, or $(0.9) \times P_0$. Over the second year, General Materials' stock price decreased by 10 percent, or $(0.9)(1.1) \times P_0$, while Standard Fixtures' stock price increased by 10 percent, or $(1.1)(0.9) \times P_0$. Today, each of the stocks is worth 99 percent of its original value.

|                   | 2 years ago | 1 year ago | Today        |             |
|-------------------|-------------|------------|--------------|-------------|
| General Materials | $P_0$       | $(1.1)P_0$ | $(1.1)(0.9)P_0$ | $= (0.99)P_0$ |
| Standard Fixtures | $P_0$       | $(0.9)P_0$ | $(0.9)(1.1)P_0$ | $= (0.99)P_0$ |

8.  The stock prices are not the same. The return quoted for each stock is the arithmetic return, not the geometric return. The geometric return tells you the wealth increase from the beginning of the period to the end of the period, assuming the asset had the same return each year. As such, it is a better measure of ending wealth. To see this, assuming each stock had a beginning price of $100 per share, the ending price for each stock would be:

    Lake Minerals ending price = $100(1.10)(1.10) = $121.00
    Small Town Furniture ending price = $100(1.25)(.95) = $118.75

10-1

Whenever there is any variance in returns, the asset with the larger variance will always have the greater difference between the arithmetic and geometric return.

9. To calculate an arithmetic return, you simply sum the returns and divide by the number of returns. As such, arithmetic returns do not account for the effects of compounding. Geometric returns do account for the effects of compounding. As an investor, the more important return of an asset is the geometric return.

10. Risk premiums are about the same whether or not we account for inflation. The reason is that risk premiums are the difference between two returns, so inflation essentially nets out. Returns, risk premiums, and volatility would all be lower than we estimated because aftertax returns are smaller than pretax returns.

## Solutions to Questions and Problems

*NOTE: All end of chapter problems were solved using a spreadsheet. Many problems require multiple steps. Due to space and readability constraints, when these intermediate steps are included in this solutions manual, rounding may appear to have occurred. However, the final answer for each problem is found without rounding during any step in the problem.*

### Basic

1. The return of any asset is the increase in price, plus any dividends or cash flows, all divided by the initial price. The return of this stock is:

   $R = [(\$86 - 75) + 1.20] / \$75$
   $R = .1627$, or $16.27\%$

2. The dividend yield is the dividend divided by price at the beginning of the period, so:

   Dividend yield = \$1.20 / \$75
   Dividend yield = .0160, or 1.60%

   And the capital gains yield is the increase in price divided by the initial price, so:

   Capital gains yield = (\$86 − 75) / \$75
   Capital gains yield = .1467, or 14.67%

3. Using the equation for total return, we find:

   $R = [(\$67 - 75) + 1.20] / \$75$
   $R = -.0907$, or $-9.07\%$

   And the dividend yield and capital gains yield are:

   Dividend yield = \$1.20 / \$75
   Dividend yield = .0160, or 1.60%

Capital gains yield = ($67 – 75) / $75
Capital gains yield = –.1067, or –10.67%

Here's a question for you: Can the dividend yield ever be negative? No, that would mean you were paying the company for the privilege of owning the stock. It has happened on bonds.

4.   The total dollar return is the change in price plus the coupon payment, so:

Total dollar return = $1,063 – 1,040 + 60
Total dollar return = $83

The total nominal percentage return of the bond is:

$R$ = [($1,063 – 1,040) + 60] / $1,040
$R$ = .0798, or 7.98%

Notice here that we could have simply used the total dollar return of $83 in the numerator of this equation.

Using the Fisher equation, the real return was:

$(1 + R) = (1 + r)(1 + h)$

$r$ = (1.0798 / 1.030) – 1
$r$ = .0484, or 4.84%

5.   The nominal return is the stated return, which is 11.80 percent. Using the Fisher equation, the real return was:

$(1 + R) = (1 + r)(1 + h)$

$r$ = (1.1180)/(1.031) – 1
$r$ = .0844, or 8.44%

6.   Using the Fisher equation, the real returns for government and corporate bonds were:

$(1 + R) = (1 + r)(1 + h)$

$r_G$ = 1.061/1.031 – 1
$r_G$ = .0291, or 2.91%

$r_C$ = 1.064/1.031 – 1
$r_C$ = .0320, or 3.20%

**7.** The average return is the sum of the returns, divided by the number of returns. The average return for each stock was:

$$\overline{X} = \left[\sum_{i=1}^{N} x_i\right]\Big/ N = \frac{[.08 + .21 - .27 + .11 + .18]}{5} = .0620, \text{ or } 6.20\%$$

$$\overline{Y} = \left[\sum_{i=1}^{N} y_i\right]\Big/ N = \frac{[.12 + .27 - .32 + .18 + .24]}{5} = .0980, \text{ or } 9.80\%$$

We calculate the variance of each stock as:

$$\sigma_X^2 = \left[\sum_{i=1}^{N} (x_i - \bar{x})^2\right]\Big/ (N-1)$$

$$\sigma_X^2 = \frac{1}{5-1}\left\{(.08 - .062)^2 + (.21 - .062)^2 + (-.27 - .062)^2 + (.11 - .062)^2 + (.18 - .062)^2\right\} = .037170$$

$$\sigma_Y^2 = \frac{1}{5-1}\left\{(.12 - .098)^2 + (.27 - .098)^2 + (-.32 - .098)^2 + (.18 - .098)^2 + (.24 - .098)^2\right\} = .057920$$

The standard deviation is the square root of the variance, so the standard deviation of each stock is:

$\sigma_X = (.037170)^{1/2}$
$\sigma_X = .1928$, or 19.28%

$\sigma_Y = (.057920)^{1/2}$
$\sigma_Y = .2407$, or 24.07%

**8.** We will calculate the sum of the returns for each asset and the observed risk premium first. Doing so, we get:

| Year | Large co. stock return | T-bill return | Risk premium |
|------|------------------------|---------------|--------------|
| 1973 | −14.69% | 7.29% | −21.98% |
| 1974 | −26.47 | 7.99 | −34.46 |
| 1975 | 37.23 | 5.87 | 31.36 |
| 1976 | 23.93 | 5.07 | 18.86 |
| 1977 | −7.16 | 5.45 | −12.61 |
| 1978 | 6.57 | 7.64 | −1.07 |
| | 19.41% | 39.31% | −19.90% |

*a.* The average return for large company stocks over this period was:

Large company stock average return = 19.41% / 6
Large company stock average return = 3.24%

And the average return for T-bills over this period was:

T-bills average return = 39.31% / 6
T-bills average return = 6.55%

b. Using the equation for variance, we find the variance for large company stocks over this period was:

Variance = $1/5[(-.1469 - .0324)^2 + (-.2647 - .0324)^2 + (.3723 - .0324)^2 + (.2393 - .0324)^2 + (-.0716 - .0324)^2 + (.0657 - .0324)^2]$
Variance = 0.058136

And the standard deviation for large company stocks over this period was:

Standard deviation = $(0.058136)^{1/2}$
Standard deviation = 0.2411 or 24.11%

Using the equation for variance, we find the variance for T-bills over this period was:

Variance = $1/5[(.0729 - .0655)^2 + (.0799 - .0655)^2 + (.0587 - .0655)^2 + (.0507 - .0655)^2 + (.0545 - .0655)^2 + (.0764 - .0655)^2]$
Variance = 0.000153

And the standard deviation for T-bills over this period was:

Standard deviation = $(0.000153)^{1/2}$
Standard deviation = 0.0124 or 1.24%

c. The average observed risk premium over this period was:

Average observed risk premium = –19.90% / 6
Average observed risk premium = –3.32%

The variance of the observed risk premium was:

Variance = $1/5[(-.2198 - (-.0332))^2 + (-.3446 - (-.0332))^2 + (.3136 - (-.0332))^2 + (.1886 - (-.0332))^2 + (-.1261 - (-.0332))^2 + (-.0107 - (-.0332))^2]$
Variance = 0.062078

And the standard deviation of the observed risk premium was:

Standard deviation = $(0.06278)^{1/2}$
Standard deviation = 0.2492 or 24.92%

9. a. To find the average return, we sum all the returns and divide by the number of returns, so:

Arithmetic average return = (.27 +.13 + .18 – .14 + .09)/5
Arithmetic average return = .1060, or 10.60%

b.   Using the equation to calculate variance, we find:

Variance = 1/4[(.27 − .106)² + (.13 − .106)² + (.18 − .106)² + (−.14 − .106)² +
(.09 − .106)²]
Variance = 0.023430

So, the standard deviation is:

Standard deviation = (0.023430)^{1/2}
Standard deviation = 0.1531, or 15.31%

10.  a.   To calculate the average real return, we can use the average return of the asset and the average inflation rate in the Fisher equation. Doing so, we find:

$(1 + R) = (1 + r)(1 + h)$

$\bar{r} = (1.1060/1.042) − 1$
$\bar{r} = .0614$, or 6.14%

b.   The average risk premium is simply the average return of the asset, minus the average real risk-free rate, so, the average risk premium for this asset would be:

$\overline{RP} = \overline{R} − \overline{R}_f$
$\overline{RP} = .1060 − .0510$
$\overline{RP} = .0550$, or 5.50%

11.  We can find the average real risk-free rate using the Fisher equation. The average real risk-free rate was:

$(1 + R) = (1 + r)(1 + h)$

$\bar{r}_f = (1.051/1.042) − 1$
$\bar{r}_f = .0086$, or 0.86%

And to calculate the average real risk premium, we can subtract the average risk-free rate from the average real return. So, the average real risk premium was:

$\overline{rp} = \bar{r} − \bar{r}_f = 6.14\% − 0.86\%$
$\overline{rp} = 5.28\%$

12.  Apply the five-year holding-period return formula to calculate the total return of the stock over the five-year period, we find:

5-year holding-period return = [(1 + R₁)(1 + R₂)(1 + R₃)(1 + R₄)(1 + R₅)] − 1
5-year holding-period return = [(1 + .1612)(1 + .1211)(1 + .0583)(1 + .2614)(1 − .1319)] − 1
5-year holding-period return = 0.5086, or 50.86%

**13.** To find the return on the zero coupon bond, we first need to find the price of the bond today. Since one year has elapsed, the bond now has 24 years to maturity. Using semiannual compounding, the price today is:

$P_1 = \$1,000/1.045^{48}$
$P_1 = \$120.90$

There are no intermediate cash flows on a zero coupon bond, so the return is the capital gains, or:

$R = (\$120.90 - 109.83) / \$109.83$
$R = .1008$, or 10.08%

**14.** The return of any asset is the increase in price, plus any dividends or cash flows, all divided by the initial price. This preferred stock paid a dividend of \$4, so the return for the year was:

$R = (\$96.12 - 94.89 + 4.00) / \$94.89$
$R = .0551$, or 5.51%

**15.** The return of any asset is the increase in price, plus any dividends or cash flows, all divided by the initial price. This stock paid no dividend, so the return was:

$R = (\$46.21 - 43.18) / \$43.18$
$R = .0702$, or 7.02%

This is the return for three months, so the APR is:

APR = 4(7.02%)
APR = 28.07%

And the EAR is:

$EAR = (1 + .0702)^4 - 1$
EAR = .3116, or 31.16%

**16.** To find the real return each year, we will use the Fisher equation, which is:

$1 + R = (1 + r)(1 + h)$

Using this relationship for each year, we find:

|      | T-bills | Inflation | Real Return |
|------|---------|-----------|-------------|
| 1926 | 0.0330  | (0.0112)  | 0.0447      |
| 1927 | 0.0315  | (0.0226)  | 0.0554      |
| 1928 | 0.0405  | (0.0116)  | 0.0527      |
| 1929 | 0.0447  | 0.0058    | 0.0387      |
| 1930 | 0.0227  | (0.0640)  | 0.0926      |
| 1931 | 0.0115  | (0.0932)  | 0.1155      |
| 1932 | 0.0088  | (0.1027)  | 0.1243      |

So, the average real return was:

Average = (.0447 + .0554 + .0527 + .0387 + .0926 + .1155 + .1243) / 7
Average = .0748 or 7.48%

Notice the real return was higher than the nominal return during this period because of deflation, or negative inflation.

17. Looking at the long-term corporate bond return history in Table 10.2, we see that the mean return was 6.4 percent, with a standard deviation of 8.4 percent. The range of returns you would expect to see 68 percent of the time is the mean plus or minus 1 standard deviation, or:

$R \in \mu \pm 1\sigma = 6.4\% \pm 8.4\% = -2.00\%$ to 14.80%

The range of returns you would expect to see 95 percent of the time is the mean plus or minus 2 standard deviations, or:

$R \in \mu \pm 2\sigma = 6.4\% \pm 2(8.4\%) = -10.40\%$ to 23.20%

18. Looking at the large-company stock return history in Table 10.2, we see that the mean return was 11.8 percent, with a standard deviation of 20.3 percent. The range of returns you would expect to see 68 percent of the time is the mean plus or minus 1 standard deviation, or:

$R \in \mu \pm 1\sigma = 11.8\% \pm 20.3\% = -8.50\%$ to 32.10%

The range of returns you would expect to see 95 percent of the time is the mean plus or minus 2 standard deviations, or:

$R \in \mu \pm 2\sigma = 11.8\% \pm 2(20.3\%) = -28.80\%$ to 52.40%

*Intermediate*

19. Here we know the average stock return, and four of the five returns used to compute the average return. We can work the average return equation backward to find the missing return. The average return is calculated as:

$5(.11) = .12 - .21 + .09 + .32 + R$
$R = .23$ or 23%

The missing return has to be 23 percent. Now we can use the equation for the variance to find:

Variance $= 1/4[(.12 - .11)^2 + (-.21 - .11)^2 + (.09 - .11)^2 + (.32 - .11)^2 + (.23 - .11)^2]$
Variance $= 0.04035$

And the standard deviation is:

Standard deviation $= (0.04035)^{1/2}$
Standard deviation $= 0.2009$, or 20.09%

**20.** The arithmetic average return is the sum of the known returns divided by the number of returns, so:

Arithmetic average return = (.27 + .12 + .32 −.12 + .19 −.31) / 6
Arithmetic average return = .0783, or 7.83%

Using the equation for the geometric return, we find:

Geometric average return = $[(1 + R_1) \times (1 + R_2) \times ... \times (1 + R_T)]^{1/T} - 1$
Geometric average return = $[(1 + .27)(1 + .12)(1 + .32)(1 − .12)(1 + .19)(1 − .31)]^{(1/6)} − 1$
Geometric average return = .0522, or 5.22%

Remember, the geometric average return will always be less than the arithmetic average return if the returns have any variation.

**21.** To calculate the arithmetic and geometric average returns, we must first calculate the return for each year. The return for each year is:

$R_1$ = ($64.83 − 61.18 + 0.72) / $61.18 = .0714, or 7.14%
$R_2$ = ($72.18 − 64.83 + 0.78) / $64.83 = .1254, or 12.54%
$R_3$ = ($63.12 − 72.18 + 0.86) / $72.18 = −.1136, or −11.36%
$R_4$ = ($69.27 − 63.12 + 0.95)/ $63.12 = .1125, or 11.25%
$R_5$ = ($76.93 − 69.27 + 1.08) / $69.27 = .1262, or 12.62%

The arithmetic average return was:

$R_A$ = (0.0714 + 0.1254 − 0.1136 + 0.1125 + 0.1262)/5
$R_A$ = 0.0644, or 6.44%

And the geometric average return was:

$R_G$ = $[(1 + .0714)(1 + .1254)(1 − .1136)(1 + .1125)(1 + .1262)]^{1/5} − 1$
$R_G$ = 0.0601, or 6.01%

**22.** To find the real return we need to use the Fisher equation. Re-writing the Fisher equation to solve for the real return, we get:

$r = [(1 + R)/(1 + h)] − 1$

So, the real return each year was:

| Year | T-bill return | Inflation | Real return |
|------|---------------|-----------|-------------|
| 1973 | 0.0729 | 0.0871 | −0.0131 |
| 1974 | 0.0799 | 0.1234 | −0.0387 |
| 1975 | 0.0587 | 0.0694 | −0.0100 |
| 1976 | 0.0507 | 0.0486 | 0.0020 |
| 1977 | 0.0545 | 0.0670 | −0.0117 |
| 1978 | 0.0764 | 0.0902 | −0.0127 |
| 1979 | 0.1056 | 0.1329 | −0.0241 |
| 1980 | 0.1210 | 0.1252 | −0.0037 |
|      | 0.6197 | 0.7438 | −0.1120 |

*a.* The average return for T-bills over this period was:

Average return = 0.6197 / 8
Average return = .0775, or 7.75%

And the average inflation rate was:

Average inflation = 0.7438 / 8
Average inflation = .0930, or 9.30%

*b.* Using the equation for variance, we find the variance for T-bills over this period was:

Variance = $1/7[(.0729 - .0775)^2 + (.0799 - .0775)^2 + (.0587 - .0775)^2 + (.0507 - .0775)^2 +$
$(.0545 - .0775)^2 + (.0764 - .0775)^2 + (.1056 - .0775)^2 + (.1210 - .0775)^2]$
Variance = 0.000616

And the standard deviation for T-bills was:

Standard deviation = $(0.000616)^{1/2}$
Standard deviation = 0.0248, or 2.48%

The variance of inflation over this period was:

Variance = $1/7[(.0871 - .0930)^2 + (.1234 - .0930)^2 + (.0694 - .0930)^2 + (.0486 - .0930)^2 +$
$(.0670 - .0930)^2 + (.0902 - .0930)^2 + (.1329 - .0930)^2 + (.1252 - .0930)^2]$
Variance = 0.000971

And the standard deviation of inflation was:

Standard deviation = $(0.000971)^{1/2}$
Standard deviation = 0.0312, or 3.12%

*c.* The average observed real return over this period was:

Average observed real return = −.1122 / 8
Average observed real return = −.0140, or −1.40%

*d.* The statement that T-bills have no risk refers to the fact that there is only an extremely small chance of the government defaulting, so there is little default risk. Since T-bills are short term, there is also very limited interest rate risk. However, as this example shows, there is inflation risk, i.e. the purchasing power of the investment can actually decline over time even if the investor is earning a positive return.

**23.** To find the return on the coupon bond, we first need to find the price of the bond today. Since one year has elapsed, the bond now has six years to maturity, so the price today is:

$P_1 = \$70(PVIFA_{5.5\%,6}) + \$1,000/1.055^6$
$P_1 = \$1,074.93$

You received the coupon payments on the bond, so the nominal return was:

$R = (\$1,074.93 - 1,080.50 + 70) / \$1,080.50$
$R = .0596$, or 5.96%

And using the Fisher equation to find the real return, we get:

$r = (1.0596 / 1.032) - 1$
$r = .0268$, or 2.68%

24. Looking at the long-term government bond return history in Table 10.2, we see that the mean return was 6.1 percent, with a standard deviation of 9.8 percent. In the normal probability distribution, approximately 2/3 of the observations are within one standard deviation of the mean. This means that 1/3 of the observations are outside one standard deviation away from the mean. Or:

$\Pr(R < -3.7 \text{ or } R > 15.9) \approx \frac{1}{3}$

But we are only interested in one tail here, that is, returns less than –3.7 percent, so:

$\Pr(R < -3.7) \approx \frac{1}{6}$

You can use the z-statistic and the cumulative normal distribution table to find the answer as well. Doing so, we find:

$z = (X - \mu)/\sigma$

$z = (-3.7\% - 6.1)/9.8\% = -1.00$

Looking at the z-table, this gives a probability of 15.87%, or:

$\Pr(R < -3.3) \approx .1587$, or 15.87%

The range of returns you would expect to see 95 percent of the time is the mean plus or minus 2 standard deviations, or:

95% level: $R \in \mu \pm 2\sigma = 6.1\% \pm 2(9.8\%) = -13.50\%$ to 25.70%

The range of returns you would expect to see 99 percent of the time is the mean plus or minus 3 standard deviations, or:

99% level: $R \in \mu \pm 3\sigma = 6.1\% \pm 3(9.8\%) = -23.30\%$ to 35.50%

25. The mean return for small company stocks was 16.4 percent, with a standard deviation of 33.0 percent. Doubling your money is a 100% return, so if the return distribution is normal, we can use the z-statistic. So:

$z = (X - \mu)/\sigma$

$z = (100\% - 16.5\%)/32.5\% = 2.569$ standard deviations above the mean

This corresponds to a probability of ≈ 0.510%, or about once every 200 years. Tripling your money would be:

$$z = (200\% - 16.5\%)/32.5\% = 5.646 \text{ standard deviations above the mean.}$$

This corresponds to a probability of (much) less than 0.5%. The actual answer is ≈.00000082039%, or about once every 1 million years.

26. It is impossible to lose more than 100 percent of your investment. Therefore, return distributions are truncated on the lower tail at –100 percent.

   *Challenge*

27. Using the z-statistic, we find:

$$z = (X - \mu)/\sigma$$

$$z = (0\% - 11.8\%)/20.3\% = -0.581$$

$$\Pr(R \leq 0) \approx 28.05\%$$

28. For each of the questions asked here, we need to use the z-statistic, which is:

$$z = (X - \mu)/\sigma$$

   *a.*   $z_1 = (10\% - 6.4\%)/8.4\% = 0.4286$

   This z-statistic gives us the probability that the return is less than 10 percent, but we are looking for the probability the return is greater than 10 percent. Given that the total probability is 100 percent (or 1), the probability of a return greater than 10 percent is 1 minus the probability of a return less than 10 percent. Using the cumulative normal distribution table, we get:

$$\Pr(R \geq 10\%) = 1 - \Pr(R \leq 10\%) = 33.41\%$$

   For a return less than 0 percent:

$$z_2 = (0\% - 6.4\%)/8.4 = -0.7619$$

$$\Pr(R < 10\%) = 1 - \Pr(R > 0\%) = 22.31\%$$

   *b.*   The probability that T-bill returns will be greater than 10 percent is:

$$z_3 = (10\% - 3.6\%)/3.1\% = 2.0645$$

$$\Pr(R \geq 10\%) = 1 - \Pr(R \leq 10\%) = 1 - .9805 \approx 1.95\%$$

   And the probability that T-bill returns will be less than 0 percent is:

$$z_4 = (0\% - 3.6\%)/3.1\% = -1.1613$$

$$\Pr(R \leq 0) \approx 12.28\%$$

c.   The probability that the return on long-term corporate bonds will be less than –4.18 percent is:

$z_5 = (-4.18\% - 6.4\%)/8.4\% = -1.2595$

$\Pr(R \leq -4.18\%) \approx 10.39\%$

And the probability that T-bill returns will be greater than 10.56 percent is:

$z_6 = (10.56\% - 3.6\%)/3.1\% = 2.2452$

$\Pr(R \geq 10.56\%) = 1 - \Pr(R \leq 10.56\%) = 1 - .9876 \approx 1.24\%$

# CHAPTER 11
# RISK AND RETURN: *THE CAPITAL ASSET PRICING MODEL (CAPM)*

## Answers to Concepts Review and Critical Thinking Questions

1.  Some of the risk in holding any asset is unique to the asset in question. By investing in a variety of assets, this unique portion of the total risk can be eliminated at little cost. On the other hand, there are some risks that affect all investments. This portion of the total risk of an asset cannot be costlessly eliminated. In other words, systematic risk can be controlled, but only by a costly reduction in expected returns.

2.  *a.*  systematic
    *b.*  unsystematic
    *c.*  both; probably mostly systematic
    *d.*  unsystematic
    *e.*  unsystematic
    *f.*  systematic

3.  No to both questions. The portfolio expected return is a weighted average of the asset's returns, so it must be less than the largest asset return and greater than the smallest asset return.

4.  False. The variance of the individual assets is a measure of the total risk. The variance on a well-diversified portfolio is a function of systematic risk only.

5.  Yes, the standard deviation can be less than that of every asset in the portfolio. However, $\beta_p$ cannot be less than the smallest beta because $\beta_p$ is a weighted average of the individual asset betas.

6.  Yes. It is possible, in theory, to construct a zero beta portfolio of risky assets whose return would be equal to the risk-free rate. It is also possible to have a negative beta; the return would be less than the risk-free rate. A negative beta asset would carry a negative risk premium because of its value as a diversification instrument.

7.  The covariance is a more appropriate measure of a security's risk in a well-diversified portfolio because the covariance reflects the effect of the security on the variance of the portfolio. Investors are concerned with the variance of their portfolios and not the variance of the individual securities. Since covariance measures the impact of an individual security on the variance of the portfolio, covariance is the appropriate measure of risk.

8.  If we assume that the market has not stayed constant during the past three years, then the lack in movement of Southern Co.'s stock price only indicates that the stock either has a standard deviation or a beta that is very near to zero. The large amount of movement in Texas Instruments' stock price does not imply that the firm's beta is high. Total volatility (the price fluctuation) is a function of both systematic and unsystematic risk. The beta only reflects the systematic risk. Observing the standard deviation of price movements does not indicate whether the price changes were due to systematic factors or firm specific factors. Thus, if you observe large stock price movements like that of TI, you cannot claim that the beta of the stock is high. All you know is that the total risk of TI is high.

9.  The wide fluctuations in the price of oil stocks do not indicate that these stocks are a poor investment. If an oil stock is purchased as part of a well-diversified portfolio, only its contribution to the risk of the entire portfolio matters. This contribution is measured by systematic risk or beta. Since price fluctuations in oil stocks reflect diversifiable plus non-diversifiable risk, observing the standard deviation of price movements is not an adequate measure of the appropriateness of adding oil stocks to a portfolio.

10. The statement is false. If a security has a negative beta, investors would want to hold the asset to reduce the variability of their portfolios. Those assets will have expected returns that are lower than the risk-free rate. To see this, examine the Capital Asset Pricing Model:

$$E(R_S) = R_f + \beta_S[E(R_M) - R_f]$$

If $\beta_S < 0$, then the $E(R_S) < R_f$

## Solutions to Questions and Problems

*NOTE: All end-of-chapter problems were solved using a spreadsheet. Many problems require multiple steps. Due to space and readability constraints, when these intermediate steps are included in this solutions manual, rounding may appear to have occurred. However, the final answer for each problem is found without rounding during any step in the problem.*

*Basic*

1.  The portfolio weight of an asset is total investment in that asset divided by the total portfolio value. First, we will find the portfolio value, which is:

    Total value = 135($47) + 105($41) = $10,650

    The portfolio weight for each stock is:

    Weight$_A$ = 135($47)/$10,650 = .5958

    Weight$_B$ = 105($41)/$10,650 = .4042

2.  The expected return of a portfolio is the sum of the weight of each asset times the expected return of each asset. The total value of the portfolio is:

    Total value = $2,100 + 3,200 = $5,300

    So, the expected return of this portfolio is:

    $E(R_p)$ = ($2,100/$5,300)(0.11) + ($3,200/$5,300)(0.14) = .1281, or 12.81%

3.  The expected return of a portfolio is the sum of the weight of each asset times the expected return of each asset. So, the expected return of the portfolio is:

    $E(R_p)$ = .25(.11) + .40(.17) + .35(.14) = .1445, or 14.45%

4.  Here we are given the expected return of the portfolio and the expected return of each asset in the portfolio and are asked to find the weight of each asset. We can use the equation for the expected return of a portfolio to solve this problem. Since the total weight of a portfolio must equal 1 (100%), the weight of Stock Y must be one minus the weight of Stock X. Mathematically speaking, this means:

$$E(R_p) = .129 = .14X_X + .09(1 - X_X)$$

We can now solve this equation for the weight of Stock X as:

$.129 = .14X_X + .09 - .10X_X$
$.039 = .04X_X$
$X_X = 0.7800$

So, the dollar amount invested in Stock X is the weight of Stock X times the total portfolio value, or:

Investment in X = 0.7800($10,000) = $7,800

And the dollar amount invested in Stock Y is:

Investment in Y = (1 - 0.7800)($10,000) = $2,200

5.  The expected return of an asset is the sum of the probability of each return occurring times the probability of that return occurring. So, the expected return of each stock asset is:

$$E(R_A) = .20(.06) + .55(.07) + .25(.11) = .0780, \text{ or } 7.80\%$$

$$E(R_B) = .20(-.20) + .55(.13) + .25(.33) = .1140, \text{ or } 11.40\%$$

To calculate the standard deviation, we first need to calculate the variance. To find the variance, we find the squared deviations from the expected return. We then multiply each possible squared deviation by its probability, and then add all of these up. The result is the variance. So, the variance and standard deviation of each stock are:

$$\sigma_A^2 = .20(.06 - .0780)^2 + .55(.07 - .0780)^2 + .25(.11 - .0780)^2 = .00036$$

$$\sigma_A = (.00036)^{1/2} = .0189, \text{ or } 1.89\%$$

$$\sigma_B^2 = .20(-.20 - .1140)^2 + .55(.13 - .1140)^2 + .25(.33 - .1140)^2 = .03152$$

$$\sigma_B = (.03152)^{1/2} = .1775, \text{ or } 17.75\%$$

6.  The expected return of an asset is the sum of the probability of each return occurring times the probability of that return occurring. So, the expected return of the stock is:

$$E(R_A) = .10(-.105) + .25(.059) + .45(.130) + .20(.211) = .1050, \text{ or } 10.50\%$$

To calculate the standard deviation, we first need to calculate the variance. To find the variance, we find the squared deviations from the expected return. We then multiply each possible squared deviation by its probability, and then add all of these up. The result is the variance. So, the variance and standard deviation are:

$$\sigma^2 = .10(-.105 - .1050)^2 + .25(.059 - .1050)^2 + .45(.130 - .1050)^2 + .20(.211 - .1050)^2 = .00747$$

$$\sigma = (.00747)^{1/2} = .0864, \text{ or } 8.64\%$$

**7.** The expected return of a portfolio is the sum of the weight of each asset times the expected return of each asset. So, the expected return of the portfolio is:

$$E(R_p) = .10(.09) + .65(.11) + .25(.14) = .1155, \text{ or } 11.55\%$$

If we own this portfolio, we would expect to get a return of 11.55 percent.

**8.** *a.* To find the expected return of the portfolio, we need to find the return of the portfolio in each state of the economy. This portfolio is a special case since all three assets have the same weight. To find the expected return in an equally weighted portfolio, we can sum the returns of each asset and divide by the number of assets, so the expected return of the portfolio in each state of the economy is:

Boom: $E(R_p) = (.07 + .15 + .33)/3 = .1833$ or 18.33%
Bust: $E(R_p) = (.13 + .03 - .06)/3 = .0333$ or 3.33%

To find the expected return of the portfolio, we multiply the return in each state of the economy by the probability of that state occurring, and then sum. Doing this, we find:

$$E(R_p) = .65(.1833) + .35(.0333) = .1308, \text{ or } 13.08\%$$

*b.* This portfolio does not have an equal weight in each asset. We still need to find the return of the portfolio in each state of the economy. To do this, we will multiply the return of each asset by its portfolio weight and then sum the products to get the portfolio return in each state of the economy. Doing so, we get:

Boom: $E(R_p) = .20(.07) + .20(.15) + .60(.33) = .2420$ or 24.20%
Bust: $E(R_p) = .20(.13) + .20(.03) + .60(-.06) = -.0040$ or −0.40%

And the expected return of the portfolio is:

$$E(R_p) = .65(.2420) + .35(-.004) = .1559, \text{ or } 15.59\%$$

To find the variance, we find the squared deviations from the expected return. We then multiply each possible squared deviation by its probability, and then add all of these up. The result is the variance. So, the variance of the portfolio is:

$$\sigma_p^2 = .65(.2420 - .1559)^2 + .35(-.0040 - .1559)^2 = .013767$$

9. *a.* This portfolio does not have an equal weight in each asset. We first need to find the return of the portfolio in each state of the economy. To do this, we will multiply the return of each asset by its portfolio weight and then sum the products to get the portfolio return in each state of the economy. Doing so, we get:

Boom: $E(R_p) = .30(.24) + .40(.45) + .30(.33) = .3510$, or 35.10%
Good: $E(R_p) = .30(.09) + .40(.10) + .30(.15) = .1120$, or 11.20%
Poor: $E(R_p) = .30(.03) + .40(-.10) + .30(-.05) = -.0460$, or −4.60%
Bust: $E(R_p) = .30(-.05) + .40(-.25) + .30(-.09) = -.1420$, or −14.20%

And the expected return of the portfolio is:

$E(R_p) = .20(.3510) + .35(.1120) + .30(-.0460) + .15(-.1420) = .0743$, or 7.43%

*b.* To calculate the standard deviation, we first need to calculate the variance. To find the variance, we find the squared deviations from the expected return. We then multiply each possible squared deviation by its probability, and then add all of these up. The result is the variance. So, the variance and standard deviation the portfolio is:

$$\sigma_p^2 = .20(.3510 - .0743)^2 + .35(.1120 - .0743)^2 + .30(-.0460 - .0743)^2 + .15(-.1420 - .0743)^2$$
$$\sigma_p^2 = .02717$$

$$\sigma_p = (.02717)^{1/2} = .1648, \text{ or } 16.48\%$$

10. The beta of a portfolio is the sum of the weight of each asset times the beta of each asset. So, the beta of the portfolio is:

$\beta_p = .10(.75) + .35(1.90) + .20(1.38) + .35(1.16) = 1.42$

11. The beta of a portfolio is the sum of the weight of each asset times the beta of each asset. If the portfolio is as risky as the market it must have the same beta as the market. Since the beta of the market is one, we know the beta of our portfolio is one. We also need to remember that the beta of the risk-free asset is zero. It has to be zero since the asset has no risk. Setting up the equation for the beta of our portfolio, we get:

$\beta_p = 1.0 = {}^1/_3(0) + {}^1/_3(1.65) + {}^1/_3(\beta_X)$

Solving for the beta of Stock X, we get:

$\beta_X = 1.35$

12. CAPM states the relationship between the risk of an asset and its expected return. CAPM is:

$E(R_i) = R_f + [E(R_M) - R_f] \times \beta_i$

Substituting the values we are given, we find:

$E(R_i) = .05 + (.11 - .05)(1.15) = .1190$, or 11.90%

13. We are given the values for the CAPM except for the β of the stock. We need to substitute these values into the CAPM, and solve for the β of the stock. One important thing we need to realize is that we are given the market risk premium. The market risk premium is the expected return of the market minus the risk-free rate. We must be careful not to use this value as the expected return of the market. Using the CAPM, we find:

$$E(R_i) = .102 = .04 + .07\beta_i$$

$$\beta_i = 0.89$$

14. Here we need to find the expected return of the market using the CAPM. Substituting the values given, and solving for the expected return of the market, we find:

$$E(R_i) = .134 = .055 + [E(R_M) - .055](1.60)$$

$$E(R_M) = .1044, \text{ or } 10.44\%$$

15. Here we need to find the risk-free rate using the CAPM. Substituting the values given, and solving for the risk-free rate, we find:

$$E(R_i) = .131 = R_f + (.11 - R_f)(1.28)$$

$$.131 = R_f + .1408 - 1.28R_f$$

$$R_f = .0350, \text{ or } 3.50\%$$

16. *a.* Again, we have a special case where the portfolio is equally weighted, so we can sum the returns of each asset and divide by the number of assets. The expected return of the portfolio is:

$$E(R_p) = (.121 + .05)/2 = .0855, \text{ or } 8.55\%$$

   *b.* We need to find the portfolio weights that result in a portfolio with a β of 0.50. We know the β of the risk-free asset is zero. We also know the weight of the risk-free asset is one minus the weight of the stock since the portfolio weights must sum to one, or 100 percent. So:

$$\beta_p = 0.50 = X_S(1.13) + (1 - X_S)(0)$$
$$0.50 = 1.13X_S + 0 - 0X_S$$
$$X_S = 0.50/1.13$$
$$X_S = .4425$$

   And, the weight of the risk-free asset is:

$$X_{Rf} = 1 - .4425 = .5575$$

   *c.* We need to find the portfolio weights that result in a portfolio with an expected return of 10 percent. We also know the weight of the risk-free asset is one minus the weight of the stock since the portfolio weights must sum to one, or 100 percent. So:

$$E(R_p) = .10 = .121X_S + .05(1 - X_S)$$
$$.10 = .121X_S + .05 - .05X_S$$
$$X_S = .7042$$

So, the β of the portfolio will be:

$$\beta_p = .7042(1.13) + (1 - .7042)(0) = 0.796$$

*d.* Solving for the β of the portfolio as we did in part *b*, we find:

$$\beta_p = 2.26 = X_S(1.13) + (1 - X_S)(0)$$

$$X_S = 2.26/1.13 = 2$$

$$X_{Rf} = 1 - 2 = -1$$

The portfolio is invested 200% in the stock and –100% in the risk-free asset. This represents borrowing at the risk-free rate to buy more of the stock.

17. First, we need to find the β of the portfolio. The β of the risk-free asset is zero, and the weight of the risk-free asset is one minus the weight of the stock, so the β of the portfolio is:

$$\beta_p = X_W(1.3) + (1 - X_W)(0) = 1.3X_W$$

So, to find the β of the portfolio for any weight of the stock, we simply multiply the weight of the stock times its β.

Even though we are solving for the β and expected return of a portfolio of one stock and the risk-free asset for different portfolio weights, we are really solving for the SML. Any combination of this stock and the risk-free asset will fall on the SML. For that matter, a portfolio of any stock and the risk-free asset, or any portfolio of stocks, will fall on the SML. We know the slope of the SML line is the market risk premium, so using the CAPM and the information concerning this stock, the market risk premium is:

$$E(R_W) = .123 = .04 + MRP(1.30)$$
$$MRP = .083/1.3 = .0638, \text{ or } 6.38\%$$

So, now we know the CAPM equation for any stock is:

$$E(R_p) = .04 + .0638\beta_p$$

The slope of the SML is equal to the market risk premium, which is 0.0638. Using these equations to fill in the table, we get the following results:

| $X_W$ | $E(R_p)$ | $\beta_p$ |
|-------|----------|-----------|
| 0% | .0400 | 0 |
| 25 | .0608 | 0.325 |
| 50 | .0815 | 0.650 |
| 75 | .1023 | 0.975 |
| 100 | .1230 | 1.300 |
| 125 | .1438 | 1.625 |
| 150 | .1645 | 1.950 |

**18.** There are two ways to correctly answer this question. We will work through both. First, we can use the CAPM. Substituting in the value we are given for each stock, we find:

$$E(R_Y) = .045 + .073(1.35) = .1436, \text{ or } 14.36\%$$

It is given in the problem that the expected return of Stock Y is 14 percent, but according to the CAPM, the return of the stock based on its level of risk should be 14.36 percent. This means the stock return is too low, given its level of risk. Stock Y plots below the SML and is overvalued. In other words, its price must decrease to increase the expected return to 14.36 percent.

For Stock Z, we find:

$$E(R_Z) = .045 + .073(0.80) = .1034, \text{ or } 10.34\%$$

The return given for Stock Z is 11.5 percent, but according to the CAPM the expected return of the stock should be 10.34 percent based on its level of risk. Stock Z plots above the SML and is undervalued. In other words, its price must increase to decrease the expected return to 10.34 percent.

We can also answer this question using the reward-to-risk ratio. All assets must have the same reward-to-risk ratio, that is, every asset must have the same ratio of the asset risk premium to its beta. This follows from the linearity of the SML in Figure 11.11. The reward-to-risk ratio is the risk premium of the asset divided by its $\beta$. This is also known as the Treynor ratio or Treynor index. We are given the market risk premium, and we know the $\beta$ of the market is one, so the reward-to-risk ratio for the market is 0.073, or 7.3 percent. Calculating the reward-to-risk ratio for Stock Y, we find:

Reward-to-risk ratio Y = (.14 – .045) / 1.35 = .0704

The reward-to-risk ratio for Stock Y is too low, which means the stock plots below the SML, and the stock is overvalued. Its price must decrease until its reward-to-risk ratio is equal to the market reward-to-risk ratio. For Stock Z, we find:

Reward-to-risk ratio Z = (.115 – .045) / .80 = .0875

The reward-to-risk ratio for Stock Z is too high, which means the stock plots above the SML, and the stock is undervalued. Its price must increase until its reward-to-risk ratio is equal to the market reward-to-risk ratio.

**19.** We need to set the reward-to-risk ratios of the two assets equal to each other (see the previous problem), which is:

$$(.14 – R_f)/1.35 = (.115 – R_f)/0.80$$

We can cross multiply to get:

$$0.80(.14 – R_f) = 1.35(.115 – R_f)$$

Solving for the risk-free rate, we find:

$$0.112 – 0.80R_f = 0.15525 – 1.35R_f$$

$$R_f = .0786, \text{ or } 7.86\%$$

*Intermediate*

**20.** For a portfolio that is equally invested in large-company stocks and long-term bonds:

Return = (11.8% + 6.1%)/2 = 8.95%

For a portfolio that is equally invested in small stocks and Treasury bills:

Return = (16.5% + 3.6%)/2 = 10.05%

**21.** We know that the reward-to-risk ratios for all assets must be equal (See Question 19). This can be expressed as:

$[E(R_A) - R_f]/\beta_A = [E(R_B) - R_f]/\beta_B$

The numerator of each equation is the risk premium of the asset, so:

$RP_A/\beta_A = RP_B/\beta_B$

We can rearrange this equation to get:

$\beta_B/\beta_A = RP_B/RP_A$

If the reward-to-risk ratios are the same, the ratio of the betas of the assets is equal to the ratio of the risk premiums of the assets.

**22.** *a.* We need to find the return of the portfolio in each state of the economy. To do this, we will multiply the return of each asset by its portfolio weight and then sum the products to get the portfolio return in each state of the economy. Doing so, we get:

Boom: $E(R_p)$ = .4(.20) + .4(.25) + .2(.60) = .3000, or 30.00%
Normal: $E(R_p)$ = .4(.15) + .4(.11) + .2(.05) = .1140, or 11.40%
Bust: $E(R_p)$ = .4(.01) + .4(−.15) + .2(−.50) = −.1560, or −15.60%

And the expected return of the portfolio is:

$E(R_p)$ = .30(.30) + .45(.114) + .25(−.156) = .1023, or 10.23%

To calculate the standard deviation, we first need to calculate the variance. To find the variance, we find the squared deviations from the expected return. We then multiply each possible squared deviation by its probability, than add all of these up. The result is the variance. So, the variance and standard deviation of the portfolio is:

$\sigma^2_p$ = .30(.30 − .1023)$^2$ + .45(.114 − .1023)$^2$ + .25(−.156 − .1023)$^2$
$\sigma^2_p$ = .02847

$\sigma_p$ = (.02847)$^{1/2}$ = .1687, or 16.87%

b. The risk premium is the return of a risky asset, minus the risk-free rate. T-bills are often used as the risk-free rate, so:

$RP_i = E(R_p) - R_f = .1023 - .038 = .0643$, or 6.43%

c. The approximate expected real return is the expected nominal return minus the inflation rate, so:

Approximate expected real return = $.1023 - .035 = .0673$, or 6.73%

To find the exact real return, we will use the Fisher equation. Doing so, we get:

$1 + E(R_i) = (1 + h)[1 + e(r_i)]$
$1.1023 = (1.0350)[1 + e(r_i)]$
$e(r_i) = (1.1023/1.035) - 1 = .0650$, or 6.50%

The approximate real risk-free rate is:

Approximate expected real return = $.038 - .035 = .003$, or 0.30%

And using the Fisher effect for the exact real risk-free rate, we find:

$1 + E(R_i) = (1 + h)[1 + e(r_i)]$
$1.038 = (1.0350)[1 + e(r_i)]$
$e(r_i) = (1.038/1.035) - 1 = .0029$, or 0.29%

The approximate real risk premium is the approximate expected real return minus the risk-free rate, so:

Approximate expected real risk premium = $.0673 - .003 = .0643$, or 6.43%

The exact real risk premium is the exact real return minus the risk-free rate, so:

Exact expected real risk premium = $.0650 - .0029 = .0621$, or 6.21%

23. We know the total portfolio value and the investment of two stocks in the portfolio, so we can find the weight of these two stocks. The weights of Stock A and Stock B are:

$X_A = \$180,000 / \$1,000,000 = .18$

$X_B = \$290,000/\$1,000,000 = .29$

Since the portfolio is as risky as the market, the $\beta$ of the portfolio must be equal to one. We also know the $\beta$ of the risk-free asset is zero. We can use the equation for the $\beta$ of a portfolio to find the weight of the third stock. Doing so, we find:

$\beta_p = 1.0 = X_A(.85) + X_B(1.40) + X_C(1.45) + X_{Rf}(0)$

Solving for the weight of Stock C, we find:

$X_C = .30413793$

So, the dollar investment in Stock C must be:

Invest in Stock C = .30413793($1,000,000) = $304,137.93

We also know the total portfolio weight must be one, so the weight of the risk-free asset must be one minus the asset weight we know, or:

$1 = X_A + X_B + X_C + X_{Rf}$
$1 = .18 + .29 + .30413793 + X_{Rf}$
$X_{Rf} = .22586207$

So, the dollar investment in the risk-free asset must be:

Invest in risk-free asset = .22586207($1,000,000) = $225,862.07

24. We are given the expected return and $\beta$ of a portfolio and the expected return and $\beta$ of assets in the portfolio. We know the $\beta$ of the risk-free asset is zero. We also know the sum of the weights of each asset must be equal to one. So, the weight of the risk-free asset is one minus the weight of Stock X and the weight of Stock Y. Using this relationship, we can express the expected return of the portfolio as:

$E(R_p) = .1122 = X_X(.1535) + X_Y(.0940) + (1 - X_X - X_Y)(.045)$

And the $\beta$ of the portfolio is:

$\beta_p = .96 = X_X(1.55) + X_Y(0.70) + (1 - X_X - X_Y)(0)$

We have two equations and two unknowns. Solving these equations, we find that:

$X_X = -0.2838710$
$X_Y = 2.0000000$
$X_{Rf} = -0.7161290$

The amount to invest in Stock X is:

Investment in stock X = -0.28387($100,000) = -$28,387.10

A negative portfolio weight means that you short sell the stock. If you are not familiar with short selling, it means you borrow a stock today and sell it. You must then purchase the stock at a later date to repay the borrowed stock. If you short sell a stock, you make a profit if the stock decreases in value. The negative weight on the risk-free asset means that we borrow money to invest.

**25.** The expected return of an asset is the sum of the probability of each return occurring times the probability of that return occurring. So, the expected return of each stock is:

$$E(R_A) = .33(.102) + .33(.115) + .33(.073) = .0967, \text{ or } 9.67\%$$

$$E(R_B) = .33(-.045) + .33(.148) + .33(.233) = .1120, \text{ or } 11.20\%$$

To calculate the standard deviation, we first need to calculate the variance. To find the variance, we find the squared deviations from the expected return. We then multiply each possible squared deviation by its probability, and then add all of these up. The result is the variance. So, the variance and standard deviation of Stock A are:

$$\sigma^2 = .33(.102 - .0967)^2 + .33(.115 - .0967)^2 + .33(.073 - .0967)^2 = .00031$$

$$\sigma = (.00031)^{1/2} = .0176, \text{ or } 1.76\%$$

And the standard deviation of Stock B is:

$$\sigma^2 = .33(-.045 - .1120)^2 + .33(.148 - .1120)^2 + .33(.233 - .1120)^2 = .01353$$

$$\sigma = (.01353)^{1/2} = .1163, \text{ or } 11.63\%$$

To find the covariance, we multiply each possible state times the product of each assets' deviation from the mean in that state. The sum of these products is the covariance. So, the covariance is:

$$Cov(A,B) = .33(.102 - .0967)(-.045 - .1120) + .33(.115 - .0967)(.148 - .1120)$$
$$+ .33(.073 - .0967)(.233 - .1120)$$
$$Cov(A,B) = -.001014$$

And the correlation is:

$$\rho_{A,B} = Cov(A,B) / \sigma_A \sigma_B$$
$$\rho_{A,B} = -.001014 / (.0176)(.1163)$$
$$\rho_{A,B} = -.4964$$

**26.** The expected return of an asset is the sum of the probability of each return occurring times the probability of that return occurring. So, the expected return of each stock is:

$$E(R_A) = .25(-.020) + .60(.138) + .15(.218) = .1105, \text{ or } 11.05\%$$

$$E(R_B) = .25(.034) + .60(.062) + .15(.092) = .0595, \text{ or } 5.95\%$$

To calculate the standard deviation, we first need to calculate the variance. To find the variance, we find the squared deviations from the expected return. We then multiply each possible squared deviation by its probability, and then add all of these up. The result is the variance. So, the variance and standard deviation of Stock A are:

$$\sigma_A^2 = .25(-.020 - .1105)^2 + .60(.138 - .1105)^2 + .15(.218 - .1105)^2 = .00644$$

$$\sigma_A = (.00644)^{1/2} = .0803, \text{ or } 8.03\%$$

And the standard deviation of Stock B is:

$$\sigma_B^2 = .25(.034 - .0595)^2 + .60(.062 - .0595)^2 + .15(.092 - .0595)^2 = .00032$$

$$\sigma_B = (.00032)^{1/2} = .0180, \text{ or } 1.80\%$$

To find the covariance, we multiply each possible state times the product of each assets' deviation from the mean in that state. The sum of these products is the covariance. So, the covariance is:

$$Cov(A,B) = .25(-.020 - .1105)(.034 - .0595) + .60(.138 - .1105)(.062 - .0595)$$
$$+ .15(.218 - .1105)(.092 - .0595)$$
$$Cov(A,B) = .001397$$

And the correlation is:

$$\rho_{A,B} = Cov(A,B) / \sigma_A \sigma_B$$
$$\rho_{A,B} = .001397 / (.0803)(.0180)$$
$$\rho_{A,B} = .9658$$

**27.** *a.* The expected return of the portfolio is the sum of the weight of each asset times the expected return of each asset, so:

$$E(R_P) = X_F E(R_F) + X_G E(R_G)$$
$$E(R_P) = .30(.10) + .70(.15)$$
$$E(R_P) = .1350, \text{ or } 13.50\%$$

*b.* The variance of a portfolio of two assets can be expressed as:

$$\sigma_P^2 = X_F^2 \sigma_F^2 + X_G^2 \sigma_G^2 + 2X_F X_G \sigma_F \sigma_G \rho_{F,G}$$
$$\sigma_P^2 = .30^2(.43^2) + .70^2(.62^2) + 2(.30)(.70)(.43)(.62)(.25)$$
$$\sigma_P^2 = .23299$$

So, the standard deviation is:

$$\sigma_P = (.23299)^{1/2} = .4827, \text{ or } 48.27\%$$

**28.** *a.* The expected return of the portfolio is the sum of the weight of each asset times the expected return of each asset, so:

$$E(R_P) = X_A E(R_A) + X_B E(R_B)$$
$$E(R_P) = .35(.09) + .65(.15)$$
$$E(R_P) = .1290, \text{ or } 12.90\%$$

The variance of a portfolio of two assets can be expressed as:

$$\sigma_P^2 = X_A^2\sigma_A^2 + X_B^2\sigma_B^2 + 2X_AX_B\sigma_A\sigma_B\rho_{A,B}$$
$$\sigma_P^2 = .35^2(.36^2) + .65^2(.62^2) + 2(.35)(.65)(.36)(.62)(.50)$$
$$\sigma_P^2 = .22906$$

So, the standard deviation is:

$$\sigma_P = (.22906)^{1/2} = .4786, \text{ or } 47.86\%$$

b.   $$\sigma_P^2 = X_A^2\sigma_A^2 + X_B^2\sigma_B^2 + 2X_AX_B\sigma_A\sigma_B\rho_{A,B}$$
$$\sigma_P^2 = .35^2(.36^2) + .65^2(.62^2) + 2(.35)(.65)(.36)(.62)(-.50)$$
$$\sigma_P^2 = .12751$$

So, the standard deviation is:

$$\sigma = (.12751)^{1/2} = .3571, \text{ or } 35.71\%$$

c.   As Stock A and Stock B become less correlated, or more negatively correlated, the standard deviation of the portfolio decreases.

29.  a.   (i)   Using the equation to calculate beta, we find:

$$\beta_A = (\rho_{A,M})(\sigma_A) / \sigma_M$$
$$0.85 = (\rho_{A,M})(0.31) / 0.20$$
$$\rho_{A,M} = 0.55$$

(ii)   Using the equation to calculate beta, we find:

$$\beta_B = (\rho_{B,M})(\sigma_B) / \sigma_M$$
$$1.40 = (.50)(\sigma_B) / 0.20$$
$$\sigma_B = 0.56$$

(iii)   Using the equation to calculate beta, we find:

$$\beta_C = (\rho_{C,M})(\sigma_C) / \sigma_M$$
$$\beta_C = (.35)(.65) / 0.20$$
$$\beta_C = 1.14$$

(iv)   The market has a correlation of 1 with itself.

(v)   The beta of the market is 1.

(vi)   The risk-free asset has zero standard deviation.

(vii)   The risk-free asset has zero correlation with the market portfolio.

(viii)   The beta of the risk-free asset is 0.

b.  Using the CAPM to find the expected return of the stock, we find:

*Firm A:*

$E(R_A) = R_f + \beta_A[E(R_M) - R_f]$

$E(R_A) = 0.05 + 0.85(0.12 - 0.05)$

$E(R_A) = .1095$, or 10.95%

According to the CAPM, the expected return on Firm A's stock should be 10.95 percent. However, the expected return on Firm A's stock given in the table is only 10 percent. Therefore, Firm A's stock is overpriced, and you should sell it.

*Firm B:*

$E(R_B) = R_f + \beta_B[E(R_M) - R_f]$

$E(R_B) = 0.05 + 1.4(0.12 - 0.05)$

$E(R_B) = .1480$, or 14.80%

According to the CAPM, the expected return on Firm B's stock should be 14.80 percent. However, the expected return on Firm B's stock given in the table is 14 percent. Therefore, Firm B's stock is overpriced, and you should sell it.

*Firm C:*

$E(R_C) = R_f + \beta_C[E(R_M) - R_f]$

$E(R_C) = 0.05 + 1.14(0.12 - 0.05)$

$E(R_C) = .1296$, or 12.96%

According to the CAPM, the expected return on Firm C's stock should be 12.96 percent. However, the expected return on Firm C's stock given in the table is 16 percent. Therefore, Firm C's stock is underpriced, and you should buy it.

30. Because a well-diversified portfolio has no unsystematic risk, this portfolio should lie on the Capital Market Line (CML). The slope of the CML equals:

$Slope_{CML} = [E(R_M) - R_f] / \sigma_M$

$Slope_{CML} = (0.12 - 0.05) / 0.22$

$Slope_{CML} = 0.31818$

a.  The expected return on the portfolio equals:

$E(R_P) = R_f + Slope_{CML}(\sigma_P)$

$E(R_P) = .05 + .31818(.09)$

$E(R_P) = .0786$, or 7.86%

b.  The expected return on the portfolio equals:

$E(R_P) = R_f + Slope_{CML}(\sigma_P)$

$.20 = .05 + .31818(\sigma_P)$

$\sigma_P = .4714$, or 47.14%

31. First, we can calculate the standard deviation of the market portfolio using the Capital Market Line (CML). We know that the risk-free rate asset has a return of 4 percent and a standard deviation of zero and the portfolio has an expected return of 7 percent and a standard deviation of 10 percent. These two points must lie on the Capital Market Line. The slope of the Capital Market Line equals:

$Slope_{CML}$ = Rise / Run
$Slope_{CML}$ = Increase in expected return / Increase in standard deviation
$Slope_{CML}$ = (.07 − .04) / (.10 − 0)
$Slope_{CML}$ = .30

According to the Capital Market Line:

$E(R_I) = R_f + Slope_{CML}(\sigma_I)$

Since we know the expected return on the market portfolio, the risk-free rate, and the slope of the Capital Market Line, we can solve for the standard deviation of the market portfolio which is:

$E(R_M) = R_f + Slope_{CML}(\sigma_M)$
.12 = .04 + (.30)($\sigma_M$)
$\sigma_M$ = (.12 − .04) / .30
$\sigma_M$ = .2667, or 26.67%

Next, we can use the standard deviation of the market portfolio to solve for the beta of a security using the beta equation. Doing so, we find the beta of the security is:

$\beta_I = (\rho_{I,M})(\sigma_I) / \sigma_M$
$\beta_I$ = (.45)(.55) / .2667
$\beta_I$ = 0.93

Now we can use the beta of the security in the CAPM to find its expected return, which is:

$E(R_I) = R_f + \beta_I[E(R_M) − R_f]$
$E(R_I)$ = 0.04 + 0.93(.12 − 0.04)
$E(R_I)$ = .1143, or 11.43%

32. First, we need to find the standard deviation of the market and the portfolio, which are:

$\sigma_M = (.0382)^{1/2}$
$\sigma_M$ = .1954, or 19.54%

$\sigma_Z = (.3285)^{1/2}$
$\sigma_Z$ = .5731, or 57.31%

Now we can use the equation for beta to find the beta of the portfolio, which is:

$\beta_Z = (\rho_{Z,M})(\sigma_Z) / \sigma_M$
$\beta_Z$ = (.28)(.5731) / .1954
$\beta_Z$ = .82

Now, we can use the CAPM to find the expected return of the portfolio, which is:

$$E(R_Z) = R_f + \beta_Z[E(R_M) - R_f]$$
$$E(R_Z) = .042 + .82(.109 - .042)$$
$$E(R_Z) = .0970, \text{ or } 9.70\%$$

*Challenge*

33. The amount of systematic risk is measured by the $\beta$ of an asset. Since we know the market risk premium and the risk-free rate, if we know the expected return of the asset we can use the CAPM to solve for the $\beta$ of the asset. The expected return of Stock I is:

$$E(R_I) = .15(.11) + .55(.18) + .30(.08) = .1395, \text{ or } 13.95\%$$

Using the CAPM to find the $\beta$ of Stock I, we find:

$$.1395 = .04 + .075\beta_I$$
$$\beta_I = 1.33$$

The total risk of the asset is measured by its standard deviation, so we need to calculate the standard deviation of Stock I. Beginning with the calculation of the stock's variance, we find:

$$\sigma_I^2 = .15(.11 - .1395)^2 + .55(.18 - .1395)^2 + .30(.08 - .1395)^2$$
$$\sigma_I^2 = .00209$$

$$\sigma_I = (.00209)^{1/2} = .0458, \text{ or } 4.58\%$$

Using the same procedure for Stock II, we find the expected return to be:

$$E(R_{II}) = .15(-.25) + .55(.11) + .30(.31) = .1160$$

Using the CAPM to find the $\beta$ of Stock II, we find:

$$.1160 = .04 + .075\beta_{II}$$
$$\beta_{II} = 1.01$$

And the standard deviation of Stock II is:

$$\sigma_{II}^2 = .15(-.25 - .1160)^2 + .55(.11 - .1160)^2 + .30(.31 - .1160)^2$$
$$\sigma_{II}^2 = .03140$$

$$\sigma_{II} = (.03140)^{1/2} = .1772, \text{ or } 17.72\%$$

Although Stock II has more total risk than I, it has much less systematic risk, since its beta is much smaller than I's. Thus, I has more systematic risk, and II has more unsystematic and more total risk. Since unsystematic risk can be diversified away, I is actually the "riskier" stock despite the lack of volatility in its returns. Stock I will have a higher risk premium and a greater expected return.

**34.** Here we have the expected return and beta for two assets. We can express the returns of the two assets using CAPM. If the CAPM is true, then the security market line holds as well, which means all assets have the same risk premium. Setting the reward-to-risk ratios of the assets equal to each other and solving for the risk-free rate, we find:

$(.1228 - R_f)/1.35 = (.0854 - R_f)/.80$
$.80(.1228 - R_f) = 1.35(.0854 - R_f)$
$.09824 - .80R_f = .11529 - 1.35R_f$
$.55R_f = .01705$
$R_f = .031$, or 3.10%

Now using CAPM to find the expected return on the market with both stocks, we find:

$.1228 = .0310 + 1.35(R_M - .0310)$          $.0854 = .0310 + .80(R_M - .0310)$
$R_M = .0990$, or 9.90%                       $R_M = .0990$, or 9.90%

**35.** *a.* The expected return of an asset is the sum of the probability of each return occurring times the probability of that return occurring. To calculate the standard deviation, we first need to calculate the variance. To find the variance, we find the squared deviations from the expected return. We then multiply each possible squared deviation by its probability, and then add all of these up. The result is the variance. So, the expected return and standard deviation of each stock are:

*Asset 1:*
$E(R_1) = .15(.20) + .35(.15) + .35(.10) + .15(.05) = .1250$, or 12.50%

$\sigma_1^2 = .15(.20 - .1250)^2 + .35(.15 - .1250)^2 + .35(.10 - .1250)^2 + .15(.05 - .1250)^2 = .00213$

$\sigma_1 = (.00213)^{1/2} = .0461$ or 4.61%

*Asset 2:*
$E(R_2) = .15(.20) + .35(.10) + .35(.15) + .15(.05) = .1250$, or 12.50%

$\sigma_2^2 = .15(.20 - .1250)^2 + .35(.10 - .1250)^2 + .35(.15 - .1250)^2 + .15(.05 - .1250)^2 = .00213$

$\sigma_2 = (.00213)^{1/2} = .0461$ or 4.61%

*Asset 3:*
$E(R_3) = .15(.05) + .35(.10) + .35(.15) + .15(.20) = .1250$, or 12.50%

$\sigma_3^2 = .15(.05 - .1250)^2 + .35(.10 - .1250)^2 + .35(.15 - .1250)^2 + .15(.20 - .1250)^2 = .00213$

$\sigma_3 = (.00213)^{1/2} = .0461$ or 4.61%

b. To find the covariance, we multiply each possible state times the product of each assets' deviation from the mean in that state. The sum of these products is the covariance. The correlation is the covariance divided by the product of the two standard deviations. So, the covariance and correlation between each possible set of assets are:

*Asset 1 and Asset 2:*

$\text{Cov}(1,2) = .15(.20 - .1250)(.20 - .1250) + .35(.15 - .1250)(.10 - .1250)$
$\qquad\qquad + .35(.10 - .1250)(.15 - .1250) + .15(.05 - .1250)(.05 - .1250)$

$\text{Cov}(1,2) = .00125$

$\rho_{1,2} = \text{Cov}(1,2) / \sigma_1 \sigma_2$
$\rho_{1,2} = .00125 / (.0461)(.0461)$
$\rho_{1,2} = .5882$

*Asset 1 and Asset 3:*

$\text{Cov}(1,3) = .15(.20 - .1250)(.05 - .1250) + .35(.15 - .1250)(.10 - .1250)$
$\qquad\qquad + .35(.10 - .1250)(.15 - .1250) + .15(.05 - .1250)(.20 - .1250)$

$\text{Cov}(1,3) = -.002125$

$\rho_{1,3} = \text{Cov}(1,3) / \sigma_1 \sigma_3$
$\rho_{1,3} = -.002125 / (.0461)(.0461)$
$\rho_{1,3} = -1$

*Asset 2 and Asset 3:*

$\text{Cov}(2,3) = .15(.20 - .1250)(.05 - .1250) + .35(.10 - .1250)(.10 - .1250)$
$\qquad\qquad + .35(.15 - .1250)(.15 - .1250) + .15(.05 - .1250)(.20 - .1250)$

$\text{Cov}(2,3) = -.00125$

$\rho_{2,3} = \text{Cov}(2,3) / \sigma_2 \sigma_3$
$\rho_{2,3} = -.00125 / (.0461)(.0461)$
$\rho_{2,3} = -.5882$

c. The expected return of the portfolio is the sum of the weight of each asset times the expected return of each asset, so, for a portfolio of Asset 1 and Asset 2:

$E(R_P) = X_1 E(R_1) + X_2 E(R_2)$
$E(R_P) = .50(.1250) + .50(.1250)$
$E(R_P) = .1250$, or 12.50%

The variance of a portfolio of two assets can be expressed as:

$\sigma_P^2 = X_1^2 \sigma_1^2 + X_2^2 \sigma_2^2 + 2X_1 X_2 \sigma_1 \sigma_2 \rho_{1,2}$

$\sigma_P^2 = .50^2(.0461^2) + .50^2(.0461^2) + 2(.50)(.50)(.0461)(.0461)(.5882)$

$\sigma_P^2 = .001688$

And the standard deviation of the portfolio is:

$\sigma_P = (.001688)^{1/2}$
$\sigma_P = .0411$ or 4.11%

d. The expected return of the portfolio is the sum of the weight of each asset times the expected return of each asset, so, for a portfolio of Asset 1 and Asset 3:

$E(R_P) = X_1E(R_1) + X_3E(R_3)$
$E(R_P) = .50(.1250) + .50(.1250)$
$E(R_P) = .1250$, or 12.50%

The variance of a portfolio of two assets can be expressed as:

$\sigma_P^2 = X_1^2 \sigma_1^2 + X_3^2 \sigma_3^2 + 2X_1X_3\sigma_1\sigma_3\rho_{1,3}$
$\sigma_P^2 = .50^2(.0461^2) + .50^2(.0461^2) + 2(.50)(.50)(.0461)(.0461)(-1)$
$\sigma_P^2 = .000000$

Since the variance is zero, the standard deviation is also zero.

e. The expected return of the portfolio is the sum of the weight of each asset times the expected return of each asset, so, for a portfolio of Asset 2 and Asset 3:

$E(R_P) = X_2E(R_2) + X_3E(R_3)$
$E(R_P) = .50(.1250) + .50(.1250)$
$E(R_P) = .1250$, or 12.50%

The variance of a portfolio of two assets can be expressed as:

$\sigma_P^2 = X_2^2 \sigma_2^2 + X_3^2 \sigma_3^2 + 2X_2X_3\sigma_2\sigma_3\rho_{1,3}$
$\sigma_P^2 = .50^2(.0461^2) + .50^2(.0461^2) + 2(.50)(.50)(.0461)(.0461)(-.5882)$
$\sigma_P^2 = .000438$

And the standard deviation of the portfolio is:

$\sigma_P = (.000438)^{1/2}$
$\sigma_P = .0209$ or 2.09%

f. As long as the correlation between the returns on two securities is below 1, there is a benefit to diversification. A portfolio with negatively correlated stocks can achieve greater risk reduction than a portfolio with positively correlated stocks, holding the expected return on each stock constant. Applying proper weights on perfectly negatively correlated stocks can reduce portfolio variance to 0.

**36.** a. The expected return of an asset is the sum of the probability of each return occurring times the probability of that return occurring. So, the expected return of each stock is:

$E(R_A) = .15(-.10) + .60(.09) + .25(.32) = .1190$, or 11.90%

$E(R_B) = .15(-.08) + .60(.08) + .25(.26) = .1010$, or 10.10%

b.   We can use the expected returns we calculated to find the slope of the Security Market Line. We know that the beta of Stock A is .25 greater than the beta of Stock B. Therefore, as beta increases by .25, the expected return on a security increases by .018 (= .1190 − .1010). The slope of the security market line (SML) equals:

$Slope_{SML}$ = Rise / Run
$Slope_{SML}$ = Increase in expected return / Increase in beta
$Slope_{SML}$ = (.1190 − .1010) / .25
$Slope_{SML}$ = .0720, or 7.20%

Since the market's beta is 1 and the risk-free rate has a beta of zero, the slope of the Security Market Line equals the expected market risk premium. So, the expected market risk premium must be 7.2 percent.

We could also solve this problem using CAPM. The equations for the expected returns of the two stocks are:

$.119 = R_f + (\beta_B + .25)(MRP)$
$.101 = R_f + \beta_B(MRP)$

We can rewrite the CAPM equation for Stock A as:

$.119 = R_f + \beta_B(MRP) + .25(MRP)$

Subtracting the CAPM equation for Stock B from this equation yields:

$.018 = .25MRP$
$MRP = .0720$, or 7.20%

which is the same answer as our previous result.

37.   a.   A typical, risk-averse investor seeks high returns and low risks. For a risk-averse investor holding a well-diversified portfolio, beta is the appropriate measure of the risk of an individual security. To assess the two stocks, we need to find the expected return and beta of each of the two securities.

*Stock A:*
Since Stock A pays no dividends, the return on Stock A is simply: $(P_1 − P_0) / P_0$. So, the return for each state of the economy is:

$R_{Recession}$ = ($64 − 75) / $75 = −.147, or −14.70%
$R_{Normal}$    = ($87 − 75) / $75 = .160, or 16.00%
$R_{Expanding}$ = ($97 − 75) / $75 = .293, or 29.30%

The expected return of an asset is the sum of the probability of each return occurring times the probability of that return occurring. So, the expected return of the stock is:

$E(R_A)$ = .20(−.147) + .60(.160) + .20(.293) = .1253, or 12.53%

And the variance of the stock is:

$$\sigma_A^2 = .20(-0.147 - 0.1253)^2 + .60(.160 - .1253)^2 + .20(.293 - .1253)^2$$
$$\sigma_A^2 = 0.0212$$

Which means the standard deviation is:

$$\sigma_A = (0.0212)^{1/2}$$
$$\sigma_A = .1455, \text{ or } 14.55\%$$

Now we can calculate the stock's beta, which is:

$$\beta_A = (\rho_{A,M})(\sigma_A) / \sigma_M$$
$$\beta_A = (.70)(.1455) / .18$$
$$\beta_A = .566$$

For Stock B, we can directly calculate the beta from the information provided. So, the beta for Stock B is:

*Stock B:*

$$\beta_B = (\rho_{B,M})(\sigma_B) / \sigma_M$$
$$\beta_B = (.24)(.34) / .18$$
$$\beta_B = .453$$

The expected return on Stock B is higher than the expected return on Stock A. The risk of Stock B, as measured by its beta, is lower than the risk of Stock A. Thus, a typical risk-averse investor holding a well-diversified portfolio will prefer Stock B. Note, this situation implies that at least one of the stocks is mispriced since the higher risk (beta) stock has a lower return than the lower risk (beta) stock.

*b.* The expected return of the portfolio is the sum of the weight of each asset times the expected return of each asset, so:

$$E(R_P) = X_A E(R_A) + X_B E(R_B)$$
$$E(R_P) = .70(.1253) + .30(.14)$$
$$E(R_P) = .1297, \text{ or } 12.97\%$$

To find the standard deviation of the portfolio, we first need to calculate the variance. The variance of the portfolio is:

$$\sigma_P^2 = X_A^2 \sigma_A^2 + X_B^2 \sigma_B^2 + 2 X_A X_B \sigma_A \sigma_B \rho_{A,B}$$
$$\sigma_P^2 = (.70)^2(.1455)^2 + (.30)^2(.34)^2 + 2(.70)(.30)(.1455)(.34)(.36)$$
$$\sigma_P^2 = .02825$$

And the standard deviation of the portfolio is:

$$\sigma_P = (0.02825)^{1/2}$$
$$\sigma_P = .1681 \text{ or } 16.81\%$$

c.    The beta of a portfolio is the weighted average of the betas of its individual securities. So the beta of the portfolio is:

$\beta_P = .70(.566) + .30(0.453)$
$\beta_P = .532$

**38.** *a.*    The variance of a portfolio of two assets equals:

$$\sigma_P^2 = X_A^2 \sigma_A^2 + X_B^2 \sigma_B^2 + 2X_A X_B \text{Cov(A,B)}$$

Since the weights of the assets must sum to one, we can write the variance of the portfolio as:

$$\sigma_P^2 = X_A^2 \sigma_A^2 + (1 - X_A)^2 \sigma_B^2 + 2X_A(1 - X_A)\text{Cov(A,B)}$$

To find the minimum for any function, we find the derivative and set the derivative equal to zero. Finding the derivative of the variance function with respect to the weight of Asset A, setting the derivative equal to zero, and solving for the weight of Asset A, we find:

$$X_A = [\sigma_B^2 - \text{Cov(A,B)}] / [\sigma_A^2 + \sigma_B^2 - 2\text{Cov(A,B)}]$$

Using this expression, we find the weight of Asset A must be:

$X_A = (.62^2 - .001) / [.33^2 + .62^2 - 2(.001)]$
$X_A = .7804$

This implies the weight of Stock B is:

$X_B = 1 - X_A$
$X_B = 1 - .7804$
$X_B = .2196$

*b.*    Using the weights calculated in part *a*, the expected return of the portfolio is:

$E(R_P) = X_A E(R_A) + X_B E(R_B)$
$E(R_P) = .7804(.09) + .2196(0.15)$
$E(R_P) = 0.1032$, or 10.32%

*c.*    Using the derivative from part *a*, with the new covariance, the weight of each stock in the minimum variance portfolio is:

$X_A = [\sigma_B^2 + \text{Cov(A,B)}] / [\sigma_A^2 + \sigma_B^2 - 2\text{Cov(A,B)}]$
$X_A = (.62^2 + -.05) / [.33^2 + .62^2 - 2(-.05)]$
$X_A = .7322$

This implies the weight of Stock B is:

$X_B = 1 - X_A$
$X_B = 1 - .7322$
$X_B = .2678$

*d.* The variance of the portfolio with the weights on part *c* is:

$$\sigma_P^2 = X_A^2 \sigma_A^2 + X_B^2 \sigma_B^2 + 2X_A X_B \text{Cov(A,B)}$$
$$\sigma_P^2 = (.7322)^2(.33)^2 + (.2678)^2(.62)^2 + 2(.7322)(.2678)(-.05)$$
$$\sigma_P^2 = .0663$$

And the standard deviation of the portfolio is:

$$\sigma_P = (0.0663)^{1/2}$$
$$\sigma_P = .2576, \text{ or } 25.76\%$$

# CHAPTER 12
# AN ALTERNATIVE VIEW OF RISK AND RETURN: *THE ARBITRAGE PRICING THEORY*

**Answers to Concept Questions**

1. Systematic risk is risk that cannot be diversified away through formation of a portfolio. Generally, systematic risk factors are those factors that affect a large number of firms in the market, however, those factors will not necessarily affect all firms equally. Unsystematic risk is the type of risk that can be diversified away through portfolio formation. Unsystematic risk factors are specific to the firm or industry. Surprises in these factors will affect the returns of the firm in which you are interested, but they will have no effect on the returns of firms in a different industry and perhaps little effect on other firms in the same industry.

2. Any return can be explained with a large enough number of systematic risk factors. However, for a factor model to be useful as a practical matter, the number of factors that explain the returns on an asset must be relatively limited.

3. The market risk premium and inflation rates are probably good choices. The price of wheat, while a risk factor for Ultra Bread, is not a market risk factor and will not likely be priced as a risk factor common to all stocks. In this case, wheat would be a firm specific risk factor, not a market risk factor. A better model would employ macroeconomic risk factors such as interest rates, GDP, energy prices, and industrial production, among others.

4. 
   a. Real GNP was higher than anticipated. Since returns are positively related to the level of GNP, returns should rise based on this factor.
   b. Inflation was exactly the amount anticipated. Since there was no surprise in this announcement, it will not affect Lewis-Striden returns.
   c. Interest rates are lower than anticipated. Since returns are negatively related to interest rates, the lower than expected rate is good news. Returns should rise due to interest rates.
   d. The President's death is bad news. Although the president was expected to retire, his retirement would not be effective for six months. During that period he would still contribute to the firm. His untimely death means that those contributions will not be made. Since he was generally considered an asset to the firm, his death will cause returns to fall. However, since his departure was expected soon, the drop might not be very large.
   e. The poor research results are also bad news. Since Lewis-Striden must continue to test the drug, it will not go into production as early as expected. The delay will affect expected future earnings, and thus it will dampen returns now.
   f. The research breakthrough is positive news for Lewis Striden. Since it was unexpected, it will cause returns to rise.
   g. The competitor's announcement is also unexpected, but it is not a welcome surprise. This announcement will lower the returns on Lewis-Striden.

   The systematic factors in the list are real GNP, inflation, and interest rates. The unsystematic risk factors are the president's ability to contribute to the firm, the research results, and the competitor.

5. The main difference is that the market model assumes that only one factor, usually a stock market aggregate, is enough to explain stock returns, while a k-factor model relies on k factors to explain returns.

6. The fact that APT does not give any guidance about the factors that influence stock returns is a commonly-cited criticism. However, in choosing factors, we should choose factors that have an economically valid reason for potentially affecting stock returns. For example, a smaller company has more risk than a large company. Therefore, the size of a company can affect the returns of the company stock.

7. Assuming the market portfolio is properly scaled, it can be shown that the one-factor model is identical to the CAPM.

8. It is the weighted average of expected returns plus the weighted average of each security's beta times a factor F plus the weighted average of the unsystematic risks of the individual securities.

9. Choosing variables because they have been shown to be related to returns is data mining. The relation found between some attribute and returns can be accidental, thus overstated. For example, the occurrence of sunburns and ice cream consumption are related; however, sunburns do not necessarily cause ice cream consumption, or vice versa. For a factor to truly be related to asset returns, there should be sound economic reasoning for the relationship, not just a statistical one.

10. Using a benchmark composed of English stocks is wrong because the stocks included are not of the same style as those in a U.S. growth stock fund.

**Solutions to Questions and Problems**

*NOTE: All end-of-chapter problems were solved using a spreadsheet. Many problems require multiple steps. Due to space and readability constraints, when these intermediate steps are included in this solutions manual, rounding may appear to have occurred. However, the final answer for each problem is found without rounding during any step in the problem.*

*Basic*

1. Since we have the expected return of the stock, the revised expected return can be determined using the innovation, or surprise, in the risk factors. So, the revised expected return is:

   $R = 12\% + 1.3(3.2\% - 3.6\%) - 0.75(3.4\% - 3.1\%)$
   $R = 11.26\%$

2. *a.* If $m$ is the systematic risk portion of return, then:

   $m = \beta_{GNP}\Delta GNP + \beta_{Inflation}\Delta Inflation + \beta_r\Delta Interest\ rates$
   $m = .0006821(\$13,982 - 14,011) - 0.90(2.60\% - 2.80\%) - .32(4.60\% - 4.80\%)$
   $m = -1.73\%$

b.  The unsystematic return is the return that occurs because of a firm specific factor such as the bad news about the company. So, the unsystematic return of the stock is −1.1 percent. The total return is the expected return, plus the two components of unexpected return: the systematic risk portion of return and the unsystematic portion. So, the total return of the stock is:

$$R = \overline{R} + m + \varepsilon$$
$$R = 12.80\% - 1.73\% - 1.1\%$$
$$R = 9.97\%$$

**3.**  a.  If $m$ is the systematic risk portion of return, then:

$$m = \beta_{GNP}\Delta\%GNP + \beta_r\Delta\text{Interest rates}$$
$$m = 1.87(2.6\% - 2.1\%) - 1.32(4.8\% - 4.3\%)$$
$$m = 0.27\%$$

b.  The unsystematic return is the return that occurs because of a firm specific factor such as the increase in market share. If $\varepsilon$ is the unsystematic risk portion of the return, then:

$$\varepsilon = 0.45(27\% - 23\%)$$
$$\varepsilon = 1.80\%$$

c.  The total return is the expected return, plus the two components of unexpected return: the systematic risk portion of return and the unsystematic portion. So, the total return of the stock is:

$$R = \overline{R} + m + \varepsilon$$
$$R = 10.50\% + 0.27\% + 1.80\%$$
$$R = 12.58\%$$

**4.**  The beta for a particular risk factor in a portfolio is the weighted average of the betas of the assets. This is true whether the betas are from a single factor model or a multi-factor model. So, the betas of the portfolio are:

$$F_1 = .20(1.55) + .20(0.81) + .60(0.73)$$
$$F_1 = 0.91$$

$$F_2 = .20(0.80) + .20(1.25) + .60(-0.14)$$
$$F_2 = 0.33$$

$$F_3 = .20(0.05) + .20(-0.20) + .60(1.24)$$
$$F_3 = 0.71$$

So, the expression for the return of the portfolio is:

$$R_i = 3.2\% + 0.91F_1 + 0.33F_2 - 0.71F_3$$

Which means the return of the portfolio is:

$$R_i = 3.2\% + 0.91(6.10\%) + 0.33(5.30\%) - 0.71(5.70\%)$$
$$R_i = 6.41\%$$

*Intermediate*

**5.** We can express the multifactor model for each portfolio as:

$$E(R_P) = R_F + \beta_1 F_1 + \beta_2 F_2$$

where $F_1$ and $F_2$ are the respective risk premiums for each factor. Expressing the return equation for each portfolio, we get:

$$16\% = 4\% + 0.85F_1 + 1.15F_2$$
$$12\% = 4\% + 1.45F_1 - 0.25F_2$$

We can solve the system of two equations with two unknowns. Multiplying each equation by the respective $F_2$ factor for the other equation, we get:

$$4.00\% = 1.0\% + .2125F_1 + 0.2875F_2$$
$$13.8\% = 4.6\% + 1.6675F_1 - 0.2875F_2$$

Summing the equations and solving $F_1$ for gives us:

$$17.8\% = 5.6\% + 1.88\,F_1$$
$$F_1 = 6.49\%$$

And now, using the equation for portfolio A, we can solve for $F_2$, which is:

$$16\% = 4\% + 0.85(6.490\%) + 1.15F_2$$
$$F_2 = 5.64\%$$

**6.** *a.* The market model is specified by:

$$R = \overline{R} + \beta(R_M - \overline{R}_M) + \varepsilon$$

so applying that to each Stock:

Stock A:
$$R_A = \overline{R}_A + \beta_A(R_M - \overline{R}_M) + \varepsilon_A$$
$$R_A = 10.5\% + 1.2(R_M - 14.2\%) + \varepsilon_A$$

Stock B:
$$R_B = \overline{R}_B + \beta_B(R_M - \overline{R}_M) + \varepsilon_B$$
$$R_B = 13.0\% + 0.98(R_M - 14.2\%) + \varepsilon_B$$

Stock C:
$$R_C = \overline{R}_C + \beta_C(R_M - \overline{R}_M) + \varepsilon_C$$
$$R_C = 15.7\% + 1.37(R_M - 14.2\%) + \varepsilon_C$$

b.   Since we don't have the actual market return or unsystematic risk, we will get a formula with those values as unknowns:

$R_P = .30R_A + .45R_B + .25R_C$
$R_P = .30[10.5\% + 1.2(R_M - 14.2\%) + \varepsilon_A] + .45[13.0\% + 0.98(R_M - 14.2\%) + \varepsilon_B]$
$\qquad + .25[15.7\% + 1.37(R_M - 14.2\%) + \varepsilon_C]$
$R_P = .30(10.5\%) + .45(13\%) + .25(15.7\%) + [.30(1.2) + .45(.98) + .25(1.37)](R_M - 14.2\%)$
$\qquad + .30\varepsilon_A + .45\varepsilon_B + .25\varepsilon_C$
$R_P = 12.925\% + 1.1435(R_M - 14.2\%) + .30\varepsilon_A + .45\varepsilon_B + .25\varepsilon_C$

c.   Using the market model, if the return on the market is 15 percent and the systematic risk is zero, the return for each individual stock is:

$R_A = 10.5\% + 1.20(15\% - 14.2\%)$
$R_A = 11.46\%$

$R_B = 13\% + 0.98(15\% - 14.2\%)$
$R_B = 13.78\%$

$R_C = 15.70\% + 1.37(15\% - 14.2\%)$
$R_C = 16.80\%$

To calculate the return on the portfolio, we can use the equation from part b, so:

$R_P = 12.925\% + 1.1435(15\% - 14.2\%)$
$R_P = 13.84\%$

Alternatively, to find the portfolio return, we can use the return of each asset and its portfolio weight, or:

$R_P = X_1R_1 + X_2R_2 + X_3R_3$
$R_P = .30(11.46\%) + .45(13.78\%) + .25(16.80\%)$
$R_P = 13.84\%$

7.  a.   Since the five stocks have the same expected returns and the same betas, the portfolio also has the same expected return and beta. However, the unsystematic risks might be different, so the expected return of the portfolio is:

$\overline{R}_p = 11\% + 0.84F_1 + 1.69F_2 + (1/5)(\varepsilon_1 + \varepsilon_2 + \varepsilon_3 + \varepsilon_4 + \varepsilon_5)$

b.   Consider the expected return equation of a portfolio of five assets we calculated in part a. Since we now have a very large number of stocks in the portfolio, as:

$N \to \infty, \ \dfrac{1}{N} \to 0$

But, the $\varepsilon_j$s are infinite, so:

$(1/N)(\varepsilon_1 + \varepsilon_2 + \varepsilon_3 + \varepsilon_4 + ..... + \varepsilon_N) \to 0$

Thus:

$$\overline{R}_P = 11\% + 0.84F_1 + 1.69F_2$$

*Challenge*

8.  To determine which investment an investor would prefer, you must compute the variance of portfolios created by many stocks from either market. Because you know that diversification is good, it is reasonable to assume that once an investor has chosen the market in which she will invest, she will buy many stocks in that market.

    Known:
    $$E_F = 0 \text{ and } \sigma = 0.10$$
    $$E_\varepsilon = 0 \text{ and } S_{\varepsilon i} = 0.20 \text{ for all i}$$

    If we assume the stocks in the portfolio are equally-weighted, the weight of each stock is $\dfrac{1}{N}$, that is:

    $$X_i = \frac{1}{N} \text{ for all i}$$

    If a portfolio is composed of N stocks each forming 1/N proportion of the portfolio, the return on the portfolio is 1/N times the sum of the returns on the N stocks. To find the variance of the respective portfolios in the 2 markets, we need to use the definition of variance from Statistics:

    $$\text{Var}(x) = E[x - E(x)]^2$$

In our case:

$$\text{Var}(R_P) = E[R_P - E(R_P)]^2$$

Note however, to use this, first we must find $R_P$ and $E(R_P)$. So, using the assumption about equal weights and then substituting in the known equation for $R_i$:

$$R_P = \frac{1}{N}\sum R_i$$
$$R_P = \frac{1}{N}\sum (0.10 + \beta F + \varepsilon_i)$$
$$R_P = 0.10 + \beta F + \frac{1}{N}\sum \varepsilon_i$$

Also, recall from Statistics a property of expected value, that is:

If: $\tilde{Z} = a\tilde{X} + \tilde{Y}$

where $a$ is a constant, and $\tilde{Z}$, $\tilde{X}$, and $\tilde{Y}$ are random variables, then:

$$E(\tilde{Z}) = E(a)E(\tilde{X}) + E(\tilde{Y})$$

and

$$E(a) = a$$

Now use the above to find $E(R_P)$:

$$E(R_P) = E\left(0.10 + \beta F + \frac{1}{N}\sum \varepsilon_i\right)$$

$$E(R_P) = 0.10 + \beta E(F) + \frac{1}{N}\sum E(\varepsilon_i)$$

$$E(R_P) = 0.10 + \beta(0) + \frac{1}{N}\sum 0$$

$$E(R_P) = 0.10$$

Next, substitute both of these results into the original equation for variance:

$$Var(R_P) = E[R_P - E(R_P)]^2$$

$$Var(R_P) = E\left[0.10 + \beta F + \frac{1}{N}\sum \varepsilon_i - 0.10\right]^2$$

$$Var(R_P) = E\left[\beta F + \frac{1}{N}\sum \varepsilon\right]^2$$

$$Var(R_P) = E\left[\beta^2 F^2 + 2\beta F\frac{1}{N}\sum \varepsilon + \frac{1}{N^2}\left(\sum \varepsilon\right)^2\right]$$

$$Var(R_P) = \left[\beta^2\sigma^2 + \frac{1}{N}\sigma^2\varepsilon + \left(1 - \frac{1}{N}\right)Cov(\varepsilon_i, \varepsilon_j)\right]^2$$

Finally, since we can have as many stocks in each market as we want, in the limit, as $N \to \infty$, $\frac{1}{N} \to 0$, so we get:

$$Var(R_P) = \beta^2\sigma^2 + Cov(\varepsilon_i, \varepsilon_j)$$

and, since:

$$Cov(\varepsilon_i, \varepsilon_j) = \sigma_i\sigma_j\rho(\varepsilon_i, \varepsilon_j)$$

and the problem states that $\sigma_1 = \sigma_2 = 0.10$, so:

$$Var(R_P) = \beta^2\sigma^2 + \sigma_1\sigma_2\rho(\varepsilon_i, \varepsilon_j)$$

$$Var(R_P) = \beta^2(0.01) + 0.04\rho(\varepsilon_i, \varepsilon_j)$$

So now, summarize what we have so far:

$R_{1i} = 0.10 + 1.5F + \varepsilon_{1i}$
$R_{2i} = 0.10 + 0.5F + \varepsilon_{2i}$
$E(R_{1P}) = E(R_{2P}) = 0.10$
$Var(R_{1P}) = 0.0225 + 0.04\rho(\varepsilon_{1i},\varepsilon_{1j})$
$Var(R_{2P}) = 0.0025 + 0.04\rho(\varepsilon_{2i},\varepsilon_{2j})$

Finally we can begin answering the questions a, b, & c for various values of the correlations:

a.  Substitute $\rho(\varepsilon_{1i},\varepsilon_{1j}) = \rho(\varepsilon_{2i},\varepsilon_{2j}) = 0$ into the respective variance formulas:

$Var(R_{1P}) = 0.0225$
$Var(R_{2P}) = 0.0025$

Since $Var(R_{1P}) > Var(R_{2P})$, and expected returns are equal, a risk averse investor will prefer to invest in the second market.

b.  If we assume $\rho(\varepsilon_{1i},\varepsilon_{1j}) = 0.9$, and $\rho(\varepsilon_{2i},\varepsilon_{2j}) = 0$, the variance of each portfolio is:

$Var(R_{1P}) = 0.0225 + 0.04\rho(\varepsilon_{1i},\varepsilon_{1j})$
$Var(R_{1P}) = 0.0225 + 0.04(0.9)$
$Var(R_{1P}) = 0.0585$

$Var(R_{2P}) = 0.0025 + 0.04\rho(\varepsilon_{2i},\varepsilon_{2j})$
$Var(R_{2P}) = 0.0025 + 0.04(0)$
$Var(R_{2P}) = 0.0025$

Since $Var(R_{1P}) > Var(R_{2P})$, and expected returns are equal, a risk averse investor will prefer to invest in the second market.

c.  If we assume $\rho(\varepsilon_{1i},\varepsilon_{1j}) = 0$, and $\rho(\varepsilon_{2i},\varepsilon_{2j}) = .5$, the variance of each portfolio is:

$Var(R_{1P}) = 0.0225 + 0.04\rho(\varepsilon_{1i},\varepsilon_{1j})$
$Var(R_{1P}) = 0.0225 + 0.04(0)$
$Var(R_{1P}) = 0.0225$

$Var(R_{2P}) = 0.0025 + 0.04\rho(\varepsilon_{2i},\varepsilon_{2j})$
$Var(R_{2P}) = 0.0025 + 0.04(0.5)$
$Var(R_{2P}) = 0.0225$

Since $Var(R_{1P}) = Var(R_{2P})$, and expected returns are equal, a risk averse investor will be indifferent between the two markets.

d.  Since the expected returns are equal, indifference implies that the variances of the portfolios in the two markets are also equal. So, set the variance equations equal, and solve for the correlation of one market in terms of the other:

$Var(R_{1P}) = Var(R_{2P})$
$0.0225 + 0.04\rho(\varepsilon_{1i},\varepsilon_{1j}) = 0.0025 + 0.04\rho(\varepsilon_{2i},\varepsilon_{2j})$
$\rho(\varepsilon_{2i},\varepsilon_{2j}) = \rho(\varepsilon_{1i},\varepsilon_{1j}) + 0.5$

Therefore, for any set of correlations that have this relationship (as found in part c), a risk adverse investor will be indifferent between the two markets.

**9.**  *a.*  In order to find standard deviation, $\sigma$, you must first find the variance, since $\sigma = \sqrt{\text{Var}}$. Recall from Statistics a property of variance:

If: $\tilde{Z} = a\tilde{X} + \tilde{Y}$

where $a$ is a constant, and $\tilde{Z}$, $\tilde{X}$, and $\tilde{Y}$ are random variables, then:

$$\text{Var}(\tilde{Z}) = a^2\text{Var}(\tilde{X}) + \text{Var}(\tilde{Y})$$

and:

$$\text{Var}(a) = 0$$

The problem states that return-generation can be described by:

$$R_{i,t} = \alpha_i + \beta_i(R_M) + \varepsilon_{i,t}$$

Realize that $R_{i,t}$, $R_M$, and $\varepsilon_{i,t}$ are random variables, and $\alpha_i$ and $\beta_i$ are constants. Then, applying the above properties to this model, we get:

$$\text{Var}(R_i) = \beta_i^2\text{Var}(R_M) + \text{Var}(\varepsilon_i)$$

and now we can find the standard deviation for each asset:

$$\sigma_A^2 = 0.7^2(0.0121) + 0.01 = 0.015929$$
$$\sigma_A = \sqrt{0.015929} = .1262 \text{ or } 12.62\%$$

$$\sigma_B^2 = 1.2^2(0.0121) + 0.0144 = 0.031824$$
$$\sigma_B = \sqrt{0.031824} = .1784 \text{ or } 17.84\%$$

$$\sigma_C^2 = 1.5^2(0.0121) + 0.0225 = 0.049725$$
$$\sigma_C = \sqrt{0.049725} = .2230 \text{ or } 22.30\%$$

*b.*  From the above formula for variance, note that as $N \to \infty$, $\dfrac{\text{Var}(\varepsilon_i)}{N} \to 0$, so you get:

$$\text{Var}(R_i) = \beta_i^2\text{Var}(R_M)$$

So, the variances for the assets are:

$$\sigma_A^2 = 0.7^2(.0121) = 0.005929$$
$$\sigma_B^2 = 1.2^2(.0121) = 0.017424$$
$$\sigma_C^2 = 1.5^2(.0121) = 0.027225$$

c. We can use the model:

$$\overline{R}_i = R_F + \beta_i(\overline{R}_M - R_F)$$

which is the CAPM (or APT Model when there is one factor and that factor is the Market). So, the expected return of each asset is:

$$\overline{R}_A = 3.3\% + 0.7(10.6\% - 3.3\%) = 8.41\%$$
$$\overline{R}_B = 3.3\% + 1.2(10.6\% - 3.3\%) = 12.06\%$$
$$\overline{R}_C = 3.3\% + 1.5(10.6\% - 3.3\%) = 14.25\%$$

We can compare these results for expected asset returns as per CAPM or APT with the expected returns given in the table. This shows that assets A & B are accurately priced, but asset C is overpriced (the model shows the return *should* be higher). Thus, rational investors will not hold asset C.

d. If short selling is allowed, rational investors will sell short asset C, causing the price of asset C to decrease until no arbitrage opportunity exists. In other words, the price of asset C should decrease until the return becomes 14.25 percent.

**10.** a. Let:

$X_1$ = the proportion of Security 1 in the portfolio and
$X_2$ = the proportion of Security 2 in the portfolio

and note that since the weights must sum to 1.0,

$$X_1 = 1 - X_2$$

Recall from Chapter 10 that the beta for a portfolio (or in this case the beta for a factor) is the weighted average of the security betas, so

$$\beta_{P1} = X_1\beta_{11} + X_2\beta_{21}$$
$$\beta_{P1} = X_1\beta_{11} + (1 - X_1)\beta_{21}$$

Now, apply the condition given in the hint that the return of the portfolio does not depend on $F_1$. This means that the portfolio beta for that factor will be 0, so:

$$\beta_{P1} = 0 = X_1\beta_{11} + (1 - X_1)\beta_{21}$$
$$\beta_{P1} = 0 = X_1(1.0) + (1 - X_1)(0.5)$$

and solving for $X_1$ and $X_2$:

$$X_1 = -1$$
$$X_2 = 2$$

Thus, sell short Security 1 and buy Security 2.

To find the expected return on that portfolio, use

$$R_P = X_1 R_1 + X_2 R_2$$

so applying the above:

$$E(R_P) = -1(20\%) + 2(20\%)$$
$$E(R_P) = 20\%$$

$$\beta_{P1} = -1(1) + 2(0.5)$$
$$\beta_{P1} = 0$$

b.  Following the same logic as in part a, we have

$$\beta_{P2} = 0 = X_3\beta_{31} + (1 - X_3)\beta_{41}$$
$$\beta_{P2} = 0 = X_3(1) + (1 - X_3)(1.5)$$

and

$$X_3 = 3$$
$$X_4 = -2$$

Thus, sell short Security 4 and buy Security 3. Then,

$$E(R_{P2}) = 3(10\%) + (-2)(10\%)$$
$$E(R_{P2}) = 10\%$$

$$\beta_{P2} = 3(0.5) - 2(0.75)$$
$$\beta_{P2} = 0$$

Note that since both $\beta_{P1}$ and $\beta_{P2}$ are 0, this is a risk free portfolio!

c.  The portfolio in part b provides a risk free return of 10%, which is higher than the 5% return provided by the risk free security. To take advantage of this opportunity, borrow at the risk free rate of 5% and invest the funds in a portfolio built by selling short security four and buying security three with weights (3,–2) as in part b.

d.  First assume that the risk free security will not change. The price of security four (that everyone is trying to sell short) will decrease, and the price of security three (that everyone is trying to buy) will increase. Hence the return of security four will increase and the return of security three will decrease.

The alternative is that the prices of securities three and four will remain the same, and the price of the risk-free security drops until its return is 10%.

Finally, a combined movement of all security prices is also possible. The prices of security four and the risk-free security will decrease and the price of security three will increase until the opportunity disappears.

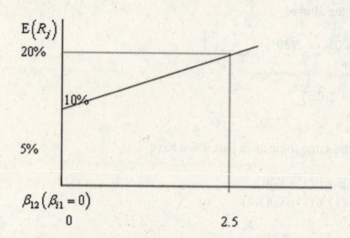

# CHAPTER 13
# RISK, COST OF CAPITAL, AND CAPITAL BUDGETING

## Answers to Concepts Review and Critical Thinking Questions

1. No. The cost of capital depends on the risk of the project, not the source of the money.

2. Interest expense is tax-deductible. There is no difference between pretax and aftertax equity costs.

3. You are assuming that the new project's risk is the same as the risk of the firm as a whole, and that the firm is financed entirely with equity.

4. Two primary advantages of the SML approach are that the model explicitly incorporates the relevant risk of the stock and the method is more widely applicable than is the DCF model, since the SML doesn't make any assumptions about the firm's dividends. The primary disadvantages of the SML method are (1) three parameters (the risk-free rate, the expected return on the market, and beta) must be estimated, and (2) the method essentially uses historical information to estimate these parameters. The risk-free rate is usually estimated to be the yield on very short maturity T-bills and is, hence, observable; the market risk premium is usually estimated from historical risk premiums and, hence, is not observable. The stock beta, which is unobservable, is usually estimated either by determining some average historical beta from the firm and the market's return data, or by using beta estimates provided by analysts and investment firms.

5. The appropriate aftertax cost of debt to the company is the interest rate it would have to pay if it were to issue new debt today. Hence, if the YTM on outstanding bonds of the company is observed, the company has an accurate estimate of its cost of debt. If the debt is privately-placed, the firm could still estimate its cost of debt by (1) looking at the cost of debt for similar firms in similar risk classes, (2) looking at the average debt cost for firms with the same credit rating (assuming the firm's private debt is rated), or (3) consulting analysts and investment bankers. Even if the debt is publicly traded, an additional complication arises when the firm has more than one issue outstanding; these issues rarely have the same yield because no two issues are ever completely homogeneous.

6.  
   *a.*   This only considers the dividend yield component of the required return on equity.  
   *b.*   This is the current yield only, not the promised yield to maturity. In addition, it is based on the book value of the liability, and it ignores taxes.  
   *c.*   Equity is inherently riskier than debt (except, perhaps, in the unusual case where a firm's assets have a negative beta). For this reason, the cost of equity exceeds the cost of debt. If taxes are considered in this case, it can be seen that at reasonable tax rates, the cost of equity does exceed the cost of debt.

**7.** $R_{Sup} = .12 + .75(.08) = .1800$ or $18.00\%$

Both should proceed. The appropriate discount rate does not depend on which company is investing; it depends on the risk of the project. Since Superior is in the business, it is closer to a pure play. Therefore, its cost of capital should be used. With an 18% cost of capital, the project has an NPV of $1 million regardless of who takes it.

**8.** If the different operating divisions were in much different risk classes, then separate cost of capital figures should be used for the different divisions; the use of a single, overall cost of capital would be inappropriate. If the single hurdle rate were used, riskier divisions would tend to receive more funds for investment projects, since their return would exceed the hurdle rate despite the fact that they may actually plot below the SML and, hence, be unprofitable projects on a risk-adjusted basis. The typical problem encountered in estimating the cost of capital for a division is that it rarely has its own securities traded on the market, so it is difficult to observe the market's valuation of the risk of the division. Two typical ways around this are to use a pure play proxy for the division, or to use subjective adjustments of the overall firm hurdle rate based on the perceived risk of the division.

**9.** The discount rate for the projects should be lower that the rate implied by the security market line. The security market line is used to calculate the cost of equity. The appropriate discount rate for projects is the firm's weighted average cost of capital. Since the firm's cost of debt is generally less that the firm's cost of equity, the rate implied by the security market line will be too high.

**10.** Beta measures the responsiveness of a security's returns to movements in the market. Beta is determined by the cyclicality of a firm's revenues. This cyclicality is magnified by the firm's operating and financial leverage. The following three factors will impact the firm's beta. (1) Revenues. The cyclicality of a firm's sales is an important factor in determining beta. In general, stock prices will rise when the economy expands and will fall when the economy contracts. As we said above, beta measures the responsiveness of a security's returns to movements in the market. Therefore, firms whose revenues are more responsive to movements in the economy will generally have higher betas than firms with less-cyclical revenues. (2) Operating leverage. Operating leverage is the percentage change in earnings before interest and taxes (EBIT) for a percentage change in sales. A firm with high operating leverage will have greater fluctuations in EBIT for a change in sales than a firm with low operating leverage. In this way, operating leverage magnifies the cyclicality of a firm's revenues, leading to a higher beta. (3) Financial leverage. Financial leverage arises from the use of debt in the firm's capital structure. A levered firm must make fixed interest payments regardless of its revenues. The effect of financial leverage on beta is analogous to the effect of operating leverage on beta. Fixed interest payments cause the percentage change in net income to be greater than the percentage change in EBIT, magnifying the cyclicality of a firm's revenues. Thus, returns on highly-levered stocks should be more responsive to movements in the market than the returns on stocks with little or no debt in their capital structure.

## Solutions to Questions and Problems

*NOTE: All end-of-chapter problems were solved using a spreadsheet. Many problems require multiple steps. Due to space and readability constraints, when these intermediate steps are included in this solutions manual, rounding may appear to have occurred. However, the final answer for each problem is found without rounding during any step in the problem.*

### Basic

1.  With the information given, we can find the cost of equity using the CAPM. The cost of equity is:

    $R_S = .035 + 1.21(.11 - .035) = .1258$, or 12.58%

2.  The pretax cost of debt is the YTM of the company's bonds, so:

    $P_0 = \$950 = \$40(PVIFA_{R\%,34}) + \$1,000(PVIF_{R\%,34})$
    $R = 4.282\%$
    $R_B = 2 \times 4.282\% = 8.56\%$

    And the aftertax cost of debt is:

    Aftertax cost of debt = 8.56%(1 − .35) = 5.57%

3.  *a.* The pretax cost of debt is the YTM of the company's bonds, so:

    $P_0 = \$1,080 = \$31.50(PVIFA_{R\%,46}) + \$1,000(PVIF_{R\%,46})$
    $R = 2.789\%$
    $R_B = 2 \times 2.789\% = 5.58\%$

    *b.* The aftertax cost of debt is:

    Aftertax cost of debt = 5.58%(1 − .35) = 3.63%

    *c.* The aftertax rate is more relevant because that is the actual cost to the company.

4.  The book value of debt is the total par value of all outstanding debt, so:

    $BV_B = \$70,000,000 + 100,000,000 = \$170,000,000$

    To find the market value of debt, we find the price of the bonds and multiply by the number of bonds. Alternatively, we can multiply the price quote of the bond times the par value of the bonds. Doing so, we find:

    $B = 1.08(\$70,000,000) + .61(\$100,000,000) = \$136,600,000$

    The YTM of the zero coupon bonds is:

    $P_Z = \$610 = \$1,000(PVIF_{R\%,24})$
    $R = 2.081\%$
    YTM = 2 × 2.081% = 4.16%

So, the aftertax cost of the zero coupon bonds is:

Aftertax cost of debt = 4.16%(1 – .35) = 2.71%

The aftertax cost of debt for the company is the weighted average of the aftertax cost of debt for all outstanding bond issues. We need to use the market value weights of the bonds. The total aftertax cost of debt for the company is:

Aftertax cost of debt = .0363[1.08($70)/$136.6] + .0271[.61($100)/$136.6] = .0321, or 3.21%

5. Using the equation to calculate the WACC, we find:

$R_{WACC}$ = .70(.13) + .30(.06)(1 – .35) = .1027, or 10.27%

6. Here we need to use the debt-equity ratio to calculate the WACC. Doing so, we find:

$R_{WACC}$ = .14(1/1.55) + .07(.55/1.55)(1 – .35) = .1065, or 10.65%

7. Here we have the WACC and need to find the debt-equity ratio of the company. Setting up the WACC equation, we find:

$R_{WACC}$ = .0980 = .13($S/V$) + .065($B/V$)(1 – .35)

Rearranging the equation, we find:

.0980($V/S$) = .13 + .065(.65)($B/S$)

Now we must realize that the V/S is just the equity multiplier, which is equal to:

$V/S$ = 1 + $B/S$

.0980($B/S$ + 1) = .13 + .04225($B/S$)

Now we can solve for B/S as:

.05575($B/S$) = .032
$B/S$ = .5740

8. a. The book value of equity is the book value per share times the number of shares, and the book value of debt is the face value of the company's debt, so:

Equity = 8,300,000($4) = $33,200,000

Debt = $70,000,000 + 60,000,000 = $130,000,000

So, the total book value of the company is:

Book value = $33,200,000 + 130,000,000 = $163,200,000

And the book value weights of equity and debt are:

Equity/Value = $33,200,000/$163,200,000 = .2034

Debt/Value = 1 – Equity/Value = .7966

b.    The market value of equity is the share price times the number of shares, so:

$S = 8,300,000(\$53) = \$439,900,000$

Using the relationship that the total market value of debt is the price quote times the par value of the bond, we find the market value of debt is:

$B = 1.083(\$70,000,000) + 1.089(\$60,000,000) = \$141,150,000$

This makes the total market value of the company:

$V = \$439,900,000 + 141,150,000 = \$581,050,000$

And the market value weights of equity and debt are:

$S/V = \$439,900,000/\$581,050,000 = .7571$

$B/V = 1 – S/V = .2429$

c.    The market value weights are more relevant.

**9.**   First, we will find the cost of equity for the company. The information provided allows us to solve for the cost of equity using the CAPM, so:

$R_S = .031 + 1.2(.07) = .1150$, or 11.50%

Next, we need to find the YTM on both bond issues. Doing so, we find:

$P_1 = \$1,083 = \$35(PVIFA_{R\%,16}) + \$1,000(PVIF_{R\%,16})$
$R = 2.847\%$
YTM = 2.847% × 2 = 5.69%

$P_2 = \$1,089 = \$37.50(PVIFA_{R\%,54}) + \$1,000(PVIF_{R\%,54})$
$R = 3.389\%$
YTM = 3.389% × 2 = 6.78%

To find the weighted average aftertax cost of debt, we need the weight of each bond as a percentage of the total debt. We find:

$X_{B1} = 1.083(\$70,000,000)/\$141,150,000 = .537$

$X_{B2} = 1.089(\$60,000,000)/\$141,150,000 = .463$

Now we can multiply the weighted average cost of debt times one minus the tax rate to find the weighted average aftertax cost of debt. This gives us:

$$R_B = (1 - .35)[(.537)(.0569) + (.463)(.0678)] = .0403, \text{ or } 4.03\%$$

Using these costs and the weight of debt we calculated earlier, the WACC is:

$$R_{WACC} = .7571(.1150) + .2429(.0403) = .0968, \text{ or } 9.68\%$$

**10.** *a.* Using the equation to calculate WACC, we find:

$$R_{WACC} = .112 = (1/1.45)(.15) + (.45/1.45)(1 - .35)R_B$$
$$R_B = .0424, \text{ or } 4.24\%$$

*b.* Using the equation to calculate WACC, we find:

$$R_{WACC} = .112 = (1/1.45)R_S + (.45/1.45)(.064)$$
$$R_S = .1336, \text{ or } 13.36\%$$

**11.** We will begin by finding the market value of each type of financing. We find:

$$B = 5,000(\$1,000)(1.05) = \$5,250,000$$
$$S = 175,000(\$58) = \$10,150,000$$

And the total market value of the firm is:

$$V = \$5,250,000 + 10,150,000 = \$15,400,000$$

Now, we can find the cost of equity using the CAPM. The cost of equity is:

$$R_S = .05 + 1.10(.07) = .1270, \text{ or } 12.70\%$$

The cost of debt is the YTM of the bonds, so:

$$P_0 = \$1,050 = \$30(PVIFA_{R\%,50}) + \$1,000(PVIF_{R\%,50})$$
$$R = 2.813\%$$
$$YTM = 2.813\% \times 2 = 5.63\%$$

And the aftertax cost of debt is:

$$R_B = (1 - .35)(.0563) = .0366, \text{ or } 3.66\%$$

Now we have all of the components to calculate the WACC. The WACC is:

$$R_{WACC} = .0366(\$5,250,000/\$15,400,000) + .1270(\$10,150,000/\$15,400,000) = .0962, \text{ or } 9.62\%$$

Notice that we didn't include the $(1 - t_C)$ term in the WACC equation. We simply used the aftertax cost of debt in the equation, so the term is not needed here.

**12.** *a.* We will begin by finding the market value of each type of financing. We find:

$B = 260,000(\$1,000)(1.04) = \$270,400,000$
$S = 9,300,000(\$34) = \$316,200,000$

And the total market value of the firm is:

$V = \$270,400,000 + 316,200,000 = \$586,600,000$

So, the market value weights of the company's financing is:

$B/V = \$270,400,000/\$586,600,000 = .4610$
$S/V = \$316,200,000/\$586,600,000 = .5390$

*b.* For projects equally as risky as the firm itself, the WACC should be used as the discount rate.

First we can find the cost of equity using the CAPM. The cost of equity is:

$R_S = .035 + 1.20(.07) = .1190$, or 11.90%

The cost of debt is the YTM of the bonds, so:

$P_0 = \$1,040 = \$34(PVIFA_{R\%,40}) + \$1,000(PVIF_{R\%,40})$
$R = 3.221\%$
$YTM = 3.221\% \times 2 = 6.44\%$

And the aftertax cost of debt is:

$R_B = (1 - .35)(.0644) = .0419$, or 4.19%

Now we can calculate the WACC as:

$R_{WACC} = .5390(.1190) + .4610(.0419) = .0834$, or 8.34%

**13.** *a.* Projects Y and Z.

*b.* Using the CAPM to consider the projects, we need to calculate the expected return of each project given its level of risk. This expected return should then be compared to the expected return of the project. If the return calculated using the CAPM is lower than the project expected return, we should accept the project; if not, we reject the project. After considering risk via the CAPM:

$E[W] = .035 + .80(.11 - .035)$     $= .0950 > .094$, so reject W
$E[X] = .035 + .95(.11 - .035)$     $= .1063 < .109$, so accept X
$E[Y] = .035 + 1.15(.11 - .035)$     $= .1213 < .13$, so accept Y
$E[Z] = .035 + 1.45(.11 - .035)$     $= .1438 > .142$, so reject Z

*c.* Project X would be incorrectly rejected; Project Z would be incorrectly accepted.

**14.** *a.* He should look at the weighted average flotation cost, not just the debt cost.

*b.* The weighted average flotation cost is the weighted average of the flotation costs for debt and equity, so:

$f_T = .03(.75/1.75) + .07(1/1.75) = .0529$, or 5.29%

*c.* The total cost of the equipment including flotation costs is:

Amount raised$(1 - .0529) = \$20,000,000$
Amount raised $= \$20,000,000/(1 - .0529) = \$21,116,139$

Even if the specific funds are actually being raised completely from debt, the flotation costs, and hence true investment cost, should be valued as if the firm's target capital structure is used.

**15.** We first need to find the weighted average flotation cost. Doing so, we find:

$f_T = .65(.08) + .05(.05) + .30(.03) = .064$, or 6.4%

And the total cost of the equipment including flotation costs is:

Amount raised$(1 - .064) = \$55,000,000$
Amount raised $= \$55,000,000/(1 - .064) = \$58,729,311$

*Intermediate*

**16.** Using the debt-equity ratio to calculate the WACC, we find:

$R_{WACC} = (.55/1.55)(.055) + (1/1.55)(.13) = .1034$, or 10.34%

Since the project is riskier than the company, we need to adjust the project discount rate for the additional risk. Using the subjective risk factor given, we find:

Project discount rate = 10.34% + 2% = 12.34%

We would accept the project if the NPV is positive. The NPV is the PV of the cash outflows plus the PV of the cash inflows. Since we have the costs, we just need to find the PV of inflows. The cash inflows are a growing perpetuity. If you remember, the equation for the PV of a growing perpetuity is the same as the dividend growth equation, so:

PV of future CF $= \$3,500,000/(.1234 - .04) = \$41,972,921$

The project should only be undertaken if its cost is less than $41,972,921 since costs less than this amount will result in a positive NPV.

**17.** We will begin by finding the market value of each type of financing. We will use B1 to represent the coupon bond, and B2 to represent the zero coupon bond. So, the market value of the firm's financing is:

$B_{B1} = 60,000(\$1,000)(1.095) = \$65,700,000$
$B_{B2} = 230,000(\$1,000)(.175) = \$40,250,000$
$P = 150,000(\$79) = \$11,850,000$
$S = 2,600,000(\$65) = \$169,000,000$

And the total market value of the firm is:

$V = \$65,700,000 + 40,250,000 + 11,850,000 + 169,000,000 = \$286,800,000$

Now, we can find the cost of equity using the CAPM. The cost of equity is:

$R_S = .04 + 1.15(.07) = .1205$, or 12.05%

The cost of debt is the YTM of the bonds, so:

$P_0 = \$1,095 = \$30(PVIFA_{R\%,40}) + \$1,000(PVIF_{R\%,40})$
$R = 2.614\%$
$YTM = 2.614\% \times 2 = 5.23\%$

And the aftertax cost of debt is:

$R_{B1} = (1 - .40)(.0523) = .0314$, or 3.14%

And the aftertax cost of the zero coupon bonds is:

$P_0 = \$175 = \$1,000(PVIF_{R\%,60})$
$R = 2.948\%$
$YTM = 2.948\% \times 2 = 5.90\%$

$R_{B2} = (1 - .40)(.0590) = .0354$, or 3.54%

Even though the zero coupon bonds make no payments, the calculation for the YTM (or price) still assumes semiannual compounding, consistent with a coupon bond. Also remember that, even though the company does not make interest payments, the accrued interest is still tax deductible for the company.

To find the required return on preferred stock, we can use the preferred stock pricing equation, which is the level perpetuity equation, so the required return on the company's preferred stock is:

$R_P = D_1 / P_0$
$R_P = \$4 / \$79$
$R_P = .0506$, or 5.06%

Notice that the required return in the preferred stock is lower than the required on the bonds. This result is not consistent with the risk levels of the two instruments, but is a common occurrence. There is a practical reason for this: Assume Company A owns stock in Company B. The tax code allows Company A to exclude at least 70 percent of the dividends received from Company B, meaning Company A does not pay taxes on this amount. In practice, much of the outstanding preferred stock is owned by other companies, who are willing to take the lower return since much of the return is effectively tax exempt for the investing company.

Now we have all of the components to calculate the WACC. The WACC is:

$R_{WACC} = .0314(\$65,700,000/\$286,800,000) + .0354(\$40,250,000/\$286,800,000)$
$\qquad + .1205(\$169,000,000/\$286,800,000) + .0506(\$11,850,000/\$286,800,000)$
$R_{WACC} = .0852$, or 8.52%

**18.** The total cost of the equipment including flotation costs was:

Total costs = \$19,000,000 + 1,150,000 = \$20,150,000

Using the equation to calculate the total cost including flotation costs, we get:

Amount raised$(1 - f_T)$ = Amount needed after flotation costs
$\$20,150,000(1 - f_T) = \$19,000,000$
$f_T = .0571$, or 5.71%

Now, we know the weighted average flotation cost. The equation to calculate the percentage flotation costs is:

$f_T = .0571 = .07(S/V) + .03(B/V)$

We can solve this equation to find the debt-equity ratio as follows:

$.0571(V/S) = .07 + .03(B/S)$

We must recognize that the $V/S$ term is the equity multiplier, which is $(1 + B/S)$, so:

$.0571(B/S + 1) = .07 + .03(B/S)$
$B/S = .4775$

**19.** *a.* Using the dividend discount model, the cost of equity is:

$R_S = [(0.95)(1.045)/\$64] + .045$
$R_S = .0605$, or 6.05%

*b.* Using the CAPM, the cost of equity is:

$R_S = .043 + 1.30(.11 - .043)$
$R_S = .1301$, or 13.01%

*c.* When using the dividend growth model or the CAPM, you must remember that both are estimates for the cost of equity. Additionally, and perhaps more importantly, each method of estimating the cost of equity depends upon different assumptions.

20. We are given the total cash flow for the current year. To value the company, we need to calculate the cash flows until the growth rate levels off at a constant perpetual rate. So, the cash flows each year will be:

Year 1: $7,500,000(1 + .08)      = $8,100,000
Year 2: $8,100,000(1 + .08)      = $8,748,000
Year 3: $8,748,000(1 + .08)      = $9,447,840
Year 4: $9,447,840(1 + .08)      = $10,203,667
Year 5: $10,203,667(1 + .08)     = $11,019,961
Year 6: $11,019,961(1 + .04)     = $11,460,759

We can calculate the terminal value in Year 5 since the cash flows begin a perpetual growth rate. Since we are valuing Arras, we need to use the cost of capital for that company since this rate is based on the risk of Arras. The cost of capital for Schultz is irrelevant in this case. So, the terminal value is:

$TV_5 = CF_6 / (R_{WACC} - g)$
$TV_5 = \$11,460,759 / (.10 - .04)$
$TV_5 = \$191,012,650$

Now we can discount the cash flows for the first 5 years as well as the terminal value back to today. Again, using the cost of capital for Arras, we find the value of the company today is:

$V_0 = \$8,100,000 / 1.08 + \$8,748,000 / 1.08^2 + \$9,447,840 / 1.08^3 + \$10,203,667 / 1.08^4$
$\qquad + (\$11,019,961 + 191,012,650) / 1.08^5$
$V_0 = \$154,107,288$

The market value of the equity is the market value of the company minus the market value of the debt, or:

$S = \$154,107,288 - 25,000,000$
$S = \$129,107,288$

To find the maximum offer price, we divide the market value of equity by the shares outstanding, or:

Share price = $129,107,288 / 3,000,000
Share price = $43.04

21. *a.* To begin the valuation of Joe's, we will begin by calculating the $R_{WACC}$ for Happy Times. Since both companies are in the same industry, it is likely that the $R_{WACC}$ for both companies will be the same. The weights of debt and equity are:

$X_B = \$140,000,000 / (\$140,000,000 + 380,000,000) = .2692$, or 26.92%
$X_S = \$380,000,000 / (\$140,000,000 + 380,000,000) = .7308$, or 73.08%

The $R_{WACC}$ for Happy Times is:

$R_{WACC} = .2692(.06)(1 - .38) + .7308(.11) = .0904$, or 9.04%

Next, we need to calculate the cash flows for each year. The EBIT will grow at 10 percent per year for 5 years. Net working capital, capital spending, and depreciation are 9 percent, 15 percent, and 8 percent of EBIT, respectively. So, the cash flows for each year over the next 5 years will be:

|  | Year 1 | Year 2 | Year 3 | Year 4 | Year 5 |
|---|---|---|---|---|---|
| EBIT | $12,500,000 | $13,750,000 | $15,125,000 | $16,637,500 | $18,301,250 |
| Taxes | 4,750,000 | 5,225,000 | 5,747,500 | 6,322,250 | 6,954,475 |
| Net income | $ 7,750,000 | $ 8,525,000 | $ 9,377,500 | $10,315,250 | $11,346,775 |
| Depreciation | 1,000,000 | 1,100,000 | 1,210,000 | 1,331,000 | 1,464,100 |
| | | | | | |
| OCF | $ 8,750,000 | $ 9,625,000 | $10,587,500 | $11,646,250 | $12,810,875 |
| – Capital spending | 1,875,000 | 2,062,500 | 2,268,750 | 2,495,625 | 2,745,188 |
| – Change in NWC | 1,125,000 | 1,237,500 | 1,361,250 | 1,497,375 | 1,647,113 |
| Cash flow from assets | $ 5,750,000 | $ 6,325,000 | $ 6,957,500 | $ 7,653,250 | $ 8,418,575 |

After Year 5 the cash flows will grow at 3 percent in perpetuity. We can find the terminal value of the company in Year 5 using the cash flow in Year 6 as:

$TV_5 = CF_6 / (R_{WACC} - g)$
$TV_5 = \$8,418,575(1 + .03) / (.0904 - .03)$
$TV_5 = \$143,561,792$

Now we can discount the cash flows and terminal value to today. Doing so, we find:

$V_0 = \$5,750,000 / 1.0904 + \$6,325,000 / 1.0904^2 + \$6,957,500 / 1.0904^3$
$\qquad + \$7,653,250 / 1.0904^4 + (\$8,418,575 + 143,561,792) / 1.0904^5$
$V_0 = \$119,969,144$

The market value of the equity is the market value of the company minus the market value of the debt, or:

$S = \$119,969,144 - 30,500,000$
$S = \$89,469,144$

To find the maximum offer price, we divide the market value of equity by the shares outstanding, or:

Share price = $89,469,144 / 1,850,000
Share price = $48.36

b. To calculate the terminal value using the EV/EBITDA multiple we need to calculate the Year 5 EBITDA, which is EBIT plus depreciation, or:

EBITDA = $18,301,250 + 1,464,100
EBITDA = $19,765,350

We can now calculate the terminal value of the company using the Year 5 EBITDA, which will be:

$TV_5 = \$19,765,350(8)$
$TV_5 = \$158,122,800$

Note, this is the terminal value in Year 5 since we used the Year 5 EBITDA. We need to calculate the present value of the cash flows for the first 4 years, plus the present value of the Year 5 terminal value. We do not need to include the Year 5 cash flow since it is included in the Year 5 terminal value. So, the value of the company today is:

$V_0 = \$5,750,000 / 1.0904 + \$6,325,000 / 1.0904^2 + \$6,957,500 / 1.0904^3$
$\qquad + \$7,653,250 / 1.0904^4 + \$158,122,800 / 1.0904^5$
$V_0 = \$123,953,986$

The market value of the equity is the market value of the company minus the market value of the debt, or:

$S = \$123,953,986 - 30,500,000$
$S = \$93,453,986$

To find the maximum offer price, we divide the market value of equity by the shares outstanding, or:

Share price = $\$93,453,986 / 1,850,000$
Share price = $\$50.52$

*Challenge*

22. We can use the debt-equity ratio to calculate the weights of equity and debt. The debt of the company has a weight for long-term debt and a weight for accounts payable. We can use the weight given for accounts payable to calculate the weight of accounts payable and the weight of long-term debt. The weight of each will be:

Accounts payable weight = $.20/1.20 = .17$
Long-term debt weight = $1/1.20 = .83$

Since the accounts payable has the same cost as the overall WACC, we can write the equation for the WACC as:

$R_{WACC} = (1/1.55)(.14) + (0.55/1.55)[(.20/1.2)\ R_{WACC} + (1/1.2)(.08)(1 - .35)]$

Solving for WACC, we find:

$R_{WACC} = .0903 + .3548[(.20/1.2)R_{WACC} + .0433]$
$R_{WACC} = .0903 + (.0591)R_{WACC} + .0154$
$(.9409)R_{WACC} = .1057$
$R_{WACC} = .1123$, or 11.23%

We will use basically the same equation to calculate the weighted average flotation cost, except we will use the flotation cost for each form of financing. Doing so, we get:

Flotation costs = $(1/1.55)(.08) + (0.55/1.55)[(.20/1.2)(0) + (1/1.2)(.04)] = .0634$, or 6.34%

The total amount we need to raise to fund the new equipment will be:

Amount raised cost = $50,000,000/(1 - .0634)$
Amount raised = $53,386,912

Since the cash flows go to perpetuity, we can calculate the present value using the equation for the PV of a perpetuity. The NPV is:

NPV = -$53,386,912 + ($6,700,000/.1123)
NPV = $6,251,949

23. We can use the debt-equity ratio to calculate the weights of equity and debt. The weight of debt in the capital structure is:

$X_B$ = .85 / 1.85 = .4595, or 45.95%

And the weight of equity is:

$X_S$ = 1 - .4595 = .5405, or 54.05%

Now we can calculate the weighted average flotation costs for the various percentages of internally raised equity. To find the portion of equity flotation costs, we can multiply the equity costs by the percentage of equity raised externally, which is one minus the percentage raised internally. So, if the company raises all equity externally, the flotation costs are:

$f_T$ = (0.5405)(.08)(1 - 0) + (0.4595)(.035)
$f_T$ = .0593, or 5.93%

The initial cash outflow for the project needs to be adjusted for the flotation costs. To account for the flotation costs:

Amount raised(1 - .0593) = $145,000,000
Amount raised = $145,000,000/(1 - .0593)
Amount raised = $154,144,519

If the company uses 60 percent internally generated equity, the flotation cost is:

$f_T$ = (0.5405)(.08)(1 - 0.60) + (0.4595)(.035)
$f_T$ = .0334, or 3.34%

And the initial cash flow will be:

Amount raised(1 - .0334) = $145,000,000
Amount raised = $145,000,000/(1 - .0334)
Amount raised = $150,006,990

If the company uses 100 percent internally generated equity, the flotation cost is:

$f_T = (0.5405)(.08)(1 - 1) + (0.4595)(.035)$
$f_T = .0161$, or 1.61%

And the initial cash flow will be:

Amount raised$(1 - .0161) = \$145,000,000$
Amount raised $= \$145,000,000/(1 - .0161)$
Amount raised $= \$147,369,867$

24. The $7.5 million cost of the land 3 years ago is a sunk cost and irrelevant; the $7.1 million appraised value of the land is an opportunity cost and is relevant. The $7.4 million land value in 5 years is a relevant cash flow as well. The fact that the company is keeping the land rather than selling it is unimportant. The land is an opportunity cost in 5 years and is a relevant cash flow for this project. The market value capitalization weights are:

$B = 260,000(\$1,000)(1.03) = \$267,800,000$
$S = 9,500,000(\$67) = \$636,500,000$
$P = 450,000(\$84) = \$37,800,000$

The total market value of the company is:

$V = \$267,800,000 + 636,500,000 + 37,800,000 = \$942,100,000$

The weight of each form of financing in the company's capital structure is:

$X_B = \$267,800,000 / \$942,100,000 = .2843$
$X_S = \$636,500,000 / \$942,100,000 = .6756$
$X_B = \$37,800,000 / \$942,100,000 = .0401$

Next we need to find the cost of funds. We have the information available to calculate the cost of equity using the CAPM, so:

$R_S = .036 + 1.25(.07) = .1235$, or 12.35%

The cost of debt is the YTM of the company's outstanding bonds, so:

$P_0 = \$1,030 = \$34(PVIFA_{R\%,50}) + \$1,000(PVIF_{R\%,50})$
$R = 3.277\%$
$YTM = 3.277\% \times 2 = 6.55\%$

And the aftertax cost of debt is:

$R_B = (1 - .35)(.0655) = .0426$, or 4.26%

The cost of preferred stock is:

$R_P = \$5.25/\$84 = .0625$, or 6.25%

a. The weighted average flotation cost is the sum of the weight of each source of funds in the capital structure of the company times the flotation costs, so:

$$f_T = .6756(.065) + .2843(.03) + .0401(.045) = .0542, \text{ or } 5.42\%$$

The initial cash outflow for the project needs to be adjusted for the flotation costs. To account for the flotation costs:

Amount raised$(1 - .0542) = \$40,000,000$
Amount raised $= \$40,000,000/(1 - .0542) = \$42,294,408$

So the cash flow at time zero will be:

$$CF_0 = -\$7,100,000 - 42,294,408 - 1,400,000 = -\$50,794,408$$

There is an important caveat to this solution. This solution assumes that the increase in net working capital does not require the company to raise outside funds; therefore the flotation costs are not included. However, this is an assumption and the company could need to raise outside funds for the NWC. If this is true, the initial cash outlay includes these flotation costs, so:

Total cost of NWC including flotation costs:

$$\$1,400,000/(1 - .0542) = \$1,480,304$$

This would make the total initial cash flow:

$$CF_0 = -\$7,100,000 - 42,294,408 - 1,480,304 = -\$50,874,712$$

b. To find the required return on this project, we first need to calculate the WACC for the company. The company's WACC is:

$$R_{WACC} = .6756(.1235) + .2843(.0426) + .0401(.0625)] = .0981, \text{ or } 9.81\%$$

The company wants to use the subjective approach to this project because it is located overseas. The adjustment factor is 2 percent, so the required return on this project is:

Project required return $= 9.81\% + 2\% = 11.81\%$

c. The annual depreciation for the equipment will be:

$$\$40,000,000/8 = \$5,000,000$$

So, the book value of the equipment at the end of five years will be:

$$BV_5 = \$40,000,000 - 5(\$5,000,000) = \$15,000,000$$

So, the aftertax salvage value will be:

Aftertax salvage value $= \$8,500,000 + .35(\$15,000,000 - 8,500,000) = \$10,775,000$

d. Using the tax shield approach, the OCF for this project is:

$$OCF = [(P - v)Q - FC](1 - t_C) + t_C D$$
$$OCF = [(\$10,900 - 9,450)(18,000) - 7,900,000](1 - .35) + .35(\$40,000,000/8) = \$13,580,000$$

e. The accounting breakeven sales figure for this project is:

$$Q_A = (FC + D)/(P - v) = (\$7,900,000 + 5,000,000)/(\$10,900 - 9,450) = 8,897 \text{ units}$$

f. We have calculated all cash flows of the project. We just need to make sure that in Year 5 we add back the aftertax salvage value and the recovery of the initial NWC. The cash flows for the project are:

| Year | Flow Cash |
|------|-----------|
| 0 | −$50,794,408 |
| 1 | 13,580,000 |
| 2 | 13,580,000 |
| 3 | 13,580,000 |
| 4 | 13,580,000 |
| 5 | 33,155,000 |

Using the required return of 11.81 percent, the NPV of the project is:

$$NPV = -\$50,794,408 + \$13,580,000(PVIFA_{11.81\%,4}) + \$33,155,000/1.1181^5$$
$$NPV = \$9,599,239.56$$

And the IRR is:

$$NPV = 0 = -\$50,794,408 + \$13,580,000(PVIFA_{IRR\%,4}) + \$33,155,000/(1 + IRR)^5$$
$$IRR = 18.17\%$$

If the initial NWC is assumed to be financed from outside sources, the cash flows are:

| Year | Flow Cash |
|------|-----------|
| 0 | −$50,874,712 |
| 1 | 13,580,000 |
| 2 | 13,580,000 |
| 3 | 13,580,000 |
| 4 | 13,580,000 |
| 5 | 33,155,000 |

With this assumption, and the required return of 11.81 percent, the NPV of the project is:

$$NPV = -\$50,874,712 + \$13,580,000(PVIFA_{11.81\%,4}) + \$33,155,000/1.1181^5$$
$$NPV = \$9,518,935.29$$

And the IRR is:

$$NPV = 0 = -\$50,874,712 + \$13,580,000(PVIFA_{IRR\%,4}) + \$33,155,000/(1 + IRR)^5$$
$$IRR = 18.11\%$$

# CHAPTER 14
# CORPORATE FINANCING DECISIONS AND EFFICIENT CAPITAL MARKETS

**Answers to Concepts Review and Critical Thinking Questions**

1.  To create value, firms should accept financing proposals with positive net present values. Firms can create valuable financing opportunities in three ways: 1) Fool investors. A firm can issue a complex security to receive more than the fair market value. Financial managers attempt to package securities to receive the greatest value. 2) Reduce costs or increase subsidies. A firm can package securities to reduce taxes. Such a security will increase the value of the firm. In addition, financing techniques involve many costs, such as accountants, lawyers, and investment bankers. Packaging securities in a way to reduce these costs will also increase the value of the firm. 3) Create a new security. A previously unsatisfied investor may pay extra for a specialized security catering to his or her needs. Corporations gain from developing unique securities by issuing these securities at premium prices.

2.  The three forms of the efficient markets hypothesis are: 1) Weak form. Market prices reflect information contained in historical prices. Investors are unable to earn abnormal returns using historical prices to predict future price movements. 2) Semi-strong form. In addition to historical data, market prices reflect all publicly-available information. Investors with insider, or private information, are able to earn abnormal returns. 3) Strong form. Market prices reflect all information, public or private. Investors are unable to earn abnormal returns using insider information or historical prices to predict future price movements.

3.  *a.*  False. Market efficiency implies that prices reflect all available information, but it does not imply certain knowledge. Many pieces of information that are available and reflected in prices are fairly uncertain. Efficiency of markets does not eliminate that uncertainty and therefore does not imply perfect forecasting ability.

    *b.*  True. Market efficiency exists when prices reflect all available information. To be efficient in the weak form, the market must incorporate all historical data into prices. Under the semi-strong form of the hypothesis, the market incorporates all publicly-available information in addition to the historical data. In strong form efficient markets, prices reflect all publicly and privately available information.

    *c.*  False. Market efficiency implies that market participants are rational. Rational people will immediately act upon new information and will bid prices up or down to reflect that information.

    *d.*  False. In efficient markets, prices reflect all available information. Thus, prices will fluctuate whenever new information becomes available.

    *e.*  True. Competition among investors results in the rapid transmission of new market information. In efficient markets, prices immediately reflect new information as investors bid the stock price up or down.

4. On average, the only return that is earned is the required return—investors buy assets with returns in excess of the required return (positive NPV), bidding up the price and thus causing the return to fall to the required return (zero NPV); investors sell assets with returns less than the required return (negative NPV), driving the price lower and thus causing the return to rise to the required return (zero NPV).

5. The market is not weak form efficient.

6. Yes, historical information is also public information; weak form efficiency is a subset of semi-strong form efficiency.

7. Ignoring trading costs, on average, such investors merely earn what the market offers; the trades all have zero NPV. If trading costs exist, then these investors lose by the amount of the costs.

8. Unlike gambling, the stock market is a positive sum game; everybody can win. Also, speculators provide liquidity to markets and thus help to promote efficiency.

9. The EMH only says, within the bounds of increasingly strong assumptions about the information processing of investors, that assets are fairly priced. An implication of this is that, on average, the typical market participant cannot earn excessive profits from a particular trading strategy. However, that does not mean that a few particular investors cannot outperform the market over a particular investment horizon. Certain investors who do well for a period of time get a lot of attention from the financial press, but the scores of investors who do not do well over the same period of time generally get considerably less attention from the financial press.

10. a. If the market is not weak form efficient, then this information could be acted on and a profit earned from following the price trend. Under (2), (3), and (4), this information is fully impounded in the current price and no abnormal profit opportunity exists.

    b. Under (2), if the market is not semi-strong form efficient, then this information could be used to buy the stock "cheap" before the rest of the market discovers the financial statement anomaly. Since (2) is stronger than (1), both imply that a profit opportunity exists; under (3) and (4), this information is fully impounded in the current price and no profit opportunity exists.

    c. Under (3), if the market is not strong form efficient, then this information could be used as a profitable trading strategy, by noting the buying activity of the insiders as a signal that the stock is underpriced or that good news is imminent. Since (1) and (2) are weaker than (3), all three imply that a profit opportunity exists. Note that this assumes the individual who sees the insider trading is the only one who sees the trading. If the information about the trades made by company management is public information, it will be discounted in the stock price and no profit opportunity exists. Under (4), this information does not signal any profit opportunity for traders; any pertinent information the manager-insiders may have is fully reflected in the current share price.

11. A technical analyst would argue that the market is not efficient. Since a technical analyst examines past prices, the market cannot be weak form efficient for technical analysis to work. If the market is not weak form efficient, it cannot be efficient under stronger assumptions about the information available.

12. Investor sentiment captures the mood of the investing public. If investors are bearish in general, it may be that the market is headed down in the future since investors are less likely to invest. If the sentiment is bullish, it would be taken as a positive signal to the market. To use investor sentiment in technical analysis, you would probably want to construct a ratio such as a bulls/bears ratio. To use

the ratio, simply compare the historical ratio to the market to determine if a certain level on the ratio indicates a market upturn or downturn. Of course, there is a group of investors called contrarians who view the market signals as reversed. That is, if the number of bearish investors reaches a certain level, the market will head up. For a contrarian, these signals are reversed.

13. Taken at face value, this fact suggests that markets have become more efficient. The increasing ease with which information is available over the Internet lends strength to this conclusion. On the other hand, during this particular period, large-capitalization growth stocks were the top performers. Value-weighted indexes such as the S&P 500 are naturally concentrated in such stocks, thus making them especially hard to beat during this period. So, it may be that the dismal record compiled by the pros is just a matter of bad luck or benchmark error.

14. It is likely the market has a better estimate of the stock price, assuming it is semistrong form efficient. However, semistrong form efficiency only states that you cannot easily profit from publicly available information. If financial statements are not available, the market can still price stocks based upon the available public information, limited though it may be. Therefore, it may have been as difficult to examine the limited public information and make an extra return.

15. *a.* Aerotech's stock price should rise immediately after the announcement of the positive news.

   *b.* Only scenario (*ii*) indicates market efficiency. In that case, the price of the stock rises immediately to the level that reflects the new information, eliminating all possibility of abnormal returns. In the other two scenarios, there are periods of time during which an investor could trade on the information and earn abnormal returns.

16. False. The stock price would have adjusted before the founder's death only if investors had perfect forecasting ability. The 12.5 percent increase in the stock price after the founder's death indicates that either the market did not anticipate the death or that the market had anticipated it imperfectly. However, the market reacted immediately to the new information, implying efficiency. It is interesting that the stock price rose after the announcement of the founder's death. This price behavior indicates that the market felt he was a liability to the firm.

17. The announcement should not deter investors from buying UPC's stock. If the market is semi-strong form efficient, the stock price will have already reflected the present value of the payments that UPC must make. The expected return after the announcement should still be equal to the expected return before the announcement. UPC's current stockholders bear the burden of the loss, since the stock price falls on the announcement. After the announcement, the expected return moves back to its original level.

18. The market is often considered to be relatively efficient up to the semi-strong form. If so, no systematic profit can be made by trading on publicly-available information. Although illegal, the lead engineer of the device can profit from purchasing the firm's stock *before* the news release on the implementation of the new technology. The price should immediately and fully adjust to the new information in the article. Thus, no abnormal return can be expected from purchasing after the publication of the article.

19. Under the semi-strong form of market efficiency, the stock price should stay the same. The accounting system changes are publicly available information. Investors would identify no changes in either the firm's current or its future cash flows. Thus, the stock price will not change after the announcement of increased earnings.

**20.** Because the number of subscribers has increased dramatically, the time it takes for information in the newsletter to be reflected in prices has shortened. With shorter adjustment periods, it becomes impossible to earn abnormal returns with the information provided by Durkin. If Durkin is using only publicly-available information in its newsletter, its ability to pick stocks is inconsistent with the efficient markets hypothesis. Under the semi-strong form of market efficiency, all publicly-available information should be reflected in stock prices. The use of private information for trading purposes is illegal.

**21.** You should not agree with your broker. The performance ratings of the small manufacturing firms were published and became public information. Prices should adjust immediately to the information, thus preventing future abnormal returns.

**22.** Stock prices should immediately and fully rise to reflect the announcement. Thus, one cannot expect abnormal returns following the announcement.

**23.** *a.* No. Earnings information is in the public domain and reflected in the current stock price.

   *b.* Possibly. If the rumors were publicly disseminated, the prices would have already adjusted for the possibility of a merger. If the rumor is information that you received from an insider, you could earn excess returns, although trading on that information is illegal.

   *c.* No. The information is already public, and thus, already reflected in the stock price.

**24.** Serial correlation occurs when the current value of a variable is related to the future value of the variable. If the market is efficient, the information about the serial correlation in the macroeconomic variable and its relationship to net earnings should already be reflected in the stock price. In other words, although there is serial correlation in the variable, there will not be serial correlation in stock returns. Therefore, knowledge of the correlation in the macroeconomic variable will not lead to abnormal returns for investors.

**25.** The statement is false because every investor has a different risk preference. Although the expected return from every well-diversified portfolio is the same after adjusting for risk, investors still need to choose funds that are consistent with their particular risk level.

**26.** The share price will decrease immediately to reflect the new information. At the time of the announcement, the price of the stock should immediately decrease to reflect the negative information.

**27.** In an efficient market, the cumulative abnormal return (CAR) for Prospectors would rise substantially at the announcement of a new discovery. The CAR falls slightly on any day when no discovery is announced. There is a small positive probability that there will be a discovery on any given day. If there is no discovery on a particular day, the price should fall slightly because the good event did not occur. The substantial price increases on the rare days of discovery should balance the small declines on the other days, leaving CARs that are horizontal over time.

**28.** Behavioral finance attempts to explain both the 1987 stock market crash and the Internet bubble by changes in investor sentiment and psychology. These changes can lead to non-random price behavior.

## Solutions to Questions and Problems

*NOTE: All end-of-chapter problems were solved using a spreadsheet. Many problems require multiple steps. Due to space and readability constraints, when these intermediate steps are included in this solutions manual, rounding may appear to have occurred. However, the final answer for each problem is found without rounding during any step in the problem.*

*Basic*

1. To find the cumulative abnormal returns, we chart the abnormal returns for each of the three airlines for the days preceding and following the announcement. The abnormal return is calculated by subtracting the market return from a stock's return on a particular day, $R_i - R_M$. Group the returns by the number of days before or after the announcement for each respective airline. Calculate the cumulative average abnormal return by adding each abnormal return to the previous day's abnormal return.

| Abnormal returns ($R_i - R_M$) | | | | | | |
|---|---|---|---|---|---|---|
| Days from announcement | Delta | United | American | Sum | Average abnormal return | Cumulative average residual |
| −4 | −0.2 | −0.2 | −0.2 | −0.6 | −0.2 | −0.2 |
| −3 | 0.2 | −0.1 | 0.2 | 0.3 | 0.1 | −0.1 |
| −2 | 0.2 | −0.2 | 0.0 | 0.0 | 0.0 | −0.1 |
| −1 | 0.2 | 0.2 | −0.4 | 0.0 | 0.0 | −0.1 |
| 0 | 3.3 | 0.2 | 1.9 | 5.4 | 1.8 | 1.7 |
| 1 | 0.2 | 0.1 | 0.0 | 0.3 | 0.1 | 1.8 |
| 2 | −0.1 | 0.0 | 0.1 | 0.0 | 0.0 | 1.8 |
| 3 | −0.2 | 0.1 | −0.2 | −0.3 | −0.1 | 1.7 |
| 4 | −0.1 | −0.1 | −0.1 | −0.3 | −0.1 | 1.6 |

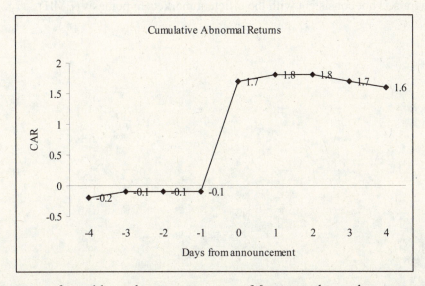

The market reacts favorably to the announcements. Moreover, the market reacts only on the day of the announcement. Before and after the event, the cumulative abnormal returns are relatively flat. This behavior is consistent with market efficiency.

2.  The diagram does not support the efficient markets hypothesis. The CAR should remain relatively flat following the announcements. The diagram reveals that the CAR rose in the first month, only to drift down to lower levels during later months. Such movement violates the semi-strong form of the efficient markets hypothesis because an investor could earn abnormal profits while the stock price gradually decreased.

3.  *a.*  Supports. The CAR remained constant after the event at time 0. This result is consistent with market efficiency, because prices adjust immediately to reflect the new information. Drops in CAR prior to an event can easily occur in an efficient capital market. For example, consider a sample of forced removals of the CEO. Since any CEO is more likely to be fired following bad rather than good stock performance, CARs are likely to be negative prior to removal. Because the firing of the CEO is announced at time 0, one cannot use this information to trade profitably *before* the announcement. Thus, price drops prior to an event are neither consistent nor inconsistent with the efficient markets hypothesis.

    *b.*  Rejects. Because the CAR increases after the event date, one can profit by buying after the event. This possibility is inconsistent with the efficient markets hypothesis.

    *c.*  Supports. The CAR does not fluctuate after the announcement at time 0. While the CAR was rising before the event, insider information would be needed for profitable trading. Thus, the graph is consistent with the semi-strong form of efficient markets.

    *d.*  Supports. The diagram indicates that the information announced at time 0 was of no value. Similar to part *a*, such movement is neither consistent nor inconsistent with the efficient markets hypothesis (EMH). Movements at the event date are neither consistent nor inconsistent with the efficient markets hypothesis.

4.  Once the verdict is reached, the diagram shows that the CAR continues to decline after the court decision, allowing investors to earn abnormal returns. The CAR should remain constant on average, even if an appeal is in progress, because no new information about the company is being revealed. Thus, the diagram is not consistent with the efficient markets hypothesis (EMH).

# CHAPTER 15
# LONG-TERM FINANCING:
## *AN INTRODUCTION*

**Answers to Concepts Review and Critical Thinking Questions**

1. The indenture is a legal contract and can run into 100 pages or more. Bond features which would be included are: the basic terms of the bond, the total amount of the bonds issued, description of the property used as security, repayment arrangements, call provisions, convertibility provisions, and details of protective covenants.

2. The differences between preferred stock and debt are:
   *a.* The dividends on preferred stock cannot be deducted as interest expense when determining taxable corporate income. From the individual investor's point of view, preferred dividends are ordinary income for tax purposes. For corporate investors, 70% of the amount they receive as dividends from preferred stock are exempt from income taxes.
   *b.* In case of liquidation (at bankruptcy), preferred stock is junior to debt and senior to common stock.
   *c.* There is no legal obligation for firms to pay out preferred dividends as opposed to the obligated payment of interest on bonds. Therefore, firms cannot be forced into default if a preferred stock dividend is not paid in a given year. Preferred dividends can be cumulative or non-cumulative, and they can also be deferred indefinitely (of course, indefinitely deferring the dividends might have an undesirable effect on the market value of the stock).

3. Some firms can benefit from issuing preferred stock. The reasons can be:
   *a.* Public utilities can pass the tax disadvantage of issuing preferred stock on to their customers, so there is a substantial amount of straight preferred stock issued by utilities.
   *b.* Firms reporting losses to the IRS already don't have positive income for any tax deductions, so they are not affected by the tax disadvantage of dividends versus interest payments. They may be willing to issue preferred stock.
   *c.* Firms that issue preferred stock can avoid the threat of bankruptcy that exists with debt financing because preferred dividends are not a legal obligation like interest payments on corporate debt.

4. The return on non-convertible preferred stock is lower than the return on corporate bonds for two reasons: 1) Corporate investors receive 70 percent tax deductibility on dividends if they hold the stock. Therefore, they are willing to pay more for the stock; that lowers its return. 2) Issuing corporations are willing and able to offer higher returns on debt since the interest on the debt reduces their tax liabilities. Preferred dividends are paid out of net income, hence they provide no tax shield.

Corporate investors are the primary holders of preferred stock since, unlike individual investors, they can deduct 70 percent of the dividend when computing their tax liabilities. Therefore, they are willing to accept the lower return that the stock generates.

5.  The following table summarizes the main difference between debt and equity:

    |                                        | Debt | Equity |
    |----------------------------------------|------|--------|
    | Repayment is an obligation of the firm | Yes  | No     |
    | Grants ownership of the firm           | No   | Yes    |
    | Provides a tax shield                  | Yes  | No     |
    | Liquidation will result if not paid    | Yes  | No     |

    Companies often issue hybrid securities because of the potential tax shield and the bankruptcy advantage. If the IRS accepts the security as debt, the firm can use it as a tax shield. If the security maintains the bankruptcy and ownership advantages of equity, the firm has the best of both worlds.

6.  There are two benefits. First, the company can take advantage of interest rate declines by calling in an issue and replacing it with a lower coupon issue. Second, a company might wish to eliminate a covenant for some reason. Calling the issue does this. The cost to the company is a higher coupon. A put provision is desirable from an investor's standpoint, so it helps the company by reducing the coupon rate on the bond. The cost to the company is that it may have to buy back the bond at an unattractive price.

7.  It is the grant of authority by a shareholder to someone else to vote his or her shares.

8.  Preferred stock is similar to both debt and common equity. Preferred shareholders receive a stated dividend only, and if the corporation is liquidated, preferred stockholders get a stated value. However, unpaid preferred dividends are not debts of a company and preferred dividends are not a tax deductible business expense.

9.  A company has to issue more debt to replace the old debt that comes due if the company wants to maintain its capital structure. There is also the possibility that the market value of a company continues to increase (we hope). This also means that to maintain a specific capital structure on a market value basis the company has to issue new debt, since the market value of existing debt generally does not increase as the value of the company increases (at least by not as much).

10. Internal financing comes from internally generated cash flows and does not require issuing securities. In contrast, external financing requires the firm to issue new securities.

11. The three basic factors that affect the decision to issue external equity are: 1) The general economic environment, specifically, business cycles. 2) The level of stock prices, and 3) The availability of positive NPV projects.

12. When a company has dual class stock, the difference in the share classes are the voting rights. Dual share classes allow minority shareholders to retain control of the company even though they do not own a majority of the total shares outstanding. Often, dual share companies were started by a family, and then taken public, but the founders want to retain control of the company.

13. The statement is true. In an efficient market, the callable bonds will be sold at a lower price than that of the non-callable bonds, other things being equal. This is because the holder of callable bonds effectively sold a call option to the bond issuer. Since the issuer holds the right to call the bonds, the price of the bonds will reflect the disadvantage to the bondholders and the advantage to the bond issuer (i.e., the bondholder has the obligation to surrender their bonds when the call option is exercised by the bond issuer.)

14. As the interest rate falls, the call option on the callable bonds is more likely to be exercised by the bond issuer. Since the non-callable bonds do not have such a drawback, the value of the bond will go up to reflect the decrease in the market rate of interest. Thus, the price of non-callable bonds will move higher than that of the callable bonds.

15. Sinking funds provide additional security to bonds. If a firm is experiencing financial difficulty, it is likely to have trouble making its sinking fund payments. Thus, the sinking fund provides an early warning system to the bondholders about the quality of the bonds. A drawback to sinking funds is that they give the firm an option that the bondholders may find distasteful. If bond prices are low, the firm may satisfy its sinking fund obligation by buying bonds in the open market. If bond prices are high though, the firm may satisfy its obligation by purchasing bonds at face value (or other fixed price, depending on the specific terms). Those bonds being repurchased are chosen through a lottery.

**Solutions to Questions and Problems**

*NOTE: All end of chapter problems were solved using a spreadsheet. Many problems require multiple steps. Due to space and readability constraints, when these intermediate steps are included in this solutions manual, rounding may appear to have occurred. However, the final answer for each problem is found without rounding during any step in the problem.*

*Basic*

1. If the company uses straight voting, the board of directors is elected one at a time. You will need to own one-half of the shares, plus one share, in order to guarantee enough votes to win the election. So, the number of shares needed to guarantee election under straight voting will be:

Shares needed = (850,000 shares / 2) + 1
Shares needed = 425,001

And the total cost to you will be the shares needed times the price per share, or:

Total cost = 425,001 × $43
Total cost = $18,275,043

If the company uses cumulative voting, the board of directors are all elected at once. You will need $1/(N + 1)$ percent of the stock (plus one share) to guarantee election, where $N$ is the number of seats up for election. So, the percentage of the company's stock you need is:

Percent of stock needed = $1/(N + 1)$
Percent of stock needed = 1 / (7 + 1)
Percent of stock needed = .1250 or 12.50%

So, the number of shares you need to purchase is:

Number of shares to purchase = (850,000 × .1250) + 1
Number of shares to purchase = 106,251

And the total cost to you will be the shares needed times the price per share, or:

Total cost = 106,251 × $43
Total cost = $4,568,793

2.  If the company uses cumulative voting, the board of directors are all elected at once. You will need $1/(N + 1)$ percent of the stock (plus one share) to guarantee election, where $N$ is the number of seats up for election. So, the percentage of the company's stock you need is:

    Percent of stock needed = $1/(N + 1)$
    Percent of stock needed = $1 / (3 + 1)$
    Percent of stock needed = .25 or 25%

    So, the number of shares you need is:

    Number of shares to purchase = $(7,600 \times .25) + 1$
    Number of shares to purchase = 1,901

    So, the number of additional shares you need to purchase is:

    New shares to purchase = 1,901 – 300
    New shares to purchase = 1,601

3.  If the company uses cumulative voting, the board of directors are all elected at once. You will need $1/(N + 1)$ percent of the stock (plus one share) to guarantee election, where $N$ is the number of seats up for election. So, the percentage of the company's stock you need is:

    Percent of stock needed = $1/(N + 1)$
    Percent of stock needed = $1 / (3 + 1)$
    Percent of stock needed = .25 or 25%

    So, the number of shares you need to purchase is:

    Number of shares to purchase = $(13,000,000 \times .25) + 1$
    Number of shares to purchase = 3,250,001

    And the total cost will be the shares needed times the price per share, or:

    Total cost = $3,250,001 \times \$10.50$
    Total cost = $34,125,011

4.  Under cumulative voting, she will need $1/(N + 1)$ percent of the stock (plus one share) to guarantee election, where $N$ is the number of seats up for election. So, the percentage of the company's stock she needs is:

    Percent of stock needed = $1/(N + 1)$
    Percent of stock needed = $1 / (6 + 1)$
    Percent of stock needed = .1429 or 14.29%

    Her nominee is guaranteed election. If the elections are staggered, the percentage of the company's stock needed is:

    Percent of stock needed = $1/(N + 1)$
    Percent of stock needed = $1 / (2 + 1)$
    Percent of stock needed = .3333, or 33.33%

    Her nominee is no longer guaranteed election.

5.   *a.*   The price of the bond today is the present value of the expected price in one year. So, the price of the bond in one year if interest rates increase will be:

$P_1 = \$40(PVIFA_{5\%,58}) + \$1,000(PVIF_{5\%,58})$
$P_1 = \$811.80$

If interest rates fall, the price if the bond in one year will be:
$P_1 = \$40(PVIFA_{3\%,58}) + \$1,000(PVIF_{3\%,58})$
$P_1 = \$1,273.31$

Now we can find the price of the bond today, which will be:

$P_0 = [.50(\$811.80) + .50(\$1,273.31)] / 1.035^2$
$P_0 = \$973.24$

For students who have studied term structure, the assumption of risk-neutrality implies that the forward rate is equal to the expected future spot rate.

   *b.*   If the bond is callable, then the bond value will be less than the amount computed in part *a*. If the bond price rises above the call price, the company will call it. Therefore, bondholders will not pay as much for a callable bond.

6.   The price of the bond today is the present value of the expected price in one year. The bond will be called whenever the price of the bond is greater than the call price of $1,150. First, we need to find the expected price in one year. If interest rates increase next year, the price of the bond will be the present value of the perpetual interest payments, plus the interest payment made in one year, so:

$P_1 = (\$100 / .12) + \$100$
$P_1 = \$933.33$

This is lower than the call price, so the bond will not be called. If the interest rates fall next year, the price of the bond will be:

$P_1 = (\$100 / .07) + \$100$
$P_1 = \$1,528.57$

This is greater than the call price, so the bond will be called. The present value of the expected value of the bond price in one year is:

$P_0 = [.60(\$933.33) + .40(\$1,150)] / 1.10$
$P_0 = \$927.27$

*Intermediate*

7.   If interest rates rise, the price of the bonds will fall. If the price of the bonds is low, the company will not call them. The firm would be foolish to pay the call price for something worth less than the call price. In this case, the bondholders will receive the coupon payment, C, plus the present value of the remaining payments. So, if interest rates rise, the price of the bonds in one year will be:

$P_1 = C + C / 0.10$

If interest rates fall, the assumption is that the bonds will be called. In this case, the bondholders will receive the call price, plus the coupon payment, C. So, the price of the bonds if interest rates fall will be:

$$P_1 = \$1,175 + C$$

The selling price today of the bonds is the PV of the expected payoffs to the bondholders. To find the coupon rate, we can set the desired issue price equal to present value of the expected value of end of year payoffs, and solve for C. Doing so, we find:

$$P_0 = \$1,000 = [.60(C + C / .10) + .40(\$1,175 + C)] / 1.09$$
$$C = \$88.57$$

So the coupon rate necessary to sell the bonds at par value will be:

Coupon rate = \$88.57 / \$1,000
Coupon rate = .0886, or 8.86%

**8.** *a.* The price of the bond today is the present value of the expected price in one year. So, the price of the bond in one year if interest rates increase will be:

$$P_1 = \$70 + \$70 / .09$$
$$P_1 = \$847.78$$

If interest rates fall, the price if the bond in one year will be:

$$P_1 = \$70 + \$70 / .06$$
$$P_1 = \$1,236.67$$

Now we can find the price of the bond today, which will be:

$$P_0 = [.35(\$847.78) + .65(\$1,236.67)] / 1.07$$
$$P_0 = \$1,028.56$$

*b.* If interest rates rise, the price of the bonds will fall. If the price of the bonds is low, the company will not call them. The firm would be foolish to pay the call price for something worth less than the call price. In this case, the bondholders will receive the coupon payment, C, plus the present value of the remaining payments. So, if interest rates rise, the price of the bonds in one year will be:

$$P_1 = C + C / .09$$

If interest rates fall, the assumption is that the bonds will be called. In this case, the bondholders will receive the call price, plus the coupon payment, C. The call premium is not fixed, but it is the same as the coupon rate, so the price of the bonds if interest rates fall will be:

$$P_1 = (\$1,000 + C) + C$$
$$P_1 = \$1,000 + 2C$$

The selling price today of the bonds is the PV of the expected payoffs to the bondholders. To find the coupon rate, we can set the desired issue price equal to present value of the expected value of end of year payoffs, and solve for C. Doing so, we find:

$P_0 = \$1,000 = [.35(C + C / .09) + .65(\$1,000 + 2C)] / 1.07$
$C = \$75.83$

So the coupon rate necessary to sell the bonds at par value will be:

Coupon rate = $\$75.83 / \$1,000$
Coupon rate = .0758, or 7.58%

c.  To the company, the value of the call provision will be given by the difference between the value of an outstanding, non-callable bond and the call provision. So, the value of a non-callable bond with the same coupon rate would be:

Non-callable bond value = $\$75.83 / 0.06 = \$1,263.79$

So, the value of the call provision to the company is:

Value = $.65(\$1,263.79 - 1,075.83) / 1.07$
Value = $\$114.18$

9.  The company should refund when the NPV of refunding is greater than zero, so we need to find the interest rate that results in a zero NPV. The NPV of the refunding is the difference between the gain from refunding and the refunding costs. The gain from refunding is the bond value times the difference in the interest rate, discounted to the present value. We must also consider that the interest payments are tax deductible, so the aftertax gain is:

NPV = PV(Gain) – PV(Cost)

The present value of the gain will be:

Gain = $\$250,000,000(.09 - R) / R$

Since refunding would cost money today, we must determine the aftertax cost of refunding, which will be:

Aftertax cost = $\$250,000,000(.10)(1 - .35)$
Aftertax cost = $\$16,250,000$

So, setting the NPV of refunding equal to zero, we find:

$0 = -\$16,250,000 + \$250,000,000(.09 - R) / R$
$R = .0845$ or 8.45%

Any interest rate below this will result in a positive NPV from refunding.

**10.** In this case, we need to find the NPV of each alternative and choose the option with the highest NPV, assuming either NPV is positive. The NPV of each decision is the gain minus the cost. So, the NPV of refunding the 8 percent perpetual bond is:

*Bond A:*

Gain = $125,000,000(.07 − .0625) / .0625
Gain = $15,000,000

Assuming the call premium is tax deductible, the aftertax cost of refunding this issue is:

Cost = $125,000,000(.075)(1 − .35) + $11,500,000(1 − .35)
Cost = $13,568,750

Note that the gain can be calculated using the pretax or aftertax cost of debt. If we calculate the gain using the aftertax cost of debt, we find:

Aftertax gain = $125,000,000[.07(1 − .35) − .0625(1 − .35)] / [.0625(1 − .35)]
Aftertax gain = $15,000,000

Thus, the inclusion of the tax rate in the calculation of the gains from refunding is irrelevant.

The NPV of refunding this bond is:

NPV = −$13,568,750 + 15,000,000
NPV = $1,431,250

The NPV of refunding the second bond is:

*Bond B:*

Gain = $132,000,000(.08 − .0710) / .0710
Gain = $16,732,394.37

Assuming the call premium is tax deductible, the aftertax cost of refunding this issue is:

Cost = ($132,000,000)(.085)(1 − .35) + $13,000,000(1 − .35)
Cost = $15,743,000

The NPV of refunding this bond is:

NPV = −$15,743,000 + 16,732,394.37
NPV = $989,394.37

Since the NPV of refunding both bonds is positive, both bond issues should be refunded.

*Challenge*

11. To calculate this, we need to set up an equation with the callable bond equal to a weighted average of the noncallable bonds. We will invest X percent of our money in the first noncallable bond, which means our investment in Bond 3 (the other noncallable bond) will be $(1 - X)$. The equation is:

$$C_2 = C_1 X + C_3(1 - X)$$
$$8.25 = 6.50 X + 12(1 - X)$$
$$8.25 = 6.50 X + 12 - 12 X$$
$$X = 0.68182$$

So, we invest about 68 percent of our money in Bond 1, and about 32 percent in Bond 3. This combination of bonds should have the same value as the callable bond, excluding the value of the call. So:

$$P_2 = 0.68182 P_1 + 0.31819 P_3$$
$$P_2 = 0.68182(106.375) + 0.31818(134.96875)$$
$$P_2 = 115.4730$$

The call value is the difference between this implied bond value and the actual bond price. So, the call value is:

Call value = 115.4730 – 103.50 = 11.9730

Assuming $1,000 par value, the call value is $119.73.

12. In general, this is not likely to happen, although it can (and did). The reason that this bond has a negative YTM is that it is a callable U.S. Treasury bond. Market participants know this. Given the high coupon rate of the bond, it is extremely likely to be called, which means the bondholder will not receive all the cash flows promised. A better measure of the return on a callable bond is the yield to call (YTC). The YTC calculation is the basically the same as the YTM calculation, but the number of periods is the number of periods until the call date. If the YTC were calculated on this bond, it would be positive.

# CHAPTER 16
# CAPITAL STRUCTURE: *BASIC CONCEPTS*

**Answers to Concepts Review and Critical Thinking Questions**

1.  Assumptions of the Modigliani-Miller theory in a world without taxes: 1) Individuals can borrow at the same interest rate at which the firm borrows. Since investors can purchase securities on margin, an individual's effective interest rate is probably no higher than that for a firm. Therefore, this assumption is reasonable when applying MM's theory to the real world. If a firm were able to borrow at a rate lower than individuals, the firm's value would increase through corporate leverage. As MM Proposition I states, this is not the case in a world with no taxes. 2) There are no taxes. In the real world, firms do pay taxes. In the presence of corporate taxes, the value of a firm is positively related to its debt level. Since interest payments are deductible, increasing debt reduces taxes and raises the value of the firm. 3) There are no costs of financial distress. In the real world, costs of financial distress can be substantial. Since stockholders eventually bear these costs, there are incentives for a firm to lower the amount of debt in its capital structure. This topic will be discussed in more detail in later chapters.

2.  False. A reduction in leverage will decrease both the risk of the stock and its expected return. Modigliani and Miller state that, in the absence of taxes, these two effects exactly cancel each other out and leave the price of the stock and the overall value of the firm unchanged.

3.  False. Modigliani-Miller Proposition II (No Taxes) states that the required return on a firm's equity is positively related to the firm's debt-equity ratio [$R_S = R_0 + (B/S)(R_0 - R_B)$]. Therefore, any increase in the amount of debt in a firm's capital structure will increase the required return on the firm's equity.

4.  Interest payments are tax deductible, where payments to shareholders (dividends) are not tax deductible.

5.  Business risk is the equity risk arising from the nature of the firm's operating activity, and is directly related to the systematic risk of the firm's assets. Financial risk is the equity risk that is due entirely to the firm's chosen capital structure. As financial leverage, or the use of debt financing, increases, so does financial risk and, hence, the overall risk of the equity. Thus, Firm B could have a higher cost of equity if it uses greater leverage.

6.  No, it doesn't follow. While it is true that the equity and debt costs are rising, the key thing to remember is that the cost of debt is still less than the cost of equity. Since we are using more and more debt, the WACC does not necessarily rise.

7.  Because many relevant factors such as bankruptcy costs, tax asymmetries, and agency costs cannot easily be identified or quantified, it is practically impossible to determine the precise debt/equity ratio that maximizes the value of the firm. However, if the firm's cost of new debt suddenly becomes much more expensive, it's probably true that the firm is too highly leveraged.

8.  It's called leverage (or "gearing" in the UK) because it magnifies gains or losses.

9.  Homemade leverage refers to the use of borrowing on the personal level as opposed to the corporate level.

10. The basic goal is to minimize the value of non-marketed claims.

**Solutions to Questions and Problems**

*NOTE: All end-of-chapter problems were solved using a spreadsheet. Many problems require multiple steps. Due to space and readability constraints, when these intermediate steps are included in this solutions manual, rounding may appear to have occurred. However, the final answer for each problem is found without rounding during any step in the problem.*

*Basic*

1.  *a.*  A table outlining the income statement for the three possible states of the economy is shown below. The EPS is the net income divided by the 5,000 shares outstanding. The last row shows the percentage change in EPS the company will experience in a recession or an expansion economy.

|  | Recession | Normal | Expansion |
|---|---|---|---|
| EBIT | $12,600 | $21,000 | $26,250 |
| Interest | 0 | 0 | 0 |
| NI | $12,600 | $21,000 | $26,250 |
| EPS | $ 2.52 | $ 4.20 | $ 5.25 |
| %ΔEPS | −40 | — | +25 |

*b.*  If the company undergoes the proposed recapitalization, it will repurchase:

Share price = Equity / Shares outstanding
Share price = $275,000/5,000
Share price = $55

Shares repurchased = Debt issued / Share price
Shares repurchased =$99,000/$45
Shares repurchased = 1,800

The interest payment each year under all three scenarios will be:

Interest payment = $99,000(.08) = $7,920

The last row shows the percentage change in EPS the company will experience in a recession or an expansion economy under the proposed recapitalization.

|  | Recession | Normal | Expansion |
|---|---|---|---|
| EBIT | $12,600 | $21,000 | $26,250 |
| Interest | 7,920 | 7,920 | 7,920 |
| NI | $ 4,680 | $13,080 | $18,330 |
| EPS | $1.46 | $ 4.09 | $ 5.73 |
| %ΔEPS | −64.22 | — | +40.14 |

2.  *a.*  A table outlining the income statement with taxes for the three possible states of the economy is shown below. The share price is $55, and there are 5,000 shares outstanding. The last row shows the percentage change in EPS the company will experience in a recession or an expansion economy.

|       | Recession | Normal   | Expansion |
|-------|-----------|----------|-----------|
| EBIT  | $12,600   | $21,000  | $26,250   |
| Interest | 0      | 0        | 0         |
| Taxes | 4,410     | 7,350    | 9,188     |
| NI    | $ 8,190   | $13,650  | $17,063   |
| EPS   | $   1.64  | $   2.73 | $   3.41  |
| %ΔEPS | −40       | —        | +25       |

*b.*  A table outlining the income statement with taxes for the three possible states of the economy and assuming the company undertakes the proposed capitalization is shown below. The interest payment and shares repurchased are the same as in part *b* of Problem 1.

|       | Recession | Normal   | Expansion |
|-------|-----------|----------|-----------|
| EBIT  | $12,600   | $21,000  | $26,250   |
| Interest | 7,920  | 7,920    | 7,920     |
| Taxes | 1,638     | 4,578    | 6,416     |
| NI    | $ 3,042   | $ 8,502  | $11,915   |
| EPS   | $   0.95  | $   2.66 | $   3.72  |
| %ΔEPS | −64.22    | —        | +40.14    |

Notice that the percentage change in EPS is the same both with and without taxes.

3.  *a.*  Since the company has a market-to-book ratio of 1.0, the total equity of the firm is equal to the market value of equity. Using the equation for ROE:

ROE = NI/$275,000

The ROE for each state of the economy under the current capital structure and no taxes is:

|       | Recession | Normal | Expansion |
|-------|-----------|--------|-----------|
| ROE   | 4.58%     | 7.64%  | 9.55%     |
| %ΔROE | −40       | —      | +25       |

The second row shows the percentage change in ROE from the normal economy.

*b.*  If the company undertakes the proposed recapitalization, the new equity value will be:

Equity = $275,000 − 99,000
Equity = $176,000

So, the ROE for each state of the economy is:

ROE = NI/$176,000

|       | Recession | Normal | Expansion |
|-------|-----------|--------|-----------|
| ROE   | 2.66%     | 7.43%  | 10.41%    |
| %ΔROE | −64.22    | —      | +40.14    |

    *c.*    If there are corporate taxes and the company maintains its current capital structure, the ROE is:

| ROE | 2.98% | 4.96% | 6.20% |
|---|---|---|---|
| %ΔROE | –40 | —— | +25 |

If the company undertakes the proposed recapitalization, and there are corporate taxes, the ROE for each state of the economy is:

| ROE | 1.73% | 4.83% | 6.77% |
|---|---|---|---|
| %ΔROE | –64.22 | —— | +40.14 |

Notice that the percentage change in ROE is the same as the percentage change in EPS. The percentage change in ROE is also the same with or without taxes.

**4.**    *a.*    Under Plan I, the unlevered company, net income is the same as EBIT with no corporate tax. The EPS under this capitalization will be:

EPS = \$750,000/265,000 shares
EPS = \$2.83

Under Plan II, the levered company, EBIT will be reduced by the interest payment. The interest payment is the amount of debt times the interest rate, so:

NI = \$750,000 – .10(\$2,800,000)
NI = \$470,000

And the EPS will be:

EPS = \$470,000/185,000 shares
EPS = \$2.54

Plan I has the higher EPS when EBIT is \$750,000.

    *b.*    Under Plan I, the net income is \$1,500,000 and the EPS is:

EPS = \$1,500,000/265,000 shares
EPS = \$5.66

Under Plan II, the net income is:

NI = \$1,500,000 – .10(\$2,800,000)
NI = \$1,220,000

And the EPS is:

EPS = \$1,220,000/185,000 shares
EPS = \$6.59

Plan II has the higher EPS when EBIT is \$1,500,000.

*c.* To find the breakeven EBIT for two different capital structures, we simply set the equations for EPS equal to each other and solve for EBIT. The breakeven EBIT is:

EBIT/265,000 = [EBIT – .10($2,800,000)]/185,000
EBIT = $927,500

5. We can find the price per share by dividing the amount of debt used to repurchase shares by the number of shares repurchased. Doing so, we find the share price is:

Share price = $2,800,000/(265,000 – 185,000)
Share price = $35.00 per share

The value of the company under the all-equity plan is:

$V = \$35(265,000 \text{ shares}) = \$9,275,000$

And the value of the company under the levered plan is:

$V = \$35(185,000 \text{ shares}) + \$2,800,000 \text{ debt} = \$9,275,000$

6. *a.* The income statement for each capitalization plan is:

|  | *I* | *II* | *All-equity* |
|---|---|---|---|
| EBIT | $8,500 | $8,500 | $8,500 |
| Interest | 6,570 | 2,920 | 0 |
| NI | $1,930 | $5,580 | $8,500 |
| EPS | $ 2.14 | $ 2.94 | $ 3.15 |

The all-equity plan has the highest EPS; Plan I has the lowest EPS.

*b.* The breakeven level of EBIT occurs when the capitalization plans result in the same EPS. The EPS is calculated as:

EPS = (EBIT – $R_BB$)/Shares outstanding

This equation calculates the interest payment ($R_BB$) and subtracts it from the EBIT, which results in the net income. Dividing by the shares outstanding gives us the EPS. For the all-equity capital structure, the interest paid is zero. To find the breakeven EBIT for two different capital structures, we simply set the equations equal to each other and solve for EBIT. The breakeven EBIT between the all-equity capital structure and Plan I is:

EBIT/2,700 = [EBIT – .10($65,700)]/900
EBIT = $9,855

And the breakeven EBIT between the all-equity capital structure and Plan II is:

EBIT/2,700 = [EBIT – .10($29,200)]/1,900
EBIT = $9,855

The break-even levels of EBIT are the same because of M&M Proposition I.

c.  Setting the equations for EPS from Plan I and Plan II equal to each other and solving for EBIT, we get:

[EBIT − .10($65,700)]/900 = [EBIT − .10($29,200)]/1,900
EBIT = $9,855

This break-even level of EBIT is the same as in part *b* again because of M&M Proposition I.

d.  The income statement for each capitalization plan with corporate income taxes is:

|  | I | II | All-equity |
|---|---|---|---|
| EBIT | $8,500 | $8,500 | $8,500 |
| Interest | 6,570 | 2,920 | 0 |
| Taxes | 772 | 2,232 | 3,400 |
| NI | $1,158 | $3,348 | $5,100 |
| EPS | $ 1.29 | $ 1.76 | $ 1.89 |

The all-equity plan has the highest EPS; Plan I has the lowest EPS.

We can calculate the EPS as:

$$EPS = [(EBIT − R_BD)(1 − t_C)]/\text{Shares outstanding}$$

This is similar to the equation we used before, except that now we need to account for taxes. Again, the interest expense term is zero in the all-equity capital structure. So, the breakeven EBIT between the all-equity plan and Plan I is:

EBIT(1 − .40)/2,700 = [EBIT − .10($65,700)](1 − .40)/900
EBIT = $9,855

The breakeven EBIT between the all-equity plan and Plan II is:

EBIT(1 − .40)/2,700 = [EBIT − .10($29,200)](1 − .40)/1,900
EBIT = $9,855

And the breakeven between Plan I and Plan II is:

[EBIT − .10($65,700)](1 − .40)/900 = [EBIT − .10($29,200)](1 − .40)/1,900
EBIT = $9,855

The break-even levels of EBIT do not change because the addition of taxes reduces the income of all three plans by the same percentage; therefore, they do not change relative to one another.

7.  To find the value per share of the stock under each capitalization plan, we can calculate the price as the value of shares repurchased divided by the number of shares repurchased. The dollar value of the shares repurchased is the increase in the value of the debt used to repurchase shares, or:

Dollar value of repurchase = $65,700 − 29,200 = $36,500

The number of shares repurchased is the decrease in shares outstanding, or:

Number of shares repurchased = 1,900 − 900 = 1,000

So, under Plan I, the value per share is:

P = $36,500/1,000 shares
P = $36.50 per share

And under Plan II, the number of shares repurchased from the all equity plan by the $29,200 in debt are:

Shares repurchased = 2,700 − 1,900 = 800

So the share price is:

P = $29,200/800 shares
P = $36.50 per share

This shows that when there are no corporate taxes, the stockholder does not care about the capital structure decision of the firm. This is M&M Proposition I without taxes.

8. *a.* The earnings per share are:

EPS = $33,000/6,000 shares
EPS = $5.50

So, the cash flow for the shareholder is:

Cash flow = $5.50(100 shares)
Cash flow = $550

*b.* To determine the cash flow to the shareholder, we need to determine the EPS of the firm under the proposed capital structure. The market value of the firm is:

V = $58(6,000)
V = $348,000

Under the proposed capital structure, the firm will raise new debt in the amount of:

B = 0.35($348,000)
B = $121,800

This means the number of shares repurchased will be:

Shares repurchased = $121,800/$58
Shares repurchased = 2,100

Under the new capital structure, the company will have to make an interest payment on the new debt. The net income with the interest payment will be:

NI = $33,000 − .08($121,800)
NI = $23,256

This means the EPS under the new capital structure will be:

EPS = $23,256 / (6,000 − 2,100 shares)
EPS = $5.96

Since all earnings are paid as dividends, the shareholder will receive:

Shareholder cash flow = $5.96(100 shares)
Shareholder cash flow = $596.31

c. To replicate the proposed capital structure, the shareholder should sell 35 percent of their shares, or 35 shares, and lend the proceeds at 8 percent. The shareholder will have an interest cash flow of:

Interest cash flow = 35($58)(.08)
Interest cash flow = $162.40

The shareholder will receive dividend payments on the remaining 65 shares, so the dividends received will be:

Dividends received = $5.96(65 shares)
Dividends received = $387.60

The total cash flow for the shareholder under these assumptions will be:

Total cash flow = $162.40 + 387.60
Total cash flow = $550

This is the same cash flow we calculated in part *a*.

d. The capital structure is irrelevant because shareholders can create their own leverage or unlever the stock to create the payoff they desire, regardless of the capital structure the firm actually chooses.

9. a. The rate of return earned will be the dividend yield. The company has debt, so it must make an interest payment. The net income for the company is:

NI = $86,000 − .08($375,000)
NI = $56,000

The investor will receive dividends in proportion to the percentage of the company's shares they own. The total dividends received by the shareholder will be:

Dividends received = $56,000($30,000/$375,000)
Dividends received = $4,480

So the return the shareholder expects is:

$R = \$4,480/\$30,000$
$R = .1493$, or 14.93%

b.  To generate exactly the same cash flows in the other company, the shareholder needs to match the capital structure of ABC. The shareholder should sell all shares in XYZ. This will net $30,000. The shareholder should then borrow $30,000. This will create an interest cash flow of:

Interest cash flow = .08 (–$30,000)
Interest cash flow = –$2,400

The investor should then use the proceeds of the stock sale and the loan to buy shares in ABC. The investor will receive dividends in proportion to the percentage of the company's share they own. The total dividends received by the shareholder will be:

Dividends received = $86,000($60,000/$750,000)
Dividends received = $6,880

The total cash flow for the shareholder will be:

Total cash flow = $6,880 – 2,400
Total cash flow = $4,480

The shareholders return in this case will be:

$R = \$4,480/\$30,000$
$R = .1493$, or 14.93%

c.  ABC is an all equity company, so:

$R_S = R_A = \$86,000/\$750,000$
$R_S = .1147$, or 11.47%

To find the cost of equity for XYZ, we need to use M&M Proposition II, so:

$R_S = R_A + (R_A - R_B)(B/S)(1 - t_C)$
$R_S = .1147 + (.1147 - .08)(1)(1)$
$R_S = .1493$, or 14.93%

d.  To find the WACC for each company, we need to use the WACC equation:

$WACC = (S/V)R_S + (B/V)R_B(1 - t_C)$

So, for ABC, the WACC is:

$WACC = (1)(.1147) + (0)(.08)$
$WACC = .1147$, or 11.47%

And for XYZ, the WACC is:

WACC = (1/2)(.1493) + (1/2)(.08)
WACC = .1147, or 11.47%

When there are no corporate taxes, the cost of capital for the firm is unaffected by the capital structure; this is M&M Proposition I without taxes.

10. With no taxes, the value of an unlevered firm is the interest rate divided by the unlevered cost of equity, so:

$V$ = EBIT/WACC
$37,000,000 = EBIT/.09
EBIT = .09($37,000,000)
EBIT = $3,330,000

11. If there are corporate taxes, the value of an unlevered firm is:

$V_U = \text{EBIT}(1 - t_C)/R_U$

Using this relationship, we can find EBIT as:

$37,000,000 = EBIT(1 - .35)/.09
EBIT = $5,123,076.92

The WACC remains at 9 percent. Due to taxes, EBIT for an all-equity firm would have to be higher for the firm to still be worth $37 million.

12. *a.* With the information provided, we can use the equation for calculating WACC to find the cost of equity. The equation for WACC is:

$$\text{WACC} = (S/V)R_S + (B/V)R_B(1 - t_C)$$

The company has a debt-equity ratio of 1.5, which implies the weight of debt is 1.5/2.5, and the weight of equity is 1/2.5, so

WACC = .11 = $(1/2.5)R_S + (1.5/2.5)(.07)(1 - .35)$
$R_S$ = .2068, or 20.68%

*b.* To find the unlevered cost of equity, we need to use M&M Proposition II with taxes, so:

$R_S = R_0 + (R_0 - R_B)(B/S)(1 - t_C)$
.2068 = $R_0 + (R_0 - .07)(1.5)(1 - .35)$
$R_0$ = .1392, or 13.92%

*c.* To find the cost of equity under different capital structures, we can again use M&M Proposition II with taxes. With a debt-equity ratio of 2, the cost of equity is:

$R_S = R_0 + (R_0 - R_B)(B/S)(1 - t_C)$
$R_S$ = .1392 + (.1392 − .07)(2)(1 − .35)
$R_S$ = .2293, or 22.93%

With a debt-equity ratio of 1.0, the cost of equity is:

$R_S = .1392 + (.1392 - .07)(1)(1 - .35)$
$R_S = .1842$, or 18.42%

And with a debt-equity ratio of 0, the cost of equity is:

$R_S = .1392 + (.1392 - .07)(0)(1 - .35)$
$R_S = R_0 = .1392$, or 13.92%

13. *a.* For an all-equity financed company:

WACC $= R_0 = R_S = .11$ or 11%

*b.* To find the cost of equity for the company with leverage, we need to use M&M Proposition II with taxes, so:

$R_S = R_0 + (R_0 - R_B)(B/S)(1 - t_C)$
$R_S = .11 + (.11 - .08)(.25/.75)(1 - .35)$
$R_S = .1165$, or 11.65%

*c.* Using M&M Proposition II with taxes again, we get:

$R_S = R_0 + (R_0 - R_B)(B/S)(1 - t_C)$
$R_S = .11 + (.11 - .08)(.50/.50)(1 - .35)$
$R_S = .1295$, or 12.95%

*d.* The WACC with 25 percent debt is:

WACC $= (S/V)R_S + (B/V)R_B(1 - t_C)$
WACC $= .75(.1165) + .25(.08)(1 - .35)$
WACC $= .1004$ or 10.04%

And the WACC with 50 percent debt is:

WACC $= (S/V)R_S + (B/V)R_D(1 - t_C)$
WACC $= .50(.1295) + .50(.08)(1 - .35)$
WACC $= .0908$ or 9.08%

14. *a.* The value of the unlevered firm is:

$V = EBIT(1 - t_C)/R_0$
$V = \$185,000(1 - .35)/.16$
$V = \$751,562.50$

*b.* The value of the levered firm is:

$V = V_U + t_C B$
$V = \$751,562.50 + .35(\$135,000)$
$V = \$798,812.50$

**15.** We can find the cost of equity using M&M Proposition II with taxes. First, we need to find the market value of equity, which is:

$V = B + S$
$\$798,812.50 = \$135,000 + S$
$S = \$663,812.50$

Now we can find the cost of equity, which is:

$R_S = R_0 + (R_0 - R_B)(B/S)(1 - t_C)$
$R_S = .16 + (.16 - .09)(\$135,000/\$663,812.50)(1 - .35)$
$R_S = .1693$, or $16.93\%$

Using this cost of equity, the WACC for the firm after recapitalization is:

$\text{WACC} = (S/V)R_S + (B/V)R_B(1 - t_C)$
$\text{WACC} = (\$663,812.50/\$798,812.50)(.1693) + (\$135,000/\$798,812.50)(.09)(1 - .35)$
$\text{WACC} = .1505$, or $15.05\%$

When there are corporate taxes, the overall cost of capital for the firm declines the more highly leveraged is the firm's capital structure. This is M&M Proposition I with taxes.

**16.** Since Unlevered is an all-equity firm, its value is equal to the market value of its outstanding shares. Unlevered has 4.5 million shares of common stock outstanding, worth $80 per share. Therefore, the value of Unlevered:

$V_U = 4,500,000(\$80) = \$360,000,000$

Modigliani-Miller Proposition I states that, in the absence of taxes, the value of a levered firm equals the value of an otherwise identical unlevered firm. Since Levered is identical to Unlevered in every way except its capital structure and neither firm pays taxes, the value of the two firms should be equal. Therefore, the market value of Levered, Inc., *should be* $360 million also. Since Levered has 2.3 million outstanding shares, worth $105 per share, the market value of Levered's equity is:

$S_L = 2,300,000(\$105) = \$241,500,000$

The market value of Levered's debt is $91 million. The value of a levered firm equals the market value of its debt plus the market value of its equity. Therefore, the current market value of Levered is:

$V_L = B + S$
$V_L = \$91,000,000 + 241,500,000$
$V_L = \$332,500,000$

The market value of Levered's equity needs to be $360 million, $27.5 million higher than its current market value of $332.5 million, for MM Proposition I to hold. Since Levered's market value is less than Unlevered's market value, Levered is relatively underpriced and an investor should buy shares of the firm's stock.

*Intermediate*

17. To find the value of the levered firm, we first need to find the value of an unlevered firm. So, the value of the unlevered firm is:

$V_U = \text{EBIT}(1 - t_C)/R_0$
$V_U = (\$57,000)(1 - .35)/.15$
$V_U = \$247,000$

Now we can find the value of the levered firm as:

$V_L = V_U + t_C B$
$V_L = \$247,000 + .35(\$90,000)$
$V_L = \$278,500$

Applying M&M Proposition I with taxes, the firm has increased its value by issuing debt. As long as M&M Proposition I holds, that is, there are no bankruptcy costs and so forth, then the company should continue to increase its debt/equity ratio to maximize the value of the firm.

18. *a.*  With no debt, we are finding the value of an unlevered firm, so:

$V = \text{EBIT}(1 - t_C)/R_0$
$V = \$19,750(1 - .35)/.15$
$V = \$85,583.33$

*b.*  The general expression for the value of a leveraged firm is:

$V_L = V_U + t_C B$

If debt is 50 percent of $V_U$, then $D = (.50) V_U$, and we have:

$V_L = V_U + t_C[(.50)V_U]$
$V_L = \$85,583.33 + .35(.50)(\$85,583.33)$
$V_L = \$100,560.42$

And if debt is 100 percent of $V_U$, then $D = (1.0) V_U$, and we have:

$V_L = V_U + t_C[(1.0)V_U]$
$V_L = \$85,583.33 + .35(1.0)(\$85,583.33)$
$V_L = \$115,537.50$

*c.*  According to M&M Proposition I with taxes:

$V_L = V_U + t_C B$

With debt being 50 percent of the value of the levered firm, $D$ must equal $(.50)V_L$, so:

$V_L = V_U + T[(.50)V_L]$
$V_L = \$85,583.33 + .35(.50)(V_L)$
$V_L = 103,737.37$

If the debt is 100 percent of the levered value, $D$ must equal $V_L$, so:

$V_L = V_U + T[(1.0)(V_L)]$
$V_L = \$85,583.33 + .35(1.0)(V_L)$
$V_L = \$131,666.67$

19. According to M&M Proposition I with taxes, the increase in the value of the company will be the present value of the interest tax shield. Since the loan will be repaid in equal installments, we need to find the loan interest and the interest tax shield each year. The loan schedule will be:

| Year | Loan Balance | Interest | Tax Shield |
|------|-------------|----------|------------|
| 0 | $1,800,000.00 | | |
| 1 | 900,000.00 | $144,000 | $50,400 |
| 2 | 0 | 72,000 | 25,200 |

So, the increase in the value of the company is:

Value increase = $50,400/1.08 + \$25,200/(1.08)^2$
Value increase = $68,271.60

20. *a.* Since Alpha Corporation is an all-equity firm, its value is equal to the market value of its outstanding shares. Alpha has 15,000 shares of common stock outstanding, worth $30 per share, so the value of Alpha Corporation is:

$V_{Alpha} = 15,000(\$30) = \$450,000$

*b.* Modigliani-Miller Proposition I states that in the absence of taxes, the value of a levered firm equals the value of an otherwise identical unlevered firm. Since Beta Corporation is identical to Alpha Corporation in every way except its capital structure and neither firm pays taxes, the value of the two firms should be equal. So, the value of Beta Corporation is $450,000 as well.

*c.* The value of a levered firm equals the market value of its debt plus the market value of its equity. So, the value of Beta's equity is:

$V_L = B + S$
$\$450,000 = \$65,000 + S$
$S = \$385,000$

*d.* The investor would need to invest 20 percent of the total market value of Alpha's equity, which is:

Amount to invest in Alpha = .20($450,000) = \$90,000

Beta has less equity outstanding, so to purchase 20 percent of Beta's equity, the investor would need:

Amount to invest in Beta = .20($385,000) = \$77,000

*e.* Alpha has no interest payments, so the dollar return to an investor who owns 20 percent of the company's equity would be:

Dollar return on Alpha investment = .20($75,000) = \$15,000

Beta Corporation has an interest payment due on its debt in the amount of:

Interest on Beta's debt = .09($65,000) = $5,850

So, the investor who owns 20 percent of the company would receive 20 percent of EBIT minus the interest expense, or:

Dollar return on Beta investment = .20($75,000 − 5,850) = $13,830

f. From part *d*, we know the initial cost of purchasing 20 percent of Alpha Corporation's equity is $90,000, but the cost to an investor of purchasing 20 percent of Beta Corporation's equity is only $77,000. In order to purchase $90,000 worth of Alpha's equity using only $77,000 of his own money, the investor must borrow $13,000 to cover the difference. The investor will receive the same dollar return from the Alpha investment, but will pay interest on the amount borrowed, so the net dollar return to the investment is:

Net dollar return = $15,000 − .09($13,000) = $13,830

Notice that this amount exactly matches the dollar return to an investor who purchases 20 percent of Beta's equity.

g. The equity of Beta Corporation is riskier. Beta must pay off its debt holders before its equity holders receive any of the firm's earnings. If the firm does not do particularly well, all of the firm's earnings may be needed to repay its debt holders, and equity holders will receive nothing.

21. a. A firm's debt-equity ratio is the market value of the firm's debt divided by the market value of a firm's equity. So, the debt-equity ratio of the company is:

Debt-equity ratio = MV of debt / MV of equity
Debt-equity ratio = $7,000,000 / $23,000,000
Debt-equity ratio = .30

b. We first need to calculate the cost of equity. To do this, we can use the CAPM, which gives us:

$R_S = R_F + \beta[E(R_M) − R_F]$
$R_S = .05 + 1.15(.12 − .05)$
$R_S = .1305$, or 13.05%

We need to remember that an assumption of the Modigliani-Miller theorem is that the company debt is risk-free, so we can use the Treasury bill rate as the cost of debt for the company. In the absence of taxes, a firm's weighted average cost of capital is equal to:

$R_{WACC} = [B / (B + S)]R_B + [S / (B + S)]R_S$
$R_{WACC} = (\$7,000,000/\$30,000,000)(.05) + (\$23,000,000/\$30,000,000)(.1305)$
$R_{WACC} = .1117$, or 11.17%

c.   According to Modigliani-Miller Proposition II with no taxes:

$R_S = R_0 + (B/S)(R_0 - R_B)$
$.1305 = R_0 + (.30)(R_0 - .05)$
$R_0 = .1117$, or 11.17%

This is consistent with Modigliani-Miller's proposition that, in the absence of taxes, the cost of capital for an all-equity firm is equal to the weighted average cost of capital of an otherwise identical levered firm.

**22.**  *a.*   To purchase 5 percent of Knight's equity, the investor would need:

Knight investment = .05($3,140,000) = $157,000

And to purchase 5 percent of Veblen without borrowing would require:

Veblen investment = .05($4,300,000) = $215,000

In order to compare dollar returns, the initial net cost of both positions should be the same. Therefore, the investor will need to borrow the difference between the two amounts, or:

Amount to borrow = $215,000 – 157,000 = $58,000

An investor who owns 5 percent of Knight's equity will be entitled to 5 percent of the firm's earnings available to common stock holders at the end of each year. While Knight's expected operating income is $550,000, it must pay $84,000 to debt holders before distributing any of its earnings to stockholders. So, the amount available to this shareholder will be:

Cash flow from Knight to shareholder = .05($550,000 – 84,000) = $23,300

Veblen will distribute all of its earnings to shareholders, so the shareholder will receive:

Cash flow from Veblen to shareholder = .05($550,000) = $27,500

However, to have the same initial cost, the investor has borrowed $58,000 to invest in Veblen, so interest must be paid on the borrowings. The net cash flow from the investment in Veblen will be:

Net cash flow from Veblen investment = $27,500 – .06($58,000) = $24,020

For the same initial cost, the investment in Veblen produces a higher dollar return.

*b.*   Both of the two strategies have the same initial cost. Since the dollar return to the investment in Veblen is higher, all investors will choose to invest in Veblen over Knight. The process of investors purchasing Veblen's equity rather than Knight's will cause the market value of Veblen's equity to rise and/or the market value of Knight's equity to fall. Any differences in the dollar returns to the two strategies will be eliminated, and the process will cease when the total market values of the two firms are equal.

**23.** *a.* Before the announcement of the stock repurchase plan, the market value of the outstanding debt is $3,600,000. Using the debt-equity ratio, we can find that the value of the outstanding equity must be:

Debt-equity ratio = $B / S$
$.35 = \$3,600,000 / S$
$S = \$10,285,714$

The value of a levered firm is equal to the sum of the market value of the firm's debt and the market value of the firm's equity, so:

$V_L = B + S$
$V_L = \$3,600,000 + 10,285,714$
$V_L = \$13,885,714$

According to MM Proposition I without taxes, changes in a firm's capital structure have no effect on the overall value of the firm. Therefore, the value of the firm will not change after the announcement of the stock repurchase plan

*b.* The expected return on a firm's equity is the ratio of annual earnings to the market value of the firm's equity, or return on equity. Before the restructuring, the company was expected to pay interest in the amount of:

Interest payment = $.08(\$3,600,000) = \$288,000$

The return on equity, which is equal to $R_S$, will be:

ROE = $R_S$ = $(\$1,350,000 - 288,000) / \$10,285,714$
$R_S = .1033$, or 10.33%

*c.* According to Modigliani-Miller Proposition II with no taxes:

$R_S = R_0 + (B/S)(R_0 - R_B)$
$.1033 = R_0 + (.35)(R_0 - .08)$
$R_0 = .0972$, or 9.72%

This problem can also be solved in the following way:

$R_0$ = Earnings before interest / $V_U$

According to Modigliani-Miller Proposition I, in a world with no taxes, the value of a levered firm equals the value of an otherwise-identical unlevered firm. Since the value of the company as a levered firm is $13,885,714 (= $3,600,000 + 10,285,714) and since the firm pays no taxes, the value of the company as an unlevered firm is also $13,885,714. So:

$R_0 = \$1,350,000 / \$13,885,714$
$R_0 = .0972$, or 9.72%

*d.* In part *c*, we calculated the cost of an all-equity firm. We can use Modigliani-Miller Proposition II with no taxes again to find the cost of equity for the firm with the new leverage ratio. The cost of equity under the stock repurchase plan will be:

$$R_S = R_0 + (B/S)(R_0 - R_B)$$
$$R_S = .1033 + (.50)(.1033 - .08)$$
$$R_S = .1058, \text{ or } 10.58\%$$

**24.** *a.* The expected return on a firm's equity is the ratio of annual aftertax earnings to the market value of the firm's equity. The amount the firm must pay each year in taxes will be:

$$\text{Taxes} = .40(\$1,500,000) = \$600,000$$

So, the return on the unlevered equity will be:

$$R_0 = (\$1,500,000 - 600,000) / \$6,300,000$$
$$R_0 = .1429, \text{ or } 14.29\%$$

Notice that perpetual annual earnings of $900,000, discounted at 14.29 percent, yields the market value of the firm's equity

*b.* The company's market value balance sheet before the announcement of the debt issue is:

|              |             |            |             |
| ------------ | ----------- | ---------- | ----------- |
|              |             | Debt       | 0           |
| Assets       | $6,300,000  | Equity     | $6,300,000  |
| Total assets | $6,300,000  | Total D&E  | $6,300,000  |

The price per share is simply the total market value of the stock divided by the shares outstanding, or:

$$\text{Price per share} = \$6,300,000 / 400,000 = \$15.75$$

*c.* Modigliani-Miller Proposition I states that in a world with corporate taxes:

$$V_L = V_U + t_C B$$

When Green announces the debt issue, the value of the firm will increase by the present value of the tax shield on the debt. The present value of the tax shield is:

$$\text{PV(Tax Shield)} = t_C B$$
$$\text{PV(Tax Shield)} = .40(\$2,000,000)$$
$$\text{PV(Tax Shield)} = \$800,000$$

Therefore, the value of Green Manufacturing will increase by $800,000 as a result of the debt issue. The value of Green Manufacturing after the repurchase announcement is:

$$V_L = V_U + t_C B$$
$$V_L = \$6,300,000 + .40(\$2,000,000)$$
$$V_L = \$7,100,000$$

Since the firm has not yet issued any debt, Green's equity is also worth $7,100,000.

Green's market value balance sheet after the announcement of the debt issue is:

| | | | |
|---|---|---|---|
| Old assets | $6,300,000 | Debt | — |
| PV(tax shield) | 800,000 | Equity | $7,100,000 |
| Total assets | $7,100,000 | Total D&E | $7,100,000 |

d.  The share price immediately after the announcement of the debt issue will be:

New share price = $7,100,000 / 400,000 = $17.75

e.  The number of shares repurchased will be the amount of the debt issue divided by the new share price, or:

Shares repurchased = $2,000,000 / $17.75 = 112,676.06

The number of shares outstanding will be the current number of shares minus the number of shares repurchased, or:

New shares outstanding = 400,000 – 112,676.06 = 287,323.94

f.  The share price will remain the same after restructuring takes place. The total market value of the outstanding equity in the company will be:

Market value of equity = $17.75(287,323.94) = $5,100,000

The market-value balance sheet after the restructuring is:

| | | | |
|---|---|---|---|
| Old assets | $6,300,000 | Debt | $2,000,000 |
| PV(tax shield) | 800,000 | Equity | 5,100,000 |
| Total assets | $7,100,000 | Total D&E | $7,100,000 |

g.  According to Modigliani-Miller Proposition II with corporate taxes

$R_S = R_0 + (B/S)(R_0 - R_B)(1 - t_C)$
$R_S = .1429 + (\$2,000,000 / \$5,100,000)(.1429 - .06)(1 - .40)$
$R_S = .1624$, or 16.24%

**25.**  a.  In a world with corporate taxes, a firm's weighted average cost of capital is equal to:

$R_{WACC} = [B / (B+S)](1 - t_C)R_B + [S / (B+S)]R_S$

We do not have the company's debt-to-value ratio or the equity-to-value ratio, but we can calculate either from the debt-to-equity ratio. With the given debt-equity ratio, we know the company has 2.5 dollars of debt for every dollar of equity. Since we only need the ratio of debt-to-value and equity-to-value, we can say:

$B / (B+S) = 2.5 / (2.5 + 1) = .7143$
$S / (B+S) = 1 / (2.5 + 1) = .2857$

We can now use the weighted average cost of capital equation to find the cost of equity, which is:

$.10 = (.7143)(1 - 0.35)(.06) + (.2857)(R_S)$
$R_S = .2525$, or 25.25%

b.  We can use Modigliani-Miller Proposition II with corporate taxes to find the unlevered cost of equity. Doing so, we find:

$R_S = R_0 + (B/S)(R_0 - R_B)(1 - t_C)$
$.2525 = R_0 + (2.5)(R_0 - .06)(1 - .35)$
$R_0 = .1333$, or 13.33%

c.  We first need to find the debt-to-value ratio and the equity-to-value ratio. We can then use the cost of levered equity equation with taxes, and finally the weighted average cost of capital equation. So:

*If debt-equity = .75*

$B / (B+S) = .75 / (.75 + 1) = .4286$
$S / (B+S) = 1 / (.75 + 1) = .5714$

The cost of levered equity will be:

$R_S = R_0 + (B/S)(R_0 - R_B)(1 - t_C)$
$R_S = .1333 + (.75)(.1333 - .06)(1 - .35)$
$R_S = .1691$, or 16.91%

And the weighted average cost of capital will be:

$R_{WACC} = [B / (B+S)](1 - t_C)R_B + [S / (B+S)]R_S$
$R_{WACC} = (.4286)(1 - .35)(.06) + (.5714)(.1691)$
$R_{WACC} = .1133$, or 11.33%

*If debt-equity =1.50*

$B / (B+S) = 1.50 / (1.50 + 1) = .6000$
$S / (B+S) = 1 / (1.50 + 1) = .4000$

The cost of levered equity will be:

$R_S = R_0 + (B/S)(R_0 - R_B)(1 - t_C)$
$R_S = .1333 + (1.50)(.1333 - .06)(1 - .35)$
$R_S = .2048$, or 20.48%

And the weighted average cost of capital will be:

$R_{WACC} = [B / (B+S)](1 - t_C)R_B + [S / (B+S)]R_S$
$R_{WACC} = (.6000)(1 - .35)(.06) + (.4000)(.2048)$
$R_{WACC} = .1053$, or 10.53%

*Challenge*

26. M&M Proposition II states:

$$R_S = R_0 + (R_0 - R_B)(B/S)(1 - t_C)$$

And the equation for WACC is:

$$\text{WACC} = (S/V)R_S + (B/V)R_B(1 - t_C)$$

Substituting the M&M Proposition II equation into the equation for WACC, we get:

$$\text{WACC} = (S/V)[R_0 + (R_0 - R_B)(B/S)(1 - t_C)] + (B/V)R_B(1 - t_C)$$

Rearranging and reducing the equation, we get:

$$\text{WACC} = R_0[(S/V) + (S/V)(B/S)(1 - t_C)] + R_B(1 - t_C)[(B/V) - (S/V)(B/S)]$$
$$\text{WACC} = R_0[(S/V) + (B/V)(1 - t_C)]$$
$$\text{WACC} = R_0[\{(S+B)/V\} - t_C(B/V)]$$
$$\text{WACC} = R_0[1 - t_C(B/V)]$$

27. The return on equity is net income divided by equity. Net income can be expressed as:

$$\text{NI} = (\text{EBIT} - R_B B)(1 - t_C)$$

So, ROE is:

$$R_S = (\text{EBIT} - R_B B)(1 - t_C)/S$$

Now we can rearrange and substitute as follows to arrive at M&M Proposition II with taxes:

$$R_S = [\text{EBIT}(1 - t_C)/S] - [R_B(B/S)(1 - t_C)]$$
$$R_S = R_0 V_U/S - [R_B(B/S)(1 - t_C)]$$
$$R_S = R_0(V_L - t_C B)/S - [R_B(B/S)(1 - t_C)]$$
$$R_S = R_0(S + B - t_C B)/S - [R_B(B/S)(1 - t_C)]$$
$$R_S = R_0 + (R_0 - R_B)(B/S)(1 - t_C)$$

28. M&M Proposition II, with no taxes is:

$$R_S = R_A + (R_A - R_f)(B/S)$$

Note that we use the risk-free rate as the return on debt. This is an important assumption of M&M Proposition II. The CAPM to calculate the cost of equity is expressed as:

$$R_S = \beta_S(R_M - R_f) + R_f$$

We can rewrite the CAPM to express the return on an unlevered company as:

$$R_0 = \beta_A(R_M - R_f) + R_f$$

We can now substitute the CAPM for an unlevered company into M&M Proposition II. Doing so and rearranging the terms we get:

$$R_S = \beta_A(R_M - R_f) + R_f + [\beta_A(R_M - R_f) + R_f - R_f](B/S)$$
$$R_S = \beta_A(R_M - R_f) + R_f + [\beta_A(R_M - R_f)](B/S)$$
$$R_S = (1 + B/S)\beta_A(R_M - R_f) + R_f$$

Now we set this equation equal to the CAPM equation to calculate the cost of equity and reduce:

$$\beta_S(R_M - R_f) + R_f = (1 + B/S)\beta_A(R_M - R_f) + R_f$$
$$\beta_S(R_M - R_f) = (1 + B/S)\beta_A(R_M - R_f)$$
$$\beta_S = \beta_A(1 + B/S)$$

**29.** Using the equation we derived in Problem 28:

$$\beta_S = \beta_A(1 + B/S)$$

The equity beta for the respective asset betas is:

| Debt-equity ratio | Equity beta |
|---|---|
| 0 | $1(1 + 0) = 1$ |
| 1 | $1(1 + 1) = 2$ |
| 5 | $1(1 + 5) = 6$ |
| 20 | $1(1 + 20) = 21$ |

The equity risk to the shareholder is composed of both business and financial risk. Even if the assets of the firm are not very risky, the risk to the shareholder can still be large if the financial leverage is high. These higher levels of risk will be reflected in the shareholder's required rate of return $R_S$, which will increase with higher debt/equity ratios.

**30.** We first need to set the cost of capital equation equal to the cost of capital for an all-equity firm, so:

$$\frac{B}{B + S} R_B + \frac{S}{B + S} R_S = R_0$$

Multiplying both sides by $(B + S)/S$ yields:

$$\frac{B}{S} R_B + R_S = \frac{B + S}{S} R_0$$

We can rewrite the right-hand side as:

$$\frac{B}{S} R_B + R_S = \frac{B}{S} R_0 + R_0$$

Moving $(B/S)R_B$ to the right-hand side and rearranging gives us:

$$R_S = R_0 + \frac{B}{S}(R_0 - R_B)$$

# CHAPTER 17
# CAPITAL STRUCTURE: *LIMITS TO THE USE OF DEBT*

## Answers to Concepts Review and Critical Thinking Questions

1.  Direct costs are potential legal and administrative costs. These are the costs associated with the litigation arising from a liquidation or bankruptcy. These costs include lawyer's fees, courtroom costs, and expert witness fees. Indirect costs include the following: 1) Impaired ability to conduct business. Firms may suffer a loss of sales due to a decrease in consumer confidence and loss of reliable supplies due to a lack of confidence by suppliers. 2) Incentive to take large risks. When faced with projects of different risk levels, managers acting in the stockholders' interest have an incentive to undertake high-risk projects. Imagine a firm with only one project, which pays $100 in an expansion and $60 in a recession. If debt payments are $60, the stockholders receive $40 (= $100 – 60) in the expansion but nothing in the recession. The bondholders receive $60 for certain. Now, alternatively imagine that the project pays $110 in an expansion but $50 in a recession. Here, the stockholders receive $50 (= $110 – 60) in the expansion but nothing in the recession. The bondholders receive only $50 in the recession because there is no more money in the firm. That is, the firm simply declares bankruptcy, leaving the bondholders "holding the bag." Thus, an increase in risk can benefit the stockholders. The key here is that the bondholders are hurt by risk, since the stockholders have limited liability. If the firm declares bankruptcy, the stockholders are not responsible for the bondholders' shortfall. 3) Incentive to under-invest. If a company is near bankruptcy, stockholders may well be hurt if they contribute equity to a new project, even if the project has a positive NPV. The reason is that some (or all) of the cash flows will go to the bondholders. Suppose a real estate developer owns a building that is likely to go bankrupt, with the bondholders receiving the property and the developer receiving nothing. Should the developer take $1 million out of his own pocket to add a new wing to a building? Perhaps not, even if the new wing will generate cash flows with a present value greater than $1 million. Since the bondholders are likely to end up with the property anyway, why would the developer pay the additional $1 million and likely end up with nothing to show for it? 4) Milking the property. In the event of bankruptcy, bondholders have the first claim to the assets of the firm. When faced with a possible bankruptcy, the stockholders have strong incentives to vote for increased dividends or other distributions. This will ensure them of getting some of the assets of the firm before the bondholders can lay claim to them.

2.  The statement is incorrect. If a firm has debt, it might be advantageous to stockholders for the firm to undertake risky projects, even those with negative net present values. This incentive results from the fact that most of the risk of failure is borne by bondholders. Therefore, value is transferred from the bondholders to the shareholders by undertaking risky projects, even if the projects have negative NPVs. This incentive is even stronger when the probability and costs of bankruptcy are high.

3.  The firm should issue equity in order to finance the project. The tax-loss carry-forwards make the firm's effective tax rate zero. Therefore, the company will not benefit from the tax shield that debt provides. Moreover, since the firm already has a moderate amount of debt in its capital structure, additional debt will likely increase the probability that the firm will face financial distress or bankruptcy. As long as there are bankruptcy costs, the firm should issue equity in order to finance the project.

4. Stockholders can undertake the following measures in order to minimize the costs of debt: 1) Use protective covenants. Firms can enter into agreements with the bondholders that are designed to decrease the cost of debt. There are two types of protective covenants. Negative covenants prohibit the company from taking actions that would expose the bondholders to potential losses. An example would be prohibiting the payment of dividends in excess of earnings. Positive covenants specify an action that the company agrees to take or a condition the company must abide by. An example would be agreeing to maintain its working capital at a minimum level. 2) Repurchase debt. A firm can eliminate the costs of bankruptcy by eliminating debt from its capital structure. 3) Consolidate debt. If a firm decreases the number of debt holders, it may be able to decrease the direct costs of bankruptcy should the firm become insolvent.

5. Modigliani and Miller's theory with corporate taxes indicates that, since there is a positive tax advantage of debt, the firm should maximize the amount of debt in its capital structure. In reality, however, no firm adopts an all-debt financing strategy. MM's theory ignores both the financial distress and agency costs of debt. The marginal costs of debt continue to increase with the amount of debt in the firm's capital structure so that, at some point, the marginal costs of additional debt will outweigh its marginal tax benefits. Therefore, there is an optimal level of debt for every firm at the point where the marginal tax benefits of the debt equal the marginal increase in financial distress and agency costs.

6. There are two major sources of the agency costs of equity: 1) Shirking. Managers with small equity holdings have a tendency to reduce their work effort, thereby hurting both the debt holders and outside equity holders. 2) Perquisites. Since management receives all the benefits of increased perquisites but only shoulder a fraction of the cost, managers have an incentive to overspend on luxury items at the expense of debt holders and outside equity holders.

7. The more capital intensive industries, such as air transport, television broadcasting stations, and hotels, tend to use greater financial leverage. Also, industries with less predictable future earnings, such as computers or drugs, tend to use less financial leverage. Such industries also have a higher concentration of growth and startup firms. Overall, the general tendency is for firms with identifiable, tangible assets and relatively more predictable future earnings to use more debt financing. These are typically the firms with the greatest need for external financing and the greatest likelihood of benefiting from the interest tax shelter.

8. One answer is that the right to file for bankruptcy is a valuable asset, and the financial manager acts in shareholders' best interest by managing this asset in ways that maximize its value. To the extent that a bankruptcy filing prevents "a race to the courthouse steps," it would seem to be a reasonable use of the process.

9. As in the previous question, it could be argued that using bankruptcy laws as a sword may simply be the best use of the asset. Creditors are aware at the time a loan is made of the possibility of bankruptcy, and the interest charged incorporates it.

10. One side is that Continental was going to go bankrupt because its costs made it uncompetitive. The bankruptcy filing enabled Continental to restructure and keep flying. The other side is that Continental abused the bankruptcy code. Rather than renegotiate labor agreements, Continental simply abrogated them to the detriment of its employees. In this, and the last several questions, an important thing to keep in mind is that the bankruptcy code is a creation of law, not economics. A strong argument can always be made that making the best use of the bankruptcy code is no different from, for example, minimizing taxes by making best use of the tax code. Indeed, a strong case can be made that it is the financial manager's duty to do so. As the case of Continental illustrates, the code can be changed if socially undesirable outcomes are a problem.

## Solutions to Questions and Problems

*NOTE: All end-of-chapter problems were solved using a spreadsheet. Many problems require multiple steps. Due to space and readability constraints, when these intermediate steps are included in this solutions manual, rounding may appear to have occurred. However, the final answer for each problem is found without rounding during any step in the problem.*

### Basic

1.  *a.*   Using M&M Proposition I with taxes, the value of a levered firm is:

$$V_L = [EBIT(1 - t_C)/R_0] + t_C B$$
$$V_L = [\$975,000(1 - .35)/.14] + .35(\$1,900,000)$$
$$V_L = \$5,191,785.71$$

   *b.*   The CFO may be correct. The value calculated in part *a* does not include the costs of any non-marketed claims, such as bankruptcy or agency costs.

2.  *a.*   *Debt issue:*

   The company needs a cash infusion of $1.3 million. If the company issues debt, the annual interest payments will be:

   Interest = $1,300,000(.08) = $104,000

   The cash flow to the owner will be the EBIT minus the interest payments, or:

   40 hour week cash flow = $550,000 – 104,000 = $446,000

   50 hour week cash flow = $625,000 – 104,000 = $521,000

   *Equity issue:*

   If the company issues equity, the company value will increase by the amount of the issue. So, the current owner's equity interest in the company will decrease to:

   Tom's ownership percentage = $3,200,000 / ($3,200,000 + 1,300,000) = .71

   So, Tom's cash flow under an equity issue will be 71 percent of EBIT, or:

   40 hour week cash flow = .71($550,000) = $391,111

   50 hour week cash flow = .71($625,000) = $444,444

   *b.*   Tom will work harder under the debt issue since his cash flows will be higher. Tom will gain more under this form of financing since the payments to bondholders are fixed. Under an equity issue, new investors share proportionally in his hard work, which will reduce his propensity for this additional work.

   *c.*   The direct cost of both issues is the payments made to new investors. The indirect costs to the debt issue include potential bankruptcy and financial distress costs. The indirect costs of an equity issue include shirking and perquisites.

3. According to M&M Proposition I with taxes, the value of the levered firm is:

$V_L = V_U + t_C B$
$V_L = \$17,850,000 + .35(\$6,000,000)$
$V_L = \$19,950,000$

We can also calculate the market value of the firm by adding the market value of the debt and equity. Using this procedure, the total market value of the firm is:

$V = B + S$
$V = \$6,000,000 + 350,000(\$38)$
$V = \$19,300,000$

With no nonmarketed claims, such as bankruptcy costs, we would expect the two values to be the same. The difference is the value of the nonmarketed claims, which are:

$V_T = V_M + V_N$
$\$19,300,000 = \$19,950,000 - V_N$
$V_N = \$650,000$

4. The president may be correct, but he may also be incorrect. It is true the interest tax shield is valuable, and adding debt can possibly increase the value of the company. However, if the company's debt is increased beyond some level, the value of the interest tax shield becomes less than the additional costs from financial distress.

*Intermediate*

5. *a.* The interest payments each year will be:

Interest payment = .09($85,000) = $7,650

This is exactly equal to the EBIT, so no cash is available for shareholders. Under this scenario, the value of equity will be zero since shareholders will never receive a payment. Since the market value of the company's debt is $85,000, and there is no probability of default, the total value of the company is the market value of debt. This implies the debt to value ratio is 1 (one).

*b.* At a growth rate of 3 percent, the earnings next year will be:

Earnings next year = $7,650(1.03) = $7,879.50

So, the cash available for shareholders is:

Payment to shareholders = $7,879.50 − 7,650 = $229.50

Since there is no risk, the required return for shareholders is the same as the required return on the company's debt. The payments to stockholders will increase at the growth rate of three percent (a growing perpetuity), so the value of these payments today is:

Value of equity = $229.50 / (.09 − .03) = $3,825.00

And the debt to value ratio now is:

Debt/Value ratio = $85,000 / ($85,000 + 3,825) = 0.957

c. At a growth rate of 7 percent, the earnings next year will be:

Earnings next year = $7,650(1.07) = $8,185.50

So, the cash available for shareholders is:

Payment to shareholders = $8,185.50 – 7,650 = $535.50

Since there is no risk, the required return for shareholders is the same as the required return on the company's debt. The payments to stockholders will increase at the growth rate of seven percent (a growing perpetuity), so the value of these payments today is:

Value of equity = $535.50 / (.09 – .07) = $26,775

And the debt to value ratio now is:

Debt/Value ratio = $85,000 / ($85,000 + 26,775) = 0.760

6. a. The total value of a firm's equity is the discounted expected cash flow to the firm's stockholders. If the expansion continues, each firm will generate earnings before interest and taxes of $2,700,000. If there is a recession, each firm will generate earnings before interest and taxes of only $1,100,000. Since Steinberg owes its bondholders $900,000 at the end of the year, its stockholders will receive $1,800,000 (= $2,700,000 – 900,000) if the expansion continues. If there is a recession, its stockholders will only receive $200,000 (= $1,100,000 – 900,000). So, assuming a discount rate of 13 percent, the market value of Steinberg's equity is:

$S_{Steinberg}$ = [.80($1,800,000) + .20($200,000)] / 1.13 = $1,309,735

Steinberg's bondholders will receive $900,000 whether there is a recession or a continuation of the expansion. So, the market value of Steinberg's debt is:

$B_{Steinberg}$ = [.80($900,000) + .20($900,000)] / 1.13 = $796,460

Since Dietrich owes its bondholders $1,200,000 at the end of the year, its stockholders will receive $1,500,000 (= $2,700,000 – 1,200,000) if the expansion continues. If there is a recession, its stockholders will receive nothing since the firm's bondholders have a more senior claim on all $1,100,000 of the firm's earnings. So, the market value of Dietrich's equity is:

$S_{Dietrich}$ = [.80($1,500,000) + .20($0)] / 1.13 = $1,061,947

Dietrich's bondholders will receive $1,200,000 if the expansion continues and $1,100,000 if there is a recession. So, the market value of Dietrich's debt is:

$B_{Dietrich}$ = [.80($1,200,000) + .20($1,100,000)] / 1.13 = $1,044,248

b. The value of company is the sum of the value of the firm's debt and equity. So, the value of Steinberg is:

$V_{Steinberg}$ = B + S
$V_{Steinberg}$ = $796,460 + 1,309,735
$V_{Steinberg}$ = $2,106,195

And value of Dietrich is:

$$V_{Dietrich} = B + S$$
$$V_{Dietrich} = \$1,044,248 + 1,061,947$$
$$V_{Dietrich} = \$2,106,195$$

You should disagree with the CEO's statement. The risk of bankruptcy *per se* does not affect a firm's value. It is the actual costs of bankruptcy that decrease the value of a firm. Note that this problem assumes that there are no bankruptcy costs.

7. *a.* The expected value of each project is the sum of the probability of each state of the economy times the value in that state of the economy. Since this is the only project for the company, the company value will be the same as the project value, so:

Low-volatility project value = .50($3,500) + .50($3,700)
Low-volatility project value = $3,600

High-volatility project value = .50($2,900) + .50($4,300)
High-volatility project value = $3,600

The low-volatility project maximizes the expected value of the firm.

*b.* The value of the equity is the residual value of the company after the bondholders are paid off. If the low-volatility project is undertaken, the firm's equity will be worth $0 if the economy is bad and $200 if the economy is good. Since each of these two scenarios is equally probable, the expected value of the firm's equity is:

Expected value of equity with low-volatility project = .50($0) + .50($200)
Expected value of equity with low-volatility project = $100

And the value of the company if the high-volatility project is undertaken will be:

Expected value of equity with high-volatility project = .50($0) + .50($800)
Expected value of equity with high-volatility project = $400

*c.* Risk-neutral investors prefer the strategy with the highest expected value. Thus, the company's stockholders prefer the high-volatility project since it maximizes the expected value of the company's equity.

*d.* In order to make stockholders indifferent between the low-volatility project and the high-volatility project, the bondholders will need to raise their required debt payment so that the expected value of equity if the high-volatility project is undertaken is equal to the expected value of equity if the low-volatility project is undertaken. As shown in part *b*, the expected value of equity if the low-volatility project is undertaken is $100. If the high-volatility project is undertaken, the value of the firm will be $2,900 if the economy is bad and $4,300 if the economy is good. If the economy is bad, the entire $2,900 will go to the bondholders and stockholders will receive nothing. If the economy is good, stockholders will receive the difference between $4,300, the total value of the firm, and the required debt payment. Let X be the debt payment that bondholders will require if the high-volatility project is undertaken. In order for stockholders to be indifferent between the two projects, the expected value of equity if the high-volatility project is undertaken must be equal to $100, so:

Expected value of equity = $100 = .50($0) + .50($4,300 – X)

X = $4,100

**8.** *a.* The expected payoff to bondholders is the face value of debt or the value of the company, whichever is less. Since the value of the company in a recession is $76,000,000 and the required debt payment in one year is $110,000,000, bondholders will receive the lesser amount, or $76,000,000.

*b.* The promised return on debt is:

Promised return = (Face value of debt / Market value of debt) – 1

Promised return = ($110,000,000 / $83,000,000) – 1

Promised return = .3253, or 32.56%

*c.* In part *a*, we determined bondholders will receive $76,000,000 in a recession. In a boom, the bondholders will receive the entire $110,000,000 promised payment since the market value of the company is greater than the payment. So, the expected value of debt is:

Expected payment to bondholders = .60($110,000,000) + .40($76,000,000)

Expected payment to bondholders = $96,400,000

So, the expected return on debt is:

Expected return = (Expected value of debt / Market value of debt) – 1

Expected return = ($96,400,000 / $83,000,000) – 1

Expected return = .1614, or 16.14%

*Challenge*

**9.** *a.* In their no tax model, MM assume that $t_C$, $t_B$, and $C(B)$ are all zero. Under these assumptions, $V_L = V_U$, signifying that the capital structure of a firm has no effect on its value. There is no optimal debt-equity ratio.

*b.* In their model with corporate taxes, MM assume that $t_C > 0$ and both $t_B$ and $C(B)$ are equal to zero. Under these assumptions, $V_L = V_U + t_C B$, implying that raising the amount of debt in a firm's capital structure will increase the overall value of the firm. This model implies that the debt-equity ratio of every firm should be infinite.

*c.* If the costs of financial distress are zero, the value of a levered firm equals:

$$V_L = V_U + \{1 - [(1 - t_C) / (1 - t_B)]\} \times B$$

Therefore, the change in the value of this all-equity firm that issues debt and uses the proceeds to repurchase equity is:

Change in value = $\{1 - [(1 - t_C) / (1 - t_B)]\} \times B$

Change in value = $\{1 - [(1 - .34) / (1 - .20)]\} \times \$1,000,000$

Change in value = $175,000

*d.* If the costs of financial distress are zero, the value of a levered firm equals:

$$V_L = V_U + \{1 - [(1 - t_C)/(1 - t_B)]\} \times B$$

Therefore, the change in the value of an all-equity firm that issues $1 of perpetual debt instead of $1 of perpetual equity is:

Change in value $= \{1 - [(1 - t_C)/(1 - t_B)]\} \times \$1$

If the firm is not able to benefit from interest deductions, the firm's taxable income will remain the same regardless of the amount of debt in its capital structure, and no tax shield will be created by issuing debt. Therefore, the firm will receive no tax benefit as a result of issuing debt in place of equity. In other words, the *effective* corporate tax rate when we consider the *change* in the value of the firm is zero. Debt will have no effect on the value of the firm since interest payments will not be tax deductible. Since this firm is unable to deduct interest payments, the change in value is:

Change in value $= \{1 - [(1 - 0)/(1 - .20)]\} \times \$1$
Change in value $= -\$0.25$

The value of the firm will decrease by $0.25 if it adds $1 of perpetual debt rather than $1 of equity.

**10.** *a.* If the company decides to retire all of its debt, it will become an unlevered firm. The value of an all-equity firm is the present value of the aftertax cash flow to equity holders, which will be:

$$V_U = (EBIT)(1 - t_C)/R_0$$
$$V_U = (\$1,300,000)(1 - .35)/.20$$
$$V_U = \$4,225,000$$

*b.* Since there are no bankruptcy costs, the value of the company as a levered firm is:

$$V_L = V_U + \{1 - [(1 - t_C)/(1 - t_B)\}] \times B$$
$$V_L = \$4,225,000 + \{1 - [(1 - .35)/(1 - .25)]\} \times \$2,500,000$$
$$V_L = \$4,558,333.33$$

*c.* The bankruptcy costs would not affect the value of the unlevered firm since it could never be forced into bankruptcy. So, the value of the levered firm with bankruptcy would be:

$$V_L = V_U + \{1 - [(1 - t_C)/(1 - t_B)\}] \times B - C(B)$$
$$V_L = (\$4,225,000 + \{1 - [(1 - .35)/(1 - .25)]\} \times \$2,500,000) - \$400,000$$
$$V_L = \$4,158,333.33$$

The company should choose the all-equity plan with this bankruptcy cost.

# CHAPTER 18
# VALUATION AND CAPITAL BUDGETING FOR THE LEVERED FIRM

## Answers to Concepts Review and Critical Thinking Questions

1. APV is equal to the NPV of the project (i.e. the value of the project for an unlevered firm) plus the NPV of financing side effects.

2. The WACC is based on a target debt level while the APV is based on the amount of debt.

3. FTE uses levered cash flow and other methods use unlevered cash flow.

4. The WACC method does not explicitly include the interest cash flows, but it does implicitly include the interest cost in the WACC. If he insists that the interest payments are explicitly shown, you should use the FTE method.

5. You can estimate the unlevered beta from a levered beta. The unlevered beta is the beta of the assets of the firm; as such, it is a measure of the business risk. Note that the unlevered beta will always be lower than the levered beta (assuming the betas are positive). The difference is due to the leverage of the company. Thus, the second risk factor measured by a levered beta is the financial risk of the company.

## Solutions to Questions and Problems

*NOTE: All end-of-chapter problems were solved using a spreadsheet. Many problems require multiple steps. Due to space and readability constraints, when these intermediate steps are included in this solutions manual, rounding may appear to have occurred. However, the final answer for each problem is found without rounding during any step in the problem.*

### Basic

1. *a.* The maximum price that the company should be willing to pay for the fleet of cars with all-equity funding is the price that makes the NPV of the transaction equal to zero. The NPV equation for the project is:

    NPV = –Purchase Price + PV[$(1 - t_C)$(EBTD)] + PV(Depreciation Tax Shield)

    If we let P equal the purchase price of the fleet, then the NPV is:

    NPV = –P + $(1 – .35)$($175,000)PVIFA$_{13\%,5}$ + $(.35)$(P/5)PVIFA$_{13\%,5}$

Setting the NPV equal to zero and solving for the purchase price, we find:

$0 = -P + (1 - .35)(\$175,000)\text{PVIFA}_{13\%,5} + (.35)(P/5)\text{PVIFA}_{13\%,5}$
$P = \$400,085.06 + (P)(.35/5)\text{PVIFA}_{13\%,5}$
$P = \$400,085.06 + .2462P$
$.7538P = \$400,085.06$
$P = \$530,761.93$

b.  The adjusted present value (APV) of a project equals the net present value of the project if it were funded completely by equity plus the net present value of any financing side effects. In this case, the NPV of financing side effects equals the after-tax present value of the cash flows resulting from the firm's debt, so:

APV = NPV(All-Equity) + NPV(Financing Side Effects)
So, the NPV of each part of the APV equation is:

NPV(All-Equity)

NPV = –Purchase Price + PV[$(1 - t_C)$(EBTD)] + PV(Depreciation Tax Shield)

The company paid $480,000 for the fleet of cars. Because this fleet will be fully depreciated over five years using the straight-line method, annual depreciation expense equals:

Depreciation = $480,000/5
Depreciation = $96,000

So, the NPV of an all-equity project is:

$\text{NPV} = -\$480,000 + (1 - .35)(\$175,000)\text{PVIFA}_{13\%,5} + (.35)(\$96,000)\text{PVIFA}_{13\%,5}$
NPV = $38,264.03

NPV(Financing Side Effects)

The net present value of financing side effects equals the after-tax present value of cash flows resulting from the firm's debt, so:

NPV = Proceeds – Aftertax PV(Interest Payments) – PV(Principal Payments)

Given a known level of debt, debt cash flows should be discounted at the pre-tax cost of debt $R_B$. So, the NPV of the financing side effects are:

$\text{NPV} = \$390,000 - (1 - .35)(.08)(\$390,000)\text{PVIFA}_{8\%,5} - \$390,000/1.08^5$
NPV = $43,600.39

So, the APV of the project is:

APV = NPV(All-Equity) + NPV(Financing Side Effects)
APV = $38,264.03 + 43,600.39
APV = $81,864.42

**2.** The adjusted present value (APV) of a project equals the net present value of the project if it were funded completely by equity plus the net present value of any financing side effects. In this case, the NPV of financing side effects equals the after-tax present value of the cash flows resulting from the firm's debt, so:

APV = NPV(All-Equity) + NPV(Financing Side Effects)

So, the NPV of each part of the APV equation is:

NPV(All-Equity)

NPV = –Purchase Price + PV[$(1 - t_C)$(EBTD)] + PV(Depreciation Tax Shield)

Since the initial investment of $1.7 million will be fully depreciated over four years using the straight-line method, annual depreciation expense is:

Depreciation = $1,700,000/4
Depreciation = $425,000

NPV = –$1,700,000 + (1 – .30)($595,000)PVIFA$_{13\%,4}$ + (.30)($425,000)PVIFA$_{9.5\%,4}$
NPV (All-equity) = –$52,561.35

NPV(Financing Side Effects)

The net present value of financing side effects equals the aftertax present value of cash flows resulting from the firm's debt. So, the NPV of the financing side effects are:

NPV = Proceeds(Net of flotation) – Aftertax PV(Interest Payments) – PV(Principal Payments)
          + PV(Flotation Cost Tax Shield)

Given a known level of debt, debt cash flows should be discounted at the pre-tax cost of debt, $R_B$. Since the flotation costs will be amortized over the life of the loan, the annual flotation costs that will be expensed each year are:

Annual flotation expense = $45,000/4
Annual flotation expense = $11,250

NPV = ($1,700,000 – 45,000) – (1 – .30)(.095)($1,700,000)PVIFA$_{9.5\%,4}$ – $1,700,000/1.095$^4$
          + .30($11,250) PVIFA$_{9.5\%,4}$
NPV = $121,072.23

So, the APV of the project is:

APV = NPV(All-Equity) + NPV(Financing Side Effects)
APV = –$52,561.35 + 121,072.23
APV = $68,510.88

**3.** *a.* In order to value a firm's equity using the flow-to-equity approach, discount the cash flows available to equity holders at the cost of the firm's levered equity. The cash flows to equity holders will be the firm's net income. Remembering that the company has three stores, we find:

| | |
|---|---|
| Sales | $3,900,000 |
| COGS | 2,010,000 |
| G & A costs | 1,215,000 |
| Interest | 123,000 |
| EBT | $ 552,000 |
| Taxes | 220,800 |
| NI | $ 331,200 |

Since this cash flow will remain the same forever, the present value of cash flows available to the firm's equity holders is a perpetuity. We can discount at the levered cost of equity, so, the value of the company's equity is:

PV(Flow-to-equity) = $331,200 / .19
PV(Flow-to-equity) = $1,743,157.89

*b.* The value of a firm is equal to the sum of the market values of its debt and equity, or:

$V_L = B + S$

We calculated the value of the company's equity in part *a*, so now we need to calculate the value of debt. The company has a debt-to-equity ratio of .40, which can be written algebraically as:

$B / S = .40$

We can substitute the value of equity and solve for the value of debt, doing so, we find:

$B / \$1,743,157.89 = .40$
$B = \$697,263.16$

So, the value of the company is:

$V = \$1,743,157.89 + 697,263.16$
$V = \$2,440,421.05$

**4.** *a.* In order to determine the cost of the firm's debt, we need to find the yield to maturity on its current bonds. With semiannual coupon payments, the yield to maturity of the company's bonds is:

$1,080 = $35 (PVIFA_{R\%,40}) + $1,000(PVIF_{R\%,40})$
$R = .03145$, or $3.145\%$

Since the coupon payments are semiannual, the YTM on the bonds is:

YTM = $3.145\% \times 2$
YTM = $6.29\%$

b.   We can use the Capital Asset Pricing Model to find the return on unlevered equity. According to the Capital Asset Pricing Model:

$$R_0 = R_F + \beta_{Unlevered}(R_M - R_F)$$
$$R_0 = 4\% + .85(11\% - 4\%)$$
$$R_0 = 9.95\%$$

Now we can find the cost of levered equity. According to Modigliani-Miller Proposition II with corporate taxes

$$R_S = R_0 + (B/S)(R_0 - R_B)(1 - t_C)$$
$$R_S = .0995 + (.40)(.0995 - .0629)(1 - .34)$$
$$R_S = .1092, \text{ or } 10.92\%$$

c.   In a world with corporate taxes, a firm's weighted average cost of capital is equal to:

$$R_{WACC} = [B / (B + S)](1 - t_C)R_B + [S / (B + S)]R_S$$

The problem does not provide either the debt-value ratio or equity-value ratio. However, the firm's debt-equity ratio is:

$$B/S = .40$$

Solving for $B$:

$$B = .4S$$

Substituting this in the debt-value ratio, we get:

$$B/V = .4S / (.4S + S)$$
$$B/V = .4 / 1.4$$
$$B/V = .29$$

And the equity-value ratio is one minus the debt-value ratio, or:

$$S/V = 1 - .29$$
$$S/V = .71$$

So, the WACC for the company is:

$$R_{WACC} = .29(1 - .34)(.0629) + .71(.1092)$$
$$R_{WACC} = .0898, \text{ or } 8.98\%$$

5.   a.   The equity beta of a firm financed entirely by equity is equal to its unlevered beta. Since each firm has an unlevered beta of 1.10, we can find the equity beta for each. Doing so, we find:

North Pole

$$\beta_{Equity} = [1 + (1 - t_C)(B/S)]\beta_{Unlevered}$$
$$\beta_{Equity} = [1 + (1 - .35)(\$2,900,000/\$3,800,000)](1.10)$$
$$\beta_{Equity} = 1.65$$

South Pole

$$\beta_{Equity} = [1 + (1 - t_C)(B/S)]\beta_{Unlevered}$$
$$\beta_{Equity} = [1 + (1 - .35)(\$3,800,000/\$2,900,000](1.10)$$
$$\beta_{Equity} = 2.04$$

b.   We can use the Capital Asset Pricing Model to find the required return on each firm's equity. Doing so, we find:

North Pole:

$$R_S = R_F + \beta_{Equity}(R_M - R_F)$$
$$R_S = 3.20\% + 1.65(10.90\% - 3.20\%)$$
$$R_S = 15.87\%$$

South Pole:

$$R_S = R_F + \beta_{Equity}(R_M - R_F)$$
$$R_S = 3.20\% + 2.04(10.90\% - 3.20\%)$$
$$R_S = 18.88\%$$

**6.**   *a.*   If flotation costs are not taken into account, the net present value of a loan equals:

$$NPV_{Loan} = \text{Gross Proceeds} - \text{Aftertax present value of interest and principal payments}$$
$$NPV_{Loan} = \$5,850,000 - .08(\$5,850,000)(1 - .40)PVIFA_{8\%,10} - \$5,850,000/1.08^{10}$$
$$NPV_{Loan} = \$1,256,127.24$$

*b.*   The flotation costs of the loan will be:

Flotation costs = $5,850,000(.025)$
Flotation costs = $146,250$

So, the annual flotation expense will be:

Annual flotation expense = $146,250 / 10$
Annual flotation expense = $14,625$

If flotation costs are taken into account, the net present value of a loan equals:

$$NPV_{Loan} = \text{Proceeds net of flotation costs} - \text{Aftertax present value of interest and principal}$$
$$\text{payments} + \text{Present value of the flotation cost tax shield}$$
$$NPV_{Loan} = (\$5,850,000 - 146,250) - .08(\$5,850,000)(1 - .40)(PVIFA_{8\%,10})$$
$$- \$5,850,000/1.08^{10} + \$14,625(.40)(PVIFA_{8\%,10})$$
$$NPV_{Loan} = \$1,149,131.21$$

**7.**   First we need to find the aftertax value of the revenues minus expenses. The aftertax value is:

Aftertax revenue = $3,200,000(1 - .40)$
Aftertax revenue = $1,920,000$

Next, we need to find the depreciation tax shield. The depreciation tax shield each year is:

Depreciation tax shield = Depreciation($t_C$)
Depreciation tax shield = ($11,400,000 / 6$)(.40)
Depreciation tax shield = $760,000

Now we can find the NPV of the project, which is:

NPV = Initial cost + PV of depreciation tax shield + PV of aftertax revenue

To find the present value of the depreciation tax shield, we should discount at the risk-free rate, and we need to discount the aftertax revenues at the cost of equity, so:

NPV = –$11,400,000 + $760,000(PVIFA$_{3.5\%,6}$) + $1,920,000(PVIFA$_{11\%,6}$)
NPV = $772,332.97

8.  Whether the company issues stock or issues equity to finance the project is irrelevant. The company's optimal capital structure determines the WACC. In a world with corporate taxes, a firm's weighted average cost of capital equals:

$R_{WACC} = [B / (B + S)](1 - t_C)R_B + [S / (B + S)]R_S$
$R_{WACC} = .80(1 - .34)(.069) + .20(.1080)$
$R_{WACC} = .0580$, or 5.80%

Now we can use the weighted average cost of capital to discount NEC's unlevered cash flows. Doing so, we find the NPV of the project is:

NPV = –$45,000,000 + $3,100,000 / .0580
NPV = $8,418,803.42

9.  a.  The company has a capital structure with three parts: long-term debt, short-term debt, and equity. Since interest payments on both long-term and short-term debt are tax-deductible, multiply the pretax costs by $(1 - t_C)$ to determine the aftertax costs to be used in the weighted average cost of capital calculation. The WACC using the book value weights is:

$R_{WACC} = (X_{STD})(R_{STD})(1 - t_C) + (X_{LTD})(R_{LTD})(1 - t_C) + (X_{Equity})(R_{Equity})$
$R_{WACC} = ($10 / $19)(.041)(1 - .35) + ($3 / $19)(.072)(1 - .35) + ($6 / $19)(.138)$
$R_{WACC} = .0650$, or 6.50%

b.  Using the market value weights, the company's WACC is:

$R_{WACC} = (X_{STD})(R_{STD})(1 - t_C) + (X_{LTD})(R_{LTD})(1 - t_C) + (X_{Equity})(R_{Equity})$
$R_{WACC} = ($11 / $40)(.041)(1 - .35) + ($10 / $40)(.072)(1 - .35) + ($26 / $40)(.138)$
$R_{WACC} = .1005$, or 10.05%

c.  Using the target debt-equity ratio, the target debt-value ratio for the company is:

$B/S = .60$
$B = .6S$

Substituting this in the debt-value ratio, we get:

$B/V = .6S / (.6S + S)$
$B/V = .6 / 1.6$
$B/V = .375$

And the equity-value ratio is one minus the debt-value ratio, or:

$S/V = 1 - .375$
$S/V = .625$

We can use the ratio of short-term debt to long-term debt in a similar manner to find the short-term debt to total debt and long-term debt to total debt. Using the short-term debt to long-term debt ratio, we get:

$STD/LTD = .20$
$STD = .2LTD$

Substituting this in the short-term debt to total debt ratio, we get:

$STD/B = .2LTD / (.2LTD + LTD)$
$STD/B = .2 / 1.2$
$STD/B = .167$

And the long-term debt to total debt ratio is one minus the short-term debt to total debt ratio, or:

$LTD/B = 1 - .167$
$LTD/B = .833$

Now we can find the short-term debt to value ratio and long-term debt to value ratio by multiplying the respective ratio by the debt-value ratio. So:

$STD/V = (STD/B)(B/V)$
$STD/V = .167(.375)$
$STD/V = .063$

And the long-term debt to value ratio is:

$LTD/V = (LTD/B)(B/V)$
$LTD/V = .833(.375)$
$LTD/V = .313$

So, using the target capital structure weights, the company's WACC is:

$R_{WACC} = (X_{STD})(R_{STD})(1 - t_C) + (X_{LTD})(R_{LTD})(1 - t_C) + (X_{Equity})(R_{Equity})$
$R_{WACC} = (.063)(.041)(1 - .35) + (.313)(.072)(1 - .35) + (.625)(.138)$
$R_{WACC} = .1025$, or 10.25%

d. The differences in the WACCs are due to the different weighting schemes. The company's WACC will most closely resemble the WACC calculated using target weights since future projects will be financed at the target ratio. Therefore, the WACC computed with target weights should be used for project evaluation.

*Intermediate*

10. The adjusted present value of a project equals the net present value of the project under all-equity financing plus the net present value of any financing side effects. In the joint venture's case, the NPV of financing side effects equals the aftertax present value of cash flows resulting from the firms' debt. So, the APV is:

$$APV = NPV(\text{All-Equity}) + NPV(\text{Financing Side Effects})$$

The NPV for an all-equity firm is:

<u>NPV(All-Equity)</u>

$$NPV = -\text{Initial Investment} + PV[(1 - t_C)(\text{EBITD})] + PV(\text{Depreciation Tax Shield})$$

Since the initial investment will be fully depreciated over five years using the straight-line method, annual depreciation expense is:

Annual depreciation = $80,000,000/5
Annual depreciation = $16,000,000

$$NPV = -\$80,000,000 + (1 - .35)(\$12,100,000)PVIFA_{13\%,20} + (.35)(\$16,000,000)PVIFA_{13\%,5}$$
$$NPV = -\$5,053,833.77$$

<u>NPV(Financing Side Effects)</u>

The NPV of financing side effects equals the after-tax present value of cash flows resulting from the firm's debt. The coupon rate on the debt is relevant to determine the interest payments, but the resulting cash flows should still be discounted at the pretax cost of debt. So, the NPV of the financing effects is:

$$NPV = \text{Proceeds} - \text{Aftertax PV(Interest Payments)} - \text{PV(Principal Repayments)}$$
$$NPV = \$25,000,000 - (1 - .35)(.05)(\$25,000,000)PVIFA_{8.5\%,15} - \$25,000,000/1.085^{15}$$
$$NPV = \$10,899,310.51$$

So, the APV of the project is:

$$APV = NPV(\text{All-Equity}) + NPV(\text{Financing Side Effects})$$
$$APV = -\$5,053,833.77 + \$10,899,310.51$$
$$APV = \$5,845,476.73$$

11. If the company had to issue debt under the terms it would normally receive, the interest rate on the debt would increase to the company's normal cost of debt. The NPV of an all-equity project would remain unchanged, but the NPV of the financing side effects would change. The NPV of the financing side effects would be:

$$NPV = \text{Proceeds} - \text{Aftertax PV(Interest Payments)} - \text{PV(Principal Repayments)}$$
$$NPV = \$25,000,000 - (1 - .35)(.085)(\$25,000,000)PVIFA_{8.5\%,15} - \$25,000,000/1.085^{15}$$
$$NPV = \$6,176,275.95$$

Using the NPV of an all-equity project from the previous problem, the new APV of the project would be:

APV = NPV(All-Equity) + NPV(Financing Side Effects)
APV = –$5,053,833.77 + $6,176,275.95
APV = $1,122,442.18

The gain to the company from issuing subsidized debt is the difference between the two APVs, so:

Gain from subsidized debt = $5,845,476.73 – 1,122,442.18
Gain from subsidized debt = $4,723,034.55

Most of the value of the project is in the form of the subsidized interest rate on the debt issue.

12. The adjusted present value of a project equals the net present value of the project under all-equity financing plus the net present value of any financing side effects. First, we need to calculate the unlevered cost of equity. According to Modigliani-Miller Proposition II with corporate taxes:

$R_S = R_0 + (B/S)(R_0 - R_B)(1 - t_C)$
$.16 = R_0 + (.50)(R_0 - .09)(1 - .40)$
$R_0 = .1438$ or 14.38%

Now we can find the NPV of an all-equity project, which is:

NPV = PV(Unlevered Cash Flows)
$NPV = -\$18,000,000 + \$5,700,000/1.1438 + \$9,500,000/(1.1438)^2 + \$8,800,000/1.1438^3$
NPV = $124,086.62

Next, we need to find the net present value of financing side effects. This is equal the aftertax present value of cash flows resulting from the firm's debt. So:

NPV = Proceeds – Aftertax PV(Interest Payments) – PV(Principal Payments)

Each year, an equal principal payment will be made, which will reduce the interest accrued during the year. Given a known level of debt, debt cash flows should be discounted at the pre-tax cost of debt, so the NPV of the financing effects is:

$NPV = \$9,300,000 - (1 - .40)(.09)(\$9,300,000) / 1.09 - \$3,100,000/1.09$
$\qquad - (1 - .40)(.09)(\$6,200,000)/1.09^2 - \$3,100,000/1.09^2$
$\qquad - (1 - .40)(.09)(\$3,100,000)/1.09^3 - \$3,100,000/1.09^3$
NPV = $581,194.61

So, the APV of project is:

APV = NPV(All-equity) + NPV(Financing side effects)
APV = $124,086.62 + 581,194.61
APV = $705,281.23

13. *a.* To calculate the NPV of the project, we first need to find the company's WACC. In a world with corporate taxes, a firm's weighted average cost of capital equals:

$R_{WACC} = [B / (B + S)](1 - t_C)R_B + [S / (B + S)]R_S$

The market value of the company's equity is:

Market value of equity = 4,500,000($25)
Market value of equity = $112,500,000

So, the debt-value ratio and equity-value ratio are:

Debt-value = $55,000,000 / ($55,000,000 + 112,500,000)
Debt-value = .3284

Equity-value = $112,500,000 / ($55,000,000 + 112,500,000)
Equity-value = .6716

Since the CEO believes its current capital structure is optimal, these values can be used as the target weights in the firm's weighted average cost of capital calculation. The yield to maturity of the company's debt is its pretax cost of debt. To find the company's cost of equity, we need to calculate the stock beta. The stock beta can be calculated as:

$\beta = \sigma_{S,M} / \sigma_M^2$
$\beta = .0415 / .20^2$
$\beta = 1.04$

Now we can use the Capital Asset Pricing Model to determine the cost of equity. The Capital Asset Pricing Model is:

$R_S = R_F + \beta(R_M - R_F)$
$R_S = 3.4\% + 1.04(7.50\%)$
$R_S = 11.18\%$

Now, we can calculate the company's WACC, which is:

$R_{WACC} = [B / (B + S)](1 - t_C)R_B + [S / (B + S)]R_S$
$R_{WACC} = .3284(1 - .35)(.065) + .6716(.1118)$
$R_{WACC} = .0890$, or 8.90%

Finally, we can use the WACC to discount the unlevered cash flows, which gives us an NPV of:

NPV = –$42,000,000 + $11,800,000(PVIFA$_{8.90\%,5}$)
NPV = $4,020,681.28

b.  The weighted average cost of capital used in part *a* will not change if the firm chooses to fund the project entirely with debt. The weighted average cost of capital is based on optimal capital structure weights. Since the current capital structure is optimal, all-debt funding for the project simply implies that the firm will have to use more equity in the future to bring the capital structure back towards the target.

14. We have four companies with comparable operations, so the industry average beta can be used as the beta for this project. So, the average unlevered beta is:

$\beta_{Unlevered} = (1.15 + 1.08 + 1.30 + 1.25) / 4$
$\beta_{Unlevered} = 1.20$

A debt-to-value ratio of .40 means that the equity-to-value ratio is .60. This implies a debt-equity ratio of .67{=.40/.60}. Since the project will be levered, we need to calculate the levered beta, which is:

$\beta_{Levered} = [1 + (1 - t_C)(Debt/Equity)]\beta_{Unlevered}$
$\beta_{Levered} = [1 + (1 - .34)(.67)]1.20$
$\beta_{Levered} = 1.72$

Now we can use the Capital Asset Pricing Model to determine the cost of equity. The Capital Asset Pricing Model is:

$R_S = R_F + \beta(R_M - R_F)$
$R_S = 3.8\% + 1.72(7.00\%)$
$R_S = 15.85\%$

Now, we can calculate the company's WACC, which is:

$R_{WACC} = [B / (B + S)](1 - t_C)R_B + [S / (B + S)]R_S$
$R_{WACC} = .40(1 - .35)(.068) + .60(.1585)$
$R_{WACC} = .1130$, or 11.30%

Finally, we can use the WACC to discount the unlevered cash flows, which gives us an NPV of:

$NPV = -\$4,500,000 + \$675,000(PVIFA_{11.30\%,20})$
$NPV = \$770,604.48$

*Challenge*

15. *a.* The company is currently an all-equity firm, so the value as an all-equity firm equals the present value of aftertax cash flows, discounted at the cost of the firm's unlevered cost of equity. So, the current value of the company is:

$V_U = [(Pretax\ earnings)(1 - t_C)] / R_0$
$V_U = [(\$21,000,000)(1 - .35)] / .16$
$V_U = \$85,312,500$

The price per share is the total value of the company divided by the shares outstanding, or:

Price per share = \$85,312,500 / 1,300,000
Price per share = \$65.63

*b.* The adjusted present value of a firm equals its value under all-equity financing plus the net present value of any financing side effects. In this case, the NPV of financing side effects equals the aftertax present value of cash flows resulting from the firm's debt. Given a known level of debt, debt cash flows can be discounted at the pretax cost of debt, so the NPV of the financing effects are:

NPV = Proceeds – Aftertax PV(Interest Payments)
NPV = \$30,000,000 – (1 – .35)(.09)(\$30,000,000) / .09
NPV = \$10,500,000

So, the value of the company after the recapitalization using the APV approach is:

$V = \$85,312,500 + 10,500,000$
$V = \$95,812,500$

Since the company has not yet issued the debt, this is also the value of equity after the announcement. So, the new price per share will be:

New share price = $\$95,812,500 / 1,300,000$
New share price = $\$73.70$

c.  The company will use the entire proceeds to repurchase equity. Using the share price we calculated in part *b*, the number of shares repurchased will be:

Shares repurchased = $\$30,000,000 / \$73.70$
Shares repurchased = 407,045

And the new number of shares outstanding will be:

New shares outstanding = $1,300,000 - 407,045$
New shares outstanding = 892,955

The value of the company increased, but part of that increase will be funded by the new debt. The value of equity after recapitalization is the total value of the company minus the value of debt, or:

New value of equity = $\$95,812,500 - 30,000,000$
New value of equity = $\$65,812,500$

So, the price per share of the company after recapitalization will be:

New share price = $\$65,812,500 / 892,955$
New share price = $\$73.70$

The price per share is unchanged.

d.  In order to value a firm's equity using the flow-to-equity approach, we must discount the cash flows available to equity holders at the cost of the firm's levered equity. According to Modigliani-Miller Proposition II with corporate taxes, the required return of levered equity is:

$R_S = R_0 + (B/S)(R_0 - R_B)(1 - t_C)$
$R_S = .16 + (\$30,000,000 / \$65,812,500)(.16 - .09)(1 - .35)$
$R_S = .1807$, or 18.07%

After the recapitalization, the net income of the company will be:

| | |
|---|---:|
| EBIT | $21,000,000 |
| Interest | 2,700,000 |
| EBT | $18,300,000 |
| Taxes | 6,405,000 |
| Net income | $11,895,000 |

The firm pays all of its earnings as dividends, so the entire net income is available to shareholders. Using the flow-to-equity approach, the value of the equity is:

$S$ = Cash flows available to equity holders / $R_S$
$S$ = \$11,895,000 / .1807
$S$ = \$65,812,500

**16.** *a.* If the company were financed entirely by equity, the value of the firm would be equal to the present value of its unlevered after-tax earnings, discounted at its unlevered cost of capital. First, we need to find the company's unlevered cash flows, which are:

| | |
|---|---|
| Sales | \$17,500,000 |
| Variable costs | 10,500,000 |
| EBT | \$ 7,000,000 |
| Tax | 2,800,000 |
| Net income | \$ 4,200,000 |

So, the value of the unlevered company is:

$V_U$ = \$4,200,000 / .13
$V_U$ = \$32,307,692.31

*b.* According to Modigliani-Miller Proposition II with corporate taxes, the value of levered equity is:

$R_S = R_0 + (B/S)(R_0 - R_B)(1 - t_C)$
$R_S = .13 + (.35)(.13 - .07)(1 - .40)$
$R_S = .1426$ or 14.26%

*c.* In a world with corporate taxes, a firm's weighted average cost of capital equals:

$R_{WACC} = [B / (B + S)](1 - t_C)R_B + [S / (B + S)]R_S$

So we need the debt-value and equity-value ratios for the company. The debt-equity ratio for the company is:

$B/S = .35$
$B = .35S$

Substituting this in the debt-value ratio, we get:

$B/V = .35S / (.35S + S)$
$B/V = .35 / 1.35$
$B/V = .26$

And the equity-value ratio is one minus the debt-value ratio, or:

$S/V = 1 - .26$
$S/V = .74$

So, using the capital structure weights, the company's WACC is:

$R_{WACC} = [B / (B + S)](1 - t_C)R_B + [S / (B + S)]R_S$
$R_{WACC} = .26(1 - .40)(.07) + .74(.1426)$
$R_{WACC} = .1165$, or 11.65%

We can use the weighted average cost of capital to discount the firm's unlevered aftertax earnings to value the company. Doing so, we find:

$V_L = \$4,200,000 / .1165$
$V_L = \$36,045,772.41$

Now we can use the debt-value ratio and equity-value ratio to find the value of debt and equity, which are:

$B = V_L$(Debt-value)
$B = \$36,045,772.41(.26)$
$B = \$9,345,200.25$

$S = V_L$(Equity-value)
$S = \$36,045,772.41(.74)$
$S = \$26,700,572.16$

d.  In order to value a firm's equity using the flow-to-equity approach, we can discount the cash flows available to equity holders at the cost of the firm's levered equity. First, we need to calculate the levered cash flows available to shareholders, which are:

| | |
|---|---:|
| Sales | $17,500,000 |
| Variable costs | 10,500,000 |
| EBIT | $ 7,000,000 |
| Interest | 654,164 |
| EBT | $ 6,345,836 |
| Tax | 2,538,334 |
| Net income | $ 3,807,502 |

So, the value of equity with the flow-to-equity method is:

$S$ = Cash flows available to equity holders / $R_S$
$S = \$3,807,502 / .1426$
$S = \$26,700,572.16$

17.  a.  Since the company is currently an all-equity firm, its value equals the present value of its unlevered after-tax earnings, discounted at its unlevered cost of capital. The cash flows to shareholders for the unlevered firm are:

| | |
|---|---:|
| EBIT | $118,000 |
| Tax | 47,200 |
| Net income | $ 70,800 |

So, the value of the company is:

$V_U = \$70,800 / .14$
$V_U = \$505,714.29$

b.  The adjusted present value of a firm equals its value under all-equity financing plus the net present value of any financing side effects. In this case, the NPV of financing side effects equals the after-tax present value of cash flows resulting from debt. Given a known level of debt, debt cash flows should be discounted at the pre-tax cost of debt, so:

NPV = Proceeds − Aftertax PV(Interest payments)
NPV = \$235,000 − (1 − .40)(.08)(\$235,000) / .08
NPV = \$94,000

So, using the APV method, the value of the company is:

APV = $V_U$ + NPV(Financing side effects)
APV = \$505,714.29 + 94,000
APV = \$599,714.29

The value of the debt is given, so the value of equity is the value of the company minus the value of the debt, or:

$S = V − B$
$S = \$599,714.29 − 235,000$
$S = \$364,714.29$

c.  According to Modigliani-Miller Proposition II with corporate taxes, the required return of levered equity is:

$R_S = R_0 + (B/S)(R_0 − R_B)(1 − t_C)$
$R_S = .14 + (\$235,000 / \$364,714.29)(.14 − .08)(1 − .40)$
$R_S = .1632$, or 16.32%

d.  In order to value a firm's equity using the flow-to-equity approach, we can discount the cash flows available to equity holders at the cost of the firm's levered equity. First, we need to calculate the levered cash flows available to shareholders, which are:

| | |
|---|---:|
| EBIT | \$118,000 |
| Interest | 18,800 |
| EBT | \$ 99,200 |
| Tax | 39,680 |
| Net income | \$ 59,520 |

So, the value of equity with the flow-to-equity method is:

$S$ = Cash flows available to equity holders / $R_S$
$S = \$59,520 / .1632$
$S = \$364,714.29$

**18.** Since the company is not publicly traded, we need to use the industry numbers to calculate the industry levered return on equity. We can then find the industry unlevered return on equity, and re-lever the industry return on equity to account for the different use of leverage. So, using the CAPM to calculate the industry levered return on equity, we find:

$R_S = R_F + \beta(MRP)$
$R_S = 5\% + 1.2(7\%)$
$R_S = 13.40\%$

Next, to find the average cost of unlevered equity in the holiday gift industry we can use Modigliani-Miller Proposition II with corporate taxes, so:

$R_S = R_0 + (B/S)(R_0 - R_B)(1 - t_C)$
$.1340 = R_0 + (.35)(R_0 - .05)(1 - .40)$
$R_0 = .1194$ or $11.94\%$

Now, we can use the Modigliani-Miller Proposition II with corporate taxes to re-lever the return on equity to account for this company's debt-equity ratio. Doing so, we find:

$R_S = R_0 + (B/S)(R_0 - R_B)(1 - t_C)$
$R_S = .1194 + (.40)(.1194 - .05)(1 - .40)$
$R_S = .1361$ or $13.61\%$

Since the project is financed at the firm's target debt-equity ratio, it must be discounted at the company's weighted average cost of capital. In a world with corporate taxes, a firm's weighted average cost of capital equals:

$R_{WACC} = [B / (B + S)](1 - t_C)R_B + [S / (B + S)]R_S$

So, we need the debt-value and equity-value ratios for the company. The debt-equity ratio for the company is:

$B/S = .40$
$B = .40S$

Substituting this in the debt-value ratio, we get:

$B/V = .40S / (.40S + S)$
$B/V = .40 / 1.40$
$B/V = .29$

And the equity-value ratio is one minus the debt-value ratio, or:

$S/V = 1 - .29$
$S/V = .71$

So, using the capital structure weights, the company's WACC is:

$R_{WACC} = [B / (B + S)](1 - t_C)R_B + [S / (B + S)]R_S$
$R_{WACC} = .29(1 - .40)(.05) + .71(.1361)$
$R_{WACC} = .1058$ or $10.58\%$

Now we need the project's cash flows. The cash flows increase for the first five years before leveling off into perpetuity. So, the cash flows from the project for the next six years are:

| | |
|---|---|
| Year 1 cash flow | $ 95,000.00 |
| Year 2 cash flow | $ 99,750.00 |
| Year 3 cash flow | $104,737.50 |
| Year 4 cash flow | $109,974.38 |
| Year 5 cash flow | $115,473.09 |
| Year 6 cash flow | $115,473.09 |

So, the NPV of the project is:

$$\text{NPV} = -\$675,000 + \$95,000/1.1058 + \$99,750/1.1058^2 + \$104,737.50/1.1058^3$$
$$+ \$109,974.38/1.1058^4 + \$115,473.09/1.1058^5 + (\$115,473.09/.1058)/1.1058^5$$
$$\text{NPV} = \$373,711.73$$

# CHAPTER 19
# DIVIDENDS AND OTHER PAYOUTS

**Answers to Concepts Review and Critical Thinking Questions**

1. Dividend policy deals with the timing of dividend payments, not the amounts ultimately paid. Dividend policy is irrelevant when the timing of dividend payments doesn't affect the present value of all future dividends.

2. A stock repurchase reduces equity while leaving debt unchanged. The debt ratio rises. A firm could, if desired, use excess cash to reduce debt instead. This is a capital structure decision.

3. The chief drawback to a strict dividend policy is the variability in dividend payments. This is a problem because investors tend to want a somewhat predictable cash flow. Also, if there is information content to dividend announcements, then the firm may be inadvertently telling the market that it is expecting a downturn in earnings prospects when it cuts a dividend, when in reality its prospects are very good. In a compromise policy, the firm maintains a relatively constant dividend. It increases dividends only when it expects earnings to remain at a sufficiently high level to pay the larger dividends, and it lowers the dividend only if it absolutely has to.

4. Friday, December 29 is the ex-dividend day. Remember not to count January 1 because it is a holiday, and the exchanges are closed. Anyone who buys the stock before December 29 is entitled to the dividend, assuming they do not sell it again before December 29.

5. No, because the money could be better invested in stocks that pay dividends in cash which benefit the fundholders directly.

6. The change in price is due to the change in dividends, not due to the change in dividend *policy*. Dividend policy can still be irrelevant without a contradiction.

7. The stock price dropped because of an expected drop in future dividends. Since the stock price is the present value of all future dividend payments, if the expected future dividend payments decrease, then the stock price will decline.

8. The plan will probably have little effect on shareholder wealth. The shareholders can reinvest on their own, and the shareholders must pay the taxes on the dividends either way. However, the shareholders who take the option may benefit at the expense of the ones who don't (because of the discount). Also as a result of the plan, the firm will be able to raise equity by paying a 10% flotation cost (the discount), which may be a smaller discount than the market flotation costs of a new issue for some companies.

9. If these firms just went public, they probably did so because they were growing and needed the additional capital. Growth firms typically pay very small cash dividends, if they pay a dividend at all. This is because they have numerous projects available, and they reinvest the earnings in the firm instead of paying cash dividends.

10. It would not be irrational to find low-dividend, high-growth stocks. The trust should be indifferent between receiving dividends or capital gains since it does not pay taxes on either one (ignoring possible restrictions on invasion of principal, etc.). It would be irrational, however, to hold municipal bonds. Since the trust does not pay taxes on the interest income it receives, it does not need the tax break associated with the municipal bonds. Therefore, it should prefer to hold higher yield, taxable bonds.

11. The stock price drop on the ex-dividend date should be lower. With taxes, stock prices should drop by the amount of the dividend, less the taxes investors must pay on the dividends. A lower tax rate lowers the investors' tax liability.

12. With a high tax on dividends and a low tax on capital gains, investors, in general, will prefer capital gains. If the dividend tax rate declines, the attractiveness of dividends increases.

13. Knowing that share price can be expressed as the present value of expected future dividends does not make dividend policy relevant. Under the growing perpetuity model, if overall corporate cash flows are unchanged, then a change in dividend policy only changes the timing of the dividends. The PV of those dividends is the same. This is true because, given that future earnings are held constant, dividend policy simply represents a transfer between current and future stockholders.

   In a more realistic context and assuming a finite holding period, the value of the shares should represent the future stock price as well as the dividends. Any cash flow not paid as a dividend will be reflected in the future stock price. As such, the PV of the cash flows will not change with shifts in dividend policy; dividend policy is still irrelevant.

14. The bird-in-the-hand argument is based upon the erroneous assumption that increased dividends make a firm less risky. If capital spending and investment spending are unchanged, the firm's overall cash flows are not affected by the dividend policy.

15. This argument is theoretically correct. In the real world, with transaction costs of security trading, home-made dividends can be more expensive than dividends directly paid out by the firms. However, the existence of financial intermediaries, such as mutual funds, reduces the transaction costs for individuals greatly. Thus, as a whole, the desire for current income shouldn't be a major factor favoring high-current-dividend policy.

16. a. Cap's past behavior suggests a preference for capital gains, while Sarah exhibits a preference for current income.
    b. Cap could show the Sarah how to construct homemade dividends through the sale of stock. Of course, Cap will also have to convince her that she lives in an MM world. Remember that homemade dividends can only be constructed under the MM assumptions.
    c. Sarah may still not invest in Neotech because of the transaction costs involved in constructing homemade dividends. Also, Sarah may desire the uncertainty resolution which comes with high dividend stocks.

17. To minimize her tax burden, your aunt should divest herself of high dividend yield stocks and invest in low dividend yield stocks. Or, if possible, she should keep her high dividend stocks, borrow an equivalent amount of money and invest that money in a tax-deferred account.

18. The capital investment needs of small, growing companies are very high. Therefore, payment of dividends could curtail their investment opportunities. Their other option is to issue stock to pay the dividend, thereby incurring issuance costs. In either case, the companies and thus their investors are better off with a zero dividend policy during the firms' rapid growth phases. This fact makes these firms attractive only to low dividend clienteles.

This example demonstrates that dividend policy is relevant when there are issuance costs. Indeed, it may be relevant whenever the assumptions behind the MM model are not met.

19. Unless there is an unsatisfied high dividend clientele, a firm cannot improve its share price by switching policies. If the market is in equilibrium, the number of people who desire high dividend payout stocks should exactly equal the number of such stocks available. The supplies and demands of each clientele will be exactly met in equilibrium. If the market is not in equilibrium, the supply of high dividend payout stocks may be less than the demand. Only in such a situation could a firm benefit from a policy shift.

20. This finding implies that firms use initial dividends to "signal" their potential growth and positive NPV prospects to the stock market. The initiation of regular cash dividends also serves to convince the market that their high current earnings are not temporary.

### Solutions to Questions and Problems

*NOTE: All end-of-chapter problems were solved using a spreadsheet. Many problems require multiple steps. Due to space and readability constraints, when these intermediate steps are included in this solutions manual, rounding may appear to have occurred. However, the final answer for each problem is found without rounding during any step in the problem.*

### *Basic*

1. The aftertax dividend is the pretax dividend times one minus the tax rate, so:

Aftertax dividend = $9.50(1 – .15) = $8.08

The stock price should drop by the aftertax dividend amount, or:

Ex-dividend price = $115 – 8.08 = $106.93

2. *a.* The shares outstanding increases by 10 percent, so:

New shares outstanding = 30,000(1.10) = 33,000

New shares issued = 3,000

Since the par value of the new shares is $1, the capital surplus per share is $36. The total capital surplus is therefore:

Capital surplus on new shares = 3,000($36) = $108,000

| Common stock ($1 par value) | $ 33,000 |
| Capital surplus | 293,000 |
| Retained earnings | 516,500 |
| | $842,500 |

  *b.* The shares outstanding increases by 25 percent, so:

   New shares outstanding = 30,000(1.25) = 37,500

   New shares issued = 7,500

   Since the par value of the new shares is $1, the capital surplus per share is $36. The total capital surplus is therefore:

   Capital surplus on new shares = 7,500($36) = $270,000

| | |
|---|---:|
| Common stock ($1 par value) | $ 37,500 |
| Capital surplus | 455,000 |
| Retained earnings | 350,000 |
| | $842,500 |

**3.** *a.* To find the new shares outstanding, we multiply the current shares outstanding times the ratio of new shares to old shares, so:

   New shares outstanding = 30,000(4/1) = 120,000

   The equity accounts are unchanged except that the par value of the stock is changed by the ratio of new shares to old shares, so the new par value is:

   New par value = $1(1/4) = $0.25 per share.

  *b.* To find the new shares outstanding, we multiply the current shares outstanding times the ratio of new shares to old shares, so:

   New shares outstanding = 30,000(1/5) = 6,000.

   The equity accounts are unchanged except that the par value of the stock is changed by the ratio of new shares to old shares, so the new par value is:

   New par value = $1(5/1) = $5.00 per share.

**4.** To find the new stock price, we multiply the current stock price by the ratio of old shares to new shares, so:

  *a.* $64(3/5) = $38.40

  *b.* $64(1/1.15) = $55.65

  *c.* $64(1/1.425) = $44.91

  *d.* $64(7/4) = $112.00

  To find the new shares outstanding, we multiply the current shares outstanding times the ratio of new shares to old shares, so:

   *a:* 330,000(5/3) = 550,000

*b:* 330,000(1.15) = 379,500

*c:* 330,000(1.425) = 470,250

*d:* 330,000(4/7) = 188,571

5. The stock price is the total market value of equity divided by the shares outstanding, so:

$P_0$ = $465,000 equity/12,000 shares = $38.75 per share

Ignoring tax effects, the stock price will drop by the amount of the dividend, so:

$P_X$ = $38.75 – 1.90 = $36.85

The total dividends paid will be:

$1.90 per share(12,000 shares) = $22,800

The equity and cash accounts will both decline by $22,800.

6. Repurchasing the shares will reduce shareholders' equity by $22,800. The shares repurchased will be the total purchase amount divided by the stock price, so:

Shares bought = $22,800/$38.75 = 588

And the new shares outstanding will be:

New shares outstanding = 12,000 – 588 = 11,412

After repurchase, the new stock price is:

Share price = $442,200/11,412 shares = $38.75

The repurchase is effectively the same as the cash dividend because you either hold a share worth $38.75 or a share worth $36.85 and $1.90 in cash. Therefore, you participate in the repurchase according to the dividend payout percentage; you are unaffected.

7. The stock price is the total market value of equity divided by the shares outstanding, so:

$P_0$ = $655,000 equity/25,000 shares = $26.20 per share

The shares outstanding will increase by 25 percent, so:

New shares outstanding = 25,000(1.25) = 31,250

The new stock price is the market value of equity divided by the new shares outstanding, so:

$P_X$ = $655,000/31,250 shares = $20.96

**8.** With a stock dividend, the shares outstanding will increase by one plus the dividend amount, so:

New shares outstanding = 410,000(1.15) = 471,500

The capital surplus is the capital paid in excess of par value, which is $1, so:

Capital surplus for new shares = 61,500($44) = $2,706,000

The new capital surplus will be the old capital surplus plus the additional capital surplus for the new shares, so:

Capital surplus = $2,150,000 + 2,706,000 = $4,856,000

The new equity portion of the balance sheet will look like this:

| | |
|---|---:|
| Common stock ($1 par value) | $ 471,500 |
| Capital surplus | 4,856,000 |
| Retained earnings | 2,552,500 |
| | $7,880,000 |

**9.** The only equity account that will be affected is the par value of the stock. The par value will change by the ratio of old shares to new shares, so:

New par value = $1(1/5) = $0.20 per share.

The total dividends paid this year will be the dividend amount times the number of shares outstanding. The company had 410,000 shares outstanding before the split. We must remember to adjust the shares outstanding for the stock split, so:

Total dividends paid this year = $0.45(410,000 shares)(5/1 split) = $922,500

The dividends increased by 10 percent, so the total dividends paid last year were:

Last year's dividends = $922,500/1.10 = $838,636.36

And to find the dividends per share, we simply divide this amount by the shares outstanding last year. Doing so, we get:

Dividends per share last year = $838,636.36/410,000 shares = $2.05

**10.** *a.* If the dividend is declared, the price of the stock will drop on the ex-dividend date by the value of the dividend, $4. It will then trade for $106.

*b.* If it is not declared, the price will remain at $110.

*c.* Mann's outflows for investments are $4,500,000. These outflows occur immediately. One year from now, the firm will realize $1,900,000 in net income and it will pay $880,000 in dividends, but the need for financing is immediate. Mann must finance $4,500,000 through the sale of shares worth $110. It must sell $4,500,000 / $110 = 40,909 shares.

*d.* The MM model is not realistic since it does not account for taxes, brokerage fees, uncertainty over future cash flows, investors' preferences, signaling effects, and agency costs.

*Intermediate*

11. The price of the stock today is the PV of the dividends, so:

$P_0 = \$1.1/1.14 + \$56/1.14^2 = \$44.06$

To find the equal two year dividends with the same present value as the price of the stock, we set up the following equation and solve for the dividend (Note: The dividend is a two year annuity, so we could solve with the annuity factor as well):

$\$44.06 = D/1.14 + D/1.14^2$
$D = \$26.75$

We now know the cash flow per share we want each of the next two years. We can find the price of stock in one year, which will be:

$P_1 = \$56/1.14 = \$49.12$

Since you own 1,000 shares, in one year you want:

Cash flow in Year one = 1,000($26.75) = $26,754.21

But you'll only get:

Dividends received in one year = 1,000($1.10) = $1,100

Thus, in one year you will need to sell additional shares in order to increase your cash flow. The number of shares to sell in year one is:

Shares to sell at time one = ($26,754.21 – 1,100)/$49.12 = 522.25 shares

At Year 2, your cash flow will be the dividend payment times the number of shares you still own, so the Year 2 cash flow is:

Year 2 cash flow = $56(1,000 – 522.25) = $26,754.21

12. If you only want $500 in Year 1, you will buy:

($1,100 – 500)/$49.12 = 12.21 shares

at Year 1. Your dividend payment in Year 2 will be:

Year 2 dividend = (1,000 + 12.21)($56) = $56,684.00

Note that the present value of each cash flow stream is the same. Below we show this by finding the present values as:

$PV = \$500/1.14 + \$56,684.00/1.14^2 = \$44,055.09$

$PV = 1,000(\$1.10)/1.14 + 1,000(\$56)/1.14^2 = \$44,055.09$

13. *a.* If the company makes a dividend payment, we can calculate the wealth of a shareholder as:

Dividend per share = $4,000/800 shares = $5.00

The stock price after the dividend payment will be:

$P_X$ = $46 – 5 = $41 per share

The shareholder will have a stock worth $41 and a $5 dividend for a total wealth of $46. If the company makes a repurchase, the company will repurchase:

Shares repurchased = $4,000/$46 = 86.96 shares

If the shareholder lets their shares be repurchased, they will have $46 in cash. If the shareholder keeps their shares, they're still worth $46.

*b.* If the company pays dividends, the current EPS is $2.1, and the P/E ratio is:

P/E = $41/$2.10 = 19.52

If the company repurchases stock, the number of shares will decrease. The total net income is the EPS times the current number of shares outstanding. Dividing net income by the new number of shares outstanding, we find the EPS under the repurchase is:

EPS = $2.10(800)/(800 – 86.96) = $2.36

The stock price will remain at $46 per share, so the P/E ratio is:

P/E = $46/$2.36 = 19.52

*c.* A share repurchase would seem to be the preferred course of action. Only those shareholders who wish to sell will do so, giving the shareholder a tax timing option that he or she doesn't get with a dividend payment.

14. *a.* Since the firm has a 100 percent payout policy, the entire net income, $85,000 will be paid as a dividend. The current value of the firm is the discounted value one year from now, plus the current income, which is:

Value = $85,000 + $1,725,000/1.12
Value = $1,625,178.57

*b.* The current stock price is the value of the firm, divided by the shares outstanding, which is:

Stock price = $1,625,178.57/25,000
Stock price = $65.01

Since the company has a 100 percent payout policy, the current dividend per share will be the company's net income, divided by the shares outstanding, or:

Current dividend = $85,000/25,000
Current dividend = $3.40

The stock price will fall by the value of the dividend to:

Ex-dividend stock price = $65.01 – 3.40
Ex-dividend stock price = $61.61

c.    i.    According to MM, it cannot be true that the low dividend is depressing the price. Since dividend policy is irrelevant, the level of the dividend should not matter. Any funds not distributed as dividends add to the value of the firm, hence the stock price. These directors merely want to change the timing of the dividends (more now, less in the future). As the calculations below indicate, the value of the firm is unchanged by their proposal. Therefore, the share price will be unchanged.

To show this, consider what would happen if the dividend were increased to $4.60. Since only the existing shareholders will get the dividend, the required dollar amount to pay the dividends is:

Total dividends = $4.60(25,000)
Total dividends = $115,000

To fund this dividend payment, the company must raise:

Dollars raised = Required funds – Net income
Dollars raised = $115,000 – 85,000
Dollars raised = $30,000

This money can only be raised with the sale of new equity to maintain the all-equity financing. Since those new shareholders must also earn 12 percent, their share of the firm one year from now is:

New shareholder value in one year = $30,000(1.12)
New shareholder value in one year = $33,600

This means that the old shareholders' interest falls to:

Old shareholder value in one year = $1,725,000 – 33,600
Old shareholder value in one year = $1,691,400

Under this scenario, the current value of the firm is:

Value = $115,000 + $1,691,400/1.12
Value = $1,625,178.57

Since the firm value is the same as in part *a*, the change in dividend policy had no effect.

ii.    The new shareholders are not entitled to receive the current dividend. They will receive only the value of the equity one year hence. The present value of those flows is:

Present value = $1,691,400/1.12
Present value = $1,510,178.57

And the current share price will be:

Current share price = $1,510,178.57/25,000
Current share price = $60.41

So, the number of new shares the company must sell will be:

Shares sold = $30,000/$60.41
Shares sold = 496.63 shares

**15.** *a.* The current price is the current cash flow of the company plus the present value of the expected cash flows, divided by the number of shares outstanding. So, the current stock price is:

Stock price = ($1,100,000 + 15,000,000) / 600,000
Stock price = $26.83

*b.* To achieve a zero dividend payout policy, he can invest the dividends back into the company's stock. The dividends per share will be:

Dividends per share = [($1,100,000)(.50)]/600,000
Dividends per share = $0.92

And the stockholder in question will receive:

Dividends paid to shareholder = $0.92(1,000)
Dividends paid to shareholder = $916.67

The new stock price after the dividends are paid will be:

Ex-dividend stock price = $26.83 − 0.92
Ex-dividend stock price = $25.92

So, the number of shares the investor will buy is:

Number of shares to buy = $916.67 / $25.92
Number of shares to buy = 35.37

**16.** *a.* Using the formula from the text proposed by Lintner:

$Div_1 = Div_0 + s(t\ EPS_1 − Div_0)$
$Div_1 = \$1.80 + .3[(.4)(\$4.95) − \$1.80]$
$Div_1 = \$1.85$

*b.* Now we use an adjustment rate of 0.60, so the dividend next year will be:

$Div_1 = Div_0 + s(t\ EPS_1 − Div_0)$
$Div_1 = \$1.80 + .6[(.4)(\$4.95) − \$1.80]$
$Div_1 = \$1.91$

*c.* The lower adjustment factor in part *a* is more conservative. The lower adjustment factor will always result in a lower future dividend.

*Challenge*

17. Assuming no capital gains tax, the aftertax return for the Gordon Company is the capital gains growth rate, plus the dividend yield times one minus the tax rate. Using the constant growth dividend model, we get:

Aftertax return $= g + D(1 - t_C) = .13$

Solving for g, we get:

$.13 = g + .055(1 - .35)$
$g = .0943$

The equivalent pretax return for Gordon Company is:

Pretax return $= g + D = .0943 + .055 = .1493$, or 14.93%

18. Using the equation for the decline in the stock price ex-dividend for each of the tax rate policies, we get:

$$(P_0 - P_X)/D = (1 - t_P)/(1 - t_G)$$

a. $P_0 - P_X = D(1 - 0)/(1 - 0)$
   $P_0 - P_X = D$

b. $P_0 - P_X = D(1 - .15)/(1 - 0)$
   $P_0 - P_X = .85D$

c. $P_0 - P_X = D(1 - .15)/(1 - .20)$
   $P_0 - P_X = 1.0625D$

d. With this tax policy, we simply need to multiply the personal tax rate times one minus the dividend exemption percentage, so:

   $P_0 - P_X = D[1 - (.35)(.30)]/(1 - .35)$
   $P_0 - P_X = 1.3769D$

e. Since different investors have widely varying tax rates on ordinary income and capital gains, dividend payments have different after-tax implications for different investors. This differential taxation among investors is one aspect of what we have called the clientele effect.

19. Since the $4,000,000 cash is after corporate tax, the full amount will be invested. So, the value of each alternative is:

*Alternative 1:*
The firm invests in T-bills or in preferred stock, and then pays out as a special dividend in 3 years

*If the firm invests in T-Bills:*

If the firm invests in T-bills, the aftertax yield of the T-bills will be:

Aftertax corporate yield $= .03(1 - .35)$
Aftertax corporate yield $= .0195$, or 1.95%

So, the future value of the corporate investment in T-bills will be:

FV of investment in T-bills = $4,000,000(1 + .0195)^3$
FV of investment in T-bills = \$4,238,592.66

Since the future value will be paid to shareholders as a dividend, the aftertax cash flow will be:

Aftertax cash flow to shareholders = \$4,238,592.66(1 − .15)
Aftertax cash flow to shareholders = \$3,602,803.76

*If the firm invests in preferred stock:*

If the firm invests in preferred stock, the assumption would be that the dividends received will be reinvested in the same preferred stock. The preferred stock will pay a dividend of:

Preferred dividend = .05(\$4,000,000)
Preferred dividend = \$200,000

Since 70 percent of the dividends are excluded from tax:

Taxable preferred dividends = (1 − .70)(\$200,000)
Taxable preferred dividends = \$60,000

And the taxes the company must pay on the preferred dividends will be:

Taxes on preferred dividends = .35(\$60,000)
Taxes on preferred dividends = \$21,000

So, the aftertax dividend for the corporation will be:

Aftertax corporate dividend = \$200,000 − 21,000
Aftertax corporate dividend = \$179,000

This means the aftertax corporate dividend yield is:

Aftertax corporate dividend yield = \$179,000 / \$4,000,000
Aftertax corporate dividend yield = .0448, or 4.48%

The future value of the company's investment in preferred stock will be:

FV of investment in preferred stock = $4,000,000(1 + .0448)^3$
FV of investment in preferred stock = \$4,561,389.21

Since the future value will be paid to shareholders as a dividend, the aftertax cash flow will be:

Aftertax cash flow to shareholders = \$4,561,389.21(1 − .15)
Aftertax cash flow to shareholders = \$3,877,180.83

*Alternative 2:*

The firm pays out dividend now, and individuals invest on their own. The aftertax cash received by shareholders now will be:

Aftertax cash received today = $4,000,000(1 – .15)
Aftertax cash received today = $3,400,000

*The individuals invest in Treasury bills:*

If the shareholders invest the current aftertax dividends in Treasury bills, the aftertax individual yield will be:

Aftertax individual yield on T-bills = .03(1 – .31)
Aftertax individual yield on T-bills = .0207, or 2.07%

So, the future value of the individual investment in Treasury bills will be:

FV of investment in T-bills = $3,400,000(1 + .0207)$^3$
FV of investment in T-bills = $3,615,540.76

*The individuals invest in preferred stock:*

If the individual invests in preferred stock, the assumption would be that the dividends received will be reinvested in the same preferred stock. The preferred stock will pay a dividend of:

Preferred dividend = .05($3,400,000)
Preferred dividend = $170,000

And the taxes on the preferred dividends will be:

Taxes on preferred dividends = .31($170,000)
Taxes on preferred dividends = $52,700

So, the aftertax preferred dividend will be:

Aftertax preferred dividend = $170,000 – 52,700
Aftertax preferred dividend = $117,300

This means the aftertax individual dividend yield is:

Aftertax individual dividend yield = $117,300 / $3,400,000
Aftertax individual dividend yield = .0345 or 3.45%

The future value of the individual investment in preferred stock will be:

FV of investment in preferred stock = $3,400,000(1 + .0345)$^3$
FV of investment in preferred stock = $3,764,180.17

The aftertax cash flow for the shareholders is maximized when the firm invests the cash in the preferred stocks and pays a special dividend later.

**20.** *a.* Let $x$ be the ordinary income tax rate. The individual receives an after-tax dividend of:

Aftertax dividend = $1,000(1 − x)$

which she invests in Treasury bonds. The Treasury bond will generate aftertax cash flows to the investor of:

Aftertax cash flow from Treasury bonds = $1,000(1 − x)[1 + .08(1 − x)]$

If the firm invests the money, its proceeds are:

Firm proceeds = $1,000[1 + .08(1 − .35)]$

And the proceeds to the investor when the firm pays a dividend will be:

Proceeds if firm invests first = $(1 − x)\{1,000[1 + .08(1 − .35)]\}$

To be indifferent, the investor's proceeds must be the same whether she invests the after-tax dividend or receives the proceeds from the firm's investment and pays taxes on that amount. To find the rate at which the investor would be indifferent, we can set the two equations equal, and solve for $x$. Doing so, we find:

$1,000(1 − x)[1 + .08(1 − x)] = (1 − x)\{1,000[1 + .08(1 − .35)]\}$
$1 + .08(1 − x) = 1 + .08(1 − .35)$
$x = .35$ or 35%

Note that this argument does not depend upon the length of time the investment is held.

*b.* Yes, this is a reasonable answer. She is only indifferent if the after-tax proceeds from the $1,000 investment in identical securities are identical. That occurs only when the tax rates are identical.

*c.* Since both investors will receive the same pre-tax return, you would expect the same answer as in part a. Yet, because the company enjoys a tax benefit from investing in stock (70 percent of income from stock is exempt from corporate taxes), the tax rate on ordinary income which induces indifference, is much lower. Again, set the two equations equal and solve for $x$:

$1,000(1 − x)[1 + .12(1 − x)] = (1 − x)(1,000\{1 + .12[.70 + (1 − .70)(1 − .35)]\})$
$1 + .12(1 − x) = 1 + .12[.70 + (1 − .70)(1 − .35)]$
$x = .1050$ or 10.50%

*d.* It is a compelling argument, but there are legal constraints, which deter firms from investing large sums in stock of other companies.

# CHAPTER 20
# ISSUING SECURITIES TO THE PUBLIC

## Answers to Concepts Review and Critical Thinking Questions

1.  A company's internally generated cash flow provides a source of equity financing. For a profitable company, outside equity may never be needed. Debt issues are larger because large companies have the greatest access to public debt markets (small companies tend to borrow more from private lenders). Equity issuers are frequently small companies going public; such issues are often quite small. Additionally, to maintain a debt-equity ratio, a company must issue new bonds when the current bonds mature.

2.  From the previous question, economies of scale are part of the answer. Beyond this, debt issues are simply easier and less risky to sell from an investment bank's perspective. The two main reasons are that very large amounts of debt securities can be sold to a relatively small number of buyers, particularly large institutional buyers such as pension funds and insurance companies, and debt securities are much easier to price.

3.  They are riskier and harder to market from an investment bank's perspective.

4.  Yields on comparable bonds can usually be readily observed, so pricing a bond issue accurately is much less difficult.

5.  It is clear that the stock was sold too cheaply, so Zipcar had reason to be unhappy.

6.  No, but in fairness, pricing the stock in such a situation is extremely difficult.

7.  It's an important factor. Only 9.68 million of the shares were underpriced. The other 30 million were, in effect, priced completely correctly.

8.  The evidence suggests that a non-underwritten rights offering might be substantially cheaper than a cash offer. However, such offerings are rare, and there may be hidden costs or other factors not yet identified or well understood by researchers.

9.  He could have done worse since his access to the oversubscribed and, presumably, underpriced issues was restricted while the bulk of his funds were allocated to stocks from the undersubscribed and, quite possibly, overpriced issues.

10. *a.* The price will probably go up because IPOs are generally underpriced. This is especially true for smaller issues such as this one.
    *b.* It is probably safe to assume that they are having trouble moving the issue, and it is likely that the issue is not substantially underpriced.

11. Competitive offer and negotiated offer are two methods to select investment bankers for underwriting. Under the competitive offers, the issuing firm can award its securities to the underwriter with the highest bid, which in turn implies the lowest cost. On the other hand, in negotiated deals, the underwriter gains much information about the issuing firm through negotiation, which helps increase the possibility of a successful offering.

12. There are two possible reasons for stock price drops on the announcement of a new equity issue: 1) Management may attempt to issue new shares of stock when the stock is over-valued, that is, the intrinsic value is lower than the market price. The price drop is the result of the downward adjustment of the overvaluation. 2) When there is an increase in the possibility of financial distress, a firm is more likely to raise capital through equity than debt. The market price drops because the market interprets the equity issue announcement as bad news.

13. If the interest of management is to increase the wealth of the current shareholders, a rights offering may be preferable because issuing costs as a percentage of capital raised are lower for rights offerings. Management does not have to worry about underpricing because shareholders get the rights, which are worth something. Rights offerings also prevent existing shareholders from losing proportionate ownership control. Finally, whether the shareholders exercise or sell their rights, they are the only beneficiaries.

14. Reasons for shelf registration include: 1) Flexibility in raising money only when necessary without incurring additional issuance costs. 2) As Bhagat, Marr and Thompson showed, shelf registration is less costly than conventional underwritten issues. 3) Issuance of securities is greatly simplified.

15. Basic empirical regularities in IPOs include: 1) underpricing of the offer price, 2) best-efforts offerings are generally used for small IPOs and firm-commitment offerings are generally used for large IPOs, 3) the underwriter price stabilization of the after market and, 4) that issuing costs are higher in negotiated deals than in competitive ones.


**Solutions to Questions and Problems**

*NOTE: All end of chapter problems were solved using a spreadsheet. Many problems require multiple steps. Due to space and readability constraints, when these intermediate steps are included in this solutions manual, rounding may appear to have occurred. However, the final answer for each problem is found without rounding during any step in the problem.*

*Basic*

1.  a.  The new market value will be the current shares outstanding times the stock price plus the rights offered times the rights price, so:

    New market value = 550,000($87) + 85,000($81) = $54,735,000

    b.  The number of rights associated with the old shares is the number of shares outstanding divided by the rights offered, so:

    Number of rights needed = 550,000 old shares/85,000 new shares = 6.47 rights per new share

    c.  The new price of the stock will be the new market value of the company divided by the total number of shares outstanding after the rights offer, which will be:

    $P_X$ = $54,735,000/(550,000 + 85,000) = $86.20

    d.  The value of the right

    Value of a right = $87.00 – 86.20 = $.80

e.  A rights offering usually costs less, it protects the proportionate interests of existing share-holders and also protects against underpricing.

**2.**  *a.*  The maximum subscription price is the current stock price, or $27. The minimum price is anything greater than $0.

*b.*  The number of new shares will be the amount raised divided by the subscription price, so:

Number of new shares = $28,000,000/$25 = 1,120,000 shares

And the number of rights needed to buy one share will be the current shares outstanding divided by the number of new shares offered, so:

Number of rights needed = 2,900,000 shares outstanding/1,120,000 new shares = 2.59

*c.*  A shareholder can buy 2.59 rights on shares for:

2.59($27) = $69.91

The shareholder can exercise these rights for $25, at a total cost of:

$69.91 + 25 = $94.91

The investor will then have:

Ex-rights shares = 1 + 2.59
Ex-rights shares = 3.59

The ex-rights price per share is:

$P_X$ = [2.59($27) + $25]/3.595 = $26.44

So, the value of a right is:

Value of a right = $27 –26.44 = $.56

*d.*  Before the offer, a shareholder will have the shares owned at the current market price, or:

Portfolio value = (1,000 shares)($27) = $27,000

After the rights offer, the share price will fall, but the shareholder will also hold the rights, so:

Portfolio value = (1,000 shares)($26.44) + (1,000 rights)($.56) = $27,000

**3.**  Using the equation we derived in Problem 2, part *c* to calculate the price of the stock ex-rights, we can find the number of shares a shareholder will have ex-rights, which is:

$P_X$ = $63.18 = [N($65) + $50]/(N + 1)
N = 7.242

The number of new shares is the amount raised divided by the per-share subscription price, so:

Number of new shares = $15,000,000/$50 = 300,000

And the number of old shares is the number of new shares times the number of shares ex-rights, so:

Number of old shares = 7.242(300,000) = 2,172,527

4. If you receive 1,000 shares of each, the profit is:

Profit = 1,000($9) – 1,000($4) = $5,000

Since you will only receive one-half of the shares of the oversubscribed issue, your profit will be:

Expected profit = 500($9) – 1,000($4) = $500

This is an example of the winner's curse.

5. Using X to stand for the required sale proceeds, the equation to calculate the total sale proceeds, including flotation costs is:

X(1 – .07) = $45,000,000
X = $48,387,097 required total proceeds from sale.

So the number of shares offered is the total amount raised divided by the offer price, which is:

Number of shares offered = $48,387,097/$31 = 1,560,874

6. This is basically the same as the previous problem, except we need to include the $1,900,000 of expenses in the amount the company needs to raise, so:

X(1 – .07) = $46,900,000
X = $50,430,108 required total proceeds from sale.

Number of shares offered = $50,430,108/$31 = 1,626,778

7. We need to calculate the net amount raised and the costs associated with the offer. The net amount raised is the number of shares offered times the price received by the company, minus the costs associated with the offer, so:

Net amount raised = (7,000,000 shares)($26.04) – 1,850,000 – 370,000 = $180,060,000

The company received $180,060,000 from the stock offering. Now we can calculate the direct costs. Part of the direct costs are given in the problem, but the company also had to pay the underwriters. The stock was offered at $28 per share, and the company received $26.04 per share. The difference, which is the underwriters spread, is also a direct cost. The total direct costs were:

Total direct costs = $1,850,000 + ($28 – 26.04)(7,000,000 shares) = $15,570,000

We are given part of the indirect costs in the problem. Another indirect cost is the immediate price appreciation. The total indirect costs were:

Total indirect costs = $370,000 + ($32.30 – 28)(7,000,000 shares) = $30,470,000

This makes the total costs:

Total costs = $15,570,000 + 30,470,000 = $46,040,000

The flotation costs as a percentage of the amount raised is the total cost divided by the amount raised, so:

Flotation cost percentage = \$46,040,000/\$180,060,000 = .2557, or 25.57%

8.  The number of rights needed per new share is:

Number of rights needed = 135,000 old shares/30,000 new shares = 4.5 rights per new share.

Using $P_{RO}$ as the rights-on price, and $P_S$ as the subscription price, we can express the price per share of the stock ex-rights as:

$P_X = [NP_{RO} + P_S]/(N + 1)$

a.  $P_X = [4.5(\$75) + \$75]/5.5 = \$75.00$;   No change

b.  $P_X = [4.5(\$75) + \$70]/5.5 = \$74.09$;   Price drops by \$.91 per share

c.  $P_X = [4.5(\$75) + \$65]/5.5 = \$73.18$;   Price drops by \$1.82 per share

9.  In general, the new price per share after the offering will be:

$$P = \frac{\text{Current market value} + \text{Proceeds from offer}}{\text{Old shares} + \text{New shares}}$$

The current market value of the company is the number of shares outstanding times the share price, or:

Market value of company = 50,000(\$40)
Market value of company = \$2,000,000

If the new shares are issued at \$40, the share price after the issue will be:

$$P = \frac{\$2,000,000 + 9,000(\$40)}{50,000 + 9,000}$$
P = \$40.00

If the new shares are issued at \$20, the share price after the issue will be:

$$P = \frac{\$2,000,000 + 9,000(\$20)}{50,000 + 9,000}$$
P = \$36.95

If the new shares are issued at \$10, the share price after the issue will be:

$$P = \frac{\$2,000,000 + 9,000(\$10)}{50,000 + 9,000}$$
P = \$35.42

*Intermediate*

**10.** *a.* The number of shares outstanding after the stock offer will be the current shares outstanding, plus the amount raised divided by the current stock price, assuming the stock price doesn't change. So:

Number of shares after offering = 7,000,000 + $30,000,000/$65 = 7,461,538

Since the par value per share is $1, the old book value of the shares is the current number of shares outstanding. From the previous solution, we can see the company will sell 461,538 shares, and these will have a book value of $65 per share. The sum of these two values will give us the total book value of the company. We divide this by the new number of shares outstanding. Doing so, we find the new book value per share will be:

New book value per share = [7,000,000($20) + 461,538($65)]/7,461,538 = $22.78

The current EPS for the company is:

$EPS_0 = NI_0/Shares_0$ = $11,500,000/7,000,000 shares = $1.64 per share

And the current P/E is:

$(P/E)_0$ = $65/$1.64 = 39.57

If the net income increases by $675,000, the new EPS will be:

$EPS_1 = NI_1/shares_1$ = $12,175,000/7,461,538 shares = $1.63 per share

Assuming the P/E remains constant, the new share price will be:

$P_1 = (P/E)_0(EPS_1)$ = 39.57($1.63) = $64.56

The current market-to-book ratio is:

Current market-to-book = $65/$20 = 3.25

Using the new share price and book value per share, the new market-to-book ratio will be:

New market-to-book = $64.56/$22.78 = 2.8336

Accounting dilution has occurred because new shares were issued when the market-to-book ratio was less than one; market value dilution has occurred because the firm financed a negative NPV project. The cost of the project is given at $30 million. The NPV of the project is the new market value of the firm minus the current market value of the firm, or:

NPV = –$30,000,000 + [7,461,538($64.56) – 7,000,000($65)] = –$3,293,478

*b.* For the price to remain unchanged when the P/E ratio is constant, EPS must remain constant. The new net income must be the new number of shares outstanding times the current EPS, which gives:

$NI_1$ = (7,461,538 shares)($1.64 per share) = $12,258,242

**11.** The current ROE of the company is:

$ROE_0 = NI_0/TE_0 = \$980,000/(\$9,400,000 - 4,100,000) = .1849$, or $18.49\%$

The new net income will be the ROE times the new total equity, or:

$NI_1 = (ROE_0)(TE_1) = .1849(\$5,300,000 + 1,500,000) = \$1,257,358$

The company's current earnings per share are:

$EPS_0 = NI_0/\text{Shares outstanding}_0 = \$980,000/65,000 \text{ shares} = \$15.08$

The number of shares the company will offer is the cost of the investment divided by the current share price, so:

Number of new shares $= \$1,500,000/\$75 = 20,000$

The earnings per share after the stock offer will be:

$EPS_1 = \$1,257,358/(65,000 + 20,000 \text{ shares}) = \$14.79$

The current P/E ratio is:

$(P/E)_0 = \$75/\$15.08 = 4.974$

Assuming the P/E remains constant, the new stock price will be:

$P_1 = 4.974(\$14.79) = \$73.58$

The current book value per share and the new book value per share are:

$BVPS_0 = TE_0/\text{shares}_0 = \$5,300,000/65,000 \text{ shares} = \$81.54 \text{ per share}$

$BVPS_1 = TE_1/\text{shares}_1 = (\$5,300,000 + 1,500,000)/85,000 \text{ shares} = \$80.00 \text{ per share}$

So the current and new market-to-book ratios are:

Market-to-book$_0 = \$75/\$81.54 = .9198$

Market-to-book$_1 = \$73.58/\$80.00 = .9198$

The NPV of the project is the new market value of the firm minus the current market value of the firm, or:

$NPV = -\$1,500,000 + [\$73.58(85,000) - \$75(65,000)] = -\$120,283$

Accounting dilution takes place here because the market-to-book ratio is less than one. Market value dilution has occurred since the firm is investing in a negative NPV project.

12.  Using the P/E ratio to find the necessary EPS after the stock issue, we get:

$P_1 = \$75 = 4.974(EPS_1)$
$EPS_1 = \$15.08$

The additional net income level must be the EPS times the new shares outstanding, so:

NI = $15.08(20,000 shares) = $301,538

And the new ROE is:

$ROE_1 = \$301,538/\$1,500,000 = .2010$, or 20.10%

Next, we need to find the NPV of the project. The NPV of the project is the new market value of the firm minus the current market value of the firm, or:

NPV = –$1,500,000 + [$75(85,000) – $75(65,000)] = $0

Accounting dilution still takes place, as BVPS still falls from $81.54 to $80.00, but no market dilution takes place because the firm is investing in a zero NPV project.

13.  *a.*  Assume you hold three shares of the company's stock. The value of your holdings before you exercise your rights is:

Value of holdings = 3($68)
Value of holdings = $204

When you exercise, you must remit the three rights you receive for owning three shares, and $11. You have increased your equity investment by $11. The value of your holdings after surrendering your rights is:

New value of holdings = $204 + 11
New value of holdings = $215

After exercise, you own four shares of stock. Thus, the price per share of your stock is:

Stock price = $215 / 4
Stock price = $53.75

*b.*  The value of a right is the difference between the rights-on price of the stock and the ex-rights price of the stock:

Value of rights = Rights-on price – Ex-rights price
Value of rights = $68 – 53.75
Value of rights = $14.25

*c.*  The price drop will occur on the ex-rights date, even though the ex-rights date is neither the expiration date nor the date on which the rights are first exercisable. If you purchase the stock before the ex-rights date, you will receive the rights. If you purchase the stock on or after the ex-rights date, you will not receive the rights. Since rights have value, the stockholder receiving the rights must pay for them. The stock price drop on the ex-rights day is similar to the stock price drop on an ex-dividend day.

**14.** *a.* The number of new shares offered through the rights offering is the existing shares divided by the rights per share, or:

New shares = 1,000,000 / 2
New shares = 500,000

And the new price per share after the offering will be:

$$P = \frac{Current\ market\ value + Proceeds\ from\ offer}{Old\ shares + New\ shares}$$

$$P = \frac{1,000,000(\$32) + \$2,000,000}{1,000,000 + 500,000}$$

P = \$22.67

The subscription price is the amount raised divided by the number of new shares offered, or:

Subscription price = \$2,000,000 / 500,000
Subscription price = \$4

And the value of a right is:

Value of a right = (Ex-rights price – Subscription price) / Rights needed to buy a share of stock
Value of a right = (\$22.67 – 4) / 2
Value of a right = \$9.33

*b.* Following the same procedure, the number of new shares offered through the rights offering is:

New shares = 1,000,000 / 4
New shares = 250,000

And the new price per share after the offering will be:

$$P = \frac{Current\ market\ value + Proceeds\ from\ offer}{Old\ shares + New\ shares}$$

$$P = \frac{1,000,000(\$32) + \$2,000,000}{1,000,000 + 250,000}$$

P = \$27.20

The subscription price is the amount raised divided by the number of number of new shares offered, or:

Subscription price = \$2,000,000 / 250,000
Subscription price = \$8

And the value of a right is:

Value of a right = (Ex-rights price – Subscription price) / Rights needed to buy a share of stock
Value of a right = (\$27.20 – 8) / 4
Value of a right = \$4.80

c.  Since rights issues are constructed so that existing shareholders' proportionate share will remain unchanged, we know that the stockholders' wealth should be the same between the two arrangements. However, a numerical example makes this clearer. Assume that an investor holds 4 shares, and will exercise under either *a* or *b*. Prior to exercise, the investor's portfolio value is:

Current portfolio value = Number of shares × Stock price
Current portfolio value = 4($32)
Current portfolio value = $128

After exercise, the value of the portfolio will be the new number of shares time the ex-rights price, less the subscription price paid. Under *a*, the investor gets 2 new shares, so portfolio value will be:

New portfolio value = 6($22.67) – 2($4)
New portfolio value = $128

Under *b*, the investor gets 1 new share, so portfolio value will be:

New portfolio value = 5($27.20) – 1($8)
New portfolio value = $128

So, the shareholder's wealth position is unchanged either by the rights issue itself, or the choice of which right's issue the firm chooses.

15. The number of new shares is the amount raised divided by the subscription price, so:

Number of new shares = $60,000,000/$P_S$

And the ex-rights number of shares (N) is equal to:

N = Old shares outstanding/New shares outstanding
N = 10,000,000/($60,000,000/$P_S$)
N = .1667$P_S$

We know the equation for the ex-rights stock price is:

$P_X = [NP_{RO} + P_S]/(N + 1)$

We can substitute in the numbers we are given, and then substitute the two previous results. Doing so, and solving for the subscription price, we get:

$P_X$ = $61 = [N($68) + $P_S]/(N + 1)$
$61 = [$68(.1667$P_S$) + $P_S]/(.1667$P_S$ + 1)
$61 = (11.333$P_S$ + $P_S$)/(1 + .1667$P_S$)
$P_S$ = $28.15

16. Using $P_{RO}$ as the rights-on price, and $P_S$ as the subscription price, we can express the price per share of the stock ex-rights as:

$P_X = [NP_{RO} + P_S]/(N + 1)$

And the equation for the value of a right is:

Value of a right = $P_{RO} - P_X$

Substituting the ex-rights price equation into the equation for the value of a right and rearranging, we get:

Value of a right = $P_{RO} - \{[NP_{RO} + P_S]/(N + 1)\}$
Value of a right = $[(N + 1)P_{RO} - NP_{RO} - P_S]/(N+1)$
Value of a right = $[P_{RO} - P_S]/(N + 1)$

17. The net proceeds to the company on a per share basis is the subscription price times one minus the underwriter spread, so:

Net proceeds to the company = $30(1 - .06) = $28.20 per share

So, to raise the required funds, the company must sell:

New shares offered = $5,375,000/$28.20 = 190,603

The number of rights needed per share is the current number of shares outstanding divided by the new shares offered, or:

Number of rights needed = 950,000 old shares/190,603 new shares
Number of rights needed = 4.98 rights per share

The ex-rights stock price will be:

$P_X = [NP_{RO} + P_S]/(N + 1)$
$P_X = [4.98($55) + 30]/5.98$
$P_X = $50.82$

So, the value of a right is:

Value of a right = $55 - 50.82 = $4.18

And your proceeds from selling your rights will be:

Proceeds from selling rights = 6,000($4.18)
Proceeds from selling rights = $25,066.07

18. Using the equation for valuing a stock ex-rights, we find:

$P_X = [NP_{RO} + P_S]/(N + 1)$
$P_X = [4($60) + $30]/5 = $54$

The stock is correctly priced. Calculating the value of a right, we find:

Value of a right = $P_{RO} - P_X$
Value of a right = $60 - 54 = $6

So, the rights are underpriced. You can create an immediate profit on the ex-rights day if the stock is selling for $54 and the rights are selling for $5 by executing the following transactions:

Buy 4 rights in the market for 4($5) = $20. Use these rights to purchase a new share at the subscription price of $30. Immediately sell this share in the market for $54, creating an instant $4 profit.

# CHAPTER 21
# LEASING

## Answers to Concepts Review and Critical Thinking Questions

1.  Some key differences are: (1) Lease payments are fully tax-deductible, but only the interest portion of the loan is; (2) The lessee does not own the asset and cannot depreciate it for tax purposes; (3) In the event of a default, the lessor cannot force bankruptcy; and (4) The lessee does not obtain title to the asset at the end of the lease (absent some additional arrangement).

2.  The less profitable one because leasing provides, among other things, a mechanism for transferring tax benefits from entities that value them less to entities that value them more.

3.  Potential problems include: (1) Care must be taken in interpreting the IRR (a high or low IRR is preferred depending on the setup of the analysis); and (2) Care must be taken to ensure the IRR under examination is *not* the implicit interest rate just based on the lease payments.

4.  *a.*   Leasing is a form of secured borrowing. It reduces a firm's cost of capital only if it is cheaper than other forms of secured borrowing. The reduction of uncertainty is not particularly relevant; what matters is the NAL.
    *b.*   The statement is not always true. For example, a lease often requires an advance lease payment or security deposit and may be implicitly secured by other assets of the firm.
    *c.*   Leasing would probably not disappear, since it does reduce the uncertainty about salvage value and the transactions costs of transferring ownership. However, the use of leasing would be greatly reduced.

5.  A lease must be disclosed on the balance sheet if one of the following criteria is met:
    *1.*   The lease transfers ownership of the asset by the end of the lease. In this case, the firm essentially owns the asset and will have access to its residual value.
    *2.*   The lessee can purchase the asset at a price below its fair market value (bargain purchase option) when the lease ends. The firm essentially owns the asset and will have access to most of its residual value.
    *3.*   The lease term is for 75% or more of the estimated economic life of the asset. The firm basically has access to the majority of the benefits of the asset, without any responsibility for the consequences of its disposal.
    *4.*   The present value of the lease payments is 90% or more of the fair market value of the asset at the start of the lease. The firm is essentially purchasing the asset on an installment basis.

6.  The lease must meet the following IRS standards for the lease payments to be tax deductible:
    *1.*   The lease term must be less than 80% of the economic life of the asset. If the term is longer, the lease is considered to be a conditional sale.
    *2.*   The lease should not contain a bargain purchase option, which the IRS interprets as an equity interest in the asset.
    *3.*   The lease payment schedule should not provide for very high payments early and very low payments late in the life of the lease. This would indicate that the lease is being used simply to avoid taxes.

4. Renewal options should be reasonable and based on the fair market value of the asset at renewal time. This indicates that the lease is for legitimate business purposes, not tax avoidance.

7. As the term implies, off-balance sheet financing involves financing arrangements that are not required to be reported on the firm's balance sheet. Such activities, if reported at all, appear only in the footnotes to the statements. Operating leases (those that do not meet the criteria in Question 6) provide off-balance sheet financing. For accounting purposes, total assets will be lower and some financial ratios may be artificially high. Financial analysts are generally not fooled by such practices. There are no economic consequences, since the cash flows of the firm are not affected by how the lease is treated for accounting purposes.

8. The lessee may not be able to take advantage of the depreciation tax shield and may not be able to obtain favorable lease arrangements for "passing on" the tax shield benefits. The lessee might also need the cash flow from the sale to meet immediate needs, but will be able to meet the lease obligation cash flows in the future.

9. Since the relevant cash flows are all aftertax, the aftertax discount rate is appropriate.

10. China Eastern Airlines' financial position was such that the package of leasing and buying probably resulted in the overall best aftertax cost. In particular, China Eastern Airlines may not have been in a position to use all of its tax credits and also may not have had the credit strength to borrow and buy the plane without facing a credit downgrade and/or substantially higher rates.

11. There is the tax motive, but, beyond this, Air Lease Corporation knows that, in the event of a default, China Eastern Airlines would relinquish the plane, which would then be re-leased. Fungible assets, such as planes, which can be readily reclaimed and redeployed are good candidates for leasing.

12. The plane will be re-leased to China Eastern Airlines or another air transportation firm, used by Air Lease Corporation, or it will simply be sold. There is an active market for used aircraft.

## Solutions to Questions and Problems

*NOTE: All end of chapter problems were solved using a spreadsheet. Many problems require multiple steps. Due to space and readability constraints, when these intermediate steps are included in this solutions manual, rounding may appear to have occurred. However, the final answer for each problem is found without rounding during any step in the problem.*

*Basic*

1. We will calculate cash flows from the depreciation tax shield first. The depreciation tax shield is:

Depreciation tax shield = ($5,200,000/4)(.35) = $455,000

The aftertax cost of the lease payments will be:

Aftertax lease payment = ($1,525,000)(1 – .35) = $991,250

So, the total cash flows from leasing are:

OCF = $455,000 + 991,250 = $1,446,250

The aftertax cost of debt is:

Aftertax debt cost = .08(1 – .35) = .052

Using all of this information, we can calculate the NAL as:

NAL = $5,200,000 – $1,446,250(PVIFA$_{5.20\%,4}$) = $95,405.02

The NAL is positive so you should lease.

2.  If we assume the lessor has the same cost of debt and the same tax rate, the NAL to the lessor is the negative of our company's NAL, so:

NAL = – $95,405.02

3.  To find the maximum lease payment that would satisfy both the lessor and the lessee, we need to find the payment that makes the NAL equal to zero. Using the NAL equation and solving for the OCF, we find:

NAL = 0 = $5,200,000 – OCF(PVIFA$_{5.20\%,4}$)
OCF = $1,473,280.45

The OCF for this lease is composed of the depreciation tax shield cash flow, as well as the aftertax lease payment. Subtracting out the depreciation tax shield cash flow we calculated earlier, we find:

Aftertax lease payment = $1,473,280.45 – 455,000 = $1,018,280.45

Since this is the aftertax lease payment, we can now calculate the breakeven pretax lease payment as:

Breakeven lease payment = $1,018,280.45/(1 – .35) = $1,566,585.31

4.  If the tax rate is zero, there is no depreciation tax shield foregone. Also, the aftertax lease payment is the same as the pretax payment, and the aftertax cost of debt is the same as the pretax cost. So:

Cost of debt = .08

Annual cost of leasing = leasing payment = $1,525,000

The NAL to leasing with these assumptions is:

NAL = $5,200,000 – $1,525,000(PVIFA$_{8\%,4}$) = $149,006.57

**5.** We already calculated the breakeven lease payment for the lessor in Problem 3. The assumptions about the lessor concerning the tax rate have not changed. So, the lessor breaks even with a payment of $1,566,585.31

For the lessee, we need to calculate the breakeven lease payment which results in a zero NAL. Using the assumptions in Problem 4, we find:

NAL = 0 = $5,200,000 – PMT(PVIFA$_{8\%,4}$)
PMT = $1,569,988.18

So, the range of lease payments that would satisfy both the lessee and the lessor are:

Total payment range = $1,566,585.31 to $1,569,988.18

**6.** The appropriate depreciation percentages for a 3-year MACRS class asset can be found in Chapter 6. The depreciation percentages are 0.3333, 0.4445, 0.1481, and 0.0741. The cash flows from leasing are:

Year 1: ($5,200,000)(.3333)(.35) + $991,250 = $1,597,856
Year 2: ($5,200,000)(.4445)(.35) + $991,250 = $1,800,240
Year 3: ($5,200,000)(.1481)(.35) + $991,250 = $1,260,792
Year 4: ($5,200,000)(.0741)(.35) + $991,250 = $1,126,112

NAL = $5,200,000 – $1,597,856/1.052 – $1,800,240/1.052$^2$ – $1,260,792/1.052$^3$ – $1,126,112/1.052$^4$
NAL = $52,107.92

The machine should still be leased. However, notice that the NAL is lower. This is because of the accelerated tax benefits due to depreciation, which represents a cost in the decision to lease compared to the decision to purchase.

**7.** We will calculate cash flows from the depreciation tax shield first. The depreciation tax shield is:

Depreciation tax shield = ($540,000/5)(.35) = $37,800

The aftertax cost of the lease payments will be:

Aftertax lease payment = ($145,000)(1 – .35) = $94,250

So, the total cash flows from leasing are:

OCF = $37,800 + 94,250 = $132,050

The aftertax cost of debt is:

Aftertax debt cost = .09(1 – .35) = .0585

Using all of this information, we can calculate the NAL as:

NAL = $540,000 – $132,050(PVIFA$_{5.85\%,5}$) = –$18,519.82

The NAL is negative, so the company should not lease.

**8.** *a.* Since the lessee has an effective tax rate of zero, there is no depreciation tax shield foregone. Also, the aftertax lease payment is the same as the pretax payment, and the aftertax cost of debt is the same as the pretax cost. To find the most the lessee would pay, we set the NAL equal to zero and solve for the payment, doing so, we find the most the lessee will pay is:

$$NAL = 0 = \$840,000 - PMT(PVIFA_{8\%,5})$$
$$PMT = \$221,589.88$$

*b.* We will calculate cash flows from the depreciation tax shield first. The depreciation tax shield is:

Depreciation tax shield = ($840,000/5)(.35) = $58,800

The aftertax cost of debt is:

Aftertax debt cost = .10(1 – .35) = .065

Using all of this information, we can calculate the minimum lease payment for the lessor as:

$$NAL = 0 = \$840,000 - PMT(1 - .35)(PVIFA_{6.50\%,5}) + \$58,800(PVIFA_{6.50\%,5})$$
$$PMT = \$220,512.33$$

*c.* A lease payment less than $220,512.33 will give the lessor a negative NAL. A payment higher than $221,589.88 will give the lessee a negative NAL. In either case, no deal will be struck. Therefore, these represent the lower and upper bounds of possible lease prices during negotiations.

*Intermediate*

**9.** The pretax cost savings are not relevant to the lease versus buy decision, since the firm will definitely use the equipment and realize the savings regardless of the financing choice made. The depreciation tax shield is:

Depreciation tax shield lost = ($8,400,000/5)(.34) = $571,200

And the aftertax lease payment is:

Aftertax lease payment = $1,950,000(1 – .34) = $1,287,000

The aftertax cost of debt is:

Aftertax debt cost = .09(1 – .34) = .0594 or 5.94%

With these cash flows, the NAL is:

$$NAL = \$8,400,000 - 1,287,000 - \$1,287,000(PVIFA_{5.94\%,4}) - \$571,200(PVIFA_{5.94\%,5}) = \$237,240.54$$

The equipment should be leased.

To find the maximum payment, we find where the NAL is equal to zero, and solve for the payment. Using X to represent the maximum payment:

$$NAL = 0 = \$8,400,000 - X(1.0594)(PVIFA_{5.94\%,5}) - \$571,200(PVIFA_{5.94\%,5})$$
$$X = \$1,340,075.47$$

So the maximum pretax lease payment is:

Pretax lease payment = $\$1,340,075.47/(1 - .34) = \$2,030,417.38$

10. The aftertax residual value of the asset is an opportunity cost to the leasing decision, occurring at the end of the project life (year 5). Also, the residual value is not really a debt-like cash flow, since there is uncertainty associated with it at year 0. Nevertheless, although a higher discount rate may be appropriate, we'll use the aftertax cost of debt to discount the residual value as is common in practice. Setting the NAL equal to zero:

$$NAL = 0 = \$8,400,000 - X(1.0594)(PVIFA_{5.94\%,5}) - 571,200(PVIFA_{5.94\%,5}) - 700,000/1.0594^5$$
$$X = \$1,222,720.05$$

So, the maximum pretax lease payment is:

Pretax lease payment = $\$1,222,720.05/(1 - .34) = \$1,852,606.14$

11. The security deposit is a cash outflow at the beginning of the lease and a cash inflow at the end of the lease when it is returned. The NAL with these assumptions is:

$$NAL = \$8,400,000 - 500,000 - 1,287,000 - \$1,287,000(PVIFA_{5.94\%,4}) - \$571,200(PVIFA_{5.94\%,5})$$
$$+ \$500,000/1.0594^5$$
$$NAL = \$111,928.87$$

With the security deposit, the firm should still lease the equipment since the NAL is greater than zero. We could also solve this problem another way. From Problem 9, we know that the NAL without the security deposit is $237,240.54, so, if we find the present value of the security deposit, we can simply add this to $237,240.54. The present value of the security deposit is:

PV of security deposit = $-\$500,000 + \$500,000/1.0594^5 = -\$125,311.67$

So, the NAL with the security deposit is:

NAL = $\$237,240.54 - 125,311.67 = \$111,928.87$

12. The decision to lease results in a debt capacity that is lowered by the present value of the aftertax lease payments. The aftertax lease payment is:

Aftertax lease payment = $\$375,000(1 - .38) = \$232,500$

The aftertax interest rate is:

Aftertax interest rate = $.08(1 - .38) = .0496$ or 4.96%

So, the reduction in debt capacity would be:

Reduction in debt capacity = $232,500(PVIFA$_{4.96\%,6}$)
Reduction in debt capacity = $1,181,609.49

**13.** *a.* Since both companies have the same tax rate, there is only one lease payment that will result in a zero NAL for each company. We will calculate cash flows from the depreciation tax shield first. The depreciation tax shield is:

Depreciation tax shield = ($550,000/3)(.34) = $62,333.33

The aftertax cost of debt is:

Aftertax debt cost = .10(1 – .34) = .0660

Using all of this information, we can calculate the lease payment as:

NAL = 0 = $550,000 – PMT(1 – .34)(PVIFA$_{6.60\%,3}$) + $62,333.33(PVIFA$_{6.60\%,3}$)
PMT = $220,780.63

*b.* To generalize the result from part *a*:

Let T$_1$ denote the lessor's tax rate.
Let T$_2$ denote the lessee's tax rate.
Let P denote the purchase price of the asset.
Let D equal the annual depreciation expense.
Let N denote the length of the lease in years.
Let R equal the pretax cost of debt.

The value to the lessor is:

$$\text{Value}_{\text{Lessor}} = -P + \sum_{t=1}^{N} \frac{L(1-T_1) + D(T_1)}{[1 + R(1-T_1)]^t}$$

And the value to the lessee is:

$$\text{Value}_{\text{Lessee}} = P - \sum_{t=1}^{N} \frac{L(1-T_2) + D(T_2)}{[1 + R(1-T_2)]^t}$$

Since all the values in both equations above are the same except T$_1$ and T$_2$, we can see that the values of the lease to its two parties will be opposite in sign only if T$_1$ = T$_2$.

*c.* Since the lessor's tax bracket is unchanged, the zero NAL lease payment is the same as we found in part *a*. The lessee will not realize the depreciation tax shield, and the aftertax cost of debt will be the same as the pretax cost of debt. So, the lessee's maximum lease payment will be:

NAL = 0 = –$550,000 + PMT(PVIFA$_{10\%,3}$)
PMT = $221,163.14

Both parties have positive NAL for lease payments between $220,780.63 and $221,163.14.

**14.** The decision to buy or lease is made by looking at the incremental cash flows. The loan offered by the bank merely helps you to establish the appropriate discount rate. Since the deal they are offering is the same as the market-wide rate, you can ignore the offer and simply use 9 percent as the pretax discount rate. In any capital budgeting project, you do not consider the financing which was to be applied to a specific project. The only exception would be if a specific and special financing deal were tied to a specific project (like a lower-than-market interest rate loan if you buy a particular car).

*a.* The incremental cash flows from leasing the machine are the lease payments, the tax savings on the lease, the lost depreciation tax shield, and the saved purchase price of the machine. The lease payments are due at the beginning of each year, so the incremental cash flows are:

|  | Year 0 | Year 1 | Year 2 | Year 3 | Year 4 |
|---|---|---|---|---|---|
| *Lease:* | | | | | |
| Lease payment | –$ 950,000 | –$950,000 | –$950,000 | –$950,000 | |
| Tax savings on lease | 332,500 | 332,500 | 332,500 | 332,500 | |
| Lost dep. tax shield | | –280,000 | –280,000 | –280,000 | –280,000 |
| Equipment cost | 3,200,000 | | | | |
| | $2,582,500 | –$897,500 | –$897,500 | –$897,500 | –$280,000 |

The aftertax discount rate is:

Aftertax discount rate = .09(1 – .35)
Aftertax discount rate = .0585 or 5.85%

So, the NAL of leasing is:

NAL = $2,582,500 – $897,500(PVIFA$_{5.85\%,3}$) – $280,00 / 1.0585$^4$
NAL = –$46,247.78

Since the NAL is negative, the company should buy the equipment.

*b.* The company is indifferent at the lease payment which makes the NAL of the lease equal to zero. The NAL equation of the lease is:

0 = $3,200,000 – PMT(1 – .35) – PMT(1 – .35)(PVIFA$_{5.85\%,3}$) – $280,000(PVIFA$_{5.85\%,4}$)
PMT = $930,668.00

**15.** *a.* The different borrowing rates are irrelevant. A basic tenant of capital budgeting is that the return of a project depends on the risk of the project. Since the lease payments are affected by the riskiness of the lessee, the lessee's cost of debt is the appropriate interest rate for the analysis by both companies.

*b.* Since both companies have the same tax rate, there is only one lease payment that will result in a zero NAL for each company. We will calculate cash flows from the depreciation tax shield first. The depreciation tax shield is:

Depreciation tax shield = ($620,000/3)(.34) = $70,266.67

The aftertax cost of debt is the lessee's cost of debt, which is:

Aftertax debt cost = .09(1 − .34) = .0594

Using all of this information, we can calculate the lease payment as:

$$NAL = 0 = \$620,000 - PMT(1 - .34)(PVIFA_{5.94\%,3}) + \$70,266.67(PVIFA_{5.94\%,3})$$
PMT = \$244,581.78

c.   Since the lessor's tax bracket is unchanged, the zero NAL lease payment is the same as we found in part *b*. The lessee will not realize the depreciation tax shield, and the aftertax cost of debt will be the same as the pretax cost of debt. So, the lessee's maximum lease payment will be:

$$NAL = 0 = -\$620,000 + PMT(PVIFA_{9\%,3})$$
PMT = \$244,933.95

Both parties have positive NAL for lease payments between \$244,581.78 and \$244,933.95.

**16.** The APR of the loan is the lease factor times 2,400, so:

APR = 0.00285(2,400) = 6.84%

To calculate the lease payment we first need the net capitalization cost, which is the base capitalized cost plus any other costs, minus any down payment or rebates. So, the net capitalized cost is:

Net capitalized cost = \$36,000 + 450 − 2,000
Net capitalized cost = \$34,450

The depreciation charge is the net capitalized cost minus the residual value, divided by the term of the lease, which is:

Depreciation charge = (\$34,450 − 21,000) / 36
Depreciation charge = \$373.61

Next, we can calculate the finance charge, which is the net capitalized cost plus the residual value, times the lease factor, or:

Finance charge = (\$34,450 + 21,000)(0.00285)
Finance charge = \$158.03

And the taxes on each monthly payment will be:

Taxes = (\$373.61 + 158.03)(0.07)
Taxes = \$37.22

The monthly lease payment is the sum of the depreciation charge, the finance charge, and taxes, which will be:

Lease payment = \$373.61 + 158.03 + 37.22
Lease payment = \$568.86

*Challenge*

17. With a four-year loan, the annual loan payment will be

$5,200,000 = PMT(PVIFA_{8\%,4})$
PMT = $1,569,988.18

The aftertax loan payment is found by:

Aftertax payment = Pretax payment – Interest tax shield

So, we need to find the interest tax shield. To find this, we need a loan amortization table since the interest payment each year is the beginning balance times the loan interest rate of 8 percent. The interest tax shield is the interest payment times the tax rate. The amortization table for this loan is:

| Year | Beginning balance | Total payment | Interest payment | Principal payment | Ending balance |
|------|------|------|------|------|------|
| 1 | $5,200,000.00 | $1,569,988.18 | $416,000.00 | $1,153,988.18 | $4,046,011.82 |
| 2 | 4,046,011.82 | 1,569,988.18 | 323,680.95 | 1,246,307.24 | 2,799,704.58 |
| 3 | 2,799,704.58 | 1,569,988.18 | 223,976.37 | 1,346,011.82 | 1,453,692.76 |
| 4 | 1,453,692.76 | 1,569,988.18 | 116,295.42 | 1,453,692.76 | 0.00 |

So, the total cash flows each year are:

| | Aftertax loan payment | | OCF | | Total cash flow |
|---|---|---|---|---|---|
| Year 1: $1,569,988 – ($416,000)(.35) | = $1,424,388.18 | – | 1,446,250 | = | –$21,861.82 |
| Year 2: $1,569,988 – ($323,680.96)(.35) | = $1,456,699.85 | – | 1,446,250 | = | 10,449.85 |
| Year 3: $1,569,988 – ($223,976.37)(.35) | = $1,491,596.45 | – | 1,446,250 | = | 45,346.45 |
| Year 4: $1,569,988 – ($116,295.42)(.35) | = $1,529,284.79 | – | 1,446,250 | = | 83,034.79 |

So, the NAL with the loan payments is:

NAL $= 0 - \$21,861.82/1.052 + \$10,449.85/1.052^2 + \$45,346.45/1.052^3 + \$83,034.79/1.052^4$
NAL = $95,405.02

The NAL is the same because the present value of the aftertax loan payments, discounted at the aftertax cost of capital (which is the aftertax cost of debt) equals $5,200,000.

18. *a.* The decision to buy or lease is made by looking at the incremental cash flows, so we need to find the cash flows for each alternative. The cash flows if the company leases are:

Cash flows from leasing:

Aftertax cost savings = $15,000(1 – .34)
Aftertax cost savings = $9,900

The tax benefit of the lease is the lease payment times the tax rate, so the tax benefit of the lease is:

Lease tax benefit = $65,000(.34)
Lease tax benefit = $22,100

We need to remember the lease payments are due at the beginning of the year. So, if the company leases, the cash flows each year will be:

| | Year 0 | Year 1 | Year 2 | Year 3 | Year 4 | Year 5 |
|---|---|---|---|---|---|---|
| Aftertax savings | | $ 9,900 | $ 9,900 | $ 9,900 | $ 9,900 | $9,900 |
| Lease payment | –$65,000 | –65,000 | –65,000 | –65,000 | –65,000 | |
| Tax benefit | 22,100 | 22,100 | 22,100 | 22,100 | 22,100 | |
| Net cash flows | –$42,900 | –$33,000 | –$33,000 | –$33,000 | –$33,000 | $9,900 |

The amount the company borrows and the repayment schedule are irrelevant since the company maintains a target debt-equity ratio. So, the cash flows from buying the machine will be:

Cash flows from purchasing:

Aftertax cost savings = $25,000(1 – .34)
Aftertax cost savings = $16,500

And the deprecation tax shield will be:

Depreciation tax shield = ($330,000 / 5)(.34)
Depreciation tax shield = $22,400

| | Year 0 | Year 1 | Year 2 | Year 3 | Year 4 | Year 5 |
|---|---|---|---|---|---|---|
| Aftertax savings | | $16,500 | $16,500 | $16,500 | $16,500 | $16,500 |
| Purchase | –$330,000 | | | | | |
| Dep. tax shield | | 22,440 | 22,440 | 22,440 | 22,440 | 22,440 |
| Net cash flows | –$330,000 | $38,940 | $38,940 | $38,940 | $38,940 | $38,940 |

Now we can calculate the incremental cash flows from leasing versus buying by subtracting the net cash flows from buying from the net cash flows from leasing. The incremental cash flows from leasing are:

| | Year 0 | Year 1 | Year 2 | Year 3 | Year 4 | Year 5 |
|---|---|---|---|---|---|---|
| Lease – Buy | $287,100 | –$71,940 | –$71,940 | –$71,940 | –$71,940 | –$29,040 |

The aftertax discount rate is:

Aftertax discount rate = .10(1 – .34)
Aftertax discount rate = .0660 or 6.60%

So, the NAL of leasing is:

$NAL = \$287,100 - \$71,940(PVIFA_{6.60\%,4}) - \$29,040 / 1.066^5$
NAL = $20,110.84

Since the NAL is positive, the company should lease the equipment.

*b.* As long as the company maintains its target debt-equity ratio, the answer does not depend upon the form of financing used for the direct purchase. A financial lease will displace debt regardless of the form of financing.

*c.* The amount of displaced debt is the PV of the incremental cash flows from year one through five.

PV = $71,940(PVIFA$_{6.60\%,4}$) + $29,040 / 1.0660$^5$
PV = $266,989.16

# CHAPTER 22
# OPTIONS AND CORPORATE FINANCE

**Answers to Concept Questions**

1. A call option confers the right, without the obligation, to buy an asset at a given price on or before a given date. A put option confers the right, without the obligation, to sell an asset at a given price on or before a given date. You would buy a call option if you expect the price of the asset to increase. You would buy a put option if you expect the price of the asset to decrease. A call option has unlimited potential profit, while a put option has limited potential profit; the underlying asset's price cannot be less than zero.

2. *a.* The buyer of a call option pays money for the right to buy....
   *b.* The buyer of a put option pays money for the right to sell....
   *c.* The seller of a call option receives money for the obligation to sell....
   *d.* The seller of a put option receives money for the obligation to buy....

3. An American option can be exercised on any date up to and including the expiration date. A European option can only be exercised on the expiration date. Since an American option gives its owner the right to exercise on any date up to and including the expiration date, it must be worth at least as much as a European option, if not more.

4. The intrinsic value of a call is Max[S – E, 0]. The intrinsic value of a put is Max[E – S, 0]. The intrinsic value of an option is the value at expiration.

5. The call is selling for less than its intrinsic value; an arbitrage opportunity exists. Buy the call for $10, exercise the call by paying $35 in return for a share of stock, and sell the stock for $50. You've made a riskless $5 profit.

6. The prices of both the call and the put option should increase. The higher level of downside risk still results in an option price of zero, but the upside potential is greater since there is a higher probability that the asset will finish in the money.

7. False. The value of a call option depends on the total variance of the underlying asset, not just the systematic variance.

8. The call option will sell for more since it provides an unlimited profit opportunity, while the potential profit from the put is limited (the stock price cannot fall below zero).

9. The value of a call option will increase, and the value of a put option will decrease.

10. The reason they don't show up is that the U.S. government uses cash accounting; i.e., only actual cash inflows and outflows are counted, not contingent cash flows. From a political perspective, they would make the deficit larger, so that is another reason not to count them! Whether they should be included depends on whether we feel cash accounting is appropriate or not, but these contingent liabilities should be measured and reported. They currently are not, at least not in a systematic fashion.

11. Increasing the time to expiration increases the value of an option. The reason is that the option gives the holder the right to buy or sell. The longer the holder has that right, the more time there is for the option to increase (or decrease in the case of a put) in value. For example, imagine an out-of-the-money option that is about to expire. Because the option is essentially worthless, increasing the time to expiration would obviously increase its value.

12. An increase in volatility acts to increase both call and put values because the greater volatility increases the possibility of favorable in-the-money payoffs.

13. A put option is insurance since it guarantees the policyholder will be able to sell the asset for a specific price. Consider homeowners insurance. If a house burns down, it is essentially worthless. In essence, the homeowner is selling the worthless house to the insurance company for the amount of insurance.

14. The equityholders of a firm financed partially with debt can be thought of as holding a call option on the assets of the firm with a strike price equal to the debt's face value and a time to expiration equal to the debt's time to maturity. If the value of the firm exceeds the face value of the debt when it matures, the firm will pay off the debtholders in full, leaving the equityholders with the firm's remaining assets. However, if the value of the firm is less than the face value of debt when it matures, the firm must liquidate all of its assets in order to pay off the debtholders, and the equityholders receive nothing. Consider the following:

Let $V_L$ = the value of a firm financed with both debt and equity
FV(debt) = the face value of the firm's outstanding debt at maturity

|  | If $V_L <$ FV(debt) | If $V_L >$ FV(debt) |
| --- | --- | --- |
| Payoff to debtholders | $V_L$ | FV(debt) |
| Payoff to equityholders | 0 | $V_L -$ FV(debt) |
|  | $V_L$ | $V_L$ |

Notice that the payoff to equityholders is identical to a call option of the form $\text{Max}(0, S_T - K)$, where the stock price at expiration ($S_T$) is equal to the value of the firm at the time of the debt's maturity and the strike price (K) is equal to the face value of outstanding debt.

15. Since you have a large number of stock options in the company, you have an incentive to accept the second project, which will increase the overall risk of the company and reduce the value of the firm's debt. However, accepting the risky project will increase your wealth, as the options are more valuable when the risk of the firm increases.

16. Rearranging the put-call parity formula, we get: $S - \text{PV}(E) = C - P$. Since we know that the stock price and exercise price are the same, assuming a positive interest rate, the left hand side of the equation must be greater than zero. This implies the price of the call must be higher than the price of the put in this situation.

17. Rearranging the put-call parity formula, we get: $S - \text{PV}(E) = C - P$. If the call and the put have the same price, we know $C - P = 0$. This must mean the stock price is equal to the present value of the exercise price, so the put is in-the-money.

18. A stock can be replicated using a long call (to capture the upside gains), a short put (to reflect the downside losses) and a T-bill (to reflect the time value component – the "wait" factor).

## Solutions to Questions and Problems

*NOTE: All end-of-chapter problems were solved using a spreadsheet. Many problems require multiple steps. Due to space and readability constraints, when these intermediate steps are included in this solutions manual, rounding may appear to have occurred. However, the final answer for each problem is found without rounding during any step in the problem.*

*Basic*

1. *a.* The value of the call is the stock price minus the present value of the exercise price, so:

   $C_0 = \$63 - [\$60/1.048] = \$5.75$

   The intrinsic value is the amount by which the stock price exceeds the exercise price of the call, so the intrinsic value is $3.

   *b.* The value of the call is the stock price minus the present value of the exercise price, so:

   $C_0 = \$63 - [\$50/1.048] = \$15.29$

   The intrinsic value is the amount by which the stock price exceeds the exercise price of the call, so the intrinsic value is $13.

   *c.* The value of the put option is $0 since there is no possibility that the put will finish in the money. The intrinsic value is also $0.

2. *a.* The calls are in the money. The intrinsic value of the calls is $3.

   *b.* The puts are out of the money. The intrinsic value of the puts is $0.

   *c.* The Mar call and the Oct put are mispriced. The call is mispriced because it is selling for less than its intrinsic value. If the option expired today, the arbitrage strategy would be to buy the call for $2.80, exercise it and pay $80 for a share of stock, and sell the stock for $83. A riskless profit of $.20 results. The October put is mispriced because it sells for less than the July put. To take advantage of this, sell the July put for $3.90 and buy the October put for $3.65, for a cash inflow of $.25. The exposure of the short position is completely covered by the long position in the October put, with a positive cash inflow today.

3. *a.* Each contract is for 100 shares, so the total cost is:

   Cost = 10(100 shares/contract)($7.60)
   Cost = $7,600

   *b.* If the stock price at expiration is $140, the payoff is:

   Payoff = 10(100)($140 – 110)
   Payoff = $30,000

   If the stock price at expiration is $125, the payoff is:

   Payoff = 10(100)($125 – 110)
   Payoff = $15,000

> *c.* Remembering that each contract is for 100 shares of stock, the cost is:
>
> Cost = 10(100)($4.70)
> Cost = $4,700
>
> The maximum gain on the put option would occur if the stock price goes to $0. We also need to subtract the initial cost, so:
>
> Maximum gain = 10(100)($110) – $4,700
> Maximum gain = $105,300
>
> If the stock price at expiration is $104, the position will have a profit of:
>
> Profit = 10(100)($110 – 104) – $4,700
> Profit = $1,300
>
> *d.* At a stock price of $103 the put is in the money. As the writer, you will make:
>
> Net loss = $4,700 – 10(100)($110 – 103)
> Net loss = –$2,300
>
> At a stock price of $132 the put is out of the money, so the writer will make the initial cost:
>
> Net gain = $4,700
>
> At the breakeven, you would recover the initial cost of $4,700, so:
>
> $4,700 = 10(100)($110 – $S_T$)
> $S_T$ = $105.30
>
> For terminal stock prices above $105.30, the writer of the put option makes a net profit (ignoring transaction costs and the effects of the time value of money).

**4.** *a.* The value of the call is the stock price minus the present value of the exercise price, so:

$C_0$ = $80 – 70/1.05
$C_0$ = $13.33

*b.* Using the equation presented in the text to prevent arbitrage, we find the value of the call is:

$80 = [($96 – 74)/($96 – 90)]$C_0$ + $74/1.05
$C_0$ = $2.60

**5.** *a.* The value of the call is the stock price minus the present value of the exercise price, so:

$C_0$ = $62 – $35/1.05
$C_0$ = $28.67

*b.* Using the equation presented in the text to prevent arbitrage, we find the value of the call is:

$62 = 2$C_0$ + $50/1.05
$C_0$ = $7.19

**6.** Using put-call parity and solving for the put price, we get:

$38 + P = $40e^{-(.026)(3/12)} + $3.80
$P = $5.54$

**7.** Using put-call parity and solving for the call price we get:

$61 + $4.89 = $65e^{-(.036)(.5)} + C$
$C = $2.05$

**8.** Using put-call parity and solving for the stock price we get:

$S + $2.40 = $85e^{-(.048)(3/12)} + $5.09$
$S = $86.68$

**9.** Using put-call parity, we can solve for the risk-free rate as follows:

$57.30 + $2.65 = $55e^{-R(2/12)} + $5.32$
$54.63 = $55e^{-R(2/12)}$
$.9932 = e^{-R(2/12)}$
$\ln(.9932) = \ln(e^{-R(2/12)})$
$-.0068 = -R(2/12)$
$R_f = 4.05\%$

**10.** Using the Black-Scholes option pricing model to find the price of the call option, we find:

$d_1 = [\ln($57/$60) + (.06 + .54^2/2) \times (3/12)] / (.54 \times \sqrt{3/12}) = .0006$

$d_2 = .0006 - (.54 \times \sqrt{3/12}) = -.2694$

$N(d_1) = .5002$

$N(d_2) = .3938$

Putting these values into the Black-Scholes model, we find the call price is:

$C = $57(.5002) - ($60e^{-.06(.25)})(.3938) = $5.24$

Using put-call parity, the put price is:

$P = $60e^{-.06(.25)} + 5.24 - 57 = $7.34$

**11.** Using the Black-Scholes option pricing model to find the price of the call option, we find:

$d_1 = [\ln($93/$90) + (.04 + .62^2/2) \times (5/12)] / (.62 \times \sqrt{5/12}) = .3237$

$d_2 = .3237 - (.62 \times \sqrt{5/12}) = -.0765$

$N(d_1) = .6269$

$N(d_2) = .4695$

Putting these values into the Black-Scholes model, we find the call price is:

$$C = \$93(.6269) - (\$90e^{-.04(5/12)})(.4695) = \$16.75$$

Using put-call parity, the put price is:

$$P = \$90e^{-.04(5/12)} + 16.75 - 93 = \$12.26$$

12. The delta of a call option is $N(d_1)$, so:

$$d_1 = [\ln(\$67/\$70) + (.05 + .49^2/2) \times .75] / (.49 \times \sqrt{.75}) = .1973$$

$$N(d_1) = .5782$$

For a call option the delta is .5782. For a put option, the delta is:

Put delta = .5782 − 1 = −.4218

The delta tells us the change in the price of an option for a $1 change in the price of the underlying asset.

13. Using the Black-Scholes option pricing model, with a 'stock' price of $1,100,000 and an exercise price of $1,250,000, the price you should receive is:

$$d_1 = [\ln(\$1,100,000/\$1,250,000) + (.05 + .25^2/2) \times (12/12)] / (.25 \times \sqrt{12/12}) = -.1863$$

$$d_2 = -.1863 - (.25 \times \sqrt{12/12}) = -.4363$$

$$N(d_1) = .4261$$

$$N(d_2) = .3313$$

Putting these values into the Black-Scholes model, we find the call price is:

$$C = \$1,100,000(.4261) - (\$1,250,000e^{-.05(1)})(.3313) = \$74,776.00$$

14. Using the call price we found in the previous problem and put-call parity, you would need to pay:

$$P = \$1,250,000e^{-.05(1)} + 74,776.00 - 1,100,000 = \$163,812.78$$

You would have to pay $163,812.78 in order to guarantee the right to sell the land for $1,250,000.

15. Using the Black-Scholes option pricing model to find the price of the call option, we find:

$$d_1 = [\ln(\$83/\$80) + (.06 + .53^2/2) \times (6/12)] / (.53 \times \sqrt{(6/12)}) = .3657$$

$$d_2 = .3657 - (.53 \times \sqrt{6/12}) = -.0091$$

$$N(d_1) = .6427$$

$$N(d_2) = .4964$$

Putting these values into the Black-Scholes model, we find the call price is:

$$C = \$83(.6427) - (\$80e^{-.06(.50)})(.4964) = \$14.81$$

Using put-call parity, we find the put price is:

$$P = \$80e^{-.06(.50)} + 14.81 - 83 = \$9.44$$

a. The intrinsic value of each option is:

Call intrinsic value = Max[$S - E$, 0] = \$3

Put intrinsic value = Max[$E - S$, 0] = \$0

b. Option value consists of time value and intrinsic value, so:

Call option value = Intrinsic value + Time value
$14.81 = \$3 + TV$
$TV = \$11.81$

Put option value = Intrinsic value + Time value
$9.44 = \$0 + TV$
$TV = \$9.44$

c. The time premium (theta) is more important for a call option than a put option; therefore, the time premium is, in general, larger for a call option.

16. The stock price can either increase 15 percent, or decrease 15 percent. The stock price at expiration will either be:

Stock price increase = $73(1 + .15) = \$83.95$

Stock price decrease = $73(1 - .15) = \$62.05$

The payoff in either state will be the maximum stock price minus the exercise price, or zero, which is:

Payoff if stock price increases = Max[$83.95 - 70, 0] = \$13.95

Payoff if stock price decreases = Max[$62.05 - 70, 0] = \$0

To get a 15 percent return, we can use the following expression to determine the risk-neutral probability of a rise in the price of the stock:

Risk-free rate = (Probability$_{Rise}$)(Return$_{Rise}$) + (Probability$_{Fall}$)(Return$_{Fall}$)
$.08 = $ (Probability$_{Rise}$)(.15) + (1 − Probability$_{Rise}$)(−.15)
Probability$_{Rise}$ = .7667

And the probability of a stock price decrease is:

Probability$_{Fall}$ = 1 − .7667 = .2333

So, the risk neutral value of a call option will be:

Call value = [(.7667 × $13.95) + (.2333 × $0)] / (1 + .08)
Call value = $9.90

17. The stock price increase, decrease, and option payoffs will remain unchanged since the stock price change is the same. The new risk neutral probability of a stock price increase is:

Risk-free rate = (Probability$_{Rise}$)(Return$_{Rise}$) + (Probability$_{Fall}$)(Return$_{Fall}$)
.05 = (Probability$_{Rise}$)(.15) + (1 − Probability$_{Rise}$)(−.15)
Probability$_{Rise}$ = .6667

And the probability of a stock price decrease is:

Probability$_{Fall}$ = 1 − .6667 = .3333

So, the risk neutral value of a call option will be:

Call value = [(.6667 × $13.95) + (.3333 × $0)] / (1 + .05)
Call value = $8.86

*Intermediate*

18. If the exercise price is equal to zero, the call price will equal the stock price, which is $75.

19. If the standard deviation is zero, $d_1$ and $d_2$ go to $+\infty$, so $N(d_1)$ and $N(d_2)$ go to 1. So:

$C = SN(d_1) - EN(d_2)e^{-rt}$
$C = \$84(1) - \$80(1)e^{-.05(6/12)} = \$5.98$

20. If the standard deviation is infinite, $d_1$ goes to positive infinity so $N(d_1)$ goes to 1, and $d_2$ goes to negative infinity so $N(d_2)$ goes to 0. In this case, the call price is equal to the stock price, which is $35.

21. We can use the Black-Scholes model to value the equity of a firm. Using the asset value of $26,300 as the stock price, and the face value of debt of $25,000 as the exercise price, the value of the firm's equity is:

$d_1 = [\ln(\$26,300/\$25,000) + (.05 + .38^2/2) \times 1] / (.38 \times \sqrt{1}) = .4550$

$d_2 = .4550 - (.38 \times \sqrt{1}) = .0750$

$N(d_1) = .6754$

$N(d_2) = .5299$

Putting these values into the Black-Scholes model, we find the equity value is:

Equity = $26,300(.6754) − ($25,000$e^{-.05(1)}$)(.5299) = $5,162.98

The value of the debt is the firm value minus the value of the equity, so:

Debt = $26,300 − 5,162.98 = $21,137.02

22. *a.* We can use the Black-Scholes model to value the equity of a firm. Using the asset value of $27,500 (the $26,300 current value of the assets plus the $1,200 project NPV) as the stock price, and the face value of debt of $25,000 as the exercise price, the value of the firm if it accepts project A is:

$d_1 = [\ln(\$27,500/\$25,000) + (.05 + .55^2/2) \times 1] / (.55 \times \sqrt{1}) = .5392$

$d_2 = .5392 − (.55 \times \sqrt{1}) = −.0108$

$N(d_1) = .7051$

$N(d_2) = .4957$

Putting these values into the Black-Scholes model, we find the equity value is:

$E_A = \$27,500(.7051) − (\$25,000e^{−.05(1)})(.4957) = \$7,603.04$

The value of the debt is the firm value minus the value of the equity, so:

$D_A = \$27,500 − 7,603.04 = \$19,896.96$

And the value of the firm if it accepts Project B is:

$d_1 = [\ln(\$27,900/\$25,000) + (.05 + .34^2/2) \times 1] / (.34 \times \sqrt{1}) = .6399$

$d_2 = .6399 − (.34 \times \sqrt{1}) = .2999$

$N(d_1) = .7389$

$N(d_2) = .6179$

Putting these values into the Black-Scholes model, we find the equity value is:

$E_B = \$27,900(.7389) − (\$25,000e^{−.05(1)})(.6179) = \$5,921.30$

The value of the debt is the firm value minus the value of the equity, so:

$D_B = \$27,900 − 5,921.30 = \$21,978.70$

*b.* Although the NPV of project B is higher, the equity value with project A is higher. While NPV represents the increase in the value of the assets of the firm, in this case, the increase in the value of the firm's assets resulting from project B is mostly allocated to the debtholders, resulting in a smaller increase in the value of the equity. Stockholders would, therefore, prefer project A even though it has a lower NPV.

   *c.* Yes. If the same group of investors have equal stakes in the firm as bondholders and stock-holders, then total firm value matters and project B should be chosen, since it increases the value of the firm to $27,900 instead of $27,500.

   *d.* Stockholders may have an incentive to take on riskier, less profitable projects if the firm is leveraged; the higher the firm's debt load, all else the same, the greater is this incentive.

**23.** We can use the Black-Scholes model to value the equity of a firm. Using the asset value of $36,400 as the stock price, and the face value of debt of $30,000 as the exercise price, the value of the firm's equity is:

$$d_1 = [\ln(\$36,400/\$30,000) + (.05 + .53^2/2) \times 1] / (.53 \times \sqrt{1}\,) = .7242$$

$$d_2 = .7242 - (.53 \times \sqrt{1}\,) = .1942$$

$$N(d_1) = .7655$$

$$N(d_2) = .5770$$

Putting these values into the Black-Scholes model, we find the equity value is:

$$\text{Equity} = \$36,400(.7655) - (\$30,000e^{-.05(1)})(.5770) = \$11,399.73$$

The value of the debt is the firm value minus the value of the equity, so:

$$\text{Debt} = \$36,400 - 11,399.73 = \$25,000.27$$

The return on the company's debt is:

$$\$25,000.27 = \$30,000e^{-R(1)}$$
$$.83334 = e^{-R}$$
$$R_D = -\ln(.83334) = .1823 \text{ or } 18.23\%$$

**24.** *a.* The combined value of equity and debt of the two firms is:

     $$\text{Equity} = \$5,162.98 + 11,399.73 = \$16,562.71$$

     $$\text{Debt} = \$21,137.02 + 25,000.27 = \$46,137.29$$

   *b.* For the new firm, the combined market value of assets is $62,700, and the combined face value of debt is $55,000. Using Black-Scholes to find the value of equity for the new firm, we find:

     $$d_1 = [\ln(\$62,700/\$55,000) + (.05 + .29^2/2) \times 1] / (.29 \times \sqrt{1}\,) = .7692$$

     $$d_2 = .7692 - (.29 \times \sqrt{1}\,) = .4792$$

     $$N(d_1) = .7791$$

     $$N(d_2) = .6841$$

Putting these values into the Black-Scholes model, we find the equity value is:

Equity $= \$62,700(.7791) - (\$55,000e^{-.05(1)})(.6841) = \$13,059.79$

The value of the debt is the firm value minus the value of the equity, so:

Debt $= \$62,700 - 13,059.79 = \$49,640.21$

c. The change in the value of the firm's equity is:

Equity value change $= \$13,059.79 - 16,562.71 = -\$3,502.92$

The change in the value of the firm's debt is:

Debt $= \$49,640.21 - 46,137.29 = \$3,502.92$

d. In a purely financial merger, when the standard deviation of the assets declines, the value of the equity declines as well. The shareholders will lose exactly the amount the bondholders gain. The bondholders gain as a result of the coinsurance effect. That is, it is less likely that the new company will default on the debt.

25. a. Using Black-Scholes model to value the equity, we get:

$d_1 = [\ln(\$13,400,000/\$15,000,000) + (.06 + .39^2/2) \times 10] / (.39 \times \sqrt{10}) = 1.0117$

$d_2 = 1.0117 - (.39 \times \sqrt{10}) = -.2216$

$N(d_1) = .8442$

$N(d_2) = .4123$

Putting these values into Black-Scholes:

Equity $= \$13,400,000(.8442) - (\$15,000,000e^{-.06(10)})(.4123) = \$7,917,466.68$

b. The value of the debt is the firm value minus the value of the equity, so:

Debt $= \$13,400,000 - 7,917,466.68 = \$5,482,533.32$

c. Using the equation for the PV of a continuously compounded lump sum, we get:

$\$5,482,533.32 = \$15,000,000e^{-R(10)}$
$.36550 = e^{-R10}$
$R_D = -(1/10)\ln(.36550) = .1006$ or $10.06\%$

  d. The new value of assets is the current asset value plus the project NPV. Using Black-Scholes model to value the equity, we get:

  $d_1 = [\ln(\$14{,}600{,}000/\$15{,}000{,}000) + (.06 + .39^2/2) \times 10] / (.39 \times \sqrt{10}) = 1.0812$

  $d_2 = 1.0812 - (.39 \times \sqrt{10}) = -.1521$

  $N(d_1) = .8602$

  $N(d_2) = .4396$

  Putting these values into Black-Scholes:

  Equity $= \$14{,}600{,}000(.8602) - (\$15{,}000{,}000e^{-.06(10)})(.4396) = \$8{,}940{,}336.91$

  e. The value of the debt is the firm value minus the value of the equity, so:

  Debt $= \$14{,}600{,}000 - 8{,}940{,}336.91 = \$5{,}659{,}663.09$

  Using the equation for the PV of a continuously compounded lump sum, we get:

  $\$5{,}659{,}663.09 = \$15{,}000{,}000e^{-R(10)}$
  $.37731 = e^{-R10}$
  $R_D = -(1/10)\ln(.37731) = .0975$ or $9.75\%$

  When the firm accepts the new project, part of the NPV accrues to bondholders. This increases the present value of the bond, thus reducing the return on the bond. Additionally, the new project makes the firm safer in the sense that it increases the value of assets, thus increasing the probability the call will end in-the-money and the bondholders will receive their payment.

26. a. In order to solve a problem using the two-state option model, we first need to draw a stock price tree containing both the current stock price and the stock's possible values at the time of the option's expiration. Next, we can draw a similar tree for the option, designating what its value will be at expiration given either of the 2 possible stock price movements.

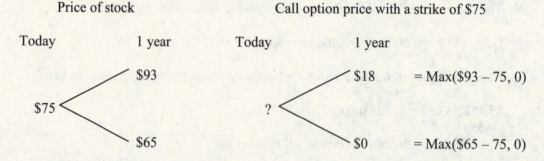

The stock price today is $75. It will either increase to $93 or decrease to $65 in one year. If the stock price rises to $93, the call will be exercised for $75 and a payoff of $18 will be received at expiration. If the stock price falls to $65, the option will not be exercised, and the payoff at expiration will be zero.

If the stock price rises, its return over the period is 19.23 percent [= ($93/$78) – 1]. If the stock price falls, its return over the period is –16.67 percent [= ($65/$78) – 1]. We can use the following expression to determine the risk-neutral probability of a rise in the price of the stock:

Risk-free rate = (Probability$_{Rise}$)(Return$_{Rise}$) + (Probability$_{Fall}$)(Return$_{Fall}$)
Risk-free rate = (Probability$_{Rise}$)(Return$_{Rise}$) + (1 – Probability$_{Rise}$)(Return$_{Fall}$)
.025          = (Probability$_{Rise}$)(.1923) + (1 – Probability$_{Rise}$)(–.1667)
Probability$_{Rise}$ = .5339 or 53.39%

This means the risk neutral probability of a stock price decrease is:

Probability$_{Fall}$ = 1 – Probability$_{Rise}$
Probability$_{Fall}$ = 1 – .5339
Probability$_{Fall}$ = .4661 or 46.61%

Using these risk-neutral probabilities, we can now determine the expected payoff of the call option at expiration. The expected payoff at expiration is:

Expected payoff at expiration = (.5339)($18) + (.4661)($0)
Expected payoff at expiration = $9.61

Since this payoff occurs 1 year from now, we must discount it back to the value today. Since we are using risk-neutral probabilities, we can use the risk-free rate, so:

PV(Expected payoff at expiration) = $9.61 / 1.025
PV(Expected payoff at expiration) = $9.38

b.  Yes, there is a way to create a synthetic call option with identical payoffs to the call option described above. In order to do this, we will need to buy shares of stock and borrow at the risk-free rate. The number of shares to buy is based on the delta of the option, where delta is defined as:

Delta = (Swing of option) / (Swing of stock)

Since the call option will be worth $18 if the stock price rises and $0 if it falls, the delta of the option is $18 (= 18 – 0). Since the stock price will either be $93 or $65 at the time of the option's expiration, the swing of the stock is $28 (= $93 – 65). With this information, the delta of the option is:

Delta = $18 / $28
Delta = .64

Therefore, the first step in creating a synthetic call option is to buy .64 of a share of the stock. Since the stock is currently trading at $78 per share, this will cost $40.77 [= (.64)($65)/(1 + .025)]. In order to determine the amount that we should borrow, compare the payoff of the actual call option to the payoff of delta shares at expiration.

Call Option
If the stock price rises to $93:        Payoff = $18
If the stock price falls to $65:        Payoff = $0

Delta Shares

| | |
|---|---|
| If the stock price rises to $93: | Payoff = (.64)($93) = $59.79 |
| If the stock price falls to $65: | Payoff = (.64)($65) = $41.79 |

The payoff of his synthetic call position should be identical to the payoff of an actual call option. However, owning .64 of a share leaves us exactly $41.79 above the payoff at expiration, regardless of whether the stock price rises or falls. In order to reduce the payoff at expiration by $41.79, we should borrow the present value of $41.79 now. In one year, the obligation to pay $41.79 will reduce the payoffs so that they exactly match those of an actual call option. So, purchase .64 of a share of stock and borrow $40.77 (= $41.79 / 1.025) in order to create a synthetic call option with a strike price of $75 and 1 year until expiration.

c.   Since the cost of the stock purchase is $50.14 to purchase .64 of a share and $40.77 is borrowed, the total cost of the synthetic call option is:

Cost of synthetic option = $50.14 – 40.77
Cost of synthetic option = $9.38

This is exactly the same price as an actual call option. Since an actual call option and a synthetic call option provide identical payoff structures, we should not expect to pay more for one than for the other.

**27.**  *a.*   In order to solve a problem using the two-state option model, we first draw a stock price tree containing both the current stock price and the stock's possible values at the time of the option's expiration. Next, we can draw a similar tree for the option, designating what its value will be at expiration given either of the 2 possible stock price movements.

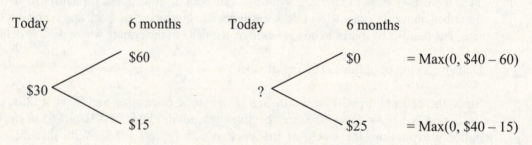

The stock price today is $30. It will either decrease to $15 or increase to $60 in six months. If the stock price falls to $15, the put will be exercised and the payoff will be $25. If the stock price rises to $60, the put will not be exercised, so the payoff will be zero.

If the stock price rises, its return over the period is 100% [= (60/30) – 1]. If the stock price falls, its return over the period is –50% [= (15/30) –1]. Use the following expression to determine the risk-neutral probability of a rise in the price of the stock:

Risk-free rate = (Probability$_{Rise}$)(Return$_{Rise}$) + (Probability$_{Fall}$)(Return$_{Fall}$)
Risk-free rate = (Probability$_{Rise}$)(Return$_{Rise}$) + (1 – Probability$_{Rise}$)(Return$_{Fall}$)

The risk-free rate over the next six months must be used in the order to match the timing of the expected stock price change. Since the risk-free rate per annum is 5 percent, the risk-free rate over the next six months is 2.47 percent [= $(1.05)^{1/2}$ –1], so.

$.0247 = (\text{Probability}_{Rise})(1) + (1 - \text{Probability}_{Rise})(-.50)$
$\text{Probability}_{Rise} = .3498 \text{ or } 34.98\%$

Which means the risk-neutral probability of a decrease in the stock price is:

$\text{Probability}_{Fall} = 1 - \text{Probability}_{Rise}$
$\text{Probability}_{Fall} = 1 - .3498$
$\text{Probability}_{Fall} = .6502 \text{ or } 65.02\%$

Using these risk-neutral probabilities, we can determine the expected payoff of the put option at expiration as:

Expected payoff at expiration = $(.3498)(\$0) + (.6502)(\$25)$
Expected payoff at expiration = $\$16.26$

Since this payoff occurs 6 months from now, we must discount it at the risk-free rate in order to find its present value, which is:

PV(Expected payoff at expiration) = $\$16.26 / (1.05)^{1/2}$
PV(Expected payoff at expiration) = $\$15.86$

b. Yes, there is a way to create a synthetic put option with identical payoffs to the put option described above. In order to do this, we need to short shares of the stock and lend at the risk-free rate. The number of shares that should be shorted is based on the delta of the option, where delta is defined as:

Delta = (Swing of option) / (Swing of stock)

Since the put option will be worth $0 if the stock price rises and $25 if it falls, the swing of the call option is –$25 (= $0 – 25). Since the stock price will either be $60 or $15 at the time of the option's expiration, the swing of the stock is $45 (= $60 – 15). Given this information, the delta of the put option is:

Delta = (Swing of option) / (Swing of stock)
Delta = $(-\$25 / \$45)$
Delta = $-.56$

Therefore, the first step in creating a synthetic put option is to short .56 of a share of stock. Since the stock is currently trading at $30 per share, the amount received will be $16.67 (= .56 × $30) as a result of the short sale. In order to determine the amount to lend, compare the payoff of the actual put option to the payoff of delta shares at expiration.

<u>Put option</u>
If the stock price rises to $60:     Payoff = $0
If the stock price falls to $15:     Payoff = $25

<u>Delta shares</u>
If the stock price rises to $60:     Payoff = $(-.56)(\$60) = -\$33.33$
If the stock price falls to $15:     Payoff = $(-.56)(\$15) = -\$8.33$

The payoff of the synthetic put position should be identical to the payoff of an actual put option. However, shorting .56 of a share leaves us exactly $33.33 below the payoff at expiration, whether the stock price rises or falls. In order to increase the payoff at expiration by $33.33, we should lend the present value of $33.33 now. In six months, we will receive $33.33, which will increase the payoffs so that they exactly match those of an actual put option. So, the amount to lend is:

Amount to lend = $33.33 / $1.05^{1/2}$
Amount to lend = $32.53

c.   Since the short sale results in a positive cash flow of $16.67 and we will lend $32.53, the total cost of the synthetic put option is:

Cost of synthetic put = $32.53 – 16.67
Cost of synthetic put = $15.86

This is exactly the same price as an actual put option. Since an actual put option and a synthetic put option provide identical payoff structures, we should not expect to pay more for one than for the other.

**28.** a.   The company would be interested in purchasing a call option on the price of gold with a strike price of $1,530 per ounce and 3 months until expiration. This option will compensate the company for any increases in the price of gold above the strike price and places a cap on the amount the firm must pay for gold at $1,530 per ounce.

b.   In order to solve a problem using the two-state option model, first draw a price tree containing both the current price of the underlying asset and the underlying asset's possible values at the time of the option's expiration. Next, draw a similar tree for the option, designating what its value will be at expiration given either of the 2 possible stock price movements.

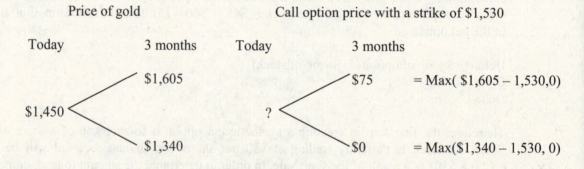

Price of gold                          Call option price with a strike of $1,530

Today           3 months      Today          3 months

                $1,605                         $75        = Max( $1,605 – 1,530,0)
$1,450                          ?
                $1,340                         $0         = Max($1,340 – 1,530, 0)

The price of gold is $1,450 per ounce today. If the price rises to $1,605, the company will exercise its call option for $1,530 and receive a payoff of $75 at expiration. If the price of gold falls to $1,340, the company will not exercise its call option, and the firm will receive no payoff at expiration. If the price of gold rises, its return over the period is 10.69 percent [= ($1,605 / $1,450) – 1]. If the price of gold falls, its return over the period is –7.59 percent [= ($1,340 / $1,450) –1]. Use the following expression to determine the risk-neutral probability of a rise in the price of gold:

Risk-free rate = $(\text{Probability}_{Rise})(\text{Return}_{Rise}) + (\text{Probability}_{Fall})(\text{Return}_{Fall})$
Risk-free rate = $(\text{Probability}_{Rise})(\text{Return}_{Rise}) + (1 - \text{Probability}_{Rise})(\text{Return}_{Fall})$

The risk-free rate over the next three months must be used in the order to match the timing of the expected price change. Since the risk-free rate per annum is 6.50 percent, the risk-free rate over the next three months is 1.59 percent $[= (1.0650)^{1/4} - 1]$, so:

$$.0159 = (Probability_{Rise})(.1069) + (1 - Probability_{Rise})(-.0759)$$
$$Probability_{Rise} = .5019 \text{ or } 50.19\%$$

And the risk-neutral probability of a price decline is:

$$Probability_{Fall} = 1 - Probability_{Rise}$$
$$Probability_{Fall} = 1 - .5019$$
$$Probability_{Fall} = .4981 \text{ or } 49.81\%$$

Using these risk-neutral probabilities, we can determine the expected payoff of the call option at expiration, which will be.

$$\text{Expected payoff at expiration} = (.5019)(\$75) + (.4981)(\$0)$$
$$\text{Expected payoff at expiration} = \$37.64$$

Since this payoff occurs 3 months from now, it must be discounted at the risk-free rate in order to find its present value. Doing so, we find:

$$\text{PV(Expected payoff at expiration)} = [\$37.64 / (1.0650)^{1/4}]$$
$$\text{PV(Expected payoff at expiration)} = \$37.06$$

Therefore, given the information about gold's price movements over the next three months, a European call option with a strike price of $1,530 and three months until expiration is worth $37.06 today.

c.   Yes, there is a way to create a synthetic call option with identical payoffs to the call option described above. In order to do this, the company will need to buy gold and borrow at the risk-free rate. The amount of gold to buy is based on the delta of the option, where delta is defined as:

Delta = (Swing of option) / (Swing of price of gold)

Since the call option will be worth $75 if the price of gold rises and $0 if it falls, the swing of the call option is $75 (= $75 − 0). Since the price of gold will either be $1,605 or $1,340 at the time of the option's expiration, the swing of the price of gold is $265 (= $1,605 − 1,340). Given this information the delta of the call option is:

Delta = (Swing of option) / (Swing of price of gold)
Delta = ($75 / $265)
Delta = .28

Therefore, the first step in creating a synthetic call option is to buy .28 of an ounce of gold. Since gold currently sells for $1,450 per ounce, the company will pay $410.38 (= .28 × $1,450) to purchase .28 of an ounce of gold. In order to determine the amount that should be borrowed, compare the payoff of the actual call option to the payoff of delta shares at expiration:

Call Option
If the price of gold rises to $1,605:    Payoff = $75
If the price of gold falls to $1,340:    Payoff = $0

Delta Shares
If the price of gold rises to $1,605:    Payoff = (.28)($1,605) = $454.25
If the price of gold falls to $1,340:    Payoff = (.28)($1,340) = $379.25

The payoff of this synthetic call position should be identical to the payoff of an actual call option. However, buying .28 of a share leaves us exactly $379.25 above the payoff at expiration, whether the price of gold rises or falls. In order to decrease the company's payoff at expiration by $379.25, it should borrow the present value of $379.25 now. In three months, the company must pay $379.25, which will decrease its payoffs so that they exactly match those of an actual call option. So, the amount to borrow today is:

Amount to borrow today = $379.25 / $1.0650^{1/4}$
Amount to borrow today = $373.32

*d.*    Since the company pays $410.38 in order to purchase gold and borrows $373.32, the total cost of the synthetic call option is $37.06 (= $410.38 – 373.32). This is exactly the same price for an actual call option. Since an actual call option and a synthetic call option provide identical payoff structures, the company should not expect to pay more for one than for the other.

29.    To construct the collar, the investor must purchase the stock, sell a call option with a high strike price, and buy a put option with a low strike price. So, to find the cost of the collar, we need to find the price of the call option and the price of the put option. We can use Black-Scholes to find the price of the call option, which will be:

*Price of call option with $95 strike price:*

$d_1 = [\ln(\$70/\$95) + (.07 + .50^2/2) \times (6/12)] / (.50 \times \sqrt{(6/12)}) = -.5880$

$d_2 = -.5880 - (.50 \times \sqrt{6/12}) = -.9415$

$N(d_1) = .2783$

$N(d_2) = .1732$

Putting these values into the Black-Scholes model, we find the call price is:

$C = \$70(.2783) - (\$95^{-.07(6/12)})(.1732) = \$3.59$

Now we can use Black-Scholes and put-call parity to find the price of the put option with a strike price of $55. Doing so, we find:

*Price of put option with $55 strike price:*

$d_1 = [\ln(\$70/\$55) + (.07 + .50^2/2) \times (6/12)] / (.50 \times \sqrt{(6/12)}) = .9579$

$d_2 = .9579 - (.50 \times \sqrt{6/12}) = .6043$

$N(d_1) = .8309$

$N(d_2) = .7272$

Putting these values into the Black-Scholes model, we find the call price is:

$C = \$70(.8309) - (\$55e^{-.07(6/12)})(.7272) = \$19.55$

Rearranging the put-call parity equation, we get:

$P = C - S + Ee^{-Rt}$
$P = \$19.55 - 70 + 55e^{-.07(6/12)}$
$P = \$2.65$

So, the investor will buy the stock, sell the call option, and buy the put option, so the total cost is:

Total cost of collar = $\$70 - 3.59 + 2.65$
Total cost of collar = $\$69.06$

*Challenge*

30.  a.  Using the equation for the PV of a continuously compounded lump sum, we get:

   $PV = \$50,000 \times e^{-.05(2)} = \$45,241.87$

   b.  Using Black-Scholes model to value the equity, we get:

   $d_1 = [\ln(\$29,000/\$50,000) + (.05 + .60^2/2) \times 2] / (.60 \times \sqrt{2}) = -.0999$

   $d_2 = -.0999 - (.60 \times \sqrt{2}) = -.9484$

   $N(d_1) = .4602$

   $N(d_2) = .1715$

   Putting these values into Black-Scholes:

   Equity = $\$29,000(.4602) - (\$50,000e^{-.05(2)})(.1715) = \$5,589.16$

   And using put-call parity, the price of the put option is:

   Put = $\$50,000e^{-.05(2)} + 5,589.16 - 29,000 = \$21,831.03$

   c.  The value of a risky bond is the value of a risk-free bond minus the value of a put option on the firm's equity, so:

   Value of risky bond = $\$45,241.87 - 21,831.03 = \$23,410.84$

   Using the equation for the PV of a continuously compounded lump sum to find the return on debt, we get:

   $\$23,410.84 = \$50,000e^{-R(2)}$
   $.46822 = e^{-R2}$
   $R_D = -(1/2)\ln(.46822) = .3794$ or 37.94%

d. The value of the debt with five years to maturity at the risk-free rate is:

PV = $50,000 × $e^{-.05(5)}$ = $38,940.04

Using Black-Scholes model to value the equity, we get:

$d_1$ = [ln($29,000/$50,000) + (.05 + $.60^2/2$) × 5] / (.60 × $\sqrt{5}$) = .4511

$d_2$ = .4511 – (.60 × $\sqrt{5}$) = –.8905

N($d_1$) = .6741

N($d_2$) = .1866

Putting these values into Black-Scholes:

Equity = $29,000(.6741) – ($50,000$e^{-.05(5)}$)(.1866) = $12,281.46

And using put-call parity, the price of the put option is:

Put = $50,000$e^{-.05(5)}$ + $12,281.46 – $29,000 = $22,221.50

The value of a risky bond is the value of a risk-free bond minus the value of a put option on the firm's equity, so:

Value of risky bond = $38,940.04 – 22,221.50 = $16,718.54

Using the equation for the PV of a continuously compounded lump sum to find the return on debt, we get:

$16,718.54 = $50,000$e^{-R(5)}$
.33437 = $e^{-R5}$
$R_D$ = –(1/5)ln(.33437) = .2191 or 21.91%

The value of the debt declines because of the time value of money, i.e., it will be longer until shareholders receive their payment. However, the required return on the debt declines. Under the current situation, it is not likely the company will have the assets to pay off bondholders. Under the new plan where the company operates for five more years, the probability of increasing the value of assets to meet or exceed the face value of debt is higher than if the company only operates for two more years.

31. a. Using the equation for the PV of a continuously compounded lump sum, we get:

PV = $60,000 × $e^{-.06(5)}$ = $44,449.09

b. Using Black-Scholes model to value the equity, we get:

$d_1$ = [ln($57,000/$60,000) + (.06 + $.50^2/2$) × 5] / (.50 × $\sqrt{5}$) = .7815

$d_2 = .7815 - (.50 \times \sqrt{5}\,) = -.3366$

$N(d_1) = .7827$

$N(d_2) = .3682$

Putting these values into Black-Scholes:

Equity $= \$57,000(.7827) - (\$60,000e^{-.06(5)})(.3682) = \$28,248.84$

And using put-call parity, the price of the put option is:

Put $= \$60,000e^{-.06(5)} + 28,248.84 - 57,000 = \$15,697.93$

c. The value of a risky bond is the value of a risk-free bond minus the value of a put option on the firm's equity, so:

Value of risky bond $= \$44,449.09 - 15,697.93 = \$28,751.16$

Using the equation for the PV of a continuously compounded lump sum to find the return on debt, we get:

$\$28,751.16 = \$60,000e^{-R(5)}$
$.47919 = e^{-R(5)}$
$R_D = -(1/5)\ln(.47919) = .1471$ or $14.71\%$

d. Using the equation for the PV of a continuously compounded lump sum, we get:

PV $= \$60,000 \times e^{-.06(5)} = \$44,449.09$

Using Black-Scholes model to value the equity, we get:

$d_1 = [\ln(\$57,000/\$60,000) + (.06 + .60^2/2) \times 5] / (.60 \times \sqrt{5}\,) = .8562$

$d_2 = .8562 - (.60 \times \sqrt{5}\,) = -.4854$

$N(d_1) = .8041$

$N(d_2) = .3137$

Putting these values into Black-Scholes:

Equity $= \$57,000(.8041) - (\$60,000e^{-.06(5)})(.3137) = \$31,888.34$

And using put-call parity, the price of the put option is:

Put $= \$60,000e^{-.06(5)} + 31,888.34 - 57,000 = \$19,337.44$

The value of a risky bond is the value of a risk-free bond minus the value of a put option on the firm's equity, so:

Value of risky bond $= \$44,449.09 - 19,337.44 = \$25,111.66$

Using the equation for the PV of a continuously compounded lump sum to find the return on debt, we get:

$25,111.66 = $60,000e^{-R(5)}$

$.41853 = e^{-R(5)}$

$R_D = -(1/5)\ln(.41853) = .1742$ or 17.42%

The value of the debt declines. Since the standard deviation of the company's assets increases, the value of the put option on the face value of the bond increases, which decreases the bond's current value.

e. From c and d, bondholders lose: $25,111.66 – 28,751.16 = –$3,639.51
From c and d, stockholders gain: $31,888.34 – 28,248.84 = $3,639.51

This is an agency problem for bondholders. Management, acting to increase shareholder wealth in this manner, will reduce bondholder wealth by the exact amount by which shareholder wealth is increased.

**32.** *a.* Since the equityholders of a firm financed partially with debt can be thought of as holding a call option on the assets of the firm with a strike price equal to the debt's face value and a time to expiration equal to the debt's time to maturity, the value of the company's equity equals a call option with a strike price of $260 million and 1 year until expiration.

In order to value this option using the two-state option model, first draw a tree containing both the current value of the firm and the firm's possible values at the time of the option's expiration. Next, draw a similar tree for the option, designating what its value will be at expiration given either of the 2 possible changes in the firm's value.

The value of the company today is $230 million. It will either increase to $280 million or decrease to $190 million in one year as a result of its new project. If the firm's value increases to $280 million, the equityholders will exercise their call option, and they will receive a payoff of $20 million at expiration. However, if the firm's value decreases to $190 million, the equityholders will not exercise their call option, and they will receive no payoff at expiration.

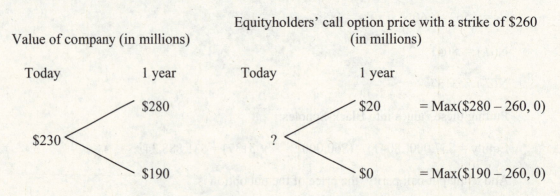

If the project is successful and the company's value rises, the percentage increase in value over the period is 21.74 percent [= ($280 / $230) – 1]. If the project is unsuccessful and the company's value falls, the percentage decrease in value over the period is –17.39 [= ($190 / $230) –1]. We can determine the risk-neutral probability of an increase in the value of the company as:

Risk-free rate = (Probability$_{Rise}$)(Return$_{Rise}$) + (Probability$_{Fall}$)(Return$_{Fall}$)
Risk-free rate = (Probability$_{Rise}$)(Return$_{Rise}$) + (1 − Probability$_{Rise}$)(Return$_{Fall}$)
.07          = (Probability$_{Rise}$)(.2174) + (1 − Probability$_{Rise}$)(−.1739)
Probability$_{Rise}$ = .6233 or 62.33%

And the risk-neutral probability of a decline in the company value is:

Probability$_{Fall}$ = 1 − Probability$_{Rise}$
Probability$_{Fall}$ = 1 − .6233
Probability$_{Fall}$ = .3767 or 37.67%

Using these risk-neutral probabilities, we can determine the expected payoff to the equityholders' call option at expiration, which will be:

Expected payoff at expiration = (.6233)($60,000,000) + (.3767)($0)
Expected payoff at expiration = $12,466,666.67

Since this payoff occurs 1 year from now, we must discount it at the risk-free rate in order to find its present value. So:

PV(Expected payoff at expiration) = ($12,466,666.67 / 1.07)
PV(Expected payoff at expiration) = $11,651,090.34

Therefore, the current value of the company's equity is $11,651,090.34. The current value of the company is equal to the value of its equity plus the value of its debt. In order to find the value of company's debt, subtract the value of the company's equity from the total value of the company:

$V_L$ = Debt + Equity
$230,000,000 = Debt + $11,651,090.34
Debt = $218,348,909.66

b.  To find the price per share, we can divide the total value of the equity by the number of shares outstanding. So, the price per share is:

Price per share = Total equity value / Shares outstanding
Price per share = $11,651,090.34 / 500,000
Price per share = $23.30

c.  The market value of the firm's debt is $218,348,909.66. The present value of the same face amount of riskless debt is $242,990,654.21 (= $260,000,000 / 1.07). The firm's debt is worth less than the present value of riskless debt since there is a risk that it will not be repaid in full. In other words, the market value of the debt takes into account the risk of default. The value of riskless debt is $242,990,654.21. Since there is a chance that the company might not repay its debtholders in full, the debt is worth less than $242,990,654.21.

d.  The value of Strudler today is $230 million. It will either increase to $315 million or decrease to $175 million in one year as a result of the new project. If the firm's value increases to $315 million, the equityholders will exercise their call option, and they will receive a payoff of $55 million at expiration. However, if the firm's value decreases to $175 million, the equityholders will not exercise their call option, and they will receive no payoff at expiration.

|  | | Equityholders' call option price with a strike of $260 |
| Value of company (in millions) | | (in millions) |

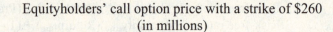

| Today | 1 year | Today | 1 year |

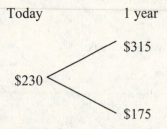

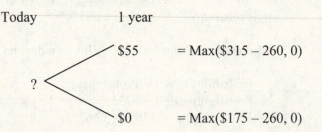

If the project is successful and the company's value rises, the increase in the value of the company over the period is 36.96 percent [= ($315 / $230) – 1]. If the project is unsuccessful and the company's value falls, the decrease in the value of the company over the period is –23.91 percent [= ($175 / $230) –1]. We can use the following expression to determine the risk-neutral probability of an increase in the value of the company:

Risk-free rate = $(\text{Probability}_\text{Rise})(\text{Return}_\text{Rise}) + (\text{Probability}_\text{Fall})(\text{Return}_\text{Fall})$

Risk-free rate = $(\text{Probability}_\text{Rise})(\text{Return}_\text{Rise}) + (1 - \text{Probability}_\text{Rise})(\text{Return}_\text{Fall})$

.07 $= (\text{Probability}_\text{Rise})(.3696) + (1 - \text{Probability}_\text{Rise})(-.2391)$

$\text{Probability}_\text{Rise} = .5079$ or 50.79%

So the risk-neutral probability of a decrease in the company value is:

$\text{Probability}_\text{Fall} = 1 - \text{Probability}_\text{Rise}$

$\text{Probability}_\text{Fall} = 1 - .5079$

$\text{Probability}_\text{Fall} = .4921$ or 49.21%

Using these risk-neutral probabilities, we can determine the expected payoff to the equityholders' call option at expiration, which is:

Expected payoff at expiration = (.5079)($55,000,000) + (.4921)($0)

Expected payoff at expiration = $27,932,142.86

Since this payoff occurs 1 year from now, we must discount it at the risk-free rate in order to find its present value. So:

PV(Expected payoff at expiration) = ($27,932,142.86 / 1.07)

PV(Expected payoff at expiration) = $26,104,806.41

Therefore, the current value of the firm's equity is $26,104,806.41.

The current value of the company is equal to the value of its equity plus the value of its debt. In order to find the value of the company's debt, we can subtract the value of the company's equity from the total value of the company, which yields:

$V_L$ = Debt + Equity

$230,000,000 = Debt + $26,104,806.41

Debt = $203,895,193.59

The riskier project increases the value of the company's equity and decreases the value of the company's debt. If the company takes on the riskier project, the company is less likely to be able to pay off its bondholders. Since the risk of default increases if the new project is undertaken, the value of the company's debt decreases. Bondholders would prefer the company to undertake the more conservative project.

33. *a.* Going back to the chapter on dividends, the price of the stock will decline by the amount of the dividend (less any tax effects). Therefore, we would expect the price of the stock to drop when a dividend is paid, reducing the upside potential of the call by the amount of the dividend. The price of a call option will decrease when the dividend yield increases.

*b.* Using the Black-Scholes model with dividends, we get:

$$d_1 = [\ln(\$93/\$90) + (.05 - .02 + .50^2/2) \times .5] / (.50 \times \sqrt{.5}) = .3119$$

$$d_2 = .3119 - (.50 \times \sqrt{.5}) = -.0416$$

$$N(d_1) = .6225$$

$$N(d_2) = .4834$$

$$C = \$93^{-(.02)(.5)}(.6225) - (\$90e^{-.05(.5)})(.4834) = \$14.88$$

34. *a.* Going back to the chapter on dividends, the price of the stock will decline by the amount of the dividend (less any tax effects). Therefore, we would expect the price of the stock to drop when a dividend is paid. The price of put option will increase when the dividend yield increases.

*b.* Using put-call parity to find the price of the put option, we get:

$$\$93e^{-.02(.5)} + P = \$90e^{-.05(.5)} + 14.88$$
$$P = \$10.58$$

35. $N(d_1)$ is the probability that "$z$" is less than or equal to $N(d_1)$, so $1 - N(d_1)$ is the probability that "$z$" is greater than $N(d_1)$. Because of the symmetry of the normal distribution, this is the same thing as the probability that "$z$" is less than $N(-d_1)$. So:

$$N(d_1) - 1 = -N(-d_1).$$

36. From put-call parity:

$$P = E \times e^{-Rt} + C - S$$

Substituting the Black-Scholes call option formula for $C$ and using the result in the previous question produces the put option formula:

$$P = E \times e^{-Rt} + C - S$$
$$P = E \times e^{-Rt} + S \times N(d_1) - E \times e^{-Rt} \times N(d_2) - S$$
$$P = S \times (N(d_1) - 1) + E \times e^{-Rt} \times (1 - N(d_2))$$
$$P = E \times e^{-Rt} \times N(-d_2) - S \times N(-d_1)$$

**37.** Based on Black-Scholes, the call option is worth $50! The reason is that present value of the exercise price is zero, so the second term disappears. Also, $d_1$ is infinite, so $N(d_1)$ is equal to one. The problem is that the call option is European with an infinite expiration, so why would you pay anything for it since you can *never* exercise it? The paradox can be resolved by examining the price of the stock. Remember that the call option formula only applies to a non-dividend paying stock. If the stock will never pay a dividend, it (and a call option to buy it at any price) must be worthless.

**38.** The delta of the call option is $N(d_1)$ and the delta of the put option is $N(d_1) - 1$. Since you are selling a put option, the delta of the portfolio is $N(d_1) - [N(d_1) - 1]$. This leaves the overall delta of your position as 1. This position will change dollar for dollar in value with the underlying asset. This position replicates the dollar "action" on the underlying asset.

# CHAPTER 23
# OPTIONS AND CORPORATE FINANCE: *EXTENSIONS AND APPLICATIONS*

## Answers to Concepts Review and Critical Thinking Questions

1.  One of the purposes to giving stock options to CEOs (instead of cash) is to tie the performance of the firm's stock with the compensation of the CEO. In this way, the CEO has an incentive to increase shareholder value.

2.  Most businesses have the option to abandon under bad conditions and the option to expand under good conditions.

3.  Virtually all projects have embedded options, which are ignored in NPV calculations and likely leads to undervaluation.

4.  As the volatility increases, the value of an option increases. As the volatility of coal and oil increases, the option to burn either increases. However, if the prices of coal and oil are highly correlated, the value of the option would decline. If coal and oil prices both increase at the same time, the option to switch becomes less valuable since the company will likely save less money.

5.  The advantage is that the value of the land may increase if you wait. Additionally, if you wait, the best use of the land other than sale may become more valuable.

6.  The company has an option to abandon the mine temporarily, which is an American put. If the option is exercised, which the company is doing by not operating the mine, it has an option to reopen the mine when it is profitable, which is an American call. Of course, if the company does reopen the mine, it has another option to abandon the mine again, which is an American put.

7.  Your colleague is correct, but the fact that an increased volatility increases the value of an option is an important part of option valuation. All else the same, a call option on a venture that has a higher volatility will be worth more since the upside potential is greater. Even though the downside is also greater, with an option, the downside is irrelevant since the option will not be exercised and will expire worthless no matter how low the asset falls. With a put option, the reverse is true in that the option becomes more valuable the further the asset falls, and if the asset increases in value, the option is allowed to expire.

8.  Real option analysis is not a technique that can be applied in isolation. The value of the asset in real option analysis is calculated using traditional cash flow techniques, and then real options are applied to the resulting cash flows.

9.  Insurance is a put option. Consider your homeowner's insurance. If your house were to burn down, you would receive the value of the policy from your insurer. In essence, you are selling your burned house ("putting") to the insurance company for the value of the policy (the strike price).

**10.** In a market with competitors, you must realize that the competitors have real options as well. The decisions made by these competitors may often change the payoffs for your company's options. For example, the first entrant into a market can often be rewarded with a larger market share because the name can become synonymous with the product (think of Q-tips and Kleenex). Thus, the option to become the first entrant can be valuable. However, we must also consider that it may be better to be a later entrant in the market. Either way, we must realize that the competitors' actions will affect our options as well.

## Solutions to Questions and Problems

*NOTE: All end-of-chapter problems were solved using a spreadsheet. Many problems require multiple steps. Due to space and readability constraints, when these intermediate steps are included in this solutions manual, rounding may appear to have occurred. However, the final answer for each problem is found without rounding during any step in the problem.*

### Basic

**1.** *a.* The inputs to the Black-Scholes model are the current price of the underlying asset (*S*), the strike price of the option (*E*), the time to expiration of the option in fractions of a year (*t*), the variance ($\sigma^2$) of the underlying asset, and the continuously-compounded risk-free interest rate (R). Since these options were granted at-the-money, the strike price of each option is equal to the current value of one share, or $50. We can use Black-Scholes to solve for the option price. Doing so, we find:

$$d_1 = [\ln(S/K) + (R + \sigma^2/2)(t)] / (\sigma^2 t)^{1/2}$$
$$d_1 = [\ln(\$50/\$50) + (.06 + .56^2/2) \times (5)] / (.56 \times \sqrt{5}) = .8657$$

$$d_2 = .8657 - (.56 \times \sqrt{5}) = -.3865$$

Find N($d_1$) and N($d_2$), the area under the normal curve from negative infinity to $d_1$ and negative infinity to $d_2$, respectively. Doing so:

$$N(d_1) = N(.8657) = .8067$$

$$N(d_2) = N(-.3865) = .3496$$

Now we can find the value of each option, which will be:

$$C = SN(d_1) - Ee^{-Rt}N(d_2)$$
$$C = \$50(.8067) - (\$50e^{-.06(5)})(.3496)$$
$$C = \$27.39$$

Since the option grant is for 30,000 options, the value of the grant is:

Grant value = 30,000($27.39)
Grant value = $821,564.00

b.  Because he is risk-neutral, you should recommend the alternative with the highest net present value. Since the expected value of the stock option package is worth more than $750,000, he would prefer to be compensated with the options rather than with the immediate bonus.

c.  If he is risk-averse, he may or may not prefer the stock option package to the immediate bonus. Even though the stock option package has a higher net present value, he may not prefer it because it is undiversified. The fact that he cannot sell his options prematurely makes it much more risky than the immediate bonus. Therefore, we cannot say which alternative he would prefer.

2.  The total compensation package consists of an annual salary in addition to 15,000 at-the-money stock options. First, we will find the present value of the salary payments. Since the payments occur at the end of the year, the payments can be valued as a three-year annuity, which will be:

PV(Salary) = $410,000(PVIFA$_{9\%,3}$)
PV(Salary) = $1,037,830.81

Next, we can use the Black-Scholes model to determine the value of the stock options. Doing so, we find:

$d_1 = [\ln(S/K) + (R + \sigma^2/2)(t)] / (\sigma^2 t)^{1/2}$
$d_1 = [\ln(\$37/\$37) + (.05 + .65^2/2) \times (3)] / (.65 \times \sqrt{3}) = .6962$

$d_2 = .6962 - (.65 \times \sqrt{3}) = -.4297$

Find N($d_1$) and N($d_2$), the area under the normal curve from negative infinity to $d_1$ and negative infinity to $d_2$, respectively. Doing so:

N($d_1$) = N(.6962) = .7568

N($d_2$) = N(−.4297) = .3337

Now we can find the value of each option, which will be:

$C = SN(d_1) - Ee^{-Rt}N(d_2)$
$C = \$37(.7568) - (\$37e^{-.05(3)})(.3337)$
$C = \$17.38$

Since the option grant is for 15,000 options, the value of the grant is:

Grant value = 15,000($17.38)
Grant value = $260,629.67

The total value of the contract is the sum of the present value of the salary, plus the option value, or:

Contract value = $1,037,830.81 + 260,629.67
Contract value = $1,298,460.48

**3.** Since the contract is to sell up to 5 million gallons, it is a call option, so we need to value the contract accordingly. Using the binomial mode, we will find the value of $u$ and $d$, which are:

$$u = e^{\sigma/\sqrt{n}}$$
$$u = e^{.58/\sqrt{12/3}}$$
$$u = 1.3364$$

$$d = 1/u$$
$$d = 1/1.3364$$
$$d = .7483$$

This implies the percentage increase if gasoline increases will be 33.64 percent, and the percentage decrease if prices fall will be 25.17 percent. So, the price in three months with an up or down move will be:

$$P_{Up} = \$3.30(1.3364)$$
$$P_{Up} = \$4.41$$

$$P_{Down} = \$3.30(.7483)$$
$$P_{Down} = \$2.47$$

The option is worthless if the price decreases. If the price increases, the value of the option per gallon is:

Value with price increase = $4.41 – 3.30
Value with price increase = $.76

Next, we need to find the risk neutral probability of a price increase or decrease, which will be:

.06 / (12/3) = .3364(Probability of rise) + –.2517(1 – Probability of rise)
Probability of rise = .4535

And the probability of a price decrease is:

Probability of decrease = 1 – .4535
Probability of decrease = .5465

The contract will not be exercised if gasoline prices fall, so the value of the contract with a price decrease is zero. So, the value per gallon of the call option contract will be:

$$C = [.4535(\$.76) + .5465(0)] / [1 + .06/(12/3)]$$
$$C = \$.340$$

This means the value of the entire contract is:

Value of contract = $.340(5,000,000)
Value of contract = $1,698,329.31

**4.** When solving a question dealing with real options, begin by identifying the option-like features of the situation. First, since the company will exercise its option to build if the value of an office building rises, the right to build the office building is similar to a call option. Second, an office building would be worth $23.5 million today. This amount can be viewed as the current price of the underlying asset ($S$). Third, it will cost $25 million to construct such an office building. This amount can be viewed as the strike price of a call option ($E$), since it is the amount that the firm must pay in order to 'exercise' its right to erect an office building. Finally, since the firm's right to build on the land lasts only 1 year, the time to expiration ($t$) of the real option is one year. We can use the two-state model to value the option to build on the land. First, we need to find the return of the land if the value rises or falls. The return will be:

$R_{Rise}$ = ($26,800,000 – 23,500,000) / $23,500,000
$R_{Rise}$ = .1404 or 14.04%

$R_{Fall}$ = ($22,000,000 – 23,500,000) / $23,500,000
$R_{Fall}$ = –.0638 or –6.38%

Now we can find the risk-neutral probability of a rise in the value of the building as:

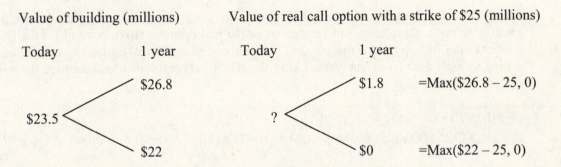

Value of building (millions)          Value of real call option with a strike of $25 (millions)

|          Today          1 year  |  Today          1 year  |

$26.8

$23.5

$22

$1.8     =Max($26.8 – 25, 0)

?

$0     =Max($22 – 25, 0)

Risk-free rate  = (Probability$_{Rise}$)(Return$_{Rise}$) + (Probability$_{Fall}$)(Return$_{Fall}$)
Risk-free rate  = (Probability$_{Rise}$)(Return$_{Rise}$) + (1 – Probability$_{Rise}$)(Return$_{Fall}$)
.048 = (Probability$_{Rise}$)(.1404) + (1 – Probability$_{Rise}$)(–.0638)
Probability$_{Rise}$ = .5475

So, a probability of a fall is:

Probability$_{Fall}$ = 1 – Probability$_{Rise}$
Probability$_{Fall}$ = 1 – .5475
Probability$_{Fall}$ = .4525

Using these risk-neutral probabilities, we can determine the expected payoff of the real option at expiration.

Expected payoff at expiration = (.5475)($1,800,000) + (.4525)($0)
Expected payoff at expiration = $985,500

Since this payoff will occur 1 year from now, it must be discounted at the risk-free rate in order to find its present value, which is:

PV = ($985,500 / 1.048)
PV = $940,362.60

Therefore, the right to build an office building over the next year is worth $940,362.60 today. Since the offer to purchase the land is less than the value of the real option to build, the company should not accept the offer.

5. When solving a question dealing with real options, begin by identifying the option-like features of the situation. First, since the company will only choose to drill and excavate if the price of oil rises, the right to drill on the land can be viewed as a call option. Second, since the land contains 475,000 barrels of oil and the current price of oil is $93 per barrel, the current price of the underlying asset (S) to be used in the Black-Scholes model is:

"Stock" price = 435,000($93)
"Stock" price = $40,455,000

Third, since the company will not drill unless the price of oil in one year will compensate its excavation costs, these costs can be viewed as the real option's strike price (E). Finally, since the winner of the auction has the right to drill for oil in one year, the real option can be viewed as having a time to expiration (t) of one year. Using the Black-Scholes model to determine the value of the option, we find:

$d_1 = [\ln(S/E) + (R + \sigma^2/2)(t)] / (\sigma^2 t)^{1/2}$
$d_1 = [\ln(\$40,455,000/\$75,000,000) + (.04 + .50^2/2) \times (1)] / (.50 \times \sqrt{1}) = -.9046$

$d_2 = -.9046 - (.50 \times \sqrt{1}) = -1.4046$

Find $N(d_1)$ and $N(d_2)$, the area under the normal curve from negative infinity to $d_1$ and negative infinity to $d_2$, respectively. Doing so:

$N(d_1) = N(-.9046) = .1828$

$N(d_2) = N(-1.4046) = .0801$

Now we can find the value of the call option, which will be:

$C = SN(d_1) - Ee^{-Rt}N(d_2)$
$C = \$40,455,000(.1828) - (\$75,000,000e^{-.04(1)})(.0801)$
$C = \$1,626,948.27$

This is the maximum bid the company should be willing to make at auction.

*Intermediate*

**6.** When solving a question dealing with real options, begin by identifying the option-like features of the situation. First, since Sardano will only choose to manufacture the steel rods if the price of steel falls, the lease, which gives the firm the ability to manufacture steel, can be viewed as a put option. Second, since the firm will receive a fixed amount of money if it chooses to manufacture the rods:

Amount received = 55,000 steel rods($29 – 18)
Amount received = $605,000

The amount received can be viewed as the put option's strike price ($E$). Third, since the project requires Sardano to purchase 500 tons of steel and the current price of steel is $670 per ton, the current price of the underlying asset ($S$) to be used in the Black-Scholes formula is:

"Stock" price = 500 tons($670 per ton)
"Stock" price = $335,000

Finally, since Sardano must decide whether to purchase the steel or not in six months, the firm's real option to manufacture steel rods can be viewed as having a time to expiration ($t$) of six months. In order to calculate the value of this real put option, we can use the Black-Scholes model to determine the value of an otherwise identical call option then infer the value of the put using put-call parity. Using the Black-Scholes model to determine the value of the option, we find:

$d_1 = [\ln(S/E) + (R + \sigma^2/2)(t)\,] / (\sigma^2 t)^{1/2}$
$d_1 = [\ln(\$335,000/\$605,000) + (.045 + .45^2/2) \times (6/12)] / (.45 \times \sqrt{6/12}\,) = -1.6278$

$d_2 = -1.6278 - (.45 \times \sqrt{6/12}\,) = -1.9460$

Find $N(d_1)$ and $N(d_2)$, the area under the normal curve from negative infinity to $d_1$ and negative infinity to $d_2$, respectively. Doing so:

$N(d_1) = N(-1.6278) = .0518$

$N(d_2) = N(-1.9460) = .0258$

Now we can find the value of call option, which will be:

$C = SN(d_1) - Ee^{-Rt}N(d_2)$
$C = \$335,000(.0518) - (\$605,000e^{-.045(6/12)})(.0258)$
$C = \$2,069.54$

Now we can use put-call parity to find the price of the put option, which is:

$C = P + S - Ee^{-Rt}$
$\$2,069.54 = P + \$335,000 - \$605,000e^{-.045(6/12)}$
$P = \$258,609.04$

This is the most the company should be willing to pay for the lease.

**7.** In one year, the company will abandon the technology if the demand is low since the value of abandonment is higher than the value of continuing operations. Since the company is selling the technology in this case, the option is a put option. The value of the put option in one year if demand is low will be:

Value of put with low demand = $9,400,000 – 8,000,000
Value of put with low demand = $1,400,000

Of course, if demand is high, the company will not sell the technology, so the put will expire worthless. We can value the put with the binomial model. In one year, the percentage gain on the project if the demand is high will be:

Percentage increase with high demand = ($14,300,000 – 12,900,000) / $12,900,000
Percentage increase with high demand = .1085 or 10.85%

And the percentage decrease in the value of the technology with low demand is:

Percentage decrease with high demand = ($8,000,000 – 12,900,000) / $12,900,000
Percentage decrease with high demand = –.3798 or –37.98%

Now we can find the risk-neutral probability of a rise in the value of the technology as:

Risk-free rate = (Probability$_{Rise}$)(Return$_{Rise}$) + (Probability$_{Fall}$)(Return$_{Fall}$)
Risk-free rate = (Probability$_{Rise}$)(Return$_{Rise}$) + (1 – Probability$_{Rise}$)(Return$_{Fall}$)
.06 = (Probability$_{Rise}$)(.1085) + (1 – Probability$_{Rise}$)(–.3798)
Probability$_{Rise}$ = .9006

So, a probability of a fall is:

Probability$_{Fall}$ = 1 – Probability$_{Rise}$
Probability$_{Fall}$ = 1 – .9006
Probability$_{Fall}$ = .0994

Using these risk-neutral probabilities, we can determine the expected payoff of the real option at expiration. With high demand, the option is worthless since the technology will not be sold, and the value of the technology with low demand is the $1.4 million we calculated previously. So, the value of the option to abandon is:

Value of option to abandon = [(.9006)(0) + (.0994)($1,400,000)] / (1 + .06)
Value of option to abandon = $131,236.90

8. Using the binomial mode, we will find the value of $u$ and $d$, which are:

$u = e^{\sigma/\sqrt{n}}$
$u = e^{.70/\sqrt{12}}$
$u = 1.2239$

$d = 1 / u$
$d = 1 / 1.2239$
$d = .8170$

This implies the percentage increase if the stock price increases will be 22.39 percent and the percentage decrease if the stock price falls will be 18.30 percent. The monthly interest rate is:

Monthly interest rate = .05/12
Monthly interest rate = .0042

Next, we need to find the risk neutral probability of a price increase or decrease, which will be:

.0042 = .2239(Probability of rise) + −.1830(1 − Probability of rise)
Probability of rise = .4599

And the probability of a price decrease is:

Probability of decrease = 1 − .4599
Probability of decrease = .5401

The following figure shows the stock price and put price for each possible move over the next two months:

|  |  |
|---|---|
| Stock price (D) | $109.36 |
| Put price | $ 0 |

| Stock price (B) | $89.35 |
|---|---|
| Put price | $ 3.77 |

| Stock price(A) | $73.00 |
|---|---|
| Put price | $12.49 |

| Stock price (E) | $ 73.00 |
|---|---|
| Put price | $ 7.00 |

| Stock price (C) | $59.64 |
|---|---|
| Put price | $20.02 |

| Stock price (F) | $ 48.73 |
|---|---|
| Put price | $ 31.27 |

The stock price at node (A) is the current stock price. The stock price at node (B) is from an up move, which means:

Stock price (B) = $73(1.2239)
Stock price (B) = $89.35

And the stock price at node (D) is two up moves, or:

Stock price (D) = $73(1.2239)(1.2239)
Stock price (D) = $109.36

The stock price at node (C) is from a down move, or:

Stock price (C) = $73(.8170)
Stock price (C) = $59.64

And the stock price at node (F) is two down moves, or:

Stock price (F) = $73(.8170)(.8170)
Stock price (F) = $48.73

Finally, the stock price at node (E) is from an up move followed by a down move, or a down move followed by an up move. Since the binomial tree recombines, both calculations yield the same result, which is:

Stock price (E) = $73(1.2239)(.8170) = $73(.8170)(1.2239)
Stock price (E) = $73.00

Now we can value the put option at the expiration nodes, namely (D), (E), and (F). The value of the put option at these nodes is the maximum of the strike price minus the stock price, or zero. So:

Put value (D) = Max($80 – 109.36, $0)
Put value (D) = $0

Put value (E) = Max($80 – 73, $0)
Put value (E) = $7

Put value (F) = Max($80 – 48.73, $0)
Put value (F) = $31.27

The value of the put at node (B) is the present value of the expected value. We find the expected value by using the value of the put at nodes (D) and (E) since those are the only two possible stock prices after node (B). So, the value of the put at node (B) is:

Put value (B) = [.4599($0) + .5401($7)] / 1.0042
Put value (B) = $3.77

Similarly, the value of the put at node (C) is the present value of the expected value of the put at nodes (E) and (F) since those are the only two possible stock prices after node (C). So, the value of the put at node (C) is:

Put value (C) = [.4599($7) + .5401($31.27)] / 1.0042
Put value (C) = $20.02

Using the put values at nodes (B) and (C), we can now find the value of the put today, which is:

Put value (A) = [.4599($3.77) + .5401($20.02)] / 1.0042
Put value (A) = $12.49

*Challenge*

9.  Since the exercise style is now American, the option can be exercised prior to expiration. At node (B), we would not want to exercise the put option since it would be out of the money at that stock price. However, if the stock price falls next month, the value of the put option if exercised is:

Value if exercised = $80 – 59.64
Value if exercised = $20.36

This is greater then the present value of waiting one month, so the option will be exercised early in one month if the stock price falls. This is the value of the put option at node (C). Using this put value, we can now find the value of the put today, which is:

Put value (A) = [.4599($3.77) + .5401($20.36)] / 1.0042
Put value (A) = $12.67

This is slightly higher than the value of the same option with a European exercise style. An American option must be worth at least as much as a European option, and can be worth more. Remember, an option always has value until it is exercised. The option to exercise early in an American option is itself an option, therefore it often has some value.

10. Using the binomial mode, we will find the value of $u$ and $d$, which are:

$$u = e^{\sigma/\sqrt{n}}$$
$$u = e^{.30/\sqrt{1/2}}$$
$$u = 1.2363$$

$$d = 1 / u$$
$$d = 1 / 1.2363$$
$$d = .8089$$

This implies the percentage increase is if the stock price increases will be 23.63 percent, and the percentage decrease if the stock price falls will be 19.11 percent. The six month interest rate is:

Six month interest rate = .06/2
Six month interest rate = .03

Next, we need to find the risk neutral probability of a price increase or decrease, which will be:

.03 = .2363(Probability of rise) + −.1911(1 − Probability of rise)
Probability of rise = .5173

And the probability of a price decrease is:

Probability of decrease = 1 − .5173
Probability of decrease = .4827

The following figure shows the stock price and call price for each possible move over each of the six month steps:

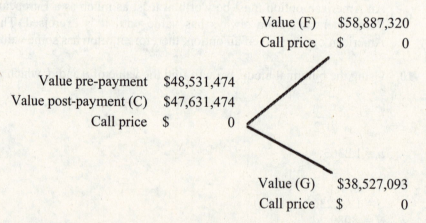

|  | Value (D) | $90,595,230 |
|---|---|---|
|  | Call price | $28,707,910 |

| Value pre-payment | $74,178,667 |
|---|---|
| Value post-payment (B) | $73,278,667 |
| Call price | $14,419,400 |

|  | Value (E) | $59,272,028 |
|---|---|---|
|  | Call price | $ 0 |

| Stock price(A) | $60,000,000 |
|---|---|
| Call price | $ 7,242,572 |

|  | Value (F) | $58,887,320 |
|---|---|---|
|  | Call price | $ 0 |

| Value pre-payment | $48,531,474 |
|---|---|
| Value post-payment (C) | $47,631,474 |
| Call price | $ 0 |

|  | Value (G) | $38,527,093 |
|---|---|---|
|  | Call price | $ 0 |

First, we need to find the building value at every step along the binomial tree. The building value at node (A) is the current building value. The building value at node (B) is from an up move, which means:

Building value (B) = $60,000,000(1.2363)
Building value (B) = $74,178,667

At node (B), the accrued rent payment will be made, so the value of the building after the payment will be reduced by the amount of the payment, which means the building value at node (B) is:

Building value (B) after payment = $74,178,667 – 900,000
Building value (B) after payment = $73,278,667

To find the building value at node (D), we multiply the after-payment building value at node (B) by the up move, or:

Building value (D) = $73,278,667(1.2363)
Building value (D) = $90,595,230

To find the building value at node (E), we multiply the after-payment building value at node (B) by the down move, or:

Building value (E) = $73,278,667(.8089)
Building value (E) = $59,272,028

The building value at node (C) is from a down move, which means the building value will be:

Building value (E) = $60,000,000(.8089)
Building value (E) = $48,531,474

At node (C), the accrued rent payment will be made, so the value of the building after the payment will be reduced by the amount of the payment, which means the building value at node (C) is:

Building value (C) after payment = $48,531,474 – 900,000
Building value (C) after payment = $47,631,474

To find the building value at node (F), we multiply the after-payment building value at node (C) by the down move, or:

Building value (F) = $47,631,474(1.2363)
Building value (F) = $58,887,320

Finally, the building value at node (G) is from a down move from node (C), so the building value is:

Building value (G) = $47,631,474(.8089)
Building value (G) = $38,527,093

Note that because of the accrued rent payment in six months, the binomial tree does not recombine during the next step. This occurs whenever a fixed payment is made during a binomial tree. For example, when using a binomial tree for a stock option, a fixed dividend payment will mean that the tree does not recombine. With the expiration values, we can value the call option at the expiration nodes, namely (D), (E), (F), and (G). The value of the call option at these nodes is the maximum of the building value minus the strike price, or zero. We do not need to account for the value of the building after the accrued rent payments in this case since if the option is exercised, you will receive the rent payment. So:

Call value (D) = Max($90,595,230 – 63,000,000, $0)
Call value (D) = $27,595,230

Call value (E) = Max($59,272,028 – 63,000,000, $0)
Call value (E) = $0

Call value (F) = Max($58,887,320 – 63,000,000, $0)
Call value (F) = $0

Call value (G) = Max($38,527,093 – 63,000,000, $0)
Call value (G) = $0

The value of the call at node (B) is the present value of the expected value. We find the expected value by using the value of the call at nodes (D) and (E) since those are the only two possible building values after node (B). So, the value of the call at node (B) is:

Call value (B) = [.5173($27,595,230) + .4827($0)] / 1.03
Call value (B) = $13,860,524

Note that you would not want to exercise the option early at node (B). The value of the option at node (B) if exercised is the value of the building including the accrued rent payment minus the strike price, or:

Option value at node (B) if exercised = $74,178,667 – 63,000,000
Option value at node (B) if exercised = $11,178,667

Since this is less than the value of the option if it left "alive", the option will not be exercised. With a call option, unless a large cash payment (dividend) is made, it is generally not valuable to exercise the call option early. The reason is that the potential gain is unlimited. In contrast, the potential gain on a put option is limited by the strike price, so it may be valuable to exercise an American put option early if it is deep in the money.

We can value the call at node (C), which will be the present value of the expected value of the call at nodes (F) and (G) since those are the only two possible building values after node (C). Since neither node has a value greater than zero, obviously the value of the option at node (C) will also be zero. Now we need to find the value of the option today, which is:

Call value (A) = [.5173($13,860,524) + .4827($0)] / 1.03
Call value (A) = $6,961,860

# CHAPTER 24
# WARRANTS AND CONVERTIBLES

**Answers to Concepts Review and Critical Thinking Questions**

1.  A warrant is issued by the company, and when a warrant is exercised, the number of shares increases. A call option is a contract between investors and does not affect the number of shares of the firm.

2.  *a.*  If the stock price is less than the exercise price of the warrant at expiration, the warrant is worthless. Prior to expiration, however, the warrant will have value as long as there is some probability that the stock price will rise above the exercise price in the time remaining until expiration. Therefore, if the stock price is below the exercise price of the warrant, the lower bound on the price of the warrant is zero.

    *b.*  If the stock price is above the exercise price of the warrant, the warrant must be worth at least the difference between these two prices. If warrants were selling for less than the difference between the current stock price and the exercise price, an investor could earn an arbitrage profit (i.e. an immediate cash inflow) by purchasing warrants, exercising them immediately, and selling the stock.

    *c.*  If the warrant is selling for more than the stock, it would be cheaper to purchase the stock than to purchase the warrant, which gives its owner the right to buy the stock. Therefore, an upper bound on the price of any warrant is the firm's current stock price.

3.  An increase in the stock price volatility increases the bond price. If the stock price becomes more volatile, the conversion option on the stock becomes more valuable.

4.  The two components of the value of a convertible bond are the straight bond value and the option value. An increase in interest rates decreases the straight value component of the convertible bond. Conversely, an increase in interest rates increases the value of the equity call option. Generally, the effect on the straight bond value will be much greater, so we would expect the bond value to fall, although not as much as the decrease in a comparable straight bond.

5.  When warrants are exercised the number of shares outstanding increases. This results in the value of the firm being spread out over a larger number of shares, often leading to a decrease in value of each individual share. The decrease in the per-share price of a company's stock due to a greater number of shares outstanding is known as dilution.

6.  In an efficient capital market the difference between the market value of a convertible bond and the value of straight bond is the fair price investors pay for the call option that the convertible or the warrant provides.

7.  There are three potential reasons: 1) To match cash flows, that is, they issue securities whose cash flows match those of the firm. 2) To bypass assessing the risk of the company (risk synergy). For example, the risk of company start-ups is hard to evaluate. 3) To reduce agency costs associated with raising money by providing a package that reduces bondholder-stockholder conflicts.

24-1

8. Because the holder of the convertible has the option to wait and perhaps do better than what is implied by current stock prices.

9. Theoretically conversion should be forced as soon as the conversion value reaches the call price because other conversion policies will reduce shareholder value. If conversion is forced when conversion values are above the call price, bondholders will be allowed to exchange less valuable bonds for more valuable common stock. In the opposite situation, shareholders are giving bondholders the excess value.

10. No, the market price of the warrant will not equal zero. Since there is a chance that the market price of the stock will rise above the $31 per share exercise price before expiration, the warrant still has some value. Its market price will be greater than zero. As a practical matter, warrants that are far out-of-the-money may sell at 0, due to transaction costs.

## Solutions to Questions and Problems

*NOTE: All end-of-chapter problems were solved using a spreadsheet. Many problems require multiple steps. Due to space and readability constraints, when these intermediate steps are included in this solutions manual, rounding may appear to have occurred. However, the final answer for each problem is found without rounding during any step in the problem.*

### *Basic*

1. The conversion price is the par value divided by the conversion ratio, or:

   Conversion price = $1,000 / 24.6
   Conversion price = $40.65

2. The conversion ratio is the par value divided by the conversion price, or:

   Conversion ratio = $1,000 / $61.50
   Conversion ratio = 16.26

3. First, we need to find the conversion price, which is the par value divided by the conversion ratio, or:

   Conversion price = $1,000 / 17.50
   Conversion price = $57.14

   The conversion premium is the necessary increase in stock price to make the bond convertible. So, the conversion premium is:

   Conversion premium = ($57.14 – 48.53) /$48.53
   Conversion premium = 0.1775 or 17.75%

4. *a.* The conversion ratio is defined as the number of shares that will be issued upon conversion. Since each bond is convertible into 21.50 shares of Hannon's common stock, the conversion ratio of the convertible bonds is 21.50.

b.  The conversion price is defined as the face amount of a convertible bond that the holder must surrender in order to receive a single share. Since the conversion ratio indicates that each bond is convertible into 21.50 shares, the conversion price is:

Conversion price = $1,000 / 21.50
Conversion price = $46.51

c.  The conversion premium is defined as the percentage difference between the conversion price of the convertible bonds and the current stock price. So, the conversion premium is:

Conversion premium = ($46.51 – 37.15) /$37.15
Conversion premium = 0.2520 or 25.20%

d.  The conversion value is defined as the amount that each convertible bond would be worth if it were immediately converted into common stock. So, the conversion value is:

Conversion value = $37.15(21.50)
Conversion value = $798.73

e.  If the stock price increases by $2, the new conversion value will be:

Conversion value = $39.15(21.50)
Conversion value = $841.73

5.  The total exercise price of each warrant is shares each warrant can purchase times the exercise price, which in this case will be:

Exercise price = 3($53)
Exercise price = $159

Since the shares of stock are selling at $58, the value of three shares is:

Value of shares = 3($58)
Value of shares = $174

Therefore, the warrant effectively gives its owner the right to buy $174 worth of stock for $159. It follows that the minimum value of the warrant is the difference between these numbers, or:

Minimum warrant value = $174 – 159
Minimum warrant value = $15

If the warrant were selling for less than $15, an investor could earn an arbitrage profit by purchasing the warrant, exercising it immediately, and selling the stock. Here, the warrant holder pays less than $15 while receiving the $15 difference between the price of three shares and the exercise price.

**6.** Since a convertible bond gives its holder the right to a fixed payment plus the right to convert, it must be worth at least as much as its straight value. Therefore, if the market value of a convertible bond is less than its straight value, there is an opportunity to make an arbitrage profit by purchasing the bond and holding it until expiration. In Scenario A, the market value of the convertible bond is $1,000. Since this amount is greater than the convertible's straight value ($900), Scenario A is feasible. In Scenario B, the market value of the convertible bond is $900. Since this amount is less than the convertible's straight value ($950), Scenario B is not feasible.

**7.**   *a.*   Using the conversion price, we can determine the conversion ratio, which is:

Conversion ratio = $1,000 / $51
Conversion ratio = 19.61

So, each bond can be exchanged for 19.61 shares of stock. This means the conversion price of the bond is:

Conversion price = 19.61($44)
Conversion price = $862.75

Therefore, the minimum price the bond should sell for is $862.75. Since the bond price is higher than this price, the bond is selling at the straight value, plus a premium for the conversion feature.

   *b.*   A convertible bond gives its owner the right to convert his bond into a fixed number of shares. The market price of a convertible bond includes a premium over the value of immediate conversion that accounts for the possibility of increases in the price of the firm's stock before the maturity of the bond. If the stock price rises, a convertible bondholder will convert and receive valuable shares of equity. If the stock price decreases, the convertible bondholder holds the bond and retains his right to a fixed interest and principal payments.

**8.** You can convert or tender the bond (i.e., surrender the bond in exchange for the call price). If you convert, you get stock worth 24.25 × $48 = $1,164. If you tender, you get $1,100 (110 percent of par). It's a no-brainer: convert.

**9.**   *a.*   Since the stock price is currently below the exercise price of the warrant, the lower bound on the price of the warrant is zero. If there is only a small probability that the firm's stock price will rise above the exercise price of the warrant, the warrant has little value. An upper bound on the price of the warrant is $51, the current price of the common stock. One would never pay more than $51 to receive the right to purchase a share of the company's stock if the firm's stock were only worth $51.

   *b.*   If the stock is trading for $58 per share, the lower bound on the price of the warrant is $3, the difference between the current stock price and the warrant's exercise price. If warrants were selling for less than this amount, an investor could earn an arbitrage profit by purchasing warrants, exercising them immediately, and selling the stock. As always, the upper bound on the price of a warrant is the current stock price. In this case, one would never pay more than $58 for the right to buy a single share of stock when he could purchase a share outright for $58.

_Intermediate_

**10.** *a.* The minimum convertible bond value is the greater of the conversion price or the straight bond price. To find the conversion price of the bond, we need to determine the conversion ratio, which is:

Conversion ratio = $1,000 / $93
Conversion ratio = 10.75

So, each bond can be exchanged for 10.75 shares of stock. This means the conversion price of the bond is:

Conversion price = 10.75($28)
Conversion price = $301.08

And the straight bond value is:

$P = \$30(\{1 - [1/(1 + .035)]^{60}\} / .035) + \$1,000[1 / (1 + .035)^{60}]$
$P = \$875.28$

So, the minimum price of the bond is $875.28

*b.* If the stock price were growing by 11 percent per year forever, each share of its stock would be worth approximately $28(1.11)$^t$ after $t$ years. Since each bond is convertible into 10.75 shares, the conversion value of the bond equals ($28)(10.75)(1.11)$^t$ after $t$ years. In order to calculate the number of years that it will take for the conversion value to equal $1,100, set up the following equation:

($28)(10.75)(1.11)$^t$ = $1,100
$t$ = 12.42 years

**11.** *a.* The percentage of the company stock currently owned by the CEO is:

Percentage of stock = 950,000 / 6,000,000
Percentage of stock = .1583 or 15.83%

*b.* The conversion price indicates that for every $38 of face value of convertible bonds outstanding, the company will be obligated to issue a new share upon conversion. So, the new number of shares the company must issue will be:

New shares issued = $40,000,000 / $38
New shares issued = 1,052,631.58

So, the new number of shares of company stock outstanding will be:

New total shares = 6,000,000 + 1,052,631.58
New total shares = 7,052,631.58

After the conversion, the percentage of company stock owned by the CEO will be:

New percentage of stock = 950,000 / 7,052,631.58
New percentage of stock = .1347 or 13.47%

**12.** *a.* Before the warrant was issued, the firm's assets were worth:

Value of assets = 9 oz of platinum($1,750 per oz)
Value of assets = $15,750

So, the price per share is:

Price per share = $15,750 / 8
Price per share = $1,968.75

*b.* When the warrant was issued, the firm received $1,750, increasing the total value of the firm's assets to $17,500 (= $15,750 + 1,750). If the 8 shares of common stock were the only outstanding claims on the firm's assets, each share would be worth $2,187.50 (= $17,500 / 8 shares). However, since the warrant gives a warrant holder a claim on the firm's assets worth $1,750, the value of the firm's assets available to stockholders is only $15,750 (= $17,500 − 1,750). Since there are 8 shares outstanding, the value per share remains at $1,968.75 (= $15,750 / 8 shares) after the warrant issue. Note that the firm uses the warrant price of $1,750 to purchase one more ounce of platinum.

*c.* If the price of platinum is $1,950 per ounce, the total value of the firm's assets is $19,500 (= 10 oz of platinum × $1,950 per oz). If the warrant is not exercised, the value of the firm's assets would remain at $19,500 and there would be 8 shares of common stock outstanding, so the stock price would be $2,437.50. If the warrant is exercised, the firm would receive the warrant's $2,000 strike price and issue one share of stock. The total value of the firm's assets would increase to $21,500 (= $19,500 + 2,000). Since there would now be 9 shares outstanding and no warrants, the price per share would be $2,388.89 (= $21,500 / 9 shares). Since the $2,437.50 value of the share that the warrant holder will receive is greater than the $2,000 exercise price of the warrant, investors will expect the warrant to be exercised. The firm's stock price will reflect this information and will be priced at $2,388.89 per share on the warrant's expiration date.

**13.** The value of the company's assets is the combined value of the stock and the warrants. So, the value of the company's assets before the warrants are exercised is:

Company value = 20,000,000($25) + 1,500,000($7)
Company value = $510,500,000

When the warrants are exercised, the value of the company will increase by the number of warrants times the exercise price, or:

Value increase = 1,500,000($19)
Value increase = $28,500,000

So, the new value of the company is:

New company value = $51,500,000 + 28,500,000
New company value = $539,000,000

This means the new stock price is:

New stock price = $539,000,000 / 21,500,000
New stock price = $25.07

Note that since the warrants were exercised when the price per warrant ($7) was above the exercise value of each warrant ($6 = $25 – 19), the stockholders gain and the warrant holders lose.

*Challenge*

14. The straight bond value today is:

Straight bond value = $58(PVIFA$_{9\%,20}$) + $1,000/1.09$^{20}$
Straight bond value = $707.89

And the conversion value of the bond today is:

Conversion value = $32.20($1,000/$150)
Conversion value = $214.67

We expect the bond to be called when the conversion value increases to $1,250, so we need to find the number of periods it will take for the current conversion value to reach the expected value at which the bond will be converted. Doing so, we find:

$214.67(1.12)$^{t}$ = $1,250
$t$ = 15.55 years.

The bond will be called in 15.55 years.

The bond value is the present value of the expected cash flows. The cash flows will be the annual coupon payments plus the conversion price. The present value of these cash flows is:

Bond value = $58(PVIFA$_{9\%,15.55}$) + $1,250/1.09$^{15.55}$ = $803.05

15. The value of a single warrant (W) equals:

$W = [\# / (\# + \#_W)] \times \text{Call}\{S = (V/\#), E = E_W\}$

where:

| | |
|---|---|
| $\#$ | = the number of shares of common stock outstanding |
| $\#_W$ | = the number of warrants outstanding |
| Call$\{S, E\}$ | = a call option on an underlying asset worth $S$ with a strike price $E$ |
| $V$ | = the firm's value net of debt |
| $E_W$ | = the strike price of each warrant |

Therefore, the value of a single warrant (W) equals:

W = [# / (# + #$_W$)] × Call{S = (V/ #), E = E$_W$}
 = [7,000,000 / (7,000,000 + 900,000) × Call{S = ($165,000,000 / 7,000,000), E = $25}
 = (.8861) × Call(S = $23.57, E = $25)

In order to value the call option, use the Black-Scholes formula. Solving for d$_1$ and d$_2$, we find

$d_1 = [\ln(S/E) + (R + ½σ^2)(t) ] / (σ^2 t)^{1/2}$
$d_1 = [\ln($23.57/25) + \{0.07 + ½(0.20)\}(1) ] / (0.20×1)^{1/2}$
$d_1 = 0.2486$

$d_2 = d_1 - (σ^2 t)^{1/2}$
$d_2 = 0.2486 - (0.20 × 1)^{1/2}$
$d_2 = -0.1987$

Next, we need to find N(d$_1$) and N(d$_2$), the area under the normal curve from negative infinity to d$_1$ and negative infinity to d$_2$, respectively.

N(d$_1$) = N(0.2486) = 0.5981

N(d$_2$) = N(–0.1987) = 0.4213

According to the Black-Scholes formula, the price of a European call option (C) on a non-dividend paying common stock is:

$C = SN(d_1) - Ee^{-Rt}N(d_2)$
$C = ($23.57)(0.5981) - (25)e^{-0.07(1)} (0.4213)$
$C = $4.28$

Therefore, the price of a single warrant (W) equals:

W = (.8861) × Call(S = $23.57, E = $25)
W = (.8861)($4.28)
W = $3.79

16. To calculate the number of warrants that the company should issue in order to pay off $18 million in six months, we can use the Black-Scholes model to find the price of a single warrant, then divide this amount into the present value of $18 million to find the number of warrants to be issued. So, the value of the liability today is:

PV of liability = $18,000,000$e^{-.06(6/12)}$
PV of liability = $17,468,019.60

The company must raise this amount from the warrant issue.

The value of the company's assets will increase by the amount of the warrant issue after the issue, but this increase in value from the warrant issue is exactly offset by the bond issue. Since the cash inflow from the warrants offsets the firm's debt, the value of the warrants will be exactly the same as if the cash from the warrants were used to immediately pay off the debt. We can use the market value of the company's assets to find the current stock price, which is:

Stock price = $240,000,000 / 2,700,000
Stock price = $88.89

The value of a single warrant (W) equals:

W = [# / (# + #$_W$)] × Call(S, K)
W = [2,700,000 / (2,700,000 + #$_W$)] × Call($88.89, $95)

Since the firm must raise $17,468,019.60 as a result of the warrant issue, we know #$_W$ × W must equal $17,468,019.60.

Therefore, it can be stated that:

$17,468,019.60 = (#$_W$)(W)
$17,468,019.60 = (#$_W$)([2,700,000 / (2,700,000 +#$_W$)] × Call($88.89, $95)

Using the Black-Scholes formula to value the warrant, which is a call option, we find:

$d_1 = [\ln(S/K) + (R + \frac{1}{2}\sigma^2)(t)\,]\,/\,(\sigma^2 t)^{1/2}$
$d_1 = [\ln($88.89\,/\,$95) + \{.06 + \frac{1}{2}(.50^2)\}(6\,/\,12)\,]\,/\,(.50^2 \times 6\,/\,12)^{1/2}$
$d_1 = .0736$

$d_2 = d_1 - (\sigma^2 t)^{1/2}$
$d_2 = .0736 - (.50^2 \times 6\,/\,12)^{1/2}$
$d_2 = -.2800$

Next, we need to find N($d_1$) and N($d_2$), the area under the normal curve from negative infinity to $d_1$ and negative infinity to $d_2$, respectively.

N($d_1$) = N(.0736) = 0.5293

N($d_2$) = N(−.2800) = 0.3897

According to the Black-Scholes formula, the price of a European call option (C) on a non-dividend paying common stock is:

$C = SN(d_1) - Ee^{-Rt}N(d_2)$
$C = ($88.89)(0.5293) - ($95)e^{-0.06(6/12)}(0.3897)$
$C = $11.12$

Using this value in the equation above, we find the number of warrants the company must sell is:

$17,468,019.60 = (#$_W$)([2,700,000 / (2,700,000 +#$_W$)] × Call($88.89, $95)
$17,468,019.60 = (#$_W$) [2,700,000 / (2,700,000 +#$_W$)] × $11.12
#$_W$ = 3,756,683

# CHAPTER 25
# DERIVATIVES AND HEDGING RISK

**Answers to Concepts Review and Critical Thinking Questions**

1.  Since the firm is selling futures, it wants to be able to deliver the lumber; therefore, it is a supplier. Since a decline in lumber prices would reduce the income of a lumber supplier, it has hedged its price risk by selling lumber futures. Losses in the spot market due to a fall in lumber prices are offset by gains on the short position in lumber futures.

2.  Buying call options gives the firm the right to purchase pork bellies; therefore, it must be a consumer of pork bellies. While a rise in pork belly prices is bad for the consumer, this risk is offset by the gain on the call options; if pork belly prices actually decline, the consumer enjoys lower costs, while the call option expires worthless.

3.  Forward contracts are usually designed by the parties involved for their specific needs and are rarely sold in the secondary market, so forwards are somewhat customized financial contracts. All gains and losses on the forward position are settled at the maturity date. Futures contracts are standardized to facilitate liquidity and to allow them to be traded on organized futures exchanges. Gains and losses on futures are marked-to-market daily. Default risk is greatly reduced with futures since the exchange acts as an intermediary between the two parties, guaranteeing performance. Default risk is also reduced because the daily settlement procedure keeps large loss positions from accumulating. You might prefer to use forwards instead of futures if your hedging needs were different from the standard contract size and maturity dates offered by the futures contract.

4.  The firm is hurt by declining oil prices, so it should sell oil futures contracts. The firm may not be able to create a perfect hedge because the quantity of oil it needs to hedge doesn't match the standard contract size on crude oil futures, or perhaps the exact settlement date the company requires isn't available on these futures. Also, the firm may produce a different grade of crude oil than that specified for delivery in the futures contract.

5.  The firm is directly exposed to fluctuations in the price of natural gas since it is a natural gas user. In addition, the firm is indirectly exposed to fluctuations in the price of oil. If oil becomes less expensive relative to natural gas, its competitors will enjoy a cost advantage relative to the firm.

6.  Buying the call options is a form of insurance policy for the firm. If cotton prices rise, the firm is protected by the call, while if prices actually decline, they can just allow the call to expire worthless. However, options hedges are costly because of the initial premium that must be paid. The futures contract can be entered into at no initial cost, with the disadvantage that the firm is locking in one price for cotton; it can't profit from cotton price declines.

7.  The put option on the bond gives the owner the right to sell the bond at the option's strike price. If bond prices decline, the owner of the put option profits. However, since bond prices and interest rates move in opposite directions, if the put owner profits from a decline in bond prices, he would also profit from a rise in interest rates. Hence, a call option on interest rates is conceptually the same thing as a put option on bond prices.

8. The company would like to lock in the current low rates, or at least be protected from a rise in rates, allowing for the possibility of benefit if rates actually fall. The former hedge could be implemented by selling bond futures; the latter could be implemented by buying put options on bond prices or buying call options on interest rates.

9. A swap contract is an agreement between parties to exchange assets over several time intervals in the future. The swap contract is usually an exchange of cash flows, but not necessarily so. Since a forward contract is also an agreement between parties to exchange assets in the future, but at a single point in time, a swap can be viewed as a series of forward contracts with different settlement dates. The firm participating in the swap agreement is exposed to the default risk of the dealer, in that the dealer may not make the cash flow payments called for in the contract. The dealer faces the same risk from the contracting party, but can more easily hedge its default risk by entering into an offsetting swap agreement with another party.

10. The firm will borrow at a fixed rate of interest, receive fixed rate payments from the dealer as part of the swap agreement, and make floating rate payments back to the dealer; the net position of the firm is that it has effectively borrowed at floating rates.

11. Transaction exposure is the short-term exposure due to uncertain prices in the near future. Economic exposure is the long-term exposure due to changes in overall economic conditions. There are a variety of instruments available to hedge transaction exposure, but very few long-term hedging instruments exist. It is much more difficult to hedge against economic exposure, since fundamental changes in the business generally must be made to offset long-run changes in the economic environment.

12. The risk is that the dollar will strengthen relative to the yen, since the fixed yen payments in the future will be worth fewer dollars. Since this implies a decline in the $/¥ exchange rate, the firm should sell yen futures. The way the interest rate is quoted will affect the calculation of which currency is strengthening.

13. *a.* Buy oil and natural gas futures contracts, since these are probably your primary resource costs. If it is a coal-fired plant, a cross-hedge might be implemented by selling natural gas futures, since coal and natural gas prices are somewhat negatively related in the market; coal and natural gas are somewhat substitutable.
    *b.* Buy sugar and cocoa futures, since these are probably your primary commodity inputs.
    *c.* Sell corn futures, since a record harvest implies low corn prices.
    *d.* Buy silver and platinum futures, since these are primary commodity inputs required in the manufacture of photographic film.
    *e.* Sell natural gas futures, since excess supply in the market implies low prices.
    *f.* Assuming the bank doesn't resell its mortgage portfolio in the secondary market, buy bond futures.
    *g.* Sell stock index futures, using an index most closely associated with the stocks in your fund, such as the S&P 100 or the Major Market Index for large blue-chip stocks.
    *h.* Buy Swiss franc futures, since the risk is that the dollar will weaken relative to the franc over the next six months, which implies a rise in the $/SFr exchange rate.
    *i.* Sell euro futures, since the risk is that the dollar will strengthen relative to the Euro over the next three months, which implies a decline in the $/€ exchange rate.

14. Sysco must have felt that the combination of fixed plus swap would result in an overall better rate. In other words, the variable rate available via a swap may have been more attractive than the rate available from issuing a floating-rate bond.

15. He is a little naïve about the capabilities of hedging. While hedging can significantly reduce the risk of changes in foreign exchange markets, it cannot completely eliminate it. Basis risk is the primary reason that hedging cannot reduce 100% of any firm's exposure to price fluctuations. Basis risk arises when the price movements of the hedging instrument do not perfectly match the price movements of the asset being hedged.

16. Kevin will be hurt if the yen loses value relative to the dollar over the next eight months. Depreciation in the yen relative to the dollar results in a decrease in the ¥/$ exchange rate. Since Kevin is hurt by a decrease in the exchange rate, he should take on a short position in yen per dollar futures contracts to hedge his risk.

## Solutions to Questions and Problems

*NOTE: All end of chapter problems were solved using a spreadsheet. Many problems require multiple steps. Due to space and readability constraints, when these intermediate steps are included in this solutions manual, rounding may appear to have occurred. However, the final answer for each problem is found without rounding during any step in the problem.*

### Basic

1. The initial price is $2,414 per metric ton and each contract is for 10 metric tons, so the initial contract value is:

   Initial contract value = ($2,414 per ton)(10 tons per contract) = $24,140

   And the final contract value is:

   Final contract value = ($2,431 per ton)(10 tons per contract) = $24,310

   You will have a gain on this futures position of:

   Gain on futures contract = $24,310 – 24,140 = $170

2. The price quote is $31.187 per ounce and each contract is for 5,000 ounces, so the initial contract value is:

   Initial contract value = ($31.187 per oz.)(5,000 oz. per contract) = $155,935

   At a final price of $31.39 per ounce, the value of the position is:

   Final contract value = ($31.39 per oz.)(5,000 oz. per contract) = $156,950

   Since this is a short position, there is a net loss of:

   5,000($31.39 – 31.187) = $1,015 per contract

   Since you sold five contracts, the net loss is:

   Net loss = 5($1,015) = $5,075

At a final price of $30.86 per ounce, the value of the position is:

Final contract value = ($30.86 per oz.)(5,000 oz. per contract) = $154,300

Since this is a short position, there is a net gain of:

5,000($31.187 – 30.86) = $1,635 per contract

Since you sold five contracts, the net gain is:

Net gain = 5($1,635) = $8,175

With a short position, you make a profit when the price falls, and incur a loss when the price rises.

3.  The call options give the manager the right to purchase oil futures contracts at a futures price of $95 per barrel. The manager will exercise the option if the price rises above $95. Selling put options obligates the manager to buy oil futures contracts at a futures price of $95 per barrel. The put holder will exercise the option if the price falls below $95. The payoffs per barrel are:

| Oil futures price: | $90 | $92 | $95 | $98 | $100 |
|---|---|---|---|---|---|
| Value of call option position: | 0 | 0 | 0 | 3 | 5 |
| Value of put option position: | –5 | –3 | 0 | 0 | 0 |
| Total value: | –$ 5 | –$ 3 | $ 0 | $ 3 | $ 5 |

The payoff profile is identical to that of a forward contract with a $95 strike price.

4.  When you purchase the contracts, the initial value is:

Initial value = 10(100)($1,580)
Initial value = $1,580,000

At the end of the first day, the value of your account is:

Day 1 account value = 10(100)($1,587)
Day 1 account value = $1,587,000

So, your cash flow is:

Day 1 cash flow = $1,587,000 – 1,580,000
Day 1 cash flow = $7,000

The day 2 account value is:

Day 2 account value = 10(100)($1,582)
Day 2 account value = $1,582,000

So, your cash flow is:

Day 2 cash flow = $1,582,000 – 1,587,000
Day 2 cash flow = –$5,000

The day 3 account value is:

Day 3 account value = 10(100)($1,573)
Day 3 account value = $1,573,000

So, your cash flow is:

Day 3 cash flow = $1,573,000 – 1,582,000
Day 3 cash flow = –$9,000

The day 4 account value is:

Day 4 account value = 10(100)($1,584)
Day 4 account value = $1,584,000

So, your cash flow is:

Day 4 cash flow = $1,584,000 – 1,573,000
Day 4 cash flow = $11,000

You total profit for the transaction is:

Profit = $1,584,000 – 1,580,000
Profit = $4,000

5.  When you purchase the contracts, your cash outflow is:

Cash outflow = 25(42,000)($2.46)
Cash outflow = $2,583,000

At the end of the first day, the value of your account is:

Day 1 account value = 25(42,000)($2.42)
Day 1 account value = $2,541,000

Remember, on a short position you gain when the price declines, and lose when the price increases. So, your cash flow is:

Day 1 cash flow = $2,583,000 – 2,541,000
Day 1 cash flow = $42,000

The day 2 account value is:

Day 2 account value = 25(42,000)($2.47)
Day 2 account value = $2,593,500

So, your cash flow is:

Day 2 cash flow = $2,541,000 – 2,593,500
Day 2 cash flow = –$52,500

The day 3 account value is:

Day 3 account value = 25(42,000)($2.50)
Day 3 account value = $2,625,000

So, your cash flow is:

Day 3 cash flow = $2,593,500 − 2,625,000
Day 3 cash flow = −$31,500

The day 4 account value is:

Day 4 account value = 25(42,000)($2.56)
Day 4 account value = $2,688,000

So, your cash flow is:

Day 4 cash flow = $2,625,000 − 2,688,000
Day 4 cash flow = −$63,000

You total profit for the transaction is:

Profit = $2,583,000 − 2,688,000
Profit = −$105,000

6. The duration of a bond is the average time to payment of the bond's cash flows, weighted by the ratio of the present value of each payment to the price of the bond. Since the bond is selling at par, the market interest rate must equal 7 percent, the annual coupon rate on the bond. The price of a bond selling at par is equal to its face value. Therefore, the price of this bond is $1,000. The relative value of each payment is the present value of the payment divided by the price of the bond. The contribution of each payment to the duration of the bond is the relative value of the payment multiplied by the amount of time (in years) until the payment occurs. So, the duration of the bond is:

| Year | PV of payment | Relative value | Payment weight |
|------|---------------|----------------|----------------|
| 1 | $65.42 | .06542 | .06542 |
| 2 | 61.14 | .06114 | .12228 |
| 3 | 873.44 | .87344 | 2.62032 |
| Price of bond | $1,000 | Duration = | 2.80802 |

7. The duration of a bond is the average time to payment of the bond's cash flows, weighted by the ratio of the present value of each payment to the price of the bond. Since the bond is selling at par, the market interest rate must equal 8 percent, the annual coupon rate on the bond. The price of a bond selling at par is equal to its face value. Therefore, the price of this bond is $1,000. The relative value of each payment is the present value of the payment divided by the price of the bond. The contribution of each payment to the duration of the bond is the relative value of the payment multiplied by the amount of time (in years) until the payment occurs. So, the duration of the bond is:

| Year | PV of payment | Relative value | Payment weight |
|------|--------------|----------------|----------------|
| 1 | $74.07 | .07407 | .07407 |
| 2 | 68.59 | .06859 | .13717 |
| 3 | 63.51 | .06351 | .19052 |
| 4 | 793.83 | .79383 | 3.17533 |
| Price of bond | $1,000 | Duration = | 3.57710 |

8. The duration of a portfolio of assets or liabilities is the weighted average of the duration of the portfolio's individual items, weighted by their relative market values.

   a. The total market value of assets in millions is:

   Market value of assets = $31 + 590 + 340 + 98 + 485
   Market value of assets = $1,544

   So, the market value weight of each asset is:

   Federal funds deposits = $31 / $1,544 = .020
   Accounts receivable = $590 / $1,544 = .382
   Short-term loans = $340 / $1,544 = .220
   Long-term loans = $98 / $1,544 = .063
   Mortgages = $485 / $1,544 = .314

   Since the duration of a group of assets is the weighted average of the durations of each individual asset in the group, the duration of assets is:

   Duration of assets = .020(0) + .382(.20) + .220(.65) + .063(5.25) + .314(12.85)
   Duration of assets = 4.59 years

   b. The total market value of liabilities in millions is:

   Market value of liabilities = $645 + 410 + 336
   Market value of liabilities = $1,391

   Note that equity is not included in this calculation since it is not a liability. So, the market value weight of each asset is:

   Checking and savings deposits = $645 / $1,391 = .464
   Certificates of deposit = $410 / $1,391 = .295
   Long-term financing = $336 / $1,391 = .242

   Since the duration of a group of liabilities is the weighted average of the durations of each individual asset in the group, the duration of liabilities is:

   Duration of liabilities = .464(0) + .295(1.60) + .242(9.80)
   Duration of liabilities = 2.84 years

   c. Since the duration of assets does not equal the duration of its liabilities, the bank is not immune from interest rate risk.

_Intermediate_

9. *a.* You're concerned about a rise in corn prices, so you would buy March contracts. Since each contract is for 5,000 bushels, the number of contracts you would need to buy is:

Number of contracts to buy = 140,000/5,000 = 28

By doing so, you're effectively locking in the settle price in March, 2012 of $6.05 per bushel of corn, or:

Total price for 140,000 bushels = 28($6.05)(5,000) = $847,000

*b.* If the price of corn at expiration is $6.13 per bushel, the value of you futures position is:

Value of futures position = ($6.13 per bu.)(5,000 bu. per contract)(28 contracts) = $858,200

Ignoring any transaction costs, your gain on the futures position will be:

Gain = $858,200 – 847,000 = $11,200

While the price of the corn your firm needs has become $11,200 more expensive since November, your profit from the futures position has netted out this higher cost.

10. *a.* XYZ has a comparative advantage relative to ABC in borrowing at fixed interest rates, while ABC has a comparative advantage relative to XYZ in borrowing at floating interest rates. Since the spread between ABC and XYZ's fixed rate costs is only 1%, while their differential is 2% in floating rate markets, there is an opportunity for a 3% total gain by entering into a fixed for floating rate swap agreement.

*b.* If the swap dealer must capture 2% of the available gain, there is 1% left for ABC and XYZ. Any division of that gain is feasible; in an actual swap deal, the divisions would probably be negotiated by the dealer. One possible combination is ½% for ABC and ½% for XYZ:

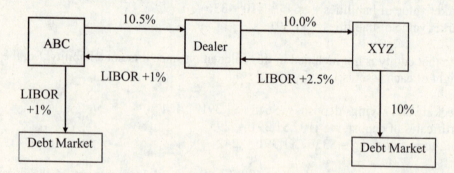

11. The duration of a liability is the average time to payment of the cash flows required to retire the liability, weighted by the ratio of the present value of each payment to the present value of all payments related to the liability. In order to determine the duration of a liability, first calculate the present value of all the payments required to retire it. Since the cost is $30,000 at the beginning of each year for four years, we can find the present value of each payment using the PV equation:

$$PV = FV / (1 + R)^t$$

So, the PV each year of college is:

Year 10 PV = $30,000 / (1.09)^{10}$ = $12,672.32
Year 11 PV = $30,000 / (1.09)^{11}$ = $11,625.99
Year 12 PV = $30,000 / (1.09)^{12}$ = $10,666.04
Year 13 PV = $30,000 / (1.09)^{13}$ = $9,785.36

So, the total PV of the college cost is:

PV of college = $12,672.32 + 11,625.99 + 10,666.04 + 9,785.36
PV of college = $44,749.71

Now, we can set up the following table to calculate the liability's duration. The relative value of each payment is the present value of the payment divided by the present value of the entire liability. The contribution of each payment to the duration of the entire liability is the relative value of the payment multiplied by the amount of time (in years) until the payment occurs.

| Year | PV of payment | Relative value | Payment weight |
|------|---------------|----------------|----------------|
| 10 | $12,672.32 | .28318 | 2.83182 |
| 11 | 11,625.99 | .25980 | 2.85780 |
| 12 | 10,666.04 | .23835 | 2.86019 |
| 13 | 9,785.36 | .21867 | 2.84269 |
| PV of college | $44,749.71 | Duration = | 11.39250 |

12. The duration of a bond is the average time to payment of the bond's cash flows, weighted by the ratio of the present value of each payment to the price of the bond. We need to find the present value of the bond's payments at the market rate. The relative value of each payment is the present value of the payment divided by the price of the bond. The contribution of each payment to the duration of the bond is the relative value of the payment multiplied by the amount of time (in years) until the payment occurs. Since this bond has semiannual coupons, the years will include half-years. So, the duration of the bond is:

| Year | PV of payment | Relative value | Payment weight |
|------|---------------|----------------|----------------|
| .5 | $ 34.15 | .03291 | .01645 |
| 1.0 | 33.31 | .03211 | .03211 |
| 1.5 | 32.50 | .03132 | .04698 |
| 2.0 | 937.66 | .90366 | 1.80733 |
| Price of bond | $1,037.62 | Duration = | 1.90287 |

**13.** Let $R$ equal the interest rate change between the initiation of the contract and the delivery of the asset.

*Cash flows from Strategy 1:*

|  | Today | 1 Year |
|---|---|---|
| Purchase silver | $-S_0$ | 0 |
| Borrow | $+S_0$ | $-S_0(1 + R)$ |
| Total cash flow | 0 | $-S_0(1 + R)$ |

*Cash flows from Strategy 2:*

|  | Today | 1 Year |
|---|---|---|
| Purchase silver | 0 | $-F$ |
| Total cash flow | 0 | $-F$ |

Notice that each strategy results in the ownership of silver in one year for no cash outflow today. Since the payoffs from both the strategies are identical, the two strategies must cost the same in order to preclude arbitrage.

The forward price (F) of a contract on an asset with no carrying costs or convenience value equals the current spot price of the asset ($S_0$) multiplied by 1 plus the appropriate interest rate change between the initiation of the contract and the delivery date of the asset.

**14.** *a.* The forward price of an asset with no carrying costs or convenience value is:

Forward price $= S_0(1 + R)$

Since you will receive the bond's face value of $1,000 in 11 years and the 11 year spot interest rate is currently 7 percent, the current price of the bond is:

Current bond price $= \$1,000 / (1.07)^{11}$
Current bond price $= \$475.09$

Since the forward contract defers delivery of the bond for one year, the appropriate interest rate to use in the forward pricing equation is the one-year spot interest rate of 5 percent:

Forward price $= \$475.09(1.05)$
Forward price $= \$498.85$

*b.* If both the 1-year and 11-year spot interest rates unexpectedly shift downward by 2 percent, the appropriate interest rates to use when pricing the bond is 5 percent, and the appropriate interest rate to use in the forward pricing equation is 3 percent. Given these changes, the new price of the bond will be:

New bond price $= \$1,000 / (1.05)^{11}$
New bond price $= \$584.68$

And the new forward price of the contract is:

Forward price $= \$584.68(1.03)$
Forward price $= \$602.22$

15.  *a.*  The forward price of an asset with no carrying costs or convenience value is:

Forward price = $S_0(1 + R)$

Since you will receive the bond's face value of $1,000 in 18 months, we can find the price of the bond today, which will be:

Current bond price = $1,000 / $(1.0473)^{3/2}$
Current bond price = $933.03

Since the forward contract defers delivery of the bond for six months, the appropriate interest rate to use in the forward pricing equation is the six month EAR, so the forward price will be:

Forward price = $933.03$(1.0361)^{1/2}$
Forward price = $949.72

*b.*  It is important to remember that 100 basis points equals 1 percent and one basis point equals .01%. Therefore, if all rates increase by 30 basis points, each rate increases by .003. So, the new price of the bond today will be:

New bond price = $1,000 / $(1 + .0473 + .003)^{3/2}$
New bond price = $929.03

Since the forward contract defers delivery of the bond for six months, the appropriate interest rate to use in the forward pricing equation is the six month EAR, increased by the interest rate change. So the new forward price will be:

Forward price = $929.03$(1 + .0361 + .003)^{1/2}$
Forward price = $947.02

*Challenge*

16.  The financial engineer can replicate the payoffs of owning a put option by selling a forward contract and buying a call. For example, suppose the forward contract has a settle price of $50 and the exercise price of the call is also $50. The payoffs below show that the position is the same as owning a put with an exercise price of $50:

| Price of coal: | $40 | $45 | $50 | $55 | $60 |
|---|---|---|---|---|---|
| Value of call option position: | 0 | 0 | 0 | 5 | 10 |
| Value of forward position: | 10 | 5 | 0 | −5 | −10 |
| Total value: | $10 | $ 5 | $ 0 | $ 0 | $ 0 |
| Value of put position: | $10 | $ 5 | $ 0 | $ 0 | $ 0 |

The payoffs for the combined position are exactly the same as those of owning a put. This means that, in general, the relationship between puts, calls, and forwards must be such that the cost of the two strategies will be the same, or an arbitrage opportunity exists. In general, given any two of the instruments, the third can be synthesized.

# CHAPTER 26
# SHORT-TERM FINANCE AND PLANNING

## Answers to Concepts Review and Critical Thinking Questions

1.  These are firms with relatively long inventory periods and/or relatively long receivables periods. Thus, such firms tend to keep inventory on hand, and they allow customers to purchase on credit and take a relatively long time to pay.

2.  These are firms that have a relatively long time between the time that purchased inventory is paid for and the time that inventory is sold and payment received. Thus, these are firms that have relatively short payables periods and/or relatively long receivable cycles.

3.  *a.*  Use:       The cash balance declined by $200 to pay the dividend.

    *b.*  Source:   The cash balance increased by $500, assuming the goods bought on payables credit were sold for cash.

    *c.*  Use:       The cash balance declined by $900 to pay for the fixed assets.

    *d.*  Use:       The cash balance declined by $625 to pay for the higher level of inventory.

    *e.*  Use:       The cash balance declined by $1,200 to pay for the redemption of debt.

4.  Carrying costs will decrease because they are not holding goods in inventory. Shortage costs will probably increase depending on how close the suppliers are and how well they can estimate need. The operating cycle will decrease because the inventory period is decreased.

5.  Since the cash cycle equals the operating cycle minus the accounts payable period, it is not possible for the cash cycle to be longer than the operating cycle if the accounts payable is positive. Moreover, it is unlikely that the accounts payable period would ever be negative since that implies the firm pays its bills before they are incurred.

6.  Shortage costs are those costs incurred by a firm when its investment in current assets is low. There are two basic types of shortage costs. 1) Trading or order costs. Order costs are the costs of placing an order for more cash or more inventory. 2) Costs related to safety reserves. These costs include lost sales, lost customer goodwill, and disruption of production schedules.

7.  A long-term growth trend in sales will require some permanent investment in current assets. Thus, in the real world, net working capital is not zero. Also, the variation across time for assets means that net working capital is unlikely to be zero at any point in time. This is a liquidity reason.

8.  It lengthened its payables period, thereby shortening its cash cycle.

9.  Their receivables period increased, thereby increasing their operating and cash cycles.

10. It is sometimes argued that large firms "take advantage of" smaller firms by threatening to take their business elsewhere. However, considering a move to another supplier to get better terms is the nature of competitive free enterprise.

11. They would like to! The payables period is a subject of much negotiation, and it is one aspect of the price a firm pays its suppliers. A firm will generally negotiate the best possible combination of payables period and price. Typically, suppliers provide strong financial incentives for rapid payment. This issue is discussed in detail in a later chapter on credit policy.

12. BlueSky will need less financing because it is essentially borrowing more from its suppliers. Among other things, BlueSky will likely need less short-term borrowing from other sources, so it will save on interest expense.

## Solutions to Questions and Problems

*NOTE: All end-of-chapter problems were solved using a spreadsheet. Many problems require multiple steps. Due to space and readability constraints, when these intermediate steps are included in this solutions manual, rounding may appear to have occurred. However, the final answer for each problem is found without rounding during any step in the problem.*

### Basic

1. *a.* No change. A dividend paid for by the sale of debt will not change cash since the cash raised from the debt offer goes immediately to shareholders.

   *b.* No change. The real estate is paid for by the cash raised from the debt, so this will not change the cash balance.

   *c.* No change. Inventory and accounts payable will increase, but neither will impact the cash account.

   *d.* Decrease. The short-term bank loan is repaid with cash, which will reduce the cash balance.

   *e.* Decrease. The payment of taxes is a cash transaction.

   *f.* Decrease. The preferred stock will be repurchased with cash.

   *g.* No change. Accounts receivable will increase, but cash will not increase until the sales are paid off.

   *h.* Decrease. The interest is paid with cash, which will reduce the cash balance.

   *i.* Increase. When payments for previous sales, or accounts receivable, are paid off, the cash balance increases since the payment must be made in cash.

   *j.* Decrease. The accounts payable are reduced through cash payments to suppliers.

   *k.* Decrease. Here the dividend payments are made with cash, which is generally the case. This is different from part *a*, where debt was raised to make the dividend payment.

*l.*   No change. The short-term note will not change the cash balance.

*m.*   Decrease. The utility bills must be paid in cash.

*n.*   Decrease. A cash payment will reduce cash.

*o.*   Increase. If marketable securities are sold, the company will receive cash from the sale.

2.   The total liabilities and equity of the company are the book value of equity, plus current liabilities and long-term debt, so:

Total liabilities and equity = $13,205 + 1,630 + 8,200
Total liabilities and equity = $23,035

We have NWC other than cash. Since NWC is current assets minus current liabilities, NWC other than cash is:

NWC other than cash = Accounts receivable + Inventory − Current liabilities
$3,205 = Accounts receivable + Inventory − $1,630
Accounts receivable + Inventory = $3,205 + 1,630
Accounts receivable + Inventory = $3,835

Since total assets must equal total liabilities and equity, we can solve for cash as:

Cash = Total assets − Fixed assets − (Accounts receivable + Inventory)
Cash = $23,035 − 18,380 − 3,835
Cash = $820

So, the current assets are:

Current assets = $820 + 3,835
Current assets = $4,655

3.   *a.*   Increase. If receivables go up, the time to collect the receivables would increase, which increases the operating cycle.

*b.*   Increase. If credit repayment times are increased, customers will take longer to pay their bills, which will lead to an increase in the operating cycle.

*c.*   Decrease. If the inventory turnover increases, the inventory period decreases.

*d.*   No change. The accounts payable period is part of the cash cycle, not the operating cycle.

*e.*   Decrease. If the receivables turnover increases, the receivables period decreases.

*f.*   No change. Payments to suppliers affects the accounts payable period, which is part of the cash cycle, not the operating cycle.

4.   *a.*   Increase; Increase. If the terms of the cash discount are made less favorable to customers, the accounts receivable period will lengthen. This will increase both the cash cycle and the operating cycle.

b.   Increase; No change. This will shorten the accounts payable period, which will increase the cash cycle. It will have no effect on the operating cycle since the accounts payable period is not part of the operating cycle.

c.   Decrease; Decrease. If more customers pay in cash, the accounts receivable period will decrease. This will decrease both the cash cycle and the operating cycle.

d.   Decrease; Decrease. Assume the accounts payable period and inventory period do not change. Fewer raw materials purchased will reduce the inventory period, which will decrease both the cash cycle and the operating cycle.

e.   Decrease; No change. If more raw materials are purchased on credit, the accounts payable period will tend to increase, which would decrease the cash cycle. We should say that this may not be the case. The accounts payable period is a decision made by the company's management. The company could increase the accounts payable account and still make the payments in the same number of days. This would leave the accounts payable period unchanged, which would leave the cash cycle unchanged. The change in purchases made on credit will not affect the inventory period or the accounts payable period, so the operating cycle will not change.

f.   Increase; Increase. If more goods are produced for inventory, the inventory period will increase. This will increase both the cash cycle and operating cycle.

**5.  a.**   A 45-day collection period implies all receivables outstanding from the previous quarter are collected in the current quarter, and:

$(90 - 45)/90 = 1/2$ of current sales are collected. So:

|                        | Q1        | Q2        | Q3        | Q4        |
|------------------------|-----------|-----------|-----------|-----------|
| Beginning receivables  | $310.00   | $370.00   | $405.00   | $390.00   |
| Sales                  | 740.00    | 810.00    | 780.00    | 940.00    |
| Cash collections       | −680.00   | −775.00   | −795.00   | −860.00   |
| Ending receivables     | $370.00   | $405.00   | $390.00   | $470.00   |

**b.**   A 60-day collection period implies all receivables outstanding from the previous quarter are collected in the current quarter, and:

$(90-60)/90 = 1/3$ of current sales are collected. So:

|                        | Q1        | Q2        | Q3        | Q4        |
|------------------------|-----------|-----------|-----------|-----------|
| Beginning receivables  | $310.00   | $493.33   | $540.00   | $520.00   |
| Sales                  | 740.00    | 810.00    | 780.00    | 940.00    |
| Cash collections       | −556.67   | −763.33   | −800.00   | −833.33   |
| Ending receivables     | $493.33   | $540.00   | $520.00   | $626.67   |

**c.**   A 30-day collection period implies all receivables outstanding from the previous quarter are collected in the current quarter, and:

(90−30)/90 = 2/3 of current sales are collected. So:

|  | Q1 | Q2 | Q3 | Q4 |
|---|---|---|---|---|
| Beginning receivables | $310.00 | $246.67 | $270.00 | $260.00 |
| Sales | 740.00 | 810.00 | 780.00 | 940.00 |
| Cash collections | −803.33 | −786.67 | −790.00 | −886.67 |
| Ending receivables | $246.67 | $270.00 | $260.00 | $313.33 |

**6.** The operating cycle is the inventory period plus the receivables period. The inventory turnover and inventory period are:

Inventory turnover = COGS/Average inventory
Inventory turnover = $140,382/[($17,385 + 19,108)/2]
Inventory turnover = 7.6936 times

Inventory period = 365 days/Inventory turnover
Inventory period = 365 days/7.6936
Inventory period = 47.44 days

And the receivables turnover and receivables period are:

Receivables turnover = Credit sales/Average receivables
Receivables turnover = $178,312/[($13,182 + 13,973)/2]
Receivables turnover = 13.1329 times

Receivables period = 365 days/Receivables turnover
Receivables period = 365 days/13.1329
Receivables period = 27.79 days

So, the operating cycle is:

Operating cycle = 47.44 days + 27.79 days
Operating cycle = 75.23 days

The cash cycle is the operating cycle minus the payables period. The payables turnover and payables period are:

Payables turnover = COGS/Average payables
Payables turnover = $140,382/[($15,385 + 16,676)/2]
Payables turnover = 8.7572 times

Payables period = 365 days/Payables turnover
Payables period = 365 days/8.7572
Payables period = 41.68 days

So, the cash cycle is:

Cash cycle = 75.23 days − 41.68 days
Cash cycle = 33.55 days

The firm is receiving cash on average 33.55 days after it pays its bills.

**7. a.** The payables period is zero since the company pays immediately. Sales in the year following this one are projected to be 15% greater in each quarter. Therefore, Q1 sales for the next year will be $620(1.15) = $713. The payment in each period is 30 percent of next period's sales, so:

| | Q1 | Q2 | Q3 | Q4 |
|---|---|---|---|---|
| Payment of accounts | $166.50 | $211.50 | $234.00 | $213.90 |

**b.** Since the payables period is 90 days, the payment in each period is 30 percent of the current period sales, so:

| | Q1 | Q2 | Q3 | Q4 |
|---|---|---|---|---|
| Payment of accounts | $186.00 | $166.50 | $211.50 | $234.00 |

**c.** Since the payables period is 60 days, the payment in each period is 2/3 of last quarter's orders, plus 1/3 of this quarter's orders, or:

Quarterly payments = 2/3(.30) times current sales + 1/3(.30) next period sales.

| | Q1 | Q2 | Q3 | Q4 |
|---|---|---|---|---|
| Payment of accounts | $179.50 | $181.50 | $219.00 | $227.30 |

**8.** Since the payables period is 60 days, the payables in each period will be:

Payables each period = 2/3 of last quarter's orders + 1/3 of this quarter's orders
Payables each period = 2/3(.75) times current sales + 1/3(.75) next period sales

| | Q1 | Q2 | Q3 | Q4 |
|---|---|---|---|---|
| Payment of accounts | $1,032.50 | $1,090.00 | $ 987.50 | $ 957.50 |
| Wages, taxes, other expenses | 264.00 | 298.00 | 276.00 | 238.00 |
| Long-term financing expenses | 73.00 | 73.00 | 73.00 | 73.00 |
| Total | $1,369.50 | $1,461.00 | $1,336.50 | $1,268.50 |

**9. a.** The November sales must have been the total uncollected sales minus the uncollected sales from December, divided by the collection rate two months after the sale, so:

November sales = ($106,800 – 76,300)/0.15
November sales = $203,333.33

**b.** The December sales are the uncollected sales from December divided by the collection rate of the previous months' sales, so:

December sales = $576,300/0.35
December sales = $218,000

**c.** The collections each month for this company are:

Collections = .15(Sales from 2 months ago) + .20(Last months sales) + .65 (Current sales)

January collections = .15($203,333.33) + .20($218,000) + .65($234,800)
January collections = $226,720

February collections = .15($218,000) + .20($234,800) + .65($249,300)
February collections = $241,705

March collections = .15($234,800) + .20($249,300) + .65($271,000)
March collections = $261,230

10. The sales collections each month will be:

Sales collections = .35(current month sales) + .60(previous month sales)

Given this collection, the cash budget will be:

|  | April | May | June |
|---|---|---|---|
| Beginning cash balance | $403,200 | $358,344 | $457,690 |
| Cash receipts |  |  |  |
| Cash collections from credit sales | 372,960 | 527,904 | 562,896 |
| Total cash available | 776,160 | 886,248 | 1,020,586 |
| Cash disbursements |  |  |  |
| Purchases | 224,640 | 211,680 | 252,720 |
| Wages, taxes, and expenses | 57,240 | 69,422 | 72,432 |
| Interest | 16,416 | 16,416 | 16,416 |
| Equipment purchases | 119,520 | 131,040 | - |
| Total cash disbursements | 417,816 | 428,558 | 341,568 |
| Ending cash balance | $358,344 | $457,690 | $679,018 |

11.

| Item | Source/Use | Amount |
|---|---|---|
| Cash | Source | $ 2,365 |
| Accounts receivable | Use | –$ 5,258 |
| Inventories | Use | –$ 6,116 |
| Property, plant, and equipment | Use | –$23,094 |
|  |  |  |
| Accounts payable | Use | –$22,126 |
| Accrued expenses | Use | –$ 1,140 |
| Long-term debt | Use | –$ 4,500 |
| Common stock | Source | $ 5,000 |
| Accumulated retained earnings | Source | $46,484 |

*Intermediate*

12. First, we need to calculate the sales from the last quarter of the previous year. Since 50 percent of the sales were collected in that quarter, the sales figure must have been:

Sales last quarter of previous year = $104,000,000 / (1 – .50)
Sales last quarter of previous year = $208,000,000

Now we can estimate the sales growth each quarter, and calculate the net sales including the seasonal adjustments. The sales figures for each quarter will be:

|  | Quarter 1 | Quarter 2 | Quarter 3 | Quarter 4 |
|---|---|---|---|---|
| Sales (basic trend) | $225,000,000 | $247,500,000 | $272,250,000 | $299,475,000 |
| Seasonal adjustment | 0 | −16,000,000 | −8,000,000 | 21,000,000 |
| Sales projection | 225,000,000 | 231,500,000 | 264,250,000 | 320,475,000 |

Since 50 percent of sales are collected in the quarter the sales are made, and 45 percent of sales are collected in the quarter after the sales are made, the cash budget is:

|  | Quarter 1 | Quarter 2 | Quarter 3 | Quarter 4 |
|---|---|---|---|---|
| Collected within quarter | $112,500,000 | $115,750,000 | $132,125,000 | $160,237,500 |
| Collection from previous quarter | 93,600,000 | 101,250,000 | 104,175,000 | 118,912,500 |
| Cash collections from sales | $206,100,000 | $217,000,000 | $236,300,000 | $279,150,000 |

**13.** *a.* A 45-day collection period means sales collections each quarter are:

Collections = 1/2 current sales + 1/2 old sales

A 36-day payables period means payables each quarter are:

Payables = 3/5 current orders + 2/5 old orders

So, the cash inflows and disbursements each quarter are:

|  | Q1 | Q2 | Q3 | Q4 |
|---|---|---|---|---|
| Beginning receivables | $34.00 | $ 52.50 | $ 45.00 | $ 61.00 |
| Sales | 105.00 | 90.00 | 122.00 | 140.00 |
| Collection of accounts | 86.50 | 97.50 | 106.00 | 131.00 |
| Ending receivables | $52.50 | $ 45.00 | $ 61.00 | $ 70.00 |
|  |  |  |  |  |
| Payment of accounts | $43.20 | $ 49.14 | $ 59.76 | $ 57.60 |
| Wages, taxes, and expenses | 31.50 | 27.00 | 36.60 | 42.00 |
| Capital expenditures |  | 40.00 |  |  |
| Interest & dividends | 6.00 | 6.00 | 6.00 | 6.00 |
| Total cash disbursements | $80.70 | $122.14 | $102.36 | $105.60 |
|  |  |  |  |  |
| Total cash collections | $86.50 | $ 97.50 | $106.00 | $131.00 |
| Total cash disbursements | 80.70 | 122.14 | 102.36 | 105.60 |
| Net cash inflow | $ 5.80 | −$ 24.64 | $ 3.64 | $ 25.40 |

The company's cash budget will be:

WILDCAT, INC.
Cash Budget
(in millions)

|  | Q1 | Q2 | Q3 | Q4 |
|---|---|---|---|---|
| Beginning cash balance | $32.00 | $37.80 | $13.16 | $16.80 |
| Net cash inflow | 5.80 | −24.64 | 3.64 | 25.40 |
| Ending cash balance | $37.80 | $13.16 | $16.80 | $42.20 |
| Minimum cash balance | −15.00 | −15.00 | −15.00 | −15.00 |
| Cumulative surplus (deficit) | $22.80 | −$ 1.84 | $ 1.80 | $27.20 |

With a $30 million minimum cash balance, the short-term financial plan will be:

WILDCAT, INC.
Short-Term Financial Plan
(in millions)

b.

|  | Q1 | Q2 | Q3 | Q4 |
|---|---|---|---|---|
| Beginning cash balance | $15.00 | $15.00 | $15.00 | $15.00 |
| Net cash inflow | 5.80 | −24.64 | 3.64 | 25.40 |
| New short-term investments | −6.14 | 0 | −2.57 | −25.45 |
| Income on short-term investments | 0.34 | 0.46 | 0 | 0.05 |
| Short-term investments sold | 0 | 23.14 | 0 | 0 |
| New short-term borrowing | 0 | 1.04 | 0 | 0 |
| Interest on short-term borrowing | 0 | 0 | −0.03 | 0 |
| Short-term borrowing repaid | 0 | 0 | −1.04 | 0 |
| Ending cash balance | $15.00 | $15.00 | $15.00 | $15.00 |
| Minimum cash balance | −15.00 | −15.00 | −15.00 | −15.00 |
| Cumulative surplus (deficit) | $   0 | $   0 | $   0 | $   0 |
|  |  |  |  |  |
| Beginning short-term investments | $17.00 | $23.14 | $   0 | $ 2.57 |
| Ending short-term investments | $23.14 | $   0 | $ 2.57 | $28.07 |
| Beginning short-term debt | $   0 | $   0 | $ 1.04 | $   0 |
| Ending short-term debt | $   0 | $ 1.04 | $   0 | $   0 |

Below you will find the interest paid (or received) for each quarter:

Q1: excess funds at start of quarter of $17 invested for 1 quarter earns .02($17) = $0.34 income

Q2: excess funds of $23.14 invested for 1 quarter earns .02($23.14) = $0.46 in income

Q3: shortage funds of $1.04 borrowed for 1 quarter costs .03($1.04) = $0.03 in interest

Q4: excess funds of $2.57 invested for 1 quarter earns .02($2.57) = $0.05 in income

Net cash cost = $0.34 + 0.46 − 0.03 + 0.05 = $0.82

**14.** *a.* With a minimum cash balance of $20 million, the short-term financial plan will be:

WILDCAT, INC.
Short-Term Financial Plan
(in millions)

|  | Q1 | Q2 | Q3 | Q4 |
|---|---|---|---|---|
| Beginning cash balance | $20.00 | $20.00 | $20.00 | $20.00 |
| Net cash inflow | 5.80 | −24.64 | 3.64 | 25.40 |
| New short-term investments | −6.04 | 0 | 0 | −22.53 |
| Income on short-term investments | 0.24 | 0.36 | 0 | 0 |
| Short-term investments sold | 0 | 18.04 | 0 | 0 |
| New short-term borrowing | 0 | 6.24 | 0 | 0 |
| Interest on short-term borrowing | 0 | 0 | −0.19 | −0.08 |
| Short-term borrowing repaid | 0 | 0 | −3.45 | −2.79 |
| Ending cash balance | $20.00 | $20.00 | $20.00 | $20.00 |
| Minimum cash balance | −20.00 | −20.00 | −20.00 | −20.00 |
| Cumulative surplus (deficit | $  0 | $  0 | $  0 | $  0 |
|  |  |  |  |  |
| Beginning short-term investments | $12.00 | $18.04 | $  0 | $  0 |
| Ending short-term investments | $18.04 | $  0 | $  0 | $22.53 |
| Beginning short-term debt | $  0 | $  0 | $ 6.24 | $ 2.79 |
| Ending short-term debt | $  0 | $ 6.24 | $ 2.79 | $  0 |

Below you will find the interest paid (or received for each quarter:

Q1: excess funds at start of quarter of $12 invested for 1 quarter earns .02($12) = $0.24 income

Q2: excess funds of $18.04 invested for 1 quarter earns .02($18.04) = $0.36 in income

Q3: shortage of funds of $6.24 borrowed for 1 quarter costs .03($6.24) = $0.19 in interest

Q4: shortage of funds of $2.79 borrowed for 1 quarter costs .03($2.79) = $0.08 in interest

Net cash cost = $0.24 + 0.36 − 0.19 − 0.08 = −$0.33

b.　And with a minimum cash balance of $10 million, the short-term financial plan will be:

### WILDCAT, INC.
#### Short-Term Financial Plan
#### (in millions

| | Q1 | Q2 | Q3 | Q4 |
|---|---|---|---|---|
| Beginning cash balance | $10.00 | $10.00 | $10.00 | $10.00 |
| Net cash inflow | 5.80 | −24.64 | 3.64 | 25.40 |
| New short-term investments | −6.24 | 0 | −3.72 | −25.56 |
| Income on short-term investments | 0.44 | 0.56 | 0.08 | 0.16 |
| Short-term investments sold | 0 | 24.08 | 0 | 0 |
| New short-term borrowing | 0 | 0 | 0 | 0 |
| Interest on short-term borrowing | 0 | 0 | 0 | 0 |
| Short-term borrowing repaid | 0 | 0 | 0 | 0 |
| Ending cash balance | $10.00 | $10.00 | $10.00 | $10.00 |
| Minimum cash balance | −10.00 | −10.00 | −10.00 | −10.00 |
| Cumulative surplus (deficit | $　0 | $　0 | $　0 | $　0 |
| | | | | |
| Beginning short-term investments | $22.00 | $28.24 | $　4.16 | $　7.89 |
| Ending short-term investments | $28.24 | $　4.16 | $　7.89 | $33.60 |
| Beginning short-term debt | $　0 | $　0 | $　0 | $　0 |
| Ending short-term debt | $　0 | $　0 | $　0 | $　0 |

Below you will find the interest paid (or received for each quarter:

Q1: excess funds at start of quarter of $22 invested for 1 quarter earns .02($22) = $0.44 income

Q2: excess funds of $28.24 invested for 1 quarter earns .02($28.24) = $0.56 in income

Q3: excess funds of $4.16 invested for 1 quarter earns .02($4.16) = $0.08 in income

Q4: excess funds of $7.89 invested for 1 quarter earns .02($7.89) = $0.16 in income

Net cash cost = $0.44 + 0.56 + 0.08 + 0.16 = $1.25

Since cash has an opportunity cost, the firm can boost its profit if it keeps its minimum cash balance low and invests the cash instead. However, the tradeoff is that in the event of unforeseen circumstances, the firm may not be able to meet its short-run obligations if enough cash is not available.

15.　a.　The current assets of Cleveland Compressor are financed largely by retained earnings. From 2011 to 2012, total current assets grew by $7,212. Only $2,126 of this increase was financed by the growth of current liabilities. Pnew York Pneumatic's current assets are largely financed by current liabilities. Bank loans are the most important of these current liabilities. They grew $3,077 to finance an increase in current assets of $8,333.

　　b.　Cleveland Compressor holds the larger investment in current assets. It has current assets of $92,616 while Pnew York Pneumatic has $78,434 in current assets. The main reason for the difference is the larger sales of Cleveland Compressor.

c.  Cleveland Compressor is more likely to incur shortage costs because the ratio of current assets to sales is 0.57. That ratio for Pnew York Pneumatic is 0.86. Similarly, Pnew York Pneumatic is incurring more carrying costs for the same reason, a higher ratio of current assets to sales.

# CHAPTER 27
# CASH MANAGEMENT

**Answers to Concepts Review and Critical Thinking Questions**

1. Yes. Once a firm has more cash than it needs for operations and planned expenditures, the excess cash has an opportunity cost. It could be invested (by shareholders) in potentially more profitable ways. Question 9 discusses another reason.

2. If it has too much cash it can simply pay a dividend, or, more likely in the current financial environment, buy back stock. It can also reduce debt. If it has insufficient cash, then it must either borrow, sell stock, or improve profitability.

3. Probably not. Creditors would probably want substantially more.

4. Cash management is associated more with the collection and disbursement of cash. Liquidity management is broader and concerns the optimal level of liquid assets needed by a firm. Thus, for example, a company's stockpiling of cash is liquidity management; whereas, evaluating a lockbox system is cash management.

5. Such instruments go by a variety of names, but the key feature is that the dividend adjusts, keeping the price relatively stable. This price stability, along with the dividend tax exemption, makes so-called adjustable rate preferred stock very attractive relative to interest-bearing instruments.

6. Net disbursement float is more desirable because the bank thinks the firm has more money than it actually does, and the firm is, therefore, receiving interest on funds it has already spent.

7. The firm has a net disbursement float of $500,000. If this is an ongoing situation, the firm may be tempted to write checks for more than it actually has in its account.

8. *a.* About the only disadvantage to holding T-bills are the generally lower yields compared to alternative money market investments.

   *b.* Some ordinary preferred stock issues pose both credit and price risks that are not consistent with most short-term cash management plans.

   *c.* The primary disadvantage of NCDs is the normally large transactions sizes, which may not be feasible for the short-term investment plans of many smaller to medium-sized corporations.

   *d.* The primary disadvantages of the commercial paper market are the higher default risk characteristics of the security and the lack of an active secondary market which may excessively restrict the flexibility of corporations to meet their liquidity adjustment needs.

   *e.* The primary disadvantages of RANs is that some possess non-trivial levels of default risk, and also, corporations are somewhat restricted in the type and amount of these tax-exempts that they can hold in their portfolios.

   *f.* The primary disadvantage of the repo market is the generally very short maturities available.

9. The concern is that excess cash on hand can lead to poorly thought-out management decisions. The thought is that keeping cash levels relatively low forces management to pay careful attention to cash flow and capital spending.

10. A potential advantage is that the quicker payment often means a better price. The disadvantage is that doing so increases the firm's cash cycle.

11. This is really a capital structure decision. If the firm has an optimal capital structure, paying off debt moves it to an under-leveraged position. However, a combination of debt reduction and stock buy-backs could be structured to leave capital structure unchanged.

12. It is unethical because you have essentially tricked the grocery store into making you an interest-free loan, and the grocery store is harmed because it could have earned interest on the money instead of loaning it to you.

## Solutions to Questions and Problems

*NOTE: All end of chapter problems were solved using a spreadsheet. Many problems require multiple steps. Due to space and readability constraints, when these intermediate steps are included in this solutions manual, rounding may appear to have occurred. However, the final answer for each problem is found without rounding during any step in the problem.*

### Basic

1. The average daily float is the average amount of checks received per day times the average number of days delay, divided by the number of days in a month. Assuming 30 days in a month, the average daily float is:

   Average daily float = 4($124,000)/30
   Average daily float = $16,533.33

2. *a.* The disbursement float is the average daily checks written times the average number of days for the checks to clear, so:

   Disbursement float = 4($17,000)
   Disbursement float = $68,000

   The collection float is the average daily checks received times the average number of days for the checks to clear, so:

   Collection float = 2(–$28,500)
   Collection float = –$57,000

   The net float is the disbursement float plus the collection float, so:

   Net float = $68,000 – 57,000
   Net float = $11,000

*b.* The new collection float will be:

Collection float = 1(–$28,500)
Collection float = –$28,500

And the new net float will be:

Net float = $68,000 – 28,500
Net float = $39,500

3. *a.* The collection float is the average daily checks received times the average number of days for the checks to clear, so:

Collection float = 3($16,000)
Collection float = $48,000

*b.* The firm should pay no more than the amount of the float, or $48,000, to eliminate the float.

*c.* The maximum daily charge the firm should be willing to pay is the collection float times the daily interest rate, so:

Maximum daily charge = $48,000(.00018)
Maximum daily charge = $8.64

4. *a.* Total float = 4($11,000) + 5($3,400)
Total float = $61,000

*b.* The average daily float is the total float divided by the number of days in a month. Assuming 30 days in a month, the average daily float is:

Average daily float = $61,000/30
Average daily float = $2,033.33

*c.* The average daily receipts are the average daily checks received divided by the number of days in a month. Assuming a 30 day month:

Average daily receipts = ($11,000 + 3,400)/30
Average daily receipts = $480.00

The weighted average delay is the sum of the days to clear a check, times the amount of the check divided by the average daily receipts, so:

Weighted average delay = 4($11,000/$14,400) + 5($3,400/$14,400)
Weighted average delay = 4.24 days

5. The average daily collections are the number of checks received times the average value of a check, so:

Average daily collections = $117(6,500)
Average daily collections = $760,500

The present value of the lockbox service is the average daily receipts times the number of days the collection is reduced, so:

PV = (2 day reduction)($760,500)
PV = $1,521,000

The daily cost is a perpetuity. The present value of the cost is the daily cost divided by the daily interest rate. So:

PV of cost = $160/.00015
PV of cost = $1,066,667

The firm should take the lockbox service. The NPV of the lockbox is the cost plus the present value of the reduction in collection time, so:

NPV = –$1,066,667 + 1,521,000
NPV = $454,333.33

The annual savings excluding the cost would be the future value of the savings minus the costs, so:

Annual savings = $1,521,000(1.00015)$^{365}$ – 1,521,000
Annual savings = $85,589.98

And the annual cost would be the future value of the daily cost, which is an annuity, so:

Annual cost = $160(FVIFA$_{365,.015\%}$)
Annual cost = $60,023.65

So, the annual net savings would be:

Annual net savings = $85,589.98 – 60,023.65
Annual net savings = $25,566.33

6.  a.  The average daily float is the sum of the percentage each check amount is of the total checks received times the number of checks received times the amount of the check times the number of days until the check clears, divided by the number of days in a month. Assuming a 30 day month, we get:

Average daily float = [.60(5,700)($55)(2) + .40(5,700)($80)(3)]/30
Average daily float = $30,780

On average, there is $30,780 that is uncollected and not available to the firm.

b.  The total collections are the sum of the percentage of each check amount received times the total checks received times the amount of the check, so:

Total collections = .60(5,700)($55) + .40(5,700)($80)
Total collections = $370,500

The weighted average delay is the sum of the average number of days a check of a specific amount is delayed, times the percentage that check amount makes up of the total checks received, so:

Weighted average delay = 2[.60(5,700)($55)/$370,500] + 3[.40(5,700)($80) /$370,500]
Weighted average delay = 2.49 days

The average daily float is the weighted average delay times the average checks received per day. Assuming a 30 day month, we get:

Average daily float = 2.49($370,500/30 days)
Average daily float = $30,780

c. The most the firm should pay is the total amount of the average float, or $30,780.

d. The average daily interest rate is:

$1.07 = (1 + R)^{365}$
R = .01854% per day

The daily cost of float is the average daily float times the daily interest rate, so:

Daily cost of the float = $30,780(.0001854)
Daily cost of the float = $5.71

e. The most the firm should pay is still the average daily float. Under the reduced collection time assumption, we get:

New average daily float = 1.5($370,500/30)
New average daily float = $18,525

7. a. The present value of adopting the system is the number of days collections are reduced times the average daily collections, so:

PV = 3(435)($975)
PV = $1,272,375

b. The NPV of adopting the system is the present value of the savings minus the cost of adopting the system. The cost of adopting the system is the present value of the fee per transaction times the number of transactions. This is a perpetuity, so:

NPV = $1,272,375 – [$.50(435)/.0002]
NPV = $184,875

c. The net cash flow is the present value of the average daily collections times the daily interest rate, minus the transaction cost per day, so:

Net cash flow per day = $1,272,375(.0002) – $.50(435)
Net cash flow per day = $36.98

The net cash flow per check is the net cash flow per day divided by the number of checks received per day, or:

Net cash flow per check = $36.98/435
Net cash flow per check = $.09

Alternatively, we could find the net cash flow per check as the number of days the system reduces collection time times the average check amount times the daily interest rate, minus the transaction cost per check. Doing so, we confirm our previous answer as:

Net cash flow per check = 3($975)(.0002) – $.50
Net cash flow per check = $.09 per check

**8.** *a.* The reduction in cash balance from adopting the lockbox is the number of days the system reduces collection time times the average daily collections, so:

Cash balance reduction = 2($135,000)
Cash balance reduction = $270,000

*b.* The dollar return that can be earned is the average daily interest rate times the cash balance reduction. The average daily interest rate is:

Average daily rate = $1.09^{1/365} - 1$
Average daily rate = .0236% per day

The daily dollar return that can be earned from the reduction in days to clear the checks is:

Daily dollar return = $270,000(.000236)
Daily dollar return = $63.76

*c.* If the company takes the lockbox, it will receive three payments early, with the first payment occurring today. We can use the daily interest rate from part *b*, so the savings are:

Savings = $135,000 + $135,000(PVIFA$_{.0236\%,2}$)
Savings = $404,904.40

If the lockbox payments occur at the end of the month, we need the effective monthly interest rate, which is:

Monthly interest rate = $1.09^{1/12} - 1$
Monthly interest rate = .7207%

Assuming the lockbox payments occur at the end of the month, the lockbox payments, which are a perpetuity, will be:

PV = C/R
$404,904.40 = C / .007207$
C = $2,918.28

It could also be assumed that the lockbox payments occur at the beginning of the month. If so, we would need to use the PV of a perpetuity due, which is:

$$PV = C + C / R$$

Solving for C:

$$C = (PV \times R) / (1 + R)$$
$$C = (\$404,904.40 \times .007207) / (1 + .007207)$$
$$C = \$2,897.39$$

9. The interest that the company could earn will be the amount of the checks times the number of days it will delay payment times the number of weeks that checks will be disbursed times the daily interest rate, so:

Interest = $58,000(7)(52/2)(.00015)
Interest = $1,583.40

10. The benefit of the new arrangement is the $3.2 million in accelerated collections since the new system will speed up collections by one day. The cost is the new compensating balance, but the company will recover the existing compensating balance, so:

NPV = $3,200,000 – ($380,000 – 350,000)
NPV = $3,170,000

The company should proceed with the new system. The savings are the NPV times the annual interest rate, so:

Net savings = $3,170,000(.05)
Net savings = $158,500

*Intermediate*

11. To find the NPV of taking the lockbox, we first need to calculate the present value of the savings. The present value of the savings will be the reduction in collection time times the average daily collections, so:

PV = 2(850)($630)
PV = $1,071,000

And the daily interest rate is:

Daily interest rate = $1.070^{1/365} - 1$
Daily interest rate = .00019 or .019% per day

The transaction costs are a perpetuity. The cost per day is the cost per transaction times the number of transactions per day, so the NPV of taking the lockbox is:

NPV = $1,071,000 – [$.22(850)/.00019]
NPV = $62,279.38

Without the fee, the lockbox system should be accepted. To calculate the NPV of the lockbox with the annual fee, we can simply use the NPV of the lockbox without the annual fee and subtract the additional cost. The annual fee is a perpetuity, so, with the fee, the NPV of taking the lockbox is:

NPV = $62,279.38 – [$5,000/.07]
NPV = –$9,149.20

With the fee, the lockbox system should not be accepted.

12.  The minimum number of payments per day needed to make the lockbox system feasible is the number of checks that makes the NPV of the decision equal to zero. The average daily interest rate is:

Daily interest rate = $1.05^{1/365} - 1$
Daily interest rate = .0134% per day

The present value of the savings is the average payment amount times the days the collection period is reduced times the number of customers. The costs are the transaction fee and the annual fee. Both are perpetuities. The total transaction costs are the transaction costs per check times the number of checks. The equation for the NPV of the project, where N is the number of checks transacted per day, is:

NPV = 0 = ($4,800)(1)N – $.10(N)/.000134 – $15,000/.05
$300,000 = $4,800N – $748.05N
$4,051.95N = $300,000
N = 74.04 ≈ 74 customers per day

# *APPENDIX 27A*

1. *a.* Decrease. This will lower the trading costs, which will cause a decrease in the target cash balance.

    *b.* Decrease. This will increase the holding cost, which will cause a decrease in the target cash balance.

    *c.* Increase. This will increase the amount of cash that the firm has to hold in non-interest bearing accounts, so they will have to raise the target cash balance to meet this requirement.

    *d.* Decrease. If the credit rating improves, then the firm can borrow more easily, allowing it to lower the target cash balance and borrow if a cash shortfall occurs.

    *e.* Increase. If the cost of borrowing increases, the firm will need to hold more cash to protect against cash shortfalls as its borrowing costs become more prohibitive.

    *f.* Either. This depends somewhat on what the fees apply to, but if direct fees are established, then the compensating balance may be lowered, thus lowering the target cash balance. If, on the other hand, fees are charged on the number of transactions, then the firm may wish to hold a higher cash balance so they are not transferring money into the account as often.

2. The target cash balance using the BAT model is:

    $$C^* = [(2T \times F)/R]^{1/2}$$
    $$C^* = [2(\$8,500)(\$25)/.06]^{1/2}$$
    $$C^* = \$2,661.45$$

    The initial balance should be $2,661.45, and whenever the balance drops to $0, another $2,661.45 should be transferred in.

3. The holding cost is the average daily cash balance times the interest rate, so:

    Holding cost = ($1,300)(.05)
    Holding cost = $65.00

    The trading costs are the total cash needed times the replenishing costs, divided by the average daily balance times two, so:

    Trading cost = [($43,000)($8)]/[($1,300)(2)]
    Trading cost = $132.31

    The total cost is the sum of the holding cost and the trading cost, so:

    Total cost = $65.00 + 132.31
    Total cost = $197.31

The target cash balance using the BAT model is:

$$C^* = [(2T \times F)/R]^{1/2}$$
$$C^* = [2(\$43,000)(\$8)/.05]^{1/2}$$
$$C^* = \$3,709.45$$

They should increase their average daily cash balance to:

New average cash balance = \$3,709.45/2
New average cash balance = \$1,854.72

This would minimize the costs. The new total cost would be:

New total cost = (\$1,854.72)(.05) + [(\$43,000)(\$8)]/[2(\$1,854.72)]
New total cost = \$185.47

**4.** *a.* The opportunity costs are the amount transferred times the interest rate, divided by two, so:

Opportunity cost = (\$1,500)(.05)/2
Opportunity cost = \$37.50

The trading costs are the total cash balance times the trading cost per transaction, divided by the amount transferred, so:

Trading cost = (\$16,000)(\$25)/\$1,500
Trading cost = \$266.67

The firm keeps too little in cash because the trading costs are much higher than the opportunity costs.

*b.* The target cash balance using the BAT model is:

$$C^* = [(2T \times F)/R]^{1/2}$$
$$C^* = [2(\$16,000)(\$25)/.05]^{1/2}$$
$$C^* = \$4,000$$

**5.** The total cash needed is the cash shortage per month times twelve months, so:

Total cash = 12(\$140,000)
Total cash = \$1,680,000

The target cash balance using the BAT model is:

$$C^* = [(2T \times F)/R]^{1/2}$$
$$C^* = [2(\$1,680,000)(\$500)/.057]^{1/2}$$
$$C^* = \$171,679.02$$

The company should invest:

Invest = \$690,000 – 171,679.02
Invest = \$518,320.98

of its current cash holdings in marketable securities to bring the cash balance down to the optimal level. Over the rest of the year, sell securities:

Sell securities = $1,680,000/$171,679.02
Sell securities = 9.79 ≈ 10 times.

6.  The lower limit is the minimum balance allowed in the account, and the upper limit is the maximum balance allowed in the account. When the account balance drops to the lower limit:

Securities sold = $80,000 − 43,000
Securities sold = $37,000

in marketable securities will be sold, and the proceeds deposited in the account. This moves the account balance back to the target cash level. When the account balance rises to the upper limit, then:

Securities purchased = $125,000 − 80,000
Securities purchased = $45,000

of marketable securities will be purchased. This expenditure brings the cash level back down to the target balance of $80,000.

7.  The target cash balance using the Miller-Orr model is:

$$C^* = L + (3/4 \times F \times \sigma^2 / R]^{1/3}$$
$$C^* = \$1,500 + [3/4(\$40)(\$70)^2/.00021]^{1/3}$$
$$C^* = \$2,387.90$$

The upper limit is:

$$U^* = 3 \times C^* - 2 \times L$$
$$U^* = 3(\$2,387.90) - 2(\$1,500)$$
$$U^* = \$4,163.71$$

When the balance in the cash account drops to $1,500, the firm sells:

Sell = $2,387.90 − 1,500
Sell = $887.90

of marketable securities. The proceeds from the sale are used to replenish the account back to the optimal target level of $C^*$. Conversely, when the upper limit is reached, the firm buys:

Buy = $4,163.71 − 2,387.90
Buy = $1,775.81

of marketable securities. This expenditure lowers the cash level back down to the optimal level of $2,387.90.

8. As variance increases, the upper limit and the spread will increase, while the lower limit remains unchanged. The lower limit does not change because it is an exogenous variable set by management. As the variance increases, however, the amount of uncertainty increases. When this happens, the target cash balance, and therefore the upper limit and the spread, will need to be higher. If the variance drops to zero, then the lower limit, the target balance, and the upper limit will all be the same.

9. The average daily interest rate is:

Daily rate = $1.07^{1/365} - 1$
Daily rate = .000185 or .0185% per day

The target cash balance using the Miller-Orr model is:

$C^* = L + (3/4 \times F \times \sigma^2 / R)^{1/3}$
$C^* = \$160,000 + [3/4(\$300)(\$890,000)/.000185]^{1/3}$
$C^* = \$170,260.47$

The upper limit is:

$U^* = 3 \times C^* - 2 \times L$
$U^* = 3(\$170,260.47) - 2(\$160,000)$
$U^* = \$190,781.41$

10. Using the BAT model and solving for R, we get:

$C^* = [(2T \times F)/R]^{1/2}$
$\$2,700 = [2(\$28,000)(\$10)/R]^{1/2}$
$R = [2(\$28,000)(\$10)]/\$2,700^2$
$R = .0768$ or 7.68%

# CHAPTER 28
# CREDIT AND INVENTORY MANAGEMENT

## Answers to Concepts Review and Critical Thinking Questions

1.  *a.*   A sight draft is a commercial draft that is payable immediately.
    *b.*   A time draft is a commercial draft that does not require immediate payment.
    *c.*   A bankers acceptance is when a bank guarantees the future payment of a commercial draft.
    *d.*   A promissory note is an IOU that the customer signs.
    *e.*   A trade acceptance is when the buyer accepts the commercial draft and promises to pay it in the future.

2.  Trade credit is usually granted on open account. The invoice is the credit instrument.

3.  Credit costs: cost of debt, probability of default, and the cash discount
    No-credit costs: lost sales
    The sum of these are the carrying costs.

4.  *1.*   Character:   determines if a customer is willing to pay his or her debts.
    *2.*   Capacity:    determines if a customer is able to pay debts out of operating cash flow.
    *3.*   Capital:     determines the customer's financial reserves in case problems occur with operating cash flow.
    *4.*   Collateral:  assets that can be liquidated to pay off the loan in case of default.
    *5.*   Conditions:  customer's ability to weather an economic downturn and whether such a downturn is likely.

5.  *1.*   Perishability and collateral value
    *2.*   Consumer demand
    *3.*   Cost, profitability, and standardization
    *4.*   Credit risk
    *5.*   The size of the account
    *6.*   Competition
    *7.*   Customer type

    If the credit period exceeds a customer's operating cycle, then the firm is financing the receivables and other aspects of the customer's business that go beyond the purchase of the selling firm's merchandise.

6.  *a.*   B:   A is likely to sell for cash only, unless the product really works. If it does, then they might grant longer credit periods to entice buyers.
    *b.*   A:   Landlords have significantly greater collateral, and that collateral is not mobile.
    *c.*   A:   Since A's customers turn over inventory less frequently, they have a longer inventory period, and thus, will most likely have a longer credit period as well.
    *d.*   B:   Since A's merchandise is perishable and B's is not, B will probably have a longer credit period.

© 2013 by McGraw-Hill Education. This is proprietary material solely for authorized instructor use. Not authorized for sale or distribution in any manner. This document may not be copied, scanned, duplicated, forwarded, distributed, or posted on a website, in whole or part.

e.   A:   Rugs are fairly standardized and they are transportable, while carpets are custom fit and are not particularly transportable.

7. The three main categories of inventory are: raw material (initial inputs to the firm's production process), work-in-progress (partially completed products), and finished goods (products ready for sale). From the firm's perspective, the demand for finished goods is independent from the demand for the other types of inventory. The demand for raw material and work-in-progress is derived from, or dependent on, the firm's needs for these inventory types in order to achieve the desired levels of finished goods.

8. JIT systems reduce inventory amounts. Assuming no adverse effects on sales, inventory turnover will increase. Since assets will decrease, total asset turnover will also increase. Recalling the DuPont equation, an increase in total asset turnover, all else being equal, has a positive effect on ROE.

9. Carrying costs should be equal to order costs. Since the carrying costs are low relative to the order costs, the firm should increase the inventory level.

10. Since the price of components can decline quickly, Dell does not have inventory which is purchased and then declines quickly in value before it is sold. If this happens, the inventory may be sold at a loss. While this approach is valuable, it is difficult to implement. For example, Dell manufacturing plants will often have areas set aside that are for the suppliers. When parts are needed, it is a matter of going across the floor to get new parts. In fact, most computer manufacturers are trying to implement similar inventory systems.

## Solutions to Questions and Problems

*NOTE: All end of chapter problems were solved using a spreadsheet. Many problems require multiple steps. Due to space and readability constraints, when these intermediate steps are included in this solutions manual, rounding may appear to have occurred. However, the final answer for each problem is found without rounding during any step in the problem.*

### Basic

1.  a.   There are 30 days until account is overdue. If you take the full period, you must remit:

Remittance = 500($135)
Remittance = $67,500

b.   There is a 1 percent discount offered, with a 10 day discount period. If you take the discount, you will only have to remit:

Remittance = (1 − .01)($67,500)
Remittance = $66,825

c.   The implicit interest is the difference between the two remittance amounts, or:

Implicit interest = $67,500 − 66,825
Implicit interest = $675

The number of days' credit offered is:

Days' credit = 30 – 10
Days' credit = 20 days

2.  The receivables turnover is:

Receivables turnover = 365/Average collection period
Receivables turnover = 365/33
Receivables turnover = 11.061 times

And the average receivables are:

Average receivables = Sales/Receivables period
Average receivables = $34,000,000 / 11.061
Average receivables = $3,073,973

3.  *a.*   The average collection period is the percentage of accounts taking the discount times the discount period, plus the percentage of accounts not taking the discount times the days' until full payment is required, so:

Average collection period = .65(15 days) + .35(30 days)
Average collection period = 20.25 days

   *b.*   And the average daily balance is:

Average balance = 1,300($1,700)(20.25)(12/365)
Average balance = $1,471,315.07

4.  The daily sales are:

Daily sales = $27,500 / 7
Daily sales = $3,928.57

Since the average collection period is 27 days, the average accounts receivable is:

Average accounts receivable = $3,928.57(27)
Average accounts receivable = $106,071.43

5.  The interest rate for the term of the discount is:

Interest rate = .01/.99
Interest rate = .0101 or 1.01%

And the interest is for:

30 – 10 = 20 days

So, using the EAR equation, the effective annual interest rate is:

$$EAR = (1 + \text{Periodic rate})^m - 1$$
$$EAR = (1.0101)^{365/20} - 1$$
$$EAR = .2013 \text{ or } 20.13\%$$

*a.* The periodic interest rate is:

Interest rate = .02/.98
Interest rate = .0204 or 2.04%

And the EAR is:

$$EAR = (1.0204)^{365/20} - 1$$
$$EAR = .4459 \text{ or } 44.59\%$$

*b.* The EAR is:

$$EAR = (1.0101)^{365/50} - 1$$
$$EAR = .0761 \text{ or } = 7.61\%$$

*c.* The EAR is:

$$EAR = (1.0101)^{365/15} - 1$$
$$EAR = .2771 \text{ or } 27.71\%$$

**6.** The receivables turnover is:

Receivables turnover = 365/Average collection period
Receivables turnover = 365/36
Receivables turnover = 10.1389 times

And the annual credit sales are:

Annual credit sales = Receivables turnover × Average daily receivables
Annual credit sales = 10.1389($58,300)
Annual credit sales = $591,097.22

**7.** The total sales of the firm are equal to the total credit sales since all sales are on credit, so:

Total credit sales = 4,900($495)
Total credit sales = $2,425,500

The average collection period is the percentage of accounts taking the discount times the discount period, plus the percentage of accounts not taking the discount times the days' until full payment is required, so:

Average collection period = .40(10) + .60(40)
Average collection period = 28 days

The receivables turnover is 365 divided by the average collection period, so:

Receivables turnover = 365/28
Receivables turnover = 13.036 times

And the average receivables are the credit sales divided by the receivables turnover so:

Average receivables = $2,425,500/13.036
Average receivables = $186,065.75

If the firm increases the cash discount, more people will pay sooner, thus lowering the average collection period. If the ACP declines, the receivables turnover increases, which will lead to a decrease in the average receivables.

8.  The average collection period is the net credit terms plus the days overdue, so:

Average collection period = 30 + 6
Average collection period = 36 days

The receivables turnover is 365 divided by the average collection period, so:

Receivables turnover = 365/36
Receivables turnover = 10.1389 times

And the average receivables are the credit sales divided by the receivables turnover so:

Average receivables = $9,300,000 / 10.1389
Average receivables = $917,260.27

9.  *a.*  The cash outlay for the credit decision is the variable cost of the engine. If this is a one-time order, the cash inflow is the present value of the sales price of the engine times one minus the default probability. So, the NPV per unit is:

NPV = –$2,400,000 + (1 – .005)($2,625,000)/1.029
NPV = $138,265.31 per unit

The company should fill the order.

*b.*  To find the breakeven probability of default, $\pi$, we simply use the NPV equation from part *a*, set it equal to zero, and solve for $\pi$. Doing so, we get:

NPV = 0 = –$2,400,000 + (1 – $\pi$)($2,625,000)/1.029
$\pi$ = .0592 or 5.92%

We would not accept the order if the default probability was higher than 5.92 percent.

    *c.*    If the customer will become a repeat customer, the cash inflow changes. The cash inflow is now one minus the default probability, times the sales price minus the variable cost. We need to use the sales price minus the variable cost since we will have to build another engine for the customer in one period. Additionally, this cash inflow is now a perpetuity, so the NPV under these assumptions is:

NPV = −$2,400,000 + (1 − .005)($2,625,000 − 2,400,000)/.029
NPV = $5,319,827.59 per unit

The company should fill the order. The breakeven default probability under these assumptions is:

NPV = 0 = −$2,400,000 + (1 − π)($2,625,000 − 2,400,000)/.029
π = .6907 or 69.07%

We would not accept the order if the default probability was higher than 69.07 percent. This default probability is much higher than in part *b* because the customer may become a repeat customer.

    *d.*    It is assumed that if a person has paid his or her bills in the past, they will pay their bills in the future. This implies that if someone doesn't default when credit is first granted, then they will be a good customer far into the future, and the possible gains from the future business outweigh the possible losses from granting credit the first time.

**10.** The cost of switching is any lost sales from the existing policy plus the incremental variable costs under the new policy, so:

Cost of switching = $720(1,100) + $495(1,140 − 1,100)
Cost of switching = $811,800

The benefit of switching is any increase in the sales price minus the variable costs per unit, times the incremental units sold, so:

Benefit of switching = ($720 − 495)(1,140 − 1,100)
Benefit of switching = $9,000

The benefit of switching is a perpetuity, so the NPV of the decision to switch is:

NPV = −$811,800 + $9,000/.0095
NPV = $135,568.42

The firm will have to bear the cost of sales for one month before they receive any revenue from credit sales, which is why the initial cost is for one month. Receivables will grow over the one month credit period and will then remain stable with payments and new sales offsetting one another.

**11.** The carrying costs are the average inventory times the cost of carrying an individual unit, so:

Carrying costs = (1,700/2)($7) = $5,950

The order costs are the number of orders times the cost of an order, so:

Order costs = (52)($725) = $37,700

The economic order quantity is:

EOQ = [(2T × F)/CC]$^{1/2}$
EOQ = [2(52)(1,700)($725)/$7]$^{1/2}$
EOQ = 4,279.19

The firm's policy is not optimal, since the carrying costs and the order costs are not equal. The company should increase the order size and decrease the number of orders.

12. The carrying costs are the average inventory times the cost of carrying an individual unit, so:

Carrying costs = (750/2)($65) = $24,375

The order costs are the number of orders times the cost of an order, so:

Restocking costs = 52($395) = $20,540

The economic order quantity is:

EOQ = [(2T × F)/CC]$^{1/2}$
EOQ = [2(52)(750)($395)/$65]$^{1/2}$
EOQ = 688.48

The number of orders per year will be the total units sold per year divided by the EOQ, so:

Number of orders per year = 52(750)/688.48
Number of orders per year = 56.65

The firm's policy is not optimal, since the carrying costs and the order costs are not equal. The company should decrease the order size and increase the number of orders.

*Intermediate*

13. The total carrying costs are:

Carrying costs = (Q/2) × CC

where CC is the carrying cost per unit. The restocking costs are:

Restocking costs = F × (T/Q)

Setting these equations equal to each other and solving for Q, we find:

CC × (Q/2) = F × (T/Q)
Q$^2$ = 2 × F × T /CC
Q = [2F × T /CC]$^{1/2}$ = EOQ

**14.** The cash flow from either policy is:

Cash flow = $(P – v)Q$

So, the cash flows from the old policy are:

Cash flow from old policy = ($104 – 47)(3,240)
Cash flow from old policy = $184,680

And the cash flow from the new policy would be:

Cash flow from new policy = ($108 – 47)(3,295)
Cash flow from new policy = $200,995

So, the incremental cash flow would be:

Incremental cash flow = $200,995 – 184,680
Incremental cash flow = $16,315

The incremental cash flow is a perpetuity. The cost of initiating the new policy is:

Cost of new policy = $–[PQ + v(Q' – Q)]$

So, the NPV of the decision to change credit policies is:

NPV = –[($104)(3,240) + ($47)(3,295 – 3,240)] + $16,315/.025
NPV = $313,055

**15.** The cash flow from the old policy is:

Cash flow from old policy = ($295 – 230)(1,105)
Cash flow from old policy = $71,825

And the cash flow from the new policy will be:

Cash flow from new policy = ($302 – 234)(1,125)
Cash flow from new policy = $76,500

The incremental cash flow, which is a perpetuity, is the difference between the old policy cash flows and the new policy cash flows, so:

Incremental cash flow = $76,500 – 71,825
Incremental cash flow = $4,675

The cost of switching credit policies is:

Cost of new policy = $–[PQ + Q(v' – v) + v'(Q' – Q)]$

In this cost equation, we need to account for the increased variable cost for all units produced. This includes the units we already sell, plus the increased variable costs for the incremental units. So, the NPV of switching credit policies is:

NPV = –[($295)(1,105) + (1,105)($234 – 230) + ($234)(1,125 – 1,105)] + ($4,675/.0095)
NPV = $157,030.26

16. If the cost of subscribing to the credit agency is less than the savings from collection of the bad debts, the company should subscribe. The cost of the subscription is:

Cost of the subscription = $750 + $10(600)
Cost of the subscription = $6,750

And the savings from having no bad debts will be:

Savings from not selling to bad credit risks = ($525)(600)(.04)
Savings from not selling to bad credit risks = $12,600

So, the company's net savings will be:

Net savings = $12,600 – 6,750
Net savings = $5,850

The company should subscribe to the credit agency.

*Challenge*

17. The cost of switching credit policies is:

Cost of new policy = –[PQ + Q(v′ – v) + v′(Q′ – Q)]

And the cash flow from switching, which is a perpetuity, is:

Cash flow from new policy = [Q′(P′ – v) – Q(P – v)]

To find the breakeven quantity sold for switching credit policies, we set the NPV equal to zero and solve for Q′. Doing so, we find:

NPV = 0 = –[($104)(3,240) + ($47)(Q′ – 3,240)] + [(Q′)($108 – 47) – (3,240)($104 – 47)]/.025
0 = –$336,960 – $47Q′ + 152,280 + $2,440Q′ – $7,387,200
$2,393Q′ = $7,571,880
Q′ = 3,164.18

18. We can use the equation for the NPV we constructed in Problem 17. Using the sales figure of 3,400 units and solving for P′, we get:

NPV = 0 = [–($104)(3,240) – ($47)(3,400 – 3,240)] + [(P′ – 47)(3,400) – ($104 – 47)(3,240)]/.025
0 = –$336,960 – 7,520 + $136,000P′ – 6,392,000 – 7,387,200
$136,000P′ = $14,123,680
P′ = $103.85

**19.** From Problem 15, the incremental cash flow from the new credit policy will be:

Incremental cash flow = Q′(P′ − v′) − Q(P − v)
And the cost of the new policy is:

Cost of new policy = −[PQ + Q(v′ − v) + v′(Q′ − Q)]

Setting the NPV equal to zero and solving for P′, we get:

NPV = 0 = −[($295)(1,105) + ($234 − 230)(1,105) + ($234)(1,125 − 1,105)] + [(1,125)(P′ − 234) − (1,105)($295 − 230)]/.0095
0 = −[$325,975 + 4,420 + 4,680] + $118,421.05P′ − 27,710,526.32 − 7,560,526.32
$118,421.05P′ = $35,606,127.64
P′ = $300.67

**20.** Since the company sells 700 suits per week, and there are 52 weeks per year, the total number of suits sold is:

Total suits sold = 700 × 52 = 36,400

And, the EOQ is 500 suits, so the number of orders per year is:

Orders per year = 36,400 / 500 = 72.80

To determine the day when the next order is placed, we need to determine when the last order was placed. Since the suits arrived on Monday and there is a 3 day delay from the time the order was placed until the suits arrive, the last order was placed Friday. Since there are five days between the orders, the next order will be placed on Wednesday

Alternatively, we could consider that the store sells 100 suits per day (700 per week / 7 days). This implies that the store will be at the safety stock of 100 suits on Saturday when it opens. Since the suits must arrive before the store opens on Saturday, they should be ordered 3 days prior to account for the delivery time, which again means the suits should be ordered in Wednesday.

**21.** The cash outlay for the credit decision is the variable cost of the engine. Since the orders can be one-time or perpetual, the NPV of the decision is the weighted average of the two potential sales streams. The initial cost is the cost for all of the engines. So, the NPV is:

NPV = −$1,425,000 + (1 − .30)(125)($13,000)/1.019 + .30(125)($13,000 − 11,400)/.019
NPV = $2,849,185.22

The company should fill the order.

**22.** The default rate will affect the value of the one-time sales as well as the perpetual sales. All future cash flows need to be adjusted by the default rate. So, the NPV now is:

NPV = −$1,425,000 + (1 − .15)[(1 − .30)(125)($13,000)/1.019 + .30(125)($13,000 − 11,400)/.019]
NPV = $2,208,057.44

The company should still fill the order.

# *APPENDIX 28A*

1.  The cash flow from the old policy is the quantity sold times the price, so:

    Cash flow from old policy = 40,000($510)
    Cash flow from old policy = $20,400,000

    The cash flow from the new policy is the quantity sold times the new price, all times one minus the default rate, so:

    Cash flow from new policy = 40,000($537)(1 – .03)
    Cash flow from new policy = $20,835,600

    The incremental cash flow is the difference in the two cash flows, so:

    Incremental cash flow = $20,835,600 – 20,400,000
    Incremental cash flow = $435,600

    The cash flows from the new policy are a perpetuity. The cost is the old cash flow, so the NPV of the decision to switch is:

    NPV = –$20,400,000 + $435,600/.025
    NPV = –$2,976,000

2.  *a.*   The old price as a percentage of the new price is:

    $90/$91.84 = .98

    So the discount is:

    Discount = 1 – .98 = .02 or 2%

    The credit terms will be:

    Credit terms: 2/15, net 30

    *b.*   We are unable to determine for certain since no information is given concerning the percentage of customers who will take the discount. However, the maximum receivables would occur if all customers took the credit, so:

    Receivables = 3,300($90)
    Receivables = $297,000 (at a maximum)

    *c.*   Since the quantity sold does not change, variable cost is the same under either plan.

    *d.*   No, because:

    d – π = .02 – .11
    d – π = –.09 or –9%

Therefore the NPV will be negative. The NPV is:

NPV = –3,300($90) + (3,300)($91.84)(.02 – .11)/(.01)
NPV = –$3,023,592

The breakeven credit price is:

P(1 + r)/(1 – $\pi$) = $90(1.01)/(.89)
P = $102.13

This implies that the breakeven discount is:

Breakeven discount = 1 – ($90/$102.13)
Breakeven discount = .1188 or 11.88%

The NPV at this discount rate is:

NPV = –3,300($90) + (3,300)($102.13)(.1188 – .11)/(.01)
NPV $\approx$ 0

3.  *a.*  The cost of the credit policy switch is the quantity sold times the variable cost. The cash inflow is the price times the quantity sold, times one minus the default rate. This is a one-time, lump sum, so we need to discount this value one period. Doing so, we find the NPV is:

NPV = –15($760) + (1 – .2)(15)($1,140)/1.02
NPV = $2,011.76

The order should be taken since the NPV is positive.

   *b.*  To find the breakeven default rate, $\pi$, we just need to set the NPV equal to zero and solve for the breakeven default rate. Doing so, we get:

NPV = 0 = –15($760) + (1 – $\pi$)(15)($1,140)/1.02
$\pi$ = .3200 or 32.00%

   *c.*  Effectively, the cash discount is:

Cash discount = ($1,140 – 1,090)/$1,140
Cash discount = .0439 or 4.39%

Since the discount rate is less than the default rate, credit should not be granted. The firm would be better off taking the $1,090 up-front than taking an 80% chance of making $1,140.

4.  *a.*  The cash discount is:

Cash discount = ($75 – 71)/$75
Cash discount = .0533 or 5.33%

The default probability is one minus the probability of payment, or:

Default probability = 1 – .90
Default probability = .10

Since the default probability is greater than the cash discount, credit should not be granted; the NPV of doing so is negative.

b.  Due to the increase in both quantity sold and credit price when credit is granted, an additional incremental cost is incurred of:

Additional cost = (6,200)($33 – 32) + (6,900 – 6,200)($33)
Additional cost = $29,300

The breakeven price under these assumptions is:

NPV = 0 = –$29,300 – (6,200)($71) + {6,900[(1 – .10)P′ – $33] – 6,200($71 – 32)}/(1.0075$^3$ – 1)
NPV = –$29,300 – 440,200 + 273,940.31P′ – 10,044,478.08 – 10,666,468.16
$21,180,446.24 = $273,940.31P′
P′ = $77.32

c.  The credit report is an additional cost, so we have to include it in our analysis. The NPV when using the credit reports is:

NPV = 6,200(32) – .90(6,900)33 – 6,200(71) – 6,900($1.50) + {6,900[.90(75 – 33) – 1.50]
          – 6,200(71 – 32)}/(1.0075$^3$ – 1)
NPV = $198,400 – 204,930 – 440,200 – 10,350 + 384,457.73
NPV = –$74,622.27

The reports should not be purchased and credit should not be granted.

5.  We can express the old cash flow as:

Old cash flow = (P – v)Q

And the new cash flow will be:

New cash flow = (P – v)(1 – $\alpha$)Q′ + $\alpha$Q′ [(1 – $\pi$)P′ – v]

So, the incremental cash flow is

Incremental cash flow = –(P – v)Q + (P – v)(1 – $\alpha$)Q′ + $\alpha$Q′ [(1 – $\pi$)P′ – v]
Incremental cash flow = (P – v)(Q′ – Q) + $\alpha$Q′ [(1 – $\pi$)P′ – P]

Thus:

$$NPV = (P – v)(Q′ – Q) – \alpha PQ′ + \left[ \frac{(P – v)(Q′ – Q) + \alpha Q′\{(1 – \pi)P′ – P\}}{R} \right]$$

# CHAPTER 29
# MERGERS AND ACQUISITIONS

## Answers to Concepts Review and Critical Thinking Questions

1.  In the purchase method, assets are recorded at market value, and goodwill is created to account for the excess of the purchase price over this recorded value. In the pooling of interests method, the balance sheets of the two firms are simply combined; no goodwill is created. The choice of accounting method has no direct impact on the cash flows of the firms. EPS will probably be lower under the purchase method because reported income is usually lower due to the required amortization of the goodwill created in the purchase.

2.  *a.*  False. Although the reasoning seems correct, in general, the new firms do not have monopoly power. This is especially true since many countries have laws limiting mergers when it would create a monopoly.

    *b.*  True. When managers act in their own interest, acquisitions are an important control device for shareholders. It appears that some acquisitions and takeovers are the consequence of underlying conflicts between managers and shareholders.

    *c.*  False. Even if markets are efficient, the presence of synergy will make the value of the combined firm different from the sum of the values of the separate firms. Incremental cash flows provide the positive NPV of the transaction.

    *d.*  False. In an efficient market, traders will value takeovers based on "fundamental factors" regardless of the time horizon. Recall that the evidence as a whole suggests efficiency in the markets. Mergers should be no different.

    *e.*  False. The tax effect of an acquisition depends on whether the merger is taxable or non-taxable. In a taxable merger, there are two opposing factors to consider, the capital gains effect and the write-up effect. The net effect is the sum of these two effects.

    *f.*  True. Because of the coinsurance effect, wealth might be transferred from the stockholders to the bondholders. Acquisition analysis usually disregards this effect and considers only the total value.

3.  Diversification doesn't create value in and of itself because diversification reduces unsystematic, not systematic, risk. As discussed in the chapter on options, there is a more subtle issue as well. Reducing unsystematic risk benefits bondholders by making default less likely. However, if a merger is done purely to diversify (i.e., no operating synergy), then the NPV of the merger is zero. If the NPV is zero, and the bondholders are better off, then stockholders must be worse off.

4.  A firm might choose to split up because the newer, smaller firms may be better able to focus on their particular markets. Thus, reverse synergy is a possibility. An added advantage is that performance evaluation becomes much easier once the split is made because the new firm's financial results (and stock prices) are no longer commingled.

5. It depends on how they are used. If they are used to protect management, then they are not good for stockholders. If they are used by management to negotiate the best possible terms of a merger, then they are good for stockholders.

6. One of the primary advantages of a taxable merger is the write-up in the basis of the target firm's assets, while one of the primary disadvantages is the capital gains tax that is payable. The situation is the reverse for a tax-free merger.

   The basic determinant of tax status is whether or not the old stockholders will continue to participate in the new company, which is usually determined by whether they get any shares in the bidding firm. An LBO is usually taxable because the acquiring group pays off the current stockholders in full, usually in cash.

7. Economies of scale occur when average cost declines as output levels increase. A merger in this particular case might make sense because Eastern and Western may need less total capital investment to handle the peak power needs, thereby reducing average generation costs.

8. Among the defensive tactics often employed by management are seeking white knights, threatening to sell the crown jewels, appealing to regulatory agencies and the courts (if possible), and targeted share repurchases. Frequently, anti-takeover charter amendments are available as well, such as poison pills, poison puts, golden parachutes, lockup agreements, and supermajority amendments, but these require shareholder approval, so they can't be immediately used if time is short. While target firm shareholders may benefit from management actively fighting acquisition bids, in that it encourages higher bidding and may solicit bids from other parties as well, there is also the danger that such defensive tactics will discourage potential bidders from seeking the firm in the first place, which harms the shareholders.

9. In a cash offer, it almost surely does not make sense. In a stock offer, management may feel that one suitor is a better long-run investment than the other, but this is only valid if the market is not efficient. In general, the highest offer is the best one.

10. Various reasons include: (1) Anticipated gains may be smaller than thought; (2) Bidding firms are typically much larger, so any gains are spread thinly across shares; (3) Management may not be acting in the shareholders' best interest with many acquisitions; (4) Competition in the market for takeovers may force prices for target firms up to the zero NPV level; and (5) Market participants may have already discounted the gains from the merger before it is announced.

**Solutions to Questions and Problems**

*NOTE: All end-of-chapter problems were solved using a spreadsheet. Many problems require multiple steps. Due to space and readability constraints, when these intermediate steps are included in this solutions manual, rounding may appear to have occurred. However, the final answer for each problem is found without rounding during any step in the problem.*

*Basic*

1. For the merger to make economic sense, the acquirer must feel the acquisition will increase value by at least the amount of the premium over the market value, so:

   Minimum economic value = $340,000,000 − 317,000,000 = $23,000,000

2.  With the purchase method, the assets of the combined firm will be the book value of Firm X, the acquiring company, plus the market value of Firm Y, the target company, so:

Assets from X = 46,800($21) = $982,800 (book value)
Assets from Y = 36,000($19) = $684,000 (market value)

The purchase price of Firm Y is the number of shares outstanding times the sum of the current stock price per share plus the premium per share, so:

Purchase price of Y = 36,000($19 + 5) = $864,000

The goodwill created will be:

Goodwill = $864,000 – 684,000 = $180,000

And the total assets of the combined company will be:

Total assets XY = Total equity XY = $982,800 + 684,000 + 180,000 = $1,846,800

3.  Since the acquisition is funded by long-term debt, the post-merger balance sheet will have long-term debt equal to the original long-term debt of Jurion's balance sheet plus the new long-term debt issue, so:

Post-merger long-term debt = $9,300 + 15,000 = $24,300

Goodwill will be created since the acquisition price is greater than the market value. The goodwill amount is equal to the purchase price minus the market value of assets. Generally, the market value of current assets is equal to the book value, so:

Goodwill created = $15,000 – $8,900 (market value FA) – $3,500 (market value CA) = $2,600

Current liabilities and equity will remain the same as the pre-merger balance sheet of the acquiring firm. Current assets will be the sum of the two firm's pre-merger balance sheet accounts, and the fixed assets will be the sum of the pre-merger fixed assets of the acquirer and the market value of fixed assets of the target firm. The post-merger balance sheet will be:

*Jurion Co., post-merger*

| | | | |
|---|---|---|---|
| Current assets | $21,500 | Current liabilities | $ 5,100 |
| Fixed assets | 41,900 | Long-term debt | 24,300 |
| Goodwill | 2,600 | Equity | 36,600 |
| Total | $66,000 | Total | $66,000 |

4.  Since the acquisition is funded by long-term debt, the post-merger balance sheet will have long-term debt equal to the original long-term debt of Jurion's balance sheet plus the new long-term debt issue, so:

Post-merger long-term debt = $9,300 + 23,000 = $32,300

Goodwill will be created since the acquisition price is greater than the market value. The goodwill amount is equal to the purchase price minus the market value of assets. Generally, the market value of current assets is equal to the book value, so:

Goodwill created = $23,000 – $15,000 (market value FA) – $3,500 (market value CA) = $4,500

Current liabilities and equity will remain the same as the pre-merger balance sheet of the acquiring firm. Current assets will be the sum of the two firm's pre-merger balance sheet accounts, and the fixed assets will be the sum of the pre-merger fixed assets of the acquirer and the market value of fixed assets of the target firm. The post-merger balance sheet will be:

*Jurion Co., post-merger*

| Current assets | $21,500 | Current liabilities | $ 5,100 |
|---|---|---|---|
| Fixed assets | 48,000 | Long-term debt | 32,300 |
| Goodwill | 4,500 | Equity | 36,600 |
| Total | $74,000 | Total | $74,000 |

5.  Since the acquisition is funded by long-term debt, the post-merger balance sheet will have long-term debt equal to the original long-term debt of Silver's balance sheet plus the new long-term debt issue, so:

Post-merger long-term debt = $3,700 + 13,800 = $17,500

Goodwill will be created since the acquisition price is greater than the market value. The goodwill amount is equal to the purchase price minus the market value of assets. Since the market value of fixed assets of the target firm is equal to the book value, and the book value of all other assets is equal to market value, we can subtract the total assets from the purchase price, so:

Goodwill created = $13,500 – ($9,150 market value TA) = $4,650

Current liabilities and equity will remain the same as the pre-merger balance sheet of the acquiring firm. Current assets and other assets will be the sum of the two firm's pre-merger balance sheet accounts, and the fixed assets will be the sum of the pre-merger fixed assets of the acquirer and the market value of fixed assets of the target firm. Note, in this case, the market value and the book value of fixed assets are the same. The post-merger balance sheet will be:

*Silver Enterprises, post-merger*

| Current assets | $ 11,100 | Current liabilities | $ 5,200 |
|---|---|---|---|
| Other assets | 2,650 | Long-term debt | 17,500 |
| Net fixed assets | 21,600 | Equity | 17,300 |
| Goodwill | 4,650 | | |
| Total | $ 40,000 | Total | $40,000 |

6.  Since the acquisition is funded by long-term debt, the post-merger balance sheet will have long-term debt equal to the original long-term debt of Silver's balance sheet plus the new long-term debt issue, so:

Post-merger long-term debt = $3,700 + 10,500 = $14,200

Goodwill will be created since the acquisition price is greater than the market value. The goodwill amount is equal to the purchase price minus the market value of assets. Since the market value of fixed assets of the target firm is equal to the book value, and the book value of all other assets is equal to market value, we can subtract the total assets from the purchase price, so:

Goodwill created = $10,500 – ($9,150 market value TA) = $1,350

Current liabilities and equity will remain the same as the pre-merger balance sheet of the acquiring firm. Current assets and other assets will be the sum of the two firm's pre-merger balance sheet accounts, and the fixed assets will be the sum of the pre-merger fixed assets of the acquirer and the market value of fixed assets of the target firm. Note, in this case, the market value and the book value of fixed assets are the same. The post-merger balance sheet will be:

*Silver Enterprises, post-merger*

| Current assets | $ 11,100 | Current liabilities | $ 5,200 |
|---|---|---|---|
| Other assets | 2,650 | Long-term debt | 14,200 |
| Net fixed assets | 21,600 | Equity | 17,300 |
| Goodwill | 1,350 | | |
| Total | $ 36,700 | Total | $36,700 |

**7.** *a.* The cash cost is the amount of cash offered, so the cash cost is $48 million.

To calculate the cost of the stock offer, we first need to calculate the value of the target to the acquirer. The value of the target firm to the acquiring firm will be the market value of the target plus the PV of the incremental cash flows generated by the target firm. The cash flows are a perpetuity, so

$V^* = \$45,000,000 + \$1,100,000/.12 = \$54,166,667$

The cost of the stock offer is the percentage of the acquiring firm given up times the sum of the market value of the acquiring firm and the value of the target firm to the acquiring firm. So, the equity cost will be:

Equity cost = .40($62,000,000 + 54,166,667) = $46,466,667

*b.* The NPV of each offer is the value of the target firm to the acquiring firm minus the cost of acquisition, so:

NPV cash = $54,166,667 – 48,000,000 = $6,166,667

NPV stock = $54,166,667 – 46,466,667 = $7,700,000

*c.* Since the NPV is greater with the stock offer, the acquisition should done with stock.

**8.** *a.* The EPS of the combined company will be the sum of the earnings of both companies divided by the shares in the combined company. Since the stock offer is one share of the acquiring firm for three shares of the target firm, new shares in the acquiring firm will increase by one-third of the number of shares of the target company. So, the new EPS will be:

EPS = ($230,000 + 690,000)/[146,000 + (1/3)(73,000)] = $5.401

The market price of Stultz will remain unchanged if it is a zero NPV acquisition. Using the P/E ratio, we find the current market price of Stultz stock, which is:

P = 12.7($690,000)/146,000 = $60.02

If the acquisition has a zero NPV, the stock price should remain unchanged. Therefore, the new PE will be:

P/E = $60.02/$5.401 = 11.11

*b.* The value of Flannery to Stultz must be the market value of the company since the NPV of the acquisition is zero. Therefore, the value is:

$V^* = $230,000(6.35) = $1,460,500$

The cost of the acquisition is the number of shares offered times the share price, so the cost is:

Cost = (1/3)(73,000)($60.02) = $1,460,500

So, the NPV of the acquisition is:

$NPV = 0 = V^* + \Delta V - Cost = $1,460,500 + \Delta V - 1,460,500$
$\Delta V = $0$

Although there is no economic value to the takeover, it is possible that Stultz is motivated to purchase Flannery for other than financial reasons.

**9.** The decision hinges upon the risk of surviving. That is, consider the wealth transfer from bondholders to stockholders when risky projects are undertaken. High-risk projects will reduce the expected value of the bondholders' claims on the firm. The telecommunications business is riskier than the utilities business.

If the total value of the firm does not change, the increase in risk should favor the stockholder. Hence, management should approve this transaction.

If the total value of the firm drops because of the transaction, and the wealth effect is lower than the reduction in total value, management should reject the project.

**10.** *a.* The NPV of the merger is the market value of the target firm, plus the value of the synergy, minus the acquisition costs, so:

NPV = 1,200($24) + $9,500 - 1,200($30) = $2,300

b.  Since the NPV goes directly to stockholders, the share price of the merged firm will be the market value of the acquiring firm plus the NPV of the acquisition, divided by the number of shares outstanding, so:

Share price = [4,800($36) + $2,300]/4,800 = $36.48

c.  The merger premium is the premium per share times the number of shares of the target firm outstanding, so the merger premium is:

Merger premium = 1,200($30 – 24) = $7,200

d.  The number of new shares will be the number of shares of the target times the exchange ratio, so:

New shares created = 1,200(4/5) = 960 new shares

The value of the merged firm will be the market value of the acquirer plus the market value of the target plus the synergy benefits, so:

$V_{BT}$ = 4,800($36) + 1,200($24) + $9,500 = $211,100

The price per share of the merged firm will be the value of the merged firm divided by the total shares of the new firm, which is:

P = $211,100/(4,800 + 960) = $36.65

e.  The NPV of the acquisition using a share exchange is the market value of the target firm plus synergy benefits, minus the cost. The cost is the value per share of the merged firm times the number of shares offered to the target firm shareholders, so:

NPV = 1,200($24) + $9,500 – 960($36.65) = $3,116.67

### Intermediate

11. The cash offer is better for the target firm shareholders since they receive $30 per share. In the share offer, the target firm's shareholders will receive:

Equity offer value = (4/5)($24) = $19.20 per share

From Problem 10, we know the value of the merged firm's assets will be $211,100. The number of shares in the new firm will be:

Shares in new firm = 4,800 + 1,200x

that is, the number of shares outstanding in the bidding firm, plus the number of shares outstanding in the target firm, times the exchange ratio. This means the post merger share price will be:

P = $211,100/(4,800 + 1,200x)

To make the target firm's shareholders indifferent, they must receive the same wealth, so:

1,200(x)P = 1,200($30)

This equation shows that the new offer is the shares outstanding in the target company times the exchange ratio times the new stock price. The value under the cash offer is the shares outstanding times the cash offer price. Solving this equation for P, we find:

P = $30 / ×

Combining the two equations, we find:

$211,100/(4,800 + 1,200x) = $30 / x
x = .8224

There is a simpler solution that requires an economic understanding of the merger terms. If the target firm's shareholders are indifferent, the bidding firm's shareholders are indifferent as well. That is, the offer is a zero sum game. Using the new stock price produced by the cash deal, we find:

Exchange ratio = $30/$36.48 = .8224

12. The cost of the acquisition is:

Cost = 300($18) = $5,400

Since the stock price of the acquiring firm is $60, the firm will have to give up:

Shares offered = $5,400/$60 = 90 shares

a.   The EPS of the merged firm will be the combined EPS of the existing firms divided by the new shares outstanding, so:

EPS = ($2,100 + 700)/(900 + 90) = $2.83

b.   The PE of the acquiring firm is:

Original P/E = $60/($2,100/900) = 25.71 times

Assuming the PE ratio does not change, the new stock price will be:

New P = $2.83(25.71) = $72.73

c.   If the market correctly analyzes the earnings, the stock price will remain unchanged since this is a zero NPV acquisition, so:

New P/E = $60/$2.83 = 21.21 times

*d.*  The new share price will be the combined market value of the two existing companies divided by the number of shares outstanding in the merged company. So:

P = [(900)($60) + 300($17)]/(900 + 90) = $59.70

And the PE ratio of the merged company will be:

P/E = $59.70/$2.83 = 21.11 times

At the proposed bid price, this is a negative NPV acquisition for A since the share price declines. They should revise their bid downward until the NPV is zero.

**13.**  Beginning with the fact that the NPV of a merger is the value of the target minus the cost, we get:

$$NPV = V_B^* - Cost$$
$$NPV = \Delta V + V_B - Cost$$
$$NPV = \Delta V - (Cost - V_B)$$
$$NPV = \Delta V - Merger\ premium$$

**14.**  *a.*  The synergy will be the present value of the incremental cash flows of the proposed purchase. Since the cash flows are perpetual, the synergy value is:

Synergy value = $390,000 / .08
Synergy value = $4,875,000

*b.*  The value of Flash-in-the-Pan to Fly-by-Night is the synergy plus the current market value of Flash-in-the-Pan, which is:

Value = $4,875,000 + 7,000,000
Value = $11,875,000

*c.*  The value of the cash option is the amount of cash paid, or $9 million. The value of the stock acquisition is the percentage of ownership in the merged company, times the value of the merged company, so:

Stock acquisition value = .30($11,875,000 + 22,000,000)
Stock acquisition value = $10,162,500

*d.*  The NPV is the value of the acquisition minus the cost, so the NPV of each alternative is:

NPV of cash offer = $11,875,000 – 9,000,000
NPV of cash offer = $2,875,000

NPV of stock offer = $11,875,000 – 10,162,500
NPV of stock offer = $1,712,500

*e.*  The acquirer should make the cash offer since its NPV is greater.

**15.** *a.* The number of shares after the acquisition will be the current number of shares outstanding for the acquiring firm, plus the number of new shares created for the acquisition, which is:

Number of shares after acquisition = 30,000,000 + 12,000,000
Number of shares after acquisition = 42,000,000

And the share price will be the value of the combined company divided by the shares outstanding, which will be:

New stock price = £590,000,000 / 42,000,000
New stock price = £14.05

*b.* Let $\alpha$ equal the fraction of ownership for the target shareholders in the new firm. We can set the percentage of ownership in the new firm equal to the value of the cash offer, so:

$\alpha$(£590,000,000) = £175,000,000
$\alpha$ = .2966 or 29.66%

So, the shareholders of the target firm would be equally as well off if they received 29.66 percent of the stock in the new company as if they received the cash offer. The ownership percentage of the target firm shareholders in the new firm can be expressed as:

Ownership = New shares issued / (New shares issued + Current shares of acquiring firm)
.2966 = New shares issued / (New shares issued + 30,000,000)
New shares issued = 12,650,602

To find the exchange ratio, we divide the new shares issued to the shareholders of the target firm by the existing number of shares in the target firm, so:

Exchange ratio = New shares / Existing shares in target firm
Exchange ratio = 12,650,602 / 18,000,000
Exchange ratio = .7028

An exchange ratio of .7028 shares of the merged company for each share of the target company owned would make the value of the stock offer equivalent to the value of the cash offer.

**16.** *a.* The value of each company is the sum of the probability of each state of the economy times the value of the company in that state of the economy, so:

Value$_{Bentley}$ = .70($290,000) + .30($110,000)
Value$_{Bentley}$ = $236,000

Value$_{Rolls}$ = .70($260,000) + .30($80,000)
Value$_{Rolls}$ = $206,000

b.  The value of each company's equity is sum of the probability of each state of the economy times the value of the equity in that state of the economy. The value of equity in each state of the economy is the maximum of total company value minus the value of debt, or zero. Since Rolls is an all equity company, the value of its equity is simply the total value of the firm, or $206,000. The value of Bentley's equity in a boom is $165,000 ($290,000 company value minus $125,000 debt value), and the value of Bentley's equity in a recession is zero since the value of its debt is greater than the value of the company in that state of the economy. So, the value of Bentley's equity is:

$$\text{Equity}_{\text{Bentley}} = .70(\$165,000) + .30(\$0)$$
$$\text{Equity}_{\text{Bentley}} = \$115,500$$

The value of Bentley's debt in a boom is the full face value of $125,000. In a recession, the value of the company's debt is $110,000 since the value of the debt cannot exceed the value of the company. So, the value of Bentley's debt today is:

$$\text{Debt}_{\text{Bentley}} = .70(\$125,000) + .30(\$110,000)$$
$$\text{Debt}_{\text{Bentley}} = \$120,500$$

Note, this is also the value of the company minus the value of the equity, or:

$$\text{Debt}_{\text{Bentley}} = \$236,000 - 115,500$$
$$\text{Debt}_{\text{Bentley}} = \$120,500$$

c.  The combined value of the companies, the combined equity value, and combined debt value is:

Combined value = $236,000 + 206,000
Combined value = $442,000

Combined equity value = $115,500 + 206,000
Combined equity value = $321,500

Combined debt value = $120,500

d.  To find the value of the merged company, we need to find the value of the merged company in each state of the economy, which is:

Boom merged value = $290,000 + 260,000
Boom merged value = $550,000

Recession merged value = $110,000 + 80,000
Recession merged value = $190,000

So, the value of the merged company today is:

Merged company value = .70($550,000) + .30($190,000)
Merged company value = $442,000

Since the merged company will still have $125,000 in debt, the value of the equity in a boom is $425,000, and the value of equity in a recession is $65,000. So, the value of the merged company's equity is:

Merged equity value = .70($425,000) + .30($65,000)
Merged equity value = $317,000

The merged company will have a value greater than the face value of debt in both states of the economy, so the value of the company's debt is $125,000.

e.   There is a wealth transfer in this case. The combined equity value before the merger was $321,500, but the value of the equity in the merged company is only $317,000, a loss of $4,500 for stockholders. The value of the debt in the combined companies was only $120,500, but the value of debt in the merged company is $125,000 since there is no chance of default. The bondholders gained $4,500, exactly the amount the stockholders lost.

f.   If the value of Bentley's debt before the merger is less than the lowest firm value, there is no coinsurance effect. Since there is no possibility of default before the merger, bondholders do not gain after the merger.

## Challenge

17.  a.   To find the value of the target to the acquirer, we need to find the share price with the new growth rate. We begin by finding the required return for shareholders of the target firm. The earnings per share of the target are:

$EPS_P$ = $960,000/750,000 = $1.28 per share

The price per share is:

$P_P$ = 10($1.28) = $12.80

And the dividends per share are:

$DPS_P$ = $470,000/750,000 = $.63

The current required return for Palmer shareholders, which incorporates the risk of the company is:

$R_E$ = [$.63(1.04)/$12.80] + .04 = .0909

The price per share of Palmer with the new growth rate is:

$P_P$ = $.63(1.06)/(.0909 − .06) = $21.49

The value of the target firm to the acquiring firm is the number of shares outstanding times the price per share under the new growth rate assumptions, so:

$V_T^*$ = 750,000($21.49) = $16,114,285.71

b. The gain to the acquiring firm will be the value of the target firm to the acquiring firm minus the market value of the target, so:

Gain = $16,114,285.71 – 750,000($12.80) = $6,514,285.71

c. The NPV of the acquisition is the value of the target firm to the acquiring firm minus the cost of the acquisition, so:

NPV = $16,114,285.71 – 750,000($20) = $1,114,285.71

d. The most the acquiring firm should be willing to pay per share is the offer price per share plus the NPV per share, so:

Maximum bid price = $20 + ($1,114,285.71/750,000) = $21.49

Notice that this is the same value we calculated earlier in part *a* as the value of the target to the acquirer.

e. The price of the stock in the merged firm would be the market value of the acquiring firm plus the value of the target to the acquirer, divided by the number of shares in the merged firm, so:

$P_{FP}$ = ($60,900,000 + 16,114,285.71)/(1,500,000 + 225,000) = $44.65

The NPV of the stock offer is the value of the target to the acquirer minus the value offered to the target shareholders. The value offered to the target shareholders is the stock price of the merged firm times the number of shares offered, so:

NPV = $16,114,285.71 – 225,000($44.65) = $6,068,944.10

f. Yes, the acquisition should go forward, and Plant should offer shares since the NPV is higher.

g. Using the new growth rate in the dividend growth model, along with the dividend and required return we calculated earlier, the price of the target under these assumptions is:

$P_P$ = $.63(1.05)/(.0909 – .05) = $16.08

And the value of the target firm to the acquiring firm is:

$V_P^*$ = 750,000($16.08) = $12,061,099.80

The gain to the acquiring firm will be:

Gain = $12,061,099.80 – 750,000($12.80) = $2,461,099.80

The NPV of the cash offer is now:

NPV cash = $12,061,099.80 – 750,000($20) = –$2,938,900.20

And the new price per share of the merged firm will be:

$P_{FP}$ = [$60,900,000 + 12,061,099.80]/(1,500,000 + 225,000) = $42.30

And the NPV of the stock offer under the new assumption will be:

NPV stock = $12,061,099.80 − 225,000($42.30) = $2,544,434.61

Even with the lower projected growth rate, the stock offer still has a positive NPV. The NPV of the stock offer is still higher. Plant should purchase Palmer with a stock offer of 225,000 shares.

18. *a.* To find the distribution of joint values, we first must find the joint probabilities. To do this, we need to find the joint probabilities for each possible combination of weather in the two towns. The weather conditions are independent; therefore, the joint probabilities are the products of the individual probabilities.

| Possible states | Joint probability |
|---|---|
| Rain-Rain | .1(.1) = .01 |
| Rain-Warm | .1(.4) = .04 |
| Rain-Hot | .1(.5) = .05 |
| Warm-Rain | .4(.1) = .04 |
| Warm-Warm | .4(.4) = .16 |
| Warm-Hot | .4(.5) = .20 |
| Hot-Rain | .5(.1) = .05 |
| Hot-Warm | .5(.4) = .20 |
| Hot-Hot | .5(.5) = .25 |

Next, note that the revenue when rainy is the same regardless of which town. So, since the state "Rain-Warm" has the same outcome (revenue) as "Warm-Rain", their probabilities can be added. The same is true of "Rain-Hot" / "Hot-Rain" and "Warm-Hot" / "Hot-Warm". Thus the joint probabilities are:

| Possible states | Joint probability |
|---|---|
| Rain-Rain | .01 |
| Rain-Warm | .08 |
| Rain-Hot | .10 |
| Warm-Warm | .16 |
| Warm-Hot | .40 |
| Hot-Hot | .25 |

Finally, the joint values are the sums of the values of the two companies for the particular state.

| Possible states | | Joint value |
|---|---|---|
| Rain-Rain | $250,000 + 250,000 = | $500,000 |
| Rain-Warm | $250,000 + 425,000 = | 675,000 |
| Rain-Hot | $250,000 + 875,000 = | 1,125,000 |
| Warm-Warm | $425,000 + 425,000 = | 850,000 |
| Warm-Hot | $425,000 + 875,000 = | 1,300,000 |
| Hot-Hot | $875,000 + 875,000 = | 1,750,000 |

b.  Recall that if a firm cannot service its debt, the bondholders receive the value of the assets. Thus, the value of the debt is reduced to the value of the company if the face value of the debt is greater than the value of the company. If the value of the company is greater than the value of the debt, the value of the debt is its face value. Here, the value of the common stock is always the residual value of the firm over the value of the debt. So, the value of the debt and the value of the stock in each state is:

| Possible states | Joint Prob. | Joint Value | Debt Value | Stock Value |
|---|---|---|---|---|
| Rain-Rain | .01 | $500,000 | $500,000 | $0 |
| Rain-Warm | .08 | 675,000 | 675,000 | 0 |
| Rain-Hot | .10 | 1,125,000 | 850,000 | 275,000 |
| Warm-Warm | .16 | 850,000 | 850,000 | 0 |
| Warm-Hot | .40 | 1,300,000 | 850,000 | 450,000 |
| Hot-Hot | .25 | 1,750,000 | 850,000 | 900,000 |

c.  The bondholders are better off if the value of the debt after the merger is greater than the value of the debt before the merger. The value of the debt is the smaller of the debt value or the company value. So, the value of the debt of each individual company before the merger in each state is:

| Possible states | Probability | Debt Value |
|---|---|---|
| Rain | .10 | $250,000 |
| Warm | .40 | 425,000 |
| Hot | .50 | 425,000 |

Individual debt value = .1($250,000) + .4($425,000) + .5($425,000)
Individual debt value = $407,500

This means the total value of the debt for both companies pre-merger must be:

Total debt value pre-merger = 2($407,500)
Total debt value pre-merger = $815,000

To get the expected debt value, post-merger, we can use the joint probabilities for each possible state and the debt values corresponding to each state we found in part c. Using this information to find the value of the debt in the post-merger firm, we get:

Total debt value post-merger = .01($500,000) + .08($675,000) + .10($850,000)
                             + .16($850,000) + .40($850,000) + .25($850,000)
Total debt value post-merger = $832,500

The bondholders are better off by $17,500. Since we have already shown that the total value of the combined company is the same as the sum of the value of the individual companies, the implication is that the stockholders are worse off by $17,500.

# CHAPTER 30
# FINANCIAL DISTRESS

**Answers to Concepts Review and Critical Thinking Questions**

1. Financial distress is often linked to insolvency. Stock-based insolvency occurs when a firm has a negative net worth. Flow-based insolvency occurs when operating cash flow is insufficient to meet current obligations.

2. Financial distress frequently can serve as a firm's "early warning" sign for trouble. Thus, it can be beneficial since it may bring about new organizational forms and new operating strategies.

3. A prepackaged bankruptcy is where the firm and most creditors agree to a private reorganization before bankruptcy takes place. After the private agreement, the firm files for formal bankruptcy. The biggest advantage is that a prepackaged bankruptcy is usually cheaper and faster than a traditional bankruptcy.

4. Just because a firm is experiencing financial distress doesn't necessarily imply the firm is worth more dead than alive.

5. Liquidation occurs when the assets of a firm are sold and payments are made to creditors (usually based upon the APR). Reorganization is the restructuring of the firm's finances.

6. The absolute priority rule is the priority rule of the distribution of the proceeds of the liquidation. It begins with the first claim to the last, in the order: administrative expenses, unsecured claims after a filing of involuntary bankruptcy petition, wages, employee benefit plans, consumer claims, taxes, secured and unsecured loans, preferred stocks and common stocks.

7. Bankruptcy allows firms to issue new debt that is senior to all previously incurred debt. This new debt is called DIP (debtor in possession) debt. If DIP loans were not senior to all other debt, a firm in bankruptcy would be unable to obtain financing necessary to continue operations while in bankruptcy since the lender would be unlikely to make the loan.

8. One answer is that the right to file for bankruptcy is a valuable asset, and the financial manager acts in shareholders' best interest by managing this asset in ways that maximize its value. To the extent that a bankruptcy filing prevents "a race to the courthouse steps," it would seem to be a reasonable use of the process.

9. As in the previous question, it could be argued that using bankruptcy laws as a sword may simply be the best use of the asset. Creditors are aware at the time a loan is made of the possibility of bankruptcy, and the interest charged incorporates it. If the only way a firm can continue to operate is to reduce labor costs, it may be a benefit to everyone, including employees.

10. There are four possible reasons why firms may choose legal bankruptcy over private workout: 1) It may be less expensive (although legal bankruptcy is usually more expensive). 2) Equity investors can use legal bankruptcy to "hold out." 3) A complicated capital structure makes private workouts more difficult. 4) Conflicts of interest between creditors, equity investors and management can make private workouts impossible.

## Solutions to Questions and Problems

*NOTE: All end of chapter problems were solved using a spreadsheet. Many problems require multiple steps. Due to space and readability constraints, when these intermediate steps are included in this solutions manual, rounding may appear to have occurred. However, the final answer for each problem is found without rounding during any step in the problem.*

### Basic

1.  Under the absolute priority rule (APR), claims are paid out in full to the extent there are assets. In this case, assets are $28,500, so you should propose the following:

    |  | Original claim | Distribution of liquidating value |
    |---|---|---|
    | Trade credit | $4,800 | $4,800 |
    | Secured mortgage notes | 8,000 | 8,000 |
    | Senior debentures | 10,000 | 10,000 |
    | Junior debentures | 15,000 | 5,700 |
    | Equity | 0 | 0 |

2.  There are many possible reorganization plans, so we will make an assumption that the mortgage bonds are fully recognized as senior debentures, the senior debentures will receive junior debentures in the value of 65 cents on the dollar, and the junior debentures will receive any remaining value as equity. With these assumptions, the reorganization plan will look like this:

    |  | Original claim |  | Reorganized claim |
    |---|---|---|---|
    | Mortgage bonds | $19,000 | Senior debenture | $19,000 |
    | Senior debentures | 9,500 | Junior debenture | 6,175 |
    | Junior debentures | 7,500 | Equity | 1,825 |

3.  Since we are given shares outstanding and a share price, the company must be publicly traded. First, we need to calculate the market value of equity, which is:

    Market value of equity = 5,000($21) = $105,000

    We also need the book value of debt. Since we have the value of total assets and the book value of equity, the book value of debt must be the difference between these two figures, or:

    Book value of debt = Total assets – Book value of equity
    Book value of debt = $75,000 – 19,000
    Book value of debt = $56,000

    Now, we can calculate the Z-score for a publicly traded company, which is:

    Z-score = 3.3(EBIT/Total assets) + 1.2(NWC/Total assets) + 1.0(Sales/Total assets)
        + .6(Market value of equity/Book value of equity)
        + 1.4(Accumulated retained earnings/Total assets)

Z-score = 3.3($6,900/$75,000) + 1.2($3,400/$75,000) + ($92,000/$75,000) + .6($105,000/$19,000)
      +1.4($16,800/$75,000)

Z-score = 5.214

4.  Since this company is private, we must use the Z-score for private companies and non-manufacturers, which is:

Z-score = 6.56(NWC/Total assets) + 3.26(Accumulated retained earnings/Total assets)
      + 1.05(EBIT/Total assets) + 6.72(Book value of equity/Total liabilities)

Z-score = 6.56($4,200/$63,000) + 3.26($16,000/$63,000) + 1.05($7,900/$63,000)
      + 6.72($18,000/$57,000)

Z-score = 3.519

# CHAPTER 31
# INTERNATIONAL CORPORATE FINANCE

## Answers to Concepts Review and Critical Thinking Questions

1. *a.* The dollar is selling at a premium because it is more expensive in the forward market than in the spot market (SF 1.11 versus SF 1.09).

   *b.* The franc is expected to depreciate relative to the dollar because it will take more francs to buy one dollar in the future than it does today.

   *c.* Inflation in Switzerland is higher than in the United States, as are nominal interest rates.

2. The exchange rate will increase, as it will take progressively more pesos to purchase a dollar. This is the relative PPP relationship.

3. *a.* The Australian dollar is expected to weaken relative to the dollar, because it will take more A\$ in the future to buy one dollar than it does today.

   *b.* The inflation rate in Australia is higher.

   *c.* Nominal interest rates in Australia are higher; relative real rates in the two countries are the same.

4. No. For example, if a country's currency strengthens, imports become cheaper (good), but its exports become more expensive for others to buy (bad). The reverse is true for currency depreciation.

5. Additional advantages include being closer to the final consumer and, thereby, saving on transportation, significantly lower wages, and less exposure to exchange rate risk. Disadvantages include political risk and costs of supervising distant operations.

6. One key thing to remember is that dividend payments are made in the home currency. More generally, it may be that the owners of the multinational are primarily domestic and are ultimately concerned about their wealth denominated in their home currency because, unlike a multinational, they are not internationally diversified.

7. *a.* False. If prices are rising faster in Great Britain, it will take more pounds to buy the same amount of goods that one dollar can buy; the pound will depreciate relative to the dollar.

   *b.* False. The forward market would already reflect the projected deterioration of the euro relative to the dollar. Only if you feel that there might be additional, unanticipated weakening of the euro that isn't reflected in forward rates today, will the forward hedge protect you against additional declines.

   *c.* True. The market would only be correct on average, while you would be correct all the time.

31-1

8. *a.* American exporters: their situation in general improves because a sale of the exported goods for a fixed number of euros will be worth more dollars.
   American importers: their situation in general worsens because the purchase of the imported goods for a fixed number of euros will cost more in dollars.

   *b.* American exporters: they would generally be better off if the British government's intentions result in a strengthened pound.
   American importers: they would generally be worse off if the pound strengthens.

   *c.* American exporters: they would generally be much worse off, because an extreme case of fiscal expansion like this one will make American goods prohibitively expensive to buy, or else Brazilian sales, if fixed in reais, would become worth an unacceptably low number of dollars.
   American importers: they would generally be much better off, because Brazilian goods will become much cheaper to purchase in dollars.

9. IRP is the most likely to hold because it presents the easiest and least costly means to exploit any arbitrage opportunities. Relative PPP is least likely to hold since it depends on the absence of market imperfections and frictions in order to hold strictly.

10. It all depends on whether the forward market expects the same appreciation over the period and whether the expectation is accurate. Assuming that the expectation is correct and that other traders do not have the same information, there will be value to hedging the currency exposure.

11. One possible reason investment in the foreign subsidiary might be preferred is if this investment provides direct diversification that shareholders could not attain by investing on their own. Another reason could be if the political climate in the foreign country was more stable than in the home country. Increased political risk can also be a reason you might prefer the home subsidiary investment. Indonesia can serve as a great example of political risk. If it cannot be diversified away, investing in this type of foreign country will increase the systematic risk. As a result, it will raise the cost of the capital, and could actually decrease the NPV of the investment.

12. Yes, the firm should undertake the foreign investment. If, after taking into consideration all risks, a project in a foreign country has a positive NPV, the firm should undertake it. Note that in practice, the stated assumption (that the adjustment to the discount rate has taken into consideration all political and diversification issues) is a huge task. But once that has been addressed, the net present value principle holds for foreign operations, just as for domestic.

13. If the foreign currency depreciates, the U.S. parent will experience an exchange rate loss when the foreign cash flow is remitted to the U.S. This problem could be overcome by selling forward contracts. Another way of overcoming this problem would be to borrow in the country where the project is located.

14. False. If the financial markets are perfectly competitive, the difference between the Eurodollar rate and the U.S. rate will be due to differences in risk and government regulation. Therefore, speculating in those markets will not be beneficial.

**Solutions to Questions and Problems**

*NOTE: All end-of-chapter problems were solved using a spreadsheet. Many problems require multiple steps. Due to space and readability constraints, when these intermediate steps are included in this solutions manual, rounding may appear to have occurred. However, the final answer for each problem is found without rounding during any step in the problem.*

*Basic*

1. Using the quotes from the table, we get:

    a.  $100(€.7310/$1) = €73.10

    b.  $1.3679

    c.  €5M($1.3679/€) = $6,839,500

    d.  New Zealand dollar

    e.  Mexican peso

    f.  (P12.8533/$1)($1.3679/€1) = P17.5820/€

       This is a cross rate.

    g.  The most valuable is the Kuwait dinar. The least valuable is the Vietnam dong.

2.  a.  You would prefer £100, since:

       (£100)($1.5862/£1) = $158.620

    b.  You would still prefer £100. Using the $/£ exchange rate and the SF/$ exchange rate to find the amount of Swiss francs £100 will buy, we get:

       (£100)($1.5862/£1)(SF .8799) = SF 139.5697

    c.  Using the quotes in the book to find the SF/£ cross rate, we find:

       (SF /$.8799)($1.5862/£1) = SF 1.3957/£1

       The £/SF exchange rate is the inverse of the SF/£ exchange rate, so:

       £1/SF 1.3957 = £.7165/SF 1

3.  a.  $F_{180}$ = ¥76.96(per $). The yen is selling at a premium because it is more expensive in the forward market than in the spot market ($.0129517 versus $.0129938).

    b.  $F_{90}$ = $.6309/£. The pound is selling at a discount because it is less expensive in the forward market than in the spot market ($1.58629 versus $1.58504).

    *c.*    The value of the dollar will fall relative to the yen, since it takes more dollars to buy one yen in the future than it does today. The value of the dollar will rise relative to the pound, because it will take less dollars to buy one pound in the future than it does today.

**4.**   *a.*    The U.S. dollar, since one Canadian dollar will buy:

    (Can$1)/(Can$1.05/$1) = $.9524

   *b.*    The cost in U.S. dollars is:

    (Can$2.19)/(Can$1.05/$1) = $2.09

    Among the reasons that absolute PPP doesn't hold are tariffs and other barriers to trade, transactions costs, taxes, and different tastes.

   *c.*    The U.S. dollar is selling at a discount, because it is less expensive in the forward market than in the spot market (Can$1.05 versus Can$1.03).

   *d.*    The Canadian dollar is expected to appreciate in value relative to the dollar, because it takes fewer Canadian dollars to buy one U.S. dollar in the future than it does today.

   *e.*    Interest rates in the United States are probably higher than they are in Canada.

**5.**   *a.*    The cross rate in ¥/£ terms is:

    (¥85/$1)($1.53/£1) = ¥130.05/£1

   *b.*    The yen is quoted high relative to the pound. Take out a loan for $1 and buy £.6536. Use the £.6536 to purchase yen at the cross-rate, which will give you:

    ¥131.4(£.6536) = ¥85.8824

    Use the pounds to buy back dollars and repay the loan. The cost to repay the loan will be:

    ¥85.8824($1/¥85) = $1.0104

    You arbitrage profit is $.0104 per dollar used.

**6.**    We can rearrange the interest rate parity condition to answer this question. The equation we will use is:

$$R_{FC} = (F_T - S_0)/S_0 + R_{US}$$

Using this relationship, we find:

Great Britain:    $R_{FC}$ = (£.6313 – £.6304)/£.6304 + .019 = .0204, or 2.04%

Japan:    $R_{FC}$ = (¥76.96 – ¥77.21)/¥77.21 + .019 = .0158, or 1.58%

Switzerland:    $R_{FC}$ = (SF .8743 – SF .8799)/SF .8799 + .019 = .0126, or 1.26%

7.    If we invest in the U.S. for the next three months, we will have:

$30,000,000(1.0021)^3 = $30,189,397.18

If we invest in Great Britain, we must exchange the dollars today for pounds, and exchange the pounds for dollars in three months. After making these transactions, the dollar amount we would have in three months would be:

($30,000,000)(£.64/$1)(1.0057)^3/(£.65/$1) = $30,046,453.81

The company should invest in the U.S.

8.    Using the relative purchasing power parity equation:

$$F_t = S_0 \times [1 + (h_{FC} - h_{US})]^t$$

We find:

$$Z3.23 = Z3.14[1 + (h_{FC} - h_{US})]^3$$
$$h_{FC} - h_{US} = (Z3.23/Z3.14)^{1/3} - 1$$
$$h_{FC} - h_{US} = .0095$$

Inflation in Poland is expected to exceed that in the U.S. by .95% annually over this period.

9.    The profit will be the quantity sold, times the sales price minus the cost of production. The production cost is in Singapore dollars, so we must convert this to U.S. dollars. Doing so, we find that if the exchange rates stay the same, the profit will be:

Profit = 30,000[$125 − {(S$141.30)/(S$1.2348/$1)}]
Profit = $317,055.39

If the exchange rate rises, we must adjust the cost by the increased exchange rate, so:

Profit = 30,000[$125 − {(S$141.30)/1.1(S$1.2348/$1)}]
Profit = $629,141.27

If the exchange rate falls, we must adjust the cost by the decreased exchange rate, so:

Profit = 30,000[$125 − {(S$141.30)/.9(S$1.2348/$1)}]
Profit = −$64,382.90

To calculate the breakeven change in the exchange rate, we need to find the exchange rate that make the cost in Singapore dollars equal to the selling price in U.S. dollars, so:

$125 = S$141.30/$S_T$
$S_T$ = S$1.1304/$1
$S_T$ = −.0845, or −8.45%

**10.** *a.* If IRP holds, then:

$$F_{180} = (\text{Kr } 5.61)[1 + (.05 - .03)]^{1/2}$$
$$F_{180} = \text{Kr } 5.6658$$

Since given $F_{180}$ is Kr 5.72, an arbitrage opportunity exists; the forward premium is too high. Borrow Kr1 today at 5% interest. Agree to a 180-day forward contract at Kr 5.72. Convert the loan proceeds into dollars:

Kr 1 ($1/Kr 5.61) = $.17825

Invest these dollars at 3%, ending up with $.18087. Convert the dollars back into krone as

$.18087(Kr 5.72/$1) = Kr 1.03458

Repay the Kr 1 loan, ending with a profit of:

Kr 1.03458 – Kr 1.02435 = Kr .01023

*b.* To find the forward rate that eliminates arbitrage, we use the interest rate parity condition, so:

$$F_{180} = (\text{Kr } 5.61)[1 + (.05 - .03)]^{1/2}$$
$$F_{180} = \text{Kr } 5.6658$$

**11.** The international Fisher effect states that the real interest rate across countries is equal. We can rearrange the international Fisher effect as follows to answer this question:

$$R_{US} - h_{US} = R_{FC} - h_{FC}$$
$$h_{FC} = R_{FC} + h_{US} - R_{US}$$

*a.* $h_{AUS} = .04 + .023 - .018$
$h_{AUS} = .045$, or 4.50%

*b.* $h_{CAN} = .06 + .023 - .018$
$h_{CAN} = .065$, or 6.50%

*c.* $h_{TAI} = .09 + .023 - .018$
$h_{TAI} = .095$, or 9.50%

**12.** *a.* The yen is expected to get stronger, since it will take fewer yen to buy one dollar in the future than it does today.

*b.* $h_{US} - h_{JAP} \approx (¥78.96 - ¥80.13)/¥80.13$
$h_{US} - h_{JAP} = -.0146$, or –1.46%

$(1 - .0146)^4 - 1 = -.0571$, or –5.71%

The approximate inflation differential between the U.S. and Japan is –5.71% annually.

13. We need to find the change in the exchange rate over time, so we need to use the relative purchasing power parity relationship:

$$F_t = S_0 \times [1 + (h_{FC} - h_{US})]^t$$

Using this relationship, we find the exchange rate in one year should be:

$F_1 = 206[1 + (.037 - .028)]^1$
$F_1 = $ HUF 207.85

The exchange rate in two years should be:

$F_2 = 206[1 + (.037 - .028)]^2$
$F_2 = $ HUF 209.72

And the exchange rate in five years should be:

$F_5 = 206[1 + (.037 - .028)]^5$
$F_5 = $ HUF 215.44

## Intermediate

14. First, we need to forecast the future spot rate for each of the next three years. From interest rate and purchasing power parity, the expected exchange rate is:

$$E(S_T) = [(1 + R_{US}) / (1 + R_{FC})]^t \, S_0$$

So:

$E(S_1) = (1.0310 / 1.0290)^1 (\$1.09/\text{€}) = \$1.0921/\text{€}$
$E(S_2) = (1.0310 / 1.0290)^2 (\$1.09/\text{€}) = \$1.0942/\text{€}$
$E(S_3) = (1.0310 / 1.0290)^3 (\$1.09/\text{€}) = \$1.0964/\text{€}$

Now we can use these future spot rates to find the dollar cash flows. The dollar cash flow each year will be:

| | |
|---|---|
| Year 0 cash flow = −€$19,000,000($1.09/€) | = −$20,710,000.00 |
| Year 1 cash flow = €3,600,000($1.0921/€) | = $3,931,626.82 |
| Year 2 cash flow = €4,100,000($1.0942/€) | = $4,486,389.09 |
| Year 3 cash flow = (€5,100,000 + 12,700,000)($1.0964/€) | = $19,515,351.22 |

And the NPV of the project will be:

NPV = −$20,710,000 + $3,931,626.82/1.105 + $4,486,389.09/1.105$^2$ + $19,515,351.22/1.105$^3$
NPV = $986,351.89

15. *a.* Implicitly, it is assumed that interest rates won't change over the life of the project, but the exchange rate is projected to decline because the Euroswiss rate is lower than the Eurodollar rate.

*b.* We can use relative purchasing power parity to calculate the dollar cash flows at each time. The equation is:

$$E[S_T] = (SF\ 1.17)[1 + (.05 - .06)]^t$$
$$E[S_T] = 1.17(.99)^t$$

So, the cash flows each year in U.S. dollar terms will be:

| $t$ | SF | $E[S_t]$ | US$ |
|---|---|---|---|
| 0 | −25,000,000 | 1.1700 | −$21,367,521.37 |
| 1 | 6,900,000 | 1.1583 | 5,957,005.96 |
| 2 | 6,900,000 | 1.1467 | 6,017,177.73 |
| 3 | 6,900,000 | 1.1352 | 6,077,957.31 |
| 4 | 6,900,000 | 1.1239 | 6,139,350.82 |
| 5 | 6,900,000 | 1.1127 | 6,201,364.46 |

And the NPV is:

$$NPV = -\$21,367,521.37 + \$5,957,005.96/1.12 + \$6,017,177.73/1.12^2 + \$6,077,957.31/1.12^3 + \$6,139,350.82/1.12^4 + \$6,201,364.46/1.12^5$$
$$NPV = \$494,750.33$$

*c.* Rearranging the relative purchasing power parity equation to find the required return in Swiss francs, we get:

$$R_{SF} = 1.12[1 + (.05 - .06)] - 1$$
$$R_{SF} = 10.88\%$$

So, the NPV in Swiss francs is:

$$NPV = -SF\ 25,000,000 + SF\ 6,900,000(PVIFA_{10.88\%,5})$$
$$NPV = SF\ 578,857.89$$

Converting the NPV to dollars at the spot rate, we get the NPV in U.S. dollars as:

$$NPV = (SF\ 578,857.89)(\$1/SF\ 1.17)$$
$$NPV = \$494,750.33$$

**16.** *a.* To construct the balance sheet in dollars, we need to convert the account balances to dollars. At the current exchange rate, we get:

Assets = solaris 34,000 × ($ / solaris 1.20) = $28,333.33
Debt = solaris 12,000 × ($ / solaris 1.20) = $10,000.00
Equity = solaris 22,000 × ($ / solaris 1.20) = $18,333.33

*b.* In one year, if the exchange rate is solaris 1.40/$, the accounts will be:

Assets = solaris 34,000 × ($ / solaris 1.40) = $24,285.71
Debt = solaris 12,000 × ($ / solaris 1.40) = $8,571.43
Equity = solaris 22,000 × ($ / solaris 1.40) = $15,714.29

*c.* If the exchange rate is solaris 1.12/$, the accounts will be:

Assets = solaris 34,000 × ($ / solaris 1.12) = $30,357.14
Debt = solaris 12,000 × ($ / solaris 1.12) = $10,714.29
Equity = solaris 22,000 × ($ / solaris 1.12) = $19,642.86

### Challenge

**17.** First, we need to construct the end of year balance sheet in solaris. Since the company has retained earnings, the equity account will increase, which necessarily implies the assets will also increase by the same amount. So, the balance sheet at the end of the year in solaris will be:

Balance Sheet (solaris)

|  |  |  |  |
|---|---|---|---|
|  |  | Liabilities | $12,000 |
|  |  | Equity | 23,750 |
| Assets | $35,750 | Total liabilities & equity | $35,750 |

Now we need to convert the balance sheet accounts to dollars, which gives us:

Assets = solaris 35,750 × ($ / solaris 1.24) = $28,830.65
Debt = solaris 12,000 × ($ / solaris 1.24) = $9,677.42
Equity = solaris 23,750 × ($ / solaris 1.24) = $19,153.23

**18.** *a.* The domestic Fisher effect is:

$1 + R_{US} = (1 + r_{US})(1 + h_{US})$
$1 + r_{US} = (1 + R_{US})/(1 + h_{US})$

This relationship must hold for any country, that is:

$1 + r_{FC} = (1 + R_{FC})/(1 + h_{FC})$

The international Fisher effect states that real rates are equal across countries, so:

$1 + r_{US} = (1 + R_{US})/(1 + h_{US}) = (1 + R_{FC})/(1 + h_{FC}) = 1 + r_{FC}$

*b.* The exact form of unbiased interest rate parity is:

$E[S_t] = F_t = S_0 [(1 + R_{FC})/(1 + R_{US})]^t$

*c.* The exact form for relative PPP is:

$E[S_t] = S_0 [(1 + h_{FC})/(1 + h_{US})]^t$

*d.* For the home currency approach, we calculate the expected currency spot rate at time t as:

$E[S_t] = (€.5)[1.07/1.05]^t = (€.5)(1.019)^t$

We then convert the euro cash flows using this equation at every time, and find the present value. Doing so, we find:

NPV $= - [€2M/(€.5)] + \{€.9M/[1.019(€.5)]\}/1.1 + \{€.9M/[1.019^2(€.5)]\}/1.1^2 +$
$\{€.9M/[1.019^3(€.5)]\}/1.1^3$
NPV = $316,230.72

For the foreign currency approach, we first find the return in the euros as:

$R_{FC} = 1.10(1.07/1.05) - 1 = .121$

Next, we find the NPV in euros as:

NPV $= - €2M + (€.9M)/1.121 + (€.9M)/1.121^2 + (€.9M)/1.121^3 = €158,115.36$

And finally, we convert the euros to dollars at the current exchange rate, which is:

NPV ($) $= €158,115.36 /€.5 = $316,230.72$